PAROCHIAL SCHOOL

PAROCHIAL SCHOOL

A Sociological Study

JOSEPH H. FICHTER, S. J.

Professor of Sociology

Loyola University of the South

UNIVERSITY OF NOTRE DAME PRESS

1958

Imprimi Potest:
Laurence O'Neill, S. J., *Praepositus Provinciae Neo Aurelianensis*
Nihil Obstat:
Arnold Wibbert, *Censor Deputatus*
Imprimatur:
✠ Leo A. Pursley, D. D., *Episcopus Wayne Castrensis*

Library of Congress Catalog Card Number 58-13614

THE LIBRARY OF CONGRESS CATALOGUING OF
THIS BOOK WILL BE FOUND ON PAGE 495.

This book is dedicated to
Genevieve, Mary Louise, Mary Therese, Marion
who among them
have had, now have, or will have
twenty-two children in the parochial school

PREFACE

THE PRESENT VOLUME represents part of a larger scheme for the sociological study of the Catholic urban parish. This research framework, as originally employed in the *Southern Parish* project, comprises four major areas of inquiry into the socio-cultural system of the parish. The first concentrates on the formal and informal patterns of religious behavior, centering around the parish church itself.[1] The second area is that of the parochial societies of lay persons. This too has been reported upon in a research study directed in a German urban parish while the author served as visiting professor of sociology at the University of Muenster, Westphalia.[2] The present work engages the third area of investigation, the parochial school. The final part of this large research scheme deals with the family life of parishioners, and has not yet been published.[3]

The financial support for this year-long study of St. Luke's parochial school was made possible through a research grant generously provided by the University of Notre Dame. Dr. John J. Kane, Chairman of the Department of Sociology, and Father Philip Moore, Vice-President for Academic Affairs, worked closely with us in initiating the study and in removing and preventing the various obstacles usually attendant upon such projects. Above all, the University provided an atmosphere of free enquiry, of intellectual inquisitiveness, of scholarly encouragement. There were no conditions or qualifications placed on this research program, nor were any theses proposed for defense or

[1] *The Dynamics of a City Church*, (Chicago: University of Chicago Press, 1951), is vol. 1 of the *Southern Parish* series.

[2] Published in German as *Soziologie der Pfarrgruppen*, (Muenster: Aschendorf, 1958).

All four major areas of research were completed in the original project in *Southern Parish*. See Paul Courtney, "The Southern Parish Case," *The Commonweal*, vol. 55, no. 8, (November 30, 1951), pp. 191–193. See also *Social Relations in the Urban Parish*, (Chicago: University of Chicago Press, 1954), chap. 15, "Major Issues in the Sociology of the Parish."

proof. This congenial scientific milieu was assured by the abiding scholarly interests of the Dean of the Graduate Division, Father Paul Beichner, and of the President of the University, Father Theodore Hesburgh.

The conception and execution of this research project, as well as the analysis of the data and the generalizations drawn from them, are my own responsibility. The gathering of data, however, was primarily the function of a research team, composed of the following persons: Edward Cahill, Thomas Coffee, Gerald Dewey, Frank Fahey, William Mitchell, Ned Tranel, Norbert Wiley, and Fathers Robert Brooks and Gordon Irving. Their reports were scrutinized and discussed when the team met every Tuesday night for several hours. Without their dedicated and dependable collaboration this study could not have been completed. My appreciation for their industry is equalled only by my admiration for their endurance.

A pseudonymous report of this kind necessarily owes a great deal to many people who cannot be named. Father Albert and his two pastoral assistants, Sister Roberta and her staff of teachers, were consistently cooperative as well as genuinely interested in the study. The parents of school children, both those attending St. Luke's and those attending the William Howard Taft Public school, were enormously helpful. The Principal of the Taft school and other public school personnel were generous with their time and talents in assisting us to obtain information. The pupils themselves seemed proud and delighted to be the center of research attention. To all of these people, nameless though they must remain, we express our enduring gratitude.

The tedious mechanics of processing research data were made tolerable by the Statistics Bureau of the University of Notre Dame. Kenneth Doty and his assistants relieved us of a heavy burden of work by running the statistics of this study through their machines. A thorough search of the literature on elementary schools, providing documentation on comparable segments of research, was carefully performed by Norbert Wiley. Most of the manual compilation of data, the checking of references and the typing of numerous versions of the manuscript, were done with unfailing good cheer by Betty Haluda.

Joseph H. Fichter

CONTENTS

PAROCHIAL SCHOOL

Chapter

ONE

INTRODUCTION: STUDYING A SCHOOL

THE DECISION to make a sociological study of a parochial school was motivated by numerous factors.[1] The importance of the parochial school system is generally taken for granted by bishops, priests, parents, teachers, and Catholic lay persons. The American laity has shown its confidence in this school system by generously financing it, without direct aid from the public treasury or from large personal endowments or philanthropic organizations.[2] At the same time this Catholic laity also pays its proportionate share to support public kindergarten, elementary, junior and senior high schools, city and state colleges, universities, and graduate schools.

In a sense, the future of Catholicism in America is being built now in the parochial school, at least for about half of the Catholic children of elementary school age. Many of the priests, sisters and parents of the next generation are here being socialized as maturing Catholics in the American culture. The loyal parishioners and devoted lay apostles of tomorrow are now being formed in the parochial schools.[3] In short, the Church and its people concentrate a tremendous amount of time and human energy and millions of dollars on the operation and maintenance of the parochial school.

This devotion and confidence bespeak an assumption that the parochial school is performing the function expected of it, yet no thorough-going, scientific examination of the parochial school has been

[1] See Arnold M. Rose, *Theory and Method in the Social Sciences* (Minneapolis: University of Minnesota Press, 1954), chap. 7, "The Selection of Problems for Research."

[2] See below, chap. 14, "Financing the School."

[3] When the data were in for the U.S. Census of 1950, Urban H. Fleege made a cautious projection of school trends in "Avalanche of Catholic Children Challenge Catholic Leadership," *The Homiletic and Pastoral Review*, vol. 53, no. 9 (June, 1953), pp. 785–791.

made to take the measure of this performance. Limited investigations have been conducted here and there; certain aspects have been scrutinized; some generalizations have been drawn. These segmental studies on discipline, lay teachers, homework, financing, and many others, employ educational concepts, terminology and approaches.[4] This limits their sociological utility. Nowhere in the literature of education or social science is there a total group study of an elementary school, private, parochial or public, in actual operation over a period of time. What the parochial school does, what it fails to do, how it functions, on the level of the schoolday program—remain unanswered questions to most Catholics and to practically all non-Catholics.

The parochial school has been an item of controversy among well-meaning people, both Catholics and non-Catholics, and most of the controversy has been carried on in the twilight zone between myths and facts.[5] Partisans of the system make some claims that cannot be substantiated. Adversaries of the parochial school make some charges that can be easily dispelled in the light of the facts. The objective social scientist does not take sides in this dispute. He presents what he has observed and makes conclusions that do not go beyond the data collected.

The main reason why we studied the parochial school is to present the scientific facts in an unbiased way. This truth, we assume, will be somehow beneficial, as truth always is, at least in the long run. Parents, priests and teachers, who are in the middle of the system may stand off with the social scientist and re-examine what they are doing. Other Catholic lay persons may re-judge the school system which they have been praising—and perhaps criticizing—and to which they contribute. People involved in public elementary education—its critics, proponents, supporters, or just ordinary onlookers—may re-assess some of the judgments they have been making about the parochial system.

Why This School?

When a social scientist selects a definite group or community for study he is inevitably asked the reasons for his choice. People want to

[4] References are made throughout this book, usually in footnotes, to the more significant of these "spot studies." For a brief historical account, including excellent bibliographical references, see Henry J. Browne, "The American Parish School in the Last Half Century," *Bulletin* of the National Catholic Educational Association, vol. 50, no. 1 (August, 1952), pp. 323–334.

[5] Anson Phelps Stokes, *Church and State in the United States* (New York: Harper, 1950), vol. 2, pp. 659–660, attempts to balance the "reasons for" and the "reasons against" the parochial schools.

know why this school, and not another, was chosen for the research site. They want to know whether this is an "average" school, and without waiting for an answer they state that another school in another city or state is different. Another perennial question put to the social science researcher is: "How far can you trust people? How do you know they are telling you the truth?" These are serious questions and they deserve serious answers.

It is conceivable that a researcher could study the parochial school in the United States by sending a questionnaire to every parochial school in the country. If twenty per cent of his questionnaires are returned he has a sample of the schools, but he has not yet seen these schools in actual operation.[6] Another reseacher might be problem-oriented, attempt to discover "what's wrong with the parochial school," and thus study only the malfunctioning schools. Both of these approaches could produce useful knowledge and reliable conclusions, but both would also suffer critical limitations.

The investigation and analysis of a single, localized parochial school, viewed in all its aspects as a social system, avoid the limitations of both the sampling and the negative approaches. All the relevant sociological data were collected day by day in St. Luke's school over the course of a normal school year, from September to June. Group research has to have a locale. The best-known sociological studies of communities like Middletown, Yankee City, Elmtown and Plainville, dealt with actual people in actual situations.[7] Southern Parish is a definite place, and there also we studied the parochial school.[8] We decided upon this Midwestern city as a place of operations not only because it appeared to typify normal, urban Catholic life, but also because it has been chosen by government agencies and by commercial enterprises as a typical American "test town." [9] Thus, as an average,

[6] See the appendix of this book where the "typicality" of St. Luke's is shown through comparison with a sample of 433 parochial elementary schools in twenty-nine states.

[7] Robert S. and Helen M. Lynd, *Middletown* and *Middletown In Transition* (New York: Harcourt, Brace, 1929, 1937); W. Loyd Warner and Paul S. Lunt, *The Social Life of a Modern Community* (New Haven: Yale University Press, 1941), and subsequent volumes in the Yankee City Series; August B. Hollingshead, *Elmtown's Youth* (New York: John Wiley, 1949); James West, *Plainville, U.S.A.* (New York: Columbia University Press, 1945).

[8] Joseph H. Fichter, *Southern Parish: Dynamics of A City Church* (Chicago: University of Chicago Press, 1951).

[9] The United States Department of the Census occasionally takes samples of this city's population, and numerous large manufacturers use it as a place to pre-test sales on their new products.

or typical city, it is neither among the best nor among the worst.

Similarly, when we chose St. Luke's parochial school as a site for research study, we looked for certain basic elements, without which the school could not operate and without which the study would not have been possible. Since the Pastor is the key person in the whole parochial set-up, we sought for one who had been in office long enough to have "settled down," who had some understanding of the meaning of research, who was willing to cooperate with us, and who believed that the research project would "be a good thing." We wanted a parish whose priests are of the diocesan clergy, since this is the more "normal" type of city parish. A parish operated by a religious order tends to have more men available to "fill in" when needed, changes its personnel more frequently, and may in someways channel the laity's energy and support away from the parish and toward the order itself.

The school we selected for study is directed by a Principal who has been in office long enough to have developed a systematic pattern of administration. She engages three lay teachers, a growing phenomenon in parochial elementary schools. St. Luke's has an adequate physical plant, with cafeteria, auditorium and playground. The school also acts as a focus for parents' activities and for extracurricular programs of the pupils. The school and the parish are not "national," nor do they present any abnormal racial, ethnic or economic differentials.[10] Finally, St. Luke's school is considered a "pretty good school" in the estimation of other pastors in the city and of interested teachers and parents from other parishes.

We selected only one school for study not only because of limitation in time, budget and personnel, but mainly because we sought to make a thorough, day-by-day sociological study. This kind of research can hardly be done in several schools by the same people at the same time. To keep an eye on 632 pupils and fourteen teachers in the classroom, on the playground, and in extracurricular activities, to learn something of their family background, and of their parents' school-related activities, is as much as one research project can competently encompass.[11] Interviews with public school teachers, and tests made

[10] The "normality" of St. Luke's parish and school is amply demonstrated from the empirical data of research below, chap. 17, "School, Parish and Community." The careful preliminary investigations we made of possible research sites were rewarded by the confirmation of our assumptions.

[11] See Daniel Katz, "Field Studies," pp. 58–97, in Leon Festinger and Daniel Katz, eds., *Research Methods in the Behavioral Sciences* (New York: Dryden Press, 1953), for a discussion of the advantages, disadvantages and procedures of a field study.

in the nearby public school, provided in some respects a "control group"—with which certain comparisons could be made.

How do we know that this book presents objective knowledge? How do we know that people were telling us the truth? This is, of course, the test question for any social scientist, and he can answer it with certainty if he has used the several devices and instruments that provide cross-checks. This is not an opinion study, although we did ask people's opinions. It is not a statistical and demographic study, although we did gather population statistics. It is not merely a recitation of observed facts, although we kept the participants under observation as much as possible. All of these approaches were used on the same objects of study and out of them has come the confidence that we were able to arrive at the truth.

Research Methods

The interview schedule for parents was devised during the first month of the study, pre-tested on more than twenty parents of children in other parochial and public schools, and then revised for use. This interview, consisting of five pages, was not put in the hands of the parents. The interview, including both poll-type and open-end questions, was held with the parents of 632 pupils of St. Luke's school and of 181 Catholic pupils of the public school. The average time consumed by each formal interview was one hour and six minutes, but beyond this we always tried to obtain informal general remarks from the parents after the formal interview ended. These were incorporated as "anecdotal material" and recorded on the last page of the interview schedule. Wherever possible, the interview was pre-arranged by telephone so that both parents could be present, and therefore, most of them took place at night, and on Saturdays and Sundays. Even with this precaution we were able to obtain only 183 interviews where both parents were present, the remainder being with 273 mothers, thirty-four fathers, and six "others," such as grandparents, uncles and aunts.[12]

Because the research team was also occupied with other aspects of the continuing project, this interviewing stretched over the months from October to the end of January. On Sunday, November 11, three weeks after we began the interviewing, an announcement was made from the pulpit of St. Luke's church, asking the people to cooperate with our researchers. During the last month of interviewing we re-

[12] Since in many cases two or more of the school children were from the same family, all 813 children were covered in 496 interviews.

ceived phone calls from impatient parents who wanted to know when we were going to visit them, and whether we had "forgotten them." This fact is indicative of the interest and cooperation that the parents demonstrated in the whole research project. Because they enjoy talking about their children we found that rapport could be fairly easily established with the interviewees.

All enquiries made of the children themselves were focused on particular aspects of the study, and for this reason we did not use a systematic, prepared interview schedule with them. For example, we always chose the key persons in any particular event or program and asked them questions: the cheerleaders, the honor patrol pupils, the Scouts and Camp Fire Girls, and many others. The children were an uninhibited and plentiful source of information, every one of them willing and anxious to "tell all." Whether we called them out of the classroom, spoke to them in passing on the corridor or playground, or interviewed them at home, the children almost invariably reported to the teachers what we had talked about. Whenever we interviewed parents we asked that the child leave the room, but on several occasions (as we discovered later) the child stood at the head of the stairs or behind a closed door, made notes on our questions, and gave them to the teacher the next day.[13]

Another and separate interview schedule was made out for the teachers, and like that of the parents, it was exactly the same for both parochial and public school teachers. Since the questions had no religious content, and in order to prevent religious difference from entering the content, we interviewed only Catholic teachers in the public schools. All of these interviews were also made by prearranged appointment. Those with parochial school teachers were completed in early October and those with public school teachers during January and February. As in the case of the parents, the identity of teachers making pejorative remarks about the school has been completely hidden, and their opinions appear in this book only as a statistic or an anecdote.

In order to probe more deeply into the behavior patterns and social relations of the parochial school we also held open-end interviews with high school students who had attended and been graduated from St. Luke's. These respondents were eleven boys and thirteen girls in the

[13] This happened when the interviews with teachers had already been completed and could no longer bias their responses. The Principal, in particular, was curious about the kinds of questions we were asking parents, and also about the answers given by the parents. For a variety of experiences in interviewing see Mark Benney and Everett Hughes, eds., *The American Journal of Sociology*, vol. 62, no. 2 (September, 1956), whole issue.

junior and senior classes. They gave us insights into the items they liked most and least about St. Luke's, and told us in what respects their academic and social preparation for high school was sufficient or deficient.

One of the most revealing devices we employed was that of the group interview, or soiree, with parents. This was an arrangement whereby one family invited four or five others for an evening of "discussion" about the parochial school. We held nine of these informal meetings, in which seventy-two parents participated, some of them more than once. The researcher simply "tossed out" general questions concerning athletics, religion, discipline, boy-girl relations, the PTA, and other pertinent aspects of the study. The records of these soirees are filled with both facts and opinions, and were extremely helpful in sounding out and verifying materials gathered through other techniques. The advantage was that the parents involved in the group stimulated each other, argued, discussed, and elaborated while the reporter was left free to jot down the main statements without interruption.[14] The interaction between interviewer and interviewee, which is a crucial phase of the single-person interview, was relatively unimportant in these soirees. Questioning, probing, cross-checking, verifying and making of transitions, were done by the participants in the normal course of discussion, while the reporter merely changed the subject from time to time.[15]

These seventy-two parents were both the most critical and the most knowledgeable of the lay people who were actively concerned about St. Luke's school. Because they put so much time and effort into the school they felt that they had the "right" to speak freely and critically, both positively and negatively, about the priests, teachers and children. On no occasion did these soirees degenerate into a "gripe session," an eventuality that is to be expected when people are disgruntled with the group or system in which they participate. These parents were selected for this experiment precisely because they knew the most about the parish and the school, its problems, history and people.[16]

[14] For a discussion of this technique see Emory S. Bogardus, *The New Social Research* (Los Angeles: Miller, 1926), chap. 4, "The Group Interview"; Robert K. Merton, Marjorie Fiske, Patricia Kendall, *The Focussed Interview* (New York: Columbia University, 1952), pp. 134–167; also James D. Thompson and N. J. Demerath, "Some Experiences with the Group Interview," *Social Forces,* vol. 31, no. 2 (December, 1952), pp. 148–154.

[15] And to interrupt the reminiscences of some parent, usually a father, who wanted to talk about what "he did when he was a boy in school."

[16] This was not a random selection. For example, when we wanted to discuss athletics, we asked the basketball coach and the former football coach, and

An average of ninety hours a week was spent by the research team in the gathering of data throughout the school year. Much of the actual research time was spent in observation of the school in operation. Every one of the fourteen classrooms was visited during the whole school day on at least eleven separate occasions. This means that we were in the classrooms on 154 of the 175 schooldays of the year. The observer arrived at St. Luke's at about eight-thirty, and sometimes for the morning Mass at eight o'clock, accompanied the children to the classroom, sat in the rear of the room, and also went out to the recess and lunch periods with them. Taking notes during this whole time provided for us a record of the total school day, the performance of the teachers, the behavior patterns of the children, the content of lessons, the relations among the children and between the teacher and her pupils.

This system of observation and note-taking was employed also at all of the extracurricular group activities of the school children, all of their athletic contests, choir singing and practice, musical and entertainment programs. Similarly, we covered the various meetings and activities of the PTA, Scouts and Cubs, Camp Fire Girls and Blue Birds, the Athletic Committee and the Patrons of St. Luke. All of the active adults in these groups were interviewed at least once concerning functions peculiar to the group. We were even able to attend some of the children's parties.

Another aspect of our research procedure was the series of tests and questionnaires administered to the pupils in both the parochial and the nearby public school. Most of these were given to the children in the sixth, seventh and eighth grades. They included the *California Test of Personality,* a series of social moral problems, questions on movie attendance, choice of great historical and contemporary persons, favorite TV programs and movie stars. We gave a sociometric friendship test to the pupils in both schools, and had them answer questionnaires concerning their bed-time, the parties they gave or attended, the music and other lessons they took outside of school hours. Whenever we administered a test or a questionnaire, we went as a team and took over the classes simultaneously with the teacher out of the room. Thus the teacher could not forewarn the children about the questions, and the pupils in one room had no opportunity to prepare those of other grades.

The autobiographies of the pupils in the upper grades, from the

---

their wives, to invite four or five other couples who were also most deeply involved in the athletic program.

fifth to the eighth grades, proved also to be a fruitful source of information. At first we experimented with this by having the child write the autobiography in the classroom without any warning or preparation. The results appeared to be rambling and inaccurate and with a minimum of factual information. We then asked the teachers to assign the autobiography as homework. Signs of parental assistance are evident in practically all of them, particularly in the matter of vital statistics, the names of places they visited as infants, and certain other features the child would have been too young to know. The children's opinions of the teachers and the school were quite frank (particularly in writing about previous teachers and grades), and their account of the highlights of their school careers helped to reconstruct the progress of a child from the kindergarten to the eighth grade.

Researchers and Researched

Detailed sociological research of this kind obviously entails social relations between the observers and the persons observed. It is in this area that the greatest caution had to be employed by the research team. It is a problem of trying to be both aloof and friendly, of attempting to be a participant but at the same time trying not to appear at all. Within a month after the start of our project practically everyone in the parish knew that we were "writing a book" about the school. The children came home to tell their parents about all the "new" regulations they had to obey because they were "being observed."

It was apparently through a misinterpretation by the children of what the teachers told them in school that the rumor flew around the parish about a "bunch of priests" who were investigating the school. Although, besides the director of the project, there were three single and four married laymen on the research team, as well as two priests, the laymen were asked by the children in the beginning of the study "are you a priest?" After a while, many of the parents apparently decided that these laymen were "at least" seminarians, and some of them were taken aback when the interviewers mentioned their own children and swapped anecdotes with the parents of St. Luke's pupils. At any rate, the talent of the interviewer, as a collector of data, did not depend upon his clerical or lay status; nor did the interpretation of the parishioners concerning the status of the researcher seem to influence in any way the giving and gathering of information.[17]

[17] We analyzed and compared the responses to key questions in 109 interviews by the clerical researchers and found no significant variations from the 387 interviews conducted by the laymen on the team. See the discussion on "Respond-

The immediate problem in this kind of situation is the question of the extent to which the presence of a research team influences the performance of the people who are being studied. There is little question but that this performance tends to improve. This was noted in the study of the Banks Wiring Room of the Hawthorne factory research, and it is unquestionably the case wherever intensive research is done.[18] When the Mother Superior of the teaching nuns visited the convent in October she said "the only thing they've talked about since I came in this afternoon was the study." She remarked also that the project had an immediate value in that the teachers were re-examining their own performance in the classroom and trying to improve it.

The teachers differed considerably in their initial reaction to the presence of the observer in the classroom. Some of them conducted the lessons as though an outside audience were an everyday occurrence; in fact they appeared to enjoy the opportunity to demonstrate their pedagogical virtuosity. A few of them were nervous, glancing frequently at the observer, and even attempting to involve him in the particular lesson at hand. This artificial atmosphere soon wore off, however, and within two months our observers could walk into any classroom without disturbing its routine. The younger children, from the first to the third grades, who are generally curious and easily distracted, continued through most of the year to squirm in their seats and to glance occasionally at the observer.

It was the constant practice of the observers to ask some of the children at recess or after school whether "there was anything different today," that is, in comparison to the day when the observer was not present. The responses were not uniform in regard to the different teachers. One boy said "she's real nice when one of you guys are in the room." A girl in another class remarked, "it was pretty much the same; some days we get more done and some days less." The children often stated that they liked to have us in the classroom; most frequently this remark came from the pupils in the upper grades, even

---

ent Reaction in the Interview Situation," Herbert H. Hyman, *et al., Interviewing in Social Research* (Chicago: University of Chicago Press, 1954), pp. 138–170.

[18] See F. J. Roethlisberger and W. J. Dickson, *Management and the Worker* (Cambridge: Harvard University Press, 1939). See the comments on this point by Marie Jahoda, Morton Deutsch and Stuart W. Cook, *Research Methods in Social Relations* (New York: Dryden, 1955), p. 60; also the well-known facts concerning social facilitation of performance in the presence of others, Otto Klineberg, *Social Psychology* (New York: Henry Holt, 1954), pp. 453–456.

though they acted quite indifferent to our presence in class, hardly noticing us, and never looking around to the back of the room. One boy ended his autobiography with the words, "Well, I will not have to tell you anything about the eighth grade because your men have been watching me so closely that I couldn't tell anything they haven't already observed."

The remarks made to us by the various teachers also lacked uniformity and agreement. One teacher said that "when you're there you are a good influence on the class; they behave better." Another said quite the opposite, "There seems to be so much more noise when one of you fellows comes into class." In their performance in the schoolroom neither of these teachers ever gave any indication that she was aware of our presence. Still another teacher, who has the children give oral reports before the class about interesting events and people, had a subtle way of calling attention to our observers. She would suggest that the pupil tell the class about the "visitor" who came to the football game, or the Camp Fire meeting, or the music recital. We were thus in the peculiar position of being observed and reported upon by the very pupils whom we were observing and about whom we were writing reports.

The research team participated through observation rather than through cooperation in the organized activities of St. Luke's. Our own opinion and counsel was asked on numerous occasions at the beginning of the survey, and our constant habit was simply to accept the statements of our questioners without making comment.[19] This was particularly important in some of the questions raised in the meetings of the PTA when there was considerable disagreement. We even had to be careful not to take a seat near one faction or the other, lest this be interpreted as sympathy or agreement.[20] There were occasions, however, when we gave physical help, as in clearing away cups and dishes after an entertainment, opening a stuck window for the teacher, wrapping a package for the Principal, helping to move chairs in the auditorium.

The cooperation of the teachers, and particularly of the Principal, was constant and complete. All of the records of the school were put

[19] See the discussion on participation and observation in Raymond L. Gold, "Roles in Sociological Field Observations," *Social Forces,* vol. 36, no. 3 (March, 1958), pp. 217–223.

[20] After the first PTA meeting at which open argument occurred our observer "went for a beer" with two of the men in order to get more details of background. The next day we had a phone call from "the other side" complaining that our observer was biased.

at our disposal; all questions were answered honestly and openly. There were times, however, when the exigencies of research touched upon delicate problems of school policy. An example of this is the whole area of boy-girl relations. We could obtain reliable information only by interviewing the children themselves, and finding out directly "who likes whom" and "who goes with whom." The children talked willingly and openly to us about this, but they also, as in other aspects of the study, talked willingly and openly to the teachers about what we had asked them. Thus, it appeared that we were arousing the interest of the children in the very subject in which the teachers were trying to discourage their interest. These interviews were completed in a few weeks, and things soon returned to normal.

There was a certain amount of involvement also of the parents in the research project. At the end of an interview we were frequently told that "this is the first time I really sat down and discussed the education of my child." Parents confessed that there were some aspects of school life that they had never before considered; and the interviews sometimes brought disagreement between husband and wife on particular items. Parents tended to reminisce about their own school days, taking it for granted that the children today "have it much easier," but indicating also in some instances that they knew very little about what is going on in the school. A latent function of the research project, as it was with the teachers, was to provide an opportunity for the parents to re-examine and "think through" the whole question of their children's education.

Parents who were at the center of the school-connected adult groups, like PTA and the Athletic Committee, demonstrated a kind of quiet pride in the fact that their parochial school was being studied. They volunteered information "to put in that book," and offered explanations on aspects that they thought we may have overlooked. In this sense some of them almost reached the status of part-time researchers for us. One of the most fruitful means for corroborating our information, or for clearing up doubtful points, were those people who said "now, don't put this in the book, but I think you ought to know it." During the last three months of the study we began to write rough drafts of certain aspects of the whole research project. By this time we had become well-acquainted with the main adult personalities in the parish. From among these we selected certain "readers" and discussants whom we judged to be both knowledgeable and critical, but above all fairly dispassionate in their views.

The adults who were involved in reading and discussing our tentative outlines and conclusions became informal collaborators in this crucial phase of the project.[21] The write-up on the Sunday School was analyzed in detail with Sister Genevieve and Miss Reickert. The sections on the athletic teams and on the area of boy-girl relations were discussed at length with Coach Bowman and his wife. Our analysis of the PTA and of the attitudes of parents toward elementary school education was thoroughly scrutinized by the O'Tooles and the Currys. Various other sections were analyzed and criticized by the Finegans, Lehrners and Glasses. This collaboration continued intermittently through the three summer months following the close of the school year, and toward the end of this period both Father Albert and Father Martin entered the research process by reviewing the whole first draft with us.

On four occasions during the school year, in November, January, February and April, we distributed in mimeographed form, a series of "Interim Observations." [22] These were eight or nine pages in length, single-spaced typing, and discussed topics like the place of the parochial school in the community, a comparison of parochial and public school administration, the problems of parent-teacher communication, and the behavior patterns of elementary school children. These reports were circulated among the priests, teachers and parents in an attempt to discover how accurately our tentative generalizations mirrored the social facts of the parochial school. This technique further involved the most active adults by stimulating their interest in the research project and by drawing them into the study as informants and commentators.

Even some of the school pupils were concerned about the gathering of data and the ultimate publication of our study, and outdid their parents in their eagerness to give us information. As a matter of fact, of all sources of data for this study, the children themselves proved to be the most thorough and reliable. The *Yearbook of Memories,* a

[21] See the similar experiences of William Foote Whyte in his research on *Street Corner Society,* discussed in his article on "Observational Field-work Methods," pp. 493–513, Maria Jahoda, Morton Deutsch and Stuart W. Cook, *Research Methods in Social Relations,* Part 2 (New York: Dryden Press, 1951).

[22] Several semi-popular articles related to this project were also published while the research team was still in the area. "Educated Catholic Women," *America,* vol. 97, no. 3 (April 20, 1957), pp. 65–66; "Parochial School Teacher," *The Catholic World,* vol. 185, no. 1,105 (April, 1957), pp. 51–55; "The Parish Today," *The Ave Maria,* vol. 85, no. 24 (June 15, 1957), pp. 8–13; "What's Wrong with Sunday School?" *The Catholic World,* vol. 185, no. 1,108 (July, 1957), pp. 246–251. See also "Lines of Communication in a Parochial School," *Bulletin* of the National Catholic Educational Association, vol. 54, no. 1 (August, 1957), pp. 214–220.

mimeographed production of the eighth graders, carried the following statement: "The interviews of the research team have made a great impression on our eighth-grade life. The statements we have made will be transposed and used in a book. Although we may pass on, someone will always remember our graduating class by this book. When we ask ourselves later on, what have we to show for our eight years at St. Luke's we can always say this book if nothing else. We should all be very proud to be a part of this book."

Statistics

The larger the number of people who think and act in the same way the more important becomes the behavior pattern that they are sharing. The statistics in our study, presented as simply as possible, are a handy guide to the variety of behavior patterns that range from those shared by most of the people to those on which there is only minor conformity. At any given point it is clear from the textual content what is a pattern of opinion and what is a pattern of action. For the most part, we were seeking data on what people actually do in situations related to the school, whether they are teachers, parents or pupils.

All parts of the interviews with parents were arranged in such wise that they could be coded and transposed to IBM cards. The open-end questions, like those pertaining to over-crowded schoolrooms, teacher shortage, and future vocation of children, presented the usual difficulties of multiple categories. These interviews were the only materials that were coded. All other interviews, tests and questionnaires were sorted, counted and classified manually.

Since the subject matter of this research project was a dynamic social unit functioning over a whole school year, certain small changes in the statistics were bound to occur. Because of residential mobility the school population itself shifted; eleven families with twenty parochial school pupils moved into the parish during the year, and eight families with seventeen pupils moved out. In spite of this mobility, involving only 2.9 per cent of the families, the school population never dropped below 630 pupils, nor went above 635. In order to have a constant universe for comparable statistics and subcategories we "froze" the school population at 632 children in the month of December, when we were more than two-thirds finished with the parents' interviews. This total figure includes 317 boys and 315 girls.

There are other small statistical variations to be accounted for. The tests and questionnaires we administered in the sixth, seventh and eighth grades of both the parochial and public schools, had to be given at different times during the year. Since there are almost always some pupils absent, and since the numbers of absentees fluctuate from day to day, there are obviously some variations in the totals of pupils giving responses on these different occasions. The final analysis of absenteeism and conduct marks could not be done until the end of the school year in June, when the pupils' permanent records were made available to us. These statistics, therefore, cover the pupil population as it was composed on the last day of school, on June 7.

It must be clear from the contents of this study that statistics were merely an instrument for the more important analyses, descriptions and generalizations of the research results. The heart of the study, so far as methods are concerned, was the daily, on-the-spot contact, communication and observation of the research team. Yet it is difficult to separate the statistical from the observational approach. How any individual child behaved in the classroom or on the playground was not so important from a sociological point of view as the extent to which his form of behavior was shared by his classmates. Recurrent, uniform, common patterns of behavior are the basic unit of the culture and their significance can be measured when they are statistically quantified and categorized.

It may be mentioned at this point that this research report is sprinkled liberally with examples and anecdotes. This is not merely a writer's technique for "livening up" otherwise monotonous materials. The quoted statements of pupils, teachers and parents are, for the most part, exemplifications of whole areas of thinking and judging. The descriptions of events in and out of the classroom are simply a picture of "what goes on" in a parochial school. Idiosyncratic behavior is also occasionally described, if for no other reason, to show the contrast between uniform and deviant patterns of conduct. These descriptions, obviously, cannot be statistically handled.

During the summer months after the close of St. Luke's school year we were fortunately able to gather further statistics on a sample of American parochial elementary schools. Teachers from these schools were in attendance at the summer session of the University of Notre Dame. In August the annual convention of the Christian Family Movement brought large numbers of parents of elementary school children to the same campus. From these parents and teachers we obtained 433 completed and usable questionnaires giving information about the operation of parochial schools.[23]

[23] These are 433 *different* schools reported on in the appendix to this book. Numerous "duplicates" of the same school from both teachers and parents were rejected.

The scientific value of this sampling device must not be overlooked. It enables us to say with confidence that St. Luke's is a representative "modal" example of the American parochial elementary school. Most of the patterns of behavior, the modes of operation, the types of group activity, that we found at St. Luke's are also characteristic of most of the other parochial schools. St. Luke's is not an "extraordinary" school when compared to the parochial schools scattered around the United States. It is "just another school," and this fact means that our generalizations and conclusions can be widely projected throughout the parochial school system. Without this statistical sample we could not be sure that St. Luke's is typical; without the day-by-day detailed study of St. Luke's we would know very little about what we were sampling.

What to Report

Since an ordinary research project of this kind is not completed until the report has been written and published, methodology includes also the problem of selection and rejection of data for the final report.[24] It is conceivable that a parish would finance a complete sociological study of its parochial school exclusively for the eyes of the pastor, or perhaps for private circulation to a few select ecclesiastical administrators. It is doubtful, however, that such a private report would contain anything more, or less, than that contained in the present report. The value of publication, however, to a wider audience is so obvious that it does not need explanation here.[25]

The social scientist picks up a great deal of information in the course of a year's research that is not sociologically relevant. This has happened in the study of St. Luke's parish. We have pruned from this report materials that may well be relevant to the psychologist, the theologian and ethician. This rejection of data is not based on the personal whim or value judgment of the researcher. It is based on the scientific prescriptions of the content of sociology as a body of knowledge.[26] While a cross-disciplinary approach to the elementary school

[24] See Joseph H. Fichter and William L. Kolb, "Ethical Limitations on Sociological Reporting," *American Sociological Review*, vol. 18, no. 5 (October, 1953), pp. 544–550; also the more extended discussion on this matter in *Social Relations in the Urban Parish* (Chicago: Chicago University Press, 1954), chap. 16, pp. 218–332.

[25] For a broad outline of suggested research projects, see Nicholas von Hoffman, "The Church: Subject of Social Research," *Social Order*, vol. 6, no. 7, (September, 1956), pp. 319–327.

[26] There exists a large literature on sociological research. For an introduction to this field see John C. McKinney, "Methodology, Procedures, and Techniques

by psychologists, economists, historians and sociologists may prove a valuable scientific project, this type of approach was not used in the study of St. Luke's. Thus, the first and principal criterion for the inclusion of research data in this report is the sociological and scientific relevance of the material.

The use of pseudonyms for persons and places has become a commonplace practice in sociological research reports, in order to "protect the anonymity" of the people involved. This practice we have followed more because it is customary—it is a "habit pattern" of sociological reporters—than because there is any need to protect the people of St. Luke's from the revelation of their own behavior. This report does not invade anyone's privacy; it does not reveal anyone's secrets. Everything in this book is already known to some people. It is the very nature of sociological research that we deal with "public facts" in the sense that repeated uniformities of behavior, shared in by a number of people, simply cannot be kept secret.

The conscientious sociological researcher and reporter, by the very nature of his scientific discipline, is prevented from "harming the reputation" of any person or group involved as objects of his study. When we imply that a certain teacher is "cranky" or that a certain officer of the PTA is "bossy" we are merely reflecting facts that are well-known by large numbers of people involved in the activities of the parochial school. If the Pastor and the Principal "come off well" in this report, or if they "come off badly," this is not the doing of either the researcher or the reporter. The whole scientific approach collapses if, after a year of painstaking and minute investigation by a research team, the final report is filled with only favorable or only unfavorable conclusions. The fact is that the term "favorable" has no place or meaning in scientific research, even in the social sciences, but it is a term that necessarily involves the norms and values of the persons and groups who are being studied.

Finally, a word must be said about the generalizations that appear at the end of each chapter. These represent an attempt to go beyond a mere summary of the chapter's content. They indicate the prevailing patterns among the other patterns that are also present in the social situation. These are conclusions in the wide sense of the term, interpretations of the research data in relation to other knowledge available in the field of sociology.

---

in Sociology," in Howard Becker and Alvin Boskoff, eds., *Modern Sociological Theory* (New York: Dryden, 1957), pp. 186–235.

Part

I

PATTERNS OF SOCIALIZATION

Chapter

TWO

THE FIRST TEN YEARS

THE SOCIALIZATION of the child is the process through which he gradually "finds himself" at home in the society and culture in which he lives.[1] He responds both to his social authorities and to his peers in the family, the neighborhood, the school and the parish. As we trace the life of the children from birth to the age of thirteen or fourteen, we find certain highlights that they remember most vividly. These similar experiences are met by most of the pupils of St. Luke's school, and they form a kind of generalized pattern, out of which we are able to reconstruct a composite biography, or life-profile. Specific experiences are, of course, unique in each case, but they are sufficiently regular and repetitive that we can draw generalizations of behavior from them.

Family Background

Only about one out of twenty (5.9%) of St. Luke's pupils is from a one-child family. Thus, the great majority of them have the advantage of experience with older or younger children in the family, and a number of them had additional baby siblings born during the school year and after the statistics from family interviews were completed. The largest single category of families from which these pupils come is that with two children, the next largest that with three children. The following table accounts for 1,184 children in these 377 families, or an average of 3.14 children per family.

These statistics show that the largest numbers of these children have some companionship at home within the immediate family. Their autobiographies tell of the happenings with younger or older siblings,

[1] See Otto Klineberg, *Social Psychology* (New York: Henry Holt, 1954), chap. 17, "The Individual in the Group," pp. 437–480; also Joseph H. Fichter, *Sociology* (Chicago: University of Chicago Press, 1957), chap. 1, "The Social Person."

particularly during the pre-school years. Three out of five of these families (60.5%) have more than two children, and almost four out of five of the children themselves (78.0%) are living in families that have three or more children. This, of course, includes the children of all ages, from pre-school to married siblings.

Children per family	Families Number	Families Per cent	Children Number	Children Per cent
One	37	9.8	37	3.1
Two	112	29.7	224	18.9
Three	97	25.7	291	24.6
Four	65	17.2	260	22.0
Five	40	10.6	200	16.9
Six	15	4.0	90	7.6
Seven	8	2.1	56	4.7
Eight	2	0.6	16	1.4
Ten	1	0.3	10	0.8
	377	100.0	1,184	100.0

The following table shows that these are largely young families, from which St. Luke's pupils come, in the sense that about four out of five (80.8%) of all the children are still of pre-highschool age. The largest number of these families were formed (83.4%), that is, the parents were married, less than twenty years ago, and 58.3 per cent of them were formed less than fifteen years ago. The following distribution of the total children shows the large concentration in the younger years.

Age-Category of children	Number	Per cent
Pre-school	266	22.5
Kindergarten	44	3.7
Elementary school	646	54.6
High school	121	10.2
Post high school	107	9.0
	1,184	100.0

The numbers of children of pre-school age and in the kindergarten indicate merely the numbers of younger siblings the pupils of St. Luke's have at home. This is no indication of the size of future first-grade registration at the school, because there are undoubtedly many "first children" of families in the parish who do not come into our statistics. Although there are forty-four children from these families in kindergarten, there were actually seventy-seven registered in April for next year's first grade at St. Luke's. The numbers of elementary school age do not correspond to St. Luke's school population of 632 pupils, because eleven of these children attend other parochial schools, and three attend a public elementary school.

St. Luke's pupils have 121 brothers and sisters of high school age, of whom sixty-four attend the Catholic high school, and the remaining fifty-seven attend public high schools. The presence of a high school student is an influence upon the younger children in the family, and some of St. Luke's pupils have spoken proudly of them in their autobiographies. There are also 107 "older" members of these families, eighteen of whom are in college while twenty-one are married. Occasionally a girl mentioned the fact that she was a "flower girl" at the wedding of her older brother or sister, and this was an outstanding event in her young life.

Only about three out of ten (29.7%) of the pupils at St. Luke's have no other member of the family present in the school. The following table shows that one-half of the families (50.1%) represented in this parochial school have two or more children there as pupils, and that the greatest proportion of pupils (60.2%) have a brother or sister in the school. This fact is an advantage not only for the children, but also for the teachers who can learn more, and exchange more information, about the family backgrounds of these children.

Children per family at St. Luke's	Families		Children	
	Number	Per cent	Number	Per cent
One	188	49.9	188	29.8
Two	136	36.1	272	43.0
Three	40	10.6	120	19.0
Four	13	3.4	52	8.2
	377	100.0	632	100.0

The early life and family experiences of these children vary somewhat according to the social class to which their parents belong. Certain observations are made by the children themselves concerning travel and vacations, the type of occupation of their father, the kinds of homes they lived in. These remarks in autobiographies do not indicate a consciousness of class status on the part of the child, but they allow the social analyst to make comparisons among the families. These comparisons were confirmed, for the most part, in the later collection of data concerning the criteria of class status among these families.[2]

[2] Class status of the family was based on a combination of six criteria: (a) education of father, (b) occupation of father, (c) birthplace of grandparents, (d)

Although the "leveling" effect of common school experiences is clearly indicated in the friendship tests in the three higher grades, and although class background appeared to have minimal effect upon the group activities of the pupils, the differentials still exist in family life. The following table shows the class distribution of the families of pupils attending St. Luke's.

Social class	Number	Per cent	
Upper-upper	23	6.1	18.9% Upper class
Lower-upper	48	12.8	
Upper-middle	100	26.5	46.1% Middle class
Lower-middle	74	19.6	
Upper-lower	98	26.0	35.0% Lower class
Lower-lower	34	9.0	

The manifestation of class among these children was hardly discernible, except at the extremes of the class range, during the school day.[3] Only a few exemplified the economic difference in their backgrounds, having obviously more expensive clothing.[4] But other factors tended to balance this off. An expensive bicycle, the amount of spending money, the possession of golf clubs, and other tangible items, could not be used as criteria to judge the class background of the child himself, because the decisions of the parents along these lines tended to defy clear-cut class expectations. The father of an upper-lower class family was sometimes more permissive in these items than the father of a higher social class.

Family Relations

By and large the pupils of St. Luke's school are fond of their parents, get along well with other members of the family and are fairly well-satisfied with conditions at home. We questioned them about many aspects of their family relations. Almost all of them answered affirmatively when asked whether the members of their family are "usually good to them." Only one boy in the sixth grade gave a negative answer

residential area, (e) condition of residence, (f) crowding of residence. See below, chap. 17, for background of all pupils.

[3] See Celia Burns Stendler, *Children of Brasstown* (Urbana: University of Illinois, 1949), for a study of the "awareness of the symbols of social class" among the children of an elementary school in a New England town. These children showed considerably more awareness of class than did St. Luke's children. (See pp. 92–95 of Stendler.)

[4] The artificial "consciousness of clothes," especially among the girls, was used as an argument in favor of school uniforms by a minority of mothers in the PTA. Their proposal was voted down by the parents.

to this question. Slightly more girls (7.7%) than boys (6.0%) feel that "no one at home loves them." More girls (11.0%) than boys (8.3%) feel that their folks "fuss at them instead of helping them," but more boys (9.5%) than girls (7.7%) think that their folks "boss them around too much." These statistics isolate the relatively small percentage of children who represent several aspects of social deviation; some have personality problems, others have not adjusted well to their home environment, and still others come from families experiencing internal difficulties.[5]

Although some of the children feel that their folks "boss" them or "fuss at" them too much, very few would be willing to exchange their parents for others. Only four per cent of them "often wish that they had some other parents," the girls being somewhat more dissatisfied (5.5%) with their parents than the boys (2.4%). The great majority (93.1%) "like both parents about the same," slightly more boys (94.0%) answering this question affirmatively than girls (92.3%). Obviously, these children think highly of their parents, and it is interesting to note how they think they are themselves esteemed by their parents. Exactly one-fifth of them answered negatively when we asked them "do your folks seem to think that you are doing well at school?" In this case the girls felt much more confidence in their parents' esteem than the boys, 91.2 per cent of them answering affirmatively as compared to only 67.9 per cent of the boys. This seems to be in accord with the generalization that parents "push" their sons more than their daughters to higher achievement.

The pride that a child feels in his home and family is indicated by his willingness to invite other children home. Only four per cent of St. Luke's pupils, more girls (6.6%) than boys (1.2%), "try to keep other children away from their homes because their homes are not as nice as the homes of the other children." This kind of attitude indicates whether they consider their home a "fit place" to which they would invite their friends. Whether their parents allow them to bring their friends home is another question, most of them (85.1%) feeling free to do so. Slightly more boys (86.9%) than girls (83.5%) said that they could "usually bring their friends home when they want to."

It is clear from these answers that most of the children are proud of their families and are at least not ashamed of the homes in which they live. Nevertheless, some of them appear to be ambitious and

[5] These questions were asked of the pupils in the three highest grades in both the parochial and the public schools, and the percentage results are approximately the same for both schools.

would like it if their family had a better residence, 58.9 per cent of them saying that they "would like to have things look better around the house." Interestingly enough, the boys were more conscious of the appearance of their homes than the girls, 61.9 per cent said they would like things looking better, as compared with fifty-six per cent of the girls.[6] While on the one hand this may indicate a certain amount of dissatisfaction with the material conditions of the residence, it is also in keeping with the cultural value of constant improvement and progress. Still, some of the children felt a kind of "pinch of poverty," 13.7 per cent of them saying that they "have a hard time because it seems that their folks hardly ever have enough money." Boys and girls are approximately the same in their answer to this question.[7]

More than one-quarter of St. Luke's pupils (26.9%) wish that their fathers had a better job. In this instance it appears that the boys are more ambitious for their father's occupational career than are the girls, 34.5 per cent of them desiring that their father get a better job, as compared with 19.8 per cent of the girls. An expected sidelight in this regard is that the older the child becomes the more likely is he to recognize and deprecate his father's occupational status. One-fifth of the sixth graders, one-fourth of the seventh graders, and thirty-five per cent of the eighth graders, answered this question in the affirmative. The general awareness of family status unquestionably increases as the child grows older.

The final question in this series concerning the family relations of the elementary school pupil was as follows: "Do you sometimes feel like running away from home?" The answers, as given in the following table, show some variations by age and type of school. This is a percentage distribution of those who answered affirmatively.

	St. Luke's	Taft School
Boys	23.8%	23.4%
Girls	23.1	34.8
Eighth grade	6.7	33.3
Seventh grade	27.5	27.1
Sixth grade	35.9	26.8
All	23.4	29.0

[6] The sex differential is even greater in the public school, 71.3 per cent of the boys saying they want things to look better around the house, as compared to 56.5 per cent of the girls.

[7] Twenty-four of the 175 pupils in the three upper grades feel that their families lack sufficient money. Thirteen of these are from lower class families, nine from the middle class, and two from the upper class.

While there is practically no sex differential among the parochial school children, the girls in the public school show considerably more discontent than the boys. More than one-third (34.8%) of the public school girls "sometimes feel like running away from home." This is in accord with the statistics of the city's juvenile aid bureau which reports annually more girl runaways than boys. The greatest contrast, however, is shown between the two schools in the grade comparison. St. Luke's pupils appear to have their greatest urge to run away from home in the sixth grade, and this decreases until in the eight grade when only 6.7 per cent have this desire. In the public school, the wish to run away from home is more evenly distributed among the three grades, but it gradually increases until the eighth grade when exactly one-third of the pupils express the desire. It is quite probable that satisfaction or dissatisfaction with school conditions also enters as a factor in these answers.

Mobility

One of the most striking features in the lives of these parochial school children is their residential mobility. Almost half of the children in the sixth, seventh and eighth grades have fathers who were in the armed services at the time the children were born. Many of them write in their autobiographies, "I did not see my father until I was two years old; and I didn't know him." One of them recalled that his father mistook a neighbor's child for his own son when he returned from the army. Sometimes mother and child travelled from one military base to another to be with the father before he went overseas. The children report in detail the places their father saw, the war experiences he had, and especially his branch of service and rank.

Military duty, however, was only one of the factors explaining the frequent moving of these children. Only twenty-six of the eighth-grade pupils had been born and baptized in St. Luke's parish. Eighteen had been born in other parishes of the state, and the remaining had been born in other states. One girl is a German-born refugee. Settling down after the war, finding larger quarters for a growing family, and occupational mobility on the part of the father, were further reasons for the fact that these children lived in different places. Obviously, the children in the higher grades have changed residence more than those in the lower grades.

Almost all of these children had been baptized before they were three weeks old. They related anecdotes about themselves which have become part of the family lore. The boy whose father is a mail carrier remarked that this time "my mother delivered the male." The usual number of mothers were disappointed because they expected a girl and the fathers because they expected a boy. Details are given concerning the weight at birth, the first tooth, the first time they walked, the first words they said.

Most of this, the children admit, is hearsay. One girl said that "I lived with my parents and little brother for quite a while before I realized I was a person. My brother and I were close pals and spent many happy hours together." Their own personal recollections appear to focus first on sickness, accidents and operations. They fell out of automobiles, gashed their heads on bicycle handles, stuck nails into various parts of their bodies. One girl playing with an Erector set even succeeded in getting a screw lodged in her nose and had to have it removed at the hospital. Almost every child recalls some kind of sickness during the pre-school period.

They speak about the birth of other children in the family and of the effect of this upon themselves. Several of them remembered that they were jealous of a new brother or sister, "because no one paid attention to me any more." Others boast about holding, feeding and taking care of the new infant. They recount their first trip on a train, usually to visit grandparents, and sometimes tell about vacation trips in the family automobile. They talk about their first neighborhood companions, the time they got lost, the games they played, the fights they had. In most cases there was also a birthday party or two which stands out in their memories. In spite of all this excitement, however, one girl remarked that "life was ordinary until I started kindergarten." Another girl stated that she spent her "whole childhood" on a farm, and then her family moved to the city so that she could attend school.[8]

The amount of mobility in the families of St. Luke's children is shown in the following table. Since the length of parents' marriage differs widely, these figures indicate the frequency of moves since the family was formed, and not since the particular school child was born. Only eleven of these families had never moved since the parents were married, fourteen of them had moved ten or more times. The following table shows the residential mobility of 374 families of St. Luke's pupils since the marriage of parents.[9]

[8] For reference to studies of early childhood see Karl C. Garrison, ed., *Growth and Development* (New York: Longmans, Green, 1952), chap. 12, Florence Heisler, "The Development of Social Behavior and Attitudes," pp. 306–338.

[9] On three of the interviews with St. Luke's families, this information was not provided.

Years married	Families Number	Per cent	Average moves per family	Average years between moves
Nine or less	77	20.6	2.65	3.04
10–14 yrs.	141	37.7	3.76	3.11
15–19 yrs.	94	25.1	3.18	5.16
20–24 yrs.	36	9.6	4.36	4.96
25 yrs. or more	26	7.0	4.11	6.84
	374	100.0	3.50	4.08

The people who have been married less than fifteen years, and who have the youngest children, move on an average of once every three years. They constitute more than half (58.3%) of all families of St. Luke's children. The following table shows the distribution of moves according to frequency.

Number of moves	Families Number	Per cent	Moves Number	Average
None	11	2.9	0	0.00
1–2	132	35.3	206	1.56
3–4	154	41.2	534	3.46
5–6	37	9.9	198	5.35
7–8	25	6.7	183	7.32
9 plus	15	4.0	188	12.53

This table shows the considerable range in residential mobility. One out of ten families (10.7%) has moved an uncommonly large number of times. More than three-quarters of them (76.5%), however, have moved between one and four times since the family was formed. In checking the school grades, we found no correlation between the amount of residential mobility and the achievement of the child in the school room.

Almost all of the St. Luke's pupils attended a public school kindergarten, with the exception of a few who moved in from other cities where parochial schools maintain kindergartens. About three out of ten (29.9%) of the pupils from the second to the eighth grades had attended another grade school before coming to St. Luke's, and less than half of these had been in the public grade school. The following table is not a record of total family mobility during the child's lifetime because it does not show the number of moves made within the parish boundaries while the child remained in the same school, nor does it show the number of different schools attended, some of the children having been at four different schools before coming to St. Luke's.[10]

Grade	Attended other schools	Other paro-chial schools	Public schools
Eighth	36.7%	21.7%	15.0%
Seventh	48.0	30.0	18.0
Sixth	44.6	27.7	16.9
Fifth	32.0	14.7	17.3
Fourth	30.5	14.7	15.8
Third	24.2	14.1	10.1
Second	10.9	4.0	6.9
Total	29.9	16.3	13.6

The Breaking-In Period

The transition from the home routine to the school routine takes place during the kindergarten and first grade.[11] This experience appears to be somewhat easier for those who have older brothers and sisters already going to school. "Before school time," said one boy, "I wanted to go to school as most kids do, but once you're in there's no getting out of it." This philosophical attitude of conformity is not gained by most children until they have been in school for at least two years. Since St. Luke's parish does not have a kindergarten, there is a kind of double transition that must take place for these children.

The first experience of shock and insecurity seems to come to the child when he must "break away" from the home, if only for a half-day, to attend kindergarten."I hated school that year," wrote one girl in her autobiography, "I would cry and make up excuses and not want to go." A boy remarked, "At first I was scared stiff. During that day almost everyone cried because it was the first time away from home." Similarly, a girl said, "I sure was scared. My mother took me the first day. When I saw all the different faces I started running home, but I didn't make it. She took me back." Another boy wrote, "I hated school and for the first few weeks I cried when my mother left me at the school."

[10] These statistics are taken from the permanent records of 545 pupils from the second to the eighth grades. They were recorded at the end of the school year and include those children who transferred to St. Luke's during the year.

[11] See Henry J. Otto, *Social Education in Elementary Schools* (New York: Rinehart, 1956), pp. 6–8, for a discussion of the social characteristics of the child entering school. For a foreign appraisal, see Geoffrey Gorer, *The American People* (New York: Norton, 1948).

The transition, at first very difficult, seemed to become easier as the weeks passed.[12] The friendliness and ability of the public school kindergarten teacher show through most of the remarks the children make. "My teacher taught me many nice things," says one girl. "We learned to play with other children, to draw with crayons and to sing songs together." The children themselves seemed to realize that this was not really school as they understood it, or as their older brothers and sisters had described school to them. "We didn't have much school; all we did was color, draw, play games, paint and learn to get along with other children." The practice of taking a nap in kindergarten every day struck some of the children as odd. "We had to bring a blanket or rug and sleep on the floor. I don't think anyone ever slept though. Everyone just laid there and whispered. " One boy said, "the thing I didn't like most about kindergarten was trying to take a nap on the hard wooden floor."

Gradually, under the ministrations and blandishments of the teacher, and despite dissatisfactions of various kinds, most of the children adjusted themselves well to the expectations of the kindergarten. One boy went so far as to say, "in kindergarten I learned more than I expected to." Another child liked the fact that the teacher used to read a lot to them from story books, "But what I liked the best was the band. I played the cymbals. We would march around the room and have a lot of fun." The father of this particular boy took the attitude that the kindergarten is not only a waste of time, but also gives the children an erroneous conception of school. "They get so used to the idea of playing and having fun that it takes two more years of school to convince them that school is a place where you study and learn."

In many instances the mother brings the child to kindergarten, but unknown terrors sometimes lurk for children who have to walk. One girl recounted the vivid memory that she was afraid of a neighbor's dog along the way to school. "I used to leave the house in the morning, go up a different street and then hide in garages until I saw the other children coming home from school." This went on for about three weeks until the teacher contacted the parents and asked about their daughter. Afterwards the girl's father brought her to school on his way to work. Other parents made better arrangements. "It was quite a long walk to kindergarten," wrote one boy. "The boy next door who was nine took me back and forth. He was paid thirty-five cents every Friday."

[12] See Ilse Forest, *Early Years at School* (New York: McGraw-Hill, 1949), chap. 4, "Establishing Routine in Early School Years."

Hardly any child enters the first grade at St. Luke's a complete stranger. Some of the other children in the classroom will have attended with him one of the three public school kindergartens within the boundaries of the parish. Some of these youngsters had already attended Sunday school and had learned something of the first-grade religion lessons. Others had previously been taken care of in the parochial nursery during the Sunday Mass, and when they were four or five years old had learned a few simple religious practices like making the Sign of the Cross and genuflecting. In our interviews with parents only nine per cent of them admitted that their child knew no prayers before entering the first grade. This appears to be a gross underestimation because the Sisters in the first grade tested the children on this point and found that 42.4 per cent could not make the Sign of the Cross and 48.4 per cent could not recite the Hail Mary.

At any rate, the transfer from the public school kindergarten to St. Luke's first grade does not carry with it all the difficulties of first entering school. The children find at least some friends in the class, and they have become somewhat accustomed to being away from home and mother for a period of time. "You have to remember that they are still practically babies," said Sister Mark. Nevertheless, they must begin to learn the processes of self-control and study. "That year we really learned something. We learned how to read, write, do arithmetic, draw and spell." The children practiced how to add and subtract, "and every Friday we worked with clay." "Sister helped me to pray, read, spell and add." "There were three groups of readers, those who were good, those who were bad, and those in the middle, like me." "Every day we had phonics. Sister had cards that had an animal on it which made the sound of the letter which the animal formed."

The fact that the first grade is a serious enterprise is impressed upon the child. Instead of a half-day of supervised play at the kindergarten he is expected to study and learn for five or six hours a day. "In the first grade I got a good look at what school was really like. It was not play but work. I also had to go a whole day." Another boy remarked that "when I started first grade I liked it very much, until some of my friends told me it was a waste of time." The first graders at St. Luke's are not expected to attend the daily Mass at eight o'clock, but many of the children come with their older brothers and sisters and are cared for by the teacher in the classroom and on the playground until the school day starts.

Since the first grader likes to play rather than study, the sucessful teacher tends to be an entertainer who changes study into play.

We have observed the manifold ingenuity of the first-grade teacher in this regard. She teaches them to count by bouncing a ball a certain number of times and then asking them the total. She has a large counting board with movable discs and lets one child after another manipulate it. The children sing out together the count to a hundred by ten's, and then by five's. Learning pronunciation is a game, the boys against the girls, with an elected scorekeeper at the blackboard. The upper and lower case letters are "mother" and "baby" letters. When flash cards are used the children get into the excitement, kneeling on their seats, standing by the desk, frantically waving hands in the air.

Numerous other techniques were employed for getting and holding the attention of these youngsters. They play a game called "fishing for words" wherein the teacher mentions a word on the page of the reader and the children look for it. Another game is "reading the wrong way," starting at the bottom right hand part of the page to discover whether children recognize words or have merely memorized the sentences. A general device is variation, so that the children are not kept at any particular thing for more than ten or fifteen minutes. The three groups of readers are taken in turns of ten minutes each at the teacher's desk while the others write in their workbooks. A favorite diversion is singing, and it appears that almost any lesson can be given in musical form.

The question of self-control and routine—to perform repeated behavior patterns in a fairly uniform way and at the same time—is a problem for both teachers and children. The six-year old has enjoyed a relatively carefree existence up to this point, and he must now learn to channel his spirit of fun and play into the regular recess periods. He must learn to walk in ranks, to hang his clothes in the closet, to keep silent during class. With some children there is still a problem of waiting to go to the rest room—even though the teacher allows them to do so without asking permission—and "accidents" are not uncommon in the first grade. In general it may be said that the routine he follows is more regular than that of his mother at home and possibly as well scheduled as that of his father in plant or office.

The first graders are the lowest rung in the lower half of the school. They play in the "little" schoolyard and only at periods when the first four grades have their recess. This protects them from the rougher play of the older boys. They tend to cling to the teacher and to form little groups around her at that time. The honor patrol girls of the eighth grade show a kind of maternal solicitude for the first graders. They look after them at the lunch period, in the corridors and after school. In a sense, these children get more attention and pampering at this time than in any later grade in their schooling.

The formation of expected behavior patterns in the first graders does not go on at an even pace. Most of the children learn to conform, some more quickly and easily than others.[13] But there is the little girl who is "an only child and spoiled," as the teacher says, and who chafes at the regularities and restraints of the schoolroom. There is the boy who is "over-bright," who learns words and gets answers twice as quickly as the others, reads ahead in the book, entertains the class with fictional narrative for ten minutes at a time. Another boy is mentally retarded, but very lively and mischievous.

In spite of these exceptions, the daily transformation of behavior in these children is almost tangible. The teacher uses many positive and religious sanctions. "If you are good today we'll read a nice new story." "The best boy and girl readers will get a prize, a little Christmas crib, on Friday." "Now write your best for the Blessed Mother." "The Baby Jesus will like you if you sit up straight." The behavioral difference in these children at the end of May, as compared to the previous September, is almost incredible. In the last months of the school year these youngsters conduct themselves quietly and attentively and in a manner that would not have seemed possible when they started in the first grade.

The Big Year

The second grade stands out in the memory of the upper graders who wrote autobiographies. They are then at the age of seven and receive the sacraments of Penance, Eucharist and Confirmation. "In the second grade Father Albert came every day and instructed us for our first Holy Communion. My first confession was very exciting. I think this was the most important year of my life—since I met the Bishop for the first time and was confirmed." A girl wrote, "that year I made my first Holy Communion. The night before I was so happy and excited I could not sleep, and was so tired in the morning. I will never forget that day."

The religious instructions take on a special significance because of this spiritual experience. The Pastor takes over the classes in the spring and tries to bring his explanations to the level of the second graders.

[13] See William E. Martin and Celia Stendler, *Child Development, The Process of Growing Up in Society* (New York: Harcourt, Brace, 1953), chap. 8, "Growing Up in Our Society," pp. 212–237.

In discussing the Last Supper he said, "the Apostles wanted to dig right in instead of waiting for the prayer." "Judas gave himself away; he goofed." "Jesus wasn't really mad at Judas; He still wanted to give him a chance." The regular teachers continue to have contests and games, for example, three boys and one girl won prizes of pious pictures for finding the largest number of titles for the Holy Spirit. The Sisters in the convent were judges for this contest.

The children receive special attention from teachers, priests and parents, a fact which impresses them with the significance of the sacraments. In April, a month before first Communion, Sister Vincent de Paul takes the boys, and Sister Bridget the girls, for "practice" daily in the church. They are arranged according to size, learn how to form the procession into and out of the church, go into the sanctuary six at a time, genuflect in unison, and approach the altar. The Pastor tries to take some of the tension out of this public reception of the sacraments by having the children go to confession several times in the preceding weeks,[14] and makes special arrangements for those who have been sick or absent.

The non-sacramental aspects of the first Communion day are also impressive in the minds of the children. All of the children in the school have individual pictures taken in early October,[15] but picture-taking, both professional and amateur, of the second graders at Communion time has become almost a form of "must-behavior." The party at home includes uncles, aunts, grandparents and other relatives, and the money gifts the child remembers range from twenty to seventy dollars. The youngsters, especially the girls, stay "dressed up" all day and remain the center of adult attention.

School work goes on progressively. "The second year was tougher than the first, and I figured it would be that way all through school." Another boy said "this year the homework began. Every night we had to at least take home one book." Still another boy who had transferred from the public school after the first grade complained that he had learned only to print. "I had a pretty hard time because I couldn't

[14] Going to confession becomes such a logical and obvious procedure for the parochial school child that he thinks everybody does it. One second grader was overheard in his backyard asking a neighbor boy, the son of a Christian Scientist, "did you make your first confession yet?"

[15] A professional photographer comes to the school to take these pictures; the teachers distribute them and collect the money for them, reminding the children that this is voluntary and "no one has to have a picture." The children want the pictures, but as in any other school practice, some of the parents think it is a waste of time and money.

write, and the teacher had to give me special attention." The children at St. Luke's begin cursive writing in the first grade. Their parents sometimes boast of this as an advantage over children in other schools who "can't even write in the second grade."

The development of memory, the recitation of poems, and learning about God, are combined in lines like the following which all the second graders learned:

"God made all things, great and small,
The fishes in the water and the little birds that call;
God made all the flowers, plants and trees.
God made the rain to help all these.
God thought of you and God thought of me,
When He thought of every bird, flower and tree."

The imagination of the children continues to be stimulated and directed by the teachers. It is a frequent practice to have the pupils "put things in their own words." When the reading lesson was on vacation time, each child was encouraged to volunteer an account of last summer's vacation. The recounting of such experiences often proved quite humorous to the class. The reading groups here are divided into boys and girls, the one reading aloud and individually, while the other writes what is being read, or writes spelling words. After five or six have read a sentence each the next child is asked to tell the others what was just read without looking at the book.

One of the spelling practices arouses interest and excitement among the children. A word in the lesson, like "bug" or "milk," or "girl," is selected to be pronounced, spelled and pronounced again, by the whole class ten times. They start each word normally, but the tempo and sound soon increase, so that on the tenth repetition the class sounds like a football cheering crowd. One of the arithmetic devices the children like most is the "family game;" in fact, they ask for it, and are allowed to have it for good behavior. A pupil stands before the room and says, "I belong to the nine family. There are three of us. What are our names?" He then calls on someone with his hand up and accepts answers like "one, one and seven," or "two, three and four." When a boy does this he invariably calls on boys to answer, and a girl always calls on girls. Telling the time of day and learning the sequence of numerals also call for demonstrations in which the pupils participate.

Songs, games and general recreation are still a part of the school life of the second graders. They appear to enjoy group singing more than any other indoor activity, and the songs they choose most frequently are: "O, Where Has My Little Dog Gone?" "Here Is Clumsy," "This Old Man," and "Dogs and Bears." Number combinations become a game, and the children answer quickly and easily such questions as "nine and two are?" and "four and eight are?" When they are given a combination like "nine, take away three, plus five," they find it harder and make more mistakes, but seem to have more fun. Like the other grades, the second grade has its own sports equipment, football and basketball for the boys, a volleyball for the girls.[16]

The patterns of conduct are expected to be better than those of the first grade, but they are in no way rigid. "The class is lively, and there is much turning around in their seats, looking out of the window and at others. Only on a couple of occasions did the Sister rebuke a child for squirming. She does try to make them keep their feet under the desks. The children laugh at others' mistakes, gasp and groan at the appropriate times and in general are not very subdued, but they do not get out of hand."[17] Children who misbehave may be penalized in several ways: standing in the corner, or in the aisle, sitting on the "little green chair," or being retained at recess. "Mary was moved to the front of the room because she was a bad girl," reported one little boy.

The second-grade children have been scolded for their misbehavior on the bus coming to school, for coming late to Mass, for talking and whispering in church. One boy and one girl are playfully named each afternoon as the "little rascals" for that day, a title that they do not seem to dislike. There are children who are less controllable than others. About one boy, the teacher said "I'd like to wring his neck," and about a girl, "she's a little minx; spoiled rotten at home; her books are all torn and marked up." There is also the girl with the "bright and shining personality," always ready and able to perform before the whole class.

An interesting aspect of the behavior of second graders is that there seems to be no sanction on so-called "cheating." When the class is given any kind of work to do, the ordinary pupil tends to turn around and look at the paper of the child in back of him, or of the child on either side of him. "This is normal curiosity," says the teacher. "They want to see how they are doing, how their answer compares with the others. We just try to get them gradually to pay attention only to their

[16] These are purchased new by the Athletic Committee, even though the coaches offered to distribute among the grades the used equipment of the varsity teams.

[17] From our observer's report for Thursday, February 21.

own work." [18] Other problems occur. The lower grades are on the first floor of the school, and during the recess of the upper grades at ten o'clock there is so much noise on the playground that the second graders must use this as a writing and study period. Their lunch period starts at eleven-twenty. The cafeteria tables are too high for them so that those who do not go home for lunch stay at their desks to eat, supervised by an eighth-grade girl who eats her own lunch at the teacher's desk.

The changed routine of the second grader, as compared to the first grader, is that he is now expected to attend daily Mass on alternate weeks, and most of them do so except in inclement weather or sickness. The two-A class attends one week, and the two-B the next week, except during Lent. Because of this added privilege they seem to feel a little more "grown-up," and they sometimes have difficulty convincing their parents that they really want to, or ought to, attend Mass. This switching from week to week, and the teacher's insistence that Mass attendance is voluntary, sometimes confuses the parents who "would like to know exactly what time the school day starts."

The Third Grade

As far as the school itself is concerned, the third grade appears to be a let-down to most of the children. In spite of the fact that this is the first time they have a lay teacher, they are very vague about school happenings. "In the third grade we had another teacher. I don't remember her name but I remember that she was nice to us." Several other children remarked, "I don't remember much about this grade." One girl wrote, "in the third grade we had a lay teacher. I don't remember very much about her. I don't remember anything I did in school that year." One boy did recall that the teacher "would give me special help because over at the public school they didn't teach righting or Arithmetic vere good there." Another child remarked that "school work was getting harder; we learned to multiply and divide and to spell bigger words."

One of the distinct differences for the pupils in the third grade is that this is the first time they have had a lay teacher since their kindergarten experiences. Since some of the parents would prefer that their children have Sisters, the Principal has allowed them no choice of

[18] See Sidonie M. Gruenberg, ed., *Our Children Today* (New York: Viking Press, 1952), chap. 10, Milton J. Senn, "Permissiveness in the Early Years," pp. 116–124.

classes in the third grade.[19] Both of the teachers are lay women and all of the children have this experience at the same time. It has been suggested that "if you have to have lay teachers this is the ideal grade for them," because the children have had such a thorough religious training in the second grade in preparation for first Communion.[20] The fact is, however, that these two lay teachers are no less spiritual in their talk and actions than are the Sisters. In some instances they appeared to be even more pious in a moralistic way than the nuns.

It is in the third grade that the children who have received Communion first begin to eat breakfast in the classroom. This continues on to the eighth grade, and it is done quietly and unobtrusively although the teacher sometimes reminds the children not to "dawdle." An average of about one-third of the children receive Communion on ordinary week days. The religious instructions become more interesting. "If there is an air show in town on Saturday when Father is hearing confessions, should you go to the air show or to confession? Can you go to Communion without going to confession?" The lines of authority are explained through the fourth commandment, from pupil to teacher to Principal to Pastor to Bishop to Pope to God. During Lent the children are told to "sacrifice" candy, save money, and buy their mother a corsage for Easter.

The teachers develop competition between boys and girls. Writing out the multiplication table, now called "number combinations," on the blackboard is a form of this, and sometimes the child simply adds to the previous sum, for example, instead of multiplying six times seven he adds seven to the total of five times seven. They compete also in reading, and in learning prefixes and suffixes.[21] The teachers tend to call on the children who do not raise their hands, and then use the hand-raisers as correctors of the others. This is not done consistently enough to form a pattern on which the children can depend.

[19] Mrs. Gordon, one of the sixth-grade teachers, was a last-minute replacement for a nun who had been assigned to St. Luke's school and then withdrawn to the mother house.

[20] A recent study showed that seventy-five per cent of the lay teachers in parochial schools are teaching classes below the fifth grade. See Edward Purcell, "The Present Status of the Lay Teacher in the Catholic Elementary Schools in Illinois" (Washington: Dissertation in the Catholic University Library, 1956).

[21] The use of competition among school children seems to have declined in favor among some educationists because universal schooling has focused attention on the less gifted pupils, who are supposedly "poor competitors." For a balanced view, see Lee J. Cronbach, *Educational Psychology* (New York: Harcourt, Brace, 1954), pp. 473–479.

The methods of controlling behavior and increasing industry also vary at this level. Children who fail in arithmetic must stay in at the morning recess and have a drill in the second-grade book. The brighter pupils are given the privilege of decorating the classroom; the poorer students are promised that they will be allowed to wash the blackboard whenever they get a hundred in spelling. "What can I do if I get a hundred?" asked one boy. He was told that he would be allowed to sweep the floor. "You see, I believe in bribes," said the teacher to our observer. A certain wry humor enters into this matter of conformity. The children were distracted by a cat that had jumped onto the windowsill, and the teacher said, "All right now, let's all look at the cat who is more interested in education than the rest of you."

Interesting little tricks are used as teaching devices although the "play" aspect used in the earlier grades is now beginning to turn into the competitive aspect. In explaining the pronunciation of words with double vowels, the teacher says, "when two vowels go walking the first does the talking." [22] A child was asked to give an example of an exclamatory sentence, and said, "O mother, the dog has his foot in the cake!" Charades and pantomiming are used to stimulate the children's imagination. Occasionally, on Wednesdays, as a reward to the class the teacher tells them "there will be no homework tonight, but watch Disneyland on TV and tell us about it tomorrow."

During the third and fourth grades the pupils gradually learn to associate better in groups.[23] Many of them still do not know the last names of their schoolmates, the two lay teachers calling them either "honey" or by their first names. The activities of the Cub Scouts keep some of the boys busy. "I received the bear and lion badges. Our den put on a little skit on the stage, the Hula Dance. You should have seen us in crepe paper grass skirts and bras. I had a time keeping mine up and doing the Hula too." Some of the girls had already started in the Blue Birds in the second grade. They put on a skit for their mothers on St. Valentine Day, depicting the life span of a woman, with the girls playing the successive roles of baby, school girl, mother, grandmother and angel. The children wore their uniforms to school for these after-school activities, many of which seemed to them to be an extension of the kindergarten and school play periods.

[22] On one occasion this teacher gave as a homework assignment the task of looking up fifty words of one syllable containing the vowels, "oa" like coat, boat, moat, and she was apparently unaware of the fact that the English language does not contain fifty words of this type.

[23] See Elizabeth B. Hurlock, *Child Development* (New York: McGraw-Hill, 1956), chap. 9, "Social Adjustments," pp. 294–320.

At the age of eight or nine the children are considered ready for camping in the summer time. Aside from those whose families can afford to keep a summer place, many of the others go to the Catholic summer camp run by the diocese, or to the Campfire or Scout camp. These vacations usually last about three weeks and are experiences which live in vivid detail in the youngster's mind. Some of the girls attend the "day camp" operated in the local public parks by the Camp Fire Girls, in which St. Luke's women leaders took regular supervisory roles. "The Blue Birds were a lot of fun," said one girl, "we used to color and draw and play games."

It appears also that around this age the children become conscious of the opposite sex in an antagonistic sort of way. One boy said that during the summer "we got up a baseball team but some were girls, and you know girls, it's got to be their way or they quit. And so we didn't have a team." Usually the boys stop completely playing any games with the girls and are fearful of being called "sissy." The teacher in the fourth grade took advantage of this feeling by using it as a threat to boys who misbehaved. "When Sister caught us talking she made us sit with a girl. We all hated that. Luckily I didn't get caught. I got to sit with a boy." The girls do not express the same kind of reluctance over this situation.[24]

The Fourth Grade

In the fourth grade St. Luke's pupils begin to take geography and history seriously.[25] They study about mountains, forests, rivers and deserts, and with the help of large roll maps are able to locate the principal countries and cities. In the history period the study of the Reformation brings a discussion on loyalty to the Holy Father, and the exploration era brings special emphasis on the role of Catholic explorers to the new world. Some of the reading periods bring together history, geography and religion, as the story of a pious girl in the midst of the trouble between Indians and French-Canadians. The children take "true-false" tests as well as "fill-in" tests.

At this level, and partly because of the over-crowded classes, the pupils correct one another's papers after tests in English and arithmetic; a perfect paper gets a score of VG, one with four or less mis-

[24] See Louis P. Thorpe, *Child Psychology and Development*, second edition (New York: Ronald Press, 1955), chap. 12, "Social Education of the Child," pp. 427–470.

[25] History and Citizenship were already studied in the third grade for eighty minutes a week, and are continued in the fourth grade, where geography is introduced for one hundred minutes a week.

takes gets G, with five or six errors an L, with seven or more a U.[26] The teacher notes these marks in her book, but also collects the test papers. If an assigned spelling word is missed, the pupil must write it fifteen times. The children learned to write paragraphs and to recognize "beginning," "middle" and "ending" sentences. They had to compose original four-line poems.[27] They studied the rules of the apostrophe, prepositions and sentence completion. The "spelldown" was a feature that the children enjoyed, but it never lasted more than ten minutes, and at the end there was always about one-third of the class still standing.

Initiative and imagination were encouraged in the fourth graders through brief, original skits, usually based on the reading lessons. A boy volunteers to dramatize Lord Baltimore, chooses his buddies to be in the play, and practices during recess. Every week one row of pupils staged a ten-minute TV Show, like the story of Attila, Julius Caesar, Pope Leo, Father Marquette. The boys and girls alternated between playing the roles in the show and announcing the "commercials" before, midway, and after the performance. During the religion period there is a daily brief report from one of the children on one of the principal holy days of the month, for example, in February they reported on Candlemas, the Apparition of Lourdes, St. Dorothy, St. Blaise, St. Valentine, and others.

The "football game" in arithmetic aroused the greatest competitive interest in the class. Each row was named after a prominent college team. There were two scorekeepers and two timekeepers. The "play" was a multiplication problem called out by the teacher. Every correct answer advanced the ball a yard. Every mistake was a "down" and after four downs the ball went over to the other team. A chart was kept on the blackboard during the fall months showing the "standing" of the teams. Another multiplication game pitted the boys against the girls.[28] The teacher held up a card with a problem on it; the pupil who missed the answer sat down; and the team with the largest number standing after ten minutes won the game. Arithmetic problems

[26] This marking system followed the new report cards, which the pupils began to understand even if the parents did not.

[27] For a sample of eighth graders' "poetry" in the *Book of Memories*, see below, chap. 10, "Boys and Girls Together."

[28] In a sense, this is both individual and group competition; some studies show that the former is a better incentive to learning than the latter. See William A. Kelly, *Educational Psychology* (Milwaukee: Bruce, 1956), pp. 292–294. For a series of discussions on "Arithmetic in the Primary Grades" by Sisters Mary Mark, M. Adelbert and Mary of the Angels, see *Bulletin* of the National Catholic Educational Association, vol. 46, no. 1 (August, 1949), pp. 451–454.

also involved long division, often done orally, "if a man bought $150 worth of bicycles for his five sons, how much did each bike cost?" They involved also percentages, "a house costs twelve thousand dollars to build; four per cent of this is profit; how much is the profit in dollars?"

The fourth grade is a kind of minor climax and transition point for the children. They are now at the "top" of the lower half of the school. They are the biggest children in the school yard during the recess periods reserved for the pupils from the first to the fourth grades. During late February and March they drop their marbles on the floor and have them confiscated for a day by the teacher.[29] During the basketball season, (February 11) Coach Bowman came in and announced basketball practice for fourth-grade boys, provided they had good grades, gym shoes and their parents' permission. Every day a different boy and a different girl are appointed to "prefect" the lavatory. "It makes them feel important," says the teacher. On a cloudy day a pupil may get up and turn on the lights without asking permission.

Among the children there was some disagreement in their opinions about the teachers. One girl remarked, "we never had much homework and would have big study periods, and for this reason I enjoyed the fourth grade very much." Another youngster felt quite the opposite and thought that the teacher was a "real disappointment. If you wanted a task she would gladly give you a wopper. She was the meanest Sister I ever saw. None of the boys in our grade got along with her." An outspoken boy told our observers that the teacher is "real nice when one of you guys are in the room." This difference of opinion is, however, a phenomenon of every class in the school, and it changes also within the year depending on the way the children react to the different actions of the teacher. By and large, however, most of the children demonstrate a high regard and affection for the teachers.

Outside Activities

The extracurricular interests of the pupils begin to take up more of their time in the fourth grade. This has been a gradual growth, however, from the first grade onward. In the fourth grade we find the largest percentage of any grade in the school taking various kinds of lessons outside the school. They are now nine or ten years old, and it seems that parents feel they are ready for music or other lessons, or

[29] Sister Vincent de Paul, of the second grade, played marbles most with the children, and she was called the "champ" by some of the fourth grade boys. For pupils' interpretation of the teacher's role see H. Otto Dahlke, *Values in Culture and Classroom* (New York: Harper, 1958), pp. 286–291.

at least, that the child be "tried out" at this time to discover any talent he may have. The autobiographies bear out this statement in a number of cases of children who told about taking lessons for a year and then giving up the effort.

One boy wrote that "when it was time for the fourth grade, mother decided it was time also for some social graces, so that I was enrolled in the local dancing group and began piano lessons. This was an all-time low for me. One year of music proved I wasn't a budding Liberace, so to my teacher's great relief, I was permitted to drop it. I am still burdened with dancing school, although I must say, the girls in the class are improving with age." As a result of such forlorn hopes, a variety of trumpets, violins, accordions and other instruments, is scattered about the homes of St. Luke's parishioners.

Music is taught as a school subject in all of the grades in the parochial school. This means mainly group singing in the lower grades, the first and second grades giving seventy-five minutes a week, and the third and fourth grades eighty minutes a week, to the actual teaching of music. While Sister Cecelia and Sister Ruth are the specialists in this field, all of the other teachers have a general competence in singing. The children themselves consider singing more a recreational than a curricular subject,[30] and they tend to look upon instrumental lessons as an extracurricular chore.[31]

The following table shows the percentage distribution of the various kinds of "outside" lessons taken by pupils from the third and fourth grades.

Type of lesson	96 Fourth graders	98 Third graders
Piano	21.9%	6.1%
Other music	7.3	2.0
Dance	15.6	7.1
Swim	43.7	3.1
Other	33.3	0.0

Only a negligible number of children in the first and second grades are taking any kind of lessons outside of school hours. Only four of

[30] For some comments on teachers' attitudes toward music, see Clifton A. Burmeister, "Music—A Fringe Activity?" *Educational Music Magazine,* vol. 33, no. 1 (September–October, 1953), pp. 8–9.

[31] The value of instrumental lessons was demonstrated through tests of fourth and fifth grade pupils by Carl B. Nelson, "The Contribution of Instrumental Instruction to General Musical Growth of All Elementary School Children," *Educational Music Magazine,* vol. 35, no. 2 (November–December, 1955), pp. 49–52.

them are practicing the piano and eleven go to dancing school. The numbers taking lessons increase in the third grade and reach their peak in the fourth grade. There are four times as many girls as boys taking piano lessons in these two grades. The most popular musical instrument, aside from the piano, is the accordion. There are twenty-one girls and only one boy in these two grades who are taking dancing lessons. Among the "other" lessons are archery, horseback riding, embroidery, French and golf.

It seems that the parents provide more parties for the children of the fourth grade than they do for those in the lower grades.[32] Forty of the ninety-six fourth-grade pupils had parties during the year to which some of their classmates were invited. Fourteen of these were attended by boys only, twenty-one by girls only, and the remaining five were mixed. In the third grade seventeen children had parties for their classmates, of which seven were attended by both boys and girls. Among the second graders there were twelve parties, four of which were mixed. This record does not include the parties to which only relatives or neighbors were invited, but it would seem that these were of relatively the same type, and that they increased in number from the first to the fourth grade.

The most interesting and time-consuming extracurricular activity for the girls from the second to the fourth grade was the program of the Blue Birds. Almost every girl who had been at St. Luke's for these grades made some reference to this group. "I became a Camp Fire Girl at the 'fly-up' ceremony of the Blue Birds at the end of the fourth grade, because that means that we fly up to a higher grade." Their weekly meetings and their well-supervised program attracted 68.7 per cent of the eligible girls in these lower grades. Cub Scouting also proved to be a drawing card for almost two out of five (38.1%) of the eligible boys in these grades. For various reasons, the boys did not participate so well as the girls in these youth movements, and their interest seemed to wane much more quickly in the later grades of the elementary school.[33]

One of the most enjoyable experiences of the third- and fourth-grade

[32] Some of the parents referred to the series of articles in *Life* magazine, describing children's parties given under the suggestions of Dr. Frances Ilg. "Celebrating the Birthday of a Four-Year Old," vol. 40, no. 6 (February 6, 1956), pp. 112–118; "The Festive Exuberance of Six-Year Olds," vol. 40, no. 10 (March 5, 1956), pp. 176–182; "Energetic Nine-Year Olds," vol. 40, no. 19 (May 7, 1956), pp. 186–192; "Helping Boys and Girls at Twelve Whoop It Up Together," vol. 40, no. 24 (June 11, 1956), pp. 168–174.

[33] For a discussion of this point, see below, chap. 7, "Youth Movements."

pupils was the train excursion to the metropolis on Sunday, April 28. Sixty-nine pupils from these grades, accompanied by Sisters Roberta, Bridget, Vincent de Paul, Martha, Ruth, Mark and Mrs. Edwards, went to the ten-thirty Mass in the big city, had a chicken dinner at a large hotel, attended a children's performance of "Sleeping Beauty," had a box lunch on the return train trip, and arrived home at eight-ten in the evening. The cost of this excursion was eight dollars to each child, and the children who experienced it "talked about nothing else for a week before and a week after it." [34] Each of the teachers had to guard ten children on the trip, and the Principal was proud that the manager of the hotel dining room and the manager of the theater said "these are the best-behaved children we've ever had here." [35]

Generalizations

1. The typical pupil of St. Luke's comes from a large, young family, averaging 3.14 children per family. More than one-quarter (26.2%) of their youngest brothers and sisters are still less than six years of age, and not yet in grade school. Six out of ten of St. Luke's pupils have one or more brothers and sisters going to the same grade school. Their family background is mainly that of middle-class urban Americans, and the class distinctions, measureable outside the school, do not appear as important factors in the school life of these children. It appears that these elementary school children are not of an age when economic and ethnic distinctions are meaningful to them.

2. The great majority of St. Luke's pupils get along well with their parents and family, but more than half of them would like their homes to look better, and more than one-quarter would like their father to have a better job. These answers indicate that the typical aspirations of the urban American drift down and take hold even among some of these pre-adolescents. The childish desire to "get away from it all" and to run away from home gradually lessens from the sixth to the eighth grade at St. Luke's, but reaches its peak among the public school eighth graders, especially the girls.

3. The families of St. Luke's pupils reflect the pattern of urban residential mobility. Three out of ten of the children from the second to the eighth grade have attended elementary schools other than St. Luke's. The average family has moved once every four years, and has

[34] Most of them clipped and saved the news photo of themselves on the train that appeared the following week in the diocesan newspaper.

[35] The manager of the theater later remarked, "we tell that to the teachers whenever we honestly can. They like to hear it."

made an average of 3.5 changes of residence since its formation. These families range from one pole, the eleven that never moved, to the other pole, the fifteen that moved nine or more times. The younger families, those in which the parents have been married less than fifteen years, and which supply 58.3 per cent of the pupils, have moved more often, about every three years.

4. The transition from home life to school life is eased for the parochial pupils by the fact that they go through the recreational experiences of the public school kindergarten. The half-day of play becomes the full day of school work, in which the study material is often presented in play form. The first grade teacher is an entertainer trying to keep the attention of her pupils by numerous ingenious teaching devices and by frequent variations of the subject matter. The transformation of behavior during this year is remarkable, so that the child in May is practically "school-broken."

5. In the second grade the child reaches the "age of reason," about seven years of age, when he is trained and expected to recognize the difference between right and wrong, and to accept the responsibility for his conduct. This important period of life is accentuated by the religious rites in which he participates, the reception of the three sacraments of Penance, Eucharist and Confirmation. During this year the child enjoys the concentrated attention of adults, parents, priests and teachers. The school day is shot through with the significance of this religious event, and the climax comes at the public ceremony of First Communion Day.

6. The third grade brings an increasing conformity in the children's behavior. They are expected to attend daily Mass promptly and regularly, and those who receive Holy Communion eat breakfast in the schoolroom during the religion lesson. There is also a gradual development of competition as an incentive to attention and industry, and the competitive aspect tends to replace during this year the "play" aspect which had prevailed in schoolwork of the first and second grades. Although the children have lay teachers in this grade for the first time at St. Luke's school, the experiences of the third grade do not stand out in the memory of the older children. This may be a "let-down" from the excitement of the First Communion year.

7. The educational horizons of the fourth-grade pupil begin to widen as he learns the lessons of history and geography, and he begins to see connections between his school work and the events portrayed on TV programs. He gets more opportunities to express himself, to give oral reports in class, and to participate in original skits built around the school lessons. Group competition becomes exciting,

sometimes the "teams" represent the rows of desks, and sometimes the boys and girls compete as groups.

8. By the time the child reaches the age of nine or ten he appears to be quite conscious of his status among his peers. This is most clearly demonstrated in classroom activities when a child can make a choice. The girl always chooses a girl, and the boy always chooses a boy, in working on a project, forming a committee, in eliciting responses in an arithmetic, reading, spelling or other contest. The fourth grader is also the biggest child at recess time, on the corridors and in the cafeteria, because the children of the first four grades are together at these times and places.

9. It is at this age also that the child is given an opportunity to test and to display his talent in music, dancing and other "outside" lessons. Extracurricular and group activities are made more available at this time. These children attend more parties than they did in the earlier grades, and the parents seem to understand that there is more enjoyment at an all-boy, or an all-girl, party than at one which both boys and girls attend. Although the boys are not yet ready for even the school's "scrub" teams, they begin to organize their own informal games. The girls concentrate most of their extracurricular group activities in the Blue Birds from which they graduate to the Camp Fire Girls at the end of the fourth grade.

Chapter

THREE

THE UPSTAIRS CLASSES

UNTIL THE new Catholic high school was built at the northwest edge of the city, the second floor of St. Luke's parochial school was used for this purpose. The eight rooms on the first floor had then contained all eight grades of the elementary school. This lower floor now has two classes of each of the first four grades, so that "moving upstairs" to the fifth grade is more than a symbolic advancement in the school child's life. Instead of having clothes closets in the back of the room "like the little kids," the pupils in the upper classes have lockers in the corridor "just like high school."

The renovation of the second floor of St. Luke's has gone on gradually room by room as the elementary school expanded. The fifth grade has taken two classrooms, as has the sixth grade. The crowded seventh and eighth grades still had one classroom apiece, but this is being changed. The former high school science laboratory was changed into a music room and is now being altered further to become another classroom. The former library will probably be subdivided next year to accommodate two classes. Up until the year of our study the upper grade girls had to go downstairs to the lavatory, but during the summer months the former football equipment room was converted into a girls' lavatory on the second floor. All other lavatories were torn out and replaced. Further expansion was anticipated during the summer when the Sisters' convent was moved to the southeast corner of the church property, and two bedrooms were added. The convent can now accommodate fourteen Sisters.

Fifth Graders

Going into the fifth grade means more than moving to a classroom on the second floor. The recess periods are now different, the upper grades going out together after the lower grades have returned to their rooms. Being on the second floor cuts down the noise and disturbance coming from the younger children on the playground. The report cards are distributed every six weeks, instead of every nine weeks as they are in the lower grades. In a sense, however, the fifth graders are again at a starting point. They are the smallest and youngest children in the upper grades, and they begin to anticipate the privileges and activities of the older children.

For the boys the big opportunity is the chance to learn the Mass prayers and to "try out" for regular positions as acolytes. It is an impressive experience that involves other members of the family. "The first time I served I was so nervous I was pacing the floor in the sacristy. My Mom was just about as nervous. She said she didn't even get one Hail Mary said the first time I served." Another boy remarked that "serving Mass for the first time was almost as big a thing as my first Holy Communion." Another said, "I won a couple of medals for serving at Mass." When Dorothy Noto saw her brother serving at the altar for the first time she too wanted to become an acolyte, so she wrote to Pope Pius XII asking why girls are not allowed to serve at Mass. Her letter was answered through the Apostolic Delegate's office in Washington, imparting His Holiness' blessing to her and her dear ones, and advising the girl to get the answer to her question from the parish priest.

In the fifth grade the religion period in the morning takes on some variation in that Father Martin gives the instructions for a half hour on Friday mornings, from nine to nine-thirty in class Five-A, and from nine-thirty to ten in Class Five-B. He spent most of the year illustrating the Christian virtues. In the discussion on the virtue of patience the children were asked to show how they could in their own daily lives imitate the patience of Christ. The virtue of forgiveness was exemplified from the words of the Lord's prayer. The positive aspects of the Christian pattern of living were stressed throughout these instructions, but the children were also reminded that the slightest venial sin committed against God is a worse evil than all the wars of the world.

It is an interesting fact that the children themselves seem to think negatively along the lines of religion and virtue. When they were asked, "what can you do to pay honor to Christ?" the best they could suggest were a series of "don'ts." "Don't quarrel at home," "Don't talk in church." "Don't cheat, steal, swear, curse, etc." All of the teachers stressed the positive during Lent, indicating actions that could be taken to please God, but the children themselves continued to think in terms of negative sacrifices, means of self-control and minor deprivations. This facet appears to be inherent in the modern urban cultural interpretation of Christianity.

During the rest of the week the Sisters continue to teach the religion period. Since the pupils are beginning to use missals at the daily Mass, more attention is paid to the study of the Mass. Outlines are placed on the blackboard; the children are asked frequently to identify the "kind" of Mass celebrated that morning. The feast of the Annunciation was given special attention, the teacher pointing out that there would have been no Incarnation, no Christmas, no Easter, if it had not been for this feast. The Bible story was read about the woman who prayed day and night in the temple; one boy volunteered the opinion that "she was crazy," while a girl insisted that "she was very holy." The children were asked what the candle symbolizes. One boy answered that "the candle reminds you of fire, and fire reminds you of ashes, and ashes remind you that we are dust of the earth."

In a discussion about Jesus one girl asked whether Christ was a Jew. Then a boy said he has a friend who was a "born Jew" and also had a Christmas tree in his house. The word "gentile" was mentioned for explanation, and a boy said that "a gentile is a fallen-away Jew." Another said "gentiles are just ordinary people." The reading lessons continued to be in large part centered around pious themes and events. Even in the history period, when the revolution was being discussed, the teacher pointed out that Benedict Arnold's disloyalty to his country was like "our disloyalty to God when we commit sins."

Various projects are devised as means to increase the children's interest in school matters. A bulletin board is maintained and the children are encouraged to bring clippings of newspaper articles and pictures highlighting current news. Various displays are made or gathered by the pupils, most of them emphasizing the children's interest in Indian and western lore—arrowheads, a canvas gold-dust bag, rocks from the Yosemite valley, and many similar items. In the fifth grade there are also miniature altars, chalices and ecclesiastical vestments, made by the pupils. An extra feature is the daily ten minutes of Latin Study, confined mainly to the memorization and interpretation of Mass prayers, the *Confiteor,* the *Gloria,* the *Credo* and other prayers. Even the first graders had learned the Latin hymn, *Adeste Fideles.* The fifth graders were taught the Sign of the Cross in Latin, and told to surprise their parents at the meal prayer by reciting it.[1]

The geography lessons in the fifth grade seemed to be confined mainly to the United States. The discussion of the New England States and their capitols brought the remark that farming is difficult in that

[1] Part of the test for the Cub Scouts earning the St. George medal was the translation of Latin phrases used in the Mass.

area. One boy rose to observe that "I was there last summer and the crops looked pretty good." The Middle Atlantic States were reported on by one girl and many questions were raised about her report. The children were constantly asking questions in geography. "Why is Australia a continent and not just a large island?" "Why is Greenland a part of North America?"

In January, the inauguration of the president aroused considerable interest. The boys were appointed to "look up" George Washington's cabinet and describe its members. The girls did the same for Eisenhower's cabinet. A girl reminded the class that she had seen some of the cabinet members on TV. Reports were given in class on the main political parties, contemporary and historical. The name of Alexander Hamilton elicited the information that he had been born in the West Indies, and his birthplace was found on the map by the third child who looked for it. The discussion of the military draft brought out the fact that "the man on TV said Elvis Presley was to be drafted."

Competition of various kinds continues in the fifth grade. Every child has an "assignment book" in which homework and assigned studies must be promptly noted. Each must also have a book mark, usually a pious picture, so that the place is not lost in the text. Various "teams," usually representing the rows of desks, compete in arithmetic, reading and spelling. Here the football team gets a touchdown when the "player" can do six successive oral problems correctly. In the reading lesson a week-long "elimination tournament" was held, the row or team surviving at the end of the week was the champion and was allowed to keep the "adoption certificates" for pagan babies that had been gained by the class in February. Another incentive was a competition between boys and girls in reading. Only the boys were told to prepare one day, and only girls the next. The group that did best did not have to prepare or recite for the third day. Thus, those who read most poorly had to prepare two out of three days, while the others prepared only one out of three days.[2]

Two different "public records" of achievement were kept in the fifth grade. The first was a large drawing of a mountain headed by the slogan "scale the heights!" Each child was represented by a flag

[2] This appears to be an example of "forced learning" in the concepts of William C. Morse and G. Max Wingo, *Psychology and Teaching* (New York: Scott, Foresman, 1955), p. 226. This is a "traditional" practice, and therefore seems to be "bad." Yet the teachers at St. Luke's also do all the things (pp. 228–231) that the authors consider "good." See also William A. Kelly, *Educational Psychology* (Milwaukee: Bruce, 1956), "Competition is an effective type of incentive with school children for stimulating achievement" (p. 294).

carrying his name, that was moved up or down the mountain according to the way in which each child completed the week's assignment. In the second part of the year this was replaced with a list of military ranks, from private to four-star general. Advance in rank came with the completion of a week's assignment. There were also demerits, as well as special awards, like the medal of honor, the distinguished service corps, and others.[3]

In the arithmetic periods the children continued multiplication and long division, fractions and percentages, but also studied the formulae for rectangles, squares, perimeters and areas. No new forms of discipline appeared. The recess periods were fifteen minutes later than they had been in the first four grades, and the children misbehaving were sometimes detained at recess, or not permitted to take the class football, basketball or volleyball to the playground. The most popular kind of school work was the singing period at the end of the day, and the teacher sometimes threatened that they would have to do arithmetic instead of music if they misbehaved.

Sports and the Sacristan

Sports begin to loom large in the sixth grade.[4] A girl remarked, "I learned to play baseball, basketball and badminton, and I learned how to ice-skate." The girls begin to practice volleyball under the tutelage of Ethel Karst, the best player in the eighth grade, who had passed the age limit for the regular team. "We have volleyball on Wednesday, Thursday and Friday, and I wish we could have it every day." In the fifth grade most of the children had already learned the "school yells" used at the various inter-school games. Now, two girls in the sixth grade are elected as fledgling cheer leaders.

The girls, however, do not get nearly so much attention in athletics as do the boys. The coaches look for prospective athletes among them, and even among the fifth- and fourth-grade boys, and attempt to develop a "feeder system" preparing them for the varsity team. Occasionally a boy from the sixth grade is allowed to "dress" for the varsity, but most of the time is devoted to practice and "scrub" operations.

[3] Sister Digna, "Motivation in Guiding the Child," *Education,* vol. 74, no. 3 (November, 1953), pp. 138–142, thinks that such public charts tend "to further flatter the bright child and to add more humiliation to the child with less ability," (p. 140) and that the teacher should try to "personalize" the education of each child.

[4] See Henry J. Otto, *Social Education in Elementary Schools* (New York: Rinehart, 1956), pp. 8–12, for a description of the social characteristics of the sixth grade child.

The coaches give the boys simple instructions concerning basic formations and plays, and now and then arrange a game with the "B" team of neighboring parochial and public schools.

The Sister Sacristan, who is a favorite with the boys because she trains the altar boys, is also a favorite with the girls because she gives them the privilege of helping in the church work. The girls even washed the church windows once a year (a job some of the parents thought should have been done by the janitor). "Sister Justin was very nice," wrote one girl, "it was great fun because the girls that worked in the sacristy got to put up the Crib for Christmas. I loved that part most because I knew that I was doing it for Jesus." Another said, "I had the privilege of working in the sacristy. On week days during lunch period I swept the sanctuary and helped in cleaning the candles. On Fridays I helped clean the holy water fonts." Still another remarked that "every Saturday I would come in the morning after Mass and clean the church with Sister Justin and Sister Dominic."

Sister Justin shares the teaching function in the sixth grade with Mrs. Gordon, who came to the school shortly after the beginning of the school year in September. They both teach religion, but on one day a week, on Thursdays, Father Martin takes over the religious instructions for a half hour. Likewise on Thursday, once a month before the first Friday, going to confession is substituted for the religion class. This is another example of "learning by doing" in which religious practice is closely integrated with religious teaching. Those children, usually five or six, who do not go to confession on that day remain in the class room and are "on their honor" to study quietly until the others come back.

Both of these teachers are also socially oriented in their class discussions and presentations. They weave the social teachings of Christianity into the various subjects.[5] In religion class a discussion on Catholic Action developed the theme of relations between the clergy and the laity, the structure of church groups, the meaning of the Christian Family Movement. In geography, a lesson on France introduced the name of Leo Harmel, the industrialist, who applied Christian so-

[5] This is a progressive and deliberately planned aspect of the elementary school curriculum and is demonstrated in the sixth-grade textbooks. The *Catholic Geography Series* is represented in this grade in the text by Frederick K. Branom and Juliana Bedier, *Neighbors in Eurasia* (New York: Sadlier, 1950), which stresses people more than places. In the reading period the *Faith and Freedom Series* text is by Sister Thomas Aquinas and Mary Synon, *This is Our Heritage* (New York: Ginn, 1943). This is more informational than literary and about three-quarters of the selections are written by the editors.

cial principles to the factory system. This was extended to an explanation of labor unions, and even the persecution of religion in France in the early part of this century. A lesson on China involved questions of famine, crop-rotation, irrigation, the work of the missionaries, the current changes made by the Communists.

The sixth graders appear to have reached a stage of intellectual growth when they are able to grasp the applications of school subjects to their everyday life and to the events of the contemporary world.[6] In the lesson on "How People Live and Work in Poland," there evolved a discussion of the "iron curtain," the recent uprisings in Poland and Hungary, refugees and immigration laws, Communists and satellite countries, the ancient religious faith of the Polish people, the destruction of Warsaw, the importance of appreciating music and musicians like Chopin and Paderewski. In relation to Russia, the teacher says, "Never condemn a whole nation, because there are some good and some bad in every people."

The interests of the teacher range over all the experiences of the children. After a big athletic contest she asks them the score of the game, which player made the most points, are they going to beat the next team they play.[7] The pupils are urged to watch the TV news shows and to make use of the public library. The sufferings of Christ lead to a serious and matter-of-fact discussion of death, burial and funerals, of the people they have known who have died. There is no glossing over the facts of life and death, no attempt to sentimentalize them, or to underemphasize them. But there are humorous moments too, as when a child stated that "priests and sisters receive Holy Orders," she was corrected with the remark that "the only holy orders received by Sisters come from their Mother Superior."

The arithmetic problems become more difficult, dealing with fractions and decimals. "Do the homework yourself," says the teacher, "because your parents have been away from decimals for quite a while." The children study like and unlike fractions, proper and mixed fractions; they convert fractions for addition, subtraction and division. The construction of a family budget absorbed the interest of the pupils, and lead to some sage remarks about a "hand to mouth" existence, about

[6] The children themselves made two contour maps which hang in the sixth-grade classroom, one of Italy and one of South America. Those were typical "group projects" and the pupils brought in small bits of cotton, iron, coal, balsa and other items to attach to the map at appropriate places.

[7] When the team wins a game the children are certain to phone or call at the convent to tell the Sisters about it. When no word comes through to the Sisters after a game they know that the team has lost.

"living from payday to payday," and even about the contribution of a fair share of income for church expenses, and about the various major items that the Pastor must worry about on the parochial budget.[8]

Looking to the future appears to be a feature also of other subjects of teaching. The conjugation of English verbs is important now because "this is the kind of thing you'll have to know when you study a foreign language later on." The children should learn to take notes now because "you'll have to do a lot of that in college." Impromptu speaking before a mock microphone was especially delightful to the children, and one little girl was told that she would have to "do that often in future years when you are president of the PTA." This public speaking exercise followed the eight rules of good speaking from the *Voyages in English*, and gave the children an opportunity to talk about favorite topics, history, spelling, turtles, kites, model ships, and even about the observers on this research study.[9]

Performing before the class seems to delight the sixth graders even more than the pupils of the lower grades. On many occasions the child is permitted to "have the floor" without interruption from the other children. One device of this kind was to have the children read a whole section in history, and have each child decide privately what the three most important questions were on the matter. They take turns standing in front of the room and acting as the teacher, asking the question and then deciding which one of the raised hands should be recognized. When the three questions have been answered the child appoints the next one (usually his or her best friend) to ask three questions.[10] They enjoy also the competitive spelling bee between the girls and the boys. One from each team goes to the blackboard. A word is called out alternately from the girls, then from the boys, and the child writing the word first and correctly on the board scores a point. Then another couple goes to the board until all have participated.

The sixth graders study Latin for about ten minutes every day, continuing the practice of the previous year, and preparing them for the

[8] The textbook used by the class, N. J. Lennes, Don C. Rogers and L. R. Traver, *Learning Arithmetic*, 6 (New York: Laidlaw Brothers, 1947), is the only one that is not part of a "Catholic Series."

[9] In a subtle way the teachers led the children onto this latter topic by asking them whether they have had visitors recently at Camp Fire or Scout meetings, music class, athletic contests and other events. Paul E. Campbell and Mary D. MacNickle, *Voyages in English* (Chicago: Loyola University Press, 1951) is a popular English textbook series used in grades third to eighth.

[10] The selections corresponded almost invariably with the friendship pairs and cliques as worked out by our sociometric tests. This was a further device for confirming our findings in this regard. See below, chap. 9, "Cliques and Clubs."

liturgical and choral participation of the seventh grade. Immediately after lunch on Mondays and Tuesdays, the two sixth-grade classes combine to practice singing under the direction of Sister Cecelia. Sometimes this lesson was held in the church, but more often in the music room. The best singers in the class were allowed to join the regular seventh-grade choir at Christmas time and then continue to sing in the parish church during the rest of the year.

The behavior of the children is kept fairly well under control but the usual penalty, the written task, is still handed out. "Careless now, careless later on," intones the teacher as she tells a child to write a misspelled word ten times. The teacher frequently calls the individual pupil "dear" and the whole class "you people." The children still compete for the privilege of doing manual tasks for the teacher. On one occasion there was almost a fist fight among some boys who wanted to be allowed to wash the windows during the noon period. The teacher commented privately about two of these boys who "are constant itches." These are also the boys who helped form the bicycle club which caused their parents some concern toward the end of the school year.[11]

"I am now a pre-teen," said one girl, "very interested in records, dancing and true friends." The interest in true friends revolved mainly around Camp Fire activities for the girls, but some of them took time out to appraise the boys in the seventh and eighth grades. In their autobiographies they mentioned parties more often than the boys did, but they were usually roller-skating and ice-skating parties. Several of the boys "discovered girls for the first time," as one of the teachers remarked, but for the most part the boys were interested in athletics and other all-male activities. They were still hardly conscious of their clothes, the boys wearing dungarees and the girls sweaters and skirts.

The Musical Year

The seventh grade is a large undivided group of fifty pupils. As we have seen, all the grades below this are split into two classes. Here all of the children come under the influence of the same teacher, Sister Cecelia, who is also the key person in the musical and entertainment programs of St. Luke's. Her influence extends over the girls from the sixth to the eighth grades. Some of the girls in the seventh grade have already come to know her because of the previous year's preliminary training for the choir.[12] As one of them wrote, "we sang our first Mass in

[11] See below, chap. 10, "Boys and Girls Together."

[12] See Paul Hume, "Music in School," *The Catholic Choirmaster*, vol. 43, no. 1 (Spring, 1957), pp. 8–11, 35. Sister Cecelia appears to be one of those nuns, who, according to the author, "are quite capable of cleaning up the Church-music situation in short order."

Advent to get practice for Christmas. During the summer we sang on weekdays and certain feasts." The nucleus of the choir, however, was the seventh grade, in which both the boys and the girls sing. In the eighth grade only girls survive, mainly because of the boys' changing voices.

Sister Cecelia's first love is music, and it is in this subject that she is undoubtedly at her best. Immediately after lunch for a half-hour on Mondays and Tuesdays she teaches music to the combined sixth-grade classes, while the sixth-grade teachers take turns at supervising the seventh-grade classroom. She takes her class over to the church to sing funeral Masses whenever a parishioner is buried on a school day. This experience substitutes for the religion class and, like the monthly confession, is another example of the integration of religious learning and religious practice.[18] On one occasion, Easter Monday morning, she brought her class to the church while she played the organ for a wedding (at which the children did not sing.) There is a small adult choir that sings the Sunday high Mass, but for all other functions Sister Cecelia's seventh grade continued to perform as the parish choir.

It has become almost a tradition at St. Luke's that the seventh grade form the nucleus of any entertainment that represents the school. The teacher plans these programs, like the presentation of songs at the PTA meeting on Tuesday, December 18; and she writes, directs, originates the choreography, and practices the participants, for the annual entertainment on the Pastor's feast day. In March and April the children practice during the lunch hour, sometimes give up their afternoon recess for rehearsals, and come for two hours on Saturday mornings, in preparation for this event. From the autobiographies of the eighth graders we could almost reconstruct the entire cast of characters, and most of the action of the operetta, "Snow White," in which they had participated in the previous year.

While the athletic teams receive an increasing amount of attention, and a few of the seventh graders "make" the varsity teams in football, basketball, baseball and volleyball, and while the Camp Fire group holds the attention of most of the girls, the undoubted highlight of the year is the operetta for the Pastor's feast day. This program was called "Melody Lane to the Land of Happiness" and it was a vehicle for the talent of both the teacher and the pupils. It is a joke around the school

[18] This occurred on twenty-four school days during the year, the first on Tuesday, September 18, and the last on Friday, June 7, when the final report cards were distributed. Sister's remark that "it seems as though twice as many people died this year as last year," is corroborated by the funeral records kept in the parish rectory.

that Father Albert has a "moveable" feast day in the sense that he fixes it on the date when Sister Cecelia thinks she will have the children ready to perform. After more than two months of practice and rehearsal the performance was set for the children on Friday afternoon, May 10, and on Sunday afternoon, May 12, for parents and other adults.

The entertainment is described as "a melodic excursion to the most interesting and thrilling land of happiness. It is a smile-provoking hour of song, dancing and frolic, put on to commemorate Father Albert's feast day and the twenty-four years that he has spent among us in hard toil." The play was in three scenes, opening as a school room in which Alice Pitre of the eighth grade is the singing teacher. The seven children in her class are music pupils from the third, fourth and fifth grades of St. Luke's. Teacher and pupils, after singing several appropriate numbers, are put to sleep with magic stardust and whisked off to the land of happiness by three singing fairies.

The second scene is the heart of the play and it gives everyone in the seventh grade a chance to perform. Most of the girls went through several dance routines; the boys appeared as clowns in typical circus formations; and the remaining girls formed "the happy brigade." This group demonstrated the theme of the play through poems and song, showing how to be happy in four simple rules: do what you must, develop the group spirit, be a steady worker, and keep smiling. The third scene was mainly a tableau, in which Emily Orsley represented a statue-still Blessed Mother on a pedestal, while Milton Tomich, the only boy with a "real part" in the play, gave a short speech in honor of the Pastor. The whole cast then sang a concluding hymn honoring Mary. The accompanists for this whole performance were three eighth-grade girls, Kathleen Duvic, Carol McEvoy and Myra Hojas.

As is almost inevitable in this kind of production there were certain disappointments among the children.[14] Since the main solos were sung by an eighth-grade girl, the girls in this class thought that the solo dances should also be done by one of their classmates; but Millie McEvoy of the seventh grade was chosen for this lead. The fact that only one boy, Milton Tomich, was chosen for a leading role, appeared to cause no friction or disappointment among the other boys. Some of the parents thought, however, that this production did not give

[14] The desire to "perform" is strong in all of the elementary school children, especially among the girls. One of the girls who danced in this program, wrote regretfully in her autobiography earlier in the year that "in my seven years of school I have been in only one play, and that was in the first grade."

sufficient opportunity for the demonstration of talent by their sons. In general, however, parents and teachers were delighted with the performance, which must be objectively judged as excellent for children at this age level. The final tableau was held on the stage while Father Albert responded to the congratulations of the children, and this made it necessary for the "statue" of the Blessed Mother to relax her pose.

The seventh grade is an efficiently operated and well-organized class, but it appears to be slightly off-normal in several ways. It is unbalanced in the proportion of only nineteen boys to thirty-one girls. In all of the tests we gave to the four upper grades the seventh grade did more poorly than the sixth or the eighth.[15] The average IQ was also lower in this grade than in the others. Aside from these items, however, the children appeared to act as normally as those in other grades, their achievement grades and their average conduct grades were, on the whole, fairly good. The teacher remarked wryly that she has had better classes in the past.

The religious instructions are taken over once a week, on Tuesday morning, by Father Martin. The text used in the regular religion period by Sister Cecelia, is called *Living for Triumph*, and the children seem to find an especial interest in it. For the first time these pupils are also taking a formal course in Church history, for which they frequently prepare two-minute oral reports on various aspects of the Church. The reports on the temporal power of the papacy, and on the extent of the papal domains, brought out the stark facts concerning the selfishness of clergy and nobility. The pupils seemed undisturbed by these facts, and accepted Sister's explanation that human failures do not destroy the divine truths of the Church. One girl asked what to do, however, in the event that a non-Catholic teacher in high school uses this information to make attacks against the Church.

In the study of English the pupils learned the use of irregular verbs, prepositions and adverbs, and the diagramming of sentences. They were expected to recognize and explain proper and common nouns and were given examples like the following: "Father William Corby gave general absolution on the battlefield at Gettysburg." They get more practice in forming paragraphs and writing short compositions of about one hundred words. Every month a kind of contest is held in composition, the children reading their productions before the class, who vote to decide the best one. Sister Cecelia is quite democratic

[15] Strangely enough, the seventh grade in the public school exhibited this same phenomenon, doing poorly on all the tests we administered.

in her classroom procedures, but she does not use this expression of popularity as the index for the marks she gives for compositions.

The geography period makes more use of maps and globes and more references to the current mass media of communication than the earlier grades. The study of Africa was highlighted by a discussion on Egypt and the Suez crisis, what Edward R. Murrow had to say about this on his TV show, "See It Now," what President Eisenhower's stand was on the problem. The arithmetic periods went into such practical questions as the opening of savings and checking accounts, the writing of checks, the balancing of business books, and to some of the more general aspects of accounting. Contests are enjoyed by the pupils, who are divided usually into three teams, all of them having both boys and girls. Problems on rates of interest and exchange value of money are called out by the teacher, and the three team representatives at the blackboard work them out as rapidly as possible. The winner makes a point for his team, and the three at the board are replaced by team mates until all have participated.

The ingenuity of Sister Cecelia and the competence of the pupils were demonstrated on one of the last days of the school year (Monday, June 3.) [16] Each girl had written a composition on religion, demonstrating what she had learned in the seventh grade. Three girls, Dotty McWellan, Marie Goheen and Maureen O'Dea, were elected as judges, who chose the ten best compositions, then ran a panel discussion before the whole class. In the afternoon the seventh grade went to the auditorium to present a "witch trial." The girls who played the parts of defendant, Joan Forshag, prosecuting attorney, Dorothy Noto, and defendant's attorney, Helen Black, had been elected by the class and had spent the week-end "reading up" on witch trials. Sister Cecelia had appointed four witnesses for and four against the defendant. Twelve girls had been elected as jurors, but since one was absent from school, Sister Roberta took her place on the jury. The children of the fourth, fifth and sixth grades formed the audience. The witch was found guilty and sentenced to wash the blackboards every day for the rest of the week.

The last week of the school year is an enjoyable one for the pupils of the seventh grade. They are now in a position to appreciate the "top spot" in the school because all of the eighth graders had departed.

[16] These programs had been planned for the following Thursday, when the Altar Boys went on a picnic; but since the public school had a holiday on June 6, St. Luke's followed suit, and the program was advanced. The eighth graders had already graduated.

All of the little jobs that had been performed by the top class were now done by the seventh graders in anticipation of the following September when they would rightfully "inherit" them. Sister Roberta, whose charges have now gone out "into the world," visits all of the classrooms, puts the records in order for the following year. For the first and only time during the year she is able to act as a full-time Principal.

No disciplinary problems of moment developed during the year in the seventh grade. The teacher was stern in a flexible manner, and could enjoy an incongruous situation even when she was involved in it. This was the case when one of the boys was unable to unroll the wall map, and Sister jerked the map sharply only to have it come off the wall on top of her. She joined in the laughter of the children. If a pupil missed an answer in prepared home study he had to stand while five or six others gave their answers. The child who forgot a book or an assignment had to write his name on the blackboard. "That's to remind me," says the teacher, "to give you some extra work."

The teacher seemed almost uncanny in her ability to detect and to prevent "foolish" questions. Like the children in the lower grades, the seventh graders delighted in expressing themselves, in "showing off." Often a question by the child was designed to seek a clue to the answer of a problem rather than to get information necessary to understand the problem. Whenever possible, the teacher left decisions to the children. For example a chairman was elected to head a decoration committee for the classroom, and ten of her friends volunteered as members. The teacher allowed them to decide what to do and how to do it, but she scolded them earnestly when they failed to carry out their own decisions. An occasional prodding of this kind kept the room fairly well decorated with seasonal posters and drawings, although the clash of colors, particularly on the shrine of the Blessed Mother, did not bespeak artistic virtuosity.[17]

The boy-girl interest increases only slightly in the seventh grade, and mainly on the part of the girls. While "pairing off" is discouraged by the teachers and by most of the parents, there are some instances of boys and girls walking home from school together. By this time all of the girls know how to dance, but they tend to dance with one another

[17] Although art is a curricular subject at St. Luke's, given sixty minutes a week from the third to the eighth grade, only a handful of pupils show proficiency in it. For the concept of a good program of art education, see Beatrice Hurley, *Curriculum for Elementary School Children* (New York: Ronald Press, 1957), chap. 13, "Adventures in Arts and Crafts," pp. 323–354; also William B. Ragan, *Modern Elementary Curriculum* (New York: Dryden Press, 1953), p. 455.

at their parties, to which boys are seldom invited. Ice-skating on Saturday afternoons provides an opportunity for boys and girls to play games together, but even in these instances it is group activity, with the girls tending to mingle more with the boys from the eighth grade and from the freshman high school class.

The Big Shots

The eighth grade appears to be the most enjoyable year for both boys and girls at St. Luke's school. "This is my big year," wrote one boy, "the tops in school, the year everybody is waiting for." The boys and girls of the honor patrol, chosen because of leadership qualities and academic achievement, feel very important in the performance of their duties. The girls operate a kind of snack bar at recess, supervise the younger children at lunch time in the classrooms, the cafeteria and on the corridors. The boys take turns selling milk to the children after Mass, and bring small cartons of milk around to the classrooms just before the noon period at eleven-twenty. These and other chores are sought after by the eighth graders, who demonstrate their sense of responsibility in performing them.

Their teacher is the Principal, Sister Roberta, the key figure in the school, and the most popular nun among both pupils and parents. "She is also a very fine teacher," said one girl, "and quite a riot. I've learned more this year than in my whole school life. She drills and drills and if anyone doesn't get it, it sure isn't her fault. She's just knocking herself out to try and teach us to be intelligent young ladies and gentlemen." One of the boys remarked that "because it is our last year at St. Luke's we try to give example to the younger children." [18] Another remarked, "Sister is very rough at times, but I think that with the kids in my class it is sometimes necessary." Another had expected life to be easier in the eighth grade. "We thought our chances of getting called on were pretty slim, there being sixty in our class, but Sister gets around the room faster than Bannister broke the four-minute mile."

As in most of the other grades, the ordinary school day starts with the religion period. Father Martin takes the class for an hour on Monday mornings. Both he and Sister Roberta make wide use of the Bible so that the pupils can quote verbatim and apply many scriptural verses. By this time they are also expected to have memorized perfectly

[18] This was emphasized by the Pastor in his exhortation to the eighth grade on Tuesday, October 16, when he distributed the first report cards of the year. He stressed their responsibilities as eighth graders "because the young ones look up to you and need your good example." During the previous week the teacher warned them to "do well because the report cards are coming out soon."

the ten commandments and the six precepts of the Church. There is a constant endeavor to "make religion practical." The children volunteer to do classroom skits on the various sacraments, on the Mass, and other Catholic ceremonies. Each day a child gives an oral report on the saint of the day and recites the oration from that day's Mass.

Religious and virtuous practices are discussed and encouraged.[19] In October the teacher asked every other day, "how many of you have persuaded your family to say the Rosary together?" The largest number to respond were thirty-three, although the rest kept promising to try. When they discussed purity, the teacher suggested that they add a "Hail Mary" to their night prayers to safeguard this virtue. In the study of the sacrament of marriage the pupils were assigned the task of writing out the ideal qualities of a mate: the boys to describe the perfect husband, and the girls the perfect wife.

One of the apparent drawbacks of the dual role of principal-teacher is turned to advantage by Sister Roberta. On the door of the eighth-grade classroom there is a notice to the effect that no salesman or business representative will be seen by the Principal during school hours. This rule is enforced, but there are numerous other occasions when Sister Roberta is called to the door, and even from the room. The children are trained to convert this time immediately into a study period and they always have standard assignments ready to be worked on. These absences from the room provide the ordinary study time for the pupils; the teacher checks up rigidly on their work; and this is the main reason why she claims that "they never really have to do any homework."

It did not take the eighth graders long to realize that Sister Roberta is serious about their studying during these periods. In the second week of school in September she detained three boys at recess to write a one hundred word essay entitled "What I Was Doing When I Should Have Been Studying." The result was carefully checked and every misspelled word had to be written correctly twenty-five times on the back of the page. Word of this kind of penalty got around the room quickly. "If they open their mouths," said Sister to one of our observers, "they have to write five hundred words." A mistake made in an arithmetic study period has to be written correctly on the blackboard ten times. The athletes have to have a minimum grade of seventy in their quizzes; otherwise they are suspended from the team for a week.

[19] For a series of discussions on religion in the seventh and eighth grades, see Cornelius Sherlock, John J. Maher and John C. Ryan, "Religion for Practical Living," *Bulletin* of the National Catholic Educational Association, vol. 46, no. 1 (August, 1949), pp. 406–413.

The eighth graders, in general, are the most alert and responsive pupils in St. Luke's school. No time is lost in the conduct of the lessons so that even the laggard is caught up in its tempo. Questions are "shot" at the class and the pupils are kept busy. "Sister is cheerful, lively, humorous, and has the class in the palm of her hand." The children like to work in small groups of their own choosing. For example, in the arithmetic period the class is divided into groups of four, three of them at the black board and the rest at their desks, working together on problems of square root. In the English period they work together composing sentences with abstract nouns as the subject, and become quite expert at diagramming sentences.

During the last two months of the school year the eighth grade made frequent delighted use of the recording machine won in the magazine subscription drive. This was used for reading and recitation, and occasionally for the spelling period. The children enjoyed the playback of their own voices and that of the teacher, and as a result made serious efforts to make correct statements, to improve their diction and to "sound better." Sister Roberta can bring the class to quiet with a brief, stern rebuke, but a joke is heartily enjoyed by all. "Sister asked Patty McDonnell for an example of a neuter noun, and the girl replied 'boys.' Everyone laughed including the teacher, who remarked 'you don't know much about boys if that's what you think.' She alluded to this several times later on, linking it with the failure of the boys to answer correctly, and in this way shifting the allusion to their ignorance." [20]

The eighth graders have all the coveted "jobs" around the school. Every morning at quarter of ten two girls quietly leave the room to attend the snack bar for the morning recess. At eleven o'clock four boys leave for the cafeteria to pick up the milk to be delivered to the various classrooms for the lunch period. All the pupils in the eighth grade take weekly "turns" in performing these functions, and the most disliked penalty in the school is to be denied this privilege. As in the other grades, the children also take turns at the various other chores, like emptying the pencil sharpeners, putting out chalk and erasers, bringing the waste paper basket around the room, adjusting the shades and windows, taking care of the bulletin board, decorating the room, and many others.[21]

Except for the annual program done by the seventh grade for the

[20] From the report on classroom observation for Thursday, April 23.

[21] There appear to be conflicting opinions among Catholic educators concerning the advisability of pupils performing these chores. See Thomas F. McNally, "The Pastor and the School," *Bulletin* of the National Catholic Educational Association, vol. 46, no. 1 (August, 1949), pp. 458–461.

Pastor's feast day, the members of the eighth grade have the most opportunities to perform before the public. The athletes attract special attention, even to the point of having write-ups in the daily paper following their games. They were given public recognition at the football banquet in early December, and at another banquet honoring basketball and volleyball players in the month of May. The principal cheerleaders for the athletic events were elected from the eighth-grade girls. There was no graduation tea dance, as in previous years, but the PTA sponsored a picnic for them, and the Award Night gave ample recognition to everyone in the class. After this excitement, the actual graduation ceremony was a relatively quiet and unostentatious affair at the eight o'clock Mass on the first Sunday in June.

One boy summed up his life with the statement that "these thirteen years of my life have been fun and excitement, and I hope the next thirteen years will be as good." A girl graduate who had spent most of her years in a public school said "I think that a Catholic school is the most wonderful school a person would ever want to go to. The kids who have gone to a Catholic school for eight years do not know how fortunate they are." In the *Yearbook of Memories* we read the following testament: "We, the graduating class of St. Luke's School, will to our benefactor, Sister Roberta, for her true blue faith in this crop of adolescents, a well-deserved vacation and a bottle of Vitamin B-12 to rebuild all the energy she burned up in her efforts to teach this group of pumpkin heads."

Book Reading

As the parochial school pupil grows older his interests expand beyond the activities of the classroom. We have seen this in the analysis of the youth movements and of the organized sports programs,[22] but there are also other areas in which they exhibit interest. These children have learned certain skills, their curiosity has been aroused, they have been encouraged by the teachers to expand their field of knowledge and experience. We have interviewed them concerning their reading habits, the parties they attend, and the kinds of "lessons" they take outside the schoolroom.

The pattern evolved along these lines is one of unevenness. All through the elementary school grades, and in every grade, there is a range from the bright alert pupil to the slow unimaginative child. Some read aloud haltingly even in the eighth grade; others read well but do not always comprehend what they read; still others "devour" books

[22] See below, chaps. 7 and 8.

from the public library. We questioned 164 children from the sixth to the eighth grades, and found that one-third of them had not drawn out or read one book from the public library during the seven months from the beginning of September to the beginning of April.[23] The following table shows this distribution.

Number of books read	Pupils		Average number read per child	
None	55	33.6%	0.0	
1–5	40	24.4	3.4	(137)
6–10	22	13.4	8.6	(190)
11–15	12	7.3	13.1	(158)
16–20	13	7.9	18.8	(245)
21 or more	22	13.4	41.8	(921)
	164	100.0	10.1	(1,651)

Given the cultural patterns of the American urban society, one would expect that girls read more than boys, and this is clearly demonstrated in the eighth and sixth grades of St. Luke's school. The above table shows that 13.4 percent of the children read well over half of all the books read by these pupils during the seven-month period, and all of these "heavy readers" (each reading about six books a month) were girls. Those who read the most are the eighth-grade girls; those who read the least are the eighth-grade boys. The seventh-grade boys, however, read on an average more than the seventh-grade girls and almost as much as the sixth-grade girls. The following table shows the sex and grade distribution of the average number of books read.[24]

School grade	78 Boys	86 Girls	164 Both
Eighth	6.5	19.3	12.5
Seventh	10.4	7.6	8.5
Sixth	7.3	10.6	8.9
	7.7	12.2	10.1

[23] Justinian Hoegerl, "Comparative Study of Leisure Time Reading by Sixth, Seventh and Eighth Grade Pupils" (Washington: Dissertation in Catholic University Library, 1956), showed that the reading habits of these children hardly differed from those reported on in several studies of the 1920–30 decade.

[24] In a reading experiment with 364 pupils from grades four through eight, each grade had access to the same set of 171 books for a period of three weeks. The mean number of books read decreased from 8.98 in the fourth grade to 1.52 in the eighth grade. See Inez L. Mauck and Esther J. Swenson, "A Study of Children's Recreational Reading," *Elementary School Journal,* vol. 50, no. 3 (November, 1949), pp. 144–150.

Since we have excluded here the reference books to which a pupil is sent for particular school assignments, we are dealing with a voluntary area where the child has relative freedom to make choices. Most of the reference books needed, like Compton's Encyclopedia, are in the classrooms of these three grades. The former high school library on the second floor of St. Luke's is used mainly as a storeroom for textbooks, and as a workshop for various extracurricular activities. For example, it was used as "headquarters" for the magazine subscription drive and for the rag drive. It contains no books that are available for loan to the school children. If the pupil wants to borrow a non-textbook he goes to the public library, and four out of five of the children (79.9%) have heeded the teachers' urging that they get a public library card. As we have seen from the above statistics, not all of these children made use of their library cards during the first seven months of the school year.

The type of book selected by the upper-graders of St. Luke's helps to indicate where their main interests lie, and also whether the central objectives of the parochial school act to arouse those interests. In general, the most popular books are sports stories, Westerns and mysteries. Books on hobbies and on special interests are also frequently mentioned. Better-known works like *Little Women, Heidi, Adventures of Alice, The Man Without A Country,* Irving's *Sketch Book* and Hans Christian Andersen's *Fairy Tales,* were read only by girls. A certain degree of sophistication is shown by two of the eighth-grade girls who mentioned as their favorite books Herman Wouk's *Marjorie Morningstar,* and Kathryn Hulme's *The Nun's Story.* These two girls are also among those who read more than twenty books during the seven month period.

Very few of the children mentioned any book that might be included in a list of so-called "Catholic literature." The exceptions are Father Rigney's *Four Years in a Red Hell,* and Father George's *God's Underground,* both of which were read by several eighth graders. Since there is no formal guidance program in reading and no formal tie-up between St. Luke's school and the Catholic Library Association,[25] the children are "on their own" in the selection of books. It is quite

[25] February is "Catholic Press Month" and it is noted in the diocesan weekly newspaper. The magazine subscription drive held in St. Luke's school made reference to Catholic literature, but there was no mention made of the National Children's Book Week, which was during the last week of November. See "Book Week Suggestions," *The Wilson Library Bulletin,* vol. 31, no. 2 (October, 1956), pp. 187–190.

likely that their selections are influenced by what their friends are reading, by the remarks made by parents at home, and by the general cultural trends, rather than by the parochial school itself. While we made no detailed inquiry of the reading habits of parents, we were frequently and regretfully told by them, especially by the husbands, that "we just don't have time to read."

A certain amount of encouragement for reading comes from the three professional librarians at the Branch Public Library two blocks down Main street from St. Luke's school. They serve the whole neighborhood, which includes two public schools as well as St. Luke's. The local library contains many volumes especially purchased for Catholic patrons and numerous reference works for the school children, like the lives of saints, the book of Catholic authors, the book on Catholic converts, the Catholic Encyclopedia and others. The children's choice of non-reference books is influenced by the displays arranged in this library and also by the librarian's suggestions.[26]

During the month of May a representative of the public library comes to all of the elementary schools, public and parochial, to explain the summer reading program for the children. Any child who reads twenty books during the summer has his name placed on the honor roll displayed in the library, and receives a small certificate attesting to this achievement. In September some of the teachers ask the children to bring these certificates to school at a kind of "show and tell" exercise. During the year of our study St. Luke's did not take advantage of the service of the public library through which it is possible to have from one to three hundred books sent to the school for a period of six weeks. These books are arranged around any type or subject that the teacher wants for her pupils and they are delivered and collected without charge to the school.

It is an interesting fact that the frequency and type of outside voluntary reading done by these children has little connection with their achievement marks or their intelligence quotients. Some of the brightest children, as measured by these two norms, did not read one book in seven months. Several others among them read only the reference

[26] It is recommended that elementary schools with two hundred or more students should have a school library. "When the school board shirks this responsibility, the public library performs a social, cultural and educational service of a very high order by giving partial or complete library service to the elementary schools." Frances Henne and Frances Spain, "The School and The Public Library," *Annals of the American Academy of Political and Social Science,* vol. 302 (November, 1955), pp. 52–59.

works that had been assigned by the teacher. On the other hand, the girl with the lowest IQ in the eighth grade read fifteen books, and the girl with the second lowest read twenty-eight books, during this period.

Parties and Lessons

Another activity in which these pupils from the upper classes participate is that of home parties. We have seen that this giving of parties for classmates gradually increased in the lower grades until in the fourth grade 41.7 per cent of the children had home parties. From the fifth to the eighth grades, however, there is no regular pattern of increase or decrease. In these four grades sixty-nine children (27.5%) gave parties to which their classmates were invited. These do not represent sixty-nine different families; for example, the Noto, Pattison, Lanius, Glass and O'Toole families, each gave two parties for their children in different school grades.

School grade	Number of pupils in grade	Number of parties attended by: Boys only	Girls only	Boys and girls
Eighth	60	2	6	3
Seventh	52	1	14	0
Sixth	65	10	8	4
Fifth	74	9	11	1
	251	22	39	8

The above table does not represent the total amount of party-going or giving by the pupils in these grades. We are speaking here only of parties held in the home of a pupil to which all or some of the classmates were invited. This gives us a further picture of the friendship cliques among the pupils, because in almost every instance the parties involved the closer friends and reciprocal social relations. In no case did the whole class attend a party, even in the three mixed parties in the eighth grade where Sister Roberta insisted, and the parents agreed, that the whole class should be invited. The seventh grade represents a peculiar pattern in that there were no mixed parties and only one party given by a boy for his male classmates. The girls in this class, however, appear to have an appreciation for recreational gatherings among themselves. Fourteen of them gave parties, and in almost every instance the girl giving the party was a member of the Camp Fire group. The boys in the sixth grade are the most "party wise" of the upper grade boys and they also have several close-knit friendship groups.

The sixth graders at St. Luke's school appear to like parties more than do the pupils in the seventh and eighth grades. When we asked the children in these three grades, "Would you rather stay away from most parties?" 22.6 per cent of the boys, and 8.8. per cent of the girls answered affirmatively. This sex differential is to be expected since there are evidences of it in many places in our study. Among the sixth graders, however, only 6.2 per cent answered affirmatively, as compared to 17.6 per cent of the seventh graders, and 23.3 per cent of the eighth graders. Quite aside from the desire to attend parties, the frequency of actually attending them is highest in the eighth grade, 88.3 per cent in this class saying that they do go to parties, as compared to 80.4 per cent of the seventh, and 81.2 per cent of the sixth-grade pupils. It appears that parental prohibitions may act as a deterrent among the younger children.

There is a similar difference of attitudes and performance in the question of dancing. Fewer boys (58.3%) than girls (83.5%) in these three upper grades say that they like to go to dances; and still fewer boys (36.9%) than girls (50.5%) say that they actually do go to dances. The general caution concerning mixed parties and dances voiced by the teachers at St. Luke's, and often confirmed by the parents, appears to inhibit the school children in these activities. While 56.7 per cent of the eighth graders say that they attend dances, this percentage drops to 35.3 per cent in the seventh grade, and to 39.1 per cent in the sixth grade.

There were also certain variations in the "content" of parties; what the children did to amuse themselves. Eating was the universal pattern at all of them; dancing was a feature of the all-girl parties as well as at the mixed parties. The girls also played recordings more at their parties than did the boys. The mixed parties of the sixth graders included two "kissing games," called post office and spin-the-bottle. These "childish" games apparently had no interest for the boys and girls in the eighth grade, or their absence may be explained by the fact that Sister Roberta quizzed the pupils in class the day after a mixed party.

These children's parties which classmates attended do not give the total picture of party-going among the pupils of the four upper grades of St. Luke's. The information concerning these parties was relatively easy to obtain, because so many of the children participated in them and could therefore corroborate each other's statements. In attempting to obtain further information, however, concerning all of the parties attended we had to question every child. The following table includes, therefore, children's parties given or attended by neighbors and relatives at the age level of the children themselves. It does not include family gatherings, parents' birthdays, picnics, Elks' Christmas parties and similar affairs.

Number of parties	111 Boys		110 Girls		221 Both	
	Per cent	Ave.	Per cent	Ave.	Per cent	Ave.
None	21.6	0.00	7.3	0.00	14.5	0.00
1–2	42.4	1.48	22.7	1.56	32.6	1.51
3–4	24.3	3.40	23.6	3.38	24.0	3.39
5–6	9.9	5.27	20.9	5.52	15.4	5.44
7 or more	1.8	9.50	25.5	8.14	13.5	8.23
	100.0	2.15	100.0	4.38	100.0	3.26

The difference between boys and girls in their party going is immediately apparent in the above table, about one out of five (21.6%) of the boys attending no parties at all, and one out of four (25.5%) of the girls attending seven or more parties. As a matter of fact, the girls average about twice as many (4.38 per girl) parties as the boys (2.15 per boy). These statistics represent the parties the children attended over an eighth-month period, from the beginning of school to the beginning of May and they show that the children averaged a little more than three (3.26) parties per child.

Another of the extra-curricular activities attracting the attention of some of the upper graders is the taking of music lessons.[27] Sisters Cecelia and Ruth teach both piano and voice, giving weekly piano lessons to thirty-two elementary pupils and six high school students, and weekly voice lessons to five of St. Luke's girls and one high school girl. At the beginning of the school year Sister Cecelia wanted to form a music club with an elected president, regular monthly business meetings and recitals. This plan did not eventuate because Sister did not have the time to devote to its organization, but she did manage to have four informal "sessions" in October, November, January and February. A formal recital was held on the afternoon of Palm Sunday before an audience of the Pastor, the faculty, and ninety-two lay adults of the parish.

The informal sessions were held in the music room after school hours and lasted from three-thirty to four-thirty. After an introduction by Sister Cecelia each child announced his or her own piece and then

[27] The "extracurricular" aspect of music is deplored, and there are many reasons why music "is often pushed to the periphery of school experiences and has remained an isolated subject matter area." See Neal E. Glenn, "Music and The Classroom Teacher," *Educational Music Magazine*, vol. 33, no. 4 (March–April, 1954), pp. 20–21, 54–56; see also Sister Mary Olive, "Music in a Unified Curriculum," *Musart*, vol. 7, no. 3 (January, 1955), pp. 4, 40–41.

played or sang it. There were also two short oral reports on the life and work of noted composers. The "stars" on these occasions were always drawn from the high school music students, who had the feature spots at the end of the program. These older children acted as an example and inspiration for the younger pupils. From twelve to fifteen of the children were able to perform on these occasions, and Sister's decision to put them on the program depended upon her satisfaction with the pupil's practice and advancement since the last meeting of the group.

At the public recital on Palm Sunday Carol McEvoy acted as Mistress of Ceremonies, giving a brief explanatory talk and then introducing the pupils in three separate groups. The first group was made up of the beginners who had started lessons during the past two years. They consisted of four boys and three girls playing piano solos, and two piano duets by girls. The second group started with a vocal duet by two sixth-grade girls, followed by piano solos by six girls and two boys and a piano duet by two girls. The third and most competent group included a boy-girl vocal duet, five piano solos by eighth-grade girls, four piano selections by high school students. The finale was the girls' quartette singing the "Hail Mary" while Emily Orsler posed on a pedestal as the Blessed Virgin.[28]

The account of this musical activity includes only those pupils who take lessons from the two Sisters at St. Luke's, and it includes also the piano and voice pupils from the lower grades. The four upstairs grades at the parochial school total 251 pupils, some of whom take music lessons outside the school, and some who take a variety of other outside lessons. The following table gives a distribution of these children according to school grade and the kind of lessons they take. This covers only regular lessons given by professionals, and not incidental instructions from parents or other adults.

Type of lesson	60 eighth graders	52 seventh graders	65 sixth graders	74 fifth graders	All pupils 251	All pupils Per cent
Piano	18	8	5	13	44	17.5
Other music	6	5	0	3	14	5.6
Dancing	5	6	6	3	20	8.0
Swim	21	8	4	10	43	17.1
Other	16	7	8	3	34	13.5

Piano is by far the most popular musical instrument for which the children take lessons. Most of the others study the accordion, although

[28] This tableau and the vocal selections of the recital were worked into the larger program for the Pastor's feast day in the following month.

the violin, guitar and flute are also played by some. The ratio of girls to boys taking piano lessons is three to one, while in dancing lessons it is four to one. The only kind of outside lessons in which the boys outnumber the girls is in swimming—twenty-seven boys to sixteen girls. In the remaining category there are nine who take golf lessons, five who take tennis lessons, and even two children in the eighth grade, one boy and one girl, who are learning to fly.

We have seen in the previous chapter that a kind of peak is reached by the children in the fourth grade. If we could follow these children through to the eighth grade we would probably see that they drop off in numbers in the outside lessons they take, particularly in music and dancing. These are the activities that demand talent and application, especially since the pupil is expected to practice about an hour every day. Children weary of these demands, and lose interest, in a way that does not seem to occur in the athletic or sports lessons they take. Proficiency in these latter activities usually involves association in groups, and not the long, lonely hours of practice needed for music and dancing.

These outside lessons of all kinds reflect also the interests that the parents have in the full development of their children's abilities. They reflect also the ability and willingness on the part of parents to pay for such instruction. The pupils taking lessons in piano, voice and dancing are over-represented in the families of the upper-middle class and higher. The parents of most of these children are fairly secure economically; they have somewhat more education and wider cultural interests than the others. Viewing the relationship of outside lessons with the social status of the child, however, must be done with caution. There are, for example, several families in the lowest social class of the parish who appear to be fiercely determined that their children shall have every advantage of such extra instruction, especially in music and dancing.[29]

Generalizations

1. At the half-way point in his elementary school career, St. Luke's pupil moves upstairs, achieves higher status, is expected to demonstrate more initiative and responsibility. Normally he is at the age of ten, and becomes eleven during the year. The symbols of advancement are all around him: religion instructions by a priest, the six-week report card, the study of Latin and greater participation in the daily Mass;

[29] See the impressionistic distinction between "genteel" and "vigorous" arts in extra-curricular lessons as related to social status, Celia Burns Stendler, *Children of Brasstown* (Urbana: University of Illinois Press, 1949), p. 93.

he now goes out to recess with the older children and takes a more direct part in the organized athletic activities. Most of this can also be said about the girls in the fifth grade, who are receiving exactly the same type of classroom training as the boys.

2. The teachers in the sixth grade appear to concentrate on the gradual social awakening of the pupils. National and world events are called to their attention. The practicality of Catholic social principles is demonstrated to them with numerous examples dealing with minority group relations. For the first time in their school careers the sixth graders seem to comprehend the interweaving of various school subjects around main areas of interest, for example, the geography lesson expands to include economic, religious, political, historical and ethical aspects. Religious doctrine and religious practice are interwoven.

3. Familiarity with the parish church and its place in education increases among both the boys and girls of the sixth grade. For the first time in their lives the girls are permitted to enter the sanctuary and sacristy regularly to assist the Sister Sacristan. This experience stands out in their autobiographies as a kind of first recognition of the female status within the religious structure. They appreciate it as an awesome and unusual opportunity to be close to the altar. The boys who make the grade as acolytes appear to have a similar initial reaction, but with the difference that they know their service will not be terminated at the end of the sixth grade. They will continue to serve at the altar until after graduation.

4. The sixth graders are for the most part beginners in activities in which they will participate more fully in the seventh and eighth grades. They are novices as choir members, receive special singing instructions on two days a week, and are sometimes allowed to sing with the school choir. Girls become official cheerleaders for the first time, two for the football season, and two for the basketball. Girls also play in an organized way and under instruction in the volleyball court. The boys play on the B team in both football and basketball, and are used for the most part to practice with the regular school teams. These activities make them feel more a part of the school, help to develop a school spirit, and tend to narrow the social distance that had previously existed before between themselves and the two grades above them.

5. From the point of view of public entertainment through music and school programs, the pupils of St. Luke's reach their peak in the seventh grade. Mainly because the music teacher is also the seventh grade teacher, but also in order to take the pressure of too much activities off the eighth grade, the principal burden of entertainment falls on these children. Although both boys and girls like to participate in

these programs, the choice roles and most of the acting are performed by girls. The kind of programs planned by Sister Cecelia, for example at Christmas and for the Pastor's feast day, are more suited to girls than to boys. This occurs even though there appears to be no dearth of singing, dancing and acting talent among the boys.

6. As the pupils advance in the parochial school the desire to express themselves seems to increase. The eagerness to answer and to ask questions is shown in the way they raise and wave their hands. They want to be heard, and they take every opportunity to speak up in class. Anyone who has watched these children from the fifth to the eighth grade will not fear the loss of initiative, competition and self-confidence among American youth. The desire for recognition and status is clearly seen in their classroom behavior. The problem of the parochial school teacher is to control and direct, rather than to stimulate these attitudes among the children.

7. One-third of the children in the three upper grades at St. Luke's do not go beyond their assignments to read books from the public library. About two out of five, however, read more than an extra book every month, while one-fifth of them read more than two books a month. Over a seven-month period the girls read an average of about twelve books per girl, as compared to almost eight books per boy. St. Luke's school does not operate a library, nor does it use the services of the Catholic Library Association, or take advantage of the professional guidance and delivery services of the city's public libraries.

8. The girls in these four upper grades attend about twice as many parties as do the boys, and they give all-girl parties more frequently than the boys give all-boy parties. Of the eight mixed parties given for classmates, four were given by parents of boys and four by parents of girls. Although the teachers urge that a mixed party should include all children in the classroom, there are always some pupils who do not attend parties. One out of five of the boys had not attended any parties, while one out of four of the girls attended seven or more parties.

9. The eighth-grade pupils get more experience in non-curricular activities than any of the other school children. They take care of chores like selling candy and delivering milk; they run messages for their teacher, the Principal; the honor patrol girls supervise the younger children at lunchtime and around the corridor; the honor patrol boys see that they make an orderly exit from the school and safely cross the street. The athletes get special attention from teachers, parents and fellow pupils. The eighth graders are the envy of the school, the most "important" persons there, and they tend to take their responsibilities seriously.

Chapter

FOUR

THE THINGS OF GOD

THE MAIN objective of St. Luke's parochial school would be destroyed if the learning process did not include religious teaching and activities. "Today for the Catholic and for other believers in organized religion the place of religion in education is very simple, very clear, and very definite. Religion, furnishing as it does a system of spiritual values of life, and a light, or guide, and a way to its ultimate purpose and destiny, is necessarily the end and objective of education. As theology it gives order to the intellectual content of education. As a philosophy of life it furnishes the guidance for the day to day experience of men. It is the one thing needful and it furnishes the sanction—the moral sanction—for all the rest of life." [1]

This concept of religious education came from the highest spokesman for the Church, Pope Pius XII, in his address to teaching Sisters. He said that "according to the Catholic concept, the object of the school and of education is the formation of the perfect Christian. Your entire school and educational system would be useless were this object not the central point of your labor." [2] The perfect Christian is, of course, a person who is developed in all his natural and supernatural capacities. The "one-sided" secular approach to education, which is said to be so wide-spread in the nation's public elementary schools, is deliberately avoided in the parochial elementary schools. The desire to train better Christians, and to counterbalance secularism, also appears to be the motivating factor in the increasing interest of Protestants in religious schools.[3]

[1] Edward A. Fitzpatrick, *How to Educate Human Beings* (Milwaukee: Bruce, 1950), p. 54.

[2] "On Educating Youth," *The Catholic Mind*, vol. 50, no. 1074 (June, 1952), p. 379.

[3] See D. Campbell Wyckoff, "The Protestant Day School," *School and Society*, vol. 82, no. 2069 (October 1, 1955) pp. 98–101, who shows the different

As we watch the teachers and pupils of the parochial school go through the daily routine of study, learning and play, we find that religion enters somehow into most of the routine. The distinctive feature of St. Luke's school is the religious or supernatural "atmosphere," which is basically a process of motivation. It is true that the children study the doctrines and practices of their Church, but they learn these with a reason. The child is learning to live in the presence of, and with the help of God. He is given all the approved cultural reasons why he should study and behave, but more is added. Silence is not just something he observes for the sake of good order, or so that he does not disturb others; it is a means of sacrifice for the souls in Purgatory; it is a means of self-control, of virtue that is pleasing to God and that brings supernatural graces to his soul. In short, religion is conceived of as guidance to the better life.[4]

External Evidences of Religion

Some of the homes of Catholic families in which we visited and interviewed during the course of our research could not be recognized as Christian homes, or as homes differing from those of non-Catholics in the neighborhood. There was no crucifix, statue, or saint's picture in sight. This could not be said of the classrooms of St. Luke's school. Every room has a crucifix hung on the wall. A list of other religious adornments, found in the seventh-grade classroom, may be taken as typical of the other rooms: "hanging on the wall was a picture of the Holy Family, one of Christ blessing the little children, one of Christ as a child in the temple, and another of the Blessed Mother; there was a large poster of Mary and the Christ Child, another of a boy being called to the priesthood by Christ, and another promoting vocations by the Fathers of the Sacred Heart. Besides these there was a small statue of the Sacred Heart, and a bust of the adult Christ. In one corner there was a small shrine containing a statue of the Virgin, before which stood a vigil candle and a vase of flowers."[5]

---

approaches, and some of the problems, of a parochial school system among Protestants. Also, Joseph Kaminetsky, "The Hebrew Day School Movement," *ibid.*, pp. 105–107, who reports on the prospects of expansion in the Jewish religious schools. For an editorialized historical view of non-Catholic schools, see Anson Phelps Stokes, *Church and State in the United States* (New York: Harper, 1950) vol. 2, pp. 671–680.

[4] See James J. Cribbin, "Guidance: Primary Function of the Catholic School," *Catholic Educational Review*, vol. 54, no. 8 (November, 1956), pp. 505–515, who points out the importance of aiding the pupil to a good life by means outside the textbook.

[5] These art objects are in the main the traditional and popular items that seem

In every classroom religious mottos, prayers and exhortations were prominently displayed. These were printed in letters about five inches high, and were affixed to the most conspicuous place in the room, the upper frame of the blackboard at the front of the room. A typical sign of this kind read: "Jesus, Mary and Joseph, I place my trust in Thee." In the lower grades these signs were made by the teachers themselves, but in the upper grades the children often made them for the class. The mottos and prayers were changed at least once a month, and were usually in keeping with the liturgical season.

It was noticeable that the theme of religious decorations and of slogans changed with the particular religious devotion of the month. October is dedicated to the Rosary, hence there were signs and slogans in all the classrooms exhorting the children to pray the Rosary, and several classes constructed small "Rosary shrines." In November the decorations changed to call attention to the souls in Purgatory; in March St. Joseph became the center of attention and in May the Blessed Mother. The lessons of Advent and Christmas, and of Lent and Easter, were pointed out to children through appropriate displays.

Some of the room adornments are specified also by the interests of the teachers. Sooner or later every nun receives as a gift a picture of the saint whose religious name she has taken. If it pleases her she may hang this also in the classroom, as was the case with the pictures of St. Robert, St. Dominic, St. Vincent de Paul and St. Bridget. Sister Justin, the sacristan and trainer of acolytes, usually had on display various miniatures reminiscent of the sanctuary. She had the boys fashion small chalices and the girls small vestments so that they learned more about the accoutrements of church services.[6] She also had a small altar with moveable figures so that the children themselves could play out the Mass and other services.

The most obvious and ever-present external manifestations of religion were the priests and teachers themselves. The clerical garb of the priests and the religious robes of the Sisters act as a constant re-

---

to have lost favor among the current experts in art education. See the collection of opinions in Sister Joanne Christie, (ed.), *Art Today in Catholic Elementary Education* (Washington: Catholic University Press, 1954), especially pp. 7–8.

[6] This comes under the general heading of "art work," for which St. Luke's has scheduled sixty minutes a week, from the third to the eighth grade. In a recent study nearly seventy per cent of elementary school teachers said that they spend from one to two hours a week on art. See Robert Kaupelis, "Art and Classroom Teachers," *School Arts*, vol. 55, no. 6 (February, 1956), pp. 17–20.

minder to the children that St. Luke's is a Catholic school. Most of them had known another kind of teacher, the lay persons in the public school kindergarten, but in the parochial school they become thoroughly accustomed to the sight of the religious garb. The autobiographies of several pupils who had transferred from public schools indicate how impressive this fact was. "It was a nice arrangement," wrote one boy of his fifth-grade experiences, "you didn't have to know any teacher's name. You just call everybody Sister." The children tend to equate the words, Sister and teacher, so that the three lay teachers in the school are occasionally answered with a "Yes, Sister," or a "No, Sister."[7] It must be noted, of course, that "there is nothing magic in a religious garb. Wearing it does not necessarily make a person a better teacher."[8]

The Three Sacraments

If we may judge accurately from the statements of the children themselves their most memorable religious experience takes place in the second grade when they receive three sacraments. "We received instructions," wrote one boy, "for confession, Holy Communion, and Confirmation. Father Albert came in every day and explained to us how these three sacraments were instituted and what they did for us. In Communion we received the Body and Blood of Christ, in confession our sins were forgiven through the absolution of the priest, in Confirmation we were made soldiers of Christ."

The parents are interested bystanders during this year. One mother remarked, "I don't think they learn anything except religion in the second grade." The father of a little girl said "they try to cram the whole religion course into them in the second grade, and I wonder whether they learn more religion in the other grades, or just repeat each year what they learned in the second grade." The fact is, of course, that the children talk more about religion at home during this year than at any other time. They realize that they must gain a certain amount of knowledge in order to be accepted for the Communion class. They study and memorize Christian doctrine at home. The parents are not

[7] The pronunciation of this word by most of the pupils is usually "Stir."

[8] William E. McManus, quoted in N.C.W.C. press release, Friday, February 15, 1957. Sister M. Madeleva, "The Preparation of Teachers of Religion," *Bulletin* of the National Catholic Educational Association, vol. 46, no. 1 (August, 1949), pp. 202–204, attacks two "heresies" and the "most grevious faults of crooked thinking," namely, that any teacher wearing a religious habit is competent to teach religion, and that training in the religious life is the ideal training for teaching religion.

allowed to forget that this is the "big year" in the lives of their children, and they become more and more involved as the day of the ceremony draws near.[9]

From the point of view of the school, however, the ordinary routine of the second grade is observed until after Christmas. During January and February, Sisters Vincent de Paul and Bridget extend the daily religion period somewhat more than the customary thirty minutes by drilling the children intensively in preparation for the time when the Pastor takes over the class. This they are able to do easily because all of the second graders are candidates for the sacraments and because on alternate weeks the children in this grade come to school while the other pupils are at the daily eight o'clock Mass.

During Lent these children were taught religion doubly, by the teacher while the Mass was going on, and by the Pastor later in the morning. Beginning on Ash Wednesday, March 6, Father Albert came to the school and taught the 2A grade from ten to ten-thirty and the 2B grade from ten-thirty to eleven. This program continued, with several exceptions when there were funerals, until the week before the children received their first Holy Communion on Sunday, May 5. It is the Pastor's personal responsibility to make sure that the youngsters have an adequate knowledge of the essential catechism material. Apparently the children learn it; as one of them remarked, "in the second grade I studied more about God than any other time because in that year I was going to make my first Holy Communion. That I think was the most important day out of my whole life."

Another boy remarked that "when I passed from the first to the second grade it was a big step of my religion. I learned that I was at the use of reason and it was bad to do wrong things." This arrival at the age of reason was noted by the Pastor. He tried to take some of the tension and excitement out of the religious experience by having these children go to confession well in advance of their Communion day. Thus, on Friday, March 22, when they were sufficiently instructed they received the sacrament of Penance for the first time,[10] and then con-

[9] Some of the parents, however, complained that the Sisters tend to "take over" all of the child's training for this important religious event, and that any direct parental involvement was discouraged by the school.

[10] The two second-grade classes, forty-nine boys and fifty-three girls, went over to the church together with the Sisters. The three priests heard confessions simultaneously, Father Thomas using a portable confessional at the altar rail. The children seemed quite excited about this experience, and although the Sisters tried to soothe them and keep them from getting tense, one little girl suffered from a "nervous stomach."

fessed on three other occasions before the Communion day. The Pastor believes that the children should get used to frequent confession and that they should not associate Penance and the Eucharist as though they were one sacrament. Some of the parents, however, were baffled on the day before the first Communion, when their children told them, "we've already been three times."

Since the reception of first Communion is a public ceremony in the church, with parents and relatives watching every movement of the child, Sister Vincent de Paul and Bridget practice the second graders in all of the external procedures.[11] "Getting toward the end of the year, Sister got us ready for Holy Communion. It was a privilege for us, but it was hard work too. We marched up and down the halls at least fifty times a day, playing like we were carrying candles." Anyone who has seen children of seven or eight years of age in a religious procession can probably appreciate the patience of the Sisters who tried to train them to walk in line with some semblance of order and without touching the lighted candle to the clothing of other children. This "marching up and down" was done in April during the religion period and at noon in the church itself.

On Saturday morning, May 4, the Pastor gave these children their final instructions, talking to them and with them for more than an hour. He repeated that this wonderful gift was from God and urged them to receive Communion frequently. "Now you are young men and women and you know what you are doing and must decide for yourselves that you will go often. Some parents go only once a year; but you must try to receive Communion weekly." He explained the importance of good preparation and thanksgiving prayers, pointed out the new laws of the Communion fast, warned them about "falling away" from the faith. Finally, he demonstrated and explained the brown scapular of the Blessed Virgin, with which they were to be invested that morning after confessions.[12]

Decision had already been made in March concerning the kinds of clothing the children would wear for first Communion day. By Sunday, March 23, the parents had already purchased the "Communion sets" (Rosary and Prayer Book) that the children were to carry. They were also instructed by the Sisters that the boys were to have blue

[11] For a comparable description of the First Holy Communion preparations, see Joseph H. Fichter, *Southern Parish*, vol. 1, *The Dynamics of A City Church*, pp. 57–62.

[12] These final instructions were repeated in the afternoon to the public school children, also to receive their first Communion the next day. See below, chap. 15, "Religion and Public School Children."

ties and trousers and white coats; the girls would wear the traditional white dress and veil of the parents' choosing. This matter of dress and appearance seems to be of concern to the little girls. "Communion day was a very important day. I realized that for the first time I was to be able to receive Jesus into my heart, but still and all, I was concerned over the way I would look in my Communion dress and if my picture would be taken."

Some of the parents came an hour before the time of Mass to be assured of a good vantage pew. Cameras were widely in evidence. In some cases the mother stayed inside to reserve the seat while the husband waited to snap pictures of the children as they came in procession from the school to the church. The children from St. Luke's filed into the front pews of the church escorted by Sisters Vincent de Paul and Bridget who knelt directly behind them. The public school children followed, accompanied by their escorts, Sisters Genevieve and Dolores.[13] The Pastor delivered a kindly and paternal sermon to the children, stressing particularly the joys of this occasion and the responsibilities that the children now had to God. "Don't depend too much on your parents. I know some of them go to Communion only once a year. Let them save their own souls, and you save yours."

Instead of receiving Communion at the altar rail, as is ordinarily done, the children had the privilege of walking up through the sanctuary and ascending the altar steps. The acolytes of the eighth grade assisted at this point in guiding the younger children to and from the altar. Flash bulbs lighted up the proceedings as parents tried to photograph their child in this memorable pose. After the Mass the children formed a procession back to the school where a certain amount of confusion ensued as parents tried to discover which of the various school exits their particular child would use. The rest of the day was a "family" day for each child, with the visits and the gifts from relatives increasing for them the significance of the occasion.

After all of this excitement, the reception of the sacrament of Confirmation on Monday evening, May 13, appeared to be almost an anticlimax. The children were intrigued, however, by the fact that they would see the Bishop, most of them for the first time, and that he would "slap them in the face." On this occasion the adult choir of the parish sang the hymns, and the Bishop spoke for twelve minutes, asking the children only four questions concerning the meaning of the sacrament of Confirmation. The children had practiced their part in the

[13] One girl, who was thought to have a communicable sickness, received her first Communion alone that day after the eleven-thirty o'clock Mass.

ceremony on the previous Sunday afternoon, together with their sponsors. They knelt at the altar rail, the boys on the epistle side, and the girls on the gospel side, with their adult sponsors standing directly behind them. They wore their finery from Communion day and conducted themselves without apparent nervousness or misapprehension. Twenty-eight adults also received the sacrament of Confirmation after the children.[14]

The Teaching of Religion

According to the weekly time schedule followed by the teachers of St. Luke's school, one hundred and fifty minutes a week are allotted to the study of religion, that is, Christian doctrine, the Bible and Church history. Unlike other subjects, where there is an increase or decrease of time given to a particular subject as the child advances from the first to the eighth grade, religion is taught for a half-hour every day in every grade. Usually this is the first period in the morning, the starting time being between eight-thirty and eight-forty-five, depending on the length of the eight o'clock Mass.

But there are exceptions to this pattern. Sister Justin in the sixth grade always has the forty-five minute arithmetic period first, on the theory that the children need their early morning alertness for this subject, and that religion might be separated as a study subject distinct from the religious attendance at Mass. The first-grade teachers start religious instructions at eight-ten, since their pupils do not attend Mass with the other children. The same arrangement is made for the second graders who attend Mass on alternate weeks during the school year, and not at all during Lent when the church is crowded with adults. Religion is taught by the regular teachers of the first four grades, with the exception of the second graders who are preparing for Holy Communion, and who receive extra instruction from the Pastor, Father Albert.

The two parish priests give supplementary religious instruction to the pupils at St. Luke's, Father Albert mainly to the first Communion class and Father Martin to the four highest grades.[15] Whenever the priests come into the classroom to give religion lessons the full-time teachers leave the room until the instructions are over. Father Martin has the regular assignment to teach religion an hour daily, except on

[14] Two public school children were absent, being with their parents on a short vacation trip.

[15] Father Thomas teaches at the Catholic high school in the city, and is thus unable to participate directly in the work of the elementary school.

Wednesday, which is his "day off." He spends an hour on Monday, nine to ten, with the eighth grade, and the same hour the next day with the seventh grade. Since the sixth and fifth grades are each split into two classes, he teaches a half-hour on Thursdays in each of the sixth grade classes, and a half-hour on Fridays in each of the fifth grade classes.

In giving these instructions Father Martin has worked out a schedule of his own that does not correspond to the material used by the regular teachers in the same classes. In the eighth grade throughout the year he teaches the sacraments, and assigns a weekly composition of one hundred words that must be turned in the following week. He teaches the Old Testament to the seventh grade, showing the connection wherever possible with the later events of the New Testament. The sixth-grade pupils learn the main happenings of Christ's life on earth, while fifth graders study the virtues needed for the good life. Father Martin does not assign a weekly composition to the seventh, sixth and fifth grades, but quizzes the children orally and briefly in each class and gives an examination at the end of January and another at the end of May.

Both the textbooks and the methods used in the teaching of religion bear little resemblance to the old-fashioned Catechism, the routine question-and-answer presentation of the Catholic faith. Repetition, as it is in all pedagogy, is still considered important, and the presentation of religion is so arranged that the pupil studies the same basic doctrine three times during his eight years at St. Luke's school. Parents and children still call the textbook "the Catechism" although the books for each grade have separate titles under the *Living My Religion Series.*[16] The first grade studies the book, *Living in God's Love,* the second grade, *Living in God's Law,* the third grade, *Living in God's Grace,* and so forth, each of the titles starting with the positive word, "living."

In spite of the new arrangement of texts[17] and of the modern method of teaching religion, these books have at their base the well-known Baltimore Catechism, the first volume of which provides the material from the first to the fifth grades, the second volume from the

[16] For an explanation of this modern approach see William Kelly, Edmund Goebel, Daniel Dougherty, M. A. Schumacker, Sister Mary Imelda, *Syllabus and Teacher's Manuals for Living My Religion Series* (New York: Benziger Brothers, 1952).

[17] See the remarks about the Commission on American Citizenship, the group established to revise the Catholic school curriculum, in Louis J. Putz (ed.), *The Catholic Church, U.S.A.* (Chicago: Fides, 1956), Frederick G. Hochwalt, "The Catholic School System in the United States," chap. 6, pp. 117–122.

sixth to the eighth grades. The teacher introduces each unit of study with a story or dramatization, gives Biblical accounts, teaches prayers and practices, and encourages projects and workbooks. Parents who follow their children's progress closely enough show great interest in this modern pedagogical approach. Some of them feel, however, that the child's interest in religion reaches a peak in the third and fourth grades and is thereafter replaced by a succession of interests in other school subjects. At any rate, most parents agree that religion is given in "a much more live way than it was in my day."

Church history is studied by the eighth-grade pupils of St. Luke's school, to provide for them an historical understanding of the doctrines and practices they learn in the religion classes. They are told that "to know and to understand the Church is a sacred duty for every Catholic. The Church is not just an organization to which we belong; it is an organism of which we are a part. Loyalty to the Church is not merely one among many loyalties. It is the one great loyalty of our lives in which all other loyalties are rooted and from which all derive their life and strength. For the Church is Christ and in the Church we are united with Him and with one another as members of one Body. Hence, a burning love for the Church must always be an outstanding characteristic of a good Catholic." [18]

It is a commonplace observation that in the parochial school religion permeates the whole curriculum, and is not confined to a single half-hour period of the day. Even arithmetic can be used as an instrument of pious thoughts, as in the case of the teacher who gave this problem to her class: "If it takes forty thousand priests and a hundred and forty thousand sisters to care for forty million Catholics in the United States, how many more priests and sisters will be needed to convert and care for the hundred million non-Catholics in the United States?" [19] The demonstration of sentence structure and of the proper use of words frequently brings some religious fact or spiritual practice before the children.

The general objective of bringing God and the supernatural into all classroom performance throughout the day is worked out at St. Luke's through the use of a set of teachers' aids. These are three volumes entitled *Guiding Growth in Christian Living*, indicating in detail how the teacher can orient the subject matter of the curriculum toward the rela-

[18] George Johnson, Jerome D. Hannan, Sister M. Dominica, *The Story of the Church, Her Founding, Mission and Progress* (New York: Benziger, 1946), p.v.

[19] Sister M. Walter, "Bridging the Vocational Gap," *The Catholic School Journal*, vol. 52, no. 3 (March, 1952), p. 79.

tionship between God and man.[20] This orientation appears to be realizable more in the children's reading performance than in any other curricular activity of the school day. The textbooks used here are the *Faith and Freedom Series*,[21] a different reader for each grade from the first to the eighth. They are especially written from a Catholic point of view, "oversaturated with religion," as one of St. Luke's teachers remarked, and allowing little opportunity for the child to become acquainted with the minor English classics read in other schools.[22]

One of the most popular forms of reading among the pupils is a series of weekly magazines, containing stories and current events, and including information about the Church and religion. Each issue contains tests about its contents and these tests were given regularly to the pupils. Five statements are made in a "Fill the Blanks" test and five in a "Take Your Choice" test; one in each of these tests always has a reference to religion, for example, "This year the theme of National Catholic Youth Week will be '—— in Youth,'" and "November 1, a holy day of obligation, is the Feast of (a) Christ the King, (b) All Saints, (c) All Souls." These magazines are published for different reading levels, the *Young Catholic Messenger* for the seventh and eighth grades, the *Junior Catholic Messenger* for the intermediary grades, and *Mine, A Magazine for the Catholic Child* in a separate edition for each of the first three grades.

This discussion of the religious permeation of the curriculum may be concluded with one further example, the comparison of the American history textbooks used in the parochial and the public school. The text used at St. Luke's[23] addresses the pupil, in part, as follows: "In this inspiring development of our country, members of the Catholic faith

[20] Sister Mary Joan and Sister Mary Nona, *Guiding Growth in Christian Social Living*, vol. 1, Primary Grades (1944), vol. 2, Intermediate Grades (1944), vol. 3, Upper Grades (1946), are not children's textbooks, but are meant for the use of the teacher in promoting a Christian curriculum in the elementary school (Washington: Catholic University Press). They propose as the goals of Christian education: physical fitness, economic competency, social virtue, cultural development, moral and spiritual perfection (vol. 1, p. 14). "Culture" is used here in the restricted sense of "refined tastes."

[21] The *Faith and Freedom Series* (New York: Ginn, 1949–1956) was planned as a series of eight books, one for each grade, but has developed into at least fourteen "reading levels" including pre-school readers, by numerous authors.

[22] One of the complaints of former St. Luke's pupils, was that they were ignorant of literature when they entered high school, partly because of these readers and partly because of the teachers' insistence on basic grammar.

[23] William Kennedy, Leonita Mulhall, Mary J. Dunn, *American History: Today and Yesterday* (New York: Benziger, 1943, with supplementary pages up to the end of 1946).

have had an important share. As we read, we shall see how much they have contributed to the progress of the nation. We may well be proud of the part they have played and resolve that in the days to come we shall prove ourselves worthy descendants of these great leaders and play an equally devoted part. May the story inspire us all to be good citizens, of whom our Church and our country may be proud." In its general index this text has fifty-five separate references under the term Catholic or Catholics. At the end of the first chapter there is a test asking the student to identify St. Patrick, St. Augustine, Vasco da Gama, St. Boniface, Leo the Great, Charlemagne, Mohammed and Diaz.

The history text used in the public school points to "the pride we Americans feel in our country. We are stirred by thoughts of her beautiful landscapes, and of the wealth and power which make the United States today the greatest nation on earth. But we are even prouder of the freedom to write, and to worship as we choose. In this book you will read the story that tells how our country grew in a short time from a group of hardy settlers to a mighty nation—a nation where millions of people have the right to lead free, useful, and happy lives. It is one of the most exciting stories you can ever read." [24] In its general index this text has nineteen references to the Church, missions and missionaries. At the end of the first chapter there is a test for identifying the following: Dark Ages, Crusades, Saracens, Mohammedans, 1498, Columbus, Far East, Diaz, da Gama, Ferdinand, Isabella, Watling Island.

Both of these history texts aim at more than giving the facts about America's past. They try to stir up pride and patriotism in the elementary school child. The nationalistic approach of the public school text is tempered somewhat in the Catholic school text by the authors' inclusion of the religious heritage of the children. One can hardly expect to find this in the necessarily neutral approach of the public school. The text used in the latter school is of more recent vintage, a technically superior book with many beautiful maps and pictures. It is used only in the eighth grade, while St. Luke's uses its textbook for both the seventh and eighth grades, paralleling the American history course with a Church history course during these two years.

From these various examples we see that the teachers of St. Luke's employ techniques and methods that channel the flow of religion into all of the subject matter in the curriculum. Religion is no longer departmentalized, a matter of brute memorization disconnected from the

[24] Howard Wilder, Robert Ludlum, Harriet McCune, *This Is America's Story* (New York: Houghton-Mifflin, 1950).

rest of the school work. The educational notion of a "general program" de-emphasizing specialization, is maintained and promoted in the parochial school. We have seen this teaching approach at work even in the three lowest grades. The teacher would occasionally have the children repeat some simple answer in chorus, but for the most part, the children were asked individually for answers, and did not have to follow the precise statement of the book. They learned prayers, however, by repeating them in unison. The children in the first grade even sang the Doxology, the Sign of the Cross,[25] and the prayer to the Guardian Angel.

How the children remember the early years of religious instruction is indicated by the following excerpt from the autobiography of a boy. "When I entered this school in the first grade eight years ago, I did not know much about my religion. In this grade, though, I learned Who made me, why and how. At this early age this did not mean much to me. It was just another lesson to learn." A seventh-grade girl recalls that "in my second, third and fourth years my Catechism questions were merely questions that had to be answered by the next day, or in consequence to be written out as a task." An eighth-grade girl who had transferred two years previously from a public school, had this to say, "I have taken into consideration the amount of religious instruction I received in the seventh and eighth grades compared with the first six years of my religious training. It seems almost impossible that you could learn as much in two years as you can in six years, but I did it."

The Practice of Religion

The parochial school is in many ways the ideal setting for the practice of religion because the patterns become set in such a way that "everybody does it." One mother, reminiscing about her own elementary school experiences, remarked, "they really made it too easy for us. The test of your faith comes afterwards when you're living with different people and in different circumstances." The child says his prayers when others do; he attends Mass when others attend; he goes to confession when others go. The extent to which he does these things meaningfully, and not simply as routine practices, depends upon his own interest and upon the teacher's ability to develop understanding in him.

The prayers recited daily in the classroom are always said in unison.

[25] In making the Sign of the Cross with the class, and facing the children, the Sisters in the first grade reversed the crossing of the right hand, moving it from the right to the left shoulder, in order not to confuse the children.

A special "salute" to the crucifix is made every morning together with the salute to the flag. "Saving cross of our Lord, Jesus Christ, Glorious Flag of the Catholic Church, I salute Thee!" The children in each class engage in group prayer at the beginning and the end of the school day, before and after the morning recess, and before and after the noon period. These prayers are the basic formulae, like the Apostles' Creed, the Acts of faith, hope, charity and contrition, the Lord's Prayer and the Angelic Salutation. At noontime they pray also the *Angelus* and the *Memorare* and the grace before and after meals. In the corridors, on the playground, and in their homes, we have sometimes asked individual children to recite some prayers and have found them almost always letter-perfect in the recitation.

It is the custom for St. Luke's pupils from the third to the eighth grade to attend the eight o'clock Mass on school days. This is not compulsory attendance, and no record is kept of absentees, yet most of the children come to Mass most of the time.[26] Many parents report that the children seem eager to attend Mass and also that they are anxious to arrive at the Church on time, and this is probably true of the older children. But the attitudes of the children seem to be mixed on this point. "When I was in the first grade," wrote one boy, "I can remember the bigger kids coming back from Church every day, and I often thought of being able to go every day too." Another boy wrote, "in the first and second grades, I thought the Mass was just a waste of time before school. Little did I know this was the greatest thing that was happening in the whole, wide world."

About twice a week, and always in preparation for an important religious feast day, the Pastor delivers a short homily to the children at Mass. This is frequently an explanation of religious practices, as in Advent and Lent, and often an exhortation to please God by performing good moral behavior. These talks are always pitched to the level of children's language and are taken seriously by them, but they are often considered somewhat amusing by adults present at the Mass. The teachers have campaigned among the children for the use of the missal at Mass and have succeeded to the point where about two-thirds of the pupils from the fourth to the eighth grade do so. About half of the

[26] In the eighth grade Sister Roberta gives a written task as a punishment for those who come late for daily Mass; they must write out the Mass from the beginning to the time they arrived in Church. There is no penalty for absentees. The result is that most of the latecomers remain in the schoolyard at the back entrance of the Church and then slip into line as their class exits.

younger children, including the second graders when they are at Mass, follow the ceremony in large-print, children's prayer books.[27]

The Mass is sung every morning by the seventh-grade choir, to which are attached most of the girls from the eighth grade and a few from the sixth. Normally they use the Gregorian chant, but when hymns are sung all of the children join in. From thirty to forty per cent of the pupils in the higher grades receive Communion daily. This percentage increases every Friday when the whole eighth grade receives the Sacrament, and also on the first Friday of every month, when all of the children from the third to the eighth grade receive Communion.[28]

The devotion to the Sacred Heart is manifested also by benediction of the Blessed Sacrament, and by the recitation of the litanies, after Mass on the first Friday of every month. On the previous day all of the children also go to confession. Father Martin hears the confessions of most of the eighth and seventh graders during the Mass which the Pastor celebrates. After breakfast the two priests return to the confessional and the children come over to the church one grade at a time. Although the teachers stress that this monthly confession is a voluntary practice, most of the children come to the church and enter the confessional. They are told that if they do not want to go to confession they may ask the priest for his blessing at this time.[29]

The children participate also in other devotions in the church during the year. The litany of the Blessed Virgin is recited after Mass during October and May. During October the sixth-grade children went to the church at noon time to recite the Rosary, but this practice was dropped after a week because it was too inconvenient. Most of the classes recite one decade of the Rosary in the classroom, a different child leading the prayer each day. During Lent the children go over to the church for the stations of the cross on Friday afternoons immediately after school.

[27] The Church is often so poorly lighted, especially on winter mornings, that it is difficult to read a prayer book during Mass.

[28] Except for the first Fridays, when breakfast is served in the cafeteria, the children who receive Communion bring their food and eat in the classroom during the first period. This practice unquestionably decreases the number of those receiving Communion, since many parents are concerned about their children "getting a good hot breakfast."

[29] We have "clocked" the confessions of the different grades and find that two priests can hear the confessions of as many as fifty children in eleven minutes.

Lenten Devotions

The way in which the Lenten season is observed at St. Luke's school is probably the most revealing indication of the intent and atmosphere of a religious school. On Shrove Tuesday, March 5, all of the teachers used the morning Catechism period to explain and discuss the meaning of Lent. They explained the symbolism of the blessed ashes, which all of the children received on the forehead the following morning. All of the teachers emphasized that Lent was a time for "giving" to God and not merely "giving up" something. They suggested "doing" things rather than "doing without" things. Many of the children resolved to receive Communion daily, and in the third grade each child has a cross made of brown paper on which he is permitted to place a gold star whenever he receives Communion. In the first and second grades the children have miniature stations of the cross, cut-outs from *Mine* magazine, and they read the appropriate prayers from a booklet while the other children are at Mass.

Despite the teachers' emphasis on the positive approach to Lent most of the practices suggested by the children themselves were acts of self-denial. They suggested giving up candy, ice cream, cokes, a favorite TV program, comic books; they resolved not to run in the corridors, not to talk in the classroom, not to copy, not to fight and so forth. One little girl in the second grade told the teacher, "I gave up throwing fits." In several classrooms each child wrote down two "penances" that could be performed by any child, like keeping silence, saying an extra prayer, helping their parents at home. These were then placed in a "penance box" from which each child drew a paper every day, read his mortification for that day, and returned the slip to the box. This custom was completely voluntary, and there was no check-up by either teacher or classmates.

On the morning of Ash Wednesday during the religion period all of the children were enrolled or re-dedicated to membership in the Pontifical Association of the Holy Childhood. Although this ceremony is performed in most places on February 2, the Feast of the Purification, the custom has grown at St. Luke's to perform it at the beginning of Lent. The children in each class recite in unison the act of consecration, as follows, "O Divine Child Jesus, we choose Thee today as the Protector of our childhood and the Model of our lives. Following Thy example, we wish to become ever more meek and humble, obedient and pious and grow in wisdom and grace to please Thee and our heavenly Father. Grateful for Thy love, we are eager to help Thee through the Holy Childhood to procure the grace of Baptism, a Christian education, and eternal salvation for little pagan children.[30] Bless us, dear Jesus, and accept our prayers and little sacrifices in their behalf. Holy Virgin Mary! Pray for us and the poor pagan children. Amen."

The school children participated also in the parish's Forty Hours' devotion to the Blessed Sacrament, conducted near the beginning of the school year, Friday to Sunday, September 21–23. Each class went over to the church in a body on Friday and spent a half-hour in prayer and adoration, except the children in the first and second grades who went for fifteen minute periods. A procession was held on both Friday and Sunday mornings, in which the little third-grade girls who had received their first Communion the previous May, acted as flower girls. Similar ceremonies were held on Maundy Thursday during Holy Week, which was a regular school day for St. Luke's children.[31]

The season of Advent in preparation for the feast of Christmas likewise provides an opportunity for the manifestation of religious practices. Mrs. Echols presented Advent wreaths to the classrooms of grades 5A and 6A, in which her boys are pupils, and it appears that this custom will spread to the other classrooms next year. In all of the grades special prayers were recited daily in preparation for the Nativity, and the classroom decoration stressed the religious meaning of the season (although in the third week of December there were many replicas of Santa Claus hung around the rooms.) In the hallway outside the classrooms of grades seven and eight the pupils constructed a small manger, empty of the figure of the Infant. Into this manger they placed daily a small piece of straw, representing the self-sacrifice they had practiced on that day.

Numerous other religious practices and devotions were fostered among the pupils of St. Luke's school. They had their throats blessed on the feast of St. Blase. They participated in the Holy Week services, in the Christmas celebration and in the Masses on holy days of obligation. They attended Mass and received Communion on the feast of St. Luke, on the Pastor's namesday, on the feast of their particular teacher, on St. Valentine's Day, St. Joseph's Day and on Mother's Day, Thanksgiving and All Souls' Day.

[30] See below, chapter 14, for an account of the drive for funds for the adoption of pagan babies. This drive was climaxed at St. Luke's school on St. Valentine's Day, but it was officially held in most other schools during the month of May. The children also sold Holy Childhood Christmas Seals.

[31] One of the parents objected strenuously to the Pastor about this "unheard of" idea of Catholic children attending school on Holy Thursday, and was given permission to keep his children at home.

The Altar Boys

All of the groups of pupils at St. Luke's school, like the total school itself, are supposed to be oriented to religious objectives: the salvation and sanctification of souls. This objective appears to be quite secondary in some of the groups, like the athletic and other recreational associations, but even these have religious overtones. The two groups that are most consistently dedicated to the service of God and the Church, are the acolytes made up of boys only, and the choir, made up mainly of girls. These are primarily religious groups, because the purpose of their existence is to give assistance in the church at the divine worship. In this sense they are "extra" to the educational function of the parochial school.

The acolytes are a continuing group of boys who keep replenishing their membership from year to year. When the eighth-grade boys graduate from the top of the membership the fifth-grade boys move in at the bottom. The criteria of admission to the altar boys presuppose good moral character, but the boy must also have written permission from his parents as well as an assurance of cooperation from them. Besides this he must learn the necessary functions of serving and memorize the Latin responses to the Mass. About half of the boys in the seventh and eighth grades (49.0%) belong to this group and 68.9 per cent of the boys in the sixth and fifth grades.

Belonging to the acolytes is a mark of prestige among St. Luke's boys. This is indicated by the fact that only one boy has voluntarily dropped out of the group in three years. It is also shown by the enthusiasm expressed in the autobiographies. "In the fifth grade I studied for serving the priest at Mass. When I finished the study of Latin, Father practiced with us for the Mass. Then finally I was officially an altar boy. When my turn came around for serving I was really happy. I am not sure how many mistakes I made, but I know I made quite a few. When I served Mass it gave me more of an appreciation of my religion." Another boy wrote, "I started serving in the fifth grade and I learned more about the priest and his work, and I learned more about the Mass and other slants on my religion."

At the beginning of the school year there were seventy-six members of this group: thirty of them with previous experience. Before Easter the remaining forty-six had also passed all the tests and were full-fledged altar boys.[32] The Latin prayers are taught to the fifth-grade

[32] The fact that these boys are permitted to perform the duties of an ordained acolyte is pointed out by Martin B. Hellriegel, "Singers and Servers," *Worship*, vol. 29, no. 2 (January, 1955), pp. 83–89.

boys by their teachers, Sister Ruth and Sister Dominic, when most of these boys are ten years old. Those who are quickest to learn Latin first are also the first to be taken for training at the noon recess by Sister Justin. Four boys are trained at a time and they are usually assisted by two veteran servers from the eighth grade.

Twelve acolytes are required to serve Mass every day, four at each of the three daily Masses. On Sundays, this number is increased to twenty boys, the school boys serving five of the Masses, while the nine-thirty Mass is served by high school students from the Junior Newman Club. A "round" of serving takes a boy through three full weeks and two extra Sundays. He starts with three companions at the six o'clock Sunday Mass and serves the six-fifteen daily during the week; the following Sunday he serves the seven-thirty Mass, and the seven o'clock during the week; then he serves the eight-thirty Mass on Sunday and the eight o'clock Mass during the week; on the fourth and fifth Sundays he serves the ten-thirty and the eleven-thirty Mass.

The whole system, as well as the group, is well organized. During the school year the list of servers' appointments is displayed in the classrooms from the fifth to the eighth grade, and another on the bulletin board in the sacristy. At the close of school in June each boy receives a copy of the complete list of summer appointments. In addition to this a boy is appointed for each month whose duty it is to telephone the four new servers every Saturday for the six o'clock Mass on the following day. At the beginning of the year the acolytes held a meeting at which they voted to pay a monthly dues of ten cents and to place a fine of twenty-five cents on anyone who failed to show up for his appointment or to get a substitute. If a boy was absent twice during the same week he had to forfeit a round of serving. If and when he reaches his fourth unexcused absence at any time during the year he was to be dropped from the group. Some fines were collected, but no individual boy failed often enough either to miss a round of serving or to be expelled from the organization.

The most faithful and competent altar boys achieved the rank of "Knights of God's Altar," and each had his name printed on a star, about two inches high and exhibited on a bulletin board inside the main entrance to the school.[33] The sixteen eighth-graders, and only three seventh-graders, became Knights during the year. These boys

[33] St. Luke's acolytes are not formally affiliated as an organization with the national movement. See Timothy J. Sullivan, "Knights of the Altar," *The American Ecclesiastical Review*, vol. 129 (September, 1953), pp. 188–191; also Gregory Gross, "Investiture of Altar Boys," *Worship*, vol. 27, no. 3 (February, 1953), pp. 146–149.

also played the most responsible roles in the larger liturgical services of the parish church, like the procession for Forty Hours in September, for Palm Sunday, Holy Thursday, Holy Saturday, and Rogation Day (April 25). They had prominent positions in the county-wide Eucharistic Hour on Sunday, October 14, and constituted the two leaders of the servers at the devotions on Wednesday and Friday evenings during Lent. On these latter occasions the appointed boys had to practice in the church during the noon recess, and were warned with the statement "if you are not in the sacristy at twelve sharp, you may find that your place has been taken by another."

The main incentive for these boys appears to be the pleasure of serving at the altar. They object strenuously if anyone tries to take their round of serving from them, or if they do not get the appointment they think they deserve to special ceremonies. The tangible rewards are not great. Twice during May the servers enjoy extra recess with candy, cokes and ice cream (purchased with the dues and fines in the treasury). On the day before the end of school, Thursday, June 6, they joined with altar boys from all over the diocese for a picnic. For this trip they paid one dollar and a half bus fare, but all other expenses were paid by the diocese.[34] Toward the end of August, Father Albert gives a general picnic on the school grounds for both the acolytes and the choir members. Finally, small religious awards, a book, medal or rosary, are given at the end of each semester for the four boys who have the highest number of "points" for serving.

The Choir

Another important systematic form of group religious behavior is that of the children's choir. "In the seventh grade we had the privilege of belonging to the choir. It was an honor to sing at the Sacrifice of the Mass." The star girl soloist in the eighth grade wrote, "we gave a great deal of glory to God by singing in the choir." A boy, who is also an outstanding basketball player, wrote "I took a step and became a member of the choir. This was an honor to be able to sing to God." The nucleus of the choir consists of the boys and girls of the seventh grade, although altar serving sometimes interferes with some of the boys and the change of voice with others. The girls from the eighth grade, trained the year before, sometimes join with the choir, and sometimes sing as a separate group. Boys and girls in the sixth grade

[34] Because only one bus was rented by Father Martin, only the seventh and eighth grade boys could go to this picnic. The younger boys complained, "we're just as much altar boys as they are. Why can't we go?"

are given preliminary training and are expected to "lead" the younger children in hymn singing at some of the Masses.

The choir is trained and led by Sister Cecelia, teacher of the seventh grade, assisted by Sister Ruth, of the fifth grade, who acts as organist. The motives behind this work are seen in the words of Sister Cecelia, "I believe it is a tremendous asset to every child's Catholic education that he be a member of the school choir and thereby receive formal training in the liturgical music of the Church. Children are made mindful of the principal feasts and different seasons of the Church year. They perceive the joy element of their faith by singing the jubilant anthems and hymns. In our limited time we attempt to acquaint the pupils with Gregorian Chant—its true beauty and usefulness in the Mass and other liturgical functions. Each sung part of the Mass is translated and explained to the pupils. The seventh grade is now making a study of the Mass as a class project." [35]

The choir from St. Luke's school is in many ways the parish choir. There is, of course, a well-functioning adult choir which sings the high Mass every Sunday and on the feasts of Christmas and Easter. All of the remaining church singing is provided by the children's choir. They sing the daily high Mass at eight o'clock, the funerals usually held at nine o'clock on school days, and an occasional wedding on Saturdays.[36] All of the Sisters form the choir at funeral Masses on Saturdays. The choir sings hymns at the low Mass at eight-thirty on Sundays, when the sixth-grade children join in. The choir sings the Forty Hours services in September, the entire Holy Week services and the Wednesday night devotions during Lent.

The children's choir sometimes "represents" St. Luke's school; for example, they participated with other parochial and public schools of the city in the "Thanksgiving Sing" on the courthouse steps. This, and a similar carol sing in the same place on Christmas eve, were

[35] On this point see the further remarks of Sister M. Joselma, "Introducing Liturgical Music to Elementary Children," *Musart*, vol. 7, no. 1 (September–October, 1955), pp. 13, 56–57; Martin B. Hellriegel, "Singers and Servers," *Worship*, vol. 29, no. 2 (January, 1955), pp. 83–89; also Mary Evangeline McSloy, "The Case for Gregorian Chant in the Curriculum of the American Catholic Elementary School" (Notre Dame; Dissertation in the University of Notre Dame Library, 1952).

[36] When there is a school-day funeral, the seven o'clock Mass is omitted, and the acolytes from that Mass serve the funeral. Sometimes, "outside talent" is hired to sing at weddings, but the children are eager and willing to perform. On Easter Monday, a school day, the seventh graders sang at a wedding, and Sister Cecelia pointed out to them that if they get married on Easter Monday they can make use of the flowers left on the altar from the day before.

televised, much to the delight of the children's parents and families. Their singing of Christmas carols also substituted for the program at the monthly meeting of the PTA on the third Tuesday of December.[37] The choir, together with the music pupils of Sister Cecelia and Sister Ruth, constituted the core of the Pastor's feast day programs on Friday, May 10, and Sunday, May 12.

Singing in the choir, like serving in the acolytes, is a voluntary activity. "The entire class is invited to sing in the choir. It is not obligatory. The children are free to discontinue if they wish to do so." The result of this choice is that four or five boys in the seventh grade feel that they "can't sing," and they stay in the library or in the body of the church when the choir sings during school hours. All of the girls in this grade participate. Recognition comes in the form of a chart hanging next to the servers' honor roll at the entrance to the school. This chart is entitled "Singing for God" and on it are the names of the choir members. Next to each name is placed a small gold star for perfect weekly attendance, a silver star if the child has been absent only once. Although there is a picnic in August for the choir, the reward for singing appears to come mainly through the pleasure derived from the function itself.

Like the altar boys, the choir girls are expected to continue their services in the parish church throughout the summer. The Sunday high Masses are discontinued in the summer months, but the daily high Mass requires the presence of an organist and some choir members. Since the Sisters leave the convent from the middle of June to the third week in August, neither Sister Cecelia nor Sister Ruth is present to serve as organist, nor is Mrs. Faulkner, organist for the adult choir, able to come for the daily Mass. Two eighth-grade graduates, Alice Pitre and Ann Burton, volunteered for this function, and they played on alternate days during the summer after graduation.[38]

A summer schedule of choir singing was made out during the second week of May. Sister Cecelia asked for volunteers among the seventh graders to "divide up" the summer for the daily Mass. About three-quarters of the girls had expectations of being away from the parish

[37] The group benefits of choir singing and the ways in which this experience can help to develop community relations, are described by Martha Pearman, "Citizenship and the School Choir," *Educational Music Magazine,* vol. 34, no. 3 (January–February, 1955), pp. 19–20.

[38] The moving of the convent building to the southeast corner of the parish property delayed the Sisters' return until September 1, and the opening of the new school year until Monday, September 9. Registration was completed on Friday, September 6, with 647 pupils starting the new year.

for vacations ranging from one to three weeks in length. They then submitted their names on a slip of paper indicating the days they would be absent from the parish. Sister constructed a twelve-week schedule, with four different girls singing the daily Mass for one week at a time. This was then mimeographed and distributed so that each girl knew when she was expected to appear in the choir loft. Because the number of girls was not large enough to complete the summer, the names of some appeared twice on the schedule. In the actual event, however, there were always more than enough singers because some appeared even when they were not scheduled.

The children from the fifth to the eighth grades receive formal training in music for one hundred minutes a week, but they do not receive marks on their report cards for this class. Most of the music they learn in these grades is hymnal and liturgical, although they also have the opportunity to express themselves in the "better" type of secular music. The result is that choir practice takes place twice a week during the noon period so that the pupils in the seventh grade can be better prepared for their work. This is a sacrifice on their part, but an even greater sacrifice by Sister Cecelia, who also gives piano lessons at noon on the remaining three school days of the week.

Other Religious Groups

We have already seen that the Holy Childhood Association exists at St. Luke's school, that the children in all grades are formally inducted into it on Ash Wednesday, and that the campaign for pagan babies was conducted in its name. This association, however, can hardly be termed a social group on the local level. It has no officers or meetings, and no continuing program within the school.

The Junior Legion of Mary is also officially established in St. Luke's parish. In May, at the end of the seventh grade, the girls are approached by Mrs. McWellan, president, and Mrs. Noto, vice-president of the Senior Legion. They are invited to one of the meetings, which take place on Wednesday evenings from six to seven o'clock. About two-thirds of the eligible girls accept the invitation, but practically all of them became auxiliary members. This requires the daily recitation of the *Catena* prayers. During the year, only one girl, Grace Kleppner, became an active member, reciting the daily prayers but also attending the weekly meeting and performing one hour of apostolic work during the week.

For her this apostolic work consisted of helping with the nursery on Sunday mornings, taking care of small children while their parents are at Mass. Between twenty-five and thirty children are brought to the nursery every Sunday. Until January it operated during the eight-thirty and nine-thirty Masses, and for the rest of the year during the nine-thirty and ten-thirty Masses. The Legionnaires call one another "Sister." The nursery is in charge of a member of the Senior Legion of Mary; the junior workers, besides Grace are all high school girls: Lynn Craft, Irene McWellan and Marie Hobetz, coach of the girls' volleyball team. These girls, occasionally joined by a few other eighth graders, teach the pre-school children a few simple religious formulae like the Sign of the Cross, the genuflection, the prayer to the guardian angel.

The failure of the Junior Legion of Mary to attract more eighth-grade girls is of some concern to Mrs. McWellan and Mrs. Noto. They felt, however, that there are several explanations, aside from the amount of self-sacrifice involved in regular membership. The time of the weekly meeting, at six o'clock on Wednesdays, is inconvenient because of the supper hour. During the winter months "it's too dark for little girls to be on the streets after meetings." Another important factor is that, except for the two mothers mentioned, all of the members of the Senior Legion are unmarried ladies. Thus, there is not the intimate interest of the mother-daughter relation (as exists in the Blue Birds and Camp Fire) to bring the young girls into the work.

Another religious group, about which some confusion existed, is the Sodality of the Blessed Virgin. Since no organized Sodality exists in either the parish or the school, the Junior Newman Club performed what is ordinarily a Sodality function, the crowning of the statue of Mary at the eight-thirty Mass on Mothers' Day, May 12. The graduating eighth graders are annually initiated into the Junior Newman Club, but a requirement for this is that they must first become Sodalists. The acceptance into the Sodality was supposed to be held on Sunday, May 19, and into the Newman Club on the following Tuesday.

The eighth-grade pupils said that Sister "forgot to tell them" on the preceding Friday about the reception into the Sodality, and the consequence was that few showed up at the eight-thirty Mass on Sunday, May 19. Nevertheless the initiation into the Newman Club took place on Tuesday evening, the children anticipating various ordeals and tasks by which they would be tested.[39] Father Martin announced that the initiation would consist of the eighth-grade boys dancing with high school girls and of the eighth-grade girls dancing with high

[39] This Tuesday was a holiday, granted by the Bishop in consequence of the Confirmation ceremonies, and employed by the Sisters in taking girls from the fifth to the eighth grade on a bus trip to their Mother House.

school boys. This was the "entrance requirement" which all of them passed. They were still not members of the Sodality. Finally, on the following Sunday, May 26, the Pastor received all of the graduating class into the Sodality, reciting with them the consecration to Mary and bringing the medal of the Blessed Mother along the altar rail so that each child could kiss it.

Religious Vocations

The Catholic elementary school is the first and earliest recruiting grounds for the future professional functionaries of the Church.[40] St. Luke's parish has a respectable record in the number of persons from the parish who are now following a religious vocation, although not all of them had their elementary training at this parochial school. These persons number nine priests and three seminarians, seventeen Sisters and two postulants to the sisterhood. Only one religious Brother has come from the parish. In the graduating class, at the end of our study, eight boys signified their intentions to study for the priesthood and three girls for the sisterhood. When we asked the children of the three upper grades to write down their future occupation, 14.3 per cent of the boys said they were going to be priests, and 13.3 per cent of the girls were going to be nuns.

There is no doubt that the teachers of St. Luke's "work on" the development of religious vocations, both in class and in individual counselling.[41] "In the sixth grade I thought I had the vocation to become a nun, but it faded away. But up until the eighth grade it kept coming back and fading away. The teachers in the sixth, seventh and eighth grades talked on the sisterhood to the class." One of the high school girls, who had graduated three years previously from St. Luke's, remarked, "if you go to Communion more often than usual, the Sisters think you've got a vocation. They pestered me so much about being a nun that I finally said I would, so that they let me alone."

This is probably the exaggerated memory of a teenager. We interviewed some of the children on this matter, particularly those who

[40] See Barnabas Mary, "Vocations Begin in the Elementary School," *The Catholic School Journal,* vol. 52, no. 3 (March, 1952), pp. 74–76. Also Thomas J. McDonnell, "Fostering Vocations in Elementary and High Schools," *ibid.,* pp. 71–73.

[41] The role of the Sisters in guiding vocations is seen in a recent study in which 86.4 per cent of aspirants said that Sisters "helped them to decide." See Sister Mary Blaise, "Fostering Vocations in Grade Six, Seven and Eight," *Bulletin* of the National Catholic Educational Association, vol. 52, no. 1 (August, 1955), pp. 103–106.

intend to follow a religious vocation. They all denied that any force or pressure was being brought to bear on them. "The Sisters talk a lot more about the priesthood and being a Sister than they do about other things, like being a lawyer or a teacher. They say you're either going to get married or be a priest, but you've got to make up your own mind with God's grace." Several of the parents, who had hopes that their own sons would some day be priests, felt that the Sisters concentrate on the girls as prospective members of their own order, and do not do enough to encourage religious vocations among boys, especially in the area of personal counselling.[42]

The teachers always send prospective vocations to Father Martin for consultation and advice. Sister Roberta says "we don't want to be guilty of pushing anyone into a vocation, but we want to encourage them as much as possible." Father Martin usually has opportunities to talk to the pupils individually every day, since the morning recess occurs immediately after his religion classes. For any extended conversation of this nature, the child comes to the priests' rectory. Father Martin resists the suggestion that he establish an office in the school, partly because he has many other regular parochial duties, and partly because he fears this would become an office of discipline and administration. Like the Pastor, he firmly believes that the teachers should run the school.

On four occasions during the year recruiting talks were given and movies shown by representatives of religious orders. Permission was obtained from the Pastor and the Principal by the Holy Cross Fathers, the Society of the Divine Word, the Fathers of the Sacred Heart, and the Maryknoll Missionary Sisters. These programs were given in the school cafeteria and each lasted for about an hour. They were usually presented in two sections, the first to the fifth and sixth graders, and the other to the seventh and eighth graders. The speakers always left some vocation literature with the teachers, a poster advertising their organization to be hung in the classrooms, and some self-addressed post cards that might be sent to them by interested pupils.

The movies presented by these visitors to the school are in color, technically excellent in photography and sound. The speakers are youthful and dynamic, and are competent in telling dramatic stories,

[42] At the elementary level there appears to be a lack of general occupational guidance for the children who anticipate careers as laics. See, on this point, Brother Philip, "Christian Vocational Guidance," *The Catholic School Journal,* vol. 52, no. 3 (March, 1952), pp. 82–83. See also Barry Fagin, "Guiding The Vocational Interests of The Child," *Education,* vol. 74, no. 3 (November, 1953), pp. 171–179.

especially about the foreign missions. The children listen with more attentiveness than they display in the classroom. The glamor of religious work tends to be played down in these movies, and its realistic hardships are described. Mrs. Gordon remarked, "the movie shown by the Maryknoll missioners was a great asset in promoting Lenten self-denial. Most of my sixth graders have no conception of what it is to want for anything. The movies of the missions in Korea seemed to have a stimulating effect on their desire to give up some of the luxuries they enjoy daily."

Another method of stimulating interest in the religious vocation is that of an annual essay contest, sponsored by the Serra Club, a men's group organized for this particular purpose. Each parochial school in the city was permitted to submit four essays from eighth graders. At St. Luke's school, eight pupils wrote essays; and four were selected for the contest by the Principal. A prize of five dollars was won by Emily Lang. The essay was entitled, "What I Would Like to Do for God if I Had a Religious Vocation." The winners from all the parochial schools of the city were guests at a banquet on Sunday, April 28, at which the Bishop presided. He gave a talk about vocations, presented the awards to each winner as well as to the boy from another school whose paper was judged the best of all the entries. The teacher of the grand prize winner was awarded ten dollars.

March is "vocation month" at St. Luke's school when special emphasis is placed on the whole question of the professional religious life.[43] Posters are made by volunteers and displayed in the various classrooms. The best ones are selected for display in the corridors, and prizes are given in each grade. Some of these are made as a group project by three or four pupils working together.[44] A pen and pencil set was the first prize in the eighth grade, won by Matthew Kronlage. The second prize, a small statue of the Christ Child, was won by Rose Lindeman. The third best poster was made by Carol McEvoy and Marjorie Zeller, each of whom received a crucifix. It is interesting to note that none of the children who won prizes in the essay and poster contests has expressed the intention of following the religious vocation.

The most elaborate concentration of attention on religious vocations is the annual bus trip to the Mother House of the teaching Sisters at

[43] See the description of vocation month activities in Matthew Vetter, "A Classroom Vocational Program," *The Catholic School Journal,* vol. 25, no. 3 (March, 1952), pp. 83–84.

[44] The social awareness of the children is indicated by one of the posters which depicted Christ embracing people of all races. It carried the statement: "Don't Let Segregation Bar Vocations."

St. Luke's. This was made on Tuesday, May 21, in two busses by more than seventy girls, mostly from the fifth to the eighth grade, with a few fourth graders included. Four Sisters rode in the busses leaving the schoolyard at seven-thirty in the morning and returning just before seven o'clock at night. The remaining seven Sisters rode in three automobiles driven by Mrs. Noto, Mrs. Bowman and Mrs. Heller.

The nuns at the Mother House use this as their annual May day celebration in honor of the Blessed Mother, and also as a picnic gathering for the teachers and pupils of the fifteen parochial schools which they staff throughout the state. The purpose of the trip is to make the young girls acquainted with the work of the Sisters and to let them see the surroundings in which the postulants and aspirants to the order live. The older girls have an opportunity to chat with former teachers, now at other schools, and with former schoolmates who are now postulants. Each child pays three dollars and fifty cents for the bus fare, and another fifty cents for lunch.[45] Games and contests of all kinds were organized for them, and in the afternoon a procession was held, each school marching as a group, with St. Luke's proudly boasting the largest representation among more than five hundred girls in attendance. The crowning of Mary's statue, a short sermon by the Bishop, and benediction of the Blessed Sacrament, concluded the program.

In preparation for this occasion the eighth-grade girls from all the parochial schools taught by these nuns were invited to compete for gold medals in an essay contest. All of the girls in the top class at St. Luke's submitted compositions on the life of a chosen saint, but none of them was selected as the winners of the three gold medals awarded for the contestants. This whole affair was a most enjoyable outing for the girls. They sang all the songs they knew during the hours on the bus ride. In their autobiographies they mention this as one of the most pleasant experiences of the year; and even the high school girls who were former pupils at St. Luke's recall this outing as a highlight of their elementary school career. The fact that this teaching order is growing in numbers and annually receiving more applicants is attested by the fact that it is now building a new $800,000 Mother House. The annual picnic may be a partial explanation of this growth.

[45] The luncheon consisted of barbecued beef, baked beans and cup cakes, and these foodstuffs were donated by the different grades in the fifteen attending schools according to a pre-arranged plan. Thus, with the fifty cents lunch charge the children were buying back their own food and at the same time making a contribution to the Mother House. There were also stands which sold religious goods and others with candy, cakes and soft drinks for sale.

Religion and Education

The question was raised at a soiree interview with a group of parents whether the various religious activities of the pupils of St. Luke's are interfering with their regular school work. The parents in general felt that the school and the church belong together and that the interflow of activities between the two would help to develop the children into good future parishioners. Attendance at the public school tends to draw the children away from the parish, or to make "second class" parishioners of them, but attendance at St. Luke's integrates the child's religion and education and brings him closer to the church.[46] As we have seen above, the children perform certain functions "for" the parish. They provide all the acolyte service, with the exception of one Mass on Sundays; the children's choir does most of the singing in the church during the year; the girls in the sixth grade help Sister Justin with work around the sacristy and sanctuary.

Do these religious, parochial activities turn the child's interest, time and energy away from the regular educational curriculum? Choir singing probably occupies more time than any of the other activities. The children from the fifth to the eighth grades are supposed to spend one hundred minutes a week in the study of music. In the seventh grade all of this time is devoted to choir practice and church music. Most of this is done in the music room, but occasionally, when there is need of the organ, the children go over to the church for practice. The sixth graders devote a little more than half of their allotted music period to church music during the week. On twenty-four occasions during the school year the seventh-grade choir sang a funeral Mass at nine o'clock on school days. The Mass requires about forty minutes and this time was subtracted about evenly from religion and music periods for the day.

The altar boys also serve at these funeral Masses and they vie with each other for the privilege because they "get out of school." But since only four boys serve at one time, and since there are seventy-six acolytes eager to serve, the average boy gets the opportunity to serve once in about a year and a half. On the Friday of Forty Hours devotion and on the Thursday of Holy Week, each altar boy, like every other child above the third grade, spends a half-hour in the church before the Blessed Sacrament. Like his classmates, the trainee server in the fifth and sixth grades receives special instructions in the Latin prayers, but he also has to memorize these prayers in his spare time.

[46] Joseph H. Fichter, *Social Relations in the Urban Parish* (Chicago: University of Chicago Press, 1954), p. 171.

Various other religious practices we have discussed in this chapter may be considered from the point of view of interference with "school work." The girls' assistance to Sister Justin in the church occurs at noon periods and after-school hours. The class prayers at different times of the day consume from one to two minutes each time. In the second semester the second graders focus their attention on preparation for the sacraments, and here again most of this occurs during the religion period. The four vocation talks given to the children from the fifth to the eighth grade, consume about one hour each.

The suggestion that there is "too much religion" in the parochial school must be looked at from the perspective of what else is done, as well as from the perspective of the school's purpose. The eighth-grade pupil spends 1,500 minutes a week in school, apportioned as follows:

Religion	10.0%	Music	6.7%
English	37.3	Science and Health	5.3
Arithmetic	15.0	Art	4.0
Social Studies	16.0	Recess and Miscellaneous	5.7

Of the twenty-five hours the eighth-grade pupil spends in school during the week, two hours and a half are spent in the study and practice of religion. This appears to be less time than is given in other elementary schools to activities like gym classes, woodwork shops for boys and cooking classes for girls. Incidental religious activities, like vocation talks, choir singing, altar serving, are of an educative nature and are oriented to the integrated and liberal purposes of the parochial school. What may be considered interference with school work, when judged by narrower norms and standards, must here be considered an integral and necessary part of the parochial child's education.

Generalizations

1. The religious motif of St. Luke's school is externally manifested in everything from the wall decorations to the nun's garb. The religious motivation of the school is recognized in the type of text books used, in the themes of study and lessons, in the reasons given for application and behavior. Religion permeates the curriculum and the child is deliberately given to understand that his relationship with God is the most important single aspect of his life on earth.

2. The central religious practice among the pupils is the daily Mass and the reception of the sacraments. The youngest children, in the first and second grades, are not permitted to attend, partly because the church building is too small. This prohibition, however, seems to have

the psychological effect of making them want to do "what the older kids do," so that they anticipate the time when they too will be allowed to attend Mass. These practices, like the prayers recited at various times of the day, are performed as a kind of group pattern in which all of the children participate together.

3. The most memorable religious experience in the life of the parochial school child occurs in the second grade, when he receives the three sacraments of Penance, Communion and Confirmation. The autobiographies of the older pupils invariably mention this experience. The preparation for this event is relatively intense (from the child's point of view,) the attention of adults—priests, teachers and parents—is focused upon him; the Communion Day itself is a time for parties and gifts. The child is told that he has now reached the age of reason, and is responsible for his behavior, and this acts as a significant transitional stage from one phase of childhood to another. It is then also that he confronts a Bishop of the Church for the first time.

4. The child is probably more liturgical-minded while he is in the parochial elementary school than he will ever again be in his life. The Church's main feast days, the lives of the saints, the liturgical seasons of Advent and Lent, all become part of his daily living and thinking. Even the classroom decorations remind him, for example, that November is the month of the Poor Souls, and March the month of St. Joseph. Habits of self-sacrifice are developed through the Advent and Lenten practices in which all the children participate.

5. The acolytes of St. Luke's form a prestige group to which the younger boys aspire and from which no boy voluntarily retires until he graduates from the eighth grade. Membership in this group is voluntary, the qualifications are rigidly maintained, and the penalties for violating the rules are voted upon by the boys themselves. The boys belonging to this organization are for the most part the better athletes, the more intelligent pupils and the best behaved. Unlike other school groups, this one continues to function during the summer.

6. Liturgical singing is considered both educational and religious. The seventh graders are in many ways the parish choir since they do most of the singing in the church. The basis of this choral work is the Gregorian chant in the sung Mass, although hymns are also sung at the low Masses. Girls in the eighth grade occasionally sing as a choir and children in the sixth grade are preparing to become choir members. The group has the opportunity to perform also as the nucleus of the program at PTA meetings, the Pastor's feastday and other occasions.

7. The parochial school of St. Luke's is considered a source of

recruitment to the religious and priestly life. Vocations are encouraged through poster and essay contests, through talks and movies by visiting priests and nuns, by the bus trip to the Mother House, and by personal counselling. Older girl graduates think the Sisters "overdo" this activity; some of the parents think there is not enough encouragement of vocations among the boys. The Sisters are intent upon getting recruits to their own teaching order, but reiterate constantly that the child must make her own choice.

8. The religious practices and groups of St. Luke's school are interwoven with the whole educational program. They are themselves educational since they are designed to assist in the promotion of the "different kind" of education that parochial school children obtain. It would be unthinkable to the teaching staff of the school to attempt to separate religion from education, or to suggest either that religion interferes with the school, or that the school interferes with religion.

Chapter

FIVE

SOCIAL ATTITUDES AND STANDARDS

ONE OF the more important functions of elementary school training is to instill in the pupils culturally approved attitudes and standards of social conduct. The effort of every elementary school in its attempts to "form character" means more than an insistence on external conformity to the rules and regulations, orderly behavior in class and playground, and friendly social relations with others.[1] It is the earnest objective of the educator that these behavior patterns will become internalized, that they will gradually result in the child's habitual acceptance of the norms that are highly valued by the school and by the total culture. The pupils are supposed to learn and accept the reasons why they should be well-behaved children.

Since the parochial school employs the sanctions of religion, permeates the whole system with a supernatural "climate," and also instills the general cultural motivation used in any other elementary school, it might be supposed that both the patterns of behavior and the norms of conduct would be higher than those in a non-religious school. This is an assumption difficult to demonstrate through known research techniques in social science. "There is no solid evidence that would lead us to conclude that the transfer of religious knowledge to ethical practice is more likely to be found among parochial school children than among public school children nurtured in religion in the church and the home."[2] Any comparative study along these lines

[1] See below, chap. 6, "Social Conformity and Conduct"; also Joseph H. Fichter, "The Development of the Individual Within the Social System," *American Catholic Sociological Review*, vol. 9, no. 3 (October, 1948), pp. 179–190.

[2] See the statement of the Board of Christian Education of the Presbyterian Church in the U.S.A., *The Church and the Schools* (Philadelphia, June, 1957), p. 18.

is handicapped by the fact that religious norms and motives must be omitted from the tests because of the great variations in the religious affiliation of public school pupils.

"The entire educational system is based on the assumption that certain types of behavior can be acquired in the social situation."[3] The entire parochial school system is also based on the assumption that certain values and norms of behavior can be acquired by the Catholic pupil through precept, example and training. We have seen the manner in which the saints are used as models of behavior, the reception of the sacraments is urged as a means of living a better life, the teaching of the Church and of the Bible is employed to raise the standards of the children of St. Luke's. A relatively broad social orientation is given to these children with the intention that prejudices be prevented and that inter-group understanding be developed.

In an attempt to test objectively the social standards, attitudes, norms and values of St. Luke's pupils, and to compare them with those of the public school children, we administered the *California Test of Personality*. This well-known instrument was employed in testing 175 pupils in the sixth, seventh and eighth grades of St. Luke's school, and 186 children in the same grades at the neighboring William Howard Taft public school. The median score for the total test was 123.2 for St. Luke's, and 121.5 for the public school. Of primary interest for our present question is the second half of the test, made up of six sections (each with twelve items) measuring the social adjustment of the child.[4]

The results of this test on social adjustment show that the parochial school children made a median score of 63.9, while those in the public school made 63.2. (The perfect score for any individual is 72.) This general similarity of the two categories of children does not lose its significance when we compare the two schools on the six sub-sections of the social adjustment test. In fact, the differences in the median scores on these smaller segments of the test become almost totally insignificant. The comparative performance of these children is as follows:

[3] Wilbur B. Brookover, *A Sociology of Education* (New York: American Book Company, 1955), chap. 13, "Socialization and Personality Adjustment in the School," p. 338.

[4] Louis Thorpe, Willis Clark, Ernest Tiegs, *California Test of Personality*, Elementary Form AA (Los Angeles: California Test Bureau, 1953).

Social adjustment as measured by:	Median scores of 175 pupils of St. Luke's	Median scores of 186 public school pupils
Social Standards	11.1	11.0
Social Skills	10.1	10.2
Freedom from Anti-Social Tendencies	10.7	10.6
Family Relations	10.7	10.8
School Relations	10.8	10.6
Community Relations	10.5	10.5

The perfect score attainable in each of these smaller segments of the test is 12. The above results show that both schools are highest in the area of social standards and lowest in the area of social skills. Since we are here concerned mainly with standards, skills and tendencies, we shall scrutinize these three sections more thoroughly and omit a discussion concerning family, school and community relations.

Social Standards, Skills and Tendencies

The median scores made by the two schools are so close that no meaningful conclusions can be drawn from their comparison. We felt, however, that there may be some differences exhibited if we compared the test in its smallest components. Each of the smaller sections of the test on social adjustment contains twelve questions, to which the child had the choice of answering only yes or no. In order to illustrate the kind of normative thinking the elementary children are doing we present here only the more pertinent and interesting samples of questions. We counted the answers on each question and compiled the percentage of pupils giving the correct answer. In some instances this answer is affirmative and in some negative.

The answers to these questions indicate that these elementary school pupils accept approximately the same norms of conduct in about the same way. They understand and accept the simple virtues of honesty, gratitude and obedience. They accept obedience to parents on a somewhat higher level than obedience to teachers. Practically all of them feel that it is morally right for them to have their parents' permission to do things, but some of them have reservations about obeying their teachers. They are in perfect agreement in their high regard for honesty and fairness in sports, but more than ten per cent of the pupils in both schools are not so honest about the lost or borrowed property of others.

Questions measuring social standards	Percentage answering correctly: St. Luke's	Taft School
Should one return things to people who won't return things they borrow?	87.4	88.2
If a person finds something, does he have a right to keep or sell it?	89.1	87.6
Do boys and girls need to do what their teachers say is right?	93.2	94.1
Is it necessary to thank those who have helped you?	98.9	99.0
Should boys and girls ask their parents permission to do things?	100.0	98.4
Is it all right to cheat in a game when the umpire is not looking?	100.0	100.0

The similarity in the responses of these children tends to reinforce the conclusions of this study concerning the common cultural background of the children in both schools.[5] There can be no question about the fact that the cultural environment is an important factor in the formation of norms and ideals of behavior, and the cultural environment has many components. These children are being educated in two different schools; and the two categories of children differ too in their religious affiliation. Each child comes from a home and family, distinct from the home and family of every other child. It appears, therefore that on the level of these simple virtues of honesty, gratitude and obedience, these three institutions of home, school, and church are sharing the common cultural values.[6] These are American norms of behavior, inculcated in the children as part of the common culture, and cross-cutting familial, educational and religious differences.

As a further index of the comparison between parochial and public school children, we select those questions dealing with social skills—the ability to get along with others. Here the questions were directed to the children themselves, asking them how they feel and what they do in concrete situations, rather than asking how a person should think and act. It is obvious that social adjustment demands social skills, and that the whole socialization process, an integral function

[5] See the discussion on this similarity below, chap. 17, "School, Parish and Community."

[6] See Francis J. Brown, *Educational Sociology* (New York: Prentice-Hall, 1954), chap. 21, "Social Attitudes," pp. 608–642; see also Sister Mary Amatora, "Molding Youth in Sanctity and Sanity," *The Catholic Educational Review*, vol. 51 (1954), pp. 649–659.

of the school, gradually teaches the child how to get along with others. A comparison of the scores on social standards and on social skills, indicates that the children in the two schools know what ought to be done, but like many adult, fully socialized persons, do not always do it.

Questions measuring social skills	Percentage answering correctly: St. Luke's	Taft School
Is it hard for you to talk to people as soon as you meet them?	51.4	59.1
Do you let people know you are right no matter what they say?	70.3	62.9
Do you usually keep from showing your temper when you are mad?	70.3	67.7
Do you usually act friendly to people you do not like?	78.3	82.8
Do you usually help other boys and girls have a good time?	96.0	95.7
Does it make you feel angry when you lose in games at parties?	97.2	98.4

This test of social skills shows somewhat more disparity between the parochial and the public school children than does the test on social standards. A relatively large percentage in both schools feel somewhat shy in meeting new people. On the other hand, almost all of the pupils know that they must be "good sports" and must not get angry when they lose at games. In general, it may be said that the pupils of St. Luke's are somewhat more polite, shy and retiring, while those from the public school are more poised, self-assured and aggressive. The public school child tends to insist on his own ideas, and does not mind letting other people know them. These are, of course, tentative generalizations, but they seem to be in accord with the statements of teachers and parents who have experience in both types of schools.

It must be pointed out, of course, that in every grade of both schools there is a range from the relatively isolated pupil to the relatively popular pupil, from the child who has few reciprocal friendships to the one who seems to be liked by almost everybody.[7] It is possible that more isolates exist in one grade than another, or in one school than another, at any given time. It is difficult to determine whether the "quality" of social relations is better in one school than in the other. Obviously, social skills are developed in both the parochial and the

[7] See the data on this point below, chap. 9, "Cliques and Clubs."

public school, since the experiences through which these skills are developed are relatively the same in both schools.[8]

The extent of a child's social adjustment can also be evaluated from the expression of anti-social tendencies. This is simply another approach to the same question of whether the pupil thinks and acts according to the acceptable norms of good human relations, but it is a negative approach. In other words, we are asking here about the patterns that a pupil should not follow, and the correct answers to the following questions are all negative.

Questions measuring anti-social tendencies	Percentage answering correctly: St. Luke's	Taft School
Have unfair people often said that you make trouble for them?	73.7	61.8
Is someone at home so mean that you often have to quarrel?	75.4	76.9
Do people often ask you to do such hard or foolish things that you won't do them?	76.6	76.3
Are people often so unfair that you lose your temper?	77.7	73.7
Is anyone at school so mean that you tear, or cut, or break things?	98.9	98.5

The pupils who answered these questions in both schools are practically unanimous in saying that they do not lose their tempers to the extent of destroying things. The self-control that is needed in positive social skills and human relations is, however, not perfect among them. About one-quarter of them in both schools find that people sometimes annoy them to the point of quarreling or to the point of refusing to conform. Anti-social tendencies are manifested not only when the child believes that others are unfair to him, but also when he wants to "do something" about it, like making trouble for the other person, or getting angry at him. This willingness to display external resentment to others appears to be slightly more prevalent among public than among parochial school pupils.

One must be careful not to read too much into the results of these tests or to make easy generalizations and conclusions from them. The practical utility of the *California Test of Personality* goes beyond the mere comparison of categories of pupils. It is most useful for the

[8] William W. Wattenberg, *The Adolescent Years* (New York: Harcourt Brace, 1955), Chap. 15, "Social Relationships," pp. 293–308, has gathered most of the studies on the problems of developing social skills.

teacher in pointing out the problem children as individuals, giving some indication of the source of their difficulties, so that the children themselves may be given helpful guidance.[9] In this sense, the test is a psychological rather than a sociological instrument. Before transmitting the results of the tests to the teachers at St. Luke's, we selected the names of the children with the two best scores and the two worst scores in each classroom, and asked the teachers what they knew about these children. Their reaction to the question was a clear proof that the test had correctly "fixed" the poles of social personalities in their classrooms.

The results of this test are nevertheless of some sociological significance because they reveal definite patterns of social behavior in elementary school children and basic similarities in the pupils from both schools. It is an interesting fact that the children from both schools score higher on the social standards test than they do on other sections dealing with actual behavior and feelings. When they are asked how they act and how they feel under certain circumstances their scores drop and they begin to show some differences between the two schools. The similarity lies in the tendency on the part of both categories of children to answer the same questions in the same general way. Where one school has a low score the other school has a low score, and this similarity follows through from the lowest to the highest scores on particular questions of the test.

Group Attitudes and Social Problems

The testing of personal and social attitudes in a general way still leaves room for an investigation of the elementary child's knowledge of broader social problems and of the child's attitudes toward minority groups. It may be assumed that one of the functions of the elementary school is to develop "social-mindedness" in the pupil although there may be some question concerning the extent to which these youngsters should be "exposed" at an early age to the paradoxes and inconsistencies of our urban American culture.[10] At any rate, there can be

[9] See Louis P. Thorpe, "Appraising Personality and Social Adjustment," *Educational Bulletin, No. 11* of the California Test Bureau, and also the earlier (1950) *Summary of Investigations,* which provides a bibliography on this test.

[10] See Paul A. Ryan, "Developing Socially-Minded Catholics," *Bulletin* of the National Catholic Educational Association, vol. 52, no. 1 (August, 1955), pp. 262–266, who maintains that "Catholics in general, are not social-minded." See also C. W. Hunnicutt and Jean D. Grambs, "The Social Studies under Fire," *The Elementary School Journal,* vol. 56, no. 5 (January, 1956), pp. 210–216.

no doubt that the modern youngster learns something about these problems, and absorbs some of the values and norms connected with them, through the mass media of communication as well as through the home and the school.

In order to discover the attitudes and knowledge of the pupils in this area we devised a series of statements on current social problems. These were deliberately couched in moral terminology in order to find out what the children considered right and wrong, and we asked them also to give their reasons for the answers. This test was administered to pupils in the sixth, seventh and eighth grades, and we were able to arrange the results in three categories: 155 pupils in St. Luke's school, 199 in the public school, and sixty-three Catholic children attending the public school. The following table shows the percentage distribution of answers according to the three categories of pupils.

Subject	Attitude	155 pupils in St. Luke's	199 pupils in Public School	63 Catholic children in Public School
1. *Refugees*	Favorable	79.4%	74.4%	69.8%
	Unfavorable	20.0	23.1	28.6
	Don't Know	0.6	2.5	1.6
2. *Foreign Aid*	Favorable	94.8	80.4	77.8
	Unfavorable	5.2	16.1	20.6
	Don't Know	0.0	3.5	1.6
3. *Negroes*	Favorable	91.0	87.9	82.5
	Unfavorable	8.4	8.1	17.5
	Don't Know	0.6	4.0	0.0
4. *Protestants*	Favorable	88.4	90.5	87.3
	Unfavorable	10.3	2.0	3.2
	Don't Know	1.3	7.5	9.5
5. *Voting*	Favorable	94.2	91.0	93.6
	Unfavorable	5.2	7.5	4.8
	Don't Know	0.6	1.5	1.6
6. *Housing*	Favorable	85.2	85.9	84.1
	Unfavorable	12.2	7.5	11.1
	Don't Know	2.6	6.6	4.8
7. *Labor Unions*	Favorable	78.1	72.9	58.7
	Unfavorable	12.2	6.0	3.2
	Don't Know	9.7	21.1	38.1

Refugees and Foreigners

The problems concerned with displaced persons and with economic aid to foreign countries have been widely discussed in America since the second World War. It is hardly possible that the children in the upper grades of these two schools have escaped some knowledge of these questions discussed either at home or at school. New troubles in Poland and the armed insurrection against the Communist regime in Hungary were only recently in the headlines when we gave these questions to the children. Hence the great majority of the pupils were able to formulate some opinion about the problem. This was not a direct question asking the pupils to distinguish among various ethnic groups and nationalities, or to indicate their "social distance" from one or another of these categories.[11]

In a minor way these questions were a test of the broad liberal and international attitudes of these children.[12] They helped to indicate the extent to which the elementary school pupils had escaped the American "Ghetto-mentality" and mid-western isolationism, about which there has been so much written. One would assume that the parochial school pupils would score better on these questions mainly because of the interest aroused in foreign missions and because of the broader and more liberal education of their own teachers. This is an assumption that was only partially and tentatively confirmed by the answers to the first two problems.

1. The problem concerning attitudes toward refugees was worded in this way: "Andrew says that we should let more refugees and immigrants come to the United States, but Anthony thinks that we already have enough of them. What do you think?"

Four-fifths of the parochial school children are in agreement that "we ought to share our prosperity and freedom with all who want to enter this country." Others said that we ought to help them "to escape persecution," that "if we make them our friends they will help us," and that "Jesus wants us to help our neighbor." One-fifth of the children reacted unfavorably to Andrew's suggestion, claiming that

[11] See E. S. Bogardus' early studies, "Social Distance and Its Origins," *Journal of Applied Sociology,* vol. 9, no. 3 (January, 1925), pp. 216–226, and "Measuring Social Distances," *op. cit.,* vol. 9, no. 4 (March, 1925), pp. 299–308; also "Changes in Racial Distances," *International Journal of Opinion and Attitude Research,* vol. 1, no. 1 (1947), pp. 55–62.

[12] See Mary Synon, "Problems of Pupils in Acquiring Christian Social Attitudes," *Bulletin* of the National Catholic Educational Association, vol. 49, no. 1 (August, 1952), pp. 415–418.

refugees "take away the jobs of American men;" they could "lower the standards of our country," and they would soon "make our country overcrowded."

Three-quarters of the non-Catholic public school pupils gave favorable answers, pointing out that "many refugees are smart and can help our scientists," that "if we didn't admit them we might get into a war," and that "we have plenty of room for them." Those who disagreed gave reasons like, "it costs too much to feed and clothe them," "Communists come in and bring foreign language and customs with them," and that we "shouldn't allow people from Asia and Africa to come here."

Almost seventy per cent of the Catholic children in public school are in favor of admitting refugees and immigrants, because "we have all the comforts of good homes for them," and "they don't need to worry about war over here." Almost three out of ten, however, had reasons for disagreeing. "They work for lower wages and cheat other workers out of a fair wage;" and "they can't speak our language," and we have to be "careful about letting Communists into our country."

2. The next problem also had to do with foreigners. "Charles thinks the United States is doing a good thing in sending billions of dollars in aid to foreign countries, but Frank disagrees with him. What do you think?"

The overwhelming majority, almost ninety-five per cent, of St. Luke's pupils are in favor of foreign aid, because we ought to "follow the Golden Rule," and "God will bless the United States for its generosity," and the people we help "will help us when we are in need." The small number disagreeing with this felt that "we can be sure they will never pay us back," and "we ought to help the people in America first."

About four-fifths of the non-Catholic children in the public school agreed with Charles. This policy of aid "strengthens international goodwill," it "makes friends and helps to avoid war," and "the money will help to feed and clothe poor people over there." Some of those expressing unfavorable attitudes said that "we need the money here to feed the Indians and to clear the slums," and "we ought to spend money here where there are droughts and floods," and that "we should give a country money only when we are indebted to them."

The majority (77.8%) of the Catholic children in the public school had favorable attitudes, saying that "other countries will consider us a friendly nation," and that "this kind of thing unites men." About one-fifth of them, however, disagreed and had in general the same reasons as their school mates.

Race and Religion

Aside from the ethnic, or national, minorities in the American society those dealt with most frequently in sociological studies are the racial and religious categories. It is a scientific fact that babies are born without prejudices and that they absorb these negative attitudes during childhood.[13] It is also a well-known fact that anti-minority biases can be developed through a socialization process in which there has been no direct contact with members of the minority. When this happens it is the most clear-cut example of the influence of teachers, parents and other social authorities.[14]

3. The next problem we proposed to the children concerned attitudes and actions in regard to Negroes. "Frances says that if a Negro family moves in next door her family is going to move away. Mary says that the best thing to do is to stay right there and make friends with the Negro family. What do you think?"

Here again the majority (91.0%) of the parochial school pupils agreed that whites should try to have friendly relations with Negroes. "A person who discriminates is guilty of grave sin." "God did not make anything bad, and the image of God is on their souls," and "we are all God's children." [15] The dissenters gave reasons like the following: "They don't keep their houses and yards neat," and "we have to watch out for inter-marriage."

Non-Catholic children in the public school also agreed in the majority (87.9%) with Mary. Some of their reasons were that "moving away would hurt the Negroes' feelings," and "it doesn't matter what skin color you have," and "everyone is equal." The few who agreed with Frances thought that "Negroes don't keep up their property and the neighborhood will be a mess," and "since we brought them over here they should be satisfied to go to separate schools and have their own areas to live in."

Catholic children in the public school had a somewhat lower score on this question. Those in favor of Mary's attitude felt that "we have to be fair to people," and "the Negro can't help it if he is colored."

[13] See Helen G. Trager and Marian R. Yarrow, *They Learn What They Live* (New York: Harper, 1952). See also Cosmas W. Novak, "A Survey of Intercultural Education," *American Catholic Sociological Review*, vol. 10, no. 3 (October, 1949), pp. 159–171.

[14] Marian Radke and Jean Sutherland, "Children's Concepts and Attitudes about Minority and Majority American Groups," *The Journal of Educational Psychology*, vol. 40, no. 8 (December, 1949), pp. 449–468.

[15] One child, who agrees with Mary, says that "Christ was not a white man."

Some of the unfavorable attitudes expressed were: "if one moves in more will come after them," and "they ought to stay in their own separate places."

4. In the next question we attempted to test opinions that might indicate Protestant-Catholic tensions. "George's father, who is a Protestant, is collecting money for fifty Protestant families in our city who are very poor. Gertrude's father, a Catholic, donates ten dollars for this cause. What do you think about it?"

The great majority (88.4%) of St. Luke's children approved of this action. They thought Gertrude's father was doing a good thing because "we must help poor people regardless of their religion," and "he performed indirectly the corporal works of mercy," but also because "he reflected credit on the Catholic Church," and "he might influence the Protestants to check into the Catholic Church and become baptized." Those who were unfavorable to the action thought that "the Protestants should support their own people," and "the money should have been given to Catholics."

Nine out of ten of the non-Catholic public school children were in favor of such behavior. "Both religions are working for the same God." This action was good because "it was helping a fellow-American," and "religion makes no difference as long as you are good." The only opinion expressed to the contrary by one of the children was that "he might make the Catholic Church mad and he would lose his Catholic friends."

The majority (87.3%) of the Catholic children in the public school also came out in favor of this donation. "Regardless of religion, he was helping the poor," and "he was giving for a good cause." The small number who thought that Gertrude's father did wrong, gave no reasons for their opinion.

Voting, Housing and Unions

The three areas in which we probed further for social attitudes and values may be treated under the general heading of "citizenship education."[16] These children had been made aware of the presidential elections during the school year; they heard a certain amount of talk about slum clearance and city cleanup campaigns, and they lived in a community where the industrial unions have been long established.

[16] *Educating for American Citizenship* (Washington: National Educational Association, 1954), pp. 51–64. See also on the same topic, Henry J. Otto, *Social Education in Elementary Schools* (New York: Rinehart, 1956), pp. 274–286.

These three subjects are, of course, only a sample of the multiplicity of social problems about which the elementary school child must later think more deeply. We can well make the assumption that he had already formed some attitudes toward them in the upper grades of the elementary school.

5. Whether or not the citizen has the duty to vote was the next problem proposed to the children. "Betty's father never votes in national, state or local elections. Ann's father says that every adult citizen has the obligation to vote. Which do you agree with, and why?"

St. Luke's children were quite positive about the importance of voting. "If we don't vote a dictator might take over the country." "Our forefathers fought for the right of freedom and it doesn't cost anything to vote;" "those who don't vote are the first to complain." Those who dissented were mainly in favor of freedom; "in a free country like this you should be allowed to vote or not vote," and "nobody can tell you that you have to vote."

Nine out of ten non-Catholic pupils in the public school thought that Ann's father is right. "Our government was formed for us to be a government by us." "We can have life, liberty and the pursuit of happiness only by voting." "Voting is a privilege people died for, and we owe it to them to vote." The relatively few dissenters also pointed out that "voting is a privilege, not an obligation." The Catholic pupils in the public school were also highly (93.6%) in favor of the duty to vote. They gave reasons similar to those of the other public school children.

6. The next problem was that of housing projects for the city's poor. "Harold says that our city ought to spend more money to build housing projects for the poor people, but Henry says the people should build their own houses without any help from the city. What do you think about it?"

About eighty-five per cent of the parochial school children are in favor of public assistance to poor people in the matter of housing. They said that we should "shelter the homeless," that "God said, 'what you do to my people, you do to me,'" and that "old houses and slums ruin the appearance of a neighborhood." Those with unfavorable attitudes thought this would be a bad thing "because there would be higher taxes," and "we ought to get the man a job so he doesn't need help."

About the same proportion of non-Catholic public school children favored public help in housing. This would be a good thing because "it would make us a more prosperous and famous city," and "poor living conditions can cause disease," and "spending money on the poor would help remove the slums." Those opposed felt that the "city would go into debt," and that "these people are too lazy to work," and "they had the same chances as other people had."

The Catholic children in the public school who were in favor of housing projects thought that "poor people deserve help from the city," and "giving them houses would improve the city." Those with unfavorable attitudes said that "the poor should learn responsibility," and "shouldn't be helped if they are lazy," and "old people should go to the old folks' home."

7. Finally, we came to the question of labor unions. "Dolores says that we ought to do away with labor unions because they cause so much trouble; but Dorothy says that we really need labor unions and should support them. What is your opinion?"

Here again, the majority (78.1%) of St. Luke's pupils were in favor of maintaining labor unions. "They give security and protection to the worker," "they keep labor united," and "the dues are small in comparison with what you get out of it." Those unfavorably disposed to unions said that "they cause strikes," and they "get the company bankrupt."

More than seven in ten (72.9%) of the non-Catholic children in the public school are in favor of supporting unions. "They help build up the country," and "give the worker protection," and "we ought to support them so that we can meet our industrial needs." Those who are against unions say that "they cause workers to riot and strike," and that "it is not fair to ask for more money and less work." A little over one-fifth of the children, however, did not have an answer.

Almost three-fifths of the Catholic children in the public school were in favor of the unions. They are "the backbone of American industry," and "they stand for what the worker wants against powerful corporations," and they "help improve working conditions." A few were opposed to unions, but most of the rest (38.1%) say that they "do not know what a labor union is."

Catholics and Jews

It may be assumed that the presence of anti-Semitic attitudes would be an anomaly among the pupils of St. Luke's school, if one were to suppose that the classroom is the only source of attitude formation. The classroom discussions on Jews in the Old and New Testament of the Bible always appeared to be carried on in an objective and even favorable way. The possibility of this prejudice in the family and the community cannot be overlooked, however, since it is obvious that group norms and stereotypes can be learned by the child in his out-of-school experiences. Many studies have been made concerning this problem and the factors of cultural environment have often been emphasized in them.[17]

8. The final problem was presented only to the Catholic children in both the parochial and the public school. It was an attempt to discover any latent prejudices the Catholic children may have against Jews. "Evelyn says that we ought not have anything to do with Jews because they are not good people. Josephine says that like any other people there are good and bad Jews, and that we ought to love everybody. What do you say?"

St. Luke's pupils were universally on the side of Josephine in this question, with the exception of one boy who did not know what to answer. Here their answers were backed up by religious and highly moral reasons. "Jesus was a Jew, and He was good." "They are all God's people." "They were the chosen people." In several answers there crept in the notion that one religion is as good as another. One boy who plans on entering the seminary said, "It does not matter about religion just so we do our part by associating with them, and also we should love our neighbor as ourselves for the love of God."

The Catholic children in the public school were also overwhelmingly in favor of Josephine's attitudes toward Jews. One boy took the opposition and only two did not know what to answer. "I think that we should like the Jews because Christ made all the people on earth." "If you were a Jew you wouldn't like it very much if other people said that they did not want to have anything to do with you." "Everyone has a right to his own religion." The lone boy who sided with Evelyn is here quoted in full: "I myself have never met very many Jews that I liked. They are good people but they don't seem to blend in right with other people. This is a touchy question to get involved in, but I think we should respect them as anybody else as long as they don't try to mingle with other people because too much of this can lead to trouble."

This boy also expressed unfavorable attitudes toward Negroes saying that if Negroes moved in next door they would soon "ruin the neighborhood." The white children at the Taft school represent a variety of religious affiliations. There are Jewish children in attendance at this public school, and one boy mentioned this as a reason for lik-

[17] See Theodore M. Newcomb, *Social Psychology* (New York: Dryden Press, 1954), pp. 587–590; also the doctoral dissertation of Sister Mary Jeanine Gruesser, *Categorical Evaluations of Jews Among Catholic Parochial School Children* (Washington: Catholic University Press, 1950).

ing them, "I go to school and play with them." There are no Jewish children in the parochial school, nor are there any Negro children at either the public or the parochial school. Yet, St. Luke's pupils were somewhat more favorably disposed toward Negroes than were either the Catholic or the non-Catholic children in the public school. This is simply further evidence of the well-known sociological fact that favorable and unfavorable attitudes can be developed among children even when they have no contact with the objects of these attitudes.[18]

Attitudes and Ignorance

On some of these social questions the attitudes of the children in the three categories differ hardly at all. They are quite similar in their attitudes on the friendly relations between Catholics and Protestants. Of course, we do not know what the result would have been among the public school children if the statement had been reversed, so that a Protestant was giving money to help poor Catholic families. Most of the children take seriously the obligation to vote. A smaller percentage of the pupils in all three categories are in favor of public housing for the poor, but the percentages favorable to it are consistent in the three types of children questioned.

It is in the remaining four social problems that the percentage differences show up. The question concerning refugees and immigrants had the highest percentage of unfavorable attitudes in all three categories, and the question concerning foreign aid had the highest percentages of unfavorable attitudes among the public school children. During the months previous to the administration of this test there was an influx of Hungarian refugees into the city. None of the children from these families entered St. Luke's school, and only a few entered the public school. In fact, there were disproportionately few children of elementary school age among the refugees.

The presence of these newcomers, the publicity given them in radio and TV programs, in public receptions, in newspaper accounts, the discussion of them at home by parents who may have felt job insecurity [19]—all of these things may be reasons why some pupils took

[18] The 1950 census showed that there were 22,012 persons living in the territory of St. Luke's parish; of these only 165 (or less than one per cent) were Negroes. All of them lived in three census tracts in the northwest section of the parish bordering the railroad tracks. One Catholic family in this area did not attend St. Luke's church and had no children of elementary school age.

[19] While the city is in general quite prosperous with fairly adequate employment opportunities, the largest factory in the city was laying off men and working

unfavorable attitudes toward both refugees and foreign aid. These factors are hardly enough, however, to explain the differences between the public and the parochial school children. It is quite likely that the attitudes of the teachers and the training of the children in the Catholic school help to account for the more favorable attitudes of the parochial school children. Many of them had selected Cardinal Mindzenty as one of the three greatest living men.[20]

The presence of unfavorable attitudes toward Negroes on the part of some Catholic children in the public school is open to speculation. About one-sixth of them were opposed to friendly and neighborly relations with Negroes. This is more than twice as much as the prejudice shown by pupils in the two other categories of pupils. A further question is raised about the apparent ambivalence of some of these children concerning Protestant-Catholic relations. Almost one-tenth of them could not make up their minds whether a Catholic was doing a good thing in helping to support the Protestant poor. This kind of reply indicates an ignorance of the principles governing such relationships, rather than an attitude for or against them.

This lack of knowledge extends particularly to the statement concerning labor unions. About one-tenth of St. Luke's pupils, one-fifth of the non-Catholic children, and almost two-fifths of the Catholics in the public school, did not know enough about labor unions to make any comment about the proposed problem, and a number of them actually confessed their ignorance. Even though about one-eighth of St. Luke's pupils demonstrated unfavorable attitudes toward labor unions, the fact is that the social principles of the so-called labor Encyclicals of the Popes have been incorporated as part of the curriculum of the parochial school. Social justice is discussed in the religion period; it is illustrated in the English Readers, and in the *Messenger* series on current events that the children read.

On this whole question of social standards and skills, of attitudes and knowledge about social problems, we found hardly any difference in the average scores of boys and girls. The following table shows the total average score on social adjustment from the *California Test of Personality* for boys and girls in both schools.

	173 Boys	181 Girls	354 Both
Social Adjustment	60.46	62.66	61.58

on short shifts. Some of the children in the area were from the families of these workers.

[20] See below, chap. 17, "School, Parish and Community." It is not clear, however, what degree of identification the children made between the Cardinal and the refugees from Eastern Europe.

Although this difference is slight, it appears to follow the general conclusions of sociologists and psychologists that females usually adapt themselves and conform more readily than males to the expectations of the culture. We have seen that the St. Luke's girl pupil is more "at home" in the school and classroom situation than is the boy. There is also the generally accepted fact that girls in the three upper grades of the elementary school are both physically and socially more mature than boys in the same grades. The following table analyzes this point somewhat further by comparing the boys and girls separately in the two schools.

	St. Luke's School			Taft School		
	84 Boys	91 Girls	175 Both	89 Boys	90 Girls	179 Both
Social Adjustment	60.87	62.36	61.65	60.08	62.96	61.53

This comparison shows that the girls score higher on social adjustment in both the parochial and the public school, and that while the boys at St. Luke's score slightly higher than the boys in the public school, the reverse is true of the girls. The public school girls appear to be slightly better adjusted than the girls from St. Luke's. It is quite clear that while there is a sex differential in this whole question of social adjustment, there is not a "school difference" in the sense that one school is a better factor of social adjustment than the other.

Similar results are found when we compare the boys of both schools with the girls of both schools on the social problems test. The following shows the percentage of students giving the three types of answers, favorable, unfavorable and don't know, on all seven problems of the test.

Attitudes on all statements:	172 Boys	182 Girls	354 Both
Favorable	84.6%	85.4%	85.03%
Unfavorable	10.2	10.3	10.21
Don't Know	5.2	4.3	4.76

This comparison shows that almost exactly the same percentage of boys and girls had unfavorable attitudes on all of the social problems. The girls, however, have a slight advantage in favorable attitudes, and they are also slightly more knowledgeable about these community problems, as indicated by the lower percentage of those who could not answer or had no opinion. The following table analyzes these differences in more detail, showing the percentage differences between the schools, and also between the sexes in each school.

Attitudes on all statements:	St. Luke's School 74 Boys	81 Girls	155 Both	Taft School 98 Boys	101 Girls	199 Both
Favorable	88.2%	86.4%	87.28%	81.9%	84.6%	83.27%
Unfavorable	9.9	10.9	10.42	10.4	9.8	10.05
Don't Know	1.9	2.7	2.30	7.7	5.6	6.68

Whatever the reasons may be, the parochial school children are several percentage points above the public school children in their favorable attitudes on these seven social problems (87.28% as compared to 83.27%). The pupils of St. Luke's apparently also have more understanding and knowledge of the problems in question, as indicated by the percentage of pupils giving no opinion (2.30% for the parochial, and 6.68% for the public school). While these differences are not great, they seem sufficient to allow the general conclusion that the parochial school succeeds in developing a deeper social awareness among the children than does the public school, and that St. Luke's children have a readier acceptance of the highest values and norms of the American culture than do the public school pupils.

This conclusion must also be examined from the point of view of the sex difference in the two schools. It is a curious fact that the boys do somewhat better than the girls at St. Luke's school, while the reverse is true in the public school. The parochial school boys have a slightly higher percentage who gave favorable answers (88.2% for boys, 86.4% for girls) and also show slightly more knowledge than the girls. Both boys and girls in the public school show lower percentages of favorable answers, but the girls score better than the boys in favorable attitudes and in knowledge of the subjects discussed.

Up to this point we have investigated the differences in these tests according to the criteria of school and of sex. We have seen that on the matter of social adjustment in the *California Test of Personality* the sex of the pupil seems a more important factor than the school attended, the girls in both schools scoring somewhat higher than the boys. In the test on social problems we have seen that the school is a more important factor than the sex of the pupil, the children of St. Luke's scoring higher consistently than the public school children. There remains then to analyze the age differences in these children, according to the grades they belong to in each school. The following table shows the distribution of scores on social adjustment.

Grade	St. Luke's School Pupils	Score	Public School Pupils	Score
Eighth	60	63.18	59	61.92
Seventh	51	60.02	68	61.04
Sixth	64	61.50	52	61.71

Here again, while the differences in the average scores are slight, we note that the eighth-grade pupils at St. Luke's are the best adjusted of any of the three grades in the two schools (scoring 63.18 out of a possible perfect score of 72). The phenomenon that we have seen in various other parts of our study appears here again, that is, that the seventh grade in both schools scores lower than either the sixth or the eighth grades. This "dip" in the seventh grade may be due simply to chance in any given school, but it seems to be quite unusual to find it in both schools. We were unable to discern any factors of stress that may have caused this variation.

The following table shows the comparison by grades in the two schools of the attitudes expressed in the test on seven social problems.

Grade	Attitude	St. Luke's School	Taft School
	Favorable	94.2%	84.0%
Eighth	Unfavorable	5.8	11.0
	Don't Know	0.0	5.0
	Favorable	80.8	78.4
Seventh	Unfavorable	12.7	11.6
	Don't Know	6.5	10.0
	Favorable	86.2	88.1
Sixth	Unfavorable	13.0	7.5
	Don't Know	0.8	4.4

The general pattern of lower seventh-grade scores that we found in the social adjustment test is confirmed also here on this test on attitudes in social problems. In both schools the lowest percentage of favorable attitudes is found in the seventh grade. An interesting variation, however, occurs in the fact that in the public school the sixth grade has the largest percentage of favorable attitudes, larger than the seventh and eighth grades of the same school. As in the case of social adjustment, so also in the matter of social attitudes, the eighth grade at St. Luke's makes up the "stars" as compared to all other school grades. They have the smallest percentage of unfavorable attitudes and they include no child who hesitated about giving an answer.

Generalizations

In this chapter we have analyzed the social standards and attitudes of the elementary school children, as expressed directly by themselves.

The conclusions we make here are drawn from the children's words, and not from our observations of their behavior, nor from various other tests we administered concerning likes and dislikes, goals and aspirations and values. Thus, we are considering here that which the children themselves consider right and wrong in social attitudes and behavior. The following general conclusions may be suggested from what they have said.

1. In areas that concern themselves, like school and play behavior, the children's standards of conduct appear to be somewhat higher than their actual patterns of conduct. They know and believe what is right, but they admit that they do not always live up to the norms. This is the obvious disparity between conscience and conduct, demonstrable not only in the lives of individuals, but also in the general disparity between the value a society professes and the level of social performance in the society. In this sense, the elementary school children are a reflection of the adult world, and perhaps provide a preview of their own future adulthood.

2. Elementary school children appear to have a more "idealized" version of cultural values in the community, and they express them in a more moralistic tone than do the adults. There is considerable difference, for example, between what the children say ought to be done about voting and about living next door to Negroes, and what the general practices in the community are in regard to these two items. The children are obviously not in a position, because of their age and status, to make concrete decisions about their own immediate performance in these areas. It is probable that their standards are higher than those of their parents because they do not have to take action concerning labor unions, displaced persons and inadequate housing.

3. There appears to be little difference between parochial and public school children in the standards of conduct, as measured by the *California Test of Personality*. This test deliberately avoids any question that would involve religious convictions and supernatural motivation, and for this reason it escapes the area in which the parochial school pupils are at their best. The children in both schools accept and demonstrate, in about the same proportions, the virtues of honesty, obedience, gratitude, self-control and kindliness. As may be expected in their sport-centered milieu, they have an abhorrence of cheating in games, or of appearing to be "poor sports."

4. There appears to be a special problem concerning social standards and attitudes among the Catholic children who attend the public school. They show the highest percentages of unfavorable attitudes

toward Negroes and refugees and toward the idea of aid to foreign countries. They also demonstrate by far the greatest ignorance concerning labor unions. This presents a peculiar unsolved problem of our research project. These children are in many ways quite similar to the Catholic children attending St. Luke's parochial school. The great difference is that although they come from Catholic families they are not experiencing the Catholic schooling of the other Catholic children in the parish.

5. The pupils of St. Luke's school demonstrated more favorable attitudes than the public school children on practically all of the statements made concerning concrete social problems of the adult world. This difference of attitude is particularly notable on the questions concerning foreign aid and labor unions. It appears that the teachers of St. Luke's are in a better position to express broader and more liberal views in these matters than are the teachers in the public school. The social philosophy behind parochial school education is less isolationist, and the texts and teachings in the parochial classroom embrace a more nearly universal view, than appears to be possible at the present time in the mid-western public elementary school.

6. The greatest difference between the two schools is in the fact that the parochial school children explain their attitudes most often with religious and supernatural reasons. They express not only the normal humanitarian, democratic and American motives for approved social attitudes and behavior, but they emphasize the idea that "God wants" this kind of thinking and behaving from His children. Since the whole parochial school revolves around religion, and since the children are constantly presented with spiritual motives for good behavior and good study habits, it is hardly unexpected that this type of reason shows up in the tests.

7. The test results show a consistent, though slight, advantage of girls over boys in both schools when we combine the totals for both sexes. It appears that the girls in the three upper grades of the elementary school are somewhat better adjusted socially than are the boys. The girls also have a slightly higher percentage of favorable attitudes than the boys in regard to the social and community problems about which we questioned them. Thus, while the school factor does not enter into the differences on social adjustment, but does enter into the differences on attitudes toward social problems, the sex factor seems to be distinguishable in both social adjustment and in social attitudes. It is likely that this difference becomes even more noticeable in later adolescence and early adulthood when differing cultural pressures are exerted on the two sexes.

8. There appears to be little question of the fact, so far as these tests extend, that the parochial school children receive a broader social education than the public school children. The confession of ignorance and the inability to give an answer, as indicated in the comparative percentages of "Don't know" replies, are found more frequently among the public school children. This kind of conclusion is contingent also on the intelligence level of the children in the two schools. We have not made a comparison of the two school populations on the basis of mental and chronological age, but as the public school Principal suggested, there is probably a factor of intelligence selectivity involved that gives a slight advantage to the parochial school children.

Chapter

SIX

SOCIAL CONFORMITY AND CONDUCT

ST. LUKE's parochial school is an on-going social system, which must not only perform its central function of educating the children, but also maintain itself in operation. As an essential requirement for its continued existence every social group must fulfill its main purpose, that is, satisfy the needs for which it exists. In order to do this it sets up certain norms of behavior, a code of regulations, either explicit or implicit, which acts as a governing control over the behavior of the persons within the structure. These norms are devised in such a manner as to assure the orderly operation of the group and to protect the welfare of the individuals composing the group.[1]

This is another way of saying that the standards and rules of conduct at St. Luke's school are not established merely for their own sake. There is not "discipline for the sake of discipline." While the school regulations, together with the discipline and social control used to enforce them, are a means of "keeping order" in the school, they are also an instrument for achieving the principal functions of the school in relation to the pupils. "Learning cannot progress effectively, individually or with respect to the class, unless good order and industrious work prevail. Classroom discipline is essential to effective teaching."[2]

There is another important aspect of this question. Not only does St. Luke's require conformity to its norms of behavior in order to keep itself in operation and to make effective teaching possible, but the teaching of the norms themselves is a benefit to the pupil. The group norms at St. Luke's reflect the values and mores of the com-

[1] For a discussion of group norms, see Theodore Newcomb, *Social Psychology* (New York: Dryden Press, 1950)), chaps. 8, 9, pp. 264–336.

[2] Brideen Lone, "A Survey of Discipline Problems in the Elementary School," *Catholic Educational Review*, vol. 54, no. 4 (April, 1956), p. 217.

munity in which it exists, and the school is helping the child to internalize the norms of the larger and adult society which he will eventually enter.[3] Respect for authority, consistent work habits, consideration for others, postponement of satisfactions—these are values in the American urban culture, and in so far as the school succeeds in inculcating them into the children it is also performing part of its role in transmitting the culture and socializing the child.

The Need to Conform

The internal maintenance of the group in operation seems to require certain essential and minimum elements. The continuous observation of St. Luke's school in action has emphasized for us the fact that it shares these minimum requirements with other forms of social systems. Like every other group (whether it is a family, a baseball team or a factory) the parochial school can keep itself going because it achieves conformity through social control, self-control and cooperation. This is another way of saying that organized group life cannot go on unless there is a mechanism for getting people to cooperate with one another and to conform to recognized rules and standards of behavior.

These observations force us to analyze more sharply the whole question of authority and independence, of obedience and self-control, of discipline and of sanctions on behavior. How much conformity is "enough" to keep the group going and fulfill its purposes? What are the best ways of promoting conformity of a voluntary nature? What areas of choice can be allowed, and even encouraged, among the pupils? Obedience to authority must exist in any orderly group, but is it operative because the person in authority says it must be so, or because the obeying persons understand the reasons for it? [4]

The concrete data which we have collected throw significant light on these questions. Research in St. Luke's school allows us to make some conclusions concerning the stereotypes about the "permissive

[3] Ruth Benedict, "Transmitting Our Democratic Heritage in the Schools," *American Journal of Sociology*, vol. 48, no. 6 (May, 1943), pp. 722–727, complains that "archaic values" like thrift and pacifism were taught to her as a child. Margaret Mead, *The School in American Culture* (Cambridge: Harvard University Press, 1951), pp. 34–35, also points out the teacher's need to know current cultural values and norms.

[4] See the findings of Sister Margaret, "Comparison of the Attitude toward Obedience of Eighth Grade Pupils in Public Schools with Those of Eighth Grade Pupils in Catholic Schools" (Washington: Dissertation in the Catholic University Library, 1956).

and reasonable" operation of the elementary school, as compared to its "authoritarian and rigid" operation. Like all stereotypes, both of these are dissipated in the intelligent observation of people in the social situation. In some form or other, social control, conformity, and cooperation must be present in all elementary schools.

Conformity and self-control are integral values of the American culture. When the individual acquires these values, he acts in a way acceptable to our social norms. Self-control, the ultimate and necessary form of social control in a democratic society, is by its nature a self-explanatory concept. With it the individual expresses conformity to social norms (the abstract agent of social control) and to the elements of authority (concrete agents of social control) so that the whole system can be maintained in order and can fulfill its functions.[5]

While we are here primarily concerned with the behavior and conformity of St. Luke's pupils, we must remember that rules and regulations exist not only for pupils, but also for the faculty and for the school as a whole. It may be said generally that the parochial school teacher has more freedom, and is less rule-bound and regimented, than the pupil school teacher.[6] The whole parochial school is more flexible, and it has more freedom of choice and action, than the public school. St. Luke's is not caught up in a bureaucratic and hierarchical system like that of the local public school. Nevertheless, the school still has norms and standards to which it must conform. Obviously, the school itself suffers fewer limitations than its functionaries and its pupils; restrictions are greater for pupils than for teachers. Kinds of action and degrees of responsibility differ on these three levels of school, faculty and children.

A merely casual acquaintance with the routine of an elementary school shows that there necessarily exists a wide area of actual and expected conformity. This is not merely a matter of personal obedience to the teacher in charge (although the children are trained to "do what teacher says") or of conscious acquiescence to the known rules

[5] See Sidonie Matsner Gruenberg, ed., *Our Children Today* (New York: Viking, 1952), Part 3, "The Meaning of Discipline." For an example of deviation in public schools, see Carl B. Rogers, "Mental-Health Findings in Three Elementary Schools," *Educational Research Bulletin*, vol. 21 (March 28, 1942), where he points out that one child in three is regarded as a problem by teachers, one in four is an intellectual misfit in his grade, one in four has serious reading deficiency, one out of six is maladjusted.

[6] See the discussion on this point below, chap. 16, "Problems of Elementary Education."

enunciated by the teacher. Conforming behavior here means mainly an acceptance of "things as they are." Each child most of the time follows the patterns of behavior that are part and parcel of the elementary school system. Patterned behavior becomes habitual, it becomes "internalized" as a segment of the socialization process. In the largest portion of their daily school activities, the children are simply acting by rote without questioning that it could be otherwise. Patterns are taken for granted.[7]

There are certain actions that the individual child performs because "everybody does it." The pupils start school and end school at a certain time of day; they line up by grades to enter the school building; [8] they attend from Monday to Friday unless they are sick or there is a holiday. The upper grades go out for recreation and for lunch periods together; the lower grades go out at another time. The children raise their hands before speaking, and stand up while speaking; at other times they know that silence is the general pattern of behavior. The children in each grade use the same textbooks, and usually study the same subject matter at the same time.[9] There is practically no choice for the child in these patterns, nor is there any indication that either the children or their parents contemplate the possibility of changing these general patterns of behavior.

Absenteeism

Conformity to behavior norms is in day-to-day practice only a relative ideal. In no group of people is there total conformity at all times by all of the members of the group. This relativism is most obviously exemplified in the generalization that "pupils of St. Luke's attend school on school days." If this were an absolute pattern there would be no behavior problem of absenteeism. Even though the state law requires compulsory school attendance, there are conditions under which pupils are excused from the law. The teachers at St. Luke's are

[7] This is, of course, a sociological commonplace, but it is more noticeable in adults than in children. The more socialized an adult is the more routinized he becomes in his behavior. See Joseph H. Fichter, *Sociology* (Chicago: University of Chicago Press, 1957), pp. 22–26.

[8] Sharp contrasts in behavior were noted by our observers. A report for Monday, December 17, reads in part: "When the bell rang ending the noon recess, I was nearly trampled by a stampeding horde of howling, screaming children, almost savage in their eagerness to get into line, where they walked quietly and serenely into the building."

[9] There are some instances, of course, when the teacher may help a few children in one subject like arithmetic while the other children are busy writing spelling words, or doing some other work.

supposed to obtain a written excuse from the parent explaining the absence of a child, but some teachers are more lenient than others, and some parents are less observant than others.

Absenteeism is not the same as truancy. A truant is a child who is absent without an excuse, and St. Luke's school, like other parochial schools in the city, may have the services of the city truant officer who is now called the "attendance officer." During the half-decade that Sister Roberta has been Principal no pupil has been reported to the truant officer. In our interviews with the children, and in their autobiographies, several of them admitted that they had "played hookey" on a number of occasions, but as far as we could discover, no disciplinary action was taken against them by the teachers. The outstanding case of truancy during the year was that of a sixth-grade boy who took literally his teacher's admonition when she said, "I don't see why you come to school when you don't study anyway." The boy built a lean-to on the river bank and lazed away eight full school days until he was discovered by his father. The latter brought him to the Pastor for a "talking to." Because this occurred in early April when many pupils were absent through sickness, the teacher had assumed the child was home sick.

Lawful absences from school are those due to illness, inclement weather or acute situations in the home which prevent attendance. "The truant is legally defined as the child who is unlawfully absent from school without the knowledge of his parents." [10] A study of New York school children showed that while only seventy-three per cent of the *absences* are lawful about ninety per cent of the absent *children* are lawfully absent. Since there were no referals to the city attendance officers, and no action taken on truancy, in St. Luke's school, we may assume that almost all who missed school were "lawfully absent." The New York study showed also that on an average day about nine out of ten pupils are actually in school, the attendance rate going as high as 92.6 per cent and as low as 87.7 per cent over the course of seventeen years. The average daily attendance rate at St. Luke's during the whole school year was 94.9 per cent.

The following table shows the distribution of the number of absences among the pupils of St. Luke's school. About six per cent of all absences were half-days, the rest were full days. The 629 children on whom we have the attendance records had 5,568 absences during the school year, of which 5,232 were full days and 336 were half-days.

[10] See *Children Absent from School* (New York: Citizens' Committee on Children, 1949), pp. 2, 3, 13.

This means that the average number of absences of each child was 8.85 times, while the average number of days of school lost for each child was 8.58 days. In the whole school, from the first to the eighth grade, thirty-eight children (6.1%) had a perfect attendance record.[11] At the other end of the scale, fifty-three children (8.4%) were absent twenty-one or more times, which meant generally that they lost more than four weeks of schooling. The girls averaged almost one absence more per year than did the boys (8.36 for the boys and 9.34 for the girls.)

Absences	314 Boys	Average	315 Girls	Average	629 Both	Average
None	8.0%	0.0	4.1%	0.0	6.1%	0.0
1–5	35.0	3.21	34.6	3.37	34.8	3.29
6–10	28.0	7.84	30.8	8.12	29.4	7.99
11–15	15.9	12.70	11.7	12.86	13.8	12.77
16–20	6.1	17.89	8.9	17.39	7.5	17.60
21–25	2.9	23.11	6.4	22.70	4.6	22.83
26–30	2.5	27.63	1.9	27.50	2.2	27.57
31 plus	1.6	35.60	1.6	40.80	1.6	38.20
Average		8.36		9.34		8.85

The majority of school pupils missed more than one week of schooling out of the thirty-five weeks (175 days) during which St. Luke's operated. This means that fifty-seven per cent of the boys, and 61.3 per cent of the girls, missed more than a week. About three out of ten, twenty-nine per cent of the boys, and 30.6 per cent of the girls, were absent from school for more than two weeks. It is clear, of course, that these absences do not all represent consecutive days on which the children failed to attend school; most of them are days and half-days scattered throughout the year. Thus, the problem of "making up work" was difficult only for those who were sick for several days at a time.

The problem of absenteeism fluctuates with general weather conditions and with the health or sickness of the whole school population. Our classroom observers noted that there were days when almost one-fifth of a given class was absent from school. This was particularly

[11] On the Award Night, when the Pastor gave the medal for perfect attendance to three boys and two girls of the graduating class, he explained that this was perfect attendance "except for sickness." Sister Roberta arose immediately to say that this meant "never absent for any reason."

noticeable in the lower grades when the inclement weather kept children at home. It was noticeable also on several occasions during the winter months, when an epidemic of colds, or of measles, appeared to strike one class after another. This was the case during January, February and March when the greatest number of absences occurred.

The following table shows the monthly fluctuations of absences in the first grade of St. Luke's school. There are eighty-five pupils included in these statistics, forty-two boys and forty-three girls. Since the number of school days varied from month to month, October having twenty-three and December only fifteen, the amount of days lost is given as a percentage of the total school days (multiplied by the number of pupils) for that month. There were 1,046 absences during the year (12.30 per child), of which 983 were full days and sixty-three half-days. The actual time lost by first graders was 1,014.5 days (11.93 per child), or 6.8 per cent of the total time they should have spent in school.

Month	Number of school days	Average days absent per child	Percentage of total time lost
September	17	0.52	3.1%
October	23	1.17	5.1
November	19	1.28	6.7
December	15	0.65	4.4
January	19	2.07	10.9
February	19	1.91	10.1
March	20	2.20	11.0
April	17	1.57	9.3
May	21	0.53	2.5
June	5	0.00	0.0
	175	11.93	6.8%

We have seen in these tables that girls miss school more than boys and that inclement weather and sickness increase the percentage of absences in the months from January to April. Absences vary, however, not only by the sex and by the month but also by the age of the children. Many of the younger children are taken to and from school by their mothers in automobiles, and this occurs also for older children who live at a distance from the school, particularly in rainy weather. Although 96.8 per cent of these families have automobiles, most of the younger children coming from the south side of the parish ride on the bus, and many of the older children use their bicycles. On a normal day there are 116 bicycles (eighty-five boys' and thirty-one girls') parked in various parts of the school yard.[12] From the point of view of absenteeism, transportation to and from school is not so great a problem, regardless of the weather, for the older children as for the younger ones. The following table gives the average number of times absent during the year, according to school grade and sex.

Grade	Boys	Girls	Both
Eighth	5.53	6.57	6.02
Seventh	6.68	7.42	7.14
Sixth	5.70	5.16	5.43
Fifth	5.93	8.32	7.01
Fourth	7.76	7.41	7.60
Third	8.17	10.34	9.33
Second	12.10	13.40	12.74
First	12.14	12.47	12.30

The several generalizations that can be drawn from these statistics are probably part of the ordinary experiences of school and family life. It appears that younger children generally are not expected to be so prompt and regular in school attendance as their older brothers and sisters. They are more easily excused from the duty of school attendance; their parents are probably more concerned about their health and about their potential for sickness and indisposition. The older children have had more experience and training. They have advanced further in the socialization process, and they are viewed as responsible and accountable persons. They are not so easily excused from the duty of attending school.

The difference in attendance between the boys and the girls does not fall into a similar explanation. It is a fact that there was more sickness among the girls than among the boys during the school year at St. Luke's. But this accounts for only part of the difference in attendance. In all other facets of behavior the girls demonstrated more regularity, and they received higher "conduct marks" than did the boys. We do not know whether cultural influences enter into these generalizations, whether, for example, the parents consider

[12] The City Council passed an ordinance that all bicycles have to carry a license. The registration was done in February, and 126 plates issued (sold) to the children at St. Luke's school in March. This is another example of the use of the elementary school as a public agency, and of the multitudinous functions performed by the Principal.

formal education more important for boys than for girls, and therefore, insist more on the regular attendance of their sons than of their daughters.[13]

Although the boys actually have a better attendance record than the girls, more of them (35.7%) than girls (20.9%) would like to "skip school" if they could. The following table shows the comparison of affirmative answers by sex, grade and school, to the question: "would you like to stay home from school a lot if it were right to do so?"

St. Luke's School		William Taft Public School	
84 boys	35.7%	94 boys	25.5%
91 girls	20.9	92 girls	6.5
175 total	28.0	186 total	16.1
60 eighth-graders	25.0	60 eighth-graders	11.7
51 seventh-graders	27.5	70 seventh-graders	14.3
64 sixth-graders	31.2	56 sixth-graders	23.2

The responses to this question in both schools bear out the generalizations that girls like to attend school more than boys do, and that the desire to absent oneself from school decreases from the sixth to the eighth grade. It appears the children come to appreciate school more as they get older. On the basis of these responses we may conclude that the public school pupils "like school" more than do St. Luke's pupils. The explanation for this difference is open to speculation: whether public school experiences are in themselves "more enjoyable," whether life there is easier and "more pleasant," or whether the public school children have a greater desire for knowledge.[14]

Marks for Conduct

Parents are interested in getting a report on how their children behave in school, and the teacher is forced to make as many judgments about conduct as she has pupils in her class. Even if her judgment were always correct, and even if all the teachers used exactly the same objective criteria of judgment, there still remain variations of behavior among the children. There is a stated attempt to obtain "uniform" good behavior from the children at St. Luke's. If the children behaved according to this ideal there would be no disci-

[13] When questioned about this, some parents declared that they are more likely to keep a daughter than a son at home "to help in emergencies."

[14] We were unable to obtain complete statistics for absences by sex and grade in the Taft school; but in grades six to eight the pupils averaged almost two days more absences than in the corresponding grades at St. Luke's.

plinary problems, there would be no difference between "trouble makers" and "good children."

Parents find it difficult to discover the "conduct grade" on a modern report card.[15] The permanent records for the pupils from the second to the eighth grade carry a grade for "citizenship" which was the nearest equivalent the parents could find for a conduct or deportment grade.[16] These grades were given in letters as follows: E for "excellent," (95–100), A (90–94), B (80–89), and C (70–79). Because a new system was used for the first grade, the following table refers only to the seven highest grades. In studying these figures we must remember that each child is supposedly compared with every other child within the class room, and that there were fourteen different teachers involved in making judgments about deportment.

Grade in school	E	A	B	C	Averages
Eighth	5.0%	55.0%	36.7%	3.3%	2.61
Seventh	0.0	33.3	58.8	7.9	2.25
Sixth	3.1	47.7	32.3	16.9	2.38
Fifth	0.0	60.0	36.0	4.0	2.56
Fourth	0.0	39.0	52.6	8.4	2.30
Third	0.0	38.5	46.1	15.4	2.23
Second	0.0	49.0	36.8	14.2	2.35
All grades	0.9	46.0	42.5	10.6	2.37

If these comparative figures were dependable indications of the behavior of children we could conclude that some of the worst behaved children were concentrated in the sixth, third and second grades, but that some of the best-behaved ones were in the eighth and sixth grades. We find that in only three grades, the eighth, sixth and fifth, did more than half of the pupils receive a mark of A or better. When these grades are transferred to a numerical scale, with the letters E to C transferred to the numbers four to one, we find that the eighth grade must be adjudged the best-behaved grade, and the third and seventh grades the poorest-behaved.

[15] See below, chap. 13 "Parents and Teachers" for an account of the confusion engendered by the new system of report cards. A recent study showed that nearly half of the Catholic schools still use "stereotyped report cards." See M. Veronice Doody, "A Critical Analysis of Procedures of Interpretation in Catholic Elementary Schools" (Washington: Dissertation in Catholic University Library, 1956).

[16] The new report card system was also used for the higher grades but the permanent records in the school files continued the old system of grading, so that the teachers were burdened with a kind of "double entry."

The conduct marks for the first grade are taken separately here because the marking system is different from that for the other grades. These new report cards carry a mark judging whether the pupil "conforms to school regulations." The translations of the new markings are as follows: E means that "the pupil *almost always* practices the trait;" G means that "the pupil acts in the manner indicated *most* of the time;" C means that "the pupil acts in the manner indicated *part* of the time;" and U means that the "pupil *seldom* acts in the manner indicated." We were unable satisfactorily to equate the two marking systems. There appears also to have been confusion in the minds of the two teachers as indicated by the great divergence in their markings. The teacher in grade 1A gave E to 47.5 per cent of the class, G to forty per cent, and C. to 12.5 per cent. The teacher in the other first grade gave E to 80.9 per cent of her class, G to the remaining 19.1 per cent, without giving the lower grade of C to anyone. The following table combines the children from both classes of the first grade.

Marks for "conformity"	Boys	Girls	Both
E	62.2%	69.0%	65.5%
G	26.7	31.0	28.7
C	11.1	0.0	5.8

These statistics show that the teachers of the first grade think highly of their pupils' conduct, judging that the majority of them (65.5%) "almost always" conform to school regulations. The fact that girls are better behaved than boys is shown by the figure that more than one-tenth of the boys, but none of the girls, were children who conform only "part" of the time. This difference between boys and girls is seen also in the other grades of the school. The following table shows these divergences according to the marking system used from the second to the eighth grades.

Marks for "citizenship"	Boys	Girls	Both
E	1.1%	0.7%	0.9%
A	33.0	58.4	46.0
B	49.8	35.6	42.5
C	16.1	5.3	10.6

While it is true that some teachers are lenient and others strict in giving conduct marks, the differential marks given along sex lines agree generally with our own observations. According to the norms employed to judge behavior in our American culture, it is a truism to remark that girls behave better than boys. The differences have been noted in the general behavior around the school. The boys appear to be more relaxed on the playground, and more uncomfortable in the classroom. The reverse was observed of the girls: they tend to be more at ease in the classroom but somewhat self-conscious and quite "ladylike" on the playground.[17] These sex differences are more noticeable in the older children, from the fourth to the eighth grades, than they are in the children of the younger grades.

Other Factors of Conduct

Besides age and sex, there are certain other items which may be correlated with the conduct marks of the pupils. We were curious to know whether there is any relation between the Intelligence Quotient and the behavior of the child. In other words, can we say that the "smartest" children tend to get the highest marks in conduct, while the "dullest" get the low marks? We selected the forty children in the sixth, seventh and eighth grades (twenty boys and twenty girls) who scored the highest in the California Mental Maturity Test. These we compared, for conduct marks, with the twenty boys and twenty girls from the same grades who scored the lowest. The following table shows the percentage distribution of this comparison.

Marks in citizenship	Highest scores (115–141)	Lowest scores (74–102)
E	7.5%	0.0%
A	45.0	32.5
B	37.5	50.0
C	10.0	17.5

More than half of the brighter pupils (52.5%) received a mark of A or better, as compared to less than one-third (32.5%) of the slow students. There are, of course, psychological as well as cultural factors at work here. Perhaps in some instances the teacher subconsciously favors the brighter child and raises his conduct marks closer to his grades for academic subjects. On the other hand, the child who is more alert mentally may often be the one who distracts the class, and "causes trouble," while the slower child may be content to "take a back seat" and cause no trouble. Still, the brighter student may also

[17] During the first weeks of our study we thought that this was a reaction to the presence of observers, the girls heeding more carefully the warnings of the teachers that they were being "observed." If there was artificial tension it soon wore off, and the girls continued to act more primly than the boys.

realize that in the competition for marks he has to "watch himself" in his behavior.

It appears that the child's lack of ability to do the lessons required in his particular class has a relation to a number of annoying characteristics of misbehavior. These are the children who often whisper or talk out loud, who are inattentive, waste time and leave their seats without permission. For the most part, these are violations of classroom regulations, and they cannot be termed serious violations of behavior when measured by objective norms of morality. Yet they are the patterns of behavior that come most to the attention of the teacher and that loom large in the marking of conduct reports.[18]

The next comparison we made is that between the popularity of the child and his conduct mark. By means of the sociometric test administered to the children of the sixth, seventh and eighth grades, we were able to select the twenty most popular children and the twenty least popular in these grades. There are ten boys and ten girls in each category.[19] We wanted to find out whether those who were most popular among their classmates were also among the "better-behaved" pupils or whether the popular ones are those who are "always cutting up," and thus receive poor conduct grades. The following table shows that the popular children tend also to be popular with the teacher when the conduct grades are given out.

Mark for citizenship	Populars	Isolates	All pupils in these grades
E	10.0%	0.0%	3.9%
A	55.0	25.0	45.5
B	30.0	55.0	41.0
C	5.0	20.0	9.6

It is clear that the popular children do better in their behavior grades than do the isolates, but they are also considerably above the average for the whole grade, just as the least popular children are considerably below the average. Three-quarters of the isolates have conduct grades of B or C, as compared to one-half (50.6%) of the total population of the three grades, and somewhat over a third (35.0%) of the popular children.

[18] M. Brideen Lone, "A Survey of Discipline Problems in the Elementary School," *Catholic Educational Review,* vol. 54, no. 4 (April, 1956), p. 227, says that "two out of every three teachers reported the child's lack of ability to do the work of the grade as a cause of one or more of their discipline problems."

[19] These two categories are made up of the same children discussed in the chapter on "Cliques and Clubs." See below, chap. 9.

Another factor that may be considered in relation to conduct marks is that of the school activities in which the pupils are involved. Participation in these activities can be measured by the number of groups and organizations to which a child belongs as well as by the amount of time he gives and the number of functions he performs in them. By these criteria we selected the thirty most active and the thirty least active among the children in the sixth, seventh and eighth grades. Each category contains fifteen boys and fifteen girls, even though there are more organized activities open for boys than for girls at St. Luke's school.

Marks for citizenship	Most active pupils	Least active pupils
E	0.0%	3.3%
A	50.0	50.0
B	43.3	33.4
C	6.7	13.3

There appears to be little mutual influence between the amount of extracurricular activities in which a child participates and the marks he receives for conduct on his report card. There is a greater range in marks for the least active pupils, one of them receiving the highest mark for conduct and four of them the lowest mark.

Strict and Lenient Teachers

There is considerable variation among the teachers of St. Luke's both in the way they distribute conduct marks and in the way they handle behavior problems in the classroom.[20] The Principal is aware of these variations, and has on occasions expressed opinions concerning the way in which the teachers live up to the norms which she sets. She knows that one teacher is "a little too old for good discipline," another is "sometimes cranky," another is "too easy" with the children. She does not hold the opinion, commonly expressed by Catholic parents, that the religious teachers have better control in the classroom than do the lay teachers of the parochial school. She does feel, however, that public school teachers are at a disadvantage in this regard; they are not "in a position" to uphold discipline mainly because the public school cannot supply the high religious motivation for good behavior.

[20] Constructive assistance, verbal appeal, censure and deprivation, are said to be the main forms of teacher response to misbehavior. See Frank Slobetz, "Elementary Teachers' Reactions to School Situations." *Journal of Educational Research,* vol. 44, no. 2 (October, 1950), pp. 81–90.

According to our own observations in the classrooms, around the school, and on the playgrounds, the most permissive, or "lenient," members of the faculty at St. Luke's are Mrs. Gordon, Sister Agatha, Sister Mark and Sister Cecelia. At the other end of the scale, the strictest disciplinarians are Sister Dominic, Mrs. Edwards, Mrs. Gerald and Sister Bridget. It is an interesting fact, however, that the parents' rating of the teachers, and the measurement of the teachers according to the conduct marks they gave, do not coincide with the rating of severity or leniency made by our observers.

The following list of teachers' names proceeds from those who may be considered the least strict (1) to the most strict (14), as measured by the percentage of parents who judged the teacher to be stricter than the parent and as measured by the conduct marks given by the teacher.

Rank		Percentage of parents rating teacher strict		Average conduct marks given by teacher *
1	Sister Mark	21.4%	Sister Roberta	2.61
2	Sister Roberta	27.1	Sister Dominic	2.56
3	Sister Ruth	28.6	Mrs. Gordon	2.55
4	Sister Justin	29.2	Sister Ruth	2.55
5	Mrs. Edwards	30.0	Sister Agatha	2.45
6	Mrs. Gerald	31.6	Sister Bridget	2.40
7	Sister Bridget	31.8	Sister Bernadette	2.35
8	Mrs. Gordon	32.0	Mrs. Edwards	2.32
9	Sister Vincent de Paul	40.9	Sister Vincent de Paul	2.30
10	Sister Cecelia	43.5	Sister Cecelia	2.25
11	Sister Martha	47.1	Sister Mark	2.23
12	Sister Bernadette	56.3	Sister Justin	2.16
13	Sister Agatha	57.7	Mrs. Gerald	2.13
14	Sister Dominic	59.1	Sister Martha	2.10

* These numerical averages are obtained by translating the marks, E, A, B, C, to the numerals, 4, 3, 2, 1, so that those with the highest numerical average were the best behaved.

Some of the teachers have the reputation among the children of being "really tough," and it appears that the parents often base their judgment on the statements and complaints the children bring home. Parents also tend to estimate the teacher on the basis of personal contact they have with her, which in the last analysis is no criterion of the way she handles the classroom discipline. When the teacher is very charming to parents, as Sister Mark and Sister Roberta are, she tends to be considered "less strict." When the teacher has a reputation among the children as the "strictest in the school," as Sister Dominic and Sister Agatha have, this too appears to make an impression on the parents. Yet, when we look at the report cards, we find that Sister Dominic tends to give high marks, and Sister Mark low marks, for conduct.

It must be pointed out, of course, that conduct marks are meant to rate the children for their behavior, and not the teacher for her attitudes and practices in maintaining discipline. In general, there appears to be little connection between the strictness of the teacher in the classroom and the low marks given to the children.[21] Regardless of the opinion expressed by parents concerning her, Mrs. Gerald is quite strict in her handling of the children and is also a "hard marker" of deportment grades. Mrs. Gordon tends to be lenient and permissive in the classroom and is also lenient in her grading on conduct. Sister Roberta, who likes to boast of the excellent conduct of her eighth graders, gives the highest marks in conduct, but as one of her boy pupils says, "she's no pushover; you can't get away with anything on her."

At a kind of half-way position in the scale from strict to lenient is Sister Vincent de Paul. She is perhaps typical of the parochial school teacher. She maintains discipline without being too severe or too easy-going. She has the confidence and poise of a person who knows that she is performing her function well.[22] Her own explanation is as follows: "I try to treat each child as an individual person. Their problems of adjustment are different. Some are nervous children who may have difficulties at home and in other situations, and with them you have to have a lot of patience. Others are normal children, but like all children they need love and attention, so I simply try to mother them. I suppose, in the long run, you have to mix authority, patience and mothering with all the children."

[21] In fact, the reverse may be said in some instances. The teacher insists upon good conduct in the classroom and the children earn good marks by behaving in accord with this insistence.

[22] See the description of approved techniques by an experienced educator, Paul E. Campbell, "Facets of School Discipline," *The Homiletic and Pastoral Review,* vol. 57, no. 9 (June, 1957), pp. 843–849. See also the statement of Percival M. Symonds, "Classroom Discipline," *Teachers' College Record,* vol. 51, no. 3 (December, 1949), "the emotionally secure teacher, feeling confident in his own strength, dares to be more informal and natural, and if at the same time he is secure in his position, or is above caring whether he is, he can afford to face possible criticism that he may invoke from his superiors" (p. 154).

From the point of view of the school child the teacher tends to personify authority; she becomes the central figure in the whole complex question of social control and conformity. There is probably no way of measuring this, but it appears that conscious conformity and obedience are focused on the person of the teacher, and that this is merely re-inforced by the expressed rules as such and by the repetitive and institutionalized patterns of behavior. The latter are necessary in the socialization process. The fact that children become creatures of custom makes the problem of social control much lighter. Nevertheless there is much evidence in our study of the strong moral influence which the teachers, both religious and lay, exert over their pupils.

By and large, the children themselves do not consider their teachers over-strict. More than three-quarters (76.6%) of the pupils in the three upper grades answered negatively the question: "Do you think the children would be happier if the teacher were not so strict?" Of the children in the same grades of the Taft Public School, 67.7 per cent answered negatively, indicating that in the opinion of the pupils the public school is stricter than the parochial school. In both schools the teachers were thought to be stricter in the sixth grade than in the seventh and eighth, and in the public school the boys seemed to be bothered more by the teacher's sternness than were the girls. The following table gives the comparison of affirmative answers by sex, grade and school.

St. Luke's School		William Taft Public School	
84 boys	23.8%	94 boys	36.2%
91 girls	23.1	92 girls	28.3
175 total	23.4	186 total	32.3
60 eighth-graders	21.7	60 eighth-graders	20.0
51 seventh-graders	23.5	70 seventh-graders	24.3
64 sixth-graders	25.0	56 sixth-graders	55.4

While a school child may like a teacher in spite of the fact that she is a strict disciplinarian, it is hardly to be expected that the child, or anyone else, for that matter, actually enjoys being disciplined. At the same time, it appears that school children have a strong sense of fairness in the teacher-pupil relation, and that they are alert to any attitude or action that is "unfair" on the part of the teacher. To put this question in their own language, we asked them whether they thought any of the teachers "have it in for" the pupils. The following table gives the comparison of affirmative answers by sex, grade and school.

St. Luke's School		William Taft Public School	
84 boys	19.0%	94 boys	44.7%
91 girls	24.2	92 girls	31.5
175 total	21.7	186 total	38.2
60 eighth-graders	13.3	60 eighth-graders	31.7
51 seventh-graders	29.4	70 seventh-graders	31.4
64 sixth-graders	23.4	56 sixth-graders	53.6

This comparison shows that St. Luke's pupils have a considerably higher regard for their teachers' sense of fairness than do the children from the public school. Almost two out of five (38.2%) of the public school pupils, and more than half (53.6%) of the sixth graders, feel that some teachers "have it in for" pupils. The girls at St. Luke's, who have sometimes said that "the boys get all the breaks," seem to feel this discrimination more (24.2%) than the boys (19.0%). In the public school this sex differential is reversed, with the boys (44.7%) claiming unfairness by the teacher to a considerable extent more than do the girls (31.5%).

A great advantage enjoyed by St. Luke's school in the matter of social control and behavior is the fact that it can afford to be selective in the admission and retention of pupils. It is known as a competent educational agency; the parents want to have their children admitted; the Church expects them to give their children Catholic schooling; and the school itself is able to set and maintain relatively high standards of conduct. Thus, there is social pressure from all sides on both parents and children that the pupils conform to the patterns of the school. Interestingly enough, we have never heard any teacher threaten to report misconduct to a child's parent.[23] It is the custom of the teachers to handle their own problems rather than to make an appeal to "higher authority."

Home Influences on Conduct

It appears to be a perennial attitudinal pattern among elementary school teachers that parents are over-indulgent of their children, and that behavior problems in the school are largely the consequence of this laxity in the home. This generalized attitude is often specified by the complaint that parents do not send their children to bed on time,

[23] We cannot be certain whether this reflects the teacher's desire to keep these matters within the school walls or her belief that the parents do not exert strong and effective control over children. Most of the teachers in both parochial and public school had a low opinion of parental laxity.

that they allow the children to attend too many movies and read too many comic books, and that they have no control over the television habits of the children. "While the impact of excessive viewing of television on the study habits of the child should not be minimized, there is a possibility that teachers may be tempted to attribute discipline problems to it unduly." [24] This statement indicates the methodological problem of distinguishing the teacher's opinions from the facts at home, and distinguishing the effects on study habits from those on behavior and discipline.

We asked the parents whether they had any regulations concerning their children's use of television, and found that these regulations fell into two general categories: the child was limited in the amount of time he could spend at the TV set (usually this meant "not till your homework is done") and also he was limited in the type of program he was allowed to view. In some instances parental regulations covered both time and type of program. The following table gives a percentage distribution of the answers and a comparison between the parochial and the public school parents.

Regulations on use of TV	St. Luke's	Public School [25]	Both
Restricted time	46.7%	43.7%	46.0%
Restricted program	13.5	15.1	13.9
Time and program	5.6	12.6	7.3
No regulations	32.4	27.7	31.3
No TV set	1.8	0.9	1.5

The apparent laxity in the censorship of types of programs by the parents seems to rest on the assumption that most daytime and late afternoon programs are not "harmful" to children. In asking the children concerning their program preferences we found that only two "children's programs," Lassie and Disneyland, were chosen among the most popular. TV programs most frequently mentioned by both

[24] "Approximately one out of two teachers looked upon children's excessive viewing of television as a cause of one or more of their discipline problems." M. Brideen Lone, "A Survey of Discipline Problems in the Elementary School," *Catholic Educational Review*, vol. 54, no. 4 (April, 1956), pp. 217–232. In another study of 230 religious educators, thirty-seven per cent thought TV is detrimental, and thirty per cent thought it is both detrimental and beneficial. Sister Noel Marie, "Statistics of Religious Educators," *The Catholic Educator*, vol. 27, no. 5 (January, 1957), pp. 291–292, 344.

[25] In this comparison the children are from three different public schools, and not only from the William Howard Taft School with which most of our comparisons were made.

parochial and public school children are those which their parents view, like I Love Lucy, Air Power, Navy Log, and Bishop Sheen. A little more than three out of ten of the parents (31.3%) said that they did not regulate their children's TV habits, and in actual daily practice, the children simply look at the same program their parents are viewing in the evening after dinner.[26]

The restriction of the time allowed for viewing TV includes also the question of a regular bedtime for the school children, especially on "school nights." According to the parental statements, the great majority of the children retire between eight and nine o'clock, but in most instances the parents admitted ruefully, "that's when they're supposed to go to bed." In order to compare parental policy with the children's practice, we asked the pupils in school one day to "write down the time you went to bed last night." The following table shows the rough comparison between the parents' and the children's answers.

Child's time of retirement	Parents' answer	Children's answer
7:30 p.m.	7.4%	8.1%
8:00 p.m.	20.2	22.3
8:30 p.m.	26.3	27.2
9:00 p.m.	24.4	25.2
9:30 p.m.	13.0	10.8
10:00 or later	8.7	6.4

In general, the children seem to claim an even earlier bedtime than their parents say they have. The parents in large numbers (70.9%) said their children retired between eight and nine o'clock, while a higher percentage (74.7%) of the children claimed this same time. There is, of course, a variation in bedtime according to the age of the children. The largest numbers in the first and second grades retire at eight o'clock, in the third and fourth grades at eight-thirty, in the fifth, sixth and seventh grades at nine o'clock and in the eighth grade at nine-thirty. This is the pattern in these classes in the sense that the modal category in each follows this time schedule. We checked their bedtime against the hour when their favorite TV programs appear, and found that most of the programs could be viewed before nine

[26] In a study of 654 elementary school children in Boston, forty-five per cent of the children said they have complete freedom of choice in selecting programs; three-quarters of them looked at TV every day and averaged from two and a half to three hours daily. Katherine Mahoney, "Elementary School Pupils' TV Habits and Choices," *Catholic Educational Review*, vol. 51, no. 4 (April, 1958), pp. 234–245.

o'clock, the two main exceptions being Playhouse 90 on Thursdays and Gunsmoke on Saturdays.[27]

So much has been written and said about the baleful effects of comic books on the behavior of children that we asked concerning them in our interviews with parents. About one-third of all parents (33.7%) say that they supervise and restrict the type of comics their children read, and one out of ten (9.7%) does not permit the children to read them at all. More than a third of the parents (36.4%) have no regulations. About one-fifth of the children (20.2%) are not interested enough in comic books either to buy, borrow or read them.[28] The following table gives the comparison between the parochial and the public school children.

Regulations on comic books	St. Luke's	Public School	Both
Restricted type	32.4%	37.8%	33.7%
None allowed	10.1	8.4	9.7
Never reads them	17.7	27.7	20.2
No regulations	39.8	26.1	36.4

The use of radio and the attendance at the movies appear to have little relation with the behavior of elementary school children. Although a small percentage (1.5%) of their homes did not have TV sets, and 2.4 per cent had no radio, many of them had at least two radios. The "extra" radio is more frequently in the kitchen for the mother's use during the day, but where the child often did his homework. Listening to the radio means mainly listening to music while doing homework, and this does not appear to distract the child. The movies, too, do not seem to be attractive to either the public or the parochial school pupils. There is no neighborhood movie house within walking distance of any part of the parish. Family attendance at the drive-in movies in the suburbs is fairly popular during the summer time, but when we asked the children during the school year we found that forty-four per cent of St. Luke's pupils, and 33.5 per cent of the Taft school children (in the sixth, seventh and eighth grades) had not been to the movies during the previous month. The TV seems

[27] See Jack Greenstein, "Effect of Television on Elementary School Grades," *Journal of Educational Research*, vol. 48, no. 3 (November, 1954), pp. 161–176, who finds no significant difference between the school grades of the viewers and the non-viewers.

[28] In a nation-wide study of twenty-thousand parochial school children from the fourth to the sixth grade, only five per cent were non-readers of comics, and forty-three per cent of parents read them. M. Gervase Glanchard, "A Survey of Comics Read by Parochial School Children," *The Catholic Educator*, vol. 21, no. 1 (September, 1950), pp. 23–26 and 31.

to have replaced the movie as the main instrument of indoor entertainment.

It appears to be a theory of child guidance that children should gradually learn responsibility by having certain assigned chores to perform around the home. We have seen that the pupils at St. Luke's are eager to "do things" for the teacher, and that otherwise menial and manual tasks are considered a privilege if done at school and for the teacher. This same attitude does not carry over successfully to the home on the part of most of the children. Some parents say "it's hard to get them to do anything around the house;" others confess that "they get it only half done," and "you feel that you've got to do it yourself anyway." On the other hand, some homes are well regulated in this regard so that the children perform their daily chores with despatch. About one-tenth of the children have no assigned chores. The following table gives the distribution of these chores.

Type of chore	St. Luke's	Public School	Both
Do dishes, set and clear table	39.5%	43.7%	40.5%
Clean up room and playthings	21.0	20.1	20.8
Remove refuse, clean walk, yard and lawn	14.0	14.3	14.1
Other chores	14.1	13.5	14.0
No chores	11.4	8.4	10.6

From the data we have gathered on these various items we must conclude that the parents do not allow nearly so much laxity as the teachers seem to believe. Most homes have regulations of various kinds meant to teach the child order and conformity. Almost seven out of ten place some restrictions on the use of TV; about four out of five set a bedtime of nine o'clock or earlier; movies and radio do not seem to be a problem; about three-quarters of the children either do not read comics or have restrictions placed upon them; approximately nine out of ten are expected to perform some kind of chores around the home. While this record of family discipline can undoubtedly be improved, and while there may be some slight exaggerations on the part of parents concerning these practices (which they admit are not always strictly adhered to) [29] the general picture of family life indicates a reasonable amount of responsibility on the part of parents.

[29] When we asked the pupils in the three upper grades, "Do you do housework?" 61.9 per cent of the boys and 93.4 per cent of the girls, answered affirmatively. The corresponding percentages for the Taft public school were 41.5

The problem of broken homes and of working mothers is of very small proportions among the families of St. Luke's pupils. The largest percentage of mothers (77.5%) are full-time homemakers or housewives. Nine per cent of the mothers have part-time employment, mainly during the hours when the children are at school. The remainder (13.5%) are gainfully employed on a full-time basis outside the home, and all of them have made daily arrangements with relatives to look after their children after school hours. In the largest number of families (94.7%) both parents are living together at home, but in 2.1 per cent of the families the parents are separated or divorced, while in the remaining 3.2 per cent one or both parents are deceased. An interesting sidelight on these statistics is the fact that no child whose mother works, or who comes from a broken family, is an outstanding "trouble-maker" at St. Luke's.

It must be remembered that the home and the school are not synonymous. They are separate social systems, and the behavioral demands of the school would be ridiculous when applied to the family. Family authority is more informal, the numbers of people involved are fewer, the functions performed are more diffuse, the social relationships are more intimate and continuous. The whole structure of family life requires a different type of discipline than that required by the school. The fact that there is more laxity in the home than in the school does not imply that home behavior has always a direct effect on school behavior. Probably the opposite is more often true in that the pressure generated by the regular routine at school is "blown off" in more permissive behavior when the child comes home. It is as unrealistic to suggest that the school class is a "large happy family" as it is to suggest that the family is a well-regulated schoolroom.

Priests and Principal

From the point of view of discipline and behavior, all authority at St. Luke's is exercised at the local level of the parish. Theoretically, the Pastor has the "last word" in any serious case of discipline, but in practice he never speaks this last word without consultation and agreement with the Principal. Father Albert points out that Sister Roberta is the head of the school, and that he wants her and the teachers to run the school without interference from either the priests or the parents. In the final analysis, it is only on two counts that they

---

and 89.1. In both schools the percentage of pupils doing housework decreases from the sixth to the eighth grade.

require his authority: the expulsion of a child from the school, and the retention of a child in the same grade for another year.

Sister Roberta confers with the Pastor on the question of expelling a child and then they both decide what to do, but she is the one who informs the parents and the child that he must go to another school. Usually the child is permitted to finish the school year so that the transfer to another school is not interpreted as expulsion. This year, however, a "trouble-maker" in the eighth grade was told in September that he really ought to go to a school closer to his home and that the eighth-grade classroom was getting too crowded.[30] He took the hint and moved to another parochial school where he became a basketball star and was roundly cheered by the St. Luke's supporters when the two teams met. He continued to be very friendly with his former teachers and classmates and occasionally came to the school grounds at the noon hour.

The Pastor was also called in for consultation with the Principal and the parents whenever there was question of demoting a child. At the mid-year, in January, the parents of three children in the second grade were advised that their children should repeat the year. They agreed that it would be best to demote them immediately to the first grade. At the beginning of May the decision was reached that fourteen pupils would be retained in the same grade during the next school year. Twenty-four other children were told that they must go to summer school in order to "make up work" if they expected to move on to the next highest grade in September. The teachers of St. Luke's do not run a summer school. The nearby Taft public school takes care of these children for six weeks at a cost of twenty-five dollars (twenty-three dollars tuition and two dollars for paper and supplies).[31]

The Pastor sometimes gets involved in the discipline of the school because the parents have called him into it. Occasionally complaints are made directly to him.[32] One mother phoned him at eight o'clock one night to say that her daughter in the third grade "is still trying to finish a punishment assignment the teacher gave." On another occasion two boys in the third grade "played hookey" in the afternoon,

[30] The original plan in September was to divide the eighth grade into two classes and to leave the sixth grade as one class, but this was reversed when late applications increased the size of the sixth grade.

[31] The only private Catholic elementary school in the city has also started a summer school for backward children, charging fifteen dollars for the six weeks' course.

[32] This practice is disliked by the teachers, who want parents to come to them rather than voice complaints either at the PTA meetings or to the priests.

went to a downtown store and stole some toy soldiers. The older boy's father came home from work early and found the boys playing with the toys on the porch.[33] He immediately brought them to the rectory for a "talk with Father." The result was that the children and their parents returned to the store, gave back the toys, and apologized to the manager.

The Pastor was called upon for disciplinary action by parents on two occasions when boys had been shoved into the shallow creek that flows two blocks west of the school,[34] and on three occasions when there were fist fights among the boys. Usually his problem in these cases is to get at the truth, and he never questions the culprit individually. "I go to the classroom and call the kids out into the hall, and stand them around me, maybe five or six of them, in a circle. Then I ask each one to tell me what happened. This way we have a discussion and I can get at the truth. Then I bawl them out, give them a warning, and send them back to the room."

The Pastor is an agent of social control in an indirect way through his general talks with the children. About twice a week he gives a short sermon at the school Mass, and almost always includes exhortations to good behavior. He personally distributes the report cards to the children in every grade of the school, starting with the eighth grade.[35] This has become a ritual. He gives a relatively short introductory talk emphasizing the importance of study, but always injecting a few remarks about conduct. The children are somewhat tense before these occasions since the significance of report cards has been "built up" by the teachers during the previous weeks. The Pastor tries to relieve the nervousness and embarrassment of the pupils by performing this function in a gentle and paternal manner. As each child comes forward for the report card, Father Albert glances at it, gives praise or makes some encouraging remark about "doing better," and often asks about the child's parents or other members of the family.

Father Martin, the assistant pastor, has no direct connection with the disciplinary procedures of the school. As moderator of the recrea-

[33] This man is a convert and has a reverent respect for the moral influence of the Church and its functionaries upon the development of his children.

[34] One boy in the second grade who slipped into this creek came home and explained the wet sleeve of his sweater by saying that "Sister wouldn't close the window when it was raining, and I had to sit there and get wet." Some months later, and only by chance, the mother mentioned the incident to the Principal, and learned that her child had a seat far removed from the window.

[35] This task takes practically the full school day. He spends about twenty minutes in each class, more in the higher grades and less in the lower grades.

tional program of the PTA, he has much informal contact with the pupils on the playground and in the teams. In this capacity he is respected and loved by the children, and is able to control them without punishments or harsh measures. He is also teacher of religion to the fifth, sixth, seventh and eighth grades. His excellence as a teacher —and the fact that he comes to each grade only once a week—reduce any behavior problems to a minimum. He is somewhat easier and more permissive than most of the regular teachers in the school.

In the actual operation of the school, and in setting the general tone of behavior, the Principal, Sister Roberta, is the most important and central figure. She has very definite ideas about conduct and discipline. "I don't believe a teacher has the right to strike a child. We should remember they are people like ourselves." Occasionally, a teacher refers a problem child to her, but she discourages this practice, mainly because as eighth grade teacher she does not have the time, but also because "after all, if I had to punish the youngsters for everything, they'd begin to think I was a monster." Thus, in actual practice each teacher must be her own disciplinarian and handle the behavior problems in her own way.

Sister Roberta was very proud of the behavior of St. Luke's children. "You can see by watching the children that they are well behaved. That's one thing I made sure we would have when I became Principal. I've been working on this for five years, and you can see the results. We absolutely demand and expect good behavior of the pupils. If some particular child shows signs of getting worse or of creating a real problem we simply tell him he cannot return here the following year. I don't want any of those things happening here that happen in the public schools, like stealing, gang fights and juvenile delinquency. We do not have one juvenile delinquent out of 632 children, and that's because we don't have any of those rough, lower type kids enrolled here." [36]

Sister Roberta's remarks indicate that she is aware of the complexity of her dual role as Principal and teacher. In her concern for the whole school, and for the children as a group, she emphasizes those forms of misconduct that would disturb the children and affect the order of the school. She wants to prevent any behavior that is socially undesirable. As a teacher she emphasizes the personal virtue

[36] These remarks were made during morning recess on the third Thursday in September. The recess was not yet over when a boy, who had been roughly knocked down by another, had to be taken to the hospital. The embarrassed Principal said that "this is the first accident like this that we've had in five years."

and morality that will improve the character of the individual. As a teacher also, she is not concerned with behavior that may inconvenience or irritate her.[37] As a Principal, however, she does not want to be known as a scold, or as she says, "a monster who is always punishing children."

Conformity in Religion and Recreation

Religious activities shared by all the children show some variation in conformity and choice. All of the seventh-grade children belong to the choir (except a few boys "who cannot sing") but the eighth-grade children may volunteer for the choir—with the result that only the eighth-grade girls do so. This is an example on the part of both sexes of conformity to peer group behavior. The girls like to sing, but the boys try to get "out of it" whenever possible. Thus, both boys and girls in the seventh grade sing because this is the traditional job of the seventh-graders, but when the choice is left open to the eighth-grade boys they prefer not to sing.[38]

Boys voluntarily serve on the altar from the fifth to the eighth grades, but once they have joined this group they must conform to all the expectations of the Mass server function. This refers only to the routine patterns in the Church itself. Appointment for times of serving, fines for absences, and so forth, are regulated by the boys themselves through suffrage. Other religious activties, like the recitation of prayers before and after class, and the study of the religious Catechism, are not open to choice by the pupils.

Daily attendance at Mass is voluntary for the school children at St. Luke's, but tardiness at this service is frowned upon and warned against by the teachers. This stricture concerning tardiness flows, however, from Church practices rather than from school patterns. When they attend Mass, Catholics are expected to attend the whole Mass from beginning to end, regardless of whether they are children or adults. The first-grade children are excused from Mass and usually go directly to the school. The second-grade children, having not yet received their first Holy Communion, attend Mass on alternate weeks except during Lent, when the eight o'clock Mass attracts many adult parishioners. Parents report that their children "act as though" the

[37] See Elmer J. Clark, "Teacher Reactions Toward Objectionable Behavior," *Elementary School Journal,* vol. 51, no. 8 (April, 1951), pp. 446–449; also Louis Kaplan, "The Annoyances of Elementary School Teachers," *Journal of Educational Research,* vol. 45, no. 9 (May, 1952), pp. 649–665.

[38] Those who "cannot sing" are the boys whose voices have changed, and no boy in the eighth grade likes to admit that he still has a child's voice when the rest of his classmates have passed this stage.

daily Mass attendance were compulsory even though they have been assured time and again that this is not the case. Children above the second grade also go to confession on the Thursday before the first Friday of each month. In all of these actions the degree of conformity by the children is very high, and it appears to be the result of training and indoctrination, as well as of the fact that "everybody does it." There are no sanctions, either penalties or awards, attached to the patterns of religious behavior.[39]

The recreational activities of the school exhibit the widest margin of choice for the children, although here also certain group patterns and regularities exist. Negative restrictions are enforced at the recess periods. In good weather the children must stay out of the halls and classrooms; they are not allowed to throw stones or snowballs; [40] they must not leave the schoolyard; no "rough play" is permitted. The play in the schoolyard is supervised by the teachers, but little of it is organized. The children are left to their own ingenuity to amuse themselves. They practice basketball shots, throw a football or volleyball around, play marbles, skip rope, and chase each other around the yard. Each class has its own sports equipment, donated by the PTA, and the play tends to be voluntarily limited to each grade level.

Other recreational patterns are much more regularized. The boy who plays on the school football, basketball or baseball team, the girl who is a cheerleader or a member of the volleyball team, must attend practice and follow the rules imposed by the game and by the coaches. Similarly, the Boy Scouts and the Camp Fire Girls must conform to the patterns of behavior set by these organizations or be subject to sanctions, or even to dismissal, from the group. It is interesting in this regard that the formal, organized groups which require the most discipline are also those which have voluntary membership.

The type of social control, the amount of conformity and the degree of cooperation involved in this patterned behavior vary according to certain observable factors. We have seen that both age and sex are factors in this regard. The children in the first and second grades do

[39] This statement requires qualification. Sister Roberta gives written tasks to those who come late for the daily Mass, but not to those who do not come to Mass at all. There is no check-up on Sunday Mass attendance of children. The teachers say that this is "conscience matter" and that no child can be asked to make a "public confession" of having missed Mass on Sunday.

[40] There is a fine of twenty-five cents levied for throwing snowballs. Some of the boys had to pay it, even though they committed the act on the way home from school. They said "there's always somebody around to snitch on you." One seventh-grade girl was fined twenty-five cents for washing the face of a boy with snow. She remarked that "it was worth the quarter."

not conform as well or as readily as those in the seventh and eighth grades. The social control exercised by the teachers is more lenient in the lower grades.[41] Another and obvious factor is the type of activity performed. Cooperation and conformity must be much more exact in the choir, in the church and in the schoolroom than in the random recreation on the school playground.

Sanctions on Behavior

We have seen that the ultimate penalty for misbehavior in St. Luke's school is dismissal, but that this is rarely invoked. Sanctions are both positive and negative, and both are effective as a threat or promise concerning expected patterns of behavior, as well as an actual punishment for transgression and a reward for conformity. Threats are sometimes used in the classrooms of St. Luke's. During the month of May the teachers frequently remind the children that those who do not do well in their studies will have to attend summer school or will have to repeat the grade next year. The football and basketball players are reminded that they must keep up in their studies or be dropped from the team.[42] The teachers, since they must handle their own problems, very seldom threaten the children that they will be reported to the Pastor, the Principal, or their parents.

Positive means of obtaining conformity include praise and promises. The teachers in the three highest grades encourage the students by telling them that "this is the best class I ever had," apparently hoping that the children will live up to such high expectations. In the lower grades, first to third, the teacher says, "if you are real good, we'll read a story after a while." It is the custom in the parochial school for each teacher to have a supply of small religious rewards, like medals, badges and pious pictures, to distribute to the children on propitious occasions. Plastic statuettes are awarded occasionally by Sister Roberta to pupils who do well in arithmetic, her favorite subject. Small gold and silver stars are pasted on the school assignments of children who have done approved work, and they appear also on lists of pupils' names posted in the classroom as recognition for steady attendance at school, at choir practice, at acolyte service.[43]

[41] The most remarkable change in behavior we observed was among the first graders whose random and sometimes erratic behavior of September becomes well patterned and regularized in May.

[42] In early October six football players in the eighth grade failed a test and were declared ineligible for the next game; but Sister Roberta relented and gave them a re-test which they passed.

[43] See the discussion on the value of rewards as a direction of impulses, in con-

The climax of this system of positive sanctions on behavior was reached on the annual Award Night, Tuesday, May 28, for the graduating class. A total of ninety-two awards was distributed to the sixty graduates.[44] Most of them were granted in relation to achievement in school work, for arithmetic, English, spelling, religion, music and art, with seven boys and eight girls receiving recognition for a general average of ninety per cent, or over, in all major subjects. In the area of conduct awards, Robert Finegan received the "citizenship award" from the Sons of the American Revolution. Three boys and two girls were awarded deportment medals; five boys and two girls received medals for perfect attendance; two girls and three boys were awarded medals for "application." No graduate went unrewarded.[45]

On an informal, daily level, to be allowed to "do things for the teacher" becomes also a sanction on behavior, as both promise and reward. Certain supererogatory patterns have developed in St. Luke's school that indicate an eagerness on the part of the pupil to please the teacher. One of the mothers said, "my children do things for the teacher that I can't get them to do at home for me." They vie with one another to be allowed to put out the chalk, empty the pencil sharpener, clean the blackboard, pull down the shades, empty the waste paper baskets, hang up the teacher's coat and so forth.[46] To some extent these actions may be motivated by a desire for recognition, or to avoid the less agreeable study tasks at hand. At any rate, the teachers know that the pupils look upon these as desirable performances which they will not be allowed to do if they misbehave.

There is a difference, of course, when one of these chores is given as a penance. Occasionally, a child who misbehaves is ordered to pick up papers in the halls or the school yard during recess. There is no glory in this because the whole class knows that it is being done as a

---

trast to punishments, which are a repression of impulses, in Percival M. Symonds, "Classroom Discipline," *Teacher's College Record,* vol. 51, no. 3 (December, 1949), pp. 147–158.

[44] These do not include the certificate of merit given to each honor patrol boy and girl.

[45] See the strictures on such practices by Paul E. Campbell, "Studying Promotion and Discipline," *The Homiletic and Pastoral Review,* vol. 55, no. 11, pp. 954–961; also Thomas J. Quigley and John B. McDowell, *Handbook of School Policies and Practices* (Diocese of Pittsburgh, 1954), which states that "there shall not be formal graduation exercises for eighth-grade students in the Diocese."

[46] Sometimes, chivalry wins out. At the end of one school day a boy and girl in the fifth grade competed to get Sister's shawl. The boy obtained it but then passed it over to the girl so that she could hand it to the teacher.

punishment. At first we suspected that all of these actions were penalties for the infringement of rules, but we were assured time and again by the children that "we asked Sister to let us do it." We have seen them during recess sweep the classrooms, arrange tables in the cafeteria and rake leaves on the playground.[47] This practice of volunteering for menial tasks may have grown out of the widespread attempt at St. Luke's school to allow as much decision-making as possible to the pupils. The area in which this can be done in an elementary school is obviously circumscribed, but it is one in which social control blends into its correlate of self-control.

The most frequently administered punishment for infraction of the rules at St. Luke's school is the written task or assignment.[48] The teacher usually speaks to the child who is misbehaving, warns him of further infractions, and finally assigns him a "task" which may be the writing of the multiplication table, a spelling list, some pages from the reader, and so forth.[49] About two-thirds of the infractions in the school are handled in this way. Detention at recess or after school is the next most frequently assigned penalty. Isolating the child from the others by making him stand in front of the room or in the corner, and setting him to certain manual tasks constitute the other normal forms of punishment.

Any penalty that indicates the disapproval of the teacher and the disesteem of the class is usually effective in controlling behavior. This general principle also governs the handling of behavior problems in the nearby public elementary school, but the ordinary forms of correction and discipline differ somewhat from those employed at St. Luke's. The most frequently employed form of penalty in the public school is the temporary isolation of a child by having him stand in the corner, at the front of the room, or out in the hallway. Almost as frequent is the deten-

[47] The bald fact also is that there is not enough janitorial service for St. Luke's school. Toward the end of January the janitor complained to Mrs. Gordon about the "dirty condition" of the sixth-grade classroom. She told the children, "you people are old enough to take care of the classroom yourselves. The janitor has too much work to do around here as it is."

[48] The manual of the Archdiocese of Chicago, *School Policies for Elementary Schools,* (no date), p. 17, says that "work of an academic nature is ineffective and destroys right attitudes," and "detention should seldom if ever be used and then only with great prudence; never prolonged after daily session, bearing in mind the services of patrol, possible home chores, concern of parents."

[49] In the beginning of the school year the traffic patrol boys punished infractions at the street intersection by assigning written tasks to the culprits. The Principal soon stopped this practice.

tion of the child for a short while after school, a practice that is convenient since the teacher has to remain at the school until four o'clock. The public school children are seldom given written tasks to perform, but they are sometimes sent to the Principal's office (a penalty not given at St. Luke's since the Principal there has no office.)[50]

A major difference in the handling of discipline is that the public school teacher occasionally resorts to corporal punishment of the pupils. This does not imply cruelty, nor does it suggest uncontrollable anger. The punishment is meted out in most instances by the Principal or in his presence, but there is also the occasional cuffing of a child in the classroom. Given the difference in attitudes, the absence of high religious motives, the inability to dismiss, or even to threaten the expulsion, of borderline cases—with all these handicaps, it is to be expected that corporal punishment is effective in the public school.[51] Some of the children who transferred to St. Luke's from a public school made autobiographical reference to earlier experiences of this kind.

The use of corporal punishment of any kind is prohibited at St. Luke's school, and neither Sister Roberta nor any of the teachers ever employ it. Other permissible sanctions are more than sufficient to keep order in the school. There were no complaints by parents to the effect that St. Luke's school is too strict or too rigid in the handling of pupils. Most of the parents agreed that the discipline at the school is relatively mild. Almost all of the parents, in reflecting on their own elementary school experiences, declared that discipline was "much rougher in the old days."[52] It is quite possible that parents tend to exaggerate the hardships, the discipline and the punishments to which they were subjected as children. This seems to be the generalization by most parents when they compare any of their own childhood ex-

[50] Elementary school teachers are forced to take some kind of action when they are confronted with a behavior problem even though mental hygienists suggest that the child be studied for causes of misbehavior before action be taken. See Celia B. Stendler, "How Well Do Elementary School Teachers Understand Child Behavior?" *The Journal of Educational Psychology,* vol. 40, no. 8 (December, 1949), pp. 489–498.

[51] See the symposium on this subject by a mother, teacher, school superintendent and guidance counsellor, Marian Kennedy, "Should The Rod Be Spared?" *National Parent Teacher,* vol. 51, no. 5 (January, 1957), pp. 16–18. See also the arguments that punishment gives people anxieties, dreads, and neuroses, Percival M. Symonds, "Classroom Discipline," *Teachers' College Record,* vol. 51, no. 3 (December, 1949), pp. 147–158.

[52] In interviews and in group discussions parents liked to reminisce about their own schooling, and it was sometimes difficult to turn the conversation back to the matter at hand, the schooling of their children.

periences with those of their offspring. This particular generation of parents of grade-school children had the common experiences of the economic depression of the thirties.

Ultimately, it is to be expected that in a religious-oriented school, the influence of moral sanctions is of great significance. The children in St. Luke's are taught that obedience, respect for authority and self-control are virtues pleasing to God. The "sacrifices" entailed in keeping silence and in following the other regulations are sublimated as means for living the good life.[53] The child is reminded in many ways through religious teachings, examples and practices that his purpose in life is to sanctify himself and to work out his eternal destiny. The response of the children to this type of spiritual appeal shows that religion provides an effective motive in the total mechanism of social control and self-control.

Generalizations

1. St. Luke's, like every elementary school and every continuing social organization, requires conformity to norms of behavior. It could not function or remain in existence without this. Teaching the child to conform is part of the function of the school, because it is implied in culture transmission and socialization. Thus, part of the learning process of the child is the internalization of the general social values and norms of conduct current in American urban society.

2. Perfect attendance at school is achieved by only six per cent of the children. Absenteeism is a normal behavior problem of the elementary school, but it is greatest in the three winter months of January, February and March, when a little more than ten per cent of the school time is lost through absenteeism. On the average the girls miss about a day more of schooling per year than do the boys. The highest rate of absenteeism is in the first and second grades, where the expectations of regular behavior are not so great as among the older children.

3. Although not so much is expected of the younger children, and their conduct when measured against the uniform norms of school life is not so well patterned as that of older children, the "conduct marks" given to them do not differ notably from those of older children. The teacher's problem of translating a judgment on behavior

[53] For example, the "sacrifices" of the children in the eighth grade were symbolized during Advent by "straws for the manger." A sack of straw was available in the classroom, and each day after school the child could take as many pieces of straw as he had made sacrifices during the day and place them in a manger in the corridor.

into a symbol given to each child is recognized in the variations of marks. Nevertheless, there is a distinct difference in the marks given to girls as compared to those given to boys. The girls appear to be more conforming; they are less troublesome; they are more "at home" in the school, than are the boys.

4. The more intelligent children and the more popular children tend to get higher marks for deportment than do the others. There is no way of discovering whether the intelligence and popularity of the child have an intangible influence on the teacher's judgment when she gives the marks. It seems probable that these children look upon deportment marks in the same competitive spirit in which they view the marks they receive for other subjects. To them and their parents "doing well" in school includes success in getting high marks for deportment. Whether a pupil is active in the various school groups or is relatively inactive, does not appear to have an influence on the deportment grade.

5. Employing the criterion of conduct marks to estimate the behavior of parochial school children implies also the recognition that the teachers differ both in their classroom practices and in their own evaluation of behavior. Some teachers are more strict than others in the way they handle their pupils. Some are more strict in the distribution of grades. This range of difference is limited at St. Luke's school in the sense that no teacher can be called an unsuccessful disciplinarian. No teacher exhibits an extreme of either rigidity or laxity.

6. The pupils themselves have quite definite ideas about the disciplinary procedures of their teachers, and are sensitive to any "unfairness" on the part of teachers. Less than one-quarter (23.4%) of St. Luke's upper-graders, as compared to more than three out of ten (32.3%) of the Taft school upper-graders, think that they would be happier if the teacher were not so strict. According to the opinion of the children themselves, who are after all most deeply involved in the teacher-pupil relationship, there is much more unfairness and discrimination toward pupils on the part of public school teachers than on the part of parochial school teachers.

7. The influence of home practices on the school behavior of the child can usually be determined in individual cases. From the very nature of the situation (the numbers involved, the type of function, authority and group) behavior must be more strictly regulated at school than at home. Thus the school cannot be as "relaxed" as the home. There is little proof to uphold the common opinion of teachers that laxity in the home is a general cause of behavior problems in the school. All parents have some sort of regulations for their children's

home behavior, but like teachers, parents differ in leniency and strictness.

8. The control of pupil conduct is the responsibility of all teachers in the parochial school. Unlike the public school, where the chief authority and responsibility for enforcement lies in the hands of the Principal, St. Luke's does not have a full-time Principal. The Pastor refuses to interfere in any way with the discipline of the school, has complete confidence in the teachers, and comes into the situation for consultation only when there is a question of expulsion or demotion. The appeal to higher authority, commonly used in the public school, is not employed at St. Luke's. The teachers do not threaten to send the child to the Principal, or to inform the parents of misconduct.

9. The extra-curricular patterns of behavior, as exhibited in religious practices and recreational activities, exhibit a latitude of conformity. In both instances there is much more freedom of choice on the part of the child, since these are voluntary rather than compulsory performances. There are, of course, institutionalized ways of behaving in both areas, and when the child enters into them he tends to "do what everybody does." Conformity becomes a matter of social pressure and of internalization of norms, as well as of conscious choice. The voluntary aspect of these behavior patterns blends in with the general expectations of behavior in a school of this type.

10. Both positive and negative sanctions of behavior are employed in the parochial school. Infractions of the rules are punished most frequently with the assignment of a written task and seldom with detention after school. The penalty system at St. Luke's differs from that of the public school where misbehavior is punished by isolation, detention and occasionally corporal punishment. The most effective and widely used positive sanction on behavior is a complicated system of rewards, ranging from religious articles and gold stars to medals and trophies for the graduating class.

Part

II

STRUCTURES OF GROUP ACTION

Chapter

SEVEN

YOUTH MOVEMENTS

BOTH PARENTS and educators commonly agree that health, bodily vigor, and physical development are of great importance to the modern elementary school, and that a consideration for this development must be an integral function of the school. We shall examine later how and to what extent the organized sports program of St. Luke's school helps to perform this function.[1] A further investigation shows that the activities of the Boy Scouts and the Camp Fire Girls are also mainly pointed in this direction. They focus upon health and welfare, upon the development of skills and crafts which are somewhat peripheral to the essential learning process of the school. In this sense they are extracurricular.

Like the athletic teams, these two youth organizations are sponsored by, and represent, St. Luke's school, but they are directly operated and controlled by lay adult parishioners. The teachers have little immediate contact with them. Father Martin is the liaison between them and the rectory and attends some of the meetings of the adult committees. The Pastor takes a benign attitude toward them and cooperates along religious and spiritual lines. These two groups have a formal connection with the PTA in that they "come under" the supervision of the Character Education Committee.

The extracurricular activities of the two youth movements are legitimized by the belief that character is built in children mainly in leisure time. The Camp Fire Girls from their inception were meant to be a character-building organization, having the "appeal of idealistic goals poetically expressed, ceremony and costume and colorful terminology." [2] Similarly, as one of the national leaders has written, "Scouting not only directs a boy's energies into harmless channels but also guides it into useful character building, for it is not merely a recreational program but an educational program as well. The

[1] See below chap. 8, "Organized Sports."

[2] *The Blue Bird Book* (New York: Camp Fire Girls, 1954), p. 2.

recreational feature serves two purposes: it gives an outlet to the surplus energy of the boy, and it serves as a sugar coating to the educational features of skills, interests, and knowledge."[3]

Limitations on Membership

Theoretically, every child in the school from the second grade on is eligible for membership in one of these two movements. This means that the potential membership of the Blue Birds, in the second, third and fourth grades, is 150 girls, and of the Camp Fire Girls, from the fifth to the eighth grade, is 125 girls. The actual membership in the younger group was 103 (68.7%), and in the older group of girls was eighty-two (65.6%). Among the boys at St. Luke's the potential membership of the Cub Pack was 147, and of the Boy Scouts, 125. The numbers belonging to these groups were fifty-six (38.1%) in the Cubs and twenty-four (19.2%) in the Scouts.

These extracurricular activities obviously attract more girls than boys. Approximately two-thirds of the available girls belong to them, and the membership stays high even in the upper grades. Only about two out of five boys in the lower grades belong to the Cubs, and this drops to one out of five by the time they reach scouting age. It is possible that in some families the cost of uniforms, dues, hikes, projects, and other items prohibits the participation of the youngster, but in so far as this is a factor in limiting membership, it ought to operate for both boys and girls. On the basis of our observations and interviews we are able to reconstruct a series of "explanations" for the lower participation of boys in Scouting.

The most frequently heard complaint by the members of the adult committee is that "there are not enough ladies willing to be den mothers." Since a Cub den operates during the daytime after school, and since the program demands adult supervision, it is obvious that the mothers of the boys involved have to serve in this capacity.[4] Mrs.

[3] Francis A. Froehlich, *The Scout Program in the Catholic Youth Apostolate* (New Brunswick: Catholic Committee on Scouting, 1956), p. 21. It is interesting to note that the argument about the "character-building" function of Scouting seems to have died down among Catholics. In a highly critical review in *Commonweal*, vol. 20, no. 26 (October 26, 1934), p. 625, of H. W. Hurt's *The Influencing of Character*, John Palmer said that "it is preposterous to claim influencing of character by purely natural means (like Scouting)." Edward R. Moore, "What Is A Boy Scout," *The Commonweal*, vol. 21, no. 10 (January 4, 1935), pp. 278–280, sprang to the defense, and made an eloquent plea for the participation of Catholics in the Scout movement.

[4] A move is under way in the parish to relieve a den mother after six months' service, and thus attract more mothers to the work. For the activities of these

Basil Gentry claimed that "we could get at least three, and probably five more dens (30–40 boys) together if the mothers would cooperate." Why the necessary volunteers were not forthcoming is answered by a list of other reasons: no available room in the house for the meetings, small children in the family to be taken care of, mother working, mother unable or unwilling to handle a group of "wild boys."

At St. Luke's there are twice as many Cubs as there are Scouts, and in the various troops in the larger city this proportion is about five to two. This mortality between the lowest and the next echelons of the movement is of great concern to the Scoutmaster and other adults interested in this work at St. Luke's. The present Scout leaders believe that the Cubs are "spoiled" by the den mothers, who help them with their projects, allow them to gain rank without really passing tests, and in general do too much for them and pamper them.[5] This implies also that the Cubs are allowed to make progress too rapidly and that they often get a taste of real Scouting while still in the Cubs and while not yet ready for it. "The strange proof of this," said Harry O'Toole, "is that Scouts who never were Cubs seem to stick to Scouting better than the others."

A crucial lack in the program at St. Luke's is the absence of the "Webelos," the organization of a transitional group between Cubbing and Scouting. The boy starts preparation for this rank at the age of ten and a half years, and is admitted to the Scouts at age eleven. This is a six months' period of training independent of both Cub meetings and Scout meetings. At this point the meetings are held early in the evening and the fathers are supposed to take over from the former maternal leadership. This step is preparatory to Scouting, and its absence means that some of the boys never take the step and that others who do go into Scouting drop out soon afterwards.

One of the former experienced leaders, Jerry Glass, said that "it has always been necessary to provide pre-tenderfoot and tenderfoot preparation before acceptance into the St. Luke's troop. If this new blood isn't introduced the troop dies as the older members leave it. We've never really mastered this problem at St. Luke's, and we seem to have formed a 'succession' of troops rather than a continuous development from Cub pack to Scout troop. It's a common problem, and other places have it too." At any rate, there are serious plans afoot

women see the picture story in *Life*, vol. 37, no. 24 (December 13, 1954), pp. 21–24, "Den Mother: Most Important Cog in the Cub Scout Movement."

[5] Cub regulations require parents to give tests and sign the child's book when each task has been accomplished. Den mothers do not give the tests for achievements.

for the formation of the Webelos during the next school year. The St. Luke's troop had a "tough" reputation in the sense that a relatively rough hazing of the new Scouts had been permitted in previous years. When Fred Nordman became Scoutmaster he put a stop to this practice.[6]

Another important hindrance to activity in the Scout troop is the emphasis on athletic sports at the parochial school. Fred Nordman, the Scoutmaster, had also coached the football team at St. Luke's up until two years ago, when he decided to focus his energies only on Scouting. This appears to have been a mistake. While he was coaching he had the boys under his influence, could keep them interested in Scouting and could avoid any conflict of schedules or programs between sports and Scouting. At the present time less than one-quarter of the eighth-grade boys are Scouts, but more than three-quarters of them play on one or more of the athletic teams. The percentage of Scouts is higher in the seventh grade where the chances of playing on the varsity are smaller. Last year the Scouts changed their meeting night to Mondays in order not to conflict with football or basketball practice, but this did not increase membership.

Still another factor is that the boy does not always clearly see the value of the functions that the Scouts perform. Often he enjoys the games, the hikes and cook-outs because of the companionship and the recreation involved in these activities. He does not like the "work" connected with the program, or with the various tests he has to pass, and the self-discipline involved in them. "So he decides to quit, and the parents are too easy on him; they let him be a quitter." Except for the Courts of Honor,[7] where the boy is the center of attention of troop members, parents and siblings, most of the Scouting functions are performed in relative privacy, or with only a few companions present. This is quite different from the opportunities he has for winning recognition through the athletic teams, which gain the attention of schoolmates, teachers and parents.

There is, furthermore, serious question whether the outdoors and crafts activities of the Scout program are consonant with the prepara-

[6] Nevertheless, a boy who breaks the regulations may still be ordered to "assume the position," which means that he bends over for an application of the paddle.

[7] The ceremonies at these Courts are symbolic and sometimes almost mystical with the candlelight and handclasps and accoutrements of a secret ritual. "It was with the avowed purpose of stimulating the interest of boys that the men behind the movement wove into the fabric of Scouting those devices which make for graphic and emotional appeal." Harold P. Levy, *Building A Popular Movement* (New York: Russell Sage Foundation, 1944), p. 28.

tion required for the enactment of adult social roles. This is a cultural question that must be asked because the American culture is constantly pressing the utilitarian motive. How often will the adult male go camping, tie knots, make campfires without matches or with green wood and damp leaves? It is true, as several of the Scout leaders pointed out, that most boys will spend some time in military service, and that the "survival techniques" learned in Scouting may become invaluable in actual combat. It is also true, however, that national leaders in the movement have long been trying to "play down" any military implication in Scouting.[8]

Besides the outdoor activities the movement offers a broad selection of merit badges, in which fathers can help their sons win achievements. Examples are: home repairs and woodwork, journalism and photography, mechanical drawing, salesmanship, public speaking and others. The deeply interested father, of whom there seem to be few in St. Luke's parish, can work with his son in these types of activities. Aside from these, the general objectives of cleanliness, cooperation, service, honor, good deeds—for which the Scouting program stands, cannot be over-emphasized as important American culture values. It appears, however, that most parents feel that these general benefits can be obtained in other programs that do not involve concentration on handicrafts and woodsmanship.

To offset this kind of thinking on the part of adults, a Catholic chaplain of Scouting writes as follows: "Other adults sometimes may humorously (actually enviously!) accuse you Scouters of trying to catch up on a frustrated childhood, or 'refusing to grow up,' of doing what you do only 'to get out of the house for a while'—but you know really why you are in Scouting. The deeper and better reason is one that you yourself may not always analyze or even recognize, but it's there. It is the same reason the nun had in mind when she mentioned that she wouldn't do the work that she was doing for a million dollars. But she would do it for the love of Christ, for the Christ Who gave Himself for others, for the Christ Who had identified Himself with those in need." [9]

[8] *Ibid.*, p. 87. In answer to the frequent objections that Scouting is either "militaristic" or for "sissies," the author says that "efforts to refute both criticisms have been varied, but much reliance has been placed in Boy Scout literature that stresses Scouting as 'red-blooded' and 'a game.' "

[9] Daniel E. Peil, "Scout Week, 1957," *Our Sunday Visitor,* February 10, 1957. See also the booklet for leadership training of seminarians, priests and laymen, by Francis A. Froehlich, *The Scout Program in the Catholic Youth Apostolate* (New Brunswick: Catholic Committee on Scouting, 1956).

The Flourishing Girls' Groups

In contrast to the failing membership in the boys' movement at St. Luke's, the membership of the Blue Birds and the Camp Fire Girls is flourishing. It represents the largest extracurricular activity for girls in the whole school, and its membership is larger than that of any other group in the school.[10] The main reason for this success seems to be that the mothers take a more active interest in their daughters in the sense that the functions of the girls' group are more familiar and more "feminine" than those of the boys' group. This does not mean that the adult committee members were satisfied; in fact, they too, claimed that they could have more girls if there were more adult leaders.

The Camp Fire Girls of the fifth, sixth, seventh and eighth grades had four leaders from among the mothers, and each of these had an adult assistant. The Blue Birds in the lower grades had seven leaders, two for the fourth grade, two for the third and three for the second. Thus, there were fifteen mothers involved in the activities and programs of the girls, as compared to only seven active den mothers for the Cub pack. The girls' movement maintains its membership almost intact as the girls move up from the Blue Birds to the Camp Fire Girls in the "Fly Up" ceremony at the end of the fourth grade. This transition is made very smoothly, and the younger girls anticipate the privilege of being allowed to graduate into the higher group. The mothers too make the transition with their daughters and "move up" from Blue Bird leader to Camp Fire leader.

One of the reasons for the maintenance of membership and for the success of this girls' movement is the lack of other groups to which the girls can belong. The girls cannot be acolytes, a function which attracts the interest of many boys from the fifth to the eighth grades. Their participation in organized sports is limited only to the volleyball team. Some of the parents remark, "we've got to have something for the girls." Several of the older girls said that "the boys get everything around here," a remark that was made in a discussion on athletics. The fact is, of course, that the balance swings heavily in favor of the girls in these outdoors and crafts movements in terms of adult attention, interest and organized program. Since there is so little else

[10] Except the Holy Childhood Association, to which every child in the school belongs. This is not a school organization, however, and has no officers or regular meetings. The only functions performed in its name during the year were the sale of Holy Childhood seals before Christmas, the dedication of members on Ash Wednesday, and the collection for pagan babies in February.

in the form of extracurricular activities for the girls to do, both they and their mothers gravitate toward the Blue Birds and Camp Fire Girls.

An important factor in attracting and maintaining membership of the girls lies in the kind of activity this group performs. In the Blue Birds the emphasis is on play and games, painting and drawing, and the general development of companionship. In a sense, this is a continuation of the play activities of the kindergarten, carried on outside the regular school program, and growing in maturity each year. Nevertheless, it is mainly recreational.[11] From the fifth grade on, however, the Camp Fire Girls perform many of the actions which are institutionalized as female patterns of behavior in our culture. They are doing the things that girls are supposed to like to do, and they are doing them with older women who know how to do them.

The functions of the Camp Fire Girls are thus preparatory to certain segments of the adult female role. Under the heading of "home crafts," they are told that "home is family, fun, friends, food. It is your house and the surroundings, inside and out. It's the way your family lives and the way its members share their happiness and problems. You can take your part in making your home run smoothly. Surprise your family with some of the good things you can cook." [12] The girls learn how to sew. They bake and cook, and even when cooking is done under primitive and inconvenient camping conditions, it is an activity that "makes sense" to them as a sample of the future domestic role. These future mothers will, however, do most of their cooking in modern kitchens. To prepare for this, the seventh grade group took a course of cooking lessons every Tuesday afternoon for six weeks beginning in early February at the Gas and Electric Company.

The crafts they learn are undoubtedly attractive to the elementary school girls and they tend to help hold these girls to the organization and its program. The things they do are more important than the peculiar symbolic terminology of the ranks they earn. None of these girls will ever in any realistic sense be a trail maker, a wood gatherer, a fire maker or a torch bearer, yet the outdoor activity that gives the name to these ranks is a very popular form of recreation for them. "Camp Fire Girls from coast to coast were asked what they liked to do best and ninety-seven per cent of them said—something out of

[11] See the description of Scouts and Camp Fire Girls as a form of leisure and play activity in Florence G. Robbins, *The Sociology of Play, Recreation, and Leisure Time* (Dubuque: William Brown, 1955), pp. 181–185.

[12] *The Book of the Camp Fire Girls* (New York: Camp Fire Girls, 1954), p. 136.

doors, like camping, hiking, cooking over an open fire. There is so much to see and do and enjoy out of doors—everything above, and on and under the earth." [13]

The Camp Fire Girls stress the social and group aspects of all their activities. "Learning a new skill is fun when you do it with a group of friends." In this sense the girls' movement tends to develop greater social solidarity within the school and to break down whatever incipient class-consciousness may appear.[14] Because it attempts to be all-inclusive, and because it more nearly achieves this aim than the boys' movement, it helps also to develop the "school spirit" of St. Luke's. These girls' groups are so large that they are unable to develop into exclusive cliques.

God and Religion

Since St. Luke's is a religious school, and since the whole structure of the parochial training is oriented toward God, it is to be expected that the two youth movements of the school would also be informed with religion. What is said of Scouting is meant also for the Camp Fire Girls and Blue Birds: "Mere character training is not enough without the inspiration and the impulse of religion. As in all branches of education, depth, vision, and power can only come from the religious motive. Therefore, the Scouting movement needs religion behind it to crown its success. Scouting is a form of education and therefore religion must be included to make it successful." [15]

The national headquarters for both groups insists that spiritual and religious development is essential to the membership. Direct encouragement is given to churches, synagogues and religious schools to form local units. St. Luke's is only one of the parochial elementary schools in the city having these groups. Several of the Protestant churches sponsor them independently of the schools. A number of the public schools also have units, but in these the religious aspect is generalized and somewhat toned down. The Y.M.C.A. has found

[13] *Ibid.*, p. 150. The St. Luke's group also liked the out of doors, but they found it almost impossible to get mothers to accompany their daughters on over-night camping.

[14] See, however, the comments of August B. Hollingshead, *Elmtown's Youth* (New York: John Wiley, 1949), pp. 290–294, giving an example of the exclusion of lower class persons by the Boy Scouts and Camp Fire Girls. The latter also resisted the organization of a senior troop of Girl Scouts in the public high school (pp. 294–297).

[15] Francis A. Froehlich, *The Scout Program in the Catholic Youth Apostolate* (New Brunswick: Catholic Committee on Scouting, 1956), p. 105.

an ingenious way of bringing religious influence into the public schools of the area by sponsoring a rival organization called the Indian Guides. This is also a kind of outdoors and crafts group in which both fathers and sons participate.

A motto of the Boy Scouts is "For God and My Country!" The boys are told what a good Scout is expected to do. "You worship God regularly with your family in your church or synagogue. You try to follow the religious teachings that you have been taught, and you are faithful in your church school duties, and help in church activities. Above all you are faithful to Almighty God's Commandments. Most great men in history have been men of deep religious faith. Washington knelt in the snow to pray at Valley Forge. Lincoln always sought Divine guidance before each important decision. Be proud of your religious faith. Remember in doing your duty to God, to be grateful to Him. Whenever you succeed in doing something well, thank Him for it. Sometimes when you look up into the starlit sky on a quiet night, and feel close to Him—thank Him as the Giver of all good things. One way to express your duty and your thankfulness to God is to help others, and this too, is a part of your Scout promise." [16]

Catholic adults interested in the Camp Fire Girls are proud of the fact that their organization received the apostolic benediction from Pope Pius XII. In a brochure especially directed to Catholic girls we read that "because Camp Fire places religion as the cornerstone in character-building, the aims of its program are closely allied with those of the Catholic youth movement. Dedicated to the purpose of developing in girls the qualities of gentleness, kindness and high ideals, Camp Fire encourages them to learn how they may best serve God, their homes and their country. Camp Fire believes that homemaking is one of woman's major responsibilities, a career that demands skillful preparation. Hence, it helps girls acquire those interests and experiences needed in building a home that is wholesome, happy, efficiently managed and best suited to the development of Christian virtues." [17]

There are certain formal religious programs in which both of these youth groups participate. On Sunday, October 14, the Catholics of the city conducted a public holy hour in honor of the Eucharist. This was held at the high school athletic field, where there was a proces-

[16] Boy Scouts of America, *Handbook for Boys* (New Brunswick: Boy Scouts of America, 1956), pp. 20–21.

[17] Brochure, *Camp Fire and the Catholic Girl* (Washington: National Catholic Welfare Conference, no date).

sion, a sermon by the Bishop and Benediction of the Blessed Sacrament. Sixteen acolytes from the sixth, seventh and eighth grades of St. Luke's, some of whom are Boy Scouts, participated dressed in cassock and surplice. The Blue Birds and Camp Fire Girls, the Cubs and Boy Scouts, all in uniform, accompanied by their adult leaders, also in uniform, walked in the procession and were identified by their parochial banners.

Each of the two youth organizations also has an annual Mass and Communion breakfast at St. Luke's. The Cubs and Scouts celebrated theirs on Sunday, February 10, but since the weather was inclement they did not have the usual marching into church in ranks. The Scouts, with their Scoutmaster, Fred Nordman, occupied the front pews of the Church and received Communion before the rest of the congregation. The breakfast was postponed for two weeks, until Sunday, February 24, when the Scouts attended the annual Mass and Communion of the Cub Pack. This was the occasion when the St. George Award was presented to thirty-three Cubs, the entire number eligible.[18] The Den mothers and the Cub master, as well as the thirteen Boy Scouts, all in uniform, also received Communion with the Cubs.

This is the third consecutive year that every eligible Cub in St. Luke's Pack won this Catholic award. One of the Scout committeemen used this as evidence that the Cubs were not being given the proper preliminary training for Scouting. He called it a "wholesale granting of undeserved awards. No pack could have one hundred per cent perfection for three years in a row unless the tests were made too easy." Nevertheless, this perfection is made possible through the intense efforts of Mrs. Echols, who trains the boys personally and rejects some children three or four times before sending them to the priest for the test.

The St. George Cub Scout Award is granted to Catholic Cubs who have passed a strictly religious test of ten requirements, from the recitation of the Ten Commandments and six precepts to the interpretation of Latin phrases used in the Mass. Only Cubs who have made their first Holy Communion and who have passed one major achievement, either Wolf, Bear or Lion, are eligible to take the test, which is administered by the Pastor. An endorsement, to the effect

[18] Certain changes have been introduced in the award system in Catholic Scouting. The St. George Award is now given to adult Scout leaders, the *Ad Altare Dei* medal continues to be the award for Boy Scouts, but the *Parvuli Dei* medal is now the official award for Cubs.

that the boy "is prepared to conduct himself as a Catholic in all ordinary situations which may confront him," must be signed by four adults: pastor, parent, cubmaster, and the chairman of the Catholic Committee for Scouting.

On this occasion Father Albert gave an impressive child-level sermon on St. George, who "was the slayer of evil and sin with his sword of faith." He informed the Cubs that it was their job to be like St. George. "First, you have to slay the evil of temptation which will trouble your own self. Then you must fight the evil outside of yourself. You must practice virtue, be square and true with all the other boys and girls, and like good Catholic Scouts you must always avoid sinful things." He then called out the names of those receiving the awards,[19] asked them to come to the Communion rail. He blessed the St. George medals and personally distributed them to each boy. The higher Catholic award, the *Ad Altare Dei* medal, for Boy Scouts, has been received by only one boy of St. Luke's parish, Martin Weston, who is a high school student.[20]

The girl movement also has its religious activities and religious awards. Sunday, March 17, the final day of the National Camp Fire Week, was designated by national leaders as "Worship God Day." The Blue Birds, Camp Fire Girls, and their adult leaders, dressed in their ceremonial garb, occupied the front pews of the church, and received Communion together before the other parishioners. On this occasion, Father Thomas celebrated the Mass, but he made no reference from the altar about the presence of the girls' group, the whole "sermon time" being taken up by reading a letter from the Bishop. Afterwards the girls marched to the school auditorium in ranks, had breakfast served by their mothers,[21] and displayed some of the hand crafts projects. The third-grade Blue Birds and the sixth-grade Camp

[19] The Pastor asked the boys to join him in thanking the Spiritual Activities Committee of the parish Holy Name Society, which donated the medals.

[20] A Deanery Scout Retreat was held on the weekend of October 19–20. Each Catholic Troop sending boys was assessed fifteen dollars, regardless of the numbers who attended. Since only three boys from St. Luke's expressed an interest in making the retreat, the adult Scout committee did not think it "worthwhile" to spend the money.

[21] This breakfast was paid for by the girls themselves out of the group treasury. In previous years each one was charged twenty-five cents, but the Pastor suggested they "earn the money." This was done through bake sales, the sales of Christmas cards and handmade objects, and the proceeds were pooled in the treasury. "Earn your own money" is a recommendation made by the organization to its members.

Fire Girls entertained with songs and skits, but the content of neither the display nor the entertainment bore any relation to the theme of the day—the worship of God.

There is no special Catholic medal or award crowning the girls' achievements in either Blue Bird or Camp Fire. But like the Scouts, these girls are constantly working for rank and passing tests. They earn "beads," the symbols of achievement in the Seven Crafts, and they earn supplementary honors by meeting specific Catholic requirements. Some of these required actions are as follows: give a spiritual bouquet to a sick person, attend Mass and receive Communion daily during Lent, assist the Altar Society for a month in the church, lead the daily recitation of the family Rosary for a month, babysit for one month for parents attending Sunday Mass, learn to use the missal.

Both the boys' and the girls' movements have camps to which they can go on weekends or for a longer period during the summer. These are operated on non-denominational lines, but the camp authorities take extra precautions that the Catholic children attend Mass on Sundays. During the summer, when the Scout camp is in constant use a priest comes regularly to offer Mass at the camp itself. On other occasions, and at the girls' camp, busses are provided on Sunday mornings to bring the children to the nearest church.

Some of the parents who have discussed the religious aspects of these two youth movements expressed the opinion that "religion is sort of added on" to the groups, and that the leaders bypass the tremendous possibility of supernatural motivation in their activities. This is in contrast to the school operation itself, where the whole cultural atmosphere is constantly laden with the spiritual. Central attention is given to the functions of the groups as outlined by the national headquarters and as patterned over the eight years' traditions at St. Luke's. Thus, the two youth groups are extracurricular in the peculiar sense that they are not essentially religious-oriented or motivated. Like the athletic and sports program, that of the two youth groups is handled by the adult leaders from the point of view of the secular culture from which it sprang. It is useful; it is important; it satisfies in an apt way certain social and personal needs of the children, but it could probably be operated just as efficiently and usefully outside the milieu of a religious elementary school.

Competition and Achievement

From the point of view of the sociological analyst the most striking feature of both these youth groups is their intense competitive orientation. The young boy fulfills his requirements as a Bobcat, and then works on his achievements to get the Wolf badge. He passes his tests in order to become a Bear cub and then a Lion cub. He then works to pass the requirements for the Webelos rank, the highest rank in Cub Scouting. Thereafter he graduates from the den and the pack to the troop, where he starts as a tenderfoot and works up the ranks from second class to first class and through the advanced awards of the Boy Scout program.[22]

The Blue Bird group is not quite so rigidly arranged in progressive steps toward the Camp Fire Girls. They progress by grades in school rather than by ranks or achievement. Beads are given instead of badges of individual achievement. They sew these beads to a sleeveless jacket, and the girl who has one-tenth of her jacket covered with beads advances along with the girl whose jacket is over-loaded with beads. Similarly, when the girl reaches the upper grades of the elementary school, she advances with her school grade through the four years of school and the four ranks of Camp Fire, from Trail Seeker to Wood Gatherer to Fire Maker and finally to Torch Bearer. In high school she may advance to membership in the Horizon Club.

This is a clear structural difference between the boys' and the girls' groups, and it appears to affect both competition and cooperation. The girls remain identified with their classmates and each grade constitutes a distinct group. The boys are identified by rank both in the Cubs and the Scouts, and it is quite possible that a boy may be in the same rank with boys who are above or below him in school.[23] Thus, they tend to be identified by membership in the Scouts rather than in the school grade. In the lower echelons, numbers are also a factor. The Den mother handles six to eight boys; the Blue Bird leader up to twenty girls. The Scout Troop is divided into small patrols; the Camp Fire Girls are divided only by the school grades in which the girls belong.

"Competition is characteristic of group life between the ages of eight and nine, and often increases past adolescence. Competition is part of our cultural pattern. Since children reproduce the pattern in their own way it is not surprising to find it among them at a very

[22] Another organizational problem at St. Luke's is the current attempt to combine the Explorers with the Scouts; the former are sometimes eighteen years old, and the latter twelve, and it is difficult to conduct a program attractive to both.

[23] For a discussion of the Cub Scouts as a formalized type of peer group, see William E. Martin and Celia Stendler, *Child Development: The Process of Growing Up in Society* (New York: Harcourt, Brace, 1953), pp. 577–581.

young age. The ideal goal, however, is cooperation, not competition. Some children love competition. It acts as a stimulant to greater effort and achievement. Some children do not seem to be affected by competitive zeal among their friends; some are greatly disturbed by it and give up. The child who wants to be the leader often must displace another child." [24]

This statement was written in relation to the Blue Birds, but it seems to be pertinent to the older girls also, as well as to all of the grade school boys in the movement. The interesting contrast in both boys' and girls' groups is that group cooperation and participation, group pride and loyalty, group identification and solidarity, are striven for, but at the same time individual achievement is urged and lauded in the attainment of rank. Theoretically, the child who does not "make the grade" on the basis of tests which require personal achievement in competition with others, is not a "good" member of the group.

There is also a certain amount of competition within each group for the attainment of group goals. For example, the need to replenish the treasuries of the girls' groups leads to competition among the members in the sale of Christmas cards, the sale of handmade rooters' dolls at the athletic games, the sale of shampoo and other items. In the matter of raising money, these girls are their mothers in miniature. They vied with one another in this, and produced results beneficial to the whole group. The Scouts are also competitive, but in a somewhat more restrained way. They had money-making projects on a small scale, and they competed in selling tickets for the Scout-O-Rama and in the paper drives.

The Scouts also have the opportunity to "show off," to uphold the "honor of St. Luke's," [25] when they compete with Scout troops from other schools and churches. The District Council promoted a "Klondike Winter Derby" at a public park on the last Sunday in January. The patrols within the troop competed as separate units and received awards according to the points they earned. St. Luke's came out second in the standings with other troops. Another area-wide competitive program was the Scout-O-Rama, held on the weekend, May 3–5, and participated in by 134 Scouting units. Each had a booth display, the St. Luke's Scouts demonstrating life-saving equipment, and the Cubs displaying "things that go," which were model planes, trains, and ships. Awards were given for outstanding booths, but St. Luke's

[24] *The Blue Bird Book* (New York: Camp Fire Girls, 1954), p. 30.

[25] The boys identify themselves more frequently by the number of their troop than by the name of their parish.

won nothing. Prizes were also given to the unit selling the most tickets—almost fifty thousand tickets were sold at twenty-five cents each throughout the county.

While play is the main function and the main attraction for both Cubs and Blue Birds, we have never attended a den meeting or a gathering of the young Blue Birds, in which there were no personal "projects" under way. These were demonstrations of achievements for awards. Similarly, the weekly meetings of the Scouts and of the Camp Fire Girls always offered a setting in which some personal task was being done or being displayed. But there were also activities in which the whole group participated, for example, the Scouts cooperated on two overnight camping trips, a tobogganing party, a Christmas party, a paper drive in conjunction with the Athletic Committee, and a summer motor tour. The Camp Fire Girls boast a parallel list of cooperative activities, performed however, by each grade group, rather than by all of the girls of the four upper grades together.

Impetus is given to individual competition through the Scouts' Courts of Honor, at which there is the awarding of merit badges and the recognition of advancement in Scout ranks, and also through the Group Council Fires at which the girls also receive public recognition for ranks and awards. This system of emulation does not stop at the level of the elementary school children. The annual appreciation dinner (Thursday, March 21) was one of the occasions during the year when awards were given to adults in the Scout movement. These were the Den Mother's Award, the Scouter's Training Award, and the Scouter's Key (which was won this year by Fred Nordman of St. Luke's Scout Troop), and the highest award of all, the Silver Beaver, which is made for "noteworthy service of exceptional character to youth in the local Council area over that normally expected in the Scouting position held by the nominee."

The girls' movement also has its system of recognition for adults at the Grand Council Fires. In previous years this had been a city-wide affair, but the Camp Fire Girls have grown to such proportions that the city is divided into districts, and the awards are given at the District Grand Council Fire. At this Fire on Friday, March 15, the motto was "Together we make tomorrow." The director of the Council Fire was Mrs. Frank Johnson, who is known in St. Luke's parish as "Mrs. Camp Fire," and who on this occasion received the national Five-Year Leadership Award. The highest Torch Bearer Award was then presented to two of St. Luke's girls, Grace Kleppner, for gardening, and Mary Fitzgerald, for homemaking. Their picture appeared in the local daily newspaper. Awarding of rank was made for Trail

Seekers and Wood Gatherers, as well as honors for ten-year, five-year, and three-year memberships.

Another form of recognition of achievement in competition is the annual "blue-gold banquet," held this year on Sunday, March 3, in the school auditorium. This was planned by the Cubmaster and the Den mothers, and consisted of a "pot-luck" meal to which each family contributed an item of food. The Pastor gave a short speech praising the adults working in this movement, and commending the Cubs who received awards. These prizes were the gold and silver arrow, the Wolf award and the Webelo award. This last mentioned award was given to Floyd Echols because his mother trained him individually for it, even though the Webelos as a group do not function at St. Luke's. This affair for the Cubs was quite distinct from the Court of Honor held at St. Luke's on the previous Monday night (April 29) to distribute awards to the Boy Scouts.

Group Service

The recognition of personal achievement which comes through public awards tends to give the erroneous impression that the immediate goal of these two youth movements is simply the development of the individual. The notion of doing a "good deed daily" has grown into our American folklore as a result of the insistence of service in the Scout movement. In both the boys' and girls' movement the various manuals make constant reference to specific actions that can be performed by the youngster for the benefit of his or her family, neighborhood, church, classmates and others. This is unquestionably a positive means to develop unselfishness in the individual child, to give him an awareness of the needs of others, and to promote a valid social awareness in him.

Aside from this spirit of individual service to others, numerous occasions are provided in the two movements for cooperative service. Sometimes this is a matter of cooperation among the members doing something for and with the group itself. For example, in early October, the fourth grade Blue Birds started preparations at their weekly meeting for a costume party to be held on the last day of the month. "Committees" were chosen by the girls themselves, under the direction of Mrs. Gentry, for refreshments, decorations and entertainment. This process of volunteering, electing and forming sub-committees within each grade group continues through the years, so that the eighth-grade Camp Fire Girls become most proficient in it. This is much more in evidence among the girls than among the boys, and practically every group program of the girls is prepared for in this way.

Service within the group was demonstrated by the "big sister" attitude taken by the older Camp Fire Girls toward the youngsters in Blue Bird. They helped out the Guardians occasionally at the Blue Bird meetings and programs. The most impressive display of this assistance was given at the "Fly-Up" for the fourth graders on the evening of May 15, when six girls from the eighth grade explained the various honors, ranks and activities, and also taught them the Camp Fire Song. They also led them in the pledge: "A Good Camp Fire Girl must: worship God, seek beauty, give aid, be happy, pursue knowledge, be trustworthy, have health, glorify work." Each new Camp Fire Girl then receives a certificate, and has the red neckerchief placed around her neck by her mother. The older girls, however, played an important role in impressing the youngsters.

Group cooperation and service to others were demonstrated in the March of Dimes by both the girl and boy movements, but the girls added something "extra" in the eighth grade. They made a scrapbook with tooled leather covers for a girl polio victim in another parish, brought it to her home and visited her as a group. In February, the sixth-grade girls prepared a meal for their parents, a task performed at some time or other by all Camp Fire groups. Here again, committees divided the work among themselves. The eighth-grade girls were most adept at preparing parties. They invited boys to a football party on October 28, to an afternoon party and dance on December 7, to a roller skating party on February 14, and another on May 23. Each of the four Camp Fire groups also went to a hospital or old peoples' home to present a carol sing at Christmas time. These are simply a few examples of the constant effort by these youth movements to "work together for others."

The Broader Community

The youth movements of St. Luke's perform certain latent functions quite aside from the clearly discernible functions and objectives mentioned thus far. They achieve what are perhaps unanticipated results in two directions; they tend to bring the interested adult parishioners, mainly parents of the children, closer together,[26] and they also tend to broaden the contacts of both children and parents with persons outside St. Luke's parish. In the first area, that of paro-

[26] The Scoutmaster, Fred Nordman, and one of the Committeemen, Walter Vogt, are unmarried. One of the Blue Bird Guardians, Mrs. Farley, does not have a child of school age, but participates actively because her little sister is in the group.

chial contact, both youth movements come under the general supervision of the Character Education Committee of the PTA. The annual dues of the adult leaders in both groups are paid by the PTA, and brief monthly reports are made concerning activities to this organization. In actual practice, however, the PTA allows the youth movements to go their own separate ways.

The women leaders of the girls' groups held quarterly meetings in November, January, March and May, under the leadership of Mrs. Basil Gentry, who with her husband is joint chairman of the Character Education Committee of the PTA. At these meetings the leaders and guardians of the girls' groups learn to know one another more intimately and to discuss in some detail the interests and problems of their young daughters. They attempt to find mutual solutions for problems like the following: only one meeting room is available for ten groups of girls and only five school days available for weekly meetings in the afternoon; [27] the buying of a coffee urn for their exclusive use (or the suggestion to have the children sell vanilla to win a forty-five cup urn); no parish group takes responsibility for keeping the kitchen of the school auditorium clean; the leaders have a key to the meeting room used by the children, but not a key to the outside door of the building; [28] the question of soliciting new membership to the girls' groups.

The boys' movement has two distinct adult committees. The Cub Pack Committee holds quarterly meetings in October, December, February, and April. Mr. Gentry, the Cubmaster, and co-chairman of the Character Education Committee of the PTA, is assisted by five other fathers, and by the Den mothers, all of whom attend the meetings. The problem of recruitment of Cubs was considered acute because of the shortage of Den mothers. Another problem was that of

[27] Even the Blue Birds meet at the school, the adult coming to the children rather than the reverse as is the case of the Cub dens. This may be a partial explanation of the larger membership and the greater success of the Blue Birds than of the Cubs. The women do not have their home disturbed by boisterous children; there is less inconvenience on the part of the child going to someone else's home after school, or as in the case of the Scout patrol to a different home each week. It is probably also one of the reasons why this girls' movement is organized nationally on a school basis.

[28] This problem of insufficient keys also plagued the athletic coach. See below, chap. 8 on "Organized Sports." The problem of the meeting room has other angles. The same room is used for both boys' and girls' meetings, and one of the Scout leaders complained that "the Blue Birds are the dirtiest kids in the school, and my boys have to clean up the meeting room after them before we can use it."

projects. The year started with a special male committee meant to plan projects; at the first meeting the whole group did this planning; but in subsequent months the Den mothers made the plans and simply told the men what they needed in the way of supplies. These adults met also on the first Monday night of every month when all of the Dens met for a joint pack meeting.

The Boy Scout Committee is made up exclusively of male membership. Its quarterly meetings were held the same Tuesday evenings on which the PTA meetings are conducted, so that even if the fathers on the Committee were interested in the PTA they would have to miss at least four of its meetings during the year. The heart of the Scout Committee's meeting is the Scoutmaster's report, but when this was completed the men usually spent a great deal of time discussing the prospective motor and camping trip for the following summer. Some of the men feared that they would "lose control" of the Scout Troop if the Pastor discovered how much money was in their treasury, or if they decided to ask the various parish organizations to help defray the expenses of the motor tour. Most of these men do not attend, or assist directly, at the regular Scout meetings of the boys, which are controlled by the Scoutmaster.

The three adult committees differ considerably in the degree of parochial solidarity which they can express, and also in the amount of actual contact they have with the children. The leaders of the girls' group meet one another most frequently in both formal and informal ways. They are also in much more direct and frequent contact with the children. In the Cub Scout committee, the men tend to allow the women to "run the show," but the general direction does remain in the hands of the Cubmaster, and the men involved do come together for the monthly pack meetings and have contact with the boys. The Boy Scout committee appears to have the least common grounds for functioning, and also the least direct relationship with the boys themselves. In this instance, the Scoutmaster acts in the manner of liaison between the adults and the youngsters.

Since both the boys' and girls' movements are units in a network of district, city, state and national organization, they must necessarily on occasion break out of the parochial boundaries.[29] This contact with "outsiders" takes a variety of forms. A district representative from

[29] The twenty-third annual Report of Progress (1956) by the Catholic Committee on Scouting showed that there were 10,390 Catholic-sponsored packs, troops and posts in nearly seven thousand parishes in 136 archdioceses and dioceses of the United States. The 1957 Report showed an increase to 11,119 units in 139 dioceses.

outside the parish attends the quarterly meetings of both the Cub and the Scout committees. The planning meetings for all city and county-wide activities like the Klondike Derby and the Scout-O-Rama, always include one or more members from St. Luke's adult committees. The annual appreciation dinner also attracts them. The Courts of Review and the Courts of Honor for the Scouts within the parish occasionally have an "outside" Scoutmaster as an honored guest. The boys themselves meet other Scouts in the various competitive affairs conducted for the city's packs and troops, but their closest contact comes at the Scouts' summer camp where they meet and live with boys from other areas.

In the girls' movement there are similar opportunities across parochial and religious lines. The women leaders have even more intensive contact with non-parishioners than do the men in the Cub and Scout committees. The Camp Fire District to which St. Luke's belongs includes five public schools and no other parochial school. The leaders in this district meet every month, except July and August, and the women from St. Luke's take an important part. Mrs. Johnson is general chairman of the District, and Mrs. Gentry is hostess chairman, Mrs. Forshag is treasurer. Each unit rotates in the function of hostess at the meetings, and this involves three or four more mothers from St. Luke's. Since the public schools are locked up nightly at nine o'clock, these meetings are held at St. Luke's and at various Protestant churches in the area.[30] The annual Camp Fire dinner, held in a downtown hotel on Wednesday, January 23, drew 553 adults from groups all over the city. Representatives from St. Luke's worked on the committees for tickets, for decorations and for hostesses.

The Blue Birds have multiplied so rapidly that the annual birthday party formerly held on a city-wide basis, is now conducted in the separate districts. In the St. Luke's district more than 350 young girls assembled to represent the six elementary schools from which they came. This was held in the local public high school on Sunday afternoon, March 17. The Council Fires, already discussed, also provide

[30] Because of the nine o'clock curfew at its own school, the Explorer Post of the local Junior High School transferred its meetings to the Methodist Church, but did not become affiliated with the congregation. In a study of "Scouting and the Public Schools," *Bulletin* of the National Association of Secondary-School Principals, vol. 38, no. 200 (February, 1954), pp. 96–97, it was shown that sixty-three per cent of public school Scouting units are sponsored by the PTA, nineteen per cent by other school groups, and eighteen per cent by service clubs and other community groups.

opportunities for meeting other girls. Unlike the Cub Scouts, the Blue Birds and Camp Fire Girls continue throughout the summer, and they have the advantage of a Day Camp, operating this year from June 24 to August 3, at the public recreational park. Three women from St. Luke's, Mrs. McWellan, Mrs. Farley, and Mrs. Gentry, acted as supervisors for this camp. Most of the girls, except those who went to the large permanent camp in another part of the state, attended this Day Camp. The City-wide Camp Fire had purchased ten acres outside the city as a campsite, but the shelters and other facilities were not yet completed.[31]

It is clear from the description of these programs and events, that the youth movements of St. Luke's parish function as a kind of channel of communication from the parish to the larger community. They tend to bring together the interested persons within the parish, and then to provide opportunities for the boys and girls to associate with other youngsters from different schools and from other parts of the city. The extent to which there is mutual influence between the parish and the community is probably not measureable. This is perhaps not so important as the fact that there is actual communication, cooperation and understanding between Catholics and non-Catholics, and that this kind of relationship identifies St. Luke's people as an integral part of the total community.

From the point of view of the broader community and of the total American culture there is the obviously present question of pluralism and unity in these youth movements. The constant attempt to fuse the objectives of Scouting and of Camp Fire programs with those of religious education has increased the number of Church-sponsored units so that Protestant, Catholic and Jewish children tend to identify the movement with their own religious faith. Thus, like most important aspects of American organizational life, these youth movements are both separatist and integrative. The Jews in Poland, like the Negroes in the South, were excluded from the Scouts, and founded their own separate Scouting units.[32] In some places class-conscious-

[31] The money to finance this camp had been raised by the girls themselves through their various projects. In general, however, the Camp Fire Girls are helped by the United Fund.

[32] See Saul Scheidlinger, "A Comparative Study of the Boy Scout Movement in Different National and Social Groups," *American Sociological Review*, vol. 13, no. 6 (December, 1948), pp. 739–750, who shows that variations in both methods and objectives occur in the Scout Movement because of specific ethnic and cultural interests of the sponsoring group.

ness operates in both the Scouts and the Camp Fire Girls to exclude children of lower-class status from membership in the movement.[33] In the ultimate analysis, it appears that the local cultural patterns are the determining factor deciding whether or not these youth movements can fulfil their inherently democratic and integrative objectives.

Generalizations

1. In the youth movements of St. Luke's school the girls are more numerous, enthusiastic and successful than the boys. The main reason for this seems to be that the girls' program of activities is centered for the most part around functions that are feminine and that fit the cultural expectations of the community. Furthermore, the girls are organized by grade in school rather than merely by rank in the group, and they hold their meetings in the school building after school hours.

2. While the girls maintain a membership of about two-thirds of their potential, the Boy Scouts decrease to about one-fifth of their potential membership. The boys do many things that are interesting and are considered fun by them, but these functions do not compete successfully with the lure and the glamor of athletics, nor are they an apprenticeship to the kinds of adult roles the boys will one day perform. Furthermore, the youngest boys are organized in Dens that are hard to manage, and the older Scouts hold their weekly patrol meetings at different homes that are sometimes inconvenient to reach.

3. The participation of adults in the youth movements varies greatly in fathers and mothers of the children. The fathers have very little systematic contact with the boys' program, and the most interested and active adults are either unmarried or do not have children in St. Luke's school. The lack of paternal participation is partly due to the fact that the fathers do not have a realistic enthusiasm about the kinds of activities the Scouts perform. The mothers, on the other hand, are able and like to do the things that their daughters perform in the movement. Some of the mothers work successfully with the Cub Scouts, but most of them do not seem to be as enthusiastic about it as they are in the help they extend to the girls.

4. Like the athletic program, these two youth movements are largely outside the social structure of the school itself. The school cooperates to the extent of allowing the use of the building; and the teachers take some small interest in the goings-on. If it were not for the parents, however, the whole organizational set-up would disap-

[33] See August B. Hollingshead, *Elmtown's Youth* (New York: John Wiley, 1949), pp. 290–297.

pear. The only structural connection is through the Character Education Committee of the PTA, but this latter organization itself tends to be merely an appendage of the school. Father Martin acts as a kind of remote moderator to the adult committees, but participates little with the children themselves.

5. Although the objective of both youth groups is avowedly the service of God, as well as of country, the religious aspects of their program appear to be more contrived than integral. Efforts are made in the way of religious demonstrations, and even of religious actions to help achieve honors. This deficiency, if it is one, shows up in the contrast between the techniques of the teacher in the classroom and those of the Den mother or Camp Fire leader. The former leans heavily on supernatural and spiritual motivation for both knowledge and behavior. This expression of motivation is almost entirely absent in the youth leader.

6. The competitive process is developed more highly and used more extensively in these two youth groups than anywhere else in St. Luke's school. A highly developed system of achievements appears in the manuals, particularly of the boys' groups, and parents of Cub Scouts attest with their signature that the child has performed the prescribed task. Tangible rewards in the form of beads, badges, ribbons and medals are given to the children who pass tests and "make rank." These items can be worn with the uniform in order to identify precisely the status of the child within the group. Group competition in the form of patrol activities appears also with the boys in the upper grades.

7. The over-riding motive of service to fellowmen appears throughout both boys' and girls' programs. Tangible rewards are given also for these various items of service, the child being able to "mark it down" as a means of advancement or as a part of a test. The children take these things seriously, as far as we could judge, but whether the isolated instances of service combine into a pattern of out-going social awareness cannot be clearly discerned. At least, this appears to be the direction in which the leaders would like to see the children develop.

8. These two youth movements provide an opportunity for social relations and cooperation among interested parents of the children. In this regard, as an instrument of parochial solidarity, they are less effective than the PTA and the school as a whole. Since the fathers do not participate to any great degree, this integrating function is performed mainly for and by the mothers. About one-third of these women are, however, also active in either the Athletic Committee

or the PTA or both. Hence, they form a core to which the other mothers are attracted and act as a channel for them over into the larger PTA.

9. Another latent function of these youth groups is that they bring both the children and their parents into contact with other people of similar interest in the larger community. This is one of the ways in which the so-called "parochialism" of Catholics is dissipated, good relations with non-Catholics are established, and mutual understanding across creedal lines is developed.

Chapter

EIGHT

ORGANIZED SPORTS

PROFESSIONAL EDUCATORS have begun to question seriously the organized athletic program on the elementary school level, especially in its highly competitive aspect and in the physical and emotional dangers that accompany it. These educators are on record as opposing highly organized competition of a varsity pattern and contact sports, like tackle football and boxing. They object to any program that exploits boys and girls or jeopardizes their health, safety or sense of values. They are in favor of instruction in physical education for all children in the school, of informal intramural competition and of occasional informal invitational games between neighboring schools.[1]

The fact that sports activities can be a means for promoting good health, and the fact that the physical and healthy development of children is now one of the functions of the elementary school, cannot be contested by any serious observer of the educational system. The question of school athletics is a relative one. How much sports is enough, and at what point does a school "go overboard" in this regard? Can the athletic program, at least in its inter-school competitive aspects, be contained as a mere "fringe" activity of the school? [2] Can it

[1] These ideas appear in a pamphlet published by the NEA, Washington, D.C., a joint committee report entitled *Desirable Athletic Competition for Children.* See pp. 5–6 for "self-checking for quality programs." As early as 1930 the White House Conference on Education adopted recommendations for an effective program of health and physical education. See *White House Conference, Addresses and Abstracts of Committee Reports* (New York: Century, 1931), p. 177; also P. R. Brammell, *National Survey of Secondary Education* (U.S. Department of the Interior, Office of Education, 1932), Monograph 28, p. 72. The suggestions made there have not been substantially altered in the intervening years. For a more sympathetic view of athletic competition on the elementary level see Earl H. Hanson, "Athletics for Children," *American School Board Journal,* vol. 128 (June, 1954), p. 31.

[2] See Harry Alexander Scott, *Competitive Sports in Schools and Colleges* (New York: Harper, 1951), chap. 13, "The Program of Competitive Sports in Elementary and Junior High Schools," where he discusses the characteristics of

be allowed to become a core activity around which the rest of the school program revolves? Or can it be integrated in its proper place alongside other functions?

Why Athletics?

There are many reasons why St. Luke's school engages in a program of athletic competition with other elementary schools. The pattern has long been set in the city at large. The public school system has a well organized league in the major sports of football, basketball, baseball and girls' volleyball. There is also a parochial school league, which imitates the public school system, and occasionally there are invitational games between certain parochial and public schools. Thus, there is a kind of social pressure for any "representative" school to follow the example of what "everybody else is doing." Furthermore, athletic competition is considered a value in the American culture, even though its alleged benefits are often only vaguely understood.[3]

The parents of the elementary school children are deeply affected by this widespread cultural value. We asked them "Are you in favor of, or against, organized athletic teams that play against other schools?" St. Luke's parents replied as follows: For—94.2%; Against—4.5%; No Answer—1.3%. Parents of public school children answered: For—95.8%; Against—2.5%; No Answer—1.7%. The relatively few parents who object to inter-school athletic competition feel that there has been an overemphasis on this aspect of education, that there are certain physical dangers involved in some of the sports, and that the children are too young to stand the excitement of strong competition.[4] Since the great majority is in favor of it, and since there is a strong nucleus of sports enthusiasts among them, the voice of the opposition is hardly heard.

As a matter of fact, if it were not for the adult Athletic Committee of the parish there would probably be no competitive sports program at St. Luke's. At the athletic banquet in early May, the Pastor publicly thanked the "wonderful Athletic Committee of the parish. Without your efforts, all this could not happen. I certainly could not do it my-

---

the child of this age, his play and athletic needs. He also speaks generally against competition, giving "Criteria Governing Inter-school Competition" (a program evaluation list) on pp. 488–89.

[3] The Protestant churches of the city sponsor an athletic league, an example not followed by the local Catholic parishes.

[4] Henry J. Otto, *Social Education in Elementary Schools* (New York: Rinehart, 1956), chap. 7, discusses the objectives of elementary physical education, as well as the physical, emotional and social benefits that can result from it.

self, and there would be no athletic program without your help." Unlike the public school where the sports program is taken as a matter of course, where the coaches are regularly employed teachers, and the school absorbs the whole financial burden, the teams of St. Luke's are coached, equipped, organized and paid for by the lay adults of the parish. In this sense, the parents, and not the teachers or priests, "run the program."

The children are also heartily in favor of the athletic teams of St. Luke's school. While relatively few of them participate as competing players, the enthusiasm for the teams spreads throughout the whole school. Even the children in the first and second grades learn the "school yells." The teachers in both parochial and public schools are overwhelmingly in favor of organized teams. (Only one public school teacher of nineteen interviewed objected to it.) Most of them, however, made certain qualifying statements to the effect that they would like to see an emphasis on intramural programs and a deemphasis of the "spirit of winning." One male teacher in the public school enthusiastically endorses football "because it teaches the boys courage and fearlessness, and makes them learn how to get along together and to cooperate as a group."

Some of the laymen think that the sports program brings prestige to St. Luke's school, and insist that prospective athletes would prefer to attend other elementary schools if St. Luke's were to give up its program. There is also the feeling that the development of competent athletes in the Catholic elementary schools will eventually improve the teams of the Catholic high school.[5] At the football banquet in November, the president of the Athletic Committee said that "these boys have worked hard to represent you people, and to bring fame to St. Luke's parish." A similar remark was made by the basketball coach at the May banquet, "We are giving these players their awards tonight because they have made many sacrifices and worked hard to bring recognition to St. Luke's school and to bring honor and glory to the whole parish."[6]

[5] Mr. Bowman, the basketball coach recognizes the desirability of a closer working arrangement with the Catholic high school. He is promoting a coaches' clinic for elementary school coaches to be conducted by the Catholic high school coach, "so that we can teach the boys what they need to know when they go there." The preliminary meeting was held in April, and the clinic scheduled for the late summer.

[6] Father Martin was somewhat more realistic in his remarks, pointing out that the adult committee worked harder than any of the children, and that the volunteer coaches made greater sacrifices than any of the players they coached.

The moral value of sports for the children was frequently emphasized by the most interested among the parents. "This is the best way to avoid delinquency," said one of the fathers. "Athletics teaches the children how to get along together. It teaches them obedience to rules since every game is made up of rules. It helps them to work off energy which they would be using in worse ways if they were not in athletics." The basketball coach took delight in repeating the statement that "the boy who shoots baskets doesn't shoot people," and when the baseball season started he liked to say that "the boy who steals second isn't stealing autos." [7]

The least enthusiastic sports fan in the parish is the Pastor. He is concerned about the possibilities of accidents to the children; he issues warnings that the program must not be "overdone" or interfere with the more serious purposes of the school; he thinks that the money raised by the Athletic Committee for the teams should be distributed so that all of the boys and girls get the benefits of athletics.[8] "I have had to take a lot of talk and a lot of reprimands about this athletic program. Some of you people think that I'm grouchy and that I'm opposed to athletics; but deep down in my heart it isn't true. What we have been doing here is very good. I say to you, use it more extensively. We should have the lower grades using the gym as much as the seventh and eighth grades." It is unquestionably a tribute to the Pastor's democratic and liberal attitudes that despite his worries and misgivings, he cooperates with the lay people in the kind of program they want most.

[7] Computing the conduct grades, A, B, C, on the report cards as 3, 2, 1, we find that the average mean grade for athletes and non-athletes is about the same; athletes: 2.14 and non-athletes: 2.19. For some views on athletics and moral behavior, see Jordan L. Larson, "Athletics and Good Citizenship," *Journal of Educational Sociology*, vol. 28 (1954–55), pp. 271–74. In the same issue see also Charles C. Noble, "The Moral and Spiritual Implications of School Athletics," pp. 260–62, and James B. Nolan, "Athletics and Juvenile Delinquency," pp. 263–65. The above are favorable to athletics as a delinquency preventer. Edwin H. Sutherland, *Principles of Criminology* (Fifth Edition), (Chicago: Lippincott, 1955), takes the position that athletics generally has no preventive effect on delinquency and can even provide occasions for it, pp. 167–68; 611–13.

[8] He expressed astonishment that the Athletic Committee "was able to spend two thousand dollars at one time for football equipment," and often refers to his own childhood when "we played on the sand lot and had just second-hand stuff to play with."

How Many Participate?

St. Luke's has an excellent modern gymnasium, which is used also and mainly as an "all-purpose" auditorium for the whole parish. At one end is a large stage; adjoining it on the right side are the kitchen and cafeteria and on the left side a large meeting room with provisions for a snack bar. In this gymnasium are held the parish bazaar, dances, plays, suppers, style shows, card parties and other general parochial activities.[9] Since there are no regular physical education classes, and no instructor for these classes, this gymnasium is hardly ever in use during the regular school hours. Since football and baseball are played out-of-doors, the gym is used only by those children who are on the boys' basketball and girls' volleyball teams.

There were no serious conflicts among these teams in the use of the gymnasium. The girls were coached by a high school student who was able to hold practice in the afternoons after school. The girls' second team was coached by an eighth grader, Ethel Karst, a volleyball star who could not play on the varsity because she reached her fifteenth birthday before the league season opened. The basketball coach came in the evening and started practice at about six-thirty o'clock. He complained, however, when the Junior Newman Club of the parish held functions at practice time, or when his players had to remove or to set up chairs for the programs of this Club. Another complaint, made also by Scout and Camp Fire leaders, was that he was not allowed to have a key to the building. "My boys have to hang around in the cold while I go scout up one of the priests to get the key." [10]

Some of the parents felt that the gymnasium should be put to more use and that a physical education program would give more of the children an opportunity to use it. Preliminary steps were taken to comply with these wishes. The PTA voted to donate one thousand dollars to furnish further equipment and to make changes in the gym. Bids were received for the work. The project was discussed by the priests, the PTA and the Athletic Association. It was finally decided that since the gym will be used for religious services during the next two years while the new church is under construction, the changes should be post-

[9] The recreation committee of the PTA tried to promote "mixed volleyball games" on Thursday evenings. Announcements were made in the Church Bulletin ("Spend an evening in the gym limbering up,") on October 21, November 18 and December 2, but the plan was abandoned because of lack of interest on the part of adult parishioners.

[10] The janitor absolutely refused to allow any lay person to use his key to the gymnasium.

poned. The Pastor also asked Mr. Bowman to consult with the physical education department of the local university, concerning the possibility of employing graduate students to teach gym classes for all the children at St. Luke's school.[11] This plan was still being discussed at the conclusion of our study, and it is likely to be put into effect in the near future.

In the three higher grades, from which the varsity teams were drawn, there were eighty-four boys. No boy in these grades was refused the opportunity to participate in athletics, even if he had little ability for the games. A total of thirty-eight boys "dressed" for football, among whom were seventeen from the sixth grade serving mainly as a scrub team against the varsity in practice sessions.[12] St. Luke's team played seven games against the other parochial schools in the league on Sunday afternoons from September 16 to October 28. St. Luke's lost its first two games and won the remaining five, ending the season in third place in the parochial school league. They also defeated two public schools in practice games.

It must be obvious that all of the boys in the three higher grades could not participate in the playing of football. There is a selectivity from the point of view of physical ability. Each child has to have a medical examination and permission from a physician; [13] he must have the permission of his parents, and finally some ability and interest in the game. There are, however, more applicants than there are berths for players. In order that competition will not be one-sided the age limit for players is fifteen years, and the weight limit for backfield men is 130 pounds. The heaviest boys on St. Luke's team were two guards and a tackle, each weighing 140 pounds; and the oldest boy was the fullback and star, Jerry Mott, age fourteen.

The Catholic basketball league comprises many more parochial school teams; the season lasts longer, but fewer pupils participate in

[11] The officials for all parochial league games were drawn from this student body, but many of the coaches were dissatisfied with their work, and are now attempting to hire only licensed officials.

[12] This group of youngsters played separate practice games against the sixth graders of four other parochial schools. They won two, lost one, and tied one. They constitute a kind of "feeder system" from which the future varsity will be drawn.

[13] This rule holds for all inter-school competitors and is enforced by the parochial school league officials. The athletes, like most of the other children at St. Luke's are covered by a blanket school accident insurance policy, issued by the Central Catholic Insurance Company, for which each child pays $1.50 per year. The Athletic Committee paid this premium for several children whose parents failed to do so.

it, than in football. The Coach had only fifteen uniforms for the first team, and issued fourteen of them to eligible players, only three of whom were seventh graders. Eighteen other boys from the seventh and sixth grades, under the direction of the assistant coach, also formed a basketball team [14] which played six games, losing one and winning one in competition with public schools, losing three and winning one against parochial school competition. The varsity played in the league with twenty other teams,[15] starting the season on November 16 and ending on March 10. They won fifteen games, and lost five, to gain the fourth place in the final league ranking.

A holiday tournament, with two days play before Christmas and two days afterward, was optional for the teams in the league. The Coach paid the seven dollars' entrance fee from the Athletic Committee's treasury only after the boys had assured him that they could "beat" the league leaders. St. Luke's was eliminated after winning two games and losing two. A final tournament, which ended on Sunday, March 24, included all the teams in the league. St. Luke's lost in the semifinals after having defeated two other teams.[16] Thus, throughout the year the basketball team engaged in twenty-seven games, winning nineteen and losing eight. During February, March and April, the coach and assistant coach taught the fundamentals of basketball to twenty-two fifth-grade boys, and also practiced the sixth- and seventh-grade boys, preparing them for next year's season. Nine boys from the fourth grade also showed up for these practice sessions.[17] Thus, a total of sixty-five boys participated in one way or another in the basketball facilities of the school.

The baseball season started for the Catholic school league as soon as the basketball season ended. St. Luke's did not enter a team in

[14] Thus, thirty-two boys were eligible to attend the banquet in May as guests of the Athletic Committee.

[15] Actually, the league is called an "inter-city league" because parochial schools from several surrounding towns are also represented in it.

[16] Sister Roberta would not believe the three girls who came immediately after the game to report that St. Luke's had been eliminated from the tournament by a weaker team which they had previously defeated. "One was crying, one was laughing hysterically, and the other stood there speechless with a dumb look on her face."

[17] The coach says that he has had numerous phone calls from mothers thanking him for giving their boys an opportunity to learn the game. He advises the mothers to have their sons do a lot of swimming during the summer and also to skip rope. The mother of one exceptional prospective athlete in the sixth grade was advised by the coach to teach her son dancing in order to increase his agility.

the league mainly because there was no coach immediately available and no plans had been made by the Athletic Committee. The eighth-grade boys liked the game and persuaded the basketball coach to "find somebody" to coach them. Finally, at the end of April, one of the men, the father of the star quarterback, second-string basketball player and regular infielder, Dick Navaro, agreed to coach the team. The boys played five practice games, and won them all, three against parochial teams and two against public school teams. Nineteen boys were on the baseball squad, five of them from the seventh grade.

Three other baseball games were rained out. Two others were canceled on Memorial Day and during the last week of school because the parents felt that the eighth graders were already engaged in too many other activities. During the summer the city's recreational commission sponsors baseball leagues for boys on the city and public school playgrounds. Thirteen boys from St. Luke's played on the teams for 12–13 year old boys, and fourteen played on teams with an age limit of eleven years. In the park centrally located in St. Luke's parish, these boys represented a little over twenty per cent of all the baseball players at both age levels. In the opinion of the City Recreational Commissioner the parochial school children are greatly underrepresented in baseball and other sports in the public playgrounds of the city.

Participation by Girls

One of the frequent complaints of girl pupils at St. Luke's school, and of the mothers of some of them, was that "the boys get all the breaks; the school spends all kinds of money on them and we get hardly anything at all." In large measure this complaint seems justified. The only organized sport for girls is volleyball. In the previous year they had almost won the league title, but this year had to be satisfied with a record of seven wins and five losses in league competition. They also won three practice games and lost the only tournament game they played.

The girls in the seventh and eighth grades showed a great deal of enthusiasm for volleyball as early as the first week of October when they began practice in the school yard. Their coach, Marie Habetz, who had previously starred at St. Luke's, came on Monday, Wednesday and Friday afternoons. At that time thirteen eighth graders and thirteen seventh graders came regularly to practice. The coach said "we'll keep them all playing until the beginning of January. As soon as I pick the regular squad of sixteen players, the rest will stop coming to practice." When the weather got colder the players moved into the gymnasium for their practice sessions.[18] By the time they were "ready" for league play there were six eighth graders and two seventh graders on the "first string," and eight substitutes mainly from the eighth grade. The other girls had had at least two months fun in the practice sessions, and they came regularly to root for St. Luke's team. From February to May the assistant coach worked with nineteen sixth graders who were aspiring to next year's team.

The Catholic volleyball league was composed of the teams from thirteen parochial schools. The teams played every Saturday from February 2 to April 27 at the Armory, the first game starting at eleven in the morning and the final game at four o'clock in the afternoon. The final tournament was held on the first Saturday in May, and when the St. Luke's team was eliminated, the coaches and players seemed relieved rather than frustrated that the long season had come to an end. There were a few tears of disappointment, but not nearly so many as were shed whenever the team lost a game during the season.

Although St. Luke's has no swimming team, coach or pool, many of the children take advantage of the two public pools.[19] On April 22, the City Recreation Department sponsored a novice swim meet for the children of the city's public and parochial schools. Applications were distributed through the schools, but the children had to fill them out and send them in individually. The response from the public school children was much greater than that from the parochial schools, three-fifths of the former being represented as compared to less than two-fifths of the latter. At St. Luke's the interest of the students was aroused through the efforts of Clare Johnson, who is also one of the most active girls in the eighth grade.[20] She got a large number of the children to apply, but only twelve of them—mostly girls—actually came to compete.

St. Luke's contingent at the April meet was poorly organized; there was no adult from the parish, teacher or parent, to help them with

[18] Both the volleyball and the basketball teams and their coaches complained about the low temperature in the gymnasium, claiming that "it is never above 58 degrees all winter long." It seems that the builder of the gymnasium advised that a window (high up which requires the use of a ladder to open and close) should be left partially open "so that the floor will not buckle." When the Pastor heard about this he said "that's a lot of nonsense; we'll just be burning fuel to heat up the schoolyard."

[19] One of these is an indoor, all-year, heated natatorium, where some of St. Luke's pupils take swimming lessons and practice weekly. The YMCA also has a pool and attracts some of St. Luke's children for swimming events.

[20] She won second place in the breath-holding event, and received this ribbon at the eighth-grade Award Night, Tuesday, May 28.

arrangements. In spite of this, seven of the entrants scored points in the meet, and St. Luke's placed ninth out of twenty-three schools in the fifth- and sixth-grade division, and seventh out of fourteen schools in the seventh- and eighth-grade division. The eighth-grade girls expected to do well in the relay race, but one of their members, Jane Walsh, failed to appear. The three others insisted that they could have won if she had been there, yet two of these three did not enter any of the other events. At any rate, the children were pleased with their showing, and boasted that in both divisions they scored more points than any of the other parochial schools entered in the meet.

The girls' participation in the athletic program at St. Luke's was enhanced by the coveted position of cheerleaders which they filled. These girls wore special jackets supplied by the Athletic Committee, but had to provide their own specially lined corduroy skirts.[21] They formed a squad of six girls, two from each of the three higher grades, elected by secret ballot of their classmates. On the Friday before the first football game Father Martin went to each of these grades and asked for volunteers, and about two-thirds of the girls raised their hands. Their names were written on the board and checked as each vote was called off. The girls, eager for this place in the spotlight, were quite excited over the election. To the surprise of Sister Roberta, the two girls elected from the eighth grade, Jane Walsh and Margie Fosullo, were pupils who had just transferred from other schools in September.

During the previous year the same cheerleaders had maintained their positions throughout the entire year. In the beginning of November, however, a rumor spread through the school that there would be a new election for basketball cheerleaders, the six previous leaders (for football) not being eligible for re-election. Sister Roberta asked Father Martin whether there should be a new election for the basketball season, and the latter consequently came over to the school on the Monday before Thanksgiving to supervise the election.[22] As with the previous group, the girl with the highest number of votes became the captain, who calls the cheers and directs them. They usually practiced on Wednesday and Friday during the recess periods by leading

[21] These skirts could be bought new for about eleven dollars, but the girls usually purchased them from previous cheerleaders for three or four dollars.

[22] There was some talk among the parents to the effect that the Principal did not like the selections made by the children for the football cheerleaders, especially the fact that some "new girls" had been elected. Sister's remark was that "so many girls want to be cheerleaders that everybody ought to get a chance."

as many of the pupils as they could gather together in the schoolyard.

At the games the cheerleaders appeared to be indefatigable. The rooters they led were mainly girls from the school, who came out in greater numbers than boys to support the teams. All of the parochial schools had squads of girl cheerleaders appropriately dressed in uniforms of the particular school's colors. The girls had relatively complicated formations and long yells, which were quite similar in all the schools. As soon as one school made an innovation, the cheerleaders from the other schools imitated it. The cheerleaders from St. Luke's were delighted with their function. Their only suggestion for improvement was that the Athletic Committee should provide light sweaters as an alternate for their warm jackets. They thought they would like these sweaters for warm days in the football season and especially for the basketball games, but when the Committee actually offered to purchase these sweaters, the girls changed their minds.

The participation of girls in the athletic program at St. Luke's is limited by factors beyond their own control. Organized girls' sports simply do not enjoy social prestige and value as the boys' sports do. The people in the parish, even the parents of girl athletes, do not take them seriously. The largest number of fans, both adults and children, came to the football games, the smallest number to the volleyball games. The football games averaged about two hundred St. Luke's rooters, the basketball games about forty, and the volleyball games about fifteen. Some of the mothers attributed the poor attendance at basketball and volleyball games to the "constant screaming and yelling of the cheerleaders." One remarked that "it's a guaranteed way of getting a quick headache."

There are other factors at work. The Armory where the girls played their games had very poor acoustics, but this was not true of the Catholic high school gymnasium, where the boys played their Sunday games. On an open date during the basketball season the boys played against an out-of-town school in St. Luke's gymnasium. The fact that a preliminary game was played at one o'clock by the second team, and the main game by the varsity team an hour later; the fact that these contests were played in the home gymnasium instead of at the other end of the city; the fact that the whole family could come right after Sunday dinner—all of these accounted for an overflow crowd on this occasion.

If the girls had been able to play their volleyball games at St. Luke's gymnasium on Sunday afternoons, they would undoubtedly have drawn a fairly large audience. Because of general housework, the mothers of girl athletes found it difficult to attend games on Saturday afternoons.[23] There is a subtle difference too, even in the mothers' attitudes toward sports. Some of the mothers push their sons into a strong competitive attitude in a way that no mother of a girl athlete did. One mother of a basketball player threatened to deprive her son of dessert for one week if he did not make a certain number of points. Fathers are much more enthusiastic about their son's athleticism than about their daughter's. One boy received a dollar from his father (and another from his grandfather) every time he made a touchdown.

This kind of parental enthusiasm was never exhibited toward the girl athletes. The parents did not make demands of the Athletic Committee for good coaching, equipment and winning teams as they did in the case of boys' sports. Most of them did not come to the meeting of the Athletic Committee when there was discussion of improving the girls' program, buying them new uniforms, arranging for their awards at the athletic banquet. It is little wonder then that the girls felt that they were being neglected, and that they were unable to participate as widely as the boys in the athletic program at St. Luke's. This helps to explain also why the girls expended so much energy and achieved so much success in the Blue Birds and the Camp Fire.

Effect of Athletics on Children

Among the parents of St. Luke's pupils, the question seldom arose whether the whole sports program was worth the time and effort expended on it. What benefit came to the parish, the school, the families, and especially to the children themselves? As we have seen above, there would be no athletic program were it not for the pressure exerted by the parents and the contributions they made in time and money. Whatever vicarious enjoyment they get in watching their own children play in these contests (and usually only the parents, brothers and sisters of the actual players attended the games) they appear to be convinced that athletics bring great benefits to the children on the teams.[24]

[23] It was the mothers who did the baking for their tired athletic daughters in preparation of the Camp Fire bake sale on Sunday, March 3.

[24] For a discussion of the benefits accruing from sports and physical education, see Henry J. Otto, *Social Education in Elementary Schools* (New York: Rinehart, 1956), chap. 7, pp. 184–201.

As far as we could ascertain, the children who actually participated as players on the athletic teams of St. Luke's school received benefits in terms of physical health and developed strength.[25] No one was seriously injured, even in football, and the minor cuts and bruises received prompt attention, and were quickly healed. The regular routine of exercise and the need to "keep in training" included sufficient hours of sleep and a proper diet, and these practices helped the child to stay physically fit.

The athletes were unquestionably under emotional and nervous strain before, during, and after every game. The coaches kept telling them that "the important thing is to play a good, hard, clean game," but they also told them with vehemence to "get out there now and win." The child who played successfully was cheered, and the child who made mistakes was chided. In a closely contested game the nervous tension built up in the child continued on through the night and allowed only fitful sleep.[26] Rivalry was strong and competition drove the individual for position on the team and the team for position in the league standing. After losing a game the St. Luke's athletes tried to smile bravely and congratulate the winners, and more often than not their tears were restrained only until they reached the privacy of the locker room.

As his contribution to the eighth-grade *Yearbook* one of the basketball players had this to say: "While playing under Coach Bowman we had to work hard in order to gain a position on the starting five. When we played we played our hearts out even though we sometimes lost. When we lost we didn't make a big issue out of it, because under our coach we learned how to lose. We went and shook hands with the opposing team and then we made up our minds to beat them if we played them again." This is a calm reflection, written several weeks after the season closed and echoing the well-drilled instructions of the coach concerning sportmanship. The boy who wrote it was probably no more emotional than the normal pupil in the school, but he

[25] Elmer D. Mitchell and Bernard S. Mason, *The Theory of Play* (New York: Barnes, 1948), discuss both theory and practice of various forms of play for different age groups. See chap. 8, "How Age and Sex Influence Play," chap. 10, "The Physical Benefits of Play," chap. 11, "Play and Mental Growth," chap. 12, "Play and Social Learning," and chap. 18, "School Athletics."

[26] After a close game, played at noontime on Saturday, the captain of the volleyball team had a restless night. She said the next day, "I was making the plays over again all night; I could hardly sleep a wink." Similar behavior had been observed by parents of other athletes and reported to us. Several of the boys had "nervous stomachs" after crucial games.

would have been probably less than normal if he were not tense and anxious during a game.[27]

The effect of athletics upon the schoolwork of the child is not clearly discernible. The coaches told the children "we don't want anybody on the team who doesn't keep up in school work. Only smart players are good players." In this they received the cooperation of the teachers; and since the boys and girls were eager to play on the teams this was a kind of incentive to do good schoolwork. Measured by the academic grades they received, the athletes showed about the same range of achievement as the non-athletes. Among the fifteen eighth-graders who at graduation received awards for having maintained a general average of ninety per cent or above, only four were non-athletes. The members of school teams spent about six hours a week in practice and two hours a week on the field or the court where the weekly game was played. This is about twice as much time as is spent on the average per week in home study by St. Luke's pupils. Our study of homework shows that the athletes do slightly more per week than do the non-athletes.[28]

Without exaggerating the claims of athletic devotees, one can say that certain beneficial social effects come from sports participation. The players learned the importance of cooperation (which is especially necessary in the school's three main sports). They maintained and developed friendships. They learned the value of self-control and fair play. There was not one incident of serious argument or loss of temper at any of the games, either with the officials, the opposing team, or with team mates.[29] The basketball team won the league's annual "best sportsmanship" trophy, donated by the Knights of Columbus. The coach pointed out that "if we got the award for the most improved team, it would be a credit to me personally; but the

[27] For a study of the emotional effects of highly competitive athletics on boys, age nine to fifteen, see Elvera Skubic, "Emotional Responses of Boys to Little League and Middle League Competitive Baseball," *The Research Quarterly*, vol. 26, no. 3 (October, 1955), pp. 345–52. The author employed the Galvanic Skin Response Test for emotionality, finding that youngsters were no more stimulated in the highly competitive league games than they were by competition in the ordinary physical education baseball games, and also that ball players tend to be less emotional than non-players.

[28] For a further discussion of homework, see below, chap. 12.

[29] At one of the basketball games, Ann Burton, a St. Luke's cheerleader, was convinced that the officials were favoring the opposing team. She maintained self-control until leaving the gymnasium when she threw her hand-bag against an auto with such force that the bag, and her eyeglasses within it, were shattered.

sportsmanship award proves that the kids learned the main thing I've been trying to teach them all season—to be honest and fair and clean."

Recognition among one's peers is a valued attribute at any age level. The players gained a certain amount of prestige as members of the various athletic teams of St. Luke's school. They felt that they were pleasing their elders too because they knew the interest and enthusiasm that the teachers and parents had for sports. This gain in status was fixed by certain symbols of achievement distributed at the two athletic banquets. Monograms were presented to the regular players on the teams. This was a "letter" to be sewn on a sweater or jacket; it was on a black background with the letters S L stitched in orange color. At the football banquet two awards were given for the best linemen, two for the best backs, one for the most valuable player. At the banquet in May fourteen monograms and five small loving cups were given to the volleyball players, besides a trophy to the most valuable player and one to the most improved player. Besides monograms to the basketball players there was also an award to the most valuable player, one to the best sportsman, and one to the team manager. The cheerleaders too were present at the banquets, which added to the prestige of those posts.

It was the Pastor's oft-stated purpose to "keep this award-giving within limits. There's such a thing as spoiling the kids by giving them too much." Were it not for his restraining influence, it is probable that the enthusiastic parents, especially the fathers, some of whom had been star athletes in their own school days, would have showered even more praise and prestige on the athletes of St. Luke's. This encouragement and recognition by adults seemed to be appreciated by the players mainly because it helped to give them status among the people who counted most—their school mates. The eighth-grade boys very clearly gained popularity by their prowess in athletics.[30]

Athletics and Adults

It is quite clear from the above that the athletic program at St. Luke's school depends for its existence upon the initiative and support of the adult parishioners. We have merely hinted at the extent of this adult cooperation. The Pastor "goes along" with the program, but

[30] Certain boys who were chosen as ones who "get along best with their classmates" did not achieve expected scores in the *California Test of Personality*. The principal variable that helped to account for their selection was their athletic ability.

his assistant, Father Martin, is officially in the middle of it. He is the moderator of all recreational activity in the parish and school. He attends the meetings of the Athletic Committee and also some of the games, but takes no active part in arranging contests, coaching or financing the teams. The teachers in the school give direct and indirect encouragement to athletics, but are very seldom in attendance at the games.

When Coach Bowman asked Sister Roberta to reserve the first two pews for his basketball players at Sunday Mass on March 24, she praised him and his athletes "for their true Christian spirit." This was the morning of the final tournament game, which the St. Luke's team lost. On two other occasions the basketball players and their coaches had gone to Mass and Communion together. Whenever Father Martin was present in the dressing room before a game the coach asked him for a blessing on the team. The priest gives the blessing and reminds the boys to "play a clean game." After winning a close game, one of the players said to him: "that was a good blessing you gave us, Father. I must have said about fifty Hail Marys too."

The football players dressed in the basement of the church before going out to their games. Under the leadership of the coaches they go upstairs and make a visit to the Blessed Sacrament and say some prayers both before and after every game. Whenever the Pastor is present on these occasions he gives them a blessing and "prays that nobody gets hurt." The influence of religious practices is noted also when a boy makes the Sign of the Cross before going into a football huddle, or before making a crucial shot on the basketball court. At the volleyball games the girls kneel on one knee in a circle around their coach and recite a brief prayer before play starts.

The volunteer coaches are the nerve center of the whole athletic system at St. Luke's school. None of them belongs to the faculty and none is a paid teacher in any sense of the term.[31] They volunteer their time and their services and, as Father Martin says, "they work harder and give more of themselves than any member of the teams." The football coach and his assistant had played on the varsity of a local public high school. Both worked every day until five o'clock, took a hurried dinner, and then coached the team three evenings a week. Coach McConnell is married and the father of two pre-school children, but even for the unmarried coach it is still a sacrifice to give up every Sunday afternoon to the children during the football season.

The basketball coach is also a regularly employed man, whose only

[31] This is quite different from the practice in the public school system and from the recommendations made by most educational agencies.

child, a son, attends St. Luke's school and whose wife is active in the parish societies. As a city fireman he has staggered work hours but his chief told him that he could take off work whenever a league game was scheduled, provided that he made up the hours at another time. One of the most enthusiastic rooters of St. Luke's team offered to pay for a substitute at the firehouse when the coach was needed at the basketball tournament. His assistant is a high school senior, who is able to coach the younger players in the afternoon after school. The baseball coach is also the father of two active athletes of St. Luke's school, and is likewise limited in his coaching to after-hours and week-ends.

The chief volleyball coach is a high school student, formerly a star on St. Luke's team. She captained the team two years earlier when they won second place in the parochial school league. Her assistant is a high school freshman, also formerly a player on St. Luke's team. These young ladies were able to coach the team in the afternoon, and could be present for games on Saturdays. Their knowledge of the game is adequate, and they have won the respect and admiration of the girl players.

These official volunteer coaches sometimes get further assistance from parents who were former athletes. Some of the men had been college football and basketball players, and they occasionally attend practice, particularly if they have a son on the team. They do not interfere with the coaches but they help individual players in mastering the intricacies of particular plays. They have been asked to take over a practice session now and then when the coach was absent or delayed. The most amusing instance of this substitution occurred when one of the fathers had to give the basketball team its pre-game pep talk and supervise the game until the coach arrived. He happened to be a non-Catholic, and he was more concerned about how the usual pre-game prayer would be recited than about any of the other details.

In the organized parochial leagues there are also numerous adults who function in different capacities. The league committee is made up of representatives from the various parishes. The officials who work the games are employed by the league and are paid three dollars per game for football and two dollars per game for basketball. Most of these officials are college students except in volleyball where some teachers and some mothers perform the function. The time keepers for boys' sports are high school athletes and for girls' sports high school girls, who are paid one dollar for each game.

This whole system of adult participation in elementary school athletics is kept in operation by the initiative and enthusiasm of the laity.[32] While there is a priest officially as a member of the league committee, and also a priest technically in charge of athletics in each of the parochial schools, in practice the whole apparatus is in the hands of lay adults. From this point of view, parochial school athletics operates outside the parochial school. The school provides the players and their parish indentification, but the lay people provide the incentive, the equipment, the facilities and the organization, necessary to maintain the athletic programs.

Generalizations

1. Unlike the public school, where the sports program is an integral part of the system, athletics in the parochial school is genuinely "extracurricular." There are no practices or games during school hours. There are no marks for achievement in sports, given under the guise of marks for physical education. The coaches are not faculty members and the school as such does not furnish the facilities or equipment. There is no physical education program for the non-athletes.

2. Pupil participation in competitive sports was limited mainly to the three higher grades of the school, although there was some opportunity for fifth graders to "prep" for next year's team. This limitation appears to be the normal procedure for athletic teams at the elementary school level (although there were a few public schools with fifth-grade teams playing one another.) The other children were limited to whatever games or sports they could devise during recess and lunch period, with the use of the sports equipment that the room mothers of the PTA had provided for each classroom. The school yard is not equipped with swings or similar play structures.

3. The boys had many more advantages than the girls in St. Luke's athletic teams. All but five boys in the eighth grade, and two-thirds of the boys in the seventh and sixth grades, were members of one or more athletic teams. This disproportion in participation obviously exists because the boys had three sports and the girls only one in which to play. The prospects for girls' teams in basketball and softball seem remote at the present time. The most inclusive extracurricular activity for female pupils is Camp Fire, while the principal activity for boys is sports.

4. Although the system operates on a volunteer and amateur basis there are certain imitations of "big-time" and professional practices.

[32] See the somewhat negative appraisal under the heading, "The School as a Vehicle of Mass Entertainment," by H. Otto Dahlke, *Values in Culture and Classroom* (New York: Harper, 1958), pp. 191–205; also the Report by the Educational Policies Commission, *School Athletics: Problems and Policies* (Washington: National Educational Association, 1954).

The attempt to develop a feeder system in the fourth and fifth grades and the tendency to think of the varsity as a preparation for high school stardom are examples of this. The coach's pep talks before games, the use of cheerleaders, the granting of monograms and other awards, are all imitations of collegiate athletic practices.

5. Even at the elementary school level athletics tend to become more work than play. The parents like to say that "the kids get a lot of fun out of it," but frequently they seem to be enjoying it more than the children do. The regular routine of practices may help greatly to develop the character of the child and to accustom him to obedience and regulations, but there is a noticeable difference between this kind of sport and the informal play in which the children indulge.

6. Adult values of competition and emulation undoubtedly work their way into the athletic program of the children. No matter how often the athletes are told that "you play the game for the sake of the game," they are still influenced by the stress to win. Anything else, however, would be practically impossible in the American culture. Competition is supposed to be a value in itself, but competition becomes meaningless to the young mind unless it leads to victory a good proportion of the time.

7. The notion that "clean living" is an accompaniment of athletics is also prevalent among the parents and teachers. The athlete is supposed to get his mind off "worse things," and to use up his energies that could otherwise be directed toward various kinds of immoralities. "If he plays games he doesn't have time for girls." Yet it was the athletic teams at St. Luke's that focused the attention of girls more closely on boys, and it provided a locus for informal relations between the sexes.

8. Can athletics be termed part of the learning process for the growing boy or girl? There is no doubt that the coaches taught these children things they did not previously know. What they learned technically was an art through practice rather than a body of knowledge in the academic sense. The by-product of the game in terms of human relations was probably more valuable than the knowledge and practice of athletic techniques.

9. The sports program functioned as a focus of cooperation and solidarity within St. Luke's school and parish. An indefinable school "spirit" develops wherever children follow the school teams with interest. This operates at its fullest when the school team is winning, and even the non-playing pupil is proud to speak of "my school." Enough has been said about parents to demonstrate that the athletic program brings them together and inspires them to work in unison for the "good of their children."

Chapter

NINE

CLIQUES AND CLUBS

THERE ARE so many subdivisions by sex, age and activity among the elementary school children that it is probably erroneous to call St. Luke's parochial school a social group in any integrated, closeknit sense of the term. The whole school, as a social unit, tends to fulfill the definition of a secondary association, but running through it is a network of smaller formal and informal cliques and primary groups.[1] These are the foundations of the social relationships existing throughout the school. Without them, the school itself would represent a loose, disjointed social structure in which essential functions could be performed only through authority and regimentation.[2]

In sociological literature the primary group is frequently alluded to as the basic form of human association, essential to the very existence and maintenance of society.[3] References are made most frequently to the intimate family circle and to the immediate play or recreational group as typical examples. The fact is, of course, that the primary group is found in all kinds of social situations, in schools, churches and political parties; and intensive research has uncovered the importance of the primary work group in industry.[4]

It is a commonplace observation that children form and reform the groups in which they associate, depending sometimes on the accessi-

[1] For the distinction between primary and secondary groups see Joseph H. Fichter, *Sociology* (Chicago: University of Chicago Press, 1957), pp. 117–119.

[2] See James Bossard, *The Sociology of Child Development* (New York: Harper, 1954), who points out that a school is a social system "with its own social structure, network of social relationships, culture and group consciousness" (p. 507).

[3] For the original formulation of this concept see C. H. Cooley, *Social Organization* (New York: Scribner, 1909). Also the treatment by Elsworth Faris, "The Primary Group: Essence and Accident," *The Nature of Human Nature* (New York: McGraw-Hill, 1937), pp. 36–45; also Theodore M. Newcomb, *Social Psychology* (New York: Dryden Press, 1950), chap. 14.

[4] See George C. Homans, *The Human Group* (New York: Harcourt, Brace, 1950), pp. 64–74; also W. Lloyd Warner and J. O. Low, *The Social System of the Modern Factory* (New Haven: Yale University Press, 1947), pp. 92–98.

bility of their age and sex peers, sometimes upon their own volatile whims and interests, or upon the kinds of personalities of their potential associates. In the pre-school years there are usually a few neighborhood children, perhaps a relative or two, with whom the child plays. Within the school society itself the children spontaneously form groups without the guidance of their elders, and there is perhaps even a point, about the sixth grade, when the "gang age" starts.[5] We have observed these small informal groups at all age levels, from the first to the eighth grade. There are also larger and well-organized groups under the supervision of adults.

In general, the large majority of the children we questioned seem to have satisfactory social relations with their schoolmates. Slightly more girls (96.7%) than boys (94.0%) in the three upper grades at St. Luke's say that the children at school "are usually nice" to them. These percentages increase from the sixth to the eighth grade, so that relations seem to be at their best in the graduating class. Most of the pupils (94.3%) are also confident that the other children consider them easy to get along with. Almost all of the girls (97.8%) and 90.5 per cent of the boys, answered affirmatively the question: "do the boys and girls seem to think that you are nice to them?" Here again, there was a gradual progression of affirmative answers from the sixth grade to the eighth grade.[6]

Friendship Cliques

A few days in the classroom at the beginning of September suffice to reveal to the teacher the more obvious pairs and cliques of friends.[7] In fact, the teachers allow the children to choose their own seating arrangements, and they thus discover who the potential talkers are, and incidentally "who likes whom." As we watched these children in the classrooms and corridors, in the playground and gymnasium, at home and in the neighborhood, we recognized the emergence of several clear characteristics. The children "gave themselves away" in their talk and actions, and we were later able to confirm our observations with friendship and sociometric tests.

[5] See the excellent study by the Children's Bureau of the Federal Security Agency, *Your Child from 6 to 12* (Washington: 1949), publication no. 324.

[6] The comparative percentages for both of these questions in the Taft public school were practically the same as those of St. Luke's.

[7] Charles A. Tonsor, "The Small Group, An Atom the School Can't Split," *The Clearing House,* vol. 29, no. 4 (December, 1954), pp. 195–198, points out that the school authorities should not manipulate the structure of the small friendship group, but try to influence its behavior through its leaders.

The informal friendship group, in which reciprocal relations exist, is very small, exclusively of one sex, and clustered around one dominant individual. As a matter of fact, most intimate friendship groups, when measured by the norm of reciprocity, were really pairs of friends. There were some three-member groups, and only a few in which each of the members considered all of the others his best friends. At St. Luke's school the children chose their friends from their own sex, and this was to be expected since practically all voluntary and compulsory activities were performed along segregated sex lines.[8] Friends probably liked to think of each other as equals but there was some inequality of prestige and social competence in every friendship pair or clique.

The behavioral expectations of these informal small primary groups were constantly being expressed in the varieties of classroom situations. The pupils, down even to the fourth and third grades, were often given the opportunity to work together on projects in groups of twos, threes and fours. In most instances they were allowed by the teachers to "bunch" with other children according to their own choices. This practice revealed not only those who wanted to work or study together, but it also indicated those who were most popular or least popular among their classmates. On numerous occasions a child was permitted to pick his or her associate or successor in asking questions of the class, playing charades and pantomiming. Invariably the child chosen would be of the same sex, and in almost every instance a "close buddy."

When the eighth grade was studying the Civil War, Sister Roberta suggested that different phases of the study could be worked out on maps and in newspaper accounts which would then be displayed on the walls. "Now we can do these different things if a few of you get together on each one of them." Hands of volunteers shot up all over the room, and the children who were called upon immediately suggested their own topic and the names of the friends who would work together. So that there would be no one left out, or unchosen, Sister would call upon the known isolates first and let them choose their co-workers.

Numerous other similar instances were observed, and only a few examples can be cited here. During Vocation Week, the seventh-graders were allowed to divide into small groups, each of which made a display poster. A pupil's ability to do "art work" entered into the

[8] See below, chap. 10, "Boys and Girls Together."

selections here but did not distort the basic structure of friendship groups. In the fifth grade a story of the early American Jesuits was read. A boy suggested to Sister Ruth that they do a skit based on the story. She agreed, put him in charge, and told him to pick the cast of characters. Naturally, he chose his best friends. Sister Justin, in the sixth grade, assigned the writing of an editorial on Mass attendance as a group project. She selected a number of "editors" and told them each to select three assistant editors; and here again the choosing of co-workers fell smoothly into the friendship pattern.

The actual production of many of these group projects was often done in the school during the study period. Sometimes, as in the preparation of a skit, it was done during the recess period. On other occasions the children were permitted to perform it over the week-end, so that they met at each other's homes after school or on Saturdays. Even in instances where the pupil had won the privilege of doing a chore for the teacher, he would frequently ask whether one or two of his best friends could help with it.

The observation of the external actions that friends perform together can be tested against the attitudes and choices that the individual pupil makes among his friends. The usual sociometric technique is to focus upon the persons chosen and to construct a chart of "cluster of friends" indicating frequency and reciprocity of choice, and showing also on the periphery of the chart those who choose but are not chosen.[9] We have used this device in a series of five friendship questions involving an invitation to the home and the willingness of the pupil to work and to study with another pupil. Thus, any individual pupil had the chance of being chosen three times by any other classmate, but he also had the opportunity to choose at most five of his classmates.

Doing Things Together

In order to discover who the child's friends were, and what the child would like to do with his friends, we asked the pupils to answer the following questions: 1. If your mother said you could invite a classmate for dinner on Friday, which one would you invite? 2. If

[9] Descriptions of such tests abound in the literature of social psychology. As a typical example concerning children see J. L. Moreno, "Changes in Sex Groupings of School Children," in G. E. Swanson (*et al.*), *Readings in Social Psychology* (New York: Holt, 1952), pp. 266–271. See also the sociograms in H. Otto Dahlke, *Values in Culture and Classroom* (New York: Harper, 1958), pp. 342–351.

this child couldn't come, whom would you ask? 3. Suppose the second person couldn't come, whom would you ask? 4. Suppose you needed help in your study and the teacher said you could ask a classmate for help, whom would you want to help you? 5. If the teacher asked you to help mend books in the library after school, whom would you want to help you? [10]

In order to obtain a clear pattern of friendship behavior within one school grade we here analyze only the various combinations of names of children in the eighth grade. These were thirty-two boys and twenty-eight girls and the way in which they chose classmates with whom they wanted to "do things" gives us a clue to the intensity of their small friendship groups. If we assume that the first name put down for the invitation home is also the name of the very best friend of the child making the choice, we may then check to note whether the child also wants to study and work with this best friend. The following table shows the distribution of these combinations.

	32 Boys	28 Girls	60 Both	(equals 100%)
Only invite home for dinner	20	5	25	41.7%
Invite for dinner but also study *and* work together	1	4	5	8.3
Invite for dinner but also study *or* work together	11	19	30	50.0

Assuming that we are correct in judging the first choice for a dinner invitation to be the best friend of the pupil doing the choosing, the results of the above table may appear surprising. One would expect that best friends who visit one another's homes would also study and work together, and this expectation is fairly well fulfilled among the girls. Almost two-thirds of the boys, however, would invite their best friends home, but would not work or study with them. If we assume, however, that each child has three best friends, the three he would invite home for dinner, we find a somewhat broader structure of the friendship group and of the actions the friends perform together. The following table is based upon three best friends.

[10] Although St. Luke's school has no functioning library, the room on the second floor where unused textbooks are stored was known to them as the library. A PTA committee sometimes mended books there, and was occasionally assisted by some of the older girls.

	96 Boys	84 Girls	180 Both	(equals 100%)
Invite home and study together	9	17	26	14.4%
Invite home and work together	18	19	37	20.6
Invite home and study and work together	3	4	7	3.9
Invite home but neither study nor work together	66	44	110	61.1
Not invited home but				
study together	18	7	25	
work together	9	9	18	
study and work together	2	0	2	

The thirty-two boys in the eighth grade each chose three different boys to invite to their homes for dinner, for a total of ninety-six choices. The twenty-eight girls therefore also had three choices each, for a total of eighty-four choices. The table above shows clearly that the girls have more association with their three best friends than do the boys. In almost half of the cases the girl will do something with her friends besides inviting them home; but with the boys this happens in less than one-third of the cases. When we asked about the one best friend, we found that 41.7 per cent of the eighth graders would invite this friend home but would not study or work with him; then when we ask about the three best friends we find that 61.1 per cent of these friends are persons whom the child would invite home, but with whom he would neither study nor work.

We must note, however, that there are also forty-five cases of children who would not be invited home by the particular person making the choice (and therefore presumably would not be among the three best friends) but they would be agreeable companions for study or work. This happens much more often with boys than with girls. The latter definitely do more things together with friends than do the former. The girls appear to have more intimate and more exclusive friendship cliques than do the boys. This is another way of saying that the boy pupil is likely to have a wider circle of friends than the girl pupil, but it is not a "closed" circle.

If we look at these data from the point of view of the persons chosen we find that some pupils are more desirable companions than others. We have seen that every child could make five choices, but could write the same friend's name down in two or even three places. Any particular child in the eighth grade could have received a number of triple, double or single choices, or not be chosen at all. As a matter of fact, the twenty-eight girls in this grade made 140 choices, the thirty-two boys in the class made 160 choices. Carl Deroche was chosen once by fourteen boys, twice by four boys and three times by one boy, for a total of twenty-five choices by nineteen boys. Clare Johnson was chosen once by six girls, twice by six girls and three times by one girl, for a total of twenty-one choices by thirteen girls. The following table shows the distribution of these friendship choices by sex in the eighth grade.[11]

Boys		Total choices	Girls		Total choices
26	received 86 single choices	86	23	received 64 single choices	64
17	received 31 double choices	62	14	received 32 double choices	64
3	received 3 triple choices	9	4	received 4 triple choices	12
4	received 0 choices	0	3	received 0 choices	0
50		157 [12]	44		140

In summarizing these data we find a certain spread in the frequency with which individual children were chosen as companions for stated activities by their eighth-grade classmates. The following table shows how the fifty choices of boys and the forty-four choices of girls are distributed from those who were not chosen at all to those who were chosen three times.

	32 Boys	28 Girls	60 Both	(equals 100%)
Not chosen at all	4	3	7	11.7%
Chosen once	26	23	49	81.7
Chosen twice	17	14	31	51.7
Chosen three times	3	4	7	11.7

While this table is not intended as an index of popularity or unpopularity among the eighth graders, it does show that seven of the children are, in this sense, social isolates and are not very close friends to any of the other pupils. These four boys and three girls would not be invited to the homes of their classmates, nor would any of the

[11] Since any particular boy or girl could be chosen two or three times the table shows that the thirty-two boys are counted fifty times and the twenty-eight girls forty-four times. The focus here is on multiple choice of individual pupils.

[12] This number is 157, instead of 160, because three girls in the class were chosen by eighth-grade boys. These are omitted from the total for girls in order to keep the statistics simple.

children ask them to study or to work with them. At the other end of the scale we find seven children who are thought of so highly that they are desirable companions in all three activities—to be invited home, to study and to work.[13] It is interesting to note, however, that in each one of these cases there was only one other child, the very best friend, with whom the child would do all three of these things.

Reciprocal Friendship

The intensity and closeness of the small friendship group are probably best demonstrated in the amount of reciprocity existing among these children. If we assume again that a child's three best friends are those whom he would invite home to dinner we may ask whether these children also consider him their best friend by inviting him home to dinner. The following table distributes the boys and girls of the eighth grade into four categories, ranging from those whose invitations were not reciprocated to those who were invited by all three of the friends whom they had invited.

Reciprocation by:	32 Boys	28 Girls	60 Both	(equals 100%)
No one	7	7	14	23.3%
One friend	11	8	19	31.7
Two friends	11	11	22	36.7
Three friends	3	2	5	8.3

This table indicates that a relatively small number (8.3%) are so closely related to their friends that they can depend upon them to reciprocate their friendship. They have good friends and they know who their friends are. Almost one-quarter of the children (23.3%), however, chose friends to invite to their home, but were not chosen in return by these same friends. The evidence shows that pairs (31.7%) and trios (36.7%) predominate among the friendship cliques of the eighth grade. This finding appears to agree with the generalizations made in other studies concerning children's informal cliques.[14]

Exactly one-fifth of the children in the three upper grades of St. Luke's answered affirmatively when we asked them, "do you have just a few friends?" The percentage was almost the same for the boys

[13] For characteristics of popular and isolate children see below, p. 229; see also Merl Bonney, *Popular and Unpopular Children* (Beacon House: Sociometry Monographs, no. 9).

[14] See Ruth Cunningham *et al.*, *Understanding Group Behavior of Boys and Girls* (New York: Columbia University Press, 1951), also William E. Martin and Celia B. Stendler, *Child Development* (New York: Harcourt, Brace, 1953), chap. 15 on children's peer groups.

as for the girls.[15] There was, however, a decrease in affirmative answers from the sixth to the eighth grade, from 25.0 per cent, to 17.6 per cent. This shows that even though the friendship circle itself grows smaller and "tighter" as the child goes into the higher grades, the child also knows more people and counts more friends. This contraction of the friendship clique, and the concomitant expansion of the number of friends, appears to be a normal experience all through adult life.

Several observations must be made about these informal friendships. They tend to become more "set" the longer the children are in school together; closer and smaller friendship circles appear among the girls than among the boys; but in neither case are the friendships so close that the children concerned will have "nothing to do" with other pupils. The following table shows how the friendship choices grow narrower as the pupil moves from the sixth to the eighth grade. In the friendship test administered to them, as we have seen, every child could select no more than five and no less than three different friends. The following table shows the variations in these friendship selections by grades:

Number of different classmates chosen	60 Eighth graders	50 Seventh graders	67 Sixth graders	177 Total
Five	15.0%	24.0%	44.8%	28.8%
Four	46.7	44.0	28.3	39.0
Three	38.3	32.0	26.9	32.2

Almost two out of five (38.3%) of the eighth graders chose only three persons for the five possible choices, while only a little over one-quarter (26.9%) of the sixth graders restricted their choices in this way. Those who chose five different classmates indicated that they have a larger "spread" of friendships, and the difference in this regard from the sixth grade (44.8%) to the eighth grade (15.0%) is quite marked. While friendship continues to shift in the eighth grade, it does not change so easily and quickly as it does among the lower grades. The sex variation in choices is shown in the following table.

Number of different classmates chosen	86 Boys	91 Girls	177 Total
Five	31.4%	26.4%	28.8%
Four	46.5	31.9	39.0
Three	22.1	41.7	32.2

[15] Only 7.6 per cent of the girls in the same grades at the Taft public school (as compared to 19.1 per cent of the boys) state that they have "just a few friends."

Here again, the "spread" of friendships is shown to be wider among the boys than among the girls, two out of five (41.7%) of the latter want to "do everything" with only their three best friends. Thus, there appears to be a general tendency among the girls to have narrower friendship circles than the boys, just as there is a similar tendency in the older children as compared with those in the lower grades. It must be noted, however, that the links of friendship go in several directions from every child, and even the member of the closest pair of friends is also the member of one or more other pairs of friends.

Informal Play Groups

While it is true that friends tend to play together, the concept of the play group is broader than that of the friendship clique. Since the children of the same grade are necessarily thrown together in the recess periods on the school grounds, their play groups are larger than their friendship groups. When the girls skip rope or play tag, there are usually ten or twelve children involved in the game. When the boys shoot baskets or toss the football around there are also a dozen or more participants. Shooting marbles or playing jacks may occur simultaneously by four or five groups in different parts of the playground, and each of them may have a circle of from five to ten players or observers. It is true, of course, that friends usually play together, but to a large extent the focus is on the game; it is the game itself, rather than the friendship, that brings them together.

Since the play in the school yard is largely self-started and self-organized by the children themselves, and since St. Luke's has no formal classes in physical education, there are always a few in every grade who are "left out of things." The only occasions on which we have seen the whole group participate in games were at the picnics, when Father Martin insisted that "everybody gets in the game." Even here there was some reluctance to participate, on the part of several boys who wanted nothing to do with boy-girl games, and on the part of two girls who were not physically well enough to join in running races.

The informal play groups of the children are not restricted in membership entirely to the children from St. Luke's school. Some of them are made up of neighborhood children, with whom the parochial school children may have attended kindergarten, or with whom they associate mainly because of residential proximity. In our interviews with parents we found that these friendships occur mainly with children in the first, second and third grades, and that in some cases a boy or girl may have a member of the opposite sex as a playmate.[16] This pattern changes quite definitely, however, at the third-grade level. From then on the friendship pairs and play groups are made up mainly of Catholic children of the same sex attending St. Luke's school.

In order to discover the extent of association of St. Luke's children with the non-Catholic children of their neighborhoods we asked the parents (and frequently supplemented this with information from the child) the names and the religion of the child's three best friends. These friends and playmates were not merely from St. Luke's school. They represent the child's immediate circle of friends from both the school and the neighborhood. The following table shows the distribution of friends and playmates by religion according to the school the child attends.

Religion of three best friends	Pupils from St. Luke's	Catholic pupils in public school
Three Catholic	49.6%	1.7%
Two Catholic	31.3	10.9
One Catholic	11.4	42.8
Three non-Catholic	3.5	37.0
No information	4.2	7.6

From this table it is quite obvious that about half (49.6%) of St. Luke's pupils have only fellow-Catholics as their best friends. A little less than a third (31.3%) of them have a close friend who is a non-Catholic, and an extremely small number (3.5%) have no Catholic child as a close friend. As we have mentioned above, the children who have non-Catholic playmates are mainly those in the lower grades of St. Luke's school, but there are also a few in the upper grades, mainly pupils who have transfered from a public school. On the other hand, about four out of five (79.8%) of the Catholic children attending the public school have either only one Catholic playmate or none.

If we look at the total number of friends these children have, counting the three best friends for each child, we may construct the following table of friendship distribution by religion.

Religion of best friends	Pupils from St. Luke's	Catholic children in public school
Catholic	74.3%	23.2%
Non-Catholic	21.5	69.2
No information	4.2	7.6

[16] The children were much more reliable than their parents in stating who their best friends were. Some of the parents could not give the names of their child's

This pattern of friendship across denominational lines may be logically expected, but it indicates also that friendships are not limited exclusively to one's own schoolmates. Approximately three-quarters (74.3%) of the playmates of St. Luke's children are Catholic, while less than one-quarter (23.2%) of the friends of Catholic children in the public school are of their own faith. This indicates that neighborhood friends are not entirely neglected in favor of schoolmates, but that the concentration of friendships is logically among the children with whom one attends school daily.[17]

The sex segregation among the friendship and play groups is observed also in the pattern of party-attendance by these children. One-quarter (25.2%) or 159, of the 632 pupils had parties given for them by their parents, and the great majority of these parties were attended only by boys (32.1%) or only by girls (52.2%) while the remaining parties (15.7%) were attended by both boys and girls. The following table shows the grade-by-grade distribution of these parties.

School grade	Number of parties given	Per cent of grade giving parties	For boys only	For girls only	For boys and girls
Eighth	11	18.3%	2	6	3
Seventh	15	28.8	1	14	0
Sixth	22	33.8	10	8	4
Fifth	21	28.4	9	11	1
Fourth	40	41.7	14	21	5
Third	17	17.3	4	6	7
Second	12	11.7	4	4	4
First	21	25.0	7	13	1
	159	25.2	51	83	25
			(32.1%)	(52.2%)	(15.7%)

While the fourth and sixth grades had the largest percentage of pupils giving parties for their classmates, there is no clear age trend in either the number or the kind of parties given. From the fifth to the eighth grade a larger percentage (27.5%) of the children had parties than was the case among the children from the first to the fourth grades (23.6% of these having parties). In the upper grades,

three best friends and most of them were not acquainted with the parents of their child's friends.

[17] Friendship selectivity among the children is a favorite target for those who attack the "divisiveness" of the parochial school system. See, for example, John W. Dykstra, "Parochial Divisions in American Life," *The Christian Century* (April 16, 1958), pp. 465–467.

however, a smaller percentage (11.6%) of the parties had both boys and girls in attendance, as compared to the lower grades, where 18.9 per cent were mixed parties.

The lists of invited guests at these various parties may be studied as a partial index of the clusters of play groups existing outside the school environment. We have seen elsewhere [18] that the girls attend parties more than twice as often as the boys, whether these are parties restricted only to schoolmates or open also to non-school friends. The frequency of party-attendance by girls helps as an instrument for identifying their best friends more than does a study of the boys' party attendance. In either case this instrument serves better in analyzing one-sex parties than mixed parties.

In the upper grades at St. Luke's it has become the custom for the teachers to urge the host or hostess of a mixed party to invite all the members of the class. This technique helped to decrease the probability of "pairing off," or even of dating, but there was always the understanding among the older children that certain couples had a mutual fondness, and there were always some who simply did not attend parties.[19] In some instances, too, when there was a party of only one sex, the child giving the party invited all the boys in the class, or all the girls; but even in these few instances there was never complete acceptance of invitations.

In all of these cases a study of the children's parties helps to identify the isolates in each classroom, children who either do not care to attend parties, or who are not really wanted as party guests by their classmates. Furthermore, it helps us also to identify the numbers of parents who were willing to go to the "trouble" to arrange a party for their children. Finally, in spite of certain efforts on the part of teachers to have these parties all-inclusive, there was always the factor of selectivity at work. The same children tended to go to parties, and to reciprocate with a party after they had been invited by someone else. This fact helped more than any other to "fix" the larger clusters of informal congeniality groups.

[18] See the appropriate sections above, chap. 2, "The First Ten Years," and chap. 3, "The Upstairs Classes."

[19] See below, chap. 10, "Boys and Girls Together;" also William Martin and Celia Stendler, *Child Development* (New York: Harcourt Brace, 1953), "Children can report on the love life of almost everyone of their classmates with considerable accuracy" (p. 226); see also the Children's Bureau Publication, no. 324, *Your Child from 6 to 12,* "Developing Wholesome Sex Attitudes," pp. 100–104; also John Connery, "Steady Dating Among Adolescents," *Theological Studies,* vol. 19, no. 1 (March, 1958), pp. 73–80.

Formal Play Groups

Besides the friendship cliques and the informal voluntary play groups there are other primary groups in St. Luke's school which center about recreational activities. The most successful of these are the various Blue Bird and Camp Fire Groups, which have carefully planned programs scaled to the interests and abilities of girls in the different age groups. Less well-organized and supervised, but also essentially recreational groups, are the Cub dens and the Boy Scout patrols. These youth movements differ from the voluntary and informal friendship circles and play groups in several ways. They are open to everyone of the same sex in the specific age category and school grade. They meet regularly at a given time and place, have planned activities and a structure of rules, and are directed by adults.[20]

Yet these youth movements within St. Luke's school have a direct bearing on the friendship cliques and play activities of the children. The uniforms that the children wear to school on meeting days tend to identify the membership apart from their classmates. Loyalty to the principles of the group is a genuine sentiment, especially among the girls. In the lower grades this tends to act as a magnet for closer friendship. In the higher grades there are strong friendships between Scouts and non-Scouts among the boys, but among the older girls the members of Camp Fire consort mainly with fellow members in their informal friendly and play activities.

The difference in size of these various groups is a factor in the development and maintenance of primary groups. The Cub dens are the smallest, averaging about eight boys in each. Since these boys are in the same grade in school and since they meet weekly in the informal atmosphere of the home of one of them, they usually form close ties within the group. This bond tends to dissipate during the summer when activities, except for the Cub-Dad camp-out on a June week-end, are held in abeyance. The twenty-four Boy Scouts at St. Luke's range from the fifth to the eighth grade and from ten to thirteen years of age. Although the Troop is subdivided into patrols, the relationship among the boys within each patrol does not seem to be so close as that existing in the Cub den.

The girls' movement is structured according to the school grade, like the Cubs, each Blue Bird group averaging fifteen members, and each Camp Fire group about twenty members. Recruitment to these groups is discussed as a problem among the adult leaders, who "want

[20] See above, chap. 7, "Youth Movements."

to get all the girls in the class into the groups." This recruiting effort never reaches more than about two-thirds of the potential members, but even with this number of members each group is too large to remain a primary group. Some of the social isolates among the girls of the four higher classes are members of Camp Fire, and some of them achieve rank with as much distinction as others; nevertheless, they remain isolates. What happens within the group of twenty girls is that a number of smaller friendship and play groups are maintained. Part of the strength of these smaller groups, however, is derived from common membership in the larger group.

The Camp Fire Girls made a distinct contribution to the extra-curricular "social life" of St. Luke's older pupils. Except for the St. Robert Club, whose activities were carried on within the school, no other group provided so much recreational opportunity at the pupil level of entertainment. Two skating parties brought the boys and girls together, as did the other "fun and dance" parties promoted by the girls. These activities did not break down the normal reserve across sex lines that was everywhere observable in St. Luke's school, but they did help to develop some of the grace and polish ordinarily lacking in shy, awkward children at this age level.[21] Of particular importance to the parents and teachers was the fact that activities were conducted in a wholesome, open and supervised atmosphere.

Another focus for the formation of play groups is the athletic program of St. Luke's school. From the point of view of organized teams in football, basketball, baseball and volleyball, this is a phenomenon quite different from the other play groups. These teams are made up of pupils from different school grades, although the nucleus is always from the eighth grade.[22] Membership on the team is based on competence in the sport itself rather than on the likes or dislikes a player may have toward the other team members. The coaches tried to develop a team spirit as well as a school spirit. Their insistence upon cooperation by the whole team, upon the need to "work as a team," rather than as individual stars, was a means of bringing the members closer together.

It may be said that friendships grow out of association on the same athletic squad, but it is difficult to pin-point the main factor in the relationships. Most of the members of the girls' volleyball team were

[21] See below, chap. 10, "Boys and Girls Together."

[22] See above, chap. 8, "Organized Sports." See also Ernest Flotow, "Charting Social Relationships of School Children," *Elementary School Journal,* vol. 46, no. 9 (May, 1946), pp. 498–504.

also in Camp Fire. Some of the football players were in the Scouts and more of them in the Acolytes. Some of the athletes had close friendships with other pupils who were non-athletes. Even within the team itself there were boys who appeared to associate closely only when they played football. Two boys, the captain and the star quarterback, do not have intimate reciprocal friendships with other boys on the team. In spite of these exceptions, however, sports act as a means of bringing young people together, and the nucleus of the team is in a strict sense a primary group, even though this group may itself be made up of several friendship cliques.

These various play groups, formal and informal, organized and unorganized, provide an insight to the whole complex network of social relations existing in St. Luke's school.[23] In analyzing these groups one may fall into the danger of overlooking the unique unity of the elementary school. There are relatively isolate individuals among the pupils, but there are no completely exclusive or isolate groups within any given classroom. Even in the friendship clique, one individual is clearly identified as a member of the group, but he may be involved with an "outside" individual, who is in turn a clearly defined member of his own friendship clique. This "crossing over" from group to group highlights the fact that social interaction permeates the school situation and gives it an integrative quality necessary for successful operation.

Populars and Isolates

From the point of view of social relations and groups the pupils in the elementary grades present a range from those who are in the midst of all activities to those who appear reluctant to join in anything.[24] There are a few children who are active in groups but not very popular, and others who are quite popular but not very active. Nor is wide popularity always correlated with intensity of relations in friendship cliques. A small group of friends may be very devoted to one another within the friendship circle, but at the same time may not be well-liked by the class at large. Thus, in employing a sociometric test to discern the most popu-

[23] See Myles Rodehaver, William Axtell and Richard Gross, *The Sociology of the School* (New York: Crowell, 1957), chap. 4, "Groups in the School." Also James Bossard, *The Sociology of Child Development* (New York: Harper, 1954), chap. 23, on the structure and function of various school groups.

[24] Some of the pupils (9.1%) do not have a high regard for their schoolmates. More boys (13.1%) than girls (5.5%) said that most of the boys and girls at school are "so bad" that they try to stay away from them. All of these were in the sixth and seventh grades.

lar and the least popular among the children, we had to disregard as much as possible the results of the friendship test.

As a criterion of popularity we used the results of the question, "Write the name of the boy (and girl) who you think gets along best with his classmates." We checked the answers to this question against the names the children had given as their three best friends. The table below shows that the boys tended to pick their best friend as the most popular boy in the class more than the girls picked their best friend as the most popular girl. The table shows also, however, that the great majority of the pupils do not equate friendship with popularity, and that they chose honestly the ones they thought "got along best with classmates."

Chose as most popular	86 Boys	91 Girls	177 Both
Best friend	25.6%	15.4%	20.4%
Second best friend	11.6	16.5	14.1
Third best friend	5.8	9.9	7.9
None of these	57.0	58.2	57.6

In order to make the comparison between popularity and social isolation we selected the twenty most popular boys and girls in the sixth, seventh and eighth grades, and compared them with the twenty least popular in the same grades. By the criterion of the question given to the children we had twenty-nine popular and thirty-six isolates but since we wanted representation from each of the grades we reduced this number to three boys and three girls from the eighth grade, the same number from the seventh grade, and four of each sex from the larger sixth grade. The isolates were those who received no votes for popularity and who were not chosen in reciprocal relations by the best friends they had named.

The outstanding external difference between these two categories is the degree of participation in the programs, activities and groups of the school. All of the populars, both boys and girls, were in some way involved in the athletic teams, the older ones tending to be the star performers on the teams. Less than half of the isolates took part in organized sports, and these mainly in a peripheral way. All of the popular girls were active in Camp Fire, as compared to sixty per cent of the girl isolates. In the non-athletic programs the popular and isolate boys were quite similar, having about the same number (about one-fifth) in the Boy Scouts, and the same proportion (about sixty per cent) in the Acolytes. Measured by the number of activities participated in, the popular boys are about twice as active as the isolates, while the popular girls are about five times more active than the isolates.

There are some differences in family background which may help to account for the differences in these two categories of children. Fifteen of the popular children come from families in which the father is either in the managerial or sales occupation, as compared to only six of the isolates. The number of organizations to which the parents belong also shows a differential, the parents of the popular children average 2.6 groups, while those of the isolates average 1.2 groups. Membership of parents in parish affiliated organizations is more than twice as frequent in the families of populars as in those of isolates. The attitudes of their parents toward the school also show a difference. The parents of sixteen of the popular pupils rate the school above average, while it is rated this high by the parents of only seven isolates.

It is difficult to discern whether the class status of the families of these children differs sufficiently to be a factor in their popularity. Although the occupational status of the fathers is somewhat higher, and the amount of education of the mothers is also slightly higher, the other indexes of social status tend to be about the same. All of the children in both categories live in the middle range of residential areas of the parish, none of them living in either the best or the poorest sections. The range in ethnic background is also quite similar, there being Irish, German, Polish and Italian names represented in both categories in about the same proportion as they are represented in the total school population. The parental connection with the school and parish, as indicated by the opinions of parents about the school and by their participation in parochial groups, appears to have some relation to the child's popularity. But cause and effect are intertwined here. We do not know whether the child's participation is a reflection of parental enthusiasm, or vice versa.

It is probably more reasonable and more fruitful to look for an explanation to the personal attributes of the children than to the cultural background of their families. One apparently significant difference in this regard shows up in the intelligence tests of the children. Popular children seem to be on the average considerably "smarter," as measured by these tests, than are the isolates.

The following table shows quite graphically that only two of the popular children scored below a hundred in the Kuhlman-Anderson Test, as compared to nine of the isolate children. On the other hand, only two of the isolates scored above 115, as compared to eleven of the popular children. The two lowest scorers among the populars are star athletes and probably owe their popularity to this ability rather than to the attributes that are commonly associated with popular personality. The brightest girl among the isolates is one who came to St. Luke's from

Range of Intelligence Quotient Scores on Kuhlman-Anderson Test

Populars		Isolates	
Boys	Girls	Boys	Girls
	140		
			139
132			
131	131		
128			
	125		
	125		
	124	124	
122			
	118		
	115		115
		114	114
113			
		110	110
		108	
		107	
	105		
103			103
103			
102			
101			
	100		100
		99	99
		98	
			95
92			
			91
	90		90
		88	
		84	
		74	

another city at the beginning of the school year and may have found it difficult for this reason to achieve status among her classmates.

We checked the scores that these forty children had made on the *California Test of Personality* and found a similar expected imbalance, with the populars scoring higher than the isolates. The following table shows the distribution. It is interesting to note that the same two popu-

Range of Scores on *California Test of Personality.*

Populars Boys	Populars Girls	Isolates Boys	Isolates Girls
142			
	137		
			132
	131		
	130		
	130		
	129		
		128	
127			
127			
	126		
	126		
	126		
	125	125	125
		125	
123			
122			
122			
119		119	119
118			
			117
112			112
		110	
		110	
108	108		
			105
			104
		103	
		100	
			93
			88
			83
		68	
		66	
112.0	126.8	105.4	107.8
119.4		106.6	

lars who scored lowest, and the same two isolates who scored highest, in the Kuhlman-Anderson Test, performed similarly in the Personality Test. In general the range was about the same in both tests, with individual children rating at about the same point in both tests.[25] Since the display of intelligence affects social relations it may also be expected to leave an effect upon one's social status with others.

The highest possible score that can be made on the Personality Test is 144. Only two of the isolates made a score over 125, as compared with eleven of the populars. On the other hand, only two of the populars scored below 110, as compared with nine of the isolates. This test helps to measure adjustment, both personal and social, and the results indicate that girls in general are somewhat better adjusted than boys. It must be noted, however, that the median score for all the children (175) at St. Luke's who took the test was 123.2. Thus, the popular boys scored somewhat below the median and the popular girls somewhat above it, but the great difference is the departure from the norm by both boy and girl isolates. The following table indicates the comparisons on the first half of the test, on personal adjustment.

	Twenty Populars			Twenty Isolates		
	Boys	Girls	Both	Boys	Girls	Both
Self-reliance	8.2	8.5	8.35	7.1	7.9	7.50
Personal worth	9.9	11.0	10.45	8.2	8.6	8.40
Personal freedom	10.2	10.0	10.10	8.5	8.2	8.35
Feeling of belonging	11.5	11.4	11.45	9.8	9.5	9.65
Withdrawing tendencies	10.0	9.7	9.85	8.2	7.6	7.90
Nervous symptoms	10.0	10.7	10.35	8.3	8.8	8.55
Personal Adjustment	*59.8*	*61.3*	*60.55*	*50.1*	*50.6*	*50.35*

These scores show the expected result that the isolates, both boys and girls, score lower on all of the attributes of personal adjustment than do the populars. But here again, we note some sex differences. The boys in both categories score slightly better on the qualities of personal freedom, on the feeling of belonging, and on freedom from withdrawing tendencies. On the other hand, the girls in both categories, score slightly better than the boys in the three qualities of self-reliance, feelings of personal worth and in freedom from nervous symptoms. These appear

[25] See a similar study made by Onas C. Scandrette, "Classroom Choice Status Related to Scores on Components of the California Test of Personality," *Journal of Educational Research*, vol. 47, no. 4 (December, 1953), pp. 291–296. Since this study was made the test has been revised, but the comparisons are still valid.

to be culturally defined characteristics and probably are an effect of different rates of maturing between the two sexes.

The following table represents the second half of the Personality Test, checking on the social adjustment of the children.

	Twenty Populars			Twenty Isolates		
	Boys	Girls	Both	Boys	Girls	Both
Social standards	10.5	11.7	11.10	10.8	11.1	10.95
Social skills	9.7	10.0	9.85	8.3	9.9	9.10
Anti-social tendencies	10.2	11.3	10.75	8.8	8.6	8.70
Family relations	10.8	10.4	10.60	8.7	8.0	8.35
School relations	10.7	11.1	10.90	9.4	9.4	9.40
Community relations	10.3	11.0	10.65	9.3	9.1	9.20
Social Adjustment	*62.2*	*65.5*	*63.85*	*55.3*	*57.2*	*56.25*

In general the isolates show lower scores than the populars in social adjustment, but the difference between the two categories is not so great in this section of the test as it is in the section on personal adjustment. This seems to indicate that the problems of the isolates are more personal than social. One of the interesting points of comparison in the above table is that both the boy and girl isolates score higher on social standards than do the boy populars. This part of the test questions the pupil on what is right and wrong morally in certain social situations, and one could expect that even an isolate who is relatively unskillful in social relations would know the answers to such questions.

Policies of Adults

There can be no doubt about the fact that the normal parent likes to see his child get along well with schoolmates, be popular among them, and to belong to groups. The teachers also encourage friendship among the pupils, and prefer to have happy, satisfied, well-adjusted children in their classrooms. Parents and teachers are also concerned about the types of groups that form and the kinds of activities they perform. There were several instances at St. Luke's school that indicated the kind of surveillance exercised by the adults.

The involvement of parents occurred most noticeably in the spontaneous formation of a "bicycle club" by thirteen boys in the sixth grade. This group evolved from a smaller circle of five friends (spotted earlier by our class observations and confirmed by the friendship test) who elected officers, made rules and began building up a treasury for use on "bike hikes" and picnics. They decided who among the sixth grade boys could be allowed to join and who were the "squares" to be kept out. All of this seemed harmless enough to the parents until at the beginning of May the boys voted to have a "coke and dance" party and to invite only the "ten best looking girls" in the sixth grade.

The interests of the boys were diverted to other channels after the parents stepped in and called a halt to these plans.[26] The club was allowed to continue on into the summer with the hope, expressed by both parents and teachers, that it would gradually disintegrate. It was this exclusive, spontaneous, identifiable kind of club that the teachers in the school also opposed. The school authorities, while announcing no formal policy on the matter, wanted no gangs or clubs formed of St. Luke's pupils unless they were supervised by the parents or the teachers. Effective means of prevention and substitution, however, were found. This was seen in the adroit handling of two "Jacket Clubs" of eighth-grade girls, which had previously existed at the school.

Our informants on this matter, high school girls who had graduated from St. Luke's, thought that the school authorities were not pleased with these clubs, but "couldn't do anything about them because it was none of their business." These girls' clubs were not "gangs" in any pejorative sense. A few close friends first formed an exclusive group, named it the "Melodettes," and bought jackets with this name stitched across the back. Then a larger group of girls formed the "Harmonettes," and soon gained greater prestige and more members than its rival. This rivalry tended to formalize, and probably aggravate, a distinct social cleavage among the eighth-grade girls.

Sister Roberta allowed the clubs to exist until the end of the school year, and then quietly laid her plans for an annually formed group embracing the whole eighth grade. At the beginning of school in September she asked the children if they wanted to start a club and "have a good time." When they agreed enthusiastically to this suggestion, she made only two stipulations: first, that membership would be voluntary, and secondly, that no pupil in the class could be excluded by the members. Everything else was decided by the children themselves: the number and persons of officers, the time of meetings, amount of dues, disposition of the dues, activities at meetings, purposes of the club, as well as the name of the club. Since this group was highly successful in preventing exclusive gangs and in developing a friendly spirit among the pupils it seems worthy of further description.[27]

This was not an on-going club, existing from year to year, which

[26] See the discussion of this event below, chap. 10, "Boys and Girls Together."
[27] The music club, moderated by Sister Cecilia, helped also to promote these social purposes. Its members were both boys and girls and it included all the

the new eighth graders joined, but was reformed yearly. Each year the organization had a different name, and this year the children voted to honor their teacher by calling it the "St. Robert Bellarmine Club."[28] They decided to receive Communion every Friday morning, pay twenty-five cents dues every month, and to use this money at the end of the year to buy a set of vestments for the church.[29] The officers of the club were William Starr, president, Clare Johnson, secretary, and Carol McEvoy, treasurer.

Part of each meeting was devoted to business and took place in the classroom. The secretary read the minutes, the treasurer gave the financial report; then there was usually a discussion of the state of finances and the programming of future meetings. The group then adjourned to the club room in the basement of the auditorium for the recreational, and major part of the meeting. At these events "everyone entertained everyone" as each took a turn at singing, playing a musical instrument, reading a poem or doing a humorous skit, alone or in a group. Once they had a short movie of the world series and once a short movie of the football highlights of the season. The meeting finally settled down to card playing and dancing, with Sister Roberta encouraging the reluctant boys to dance with the girls.[30]

The St. Robert Club seemed to take the minds of the pupils off the formation of jacket clubs, exclusive gangs, miniature sororities or fraternities, besides helping them adjust socially to the opposite sex. The parents in general were heartily in favor of this club, appreciated its spiritual orientation and praised the teacher for her ingenuity. Some of them remarked that the club helped to prevent the problems that seem to accompany spontaneous, child-originated gangs. Internally, the St. Robert Club taught the children how to conduct meetings in an organized manner, how to discuss problems and come to decisions that were satisfactory to the majority, and how to conduct themselves socially in a congenial and friendly manner.

---

music pupils from the third to the eighth grade, as well as several high school students, but its activities were not so extensive as those of the St. Robert Club.

[28] This name did not seem to mean much to the children. In their autobiographies, some of them called it the "civics club," and others simply the "eighth-grade club."

[29] George Ford, who was also the master of ceremonies at the Award Night for the graduates on Tuesday, May 29, presented this gift to the Pastor in the name of the class.

[30] These boys showed less timidity at home parties, and we may infer that the school-like atmosphere of the parish auditorium tended to inhibit them even more than usual.

As far as we could ascertain from observation of the school situation and from interviews with the pupils, the policy of the teachers toward cliques and clubs is fairly well received by the pupils themselves. We have discussed the attitudes of school authorities toward boy-girl relations in another place, but these two questions flow into one another. The school encourages group life; it devises means for the adjustment of individuals to the group, and it makes a valuable social contribution in forestalling formal, exclusive cliques.[31] Perhaps when the children attain the relative freedom of high school life, they may look back and think that they were under repression in the elementary school. During the present school year, however, they seemed to be too busy to complain.

Generalizations

1. All the informal friendship circles within St. Luke's school are of one sex. The parents of a child in the lower grades may occasionally mention a relative or neighbor of the opposite sex as one of the child's best friends, but the actual companionship around the school and in school-related activities is always with a child of the same sex. This is true also, with the exception of the eighth-grade St. Robert's Club, of all the formal and organized play groups in the school. This finding is in accord with the conclusions of other studies that peer groups of children of pre-high school age are comprised almost entirely by members of the same sex.

2. The friendship clique is small and the relations are reciprocal but not exclusive. The school is covered with a quiltwork of friendship pairs and trios, but in almost every case, even in that of "very best" friends, each member of the clique also has "outside connections." For obvious reasons, the closest friends within the school are also within the same grade. In the upper grades, however, there are more social relations across grade lines than in the lower grades. In no case, however, were these cross-grade relations developed to the point of "best friends" for the parties involved.

3. There are some children in each grade who are, in a relative sense, social isolates. They have friends among the schoolmates whom they would invite home to dinner, and with whom they would like to study and work; but the friends they chose have even better friends with

[31] See Henry J. Otto, *Social Education in Elementary Schools* (New York: Rinehart, 1956), chap. 3 on the classroom society. See also the study by Carson McGuire and Rodney Clark, "Age-Mate Acceptance and Indices of Peer Status," *Child Development*, vol. 23, no. 2 (June, 1952), pp. 141–154.

whom they would like to do these things. Thus, the term, "isolate" must be used cautiously, because no one is completely excluded from association, and even from friendship, with all of the members of the class.

4. The average girl has reciprocal relations with more girls than the average boy has with boys. The girl does more things together with these girl friends than the boy does with his boy friends. If a girl invites another girl home for dinner this friend is likely also to invite her. If a boy invites another boy for dinner, the invitation is not reciprocated as often as it is with girls. In more than two-thirds of the cases the boy who is invited home is not also the boy with whom study and work would be done. Among the girls this is true in less than half of the cases.

5. Since only Catholic children attend St. Luke's, the informal friendship and play groups within the school are limited in membership to fellow Catholics. The average school child also often has neighborhood friends who go to other schools and who are non-Catholics. In comparing the play groups of St. Luke's children with those of Catholic children attending the public school, we find that about three-quarters (74.3%) of the friends of St. Luke's pupils are Catholics, as compared to less than one-quarter (23.2%) of the friends of Catholic children in the public school. This indicates obviously that the school a child attends is a more important selector of friends than is the religion he professes.

6. Parties are the manifestation of friendship and they are a form of activity in the play group. Among the boys, almost three out of ten (27.8%) did not attend a party all year; while among the girls this proportion is only one out of twenty (4.9%). The average boy in the sixth, seventh and eighth grades attends about two parties a year, while the average girl in the same grades attends about five. The list of names of those invited to parties shows by its omissions who the isolates are in any particular class.

7. Camp Fire and Blue Birds constitute the most active play groups for girls at St. Luke's, while athletics is the main focus of play groups for the older boys, and Cub Scouts for the younger boys. There is a subtle difference of emphasis here. Friendship groups appear to be a by-product of athletics, but companionship and friendly relations are an essential ingredient mixed right into the girls' organized movement. Getting along well with other girls is a deliberately promoted objective of the Blue Birds and Camp Fire Girls.

8. It is commonly assumed that the most popular child has the largest number of friends, and this assumption was borne out in our study. The child who was voted as the one "who gets along best with classmates"

was also the child with whom others want to do things (invite home, study and work together). But friendship and popularity do not equate. About one-quarter of the boys chose their best friend as the most popular boy in class, and less than one out of six (15.4%) of the girls chose their best friend as the most popular girl. The children apparently used different criteria in judging friendship and popularity.

9. In comparing the twenty most popular with the twenty least popular children in the three higher grades, we find that the former are much more active in extracurricular programs than the latter. The populars come from families in which the parents are active in parish societies and in which the parents have a high esteem of St. Luke's school and its teachers. The populars have higher intelligence scores than the isolates and they also score higher in the testable qualities of personality.

10. The school authorities and the parents promote friendships and the formation of groups among St. Luke's pupils. Their policy, however, more clearly formulated by teachers than by parents, is to guard against the spontaneous formation by the children themselves of exclusive clubs and gangs. The eighth-grade teacher prevented this development by encouraging the formation and maintenance of a club for the whole class.

Chapter

TEN

BOYS AND GIRLS TOGETHER

THE SEGREGATION of the sexes has been traditional in the Christian religion and has been maintained to some degree even in the American Catholic schools until recently. Parochial societies and most of the larger diocesan and national organizations continue to be limited in membership to only one sex.[1] This does not mean that there are never joint activities or programs or that the more general religious services are attended by sex-segregated congregations. The trend toward the mingling of the sexes is slowly growing within the Catholic church, and the most obvious manifestation of this trend is in the schools.

This trend in the schools came to the attention of Pope Pius XI, and in his encyclical, *Christian Education of Youth,* he warned against co-education, particularly "in the most delicate and decisive period of formation, that, namely, of adolescence." The late Holy Father pointed out that a mingling of the sexes in the schools ignores the differential educational needs of male and female and exposes the young to grave moral dangers.[2] On the elementary school level in the United States—except for those relatively few parents who could afford to send their children to private schools—most parents send their children to ele-

[1] The Christian Family Movement and the Lay Retreat Movement are developing a bi-sexual program in the United States. Older movements and organizations like the Sodality, the Knights of Columbus, Knights of Peter Claver, and various others continue to be exclusively of one sex. Church choirs are supposed to be made up of only male voices, but most parishes have predominantly female choirs.

[2] Pius XI, *Christian Education of Youth* (New York: The Paulist Press, no date), p. 26. This danger is adverted to by William F. Cunningham, *The Pivotal Problems of Education* (New York: Macmillan, 1940), p. 185 where he says "it is the theory of many educators that if young people are thrown together in school life, any training necessary for social adjustment will automatically take care of itself. This method, particularly in the adolescent age, is equivalent to bringing high explosives closely together and expecting them to fuse."

mentary schools attended by both boys and girls. This is the pattern for both public and parochial schools, although it differs from private schools, which are often of only one sex.

This problem of the association of school children across sex lines, especially in the matter of "steady" friendships and dating, has engaged the attention of some members of the American hierarchy. The Archbishop of New Orleans showed his concern about such practices in the Catholic schools when he said that "we may have to reach the point of forbidding association of boys and girls in grade schools and high schools." The school itself is not responsible for the fact that they "go steady" but it is the meeting place of boys and girls. Their friendship begins at school but it becomes more manifest when they walk home together and in their recreational activities. His Excellency points out that this is a danger that must be warded off by the cooperative endeavor of family, church and school. "Occasional talks on these matters are given in the classroom, usually by priests on moral matters, but this does not dispense the teachers from doing their share. We have come to the point at which something must be done. It will have to be a strong appeal for cooperation not only to teachers but also to parents." [3]

Toward the end of our study the pastors of the Peoria, Illinois area drew up a code of conduct for their grade school pupils, to go into effect in the following September. The code consisted of the following prohibitions: 1. No grade school dances. 2. No mixed parties other than school-sponsored functions. 3. No social activity of a group of boys, or a group of girls, should occur unless chaperoned by parents at all times. 4. No dating at the grade school level (this includes "pairing off" at movies, skating rinks, etc.) 5. No formals, corsages, or make-up in school or church activities. Simplicity and modesty of dress should be insisted upon at all times.[4]

[3] NCWC news release, March 17, 1957. On the moral aspects of "going steady" see Francis J. Connell, "Juvenile Courtships," *The American Ecclesiastical Review,* vol. 132 (March, 1955), pp. 181–190, where he presents a theological argument that going steady for those extremely remote from the possibility of marriage is a proximate occasion of sin, hence the practice itself is sinful.

[4] Reported in the Peoria edition of *The Register,* Sunday, May 19, 1957, and subsequently reported and commented upon by most of the Catholic diocesan weekly newspapers throughout the country. A voluntary code of behavior was adopted by the seventh and eighth graders of the public school in Cedar Grove, New Jersey, banning dungarees except on gym dates, ending dances by ten-thirty, and advising against single dating. (A.P. News Release, February 8, 1957.) Most of the magazine and newspaper articles discussed these problems among high school students rather than among elementary pupils.

Voluntary and Imposed Mingling

In the formal organization of St. Luke's school the boys and girls receive the same basic education. Informally, there are some distinctions made, but the content matter of the class is, and must be, the same for both since they sit in the same classrooms together. Thus there is no direct attention paid to "differing educational needs" of the sexes. Whether or not the children are exposed to "grave moral dangers" seems to depend upon a number of conditions, one of which is the period of puberty and early adolescence among the grade-school children. From this point of view the papal directive would seem to apply only to most children in the eighth grade, some in the seventh grade, and to a few girls in the sixth grade who matured early.

The seating arrangements in the classrooms of St. Luke's school present some interesting contrasts in the mingling of the sexes. With the exception of the first and second grades which need some guidance, the teachers in the beginning of the year allow the children to choose their own places. The class invariably and voluntarily falls into a segregated sex pattern, and each child wants to sit by his or her best friend. Since young friends tend to talk too much and to pay more attention to each other than to the lesson or the teacher, this whole pattern is soon broken up. "When we misbehaved Sister would make us sit by a boy," said one fourth-grade girl, "we sure hated that." Sometimes a boy-talker would be placed in the center of several well-behaved girls.[5]

In the higher grades the reluctance to sit next to a pupil of the opposite sex does not always appear to be genuine. The mixed seating pattern creates a mild kind of bantering, a sort of embarrassed, "giggling" attitude of contravention that cannot be called antagonism or conflict. One gets the impression from observation that a genuine regard exists between the boys and girls of the eighth grade, but that all are careful not to allow open expression of it. The following excerpts from the "Class Poem" of the graduating class give a hint of this subsurface friendliness, enjoyable to all concerned.

> In his head Bob is sort of hazy,
> All his talk drives Jo Anne crazy.

[5] Reactions seem to depend upon the situation. A third-grade boy had no spelling book and was told to sit with someone who did. He voluntarily sat with the nearest girl, and no notice was taken of this by children or teacher. Yet, in the second grade a boy and girl talking were made to sit together as a punishment. They appeared to be embarrassed, and sat on opposite edges of the seat gazing intently at their readers.

Barbara among the boys does sit,
Sometimes she could throw a fit.

Mary Anne's shoes are worn and scuffed,
Her ruler bent and cracked,
From hitting the boy who annoys her so,
With a great big fabulous wack.

Melanie by Noto she does sit,
And really dislikes the thought of it.

In shifting the children around the room the teacher does not always put the trouble maker up in the front row, especially if he or she is an amateur comedian and distracts the rest of the class. Sometimes, not for reasons of discipline, but to encourage a backward child, the teacher places a popular and an isolate child together. Occasionally the children have asked the teacher to change all the seats, and have even voted on this. The teachers think that the children, especially those in the higher grades, get bored sitting in the same places for too long a time.[6]

The result of this moving around within the classroom is that there is no similar seating pattern followed in all fourteen classrooms of St. Luke's school. In seven of the classrooms the children are indiscriminately mixed and the extent of the distribution depends on whether males or females are more numerous in the class (2B, 3A, 3B, 4B, 6B, 7, 8). In five of the grades (1A, 1B, 4A, 5A, 6A) the pupils are seated in alternate rows of boys and girls. In only two rooms (2A, 5B) are the children segregated by sex, with the boys occupying the front half of the room and the girls the back half.

This practical solution, dictated by the experiences in each classroom and by the teacher's need to keep the class operating smoothly and efficiently, appears to result in a mingling rather than a segregation of the sexes. It resists the desires of the pupils to maintain separate seating arrangements. It acts as a curb on their talkativeness, and as an encouragement of attention to the teacher and the lesson at hand. Even the pattern of alternate rows of boys and girls, which appears to be a separation of the sexes, is in reality a separation of boy from

[6] Moving one's place is a simple change except in the eighth-grade classroom which is the only one with movable and adjustable desks. These were newly installed in September and each child was held responsible for any cuts, marks or ink spots on the desk. Moving a place in this class meant moving the desks around, an event of considerable noise and distraction. In all other classrooms the desks are permanently fixed on "runners."

boy and girl from girl. It prevents the members of the same sex from talking with one another.

In almost every other activity in which the children engage in and around the school there is a separation of the sexes. This extends even to the annual custom of gift-giving at the Christmas party held in each grade. Each boy brings one boy's gift, and each girl a girl's gift, and these are deposited in two separate piles in front of the room. The tallest boy in the class acts as Santa Claus, and as the names are called out, he distributes the gifts, first to the boys, then to the girls. Most of these names are drawn blind and the price limit is fifty cents, but in the eighth grade Sister Roberta allowed certain special friends to exchange gifts and to fix their own price limit. All other gifts were distributed indiscriminately by name, but discriminately by sex.

When the children leave the classroom, regardless of where they sit, the boys file out first and the girls after them.[7] This same arrangement pertains in lining up outside the school to return to the classroom (except for Sister Vincent de Paul's second grade, where the boys and girls walk abreast). In the schoolyard the girls stay on "their side" and the boys on theirs. This is a spontaneous and voluntary separation of the sexes for there is no fence between the two sections, there is no school regulation to this effect, and there are no orders given by the teachers to maintain this separation.[8] This is simply a further demonstration of the well-known fact, derived from daily observation, that children of elementary school age prefer the companionship of persons of their own sex.

Voluntary and Imposed Segregation

The informal games played by the children also resist any mingling of the sexes because the children normally follow the cultural definition of boys' and girls' games. This separation obviously extends to the organized sports like football for the boys and volleyball for the girls. At St. Luke's the latter is a "girl's game," but in the early spring the

[7] An amusing reversal of chivalry is the fact that this pattern of "males first" is followed in the fire drills which occur at intervals during the school year. In order to "make a good showing" before the inspecting fireman, the Principal informs all of the teachers ahead of time and has the children lined up in the classroom before the fire alarm sounds.

[8] A boy in the second grade said that Sister threatened to make him carry a doll or wear a hair ribbon if he did not stay away from the girls' side of the playground. At one morning recess at the end of February eleven girls and two boys surrounded Sister Cecelia in the schoolyard, exchanging pleasantries with her. "Sister called the boys 'sissies' for hanging around the girls' schoolyard, and told them in a kindly way to resume play with the other boys."

boys played volleyball against the girls several times. Father Martin put a stop to this, and the girls grumbled about the prohibition. They wanted this experience because "it was such good practice for our team." At the eighth-grade picnic the girls challenged the boys to a game of softball, which did not quite last one full inning. The girls' side was quickly retired. The boys continued to bat and to make runs until Father Martin blew the whistle to announce lunch.

The girls are more enthusiastic rooters for the school teams than are the boys. The six girl cheerleaders are always "backed up" by girl rooters, who know all the school yells and who use them vociferously especially at football games. The pupils' attendance at basketball games is always less than at football games, but here again the girl rooters outnumber the boys. During the volleyball season the girls complained that the boys never supported their games. One Saturday afternoon the coach rounded up his basketball players and took them to root for St. Luke's volleyball team. The boys were extremely noisy and rooted at the top of their voices. One of the substitute players, Marie DeBlanc, told our observer, "They make us nervous when they do that; and I don't like boys anyway." [9]

The spontaneous and voluntary separation of the sexes was especially noticeable at the two school picnics held at the end of May, one for Mrs. Gordon's sixth grade and one for the eighth grade. When the food was distributed by some of the mothers the boys automatically lined up on the right and the girls on the left. The boys then drifted to three picnic tables on one side and the girls to the tables on the other side. While they were eating the girls started a cheer: "Rah, Rah, Rah, eighth-grade girls!" The boys responded to this with "Boo, Boo, Boo, eighth-grade girls!" and then gave a cheer for themselves. This kind of playful banter and raillery went on during most of the meal until it was effectively stopped by the girls with a yell: "Two bits, four bits, six bits, a dollar! All for the eighth-grade boys stand up and holler!" Then all the girls stood up and cheered. The boys seemed non-plussed by this kind of unorthodox behavior and were silenced by it. "That'll make 'em feel cheap," said one of the girls.

The picnic games were planned and supervised by Father Martin and some of the mothers present. Every child participated individually in the sack race and the bean-carrying race. Three teams, each made up of both boys and girls, competed in the tug-of-war (although the boys wanted to form one team against the girls). Two games were

[9] To which her girl friend, Dorothy Ellis remarked, "Oh yeah, you ought to see her in school with the boys."

only reluctantly entered into by some of the boys; these were an orange-passing game and a marshmallow game, in which some contact was possible between boys and girls. The dodge ball game proceeded to the point where one boy and one girl remained in the circle. In the excitement one of the boys threw the ball and hit the remaining boy, thus eliminating him. Several boys immediately jumped on the offender and pummeled him, shouting, "You dope, you let the girls win!" The final game, an egg-throwing contest had been anticipated by the boys, who wanted to throw eggs at the girls. This was avoided by Father Martin, who ruled that no mixed pairs would compete in the contest.

Since St. Luke's school is intimately connected with the parish church, there are numerous occasions when the children are in church together. At the daily Mass and at other services the girls always occupy the pews on the gospel side of the church and the boys on the epistle side. The school choir, however, is made up of both sexes of the children of the seventh grade, but even here there is a rough division with the boys on one side of the organ and the girls on the other. At the reception of the sacraments, first Communion and Confirmation, the boys go up to the altar first, and the girls afterward. This arrangement is followed also in church processions.

On the Sunday morning, when the eighth grade graduated, the children lined up outside the school, the boys in front followed by the girls. They marched down the street, around the corner and into the church in this order; the boys filed into the first three pews on both sides of the main aisle, with the girls seated in back of them. There was an interesting variation of this on the Award Night (May 28), the Tuesday before graduation. The children lined up as boy-girl pairs at the back of the auditorium. They walked up the aisle, the boy on the left, the girl on the right, and then separated to go to either side. Thus, during the whole ceremony the segregation was complete. When a girl sang or played the accordion, she was always accompanied on the piano by a girl; when a boy performed he was accompanied by a boy.[10]

With the exception of the St. Robert Club, which comprised all members of the eighth grade, all other groups and organizations in the school were uni-sexual. The acolytes could be only boys, and the children who helped Sister Justin in the sanctuary and sacristy were only

[10] A study made in the New York City schools before the War showed that sex cleavage is a stronger factor then color cleavage, especially in the lower grades. See Joan Criswell, "A Sociometric Study of Race Cleavage in the Classroom," *Archives of Psychology*, no. 235 (1938–39).

girls. The Scouting and Camp Fire organizations are everywhere separated by sex lines. We have seen also that the friendship cliques and informal groupings were always exclusively comprised of either boys or girls. This was especially true of the jacket clubs that used to exist in former eighth grades, and of the bicycle club which formed this year among the sixth-grade boys.

These various forms of segregation appear to have different functions at the different grade levels and, within the grades, from situation to situation. The imposed segregation is largely a matter of convenience in the lower grades, where sex attraction is not operating at all. In the younger groups the boys and girls are kept separate for accounting purposes, for safety and order, to respect the children's lack of attraction across sex lines, and to acculturate them to an identity with their own sex. In the upper grades a further purpose is added—to prevent them from getting too interested in each other.

The voluntary segregation seems to work similarly in the lower grades. Here the boys and girls are uninterested in each other and they naturally drift into and stay in separate groups.[11] The children in the upper grades, especially the girls, are developing some interest in the opposite sex, but it seems to require several years to learn how to act out this interest with confidence, smoothness and "social grace." Therefore, voluntary segregation continues for the most part, but with a modification. The children tend to act out their interest in the other sex on a group basis. The girls may group with the girls, and the boys with the boys, at a picnic, at a ball game, on the playground, and in this way find security against embarrassment. Communication then transpires from group to group, instead of from individual to individual, and this is expressed in the taunting, cheering, bantering or trick-playing that flows from one sex group to the other.

The athletic program at St. Luke's school performs a double function of segregation and congregation between the sexes. Athletics, especially for boys, is often designed as a means of "working off steam," and of keeping them from becoming too interested in the opposite sex at an early age. The practice sessions and games of the football, basketball and baseball teams, consume a great deal of the boys' time, energy and attention. Volleyball occupies the upper grade girls from October on, even though the league games do not begin until

[11] For example, in the third grade there are two pencil sharpeners and no rule was ever laid down about their use, but the boys always use one and the girls the other. Only when one of them was broken did the boys and girls mingle to use the remaining sharpener.

January. All of this is "good, healthy exercise," and is intended, in part at least, to develop clean living and a healthy state of mind.[12]

Athletics has, however, another bearing on boy-girl relations at St. Luke's school. Sometimes the practice session, but especially the games of the boys' teams, provide an occasion for the boys and girls to assemble and to engage in limited contact and communication. At a football game on a Sunday afternoon many of the seventh- and eighth-grade girls are on the sidelines among the spectators. In their Sunday clothes, and sometimes wearing a touch of lipstick, these girls look somewhat more mature and attractive than they do in the school room. They bantered back and forth with the players, and especially with the substitutes.[13] Attending the basketball games, although the physical distance was somewhat greater between players and girl spectators, gave similar opportunities.[14]

The athletic program, then, appears to have two influences on boy-girl relations. It segregates the children in the actual playing of the game and provides a release for energies that might otherwise be spent in pursuing the opposite sex. On the other hand, it brings them together in an atmosphere that is somewhat more relaxed than that of the school room and play ground. It provides an opportunity for the boys to display prowess before the girls, and for the girls to banter back and forth with the boys.

Boy Friends and Girl Friends

In spite of the various forms of imposed segregation and the voluntary grouping by sex, these children are living in the midst of an urban culture where boy-girl interests develop young. Parents and teachers are aware of this interest, and some of the children manifest it as early as the fifth grade. The girls begin to notice boys, especially boys in a higher grade, at a younger age than the boys notice the girls.[15] The teacher in the sixth grade can point out several girls who

[12] See the discussion of the effects of athletics, above, chap. 8, "Organized Sports."

[13] Some of the substitutes, lying on the ground at the sidelines, occasionally made approving remarks about the "shape" displayed by the girl cheer leaders for the opposing team across the field, when their skirts flared out in leading the cheers.

[14] One of the parents mentioned that her eighth-grade daughter "cried her eyes out" on one occasion when she was unable to get to an important basketball game.

[15] The sixth-grade teacher told about a boy in her class who has been interested in a girl classmate "for almost five years." A girl in the third grade informed our reporter that she is "engaged" to a high school student, and that in her neighborhood the boys "chase the girls and try to kiss them."

are "boy crazy" and several boys who "have just discovered girls." The great majority of the children in the sixth grade, however, and about half in the seventh grade, pretend that they do not like children of the opposite sex (although many of these do give occasional evidence of interest in a particular member of the opposite sex).

Several of our eighth-grade informants told us that every member of the class has someone he or she "likes better than anyone else." One girl said "you don't like to tell who he is because you get teased so much." Usually a girl will confide only to her closest friend the name of the boy she likes most, and thus the word spreads around the class. We have observed a certain amount of note-passing between boys and girls in the classroom and on the play ground and have found that the participants follow a pattern of boy-girl relations verified by evidence from teachers, parents and other children. There are, of course, varying degrees in this sort of relationship: there are "boy-haters" and "girl-haters," those who admire each other only at a distance, those whose interest in the other sex is unrequited, those who show a certain amount of fondness for each other, and a few who are "almost" going steady.

The existence of "crushes" is recognized by Sister Roberta in the eighth grade, and she combats it by ridicule, embarrassment and the insistence on frankness. At the beginning of the year she joked about the pairing off of boys and girls. "Now, we're going to put all the sweethearts next to each other here in the front row. This will be lovers' lane. Pretty soon they'll get so sick of looking at each other that they will want their places changed." The children believed that she would have done this, and no couple in the class would have dared to become so obviously smitten that they would have qualified for a place in lovers' lane. Still, Sister knew accurately those who were fond of each other. At an entertainment she would say to our observer, "Now watch how Jerry looks at Alice when she sings. He's crazy about her." At a basketball game she says, "Look at how Nancy yells and claps when Walter makes a basket."

Ridicule and embarrassment were not the only weapons used by the teachers as a preventive of overfondness across sex lines. The teachers displayed understanding and sympathy in handling this question. They devised a technic for Valentine's Day which was meant to sublimate and re-direct the ordinary romantic implications of this day. They asked the children in all the grades to save the money they would ordinarily use for buying Valentine cards and gifts and to put it in the mite boxes for pagan babies. In previous years the custom had been for each child to make, or buy, a Valentine for every other child in the class, and to distribute these within the room. This practice was discontinued with the result that the children contributed one hundred and ninety-five dollars for the "adoption" of thirty-nine babies in the foreign missions.[16] This did not prevent the sending of Valentines through the mails, but it tended to give a new dimension to the meaning of "love" and St. Valentine. More than two hundred and fifty children received Holy Communion that morning as a mark of their love of God and fellowman.

The teachers of both the seventh and the eighth grade mentioned frequently that the children are "too young to be pairing off." They insisted on knowing about any parties that were to be held *before* the event, and they always conducted a public discussion in class the next day, asking what games were played, who danced with whom, what time they went home, and so forth. One of the boys in the eighth grade had a birthday party, at which the girls told his mother, "Sister is going to give it to us tomorrow." The lady told them they were mistaken because she had called up Sister Roberta and obtained her approval before she arranged the party. The girls replied, "It isn't that she scolds us. She just asks all kinds of embarrassing questions and wants to know everything that goes on."

This kind of openness about dating, dancing and parties was probably the best antidote to anything "going wrong" in the boy-girl relations. Some of the children resented it and said that the Sisters "can't really tell us what to do after school hours." As a matter of fact, this is precisely what the teachers did, but in a jocular, bantering and ridiculing way. They had the support of most of the parents in this sort of indirect control because the parents themselves often seemed bewildered about how to cope with this situation. They were glad that the school, the Sisters and the priests took a strict view on mixed parties and dancing and absolutely forbade "going steady." Only 3.2 per cent of the parents interviewed thought that St. Luke's school should provide "more social activities" for the children.

For those children who are interested in the opposite sex[17] there is a kind of gradual development in forms of behavior evidencing this interest from the sixth to the eighth grade. In the sixth grade most of it is simply "talk." The girls talk among themselves about "who is

[16] See a further account of this campaign for pagan babies below, chap. 14, on "Financing the School."

[17] A summary of the development of interest in the opposite sex, from age ten to sixteen, is given by Arnold Gesell *et al.*, *Youth: The Years from Ten to Sixteen* (New York: Harper, 1956), pp. 413–422. See also the discussion on coeducation in Edward A. Fitzpatrick, *Philosophy of Education* (Milwaukee: Bruce, 1953), pp. 79–80.

the cutest boy," and "who they like the most." A girl rides on her bicycle by a boy's house and shouts at him. A couple of boys walk home from school a few paces behind a couple of girls, and make remarks, sometimes mild insults, about them. This is supposed to indicate their interest, and perhaps, affection. There were two informal "coke and dance" parties in the Spring which only fifteen sixth graders attended and which were generally disapproved by the parents.

In the seventh grade there were almost twice as many girls as boys. The latter thought that their girl classmates were all "squares." They did not want to "fool around with the little kids" in the sixth grade, and they were rejected as "pests" by the eighth-grade girls whom they liked and teased. But there were three girls in this class who were very fond of boys in the eighth grade. Janet Baxter liked George Reineck, the captain of the football team and of the Patrol Boys. After his traffic duty he often walked her the three blocks home, even though she lived in the opposite direction, and he talked to her on the phone at least once a week. Another eighth-grade boy, Richard Navaro, used to leave his bike a block from the school and make his younger brother take it home whenever he had a chance to carry a seventh-grade girl's books. The daily walk home was taken by Carl Deroche (who was liked by all the girls "because he is so polite and such a gentleman,") and a seventh grader, Mary O'Toole. Her mother insisted that he should walk all the way home and come into the house. This seemed to give a kind of tacit approval to the arrangement. The boy gave her a gift at Christmas and a box of candy on Valentine's Day.

There were also three eighth-grade girls who had frequent telephone contacts with high school freshmen. On several occasions they went to high school dances, and during the ice-skating season were together on every available Saturday and Sunday afternoon. The teachers tried to keep these relations under control mainly by "exposing" them and by asking the girls openly in class about their "boy friends." During the previous year there had been a well-known case of "going steady" between the star football player and a girl in first year high school. Some of the parents thought it was "scandalous" that she should come over to the school every day and walk home hand-in-hand with him. One of their "love letters" was intercepted, and Father Martin was called in to handle the "case." The boy is on the honor roll in high school and the couple continues to "go steady."

Besides these inter-class and inter-school relationships there is also a certain amount of "pairing-off" within the eighth grade. It is in most instances, however, a fluid situation. It is more a question of "who likes whom," rather than "who goes with whom." Patty McDonnell is the best dancer in the class and she is fond of a boy who likes a seventh-grade girl, but she is so popular that another one of the boys asked her to "go steady." The most involved kind of situations occur, like the following: Sue said, "Nancy likes Mike, they kid around together—and Pat likes Nancy—but Mike doesn't like Nancy, he likes me, but I don't like him; I like Jim. He walked me home sometimes and asked me to go to the coke party with him; but I'm going to the party with Dick."

What the children do in this regard after school hours and away from the school is presumably more the concern of the parents than of the teachers. Yet the reputation of the school is involved and there is little in the lives of these pupils that escapes the attention of the teachers. For example, the latter are happy that there is no "hang-out" for St. Luke's pupils in the form of a candy store or ice cream parlor in the immediate vicinity. Nor is there any neighborhood movie within the parish boundaries where the children can "get into trouble." The nearest drug store, two blocks north of the school, does not have booths in which the children can congregate. In the other direction, three blocks south of the school, is a small restaurant owned by a parishioner, where the children sometimes go in small groups for ice cream, cokes and pie. By the testimony of the waitresses, and by our own observation, St. Luke's pupils talk and act there in a more restrained manner than do the children from the nearby public school. Still further south on Main Street, six blocks from the school, is a large drug store, the favorite meeting place of high schoolers, to which a few of the eighth-grade girls occasionally go to meet their high school friends.

It appears significant in this regard that at St. Luke's the children do not ordinarily think of a member of the opposite sex as part of the circle of "best friends." We administered a Friendship Test to the pupils in the sixth, seventh and eighth grades, stating a series of activities and asking for the names of those with whom he would like to do these things (sort books in the library, work arithmetic problems, go to the movies, invite home for dinner).[18] No girl in the three grades chose a boy with whom to do these things. A boy in the eighth grade chose his sister to help him in arithmetic. One boy in the sixth grade chose three different girls, and two boys in the same grade each chose one girl (the same girl).

The results of the same test showed up very differently when administered in the sixth, seventh and eighth grades of the neighboring public school. The following table shows the percentage of each sex in every grade, choosing their friends from the opposite sex.

[18] See above, chap. 9, "Cliques and Clubs," for a discussion of this test.

Grade	Boys	Girls	Both
Eighth	0.0%	13.3%	6.7%
Seventh	39.0	25.8	33.3
Sixth	43.2	10.3	28.8

Whatever the factors and the circumstances leading to this situation, it is clearly demonstrable that the public school pupil evidences more interest in the opposite sex than does St. Luke's pupil.[19] It is probable that the parents of these children are more permissive than the parents of St. Luke's children, but it is much more likely that the whole tone of the public school, the attitude of its teachers, the encouragement of weekly dances, the sponsoring of frequent bi-sexual programs, the absence of religion and spiritual motivation—all of these combine to account for the difference in interest across sex lines.

Parties and Dances

It must be remembered that these boys and girls are from eleven to thirteen years old (some of them fourteen toward the end of the school year). They are, in a sense, at a physiological and psychological turning point in their lives.[20] They are early teen-agers, surrounded in their out-of-school hours by sentimental song hits, interested in TV programs and performers, and they are becoming more aware of the expectations of the American culture in the boy-girl relationships. Whatever the causes or conditions, the fact is that some boys become interested in some girls, and more girls become interested in some boys. The qualifying adjective "some" must be employed here, for in each of the upper grades are to be found a substantial number of "boy-avoiders" and "girl-haters," children who identify with their own age and sex group. In fact, the majority of the youngsters identify more readily and more frequently with peers of their own sex, and commit themselves more whole-heartedly to the cliques, play groups and gangs of their own sex than to pair relationships.

Nevertheless, practically all of the older children felt that the ability

[19] The St. Luke's girls appear to be more shy than those from the Taft public school. In answer to the question, "do you talk to new boys?" 59.3 per cent of St. Luke's girls, and 87.0 per cent of Taft's girls, answered affirmatively. The corresponding figures for boys were 75.0 per cent and 68.1 per cent.

[20] For studies on sex development and problems during puberty and adolescence, see William W. Wattenberg, *The Adolescent Years* (New York: Harcourt Brace, 1955) chap. 14, "Sex;" also Marguerite Malm and Otis G. Jamison, *Adolescence* (New York: McGraw-Hill, 1952), chap. 6, "Heterosexual Adjustment."

to dance had to be acquired, some taking real pleasure in this activity, and others, especially among the boys, performing it with reluctance and with a sense only of cultural obligation. All of the girls, and most of the boys, in the eighth grade had at least an elementary ability to dance with a partner of the opposite sex. The following table shows their answers to the question, "who taught you how to dance?"

	Boys	Girls
Do not dance	6	0
Self-taught	7	0
Professional instructor	5	4
Brother or sister	2	10
A boy	1	0
A girl	1	5
Parents or aunt	10	9
	32	28

A relatively small percentage of the parents send their children to dancing school, mainly for ballroom dancing, but some also for tap dancing. George Reineck, captain of the football team, performed at the Award Night with a tap routine. In an informal soiree with some of the parents in the middle of January (January 11) the parents expressed themselves in favor of some kind of supervised dance sessions at St. Luke's school. They cited the example of a parochial school in another state where a professional instructor teaches the eighth-grade children folk dances and square dancing in the first semester and ballroom dancing in the second semester. Two years before our study, the Junior Newman Club, made up of high schoolers from the parish, ran a regular Sunday afternoon class to teach the eighth graders how to dance. This has since been abolished, the parents saying that Father Martin is now too busy to supervise it, Father Martin saying that "it was a waste of time; most of them already knew how to dance." There is no indication that this was discontinued because of objections by priests, teachers or parents.

St. Luke's school did not hold any dances for the grade school children throughout the year. This is quite different from the neighboring public school which sponsors a dance for the pupils every Friday evening. The St. Robert Club had the opportunity to dance once a month at the meetings, and the Principal in past years had insisted that the eighth-graders must learn to dance before their annual graduation tea. One mother, reminiscing about this tea, said that "the children were stiff and shy and awkward. The boys sat on one side of the room and the girls on the other. You had to coax them to dance.[21] You can't tell me they were having a good time." By vote of the graduating class this year the annual tea dance was replaced by a picnic, sponsored by the PTA.

During the summer the Rosary Society sponsored square dancing in the school yard for the whole parish. Some of the seventh and eighth graders attended and enjoyed these affairs. On the Friday after graduation (the last day of school for the lower grades) the Junior Newman Club held a semi-formal dance in the auditorium. A hired orchestra played from the stage, the lights were turned low, the hall decorated on a Japanese theme since the affair was named "The Emperor's Dance." The recently graduated pupils were invited, at a cost of two dollars per couple. Four of the girl graduates, dressed in Japanese kimonos and with heavy facial make-up, took tickets at the door and served punch. Four others were there with dates. Ann Burton came with George Reineck of the graduating class, while Suzanne Keller, Margie Fasullo and Patty McDonnell were with their "boy friends" from high school.

The remarks of the girls concerning this dance provides an insight into the boy-girl relations at St. Luke's school. They thought it was "too elaborate" and "too grown up" for them. Aside from Dr. and Mrs. Stanley Miklaus and Mr. and Mrs. Vincent O'Connell, the chaperones, there were only thirty-six couples in attendance, most of them high school seniors and a few of post-high school age. There was a noticeable age differential between recently graduated eighth graders and the older persons present. The girls said the attendance showed that there had been no "real dating" by eighth graders during the school year. They remarked that a "sock hop" which could be attended "stag," or a "free" dance, like the one held that same night at the Park Recreational Center, would have brought out more of St. Luke's pupils.

There were no Christmas parties and no graduation parties among the eighth graders of St. Luke's during this year. This was pointed out as being an unusual situation by some of the parents who had had experience with older children graduating in previous years. Mrs. Egan remarked that her daughter attended three graduation parties in the previous year, but that her son graduating this year said that no parties were planned. Parents who had nephews or nieces in two other parochial schools in the city said that "the eighth-grade children had

[21] We asked the pupils in the three upper grades whether they "like to dance," and had affirmative answers from 58.3 per cent of the boys and from 83.5 per cent of the girls. The corresponding percentages at the Taft school were 68.1 for boys and 81.1 for girls.

a regular round of parties during the Christmas season—almost every night at a different house."

Whenever the teachers knew ahead of time that a mixed party was to be held they asked those responsible for the party to invite all the children in the particular class. This could be done for birthday parties of children in the higher grades when the child or the mother told the teacher about the party. There were several parties given for children in the fourth, fifth and sixth grades, in which this procedure was not followed. This may have been because the parents involved had not yet been "indoctrinated" in the policy of the school, or because the children themselves never thought about having the matter cleared with the teacher. At any rate, these few parties had limited attendance because invitations had been issued only to particular friends.

Most of the parties throughout all the grades of the school were either exclusively for girls, or exclusively for boys. From our records,[22] we conclude that the girls had about three times as many parties as the boys. From the first to the fourth grades the girls' parties were a matter of "eating and playing games." From the fifth to the eighth grade the girls "ate, danced, played games and listened to records." From the first to the eighth grade the boys' parties were almost exclusively devoted to "eating and playing games." All of these parties were held in the home of the person giving the party. Occasionally there was a so-called "party" in the classroom itself, especially in the lower grades, when a mother would send cake and candy to the school for all the classmates on her child's birthday. The teachers were not in favor of this arrangement because they did not want a pattern established according to which parents would feel they had to provide the "makings" of a party.

Members of the Camp Fire Girls are required to give a mixed party as "part of rank." This requirement is for the achievement of the third rank, that of Fire-Maker, after the girls have passed all the earlier tests as Trail-Seekers and Wood-Gatherers.[23] This they did at the home of Clare Johnson in honor of the football team after the final victory of the season. The football players later reciprocated with a

[22] We were not able to keep track of, much less attend, all home parties given for or by the children. Therefore, toward the end of the school year we had the children in all the grades write down for us the number of parties they attended since the beginning of school in September, who gave the party, who were present, what they did at the party. We then eliminated the relatively few parties which were attended only by members of the family or by neighbors.

[23] *The Book of the Camp Fire Girls*, revised edition (New York: Camp Fire Girls, 1954), p. 91.

party at Bill Lanius' home. These two parties and Anthony Noto's birthday party were given with the knowledge and approval of Sister Roberta. The Camp Fire Girls, however, ran into trouble when planning another party to be held in the school club room. The Principal chided the girls for not telling her about it "in time" but she finally gave her consent. The girls did not think that this party was quite successful, and they appear to find the informal and relaxed atmosphere of the home more enjoyable than the routine and supervised situation at school. This group also ran a mixed roller skating party after school on St. Valentine's Day.

Our observer's report of the party held in honor of the football players gives an insight into the kind of relationship existing between these boys and girls. "The party lasted from five to eight on the Sunday of the final football game. Twelve boys and twelve girls were present, most of the boys having been invited by individual girls.[24] The girls wore their best party dresses but the boys wore informal sports clothes. Mr. and Mrs. Johnson supervised in an unobtrusive way, but had to help to 'get things going.' The time was about equally apportioned to playing games, eating and dancing."

"A typical game was the 'feather game.' A boy and a girl stand at one end of a card table and try to blow a feather toward the opposite end, where another couple is blowing against them. The game caused a great deal of giggling and laughing, and teamed up one couple in sporting cooperation against another couple. Other games were: dancing in couples while balancing an apple held between the foreheads of the couple, the boys scrambling for the matching shoe of a girl in the whole pile of shoes, raffling off a paper football signed by all members of the party, the granting of facetious awards to each of the football players.[25] The boys had to be prodded a bit to enter these games, which they seemed to look on at first as something childish or sissy. But they appeared to enjoy themselves immensely once the games started."

"The dancing began very slowly with only a few boys getting into it. Gradually nearly every boy danced and the party settled down to music and dance. The girls served a light supper, which they had themselves prepared as part of the Camp Fire Girl requirement. After more dancing the party was called to a close by Mrs. Johnson, who simply announced, 'O.K., now, this is the last dance.' The children

[24] This practice of individual invitations is an example of "pairing off" that was frowned upon by the teachers.

[25] One award, for example, was a dog biscuit, presented with the words, "For you, Jimmy, since you always seem so hungry in school, we have something you can eat for Monday's lunch."

then made the finish more exciting by ripping down all the elaborate decorations including the 'goal posts.' They walked toward home in a group and each left the main group as his street was reached. No one 'walked home' anyone else."

Sex Instructions

The pupils of St. Luke's achieve the ordinary amount of knowledge concerning the moral aspects of sex in the catechism treatment of the sixth and ninth commandments. They appear to understand quite well the meaning of chastity and the importance of avoiding impure acts and "dirty" thoughts and words. The girls are taught to be "ladies" and are warned that even when they skip rope they must be modest and not let their skirts fly too high. The boys are told to pray for the virtue of purity, and that a pure heart is what really makes a person manly. These are part of the ordinary routine of teaching the religious aspects of sexuality. Prayers and devotion to the Mother of God are often specifically stressed as means to the preservation of chastity.

Occasionally the Pastor mentions these points in his talks at the morning Mass for the children. The tenor of these talks may be illustrated by the following parting words of advice given to the eighth-grade girls on the last day of school. "When I was a kid girls didn't go around with short hair like yours. If they wore short hair and lipstick they were thought of as bar girls, or even as street girls. And the girl who smoked cigarettes, that was terrible in those days. Nowadays, I suppose we get used to these things; maybe we also get used to sin and to temptation."

"You know you are all prone to evil. We have the inclination to evil. And I want you girls to listen to this. The boy will give you a bottle of coke and then try to squeeze it out of you, as they say. He spends money on a girl but he wants to get something out of it. He has evil intentions. He may buy you a box of candy, and then say, 'You think I'm giving it to you for nothing?' That's when things get bad. You always have to be on the look-out. Now this is when you have to watch out, because giving in is bad. It's sinful. The sin of impurity takes two people, you know. Of course, there are solitary sins of impurity, but they are like freaks of nature."

"Now you have learned the same principles as I have. As you grow older these urges develop in you. They get stronger and you have to be careful about them. You know, it's like taking a lion cub and making a pet out of him, but you can't do that when he's five or six years old. You know that sex desires are not bad in themselves, but these desires grow stronger and they can become an occasion of evil for you. Everything must be used in moderation, but using them in over-moderation we make pigs of ourselves. We have to suppress them. We have to chain and manacle them. Sex is not bad in itself. If it were not for the urges of the flesh, none of us would be here today. I wouldn't be here and you wouldn't be here. But you must wait to start the process of procreation."

These words are only a portion of the final talk given to both the boys and the girls in the classroom, and they represent a certain degree of circumlocution that is probably necessary in addressing a mixed audience. The children unquestionably need also a different kind of instruction, which many apparently do not receive from their parents. Sister Roberta illustrates this failure of parents with the example of the girl who asked her mother the meaning of adultery. The mother said it is "sleeping with the iceman when your husband is not home." And Sister remarks "apparently it is not adultery if the husband is home." On the other hand, the failure of the school in teaching these matters was illustrated by the mother of a fifth-grade boy. "My cousin was over to the house one rainy night, and I asked my husband to drive her home. The next day the boy asked me if Daddy had committed adultery the night before, and when I pressed him for an explanation he said that he learned in school that adultery means 'going out with another woman.' "

The whole question of sex instructions to young children has been widely discussed for several decades, and it appears that the school authorities at St. Luke's have introduced a practical and successful solution. The instructions are given to groups and with all of the prudence and caution suggested by the Holy Father,[26] although the children may obtain also individual clarification from the teachers. The Bishops of the United States have urged that it is the duty of parents to perform this function. "Fathers and mothers have a natural competence to instruct their children with regard to sex. False modesty should not deter them from doing their duty in this regard." The Bishops are opposed to public instructions. "We protest in the strongest possible terms against the introduction of sex education into the

[26] Pius XI, *Christian Education of Youth* (Washington: National Catholic Welfare Council, 1936), p. 25. See also Francis F. Brown, "Forming Proper Sex Attitudes," *The Catholic Educator*, vol. 27, no. 1 (September, 1956), pp. 33–35, where he says that "on the grounds then that parents have not only failed to prepare their children through proper training in chastity, but also paved their way to spiritual perdition by relaxing discipline during the crucial adolescence and post-adolescence—on these grounds, it becomes urgent for the teacher to take responsibility" (p. 35). See also Mary Anthony Wagner, "Sex Education and the Catholic Girl," *The Catholic Educator*, vol. 20, no. 5 (January, 1950), pp. 250–253.

schools. To be of benefit such instruction should be far broader than the imparting of information, and must be given individually."[27]

In an effort to correct the erroneous notions gained in the lower grades, and with the knowledge that some parents do not instruct their children in the facts of life,[28] St. Luke's provides annual sex instructions to the pupils of the seventh and eighth grades. During Lent, in the week beginning March 25, Father Martin replaced the morning religious period with sex instructions for the boys of the seventh and eighth grades on Monday, Tuesday, Thursday and Friday. Sister Roberta gave similar instructions to the girls at the same periods on Monday, Tuesday and Thursday. A booklet, *Accent on Purity,*[29] was used as a starting point by Father Martin for these classes. Sister Roberta contented herself mainly with reading directly from this booklet to the girls.

This short course of lessons was introduced by a talk on the divine purpose of sex, explaining that all of God's creations are good, and that human beings are meant to use sex in God's way. A detailed explanation was then given, in simple but technically correct language, of the physiology of sexual reproduction in human beings; the difference of the structure of the male and female form, and how they complement one another; the way in which babies are conceived and born and nourished. The course was concluded with a series of recommendations to aid in the preservation and development of purity.

The contrast between the girls' instructions and those of the boys indicates not only a sex difference in attitudes of the children, but also in the manner in which the instructions were given. Sister Roberta finished the series in three periods, and arranged for the girls to have

[27] Annual Statement of the Bishops of the United States, "The Child: Citizen of Two Worlds," *Catholic Mind,* vol. 49, no. 1058 (February, 1951), pp. 137–144 (p. 142). A Joint Pastoral Letter of the Archbishops and Bishops of England and Wales, "The Catholic Attitude to Sex Education" (London: Catholic Truth Society, 1944), states that "teachers have no strict right to arrogate to themselves parental duties; if called upon by the parents to deputize for them in this delicate matter, they may very properly do so" (p. 4).

[28] This was acknowledged by some of the parents in our soiree group interviews. One mother whose fourth child, a daughter, was then in the seventh grade, had not instructed her children, and had never been told by them that sex instructions were being given at St. Luke's. Others were happy that the school had "taken the job off our hands." Still another mother, a trained obstetrician, had objected to the "misinformation" her daughter received at the school, and offered to give the instructions for the teachers. She was somewhat nettled that her offer was rejected.

[29] Joseph E. Haley, *Accent on Purity,* third edition (Chicago: Fides, 1952). A fourth and illustrated edition has since appeared (1957).

a study period on Friday morning while the boys were receiving the last instruction from Father Martin. The eighth-grade girls, as contrasted with those from the seventh grade, treated the talks in a nonchalant and disinterested way. "This was old stuff to them" writes our reporter. "They had heard it the year before, hardly paid any attention and asked few questions. Most of them were reading, doing arithmetic problems, or studying lessons. The seventh-grade girls listened attentively, but appeared to be reluctant to ask questions, either because of embarrassment or because they sensed that the teacher herself did not want to go into further details." In telling their mothers about these instructions some of the girls seemed to remember most vividly the remark of the teacher that "if young girls knew how terrible and painful childbirth is, the convents would be full of vocations."

In their classes with Father Martin, the boys had so many questions that there was not enough time to answer them all. The priest spoke in a matter-of-course fashion, allowing neither a frivolous nor a frightened atmosphere to develop. Except for two boys at the back of the room who exchanged knowing smiles and snickers when the teacher turned to the blackboard, the pupils reacted to him in an open and interested way. Many of the questions were directed at the difference between sinful and permissible acts in the area of sex, but others sought technical information about Cesarean section, miscarriage, breast-feeding and similar matters. The impression made by these talks may be summed up in the remarks of two of the boys at home. The father of one asked him what was said in class; his reply was, "Oh, we talked about our bodies." Another boy told his mother in more detail about the instructions, and concluded "It's a wonderful way the Lord works things out; you know, there's nothing dirty about all this."

The children had been told at the beginning of the instructions that they must not discuss these matters among themselves, but only with the teacher or with their parents. As far as we could ascertain from observation and interviews, this warning was carefully heeded. There was certainly no general wave of sex talk around the school and there was no individual boy or girl who appeared to be prurient or overtalkative about sex.[30] The desire that children have to maintain reputa-

[30] Pupils liked to be singled out for individual interviews and seemed anxious to "tell all." Our observations about boy-girl relations in the school were confirmed in these interviews, and most of the informal details about friendships, cliques, dating and out-of-school activities came from them.

tion among their peers seemed to be at work here. This kind of thing "simply wasn't done." We checked more deeply in this area in our interviews with high school students, former pupils of St. Luke's. Said one freshman, "the kids over there are pretty decent in their talk; you never hear any dirty stuff. You should have heard them in the public school where I was in the sixth grade."

Adult Control and Attitudes

The boy-girl relation at St. Luke's school, and all it involves in the matter of parties, dances, dating and sex knowledge, appears to be as well under control as one can expect in this kind of urban environment. The children themselves seem to accept the situation as part of the restraints of home and school normal to their age level. Some of the more "socially conscious" among the older children grumble at these restrictions, some are not bothered because they are not interested in the opposite sex, and the great majority go along with what their parents and teachers think best for them. Those who have graduated from St. Luke's and are in high school feel now that the restrictions in the parochial school were somewhat too great. They said they were "not prepared" for the mingling of the sexes in high school and were quite "shy" for the first few months.[31]

The priests and the teachers are well aware of the problems involved in the boy-girl relationship and take a realistic attitude toward them. They constantly say they want everything "open and above-board." When the Camp Fire Girls were discouraged by the teachers from having a mixed party at Halloween, they went to the Pastor about it. He seemed unwilling to make a decision and did not express direct disapproval. "We shouldn't have too many of these things," he told the girls. "Some of the people in the parish are objecting to such parties for school children. We musn't start this sort of thing too early." We have seen that both Father Martin and Sister Roberta take a healthy view of parties, picnics and dances where the boys and girls are together. They have also stressed the importance of modesty and purity for both sexes, and the dangers of pairing off.

The sixth-grade teachers, who are in a position to see the beginnings of boy-girl interests, are particularly concerned about developing

[31] Those attending Catholic high school where the segregation of the sexes is still continued seem to duplicate the same attitudes which they had in elementary school. More of them, however, especially the girls, resent the imposed segregation. One high school junior said, "Sister threatens to pull the shade down and give us a penance when we look out of the window at the boys practicing track."

healthy attitudes in the children in this regard. They feel that the patterns set here will tend to continue through the next two years. In this sense both teachers and parents consider the sixth grade the "problem year." Note-passing begins in the classroom and on the play ground, and at this point the teachers know that they must point out the proprieties and improprieties of such conduct. A certain amount of excitement was triggered on the occasion of a sixth-grade girl's birthday party which a few of the boys "crashed." They enjoyed it so much that they decided to form a small club, and run a coke and dance party to which "only the ten best-looking girls in the sixth grade would be invited."

The mothers of the boys became involved when the boys had to decide whose house would be the site of the party. There was a great deal of phone-calling among the mothers, who agreed that "they're pretty young to be starting that sort of thing. What do you think we ought to do about it? I'm sure they haven't done anything wrong, and don't intend to do wrong. But, we can't make such parties look like great big forbidden fruit. Please don't let on that we talked about it; my boy wouldn't want me prying in his affairs. It's so hard to deny them anything." The result of these telephone conversations was an informal meeting of the parents involved after the eight-thirty Mass in the school on the fourth Sunday of May. Only five people showed up (there were only thirteen boys involved) and they all agreed that such a party must be planned and supervised by the parents. One father said, "We can't let them run on unorganized. Maybe the whole thing should be called to a screeching halt and the boys' energies directed to sports instead of girls." Finally, Mrs. Echols took a strong stand in complete opposition to the party. The other parents seemed to be relieved that someone had made a definite decision, because none of them wanted to go through with it yet no one wanted "to be the one to spoil the kids' fun." Later, one of the boys said that the parents "lowered the boom" but neither he nor any of the others seemed to be disappointed at the decision.

As we have seen, only a very small number of parents (3.2%) believed that there should be more "social activity" for the children of St. Luke's school.[32] The great majority seemed to feel that there is an influence from the public school pattern, where there are weekly

[32] See Alice Crow, "Parental Attitudes Toward Boy-Girl Relations," *Journal of Educational Sociology*, vol. 29 (November, 1955), pp. 126–133, where she describes how adults "push" children into boy-girl consciousness. "The sex factor is not likely to affect children's attitudes toward one another unless adults

dances and where the children themselves have both a dance band and a marching band. It was a common statement by both elementary school children and by former pupils of St. Luke's that "there is much more boy-girl stuff in the public schools." [33] The Catholic parents of public school pupils appear to be somewhat more permissive along these lines than are the parents of St. Luke's children, but they are also somewhat more worried about the problems involved.

It seems clear that neither of the two groups of adults, the teachers and the parents, who might be expected to guide the sexual awakening of the children, is taking a positive, formal and supervisory role in this process. The priests and teachers must act on a piecemeal basis, advising against or for a certain party or dance, discouraging some specific case of "puppy love," giving group instructions on sex and morality, and applying their own principles to the extent that limited access to the individual child permits. While the school authorities have the advantage of contacting the total group of pupils, the boys and girls see each other after school and they are living in families and neighborhoods, where other factors are at work. There is, from this point of view, another disadvantage in the fact that the school authorities, except for the three lay teachers, are unmarried and live a semi-monastic life. To some extent this limits their abilities to understand and to get close to the child in puberty.

The parents, of course, also exercise guidance of their children, but they contact only their own children and a few of the child's friends. A parent can decide whether his child will be allowed to attend or give a party, whether or when he will be allowed to date, and can also instill in the child general attitudes toward the opposite sex. Many of the parents had specific rules for their children concerning dating, parties and hours, but many did not. In some instances the parent contacted the teacher about giving a party, or phoned another parent. This is a form of supervision but it does not seem to grapple with the problem.

The parents have the advantage over the teacher in being physically and perhaps sympathetically closer to their children, but they can legislate only for their own children, and not for the children's class-

---

encourage the youngsters to differentiate between their boy and girl companions. By their supposedly jesting remarks, adults may develop attitudes of self-consciousness in the growing child" (p. 128).

[33] One of the boys in the eighth grade is the only parochial school member of a regular swimming class at the City Natatorium. He says, "That's all those public school kids talk about; they're girl crazy." This greater interest across sex lines is indicated also in the Friendship Test, mentioned above, pp. 251 f.

mates. The children are adept, of course, at exploiting this weakness with the old and potent argument, "everybody else is doing it." In a cultural setting where parents simply do not know and cannot follow what "everybody else is doing" there is a necessity for parents to communicate with each other. This is done more often where a group of one sex is concerned, for example, in preparing for the girls who danced at the Pastor's feast day entertainment, or in working out plans for the boys' football banquet. In the matter of boy-girl relations there was much informal telephone contact, as well as the meeting of parents after Sunday Mass to discuss the proposed sixth-grade party.

The main agency of parent communication is the PTA, but it has not directly confronted the problem of aiding boys and girls in adjustment to each other. Each parent seems to have his own ideas, and they do not present a common front because they have none.[34] As one of its objectives the PTA at St. Luke's is trying to "secure for every child the highest advantages in physical, mental, social and spiritual education," and it currently includes committees for Character Education, Recreation, Citizenship, Spiritual Education, Home and Family, among others. It has no committee or program specifically aimed at the problem of boy-girl adjustment.

The adult committee supervising the Camp Fire Girls is the nearest thing to a boy-girl guidance committee that St. Luke's school has. The Camp Fire group is the only agency in the parish that has a clear-cut program for the child of puberty and adolescence. The Boy Scout program seems to pretend "officially" that girls do not exist. The Camp Fire group is interested in the social competence of the girls. Participating in a mixed gathering under the supervision of adults, is a necessary requirement for advancing in rank.

Within this informal framework of supervisory agencies the boys and girls themselves seem to be making the transition into adolescence without any notable trauma. The counselling of the confessional, which is open to all of them, and the fact that friendly teachers can and do give time to individual children, seems to cushion the absence of more formalized technics. There were no cases of sexual misconduct that came to our attention all year, nor did there appear to be an excessive amount of fears and withdrawal from the opposite sex. High spiritual

[34] This was clearly demonstrated in group interviews with parents, and it does not follow sex lines. One husband is opposed to anything like boy-girl interest on the elementary level, while his wife favors it. In another couple the wife says, "They have lots of time for these things when they reach high school," but the husband contests that they "ought to learn how to get along with each other right now in the grade school."

motivation, the use of prayer and the sacraments, mingle with the numerous natural and cultural influences, to affect a relatively healthy, normal boy-girl adjustment at St. Luke's school.

Generalizations

1. The empirical evidence points unquestionably to the fact that parochial elementary school children, even in the higher grades, prefer segregation to mingling across sex lines. This is clearly observable in their preferences in class seating arrangements, in their after-school behavior at home and in the neighborhood. It is also shown by the fact that putting children of opposite sexes together, as in the classroom seating, is considered a "punishment" by the child and is often used by the teacher for the sake of good order and a quiet classroom.

2. The child identifies primarily with its own sex group. The boy-boy relationship and the girl-girl relationship remain the basis for friendships and group formation outside the family. This is an expected phenomenon since sharing of the same sex is the focus of an important segment of organized adult society. Nevertheless, there are "group relations" across sex lines in the parochial school. The child in the group focuses on the other sex as a group rather than as an individual. Thus, these boy-girl relations are not personal and individual. They appear to be a friendly, healthy, awkward, shy, bantering type of relation.

3. Group relations across sex lines are specified by the type of activity involved in them. Both boys and girls at St. Luke's have an intense interest in athletics, which in varying degrees brings them together. The girls *also* like dancing and are much more proficient in this art than are the boys. The latter have to be coaxed to dance and their ineptitude gives the girls an advantage. On the other hand, the boy's superiority in sports gives him in this activity an opportunity to show off and he has the advantage.

4. Parties in general tend to be labeled as female activities by the boys of St. Luke's. Here again, the girl does this better than the boy. For the most part the boys in the upper grades have to be "pushed" into parties by the girls and their mothers. The relatively few instances of mixed parties given by boys were in fact given as a reaction to, or in reciprocation for, previous parties to which the girls invited the boys.

5. The general attitude of adults—priests, teachers and parents—toward mixed parties on the grade school level is a negative one. They tend to regard these parties as a concession to cultural compulsion, to the vague idea that boys and girls ought to have them as a means of

learning to adjust to one another. The school authorities have a fairly definite, but reluctant, policy of permitting mixed parties, provided that everything is "open and above-board," the invitations are issued to the whole class rather than to individuals, that there be no pairing-off, and that a full account be given of what went on.

6. There is no positive program in the parochial school, specifically designed to teach the boys and girls how to adjust to one another in this early adolescent period. Except for one aspect of the Camp Fire program, the activities which help to achieve this adjustment just seem to "happen." There is a great deal of talk about it on the part of parents, and some worry, but they do practically nothing about it in an organized and systematic way, either as parents alone or in cooperation with teachers and priests.

7. The public school children demonstrate a greater interest in the opposite sex than do the children of St. Luke's. The latter almost invariably name a person of their own sex as "best friend," while the public school children frequently choose a best friend from the other sex. The public school children discuss boy friends and girl friends much more, they have many more school-sponsored dances, and they appear to mingle much more across sex lines after school hours, than do the children from St. Luke's.

8. A small amount of pairing-off of a casual nature takes place among the seventh and eighth graders. This is more in their talk and in their minds than it is in their external behavior. Some walk home together; they may telephone occasionally; they may happen to meet at the skating rink when the "whole gang" is there. There is practically no pre-arranged dating, except for three eighth-grade girls who have had "dates" with high school freshmen. A boy may admit that he likes a certain girl, but he would never speak of her as "my girl."

9. Pairing-off, or identification of a particular friendship between a boy and a girl, is discouraged by ridicule and embarrassing statements on the part of teachers. Any symptom of it is also given immediate publicity by classmates, and this jeering publicity by one's peers seems to be more effective in slowing down the practice of pairing-off than anything done by teachers and parents.

10. The emphasis on modesty and chastity, and the whole religious atmosphere of the school, are unquestionably effective in providing positive and wholesome attitudes between the sexes. The fact that the St. Robert Club in the eighth grade voted to receive Communion every Friday morning, is an indication these children take the virtuous life seriously. They know from their religious instruction what is sinful and what is virtuous in regard to sex. In this respect they have also the

advantage of group pressure because they know that decency and "proper" behavior are expected of them by their classmates, and that anything else is considered "sneaky" and underhand by them.

11. It is at this same level that sex instructions are given to the children of the upper grades. A clear, factual description of the physiological aspects of sex is presented, but this is only a part of the sex instructions. The technical and accurate biological information, that might be given by a physician or nurse, is here contained within the whole Christian philosophy of sex. The calm way in which the pupils react to these instructions is partly a consequence of the manner in which they are given and partly of the general spiritual framework of the whole school.

Part

III

AGENCIES OF CONTROL

Chapter

ELEVEN

THE TEACHERS OF ST. LUKE'S

THE ELEMENTARY school teacher is a pivotal person in the socialization of children. She represents the principal institutionalized channel through which the cultural heritage flows. Parents are temporary educators who "finish their job" when their own children grow up, but the teacher plays a permanent role in reproducing and maintaining the cultural values to each succeeding grade and even to succeeding generations. "The American teacher has long been in a strangely paradoxical position in our society. Regarded as a sort of bulwark of that society, a person whose virtues are often extolled and whose service is frequently eulogized, she has at the same time been underpaid, has enjoyed little prestige, and has been fenced in with all sorts of social restrictions and encumbrances." [1]

The teacher in the parochial school system is entrusted with the direct transmission of values that are fully cultural. The facts and ideals she teaches to her pupils are not limited only to so-called secular knowledge. She hands on the fullness of the culture in so far as the child's capacity can receive it, and this includes the significant area of spiritual and religious values. Thus, in fulfilling the social function of the teacher's role, she is able to act as a full transmitter of the Christian American culture.[2] She is able, and indeed obliged, to teach the fullness of truth, and thus does not suffer the restrictions on freedom of thought and expression that are sometimes placed upon the public school teacher in the secular society.[3]

[1] Blaine E. Mercer and Edwin R. Carr, *Education and the Social Order* (New York: Rinehart, 1957), p. 374.

[2] See Sister M. Bernard McGrath, *The Compatibility of Catholic Schools and Democratic Standards* (Washington: Catholic University Press, 1948), chap. 4, "The Curriculum and Educational Procedures," pp. 74–99.

[3] In the absence of empirical research it is possible to develop the caricature of parochial school teaching that appears in Paul Blanshard, *American Freedom*

Autonomy and Standards

From the point of view of authority and function, the teaching personnel of St. Luke's constitutes a relatively "self-contained" unit. The Pastor is ultimately responsible to the Bishop for the successful maintenance of the school, but the Bishop does not interfere with the Pastor just as the Pastor does not interfere with the Principal. The formal structural link between the school and the Bishop is the office of the diocesan superintendent of schools, who is a busy Pastor in a distant city. He did not visit St. Luke's during our study, and the extent of his communication was four routine items: the weekly time schedule of subjects, the school year calendar, the uniform report cards, and the list of recommended textbooks.[4] All of these were accepted more as guides, rather than as authoritative directives, by the Pastor and the Principal.[5] Ultimately, all decisions concerning the school were made locally by the Principal with the explicit or implicit approval of the Pastor.

The drive for standardization in elementary schools, particularly for the purpose of "raising standards," which has resulted in the publication of teachers' handbooks in the larger archdioceses and dioceses, has not occurred in the diocese where St. Luke's school is located. Unlike some of the larger teaching orders of Sisters, the congregation that supplies the Sisters to St. Luke's, has not distributed among its members a formalized manual for teachers. Thus, neither the diocese, through the superintendent of schools, nor the teaching order, through its Mother Provincial, exerts any direct authority over classroom and school procedures at St. Luke's.

The school and its faculty are similarly independent of city, county and state boards of education. The multiple and increasingly rigid school regulations issuing from these authorities do not reach down to the level of the elementary parochial school.[6] St. Luke's faculty belongs to St. Luke's parish. It is dedicated to the task of making good

---

and Catholic Power (Boston: Beacon Press, 1949), p. 69. For a balanced and intelligent criticism, see Gerard S. Sloyan, *The Recognition of Certain Christian Concepts in the Social Studies in Catholic Elementary Education* (Washington: Catholic University Press, 1948), pp. 177–180.

[4] For comparable information from over ninety dioceses, see Richard O. Wilson, "The Diocesan Superintendent's Office: Its Structure, Personnel, and Finance" (Washington: Dissertation in Catholic University Library, 1953).

[5] For a further discussion of these items see below, chap. 16, "Problems of Elementary Education," and chap. 13, "Parents and Teachers."

[6] See the complaint of Lydia Stout, "What Strangles American Teaching." *The Atlantic Monthly*, vol. 201, no. 4 (April, 1958) pp. 59–63.

practicing Catholics and exemplary American citizens out of the children of the parish. This means obviously that these teachers recognize certain standards both of methods and of achievement. In the absence of handbooks and of directives from above, they appear to find these standards in their common training and shared experience.

Several points must be made about the actual development of standards by each individual teacher at St. Luke's. During the period of her college training each has had the advantage of the normal education courses in teaching methods. These supply the usual formulae of techniques which are then tested in practice teaching under supervision. Each of them also makes use of the various manuals supplied by the publishers of the textbooks in use at St. Luke's school. These supply norms of coverage of materials as well as some hints on teaching techniques. Except for the arithmetic texts, all of the others are deliberately written from the "Catholic point of view," and this means that the over-arching and unifying standard of education is religion. As a result of these combined factors, the teaching at St. Luke's is neither traditional nor radical. It is an eclectic type of "vitalized formality." [7]

Our observation of classroom techniques, investigation of textbooks and testing of pupils, have forced the conclusion that the teaching procedures at St. Luke's school are standardized in a flexible way. The descriptions given throughout this book show that there is a range of teacher competence—as there is in any school—but that in general an integrated body of knowledge is presented to the children at their own level of capacities and interests.[8] If one is seeking a label, this whole arrangement can probably be called a "core curriculum" and its operative technique appears to be the "Herbartian method" as modified by Morrison.[9] Neither teachers nor parents, however, are deeply concerned about such labels.

[7] See a balanced discussion of this synthesis of traditionalism and progressivism in Benjamin Brickman, "Merging the 'Old' and the 'New' in a Child's Education—An Eclectic View," *The Elementary School Journal,* vol. 56, no. 7 (March, 1956), pp. 299–302.

[8] Research projects in the field of education abound in questionnaires and interviews and checklists, with a notable lack of direct empirical observation and field work. One of the few exceptions is the study by W. A. Oliver, "Teachers' Educational Beliefs Versus Their Classroom Practices," *Journal of Educational Research,* vol. 47, no. 1 (September, 1953), pp. 47–55, who attempts to demonstrate that public school teachers are still employing "old-fashioned" techniques.

[9] See the discussion on these items in Chris. A. DeYoung, *Introduction to American Public Education* (New York: McGraw-Hill, 1955), pp. 421–425.

The ultimate criterion for discovering whether St. Luke's school is reaching, or even surpassing, the standards exhibited by other elementary schools is found in the achievement of pupils. The results of the comparative tests given to the children of both the parochial and public schools are scattered throughout this book. The graduates of St. Luke's school do as well as, and in some instances slightly better than, their classmates in both public and Catholic high schools of the city. Standardized tests are administered each year at St. Luke's to the pupils of the first, fourth and seventh grades.[10] In previous years the *California Short Form Test of Mental Maturity,* and on one occasion the *Pintner-Cunningham Test,* was administered. In the year of our study both the *Kuhlman-Anderson Intelligence Test* and the *American School Achievement Test* were given to the pupils.

Who They Are

Two priests, eleven nuns and three lay women do all of the teaching in the classrooms of St. Luke's.[11] The priests are really only part-time teachers, specializing in religious instruction for some of the grades in the school. The lay teachers are married women, apostolic parishioners, who have "returned to teaching" at a sacrifice of time and money in order to help alleviate the teacher shortage. The Sisters are members of a teaching order, with its provincial house in the adjoining diocese. They are appointed to the mission of teaching in this school by their Mother Superior.

The teachers at St. Luke's are in theory recruited on a one-year basis, but in practice their tenure continues over a period of years. The three lay teachers are hired on one-year contracts, but since they are so desperately needed, they have no fear of "losing their jobs." [12] They are

[10] For samples of frequency and types of standardized tests, see Roscoe A. Boyer and Merrill T. Eaton, "Standardized Testing in the Schools of Indiana," *Bulletin* of the School of Education, Indiana University, vol. 27, no. 1 (January, 1951); also F. E. Heinemann, "Approval and Accrediting Standards in Minnesota," *Bulletin* of the National Association of Secondary School Principals, vol. 36, no. 168 (April, 1952), pp. 205–208.

[11] For the comparative statistics on expanding elementary schools and faculties, see John P. Sullivan, "The Growth of Catholic Schools," *America,* vol. 98, no. 7 (November 16, 1957), pp. 201–205. In seven years, since 1950, the proportion of lay teachers had increased from 9.9 per cent to 17.5 per cent.

[12] Mrs. Gordon retired from teaching at the end of the year in order to devote more time to her children. She was replaced by another lay teacher. Another nun was also added to the faculty so that St. Luke's had twelve Sisters and three lay teachers for the next school term.

hired by the Principal and paid by the Pastor. The teaching appointments of the nuns are made each year in the middle of August, just after they have finished their annual retreat at the provincial house. Sealed envelopes are placed on the altar rail and each contains the assignment for that particular nun for the coming year. Theoretically, the nuns must be ready to go wherever obedience assigns them, but in practice the teachers are returned to the same school as consistently as possible. An exception is the local superior who is also often the Principal, whose assignment is for a three-year term, and who may have this assignment renewed only three times at the same school.

Sister Justin and Sister Roberta have been at St. Luke's nine and eight years respectively. Sister Agatha has taught there for six years, while three nuns, Sisters Cecelia, Vincent de Paul and Bridget have been at the school for five years each. Only one member of the faculty is a beginning teacher, Sister Mark. If we omit the four teachers who started in September, the total tenure at St. Luke's of the remaining ten faculty members is forty-seven years, or an average of 4.7 years per teacher. The following table shows the total teaching experience of this faculty both at St. Luke's and elsewhere.

Name of teacher	Years at St. Luke's	Years at other schools	Total years teaching
Sister Justin	9	7	16
Sister Roberta	8	26	34
Sister Agatha	6	34	40
Sister Cecelia	5	2	7
Sister Vincent de Paul	5	2	7
Sister Bridget	5	2	7
Sister Ruth	3	2	5
Sister Dominic	2	3	5
Sister Martha	2	2	4
Mrs. Edwards	2	0	2
Mrs. Gerald	1	10	11
Sister Bernadette	1	7	8
Mrs. Gordon	1	1	2
Sister Mark	1	0	1

The three teachers who have been at St. Luke's for the longest period are also the most experienced teachers, totaling ninety years of teaching among them. The remaining teachers average a little more than five years each in teaching experience. It is difficult to assess the problem of teacher "turnover" in a school like St. Luke's which has expanded from nine to fourteen classrooms and has increased its school population about one-third in the period of four years, and where the decision to remain or to change positions is not entirely in the hands of the teacher. The length of service of any particular nun at any particular school may depend upon the needs of other schools operated by the teaching order as well as upon the local conditions under which the Sisters live. The assignment to St. Luke's is considered a "good spot" in the current informal opinion within this teaching order, and a contented nun is not quickly and easily removed by her Superior Provincial.

What They Do

The fourteen teachers at St. Luke's school are with the children from eight in the morning till three in the afternoon. They attend the daily Mass with them, look after them at recess and at the lunch period, and teach all of the curriculum to the entire class. Every teacher is expected to be competent in every subject, English, arithmetic, religion, even art and music. Emphases change on these subjects in the different grades, for example, the first grade has three times as much reading as the eighth grade, and the fourth grade has twice as much arithmetic as the first grade. The second grade concentrates on religion, the seventh grade on music.

St. Luke's teachers are thus expected to be liberal and well-rounded educators, but there are also some specialists among them. Sisters Cecelia and Ruth are competent musicians, Sister Justin is a Latin teacher, Sister Dominic is an expert typist and the best artist among the teachers. Fathers Albert and Martin are also teaching specialists since they handle part of the religious instructions for some of the grades. Sister Roberta, the principal, is administrator, business woman, and ultimate disciplinarian of the school. Every teacher carries a full load in the classroom, teaching the same group of children all day, and none of them is engaged in so-called departmental teaching.

There are certain general tasks in which all of the teachers engage. The most common of these is the sharing of playground and cafeteria supervision at the noon period. This requires six teachers every day, and they operate in shifts of three, since the lunch period is staggered for the lower and the upper grades. One teacher supervises the boys' playground, another the girls' and a third the northwest playground for the smaller children. At the beginning of the year the teachers are given their choice of playground, and a schedule is worked out so that there is time for the teacher's own lunch. Thus each teacher has every alternate week free of the playground supervision.[13] At the beginning of the year in September there was a plan afoot that volunteer mothers from the PTA would take over this noon-time task, but it never materialized.

The first and second grades have ten-minute recess periods both morning and afternoon. From the third to the sixth grade the afternoon recess is limited to five minutes, and in the seventh and eighth grades it is omitted entirely. At these recess periods the teacher accompanies her own class to the playground, or in inclement weather, stays with them inside the building. The relatively small playground makes it necessary to stagger the recess periods, and since most of the classes are on the east side of the building, next to the playground, the noise of children shouting is a handicap to teaching for those remaining in the classrooms. The teachers usually assign a study period when this occurs.

We have seen that Sister Justin is often occupied at the noon period with the training of altar boys.[14] Since she is also the sacristan of the parish, she works in the sanctuary sometimes at noon, but more often after school hours and on Saturdays with the help of Sister Dominic and some of the sixth-grade girls. Sister Justin is thus faced with a twofold extracurricular task. She has the responsibility of seeing that altar boys are appointed for both regular and special services in the church and that the lists of appointees are hung in the sacristy and in the upper grades. She must also perform whatever organizational and supervisory functions the acolytes' group requires. Since she is an expert in liturgical practices she must see to it that the equipment for services, the Crib for Christmas, palms for Palm Sunday, the oils of Confirmation, and so forth, are prepared in advance.

The two music teachers of the school are Sisters Cecelia and Ruth. Besides the singing instructions which they and all the teachers give in all of the classrooms, these two Sisters also give private lessons every afternoon after school and on Saturdays. Piano lessons are given to thirty-two pupils from the third to the eighth grade and to six high school students. Five children from the fifth to the eighth grades take private singing lessons from these Sisters. All lessons are given in the convent parlor or in classrooms.

Choir practices are conducted for the most part during the daily music period. Both Sisters Cecelia and Ruth play the organ at the daily

[13] The honor patrol girls of the eighth grade share much of this burden with the teachers by supervising the younger children in the corridors.

[14] See the discussion on the Sacristan, above, chap. 3, "The Upstairs Classes."

Mass when the children sing, although this chore is also sometimes performed by Alice Pitre. Another activity which falls to the responsibility of Sister Cecelia is the preparation for all school plays and entertainments in which the children participate and in which her own music pupils are the star performers.[15] The annual program for the Pastor's feast day is the largest of this kind. In the year before our study she presented "Snow White and the Seven Dwarfs," while this year she staged an original play entitled, "Melody Lane to Happiness." This required practice and rehearsals every day during the Spring vacation, April 1–5, and on every Saturday afternoon until the performances on Friday and Sunday, May 10 and 12.

All of the teachers have assumed a kind of janitorial responsibility for their individual classrooms. This is not time-consuming to any great degree. It means that each child "picks up" in the area of his desk before going out to lunch and before final dismissal for the day. Picking up papers around the corridors and on the schoolyard is occasionally given as a penance to pupils who have misbehaved. Sweeping the classroom and washing the blackboards are chores that the children vie with one another to perform. There is only one janitor for the whole parish plant, and he is able to give each classroom a thorough cleaning only about once a week.

The amount of time spent after hours in the correction of papers and in preparation for the next day's work varies according to the industry of the individual teacher and the size of her class. It is at this point that the difference between the lay teachers and the religious teachers must be noted. The lay teachers spend the same amount of time in the classroom as the religious teachers. They share equally in the supervisory duties at recess and at the lunch periods; they have the same janitorial duties and the same obligation to prepare lessons for the next day's classes. They are also present at the daily morning Mass. The lay teachers do not have charge of any of the groups and organizations to which the pupils belong. When all this has been done they are free to return to their homes and families.

On the basis of our data we are able to reconstruct the normal school day of the teaching Sister at St. Luke's school.[16] She rises at 4:50 in the morning and retires at 9:20 at night. She is with the school

[15] See *ibid.*, the section on "parties and lessons."

[16] Mother Mary Magdalen, Superior General, Sisters of the Humility of Mary, "Adaptation of the Horarium," *Sister Formation Bulletin,* vol. 2, no. 2 (December, 1955), pp. 11–12, shows how in her order the daily schedule was adapted to the modern needs of the parochial school teachers.

children about six and a half hours, including attendance at the children's Mass and supervision of noon period on the playground. She spends about three hours in prayer and meditation, including the early morning Mass when the Sisters receive Communion. The three daily meals require about one and a quarter hours; the housework on a school day takes about a half-hour, and in the evening another half-hour is given to community recreation among the Sisters.

If the Sister has no extracurricular activity, like sacristan work, play practice, music lessons, meetings with parents, to attend to in the afternoon, she has a period of an hour and a half between the end of school and supper time, in which to correct papers and prepare lessons. Similarly in the evenings she has a period of an hour and three-quarters in which to study, read and write correspondence. There are, of course, variations in this routine. The Sisters have a part-time cook who prepares their meals, but they themselves rotate other household chores from week to week, like washing dishes, sweeping, running the electric washer, answering the telephone, and others. Most of the Sisters go over to the school in the morning for a half-hour of immediate preparation before the children's Mass at eight o'clock.[17]

Saturday appears to be the most variable day of the week for the Sisters. They concentrate on major tasks of housework and are able also to read and study. During the spring vacation they washed all the walls and ceilings of the convent. Two of the Sisters are taking correspondence extension courses from the State University. One day a month, the last Sunday, is a day of spiritual recollection, when one of the priests comes over for a conference in the afternoon. Sunday afternoons are also the best time for visits from the relatives of the nuns, and occasionally a few of the Sisters will go for an automobile ride with ladies of the parish.[18] Several times during the year the Sisters have an all-day outing to the Mother House of their order.

[17] Mary C. Werner, *An Analysis and Evaluation of the Problems Arising from the Extra-Class Activities Assigned Religious Teachers in Parochial Schools* (Cleveland: St. John College, 1956, unpublished Master's thesis), shows that the daily schedule of the Sister, based on a seven-day week has three hours and twenty-one minutes for religious obligations, four hours and fourteen minutes for community and personal care, five hours and fifty-five minutes for professional duties, three hours and twenty-eight minutes for extra-class activities (p. 109).

[18] These women are from among the parents of St. Luke's children and are in many ways the closest lay friends the nuns have. They have an informal agreement to give service of this kind whenever the nuns wish it. Most of the time, they say, they have to persuade the Sisters to "take some time off."

What They Think

The teachers appear to be fairly well satisfied with their work and with the way in which St. Luke's school is operated. Nine of them, and this included mainly those who have had the most experience in teaching, rated the school an "average" elementary school. The remaining five who rated the school "above average" include the two lay teachers of the third grade. Generally speaking, the younger teachers seem to be more optimistic and to have a higher regard for the school than do the older and more experienced teachers. None of the teachers rated the school "below average," but when we asked them to compare St. Luke's with schools at which they had previously taught, one Sister said that St. Luke's is not so good as the others. The Principal, the two teachers of the second grade, and Mrs. Gerald, stated that St. Luke's is a better school than the ones in which they have had previous experience.

When we asked them what they thought about their pupils the great majority of teachers said that the children were average both in their studies and in their behavior. We must remember that in this case each teacher was judging only the children she had in her own classroom. Every experienced teacher knows that there are fluctuations in the quality of pupils she has from year to year; the general tone may be above average one year and below average the next. Sister Roberta thinks that her eighth graders are above average in behavior, and this opinion, incidentally, is shared by parents who have observed the succeeding graduating classes over the years. Only one Sister believes that the children in her class are below average in behavior.[19]

Only two teachers, one of them a lay woman, consider their pupils above average in intelligence and studies. Only one Sister thinks that her class is below average in studies. "I find it extremely difficult to become adjusted to my present group. They are far below average, and to make it worse, they seem so indifferent about their work that I find it discouraging at times to continue teaching. It seems harder to teach here than it is in a small city." All of the remaining eleven teachers feel that in general their pupils are no better and no worse in their studies than the average elementary school child.

When asked what they liked most about their present teaching position two of the lay teachers praised specifically the congeniality

[19] Mr. Bowman and his wife, who probably know the pupils at St. Luke's better than any other parents, remarked quite independently that "they're going to have trouble with the kids in that class later on."

and excellent relations between the religious and the lay teachers.[20] Most of the Sisters mentioned the systematic way in which the school is run as the most pleasing quality. "The good order and discipline mean more to me than anything else. Each teacher knows the schedule and her duties, and the cooperation of all makes the program work very smoothly." Another Sister said, "the school is run very systematically. We are given a definite time for study and for preparing our lesson plans each evening." Some of them remarked that they liked certain subjects they are teaching, and others that they enjoyed working with children of the particular age level of their class.

The teachers, like the parents, hesitate to find fault with the school. We asked them what they "like least" about their present teaching position. Four of them had no comments to make to this question. Four others declared that their particular classroom is overcrowded. Three others deplored the fact that "there is not enough time" in the day to do all the things they want to do, or are expected to do. This complaint referred only to after-school hours. One teacher dislikes the numerous extracurricular activities of the children, "the clubs! Every day there is a meeting of some sort. All the children think of is what is going to happen after school."

One of the lay teachers dislikes "my daily stint at noon supervising the playground." In this regard, she spoke up also on behalf of the Sisters, none of whom complained about this duty. "I feel that it is a shame that the Sisters particularly must spend their so-called rest and lunch period patroling the school yard. The Sister must return to her afternoon classes more fatigued than she left it." The only other dissatisfaction expressed was that of the teacher who thought her pupils were indifferent to study and were far below the average as students.

Although only four teachers complained about over-crowding in their classrooms, most of the other teachers made statements that would lead to the conclusion that they consider St. Luke's to be overcrowded. We asked them, "In your opinion, how many pupils can a teacher handle efficiently in one class?" Then, we compared this to the answer they gave to the question, "How many pupils do you have in your class?" The two sixth-grade classes and the two fifth-grade classes are

[20] See Sister Marie Theresa, "The Principal and the Lay Teacher," *Bulletin* of the National Catholic Educational Association, vol. 50, no. 1 (August, 1953), pp. 358–364; for a broader discussion of the lay teacher by Henry M. Hald, Sylvester J. Holbel and Mrs. James Welch, see vol. 51, no. 1 (August, 1954), pp. 547–557.

the smallest in the school, averaging thirty-five children in each. In none of these classes did the teachers state, explicitly or implicitly, that their rooms were crowded. If the "ideal number" could be achieved for each of the fourteen teachers, there would be 505 pupils (thirty-six per teacher) in the school, instead of the present number of 632 (45.1 per teacher).

The following table shows the relativity of the crowding problem both in the minds of the teacher and in the actual variations from class to class. One teacher thought she could handle forty-five pupils, but has thirty-eight in her class. Four teachers think that forty pupils constitute the right number, but they average fifty-two in their classes. Six teachers would like to have thirty-five children, but they average 41.5 per classroom. Three teachers think that thirty would be the ideal number, but they average 45.6 pupils per class.

Grade	Teacher can handle	Children in class	Extent of overcrowding	Average overcrowding
Five-B	45	38	—7	—7
Eight	40	60	20	12
Three-A	40	52	12	
Four-B	40	50	10	
Three-B	40	46	6	
Seven	35	52	17	11
Two-A	35	51	16	
One-B	35	45	10	
Five-A	35	36	1	
Six-B	35	33	—2	—2.5
Six-A	35	32	—3	
Two-B	30	52	22	15.7
Four-A	30	46	16	
One-A	30	39	9	
	505	632	127	9.1

We asked the teachers how they thought St. Luke's school compares with the elementary school they had themselves attended as children. Nine of them, including the three lay teachers, feel that St. Luke's is better than the school they attended. The reasons they gave were numerous: modern conveniences, better trained teachers, more interest in the child as an individual, more intelligent discipline, more relaxed atmosphere, better books and teaching aids. Three of the teachers thought that St. Luke's is neither better nor worse than the one they attended. The two Sisters who believe that their own childhood school was better than St. Luke's found fault with today's children who are "restless and inattentive;" they have "too many distractions," and they do not study as much as children used to.

The teachers at St. Luke's are unanimously in favor of the organized athletic teams like football, basketball, baseball and volleyball. They make no qualifications whatsoever on this point, but when they were asked what further "outside" activities and programs the school should provide, exactly half of them said that the school already provides everything and that the children have "more than enough." The remaining seven teachers gave no answer to this question. As far as home and family recreation were concerned the teachers were also unanimous that parents should make regulations and exercise censorship in the use of TV and radio, in going to the movies and reading comic books. They believe that every child should have definite chores to do around the house, and should have a regular hour for retiring.

Although the teachers attended only the first two meetings of the year in the PTA, and at these meetings there was some dissension involving the faculty, five of them esteem the PTA above average, and none of the rest considers it below average. When asked what should be done in order to improve the PTA, ten of them had no suggestions to make. Two of the Sisters remarked that more men should be attracted to the meetings, and should be elected to office, because "men are more reasonable than women." One teacher suggested that the "trouble makers be eliminated from the organization," and another suggested that "questions of education should be discussed with the Pastor and the Principal and not at the PTA meetings." [21]

What Parents Think of Teachers

The general attitude of the people toward the teachers, both lay and religious, is one of respect and admiration. This has been observed particularly in regard to the Sisters who are the recipients of abundant generosity and kindness on the part of parents.[22] The general appreciation for the teachers of St. Luke's as a group of dedicated women does not blind the parents to the fact that as individuals they vary in competence and personality. This discernment on the part of parents is shown in the judgment of 57.3 per cent that the school itself is above average, while a lower percentage (52.3) thought that the teachers were above average. Thirty-five per cent of the parents thought that the teachers are of average competence, while only 1.3 per cent con-

[21] See below, chap. 13, on "Parents and Teachers."
[22] See below, chap. 14, "Financing the School."

sidered some particular teacher below average. The rest did not answer the question.

These percentages, however, refer only to the teachers in general and give no indication of what parents thought of individual teachers. Six of the teachers were considered above average by more than half of the parents of their pupils. The following table indicates their rank in this process of rating by parents.

Name of teacher	Considered above average by this percentage of parents
Sister Roberta	79.7%
Sister Ruth	60.7
Sister Mark	57.1
Sister Cecelia	56.5
Sister Bernadette	56.3
Mrs. Gordon	52.0

When we asked the parents what they liked most about their child's teacher, more than one-quarter of them (26.5%) had no comment to make, and about one-fifth (20.7%) of them said that she had a pleasant personality, is easy to talk to, is friendly and cheerful.[23] More than one-third of the parents (34.6%) praised the teacher's ability in understanding children, in getting them to learn, and in being interested in the individual. Another segment (11.9%) of the parents praised the teachers for maintaining discipline, making the children work, being open-minded and playing no favorites. The remaining parents who commented on the good qualities of the teacher had a scattering of complimentary remarks to make.

Since the parents do not visit the classrooms during school hours at St. Luke's, the opinions they express concerning the teacher are largely impressionistic. This is important, of course, because the relationship between teacher and parent depends mainly on the attitudes they have toward one another. It is probable that the uncomplimentary attitude of the parent toward the teacher is based mostly on hearsay in the sense that the children may complain at home. The complimentary attitudes, on the other hand, appear to come from personal contact. At any rate, neither kind of opinion is really a direct judgment of the teacher's performance in the classroom.

[23] The traits that teachers themselves rate highest in other teachers are the following: (1) honesty and fairness, (2) sincerity, (3) courtesy and politeness, and (4) common sense. See Sister Mary Amatora, "Highs and Lows in the Teacher Personality," *Journal of Educational Research*, vol. 48, no. 9 (May, 1955), pp. 693–698.

The difference between hearsay and personal contact as a source of parental attitude toward teachers is demonstrated when we compare the parent's rating of the teacher with the frequency of contact between parent and teacher. The following table shows that those who have no communication with the teacher do not rate her above average as often as those who have met the teacher several times.

Number of contacts	Percentage of parents rating teacher above average
None	34.5%
One	52.2
Two	55.7
Three	64.3
Four or more	61.9

It appears to be a valid generalization that the parent's opinion of the teacher improves in proportion to the number of personal contacts made between the two. It may be that the less competent teacher is the more reluctant to meet the parent, and thus the parent has the opportunity more often to judge only the better teachers. At any rate, the increase of understanding between home and school seems to demand more frequent personal contact between parent and teacher. If this were merely a desire for popularity on the part of the teacher, it would be relatively unimportant; but in so far as it increases understanding of the child and his problems, the communication between teacher and parent seems important.

If it were possible to offer a composite picture of the teachers at St. Luke's the above statements would form a description of that which almost three-quarters of the parents think of their children's teacher. Certainly, the six most highly rated teachers in the school would fit this description: "a pleasant personality, interested in the children as individuals, able to impart knowledge and to control behavior in an impartial manner." [24] The parents' estimation of the teacher as above average seems to be correlated also with the parents' satisfaction that their child is learning well under the guidance of the teacher. Almost four out of five (79.0%) of all parents think their children are "learning enough," but of those who rate the teacher above average, 83.2 per cent say this, while of those who rate the teacher as average, 75.6 per cent say their child is learning enough. A very small minority, only 2.9

[24] For a series of teaching qualities desired by parents, see John J. Gallen, "A Parent Speaks to the Teacher," *Bulletin* of the National Catholic Educational Association, vol. 46, no. 1 (August, 1949), pp. 451–454.

per cent of all parents, said that incompetent teaching was the reason for the child's failure to learn well. Interestingly enough, this is more than twice as high as the small percentage (1.3%) of parents who rated their child's teacher below average.

When we asked the parents what they liked least about their child's teacher, we found that more than four-fifths of them (82.8%) had no comment to make, or simply declared that the teacher has no bad qualities. Those who did make complaints varied so widely in their comments that it is practically impossible to categorize their responses. The so-called bad qualities of the teacher did not cluster around one or a few particular items. They ranged from the statement that the teacher is too strict to that she is too lenient; one gives too much homework and another not enough; one favors the boys and one favors the girls; one is too old and one is too young. A little more than one-sixth of the parents (17.2%) found some fault with the teacher of their child, but the actual list of complaints is so diverse that no general or principal fault can be isolated. The complaint made most frequently (2.7%) is that the teacher is a "poor disciplinarian."

The teachers were almost unanimous in their belief that the parents are more lenient with the children than the teachers are. The lone exception was the Sister who said that parents are stricter than teachers in the sense that they use corporal punishment on their children, while the teachers never do this. The parents, however, were in no wise unanimous in answering the same question. Less than two out of five (37.7%) agree that they are more lenient than the teachers. The largest number (40.3%) feel that the teacher handles the child in about the same way the parent does. One out of eight (12.7%) actually maintains that the teacher is more lenient than the parent. The remaining 9.3 per cent were unwilling or unable to answer this question.

The problem of evaluating the parents' opinions of the strictness of the teacher lies in two directions: first, whether leniency or strictness is considered a "good quality," and secondly, whether the parents' own handling of the child was strict or lenient. The teachers definitely believe that parents are "too easy" with their children. Most of the parents, when queried on this point, also felt that they themselves were too lenient with their children. They admit that they allow the children to "get away with too much," do not keep hard and fast rules about bed time, home chores and the use of television. Thus, it would seem that those parents (40.3%) who said that the teacher handles the child in about the same way as the parent does, were really suggesting that the teacher is too lenient. On this basis, it could be assumed that those parents (37.7%) who think the teacher is stricter than the parent are trying to say something favorable about the teacher. Since, however, only four parents think that the teacher is "too strict" it cannot be said that "over-discipline" is either a problem at St. Luke's or that the parents in general consider it a fault in the teachers.

Pupils' Opinions of Teachers

There is a free and easy extracurricular friendship existing between most of the pupils and most of the teachers at St. Luke's. The Principal wants to be "everybody's friend." She tells the teachers to handle their own disciplinary problems, and refuses to act as head disciplinarian, lest the children think of her as a "monster." She calls the children "honey," and has built up such a reputation for cheerfulness and kindliness that many pupils in the lower grades look forward to the time when they will be eighth graders. When they are talking among themselves the older children call her "Bobby" in an affectionate way. "Nothing escapes her," says one of the mothers. This nickname pleases her.

Toward the end of our study one of our observers evaluated her as follows: "Sister Roberta is a remarkably accomplished teacher and administrator. She teaches with finesse; she disciplines almost without effort, without 'breaking stride,' and has utter confidence (and near-perfect results) in this. She is loved and respected by her pupils and confreres, and widely admired by the parents. She is patient, friendly and winsome, and seems to be totally dedicated to God and His work. Her personality has an outstanding poise, stability and order, and this order is reflected throughout the school."

The autobiographies of her pupils indicate that these children are discerning beyond the general remarks about this "wonderful teacher" and this "very nice person." They say that she works hard, keeps order and makes the children learn. "You don't get away with anything in this grade," said one boy. "She keeps her eye on everybody all the time, so you can't get into much trouble," said another. One girl remarked that "anybody who doesn't learn from Sister Roberta is either too dumb to try or too dumb to learn." One boy wrote that "she is both tough on us and fair to us, and really makes us study."

Another teacher whose influence is widespread through the school is Sister Cecelia, called "the Maestro" by some of her more sophisticated pupils, but generally known around the school as "Lulu." As one of our observers remarked, "Sister has demonstrated ability and initiative in coaching the choir, giving music lessons and directing the annual operetta. Perhaps it is the leadership and sophistication she brings to these outside activities that so captures the children's affection for her and permits her to have a well-organized class in spite of not being a particularly 'tough' disciplinarian or traditionally demanding teacher. She is not the most skilled teacher in the school, and sometimes the interest of the class lags, yet she 'has something' that inspires the devotion of the children."

One of the girls in the seventh grade paid Sister Cecelia the highest compliment of all, the desire to imitate her. "I enjoyed her most of all the teachers. I would like to be a nun just like her." One boy said that, "although I generally don't like school, I do like her best of all." Others remarked about her great patience in working with the children inside and outside the classroom. As one boy said, "she was the first one who really convinced me that I could get the school work as good as anybody else." Her music pupils and others who have been in the school plays she directed have developed a great respect and admiration for her through these experiences.

Sister Justin, who trains the altar boys and takes care of the sacristy is described by one of her former pupils as "tops." Our observer in her class remarks that "she performs well on all fronts. She is a good teacher, full of interesting techniques to buoy up lagging attention, and the class responds in an interested way. Her class is not a quiet one, but the noise is busy and interested, and seems to reflect the high motivation of the pupils. She shows a concern for extracurricular activities, asking about the latest football or basketball game, or about the hobbies and trips of the pupils. It is her opinion that the textbooks, with their heavily religious stress, are too far removed from the children's daily experiences. She has a high degree of awareness of the larger problems of education, like teacher shortage and overcrowding, and is articulate about them."

The theme of Sister Justin's religious influence is often repeated by the children. It is the altar of God and His service. "She taught me to be an altar boy. One of the biggest thrills of my life was serving my first Mass." As sacristan she allows the girls to work with her around the church. "Sister Justin was very nice. It was great fun because the girls that worked in the sacristy got to put up the crib for Christmas." She is recognized as the "jolly" type of nun. "She always had jokes and stories to tell us at recess, and she'd want to hear the latest jokes we had. She laughed even when they were corny." She appears to be an important factor in preventing religion from becoming a "gloomy" experience among St. Luke's pupils.

The three teachers we have so far discussed are working with the upper grades, with pupils who are more able to express their views than are the younger children. While space does not permit a similar analysis of all fourteen teachers in the school, it may broaden the picture of the faculty somewhat if we look briefly at some of the teachers in the lower grades. Remarks about these teachers are also made by older children in their autobiographies, but we have also had some forthright and revealing interviews with the youngest children, even with first graders.

The children in the first grade are very fond of Sister Bernadette, irreverently called "Bernie" by some of the fourth graders, even though none of these has had her as a teacher. The integrity of her teaching mannerisms sets her apart. She has the expected traits of a first-grade teacher: patience, motherliness and simple kindness, but "beyond this," writes our observer, "is her childlike approach to teaching. One of the things that illustrates this is the way she moralizes. There is no jarring transition when she moves from the subject matter to make a moral application. These transitions are quite plausible and natural. In fact, there never really seems to be any departure from religion. She is the most expert of all the faculty in fusing religion and morality with the subject matter at hand."

"The kids didn't like her at first," said one little boy in May, "but now they want to have her next year too." One girl summed up her appreciation of Sister Bernadette with the words, "she's funny." This remark points at the artful touch Sister has in exacting correct conduct. When she reprimands the children it is often in a facetious way, for example, a noisy class is quieted by her question: "What am I allergic to?" the loud, chorused response being, "Noise!" The child who forgets to write his name at the head of the assignment is called "Mr. Nobody," to the delight of all the children.

Sister Bernadette controls and promotes the wealth of spontaneity that appears to be characteristic of these first-grade children by permitting them to tell stories, sing songs, or do dances in solo fashion before the whole class. She gives the children a fair amount of decision-making freedom for this age level. Occasionally, the children are allowed the opportunity to decide whether they want to stay in or go out for recess, whether there shall be a singing or story-telling session, and what songs or stories are to be enjoyed. Her virtuosity in getting results from the children sometimes amazes the parents. One child came home and sang Brahm's *Lullaby* for her mother; another little boy recited the whole *Memorare* for his parents.

One of the Sisters in the second grade (who shall be nameless here) is well-remembered by her former pupils and tends to have contact with the parents of those who receive the first Communion. One boy remembered her as "the only teacher I didn't like," but gave no reason for his dislike. A girl claimed that she "got headaches because Sister shouted so much at us," and through the intervention of her mother was transferred to the other second-grade class. Nevertheless, there are many children who speak of her with great fondness as the one who led them closer to God and also the one who was "so much fun at recess and on the playground." Most of the children like her because she is a competent art instructor and gives them the opportunity to express their own imagination in art work.

Sister's cheerfulness appears to be reserved for contacts outside the classroom. "Her most noticeable characteristic is that she sometimes raises her voice loudly and is given to the use of sarcasm. In general, she is on the stern side and sometimes corrects the children who answer erroneously by reprimanding them. She seems to be somewhat moody. One day she is in the best of spirits, handling her class with a fine touch; another day she seems to be almost disorganized, reprimanding severely such things as coughing. Part of her problem is the size of her class—over fifty pupils. Often the classroom pace drags and the children are restless."

The parents seem to delight in the "stories" the children bring home about this Sister. A report from a soiree interview with parents says, "she is less reserved, and in this sense different from the other Sisters. She is high strung and the children are often pretty tense when they come home from school. She does much better in October than in April and seems to wear down during the course of the year." One of her reputed remarks in the classroom had become almost legendary among the parents. She is supposed to have told the children that "you must listen to what I tell you, and I want you to know that I'm not afraid of any of your parents."

There are two lay teachers in the third grade, and similar critical remarks are made about one of them. "Her teaching is without inspiration—slow, plodding and uninteresting. She is stern, almost regimenting, and quick to issue large threats. Yet she does not get good order and discipline from her pupils. Her scoldings are given in a personal way, as though the child had insulted her. This sometimes borders on the theatrical." This teacher's attempts at humor are sometimes cynical, for example, after the children marked their own papers for a test she asked, "How many got a hundred in spelling?" and the hands shot up all over the room. Then she said, "O. K. Now, how many changed their papers to get a hundred in spelling?"

The children do not appear to be negatively affected by such practices. "We don't take her too seriously," said one precocious third grader. "She's got bats," said another. This lay woman is an interesting contrast to most of the nuns in two directions. She introduces daily life experience into the classroom, giving meaning and concreteness to the lessons. She can do this in a somewhat more realistic way that appears to be appreciated by the children. On the other hand is her somewhat artificial injection of piety and moralizing into the subject matter. For example, from the spelling word, "careless," there issued a ten-minute sermon on the importance of obeying parents, brushing teeth, going to bed on time, and so forth. A misbehaving child is often reprimanded for "hurting Jesus." On one occasion when a bottle of liquid lip rouge was found in the room she threatened to keep the whole class in until she found out who committed this "sin," and the even "worse sin" of not admitting guilt.

The Lay Teachers

In discussing the problem of overcrowding in the parochial school Sister Roberta remarked that "the lay teachers are with us to stay. I would suggest that each school have at least one lay teacher for every five Sisters." [25] Sister Justin said that "we ought to accept lay teachers and make them feel that they belong. The PTA should pay special attention to lay teachers and invite them frequently to social activities." None of the Sisters expressed reluctance to accept lay teachers at St. Luke's; and the three lay teachers are enthusiastic about the cooperation and cordial relations existing between them and the nuns.

According to the estimation of all the teachers, St. Luke's school is over-crowded to the extent of an excess of 127 pupils. If an attempt were made to redistribute these children so that each teacher would have a more or less "normal" teaching load, the school would need at least three more teachers. Since religious Sisters are not available to fill these posts, the school would necessarily have to hire more lay teachers. Mrs. Gordon feels that parishioners who have had some experience in teaching should look upon this as an apostolic opportunity. But it is difficult to attract lay teachers to parochial schools; the salary is usually lower than that in the public school; there are no tenure, promotion or pension plans.[26] Many parishes are financially unable to

[25] The proportion is actually four to one (81.2% religious, 18.8% lay) in the fifteen parochial elementary schools of the city where St. Luke's is located. According to the 1956–57 statistics in Kenedy's *Catholic Directory*, 75.3 per cent of elementary teachers in Catholic schools are Sisters, while the remaining 24.7 per cent are lay persons. It is seven to one in the report by Sister Noel Marie, "Statistics of Religious Educators," *The Catholic Educator*, vol. 27, no. 5 (January, 1957), pp. 291–292 and 344.

[26] See Harold Gluck, "Lay Teacher Morale in Catholic Schools," *Catholic Educational Review*, vol. 52, no. 9 (November, 1954), pp. 537–541, where a sum-

procure such teachers, and some pastors are reluctant to hire them.

The parents have a peculiarly ambivalent attitude toward the three lay teachers at St. Luke's. When asked about the particular teacher who has their child in class they respond in about the same way they do when asked about a religious teacher. They find mainly good qualities and few faults in her. But when they are asked about lay teachers in general some seem to think that they are a "necessary evil," and that "if you don't have Sisters for the children you might as well send them to the public school." [27] Since the Principal knows these attitudes of parents she arranged that there could be no choice of teachers in the third grade. All the children must have this same experience at the same time. Her anticipation of parents' complaints was, however, unfounded in the sixth grade, where no parents asked that their child be transferred from the lay teacher's class to the Sister's class.

One of the girls in the seventh grade was probably reflecting the remarks of her parents when she wrote, "I appreciate the meaning of having Sisters instead of teachers. Sisters to me are people who have been given a very wonderful gift and have used their talents to the utmost that the good Lord gave them. Lay teachers have nothing to give up but time, and that isn't very valuable considering it is their jobs and not their lives. I do in all circumstances respect both for they have to contend with *us*, and that's not as easy as it sounds, for we can be, and sometimes are, very difficult."

This kind of statement indicates that the lay teacher is at a disadvantage in the parochial school competing for the respect and devotion of the children. On the other hand, as one of the fathers pointed out, "it is an advantage to be judged only on your merits as a teacher. If the children like a religious teacher it may be because she is an inspiring nun. But when they like Mrs. Gordon, it's because she is a good teacher." Many of the girls in the class consider Mrs. Gordon

---

mary of recommendations is offered. See a list of complaints in Eileen Z. Silbermann, "Lay Teachers Speak Their Mind," *The Catholic Educator*, vol. 25, no. 6 (February, 1955), pp. 363–364; also John F. Reilly, "What About the Lay Teacher?" *The Catholic Educator*, vol. 24, no. 10 (June, 1954), pp. 541–542 and 555.

[27] A study of six parochial schools in Cleveland showed that attitudes toward lay teachers were favorable; only three per cent agreed with the statement that "lay teachers are a necessary evil." See Mary Delrey, "Attitude of Parents Toward Lay Teachers," *Catholic Educational Review*, vol. 54, no. 8 (October, 1956), pp. 459–466. See also, Carl J. Ryan, "The Lay Teacher in the Catholic School," *The Homiletic and Pastoral Review*, vol. 48, no. 8 (May, 1948), pp. 575–581, who argues that on some grounds lay teachers are even better than Sisters.

the "nicest and most friendly teacher." The boys like her, but for other reasons. "She doesn't give us long homework assignments; she has nice long study periods; and she doesn't hand out too many tasks."

From the point of view of formal schooling the three lay teachers are among the best educated women on St. Luke's faculty. Only three of the Sisters have had more years of professional teaching experience than Mrs. Gerald. The younger nuns on the faculty are still pursuing the Bachelor's degree by taking university extension courses and by attending summer school every year. It is an index of the pressure placed on religious superiors, and perhaps also of the need for lay teachers, that only the older Sisters at St. Luke's have a college education.[28] Most of the parents seem to be unaware of this fact. They tend to look upon the nun as the better type of teacher mainly because she is a nun; and who can say that they are completely in error? Teaching in an elementary school is probably more a matter of skill than of scholarship, and teaching in a parochial school seems to require a certain kind of religious skill as well.

Since there are no "extra" nuns upon whom the Principal can call, the problem of substitute teachers is solved by lay women of the parish. When we asked Sister Roberta about this problem at the beginning of the year, she jokingly replied that "the teachers here get sick only on Saturdays and Sundays." Then she showed us a list of six parishioners, all former teachers, who volunteered to "come in for a day or two when needed." Mrs. McWellan substituted ten days for Mrs. Gerald in the spring, and said she did not "feel complimented" when the children applauded the announcement of their regular teacher's impending return. Sister Dominic continued teaching for several days even though feeling badly. When she discovered she had the measles, she reassured herself with the knowledge that all the children in her class had them, and stayed on in the classroom. Sister Roberta missed one day of class through illness, and her eighth graders had to be dismissed when a substitute could not be found.[29] During the last few days of school, after graduation, Roberta Suhor took over Sister Bernadette's first grade. By and large, however, the teachers of St.

[28] A study of elementary teachers, using the Minnesota Teacher Attitude Inventory, showed that teachers who are university graduates maintain a more "harmonious relationship with children" than do the graduates of either Teachers' Colleges or Liberal Arts Colleges. See Nolan C. Kearney and Patrick D. Rocchio, "The Effect of Teacher Education on the Teacher's Attitude," *Journal of Educational Research,* vol. 49, no. 9 (May, 1956), pp. 703–708.

[29] The boys in her class immediately bought her a box of candy and a "get well" card. The girls then imitated them by sending Sister a bouquet of flowers.

Luke's proved themselves to be very durable and healthy persons during the whole year.

Generalizations

1. As in all elementary schools, both public and parochial, the teachers of St. Luke's show a wide range of experience. There are veterans, and there are novices—and those in between. All except two of the teachers, one Sister and one lay woman, have taught at other elementary schools. There is a certain amount of turnover since the school has expanded by about one-third during the last four years.

2. Each member of the teaching staff must be able to teach all of the subjects to her class. This is common practice in the lower elementary grades, but it is continued at St. Luke's up to and including the eighth grade. There is no departmentalization according to subject matter. Some of the teachers, however, may be called specialists in a relative sense, like those who exercise their competence in teaching music, Latin and the liturgy, Communion preparation, and art work. From their past record it is evident too that teachers may specialize at a certain grade level and teach only the second grade or the fifth grade.

3. Certain extracurricular tasks are shared in general by the teachers, like attending Mass with the children, supervising recess and noon period. The supervision of the playground and the cafeteria is rotated among the teachers, and they are assisted in this by the honor patrol girls of the eighth grade. The Sisters also share the household tasks of the convent. Some extra duties are performed by only one individual Sister, like those of the Principal, the two music teachers, the sacristan and her assistant.

4. Most of the teachers at St. Luke's seem to believe that the school is a normal elementary school, that is just about as good as the other schools at which they had previously taught. For the most they consider the pupils of average mental ability, normal in their study habits and conduct. It must be noted that the norm they are using here is their own knowledge and experience of children in parochial schools, and they were not making any comparisons with the pupils of either public or private schools.

5. According to most of the teachers the classrooms of St. Luke's school are overcrowded. They differ on their estimation of an ideal number of pupils, from thirty to forty-five per teacher, but the average suggestion is thirty-six pupils per teacher. Actually the present pupil-teacher ratio is 45.1 per teacher, which is an average of 9.1 pupils higher than the stated ideal. But this problem of crowding fluctuates from classroom to classroom. Some of the classes actually have less than the

norm set by the teacher, but nine classrooms are overcrowded, having from nine to twenty-two pupils more than the teacher thinks she can handle.

6. The teachers are generally in favor of the children's extracurricular activities, being unanimously in favor of the organized athletic teams competing with other schools. But none of them is in favor of adding further activities for the children. While they do not believe that the children are spoiled, as far as the school has control over these activities, they think that the parents tend to spoil the children. To their mind, the parents are much more lenient than the teachers are. Most of the parents agree with this.

7. The teachers, as a group, are popular with the parents of their pupils. The parents rate them for "good qualities" in the following order: teaching competence, pleasant personality, and ability to maintain order. Variations in ability are noted, not only from the opinions of parents, but also from daily observation of the teacher in the classroom. Six of St. Luke's teachers are rated above average by more than half of their pupils' parents. The parents in general do not believe that the teachers are "over-strict." Most of them have no complaints to make, and the complaints that are made do not cluster around one or a few items.

8. Cordial, easy and respectful relations exist between most of the pupils and most of the teachers. The better-known teachers in the school tend to have the highest rating and the most friends among the pupils. This popularity cross-cuts classroom lines, particularly in the case of the Principal, the sacristan and the music teachers. These teachers have broader contacts than the others with both pupils and parents; and there appears to be a correlation between the teacher's popularity and the number and frequency of the contacts she has. The better-known teachers are the better-liked teachers.

9. The three lay teachers at St. Luke's feel at home in the school. They have cordial reciprocal relations with the religious teachers. They appear to be able to teach the religion classes as competently as most of the nuns. Parents in general hold the traditional view that "it would be better if we could have nuns," when they speak of lay teachers as a category. But when they speak of these three lay teachers as individuals who have the care of their children, they tend to rate them highly on the basis of their teaching competence.

Chapter

TWELVE

WHAT PARENTS WANT IN EDUCATION

IT IS ONE of the major theses of Catholic educators that the parochial elementary school is the joint enterprise of parents, teachers and priests, and that the education given the child at this age level is the product of the combined efforts of home, school, and church. In other parts of this book we have discussed the extent and kind of participation given by the priests and parents in St. Luke's parochial school. It extends from catechism teaching by the priests to the equipment of athletic teams by the parents. The question dealt with in the present chapter concerns the parents' ideas about elementary education. Why do they send their child to this particular school? What do they like or dislike about the way the school operates?

The opinion of parents is crucial in the ultimate objectives rather than in the methods and techniques of the schools. A society gets the kind of schools it deserves, and the society is made up mainly of "lay" people, as contrasted to professional educators. Since the whole educational institution is a basic segment of the total culture, it is bound to be influenced by, and to influence, the kind of culture which is developing in America.[1] In a less direct sense this is true of Catholic elementary schools, where the curriculum—if not the teaching methods—tends to be more stable and traditional than it is in the public schools. Nevertheless, just as the "lay public" has an influence on the public school educators, so also—in a mediate and indirect way—do the lay parishioners, the parents, have an influence on the parochial school.[2]

[1] The present study is evidence of the fact that this is not a mutually equal influence. For a discussion of the influence of the general culture upon the school, see William H. Whyte, *The Organization Man* (New York: Simon and Schuster, 1956), chap. 28, "The Organization Children"; also David Riesman, *The Lonely Crowd* (New York: Doubleday, 1953), pp. 54–85.

[2] See below, chaps. 13 and 17. See also James R. Curtin, *Attitudes of Parents Toward Catholic Education* (Washington: Catholic University Press, 1954), pp. 34–35.

An eminent Catholic educator has pointed out some difficulties in this regard. "Many an educator finds it difficult to embrace a policy of community participation in the school. He says 'parents today simply are not interested in what we are trying to do.' The unfortunate fact is that many school administrators today are reaping the sour fruit of an early policy which reflected the attitude, 'stick to your knitting and leave the schools alone.'"[3] Another educator, a public school administrator, remarks that even now the general citizenry helps to shape the aims and objectives of education, while the experts and professionals decide upon the means for achieving them. "Lay citizens are going to have more to say about what we teach and how we teach in the future than they have ever had in the past."[4]

The existence and maintenance of the parochial school depend upon the attitudes of cooperation by the parents in a more subtle way than may be shown in the moral obligation to give their children a Catholic education. Catholic parents can, and do, give, withhold, or vary their financial contributions that support the school.[5] They can, and do, for reasons of teacher incompetence, overcrowding and other pedagogical defects—quite aside from the question of religious instruction—choose to send their children to some school other than the local parochial school. If the parents of public school children do not like the school, they have no recourse except to try to change the policies of the school. Catholic parents have the alternative of sending their children to public schools. Although Catholics have a moral obligation to use the Catholic schools, yet these schools depend on the good will of these parents.[6]

Why This School?

It appears from our study that most parents do not really know why they are sending their children to school. They realize, of course, that it is "the thing to do," that "everybody has to go to school." Thus, there

[3] Urban H. Fleege, "Participation, the Key to Good School-Community Relations," *The Catholic Educator,* vol. 24, no. 4 (December, 1953), pp. 242–245.

[4] Paul J. Misner, "Citizens and Teachers Plan the Curriculum," *National Parent Teacher,* vol. 50, no. 9 (May, 1956), pp. 26–27. For a widely cited "internal controversy" on the parochial school, see Pat Somers Cronin, "A Mother Complains," and Sister Mary Ransom, "A Nun Replies," *America,* vol. 99, no. 15 (July 12, 1958), pp. 410–412, and the variety of opinions later expressed in *America,* vol. 99, no. 19 (August 9, 1958), pp. 491–494.

[5] See below, chap. 14, "Financing the School."

[6] Carl J. Ryan, Superintendent of parochial schools in the Cincinnati diocese. "Parochial Schools Rest on Good Will," *The Catholic Educator,* vol. 26, no. 8 (April, 1956), pp. 493–494.

is the usual, but often unrecognized social pressure in the community, as well as the state law that makes education compulsory for children up to a certain age. One parent remarked, that "nowadays you can't get along without education." Another said that "if you want to get anywhere in life today, you have to have an education." This latter remark referred to "more education" in the sense of college studies.

We asked the parents more specifically "why did you send your child to this school rather than any other?" For Catholic parents, there was a choice between the parochial school of St. Luke's parish and one of the three public schools existing closest to their homes.[7] The following table shows the distribution of reasons given by Catholic parents for sending their children to St. Luke's parochial school.

Want Catholic education for child	59.4%
Members of this parish	22.3
Obligation to educate child as Catholic	8.8
Sisters are better teachers	4.8
Better discipline	2.4
Other reasons	2.3

It is obvious from these answers given by Catholic parents that training in religion is uppermost in their minds as a reason for sending their children to St. Luke's school. They felt that this was expected of them as Catholics and as parishioners, and most of them reacted to our question as though they had never even thought of anything except the parochial school for their children. They appeared to be quite satisfied with their choice, as is seen in the table below, comparing the parents in the rating of the parochial and the public school.

	St. Luke's School	Public School
Above average	57.3%	52.1%
Average	37.9	41.2
Below average	2.1	3.4
No answer	2.7	3.3

The parents' rating of the school indicates that the great majority were satisfied with the way their children were receiving elementary education. Parents of parochial school children seem more satisfied than parents of public school children. This differential was shown also when

[7] Most of the non-Catholic children living in St. Luke's parochial territory attended the two public schools located a few blocks in either direction, east and west, of St. Luke's school. A third public school, within the southern boundaries of the parish, drew the rest.

we asked the parents what educational improvements they would suggest, and whether they had any complaints to make about the school itself. Here again large numbers of parents in both instances had no suggestions to make (41.9% parochial and 40.3% public). For the most part, their suggestions for improvement had to do with the physical conditions, the over-crowding, the use of cafeteria, gymnasium and playground.

When we asked the parents of public school children why they sent their child to this school their principal reason was that the parochial school was too far from home, "the child could walk to the public school from home," but would have to use means of transportation to reach St. Luke's.[8] Some said that the child did not want to change once he had made friends in the kindergarten, first and second grades. Occasionally a parent had a relative or friend teaching in the near-by school and felt that the child would thus get good care and supervision. The statement about proximity was given by 70.6 per cent of these Catholic parents of public school children, and it was used about as frequently for pupils from the fifth to the eighth grade as it was for the younger children.

There were other reasons given for sending the Catholic child to the public school. In 9.2 per cent of the interviews the parents said that the public school is less crowded. In 5.9 per cent of the interviews the non-Catholic parent, usually the father, thought that public school education is better than parochial because "there is less work and less religion," and because he or she resented the nuns and priests. In some instances (3.4%) the child had entered the kindergarten at the mid-term in January and had continued through the grades under this arrangement. Transferring to St. Luke's would have meant the loss of a semester.

In the remaining interviews (10.9%) there were many scattered reasons given: there is more social life in the public school; it costs less to send the child there; it is more lenient; classes in speech correction are given; the physical education program is better, and so forth. These and many other statements were made, but they are more or less isolated reasons, given by no more than two interviewees.

The transfer of children from one elementary school to another provides only a partial hint concerning the reasons why parents chose one

[8] We did not ask the question, "Why didn't you send your child to St. Luke's school?" Many of the parents, however, appeared to be on the defensive and to think that this was our implication. See Gerald Schnepp, *Leakage from a Catholic Parish* (Washington: Catholic University Press, 1942), pp. 173–189, for ten reasons why Catholics send their children to public schools.

school over another. Some of these transfers are due simply to family mobility, which is a typical phenomenon of urban living, and here again proximity of the school to the home plays an important part.[9] From the evidence we could gather, however, there seems to be more shifting of Catholic pupils from the public school to the parochial school than vice versa. Almost three out of ten (29.7%) of the 545 pupils in the grades from second to eighth at St. Luke's school had previously attended one or more other elementary schools. The transfer from a public school was made by 13.6 per cent of them, and from another Catholic school by 16.1 per cent. Among the Catholic children in the same grades of the public school we found that 32.4 per cent had changed schools one or more times. The transfer from another public school was made by 20.5 per cent of them, while only 11.9 per cent of them had switched from a parochial school to the public school.

There was thus a total of 211 Catholic children in both schools whose parents had transferred them from other schools. In these cases we asked the parent to make a comparison between the present and the previous school the child attended. The question was, "is your child's present school better than, as good as, or not so good as, the school he previously attended?" The following table shows the distribution of answers and refers again only to children from the second to the eighth grades.

	School the child now attends is:				
	Better	Same	Worse	No opinion	(Total children)
Child now attends St. Luke's School	52.5%	32.7%	5.5%	9.3%	(162)
Child now attends public school	44.9	24.5	16.3	14.3	(49)

This comparison adds confirmation to the generalization that parochial school parents are more satisfied than are the parents of the public school children. Only a small percentage (5.5%) thought that St. Luke's is not so good as the school their child previously attended, while almost one-sixth (16.3%) of the public school parents think their present school is worse than the previous one. We checked further to note whether the school from which the child transferred was a Catholic or public school. In this way, although the categories become

[9] For data in the mobility of St. Luke's pupils, see above chap. 2, "The First Ten Years."

quite small, we have an indication of the parents' own comparative opinion of the two kinds of schools. The following table shows that St. Luke's parents have a proportionately higher regard for parochial than for public schools.

Child now in St. Luke's transfer from:	*St. Luke's School is:*				
	Better	Same	Worse	No opinion	(Total children)
Another parochial school	40.9%	43.2%	4.5%	11.4%	(88)
A public school	66.2	20.3	6.7	6.8	(74)

Those who said that St. Luke's is worse than the parochial school the child previously attended were making the comparison to three parochial schools in the same city where St. Luke's exists. In their opinion, at least, there were three other parishes in the same city that are more successful in providing elementary education for their children than is St. Luke's. Four-fifths of the respondents, however, thought that the other parochial schools are about the same, or not so good as, St. Luke's. Those who had transferred their child from a public school were quite definite in their opinion, two-thirds of them maintaining that St. Luke's is better than, and one-fifth saying it is as good as the previous public school.[10]

Child now in public school, transfer from:	*Public school is:*				
	Better	Same	Worse	No opinion	(Total children)
A parochial school	50.0%	33.3%	16.7%	0.0%	(18)
Another public school	41.9	19.4	16.1	22.6	(31)

Here, in the answers of parents of public school children we find a relatively high percentage of dissatisfaction with the public school, almost one-sixth of the parents in both categories saying that the present school is worse than the previous one. Nevertheless, half of the parents thought that the present public school is better than the previous parochial school. Most of these parents had previously sent

[10] See above, chap. 11, "The Teachers of St. Luke's," for the opinions of both parents and pupils.

their children to St. Luke's school and to that extent their opinions are a direct comparison between St. Luke's and the public school.

Attitudes on Discipline

Do the parents want a strict school or a lenient school for their children? What type of punishment do they approve for their children? Most parents realize that a certain amount of disciplinary action must be taken by the teachers to maintain order in the classroom. Some of these parents think that the teacher is stricter than they, the parents, in the handling of the child. Generally speaking, more of the public school than the Catholic school parents believed that the teacher is more lenient than the parent. The following table shows the variations in the opinions of parents on this matter.

Parents believe teacher is:	St. Luke's School	Public School
stricter	37.7%	29.4%
about the same	40.3	32.7
more lenient	12.7	27.7
no answer	9.3	10.2

It is difficult to conclude from these opinions whether the parents approve strictness or leniency in the school handling of their children. The impression is, however, that the parents of St. Luke's children tend to visualize the school situation in terms of strictness rather than of leniency. Many of the parents of public school pupils, on the other hand, tend to think of the public school in terms of leniency. In the mind of parents, the public school teachers appear generally more lenient than the parochial school teachers. Many of the parents evidenced great sympathy for the teachers in this regard. They felt that the very nature of the school situation, since the teacher has to handle large numbers of children, makes it necessary for her to be more strict than the parent. "I don't see how she can do it," said one mother, "I have trouble trying to keep just three children in line."

What the parents want in the matter of school discipline can be deduced more clearly from the statements they made concerning the kinds of punishment they approved for the school room. We asked them the open-end question, "In general what do you consider the most effective kind of punishment for children when they get out of hand in school?" The following table shows the variation in their answers, and also gives the comparison between the two types of schools.

Type of punishment suggested by parents:	St. Luke's	Public School
Detention at recess or after school	35.0%	32.8%
Written tasks	23.6	10.1
Corporal punishment	8.2	16.0
Verbal reprimand	4.0	5.9
Stand in hall, corner, in front of room	3.7	6.7
Inform parents	3.7	9.3
Other suggestions	3.2	1.5
No suggestions	18.6	17.7

It appears that parents of children in both types of schools are in favor of depriving the pupils of recreation when they have misbehaved. This means depriving the child of privileges that he would enjoy, and this is probably the type of punishment that the parents themselves mete out most at home. The assignment of written tasks to the offending child is favored much more by the parents of St. Luke's children, while the administering of corporal punishment is more favored by the parents of public school children.[11] This difference is probably related to the fact that the parents of the public school children tend to think that the public school "could use a little more strictness," while the parents of St. Luke's children tend to see their school as already stricter than the home.

The fact is that the public school teachers "shake up" and "paddle" their pupils on occasion, a practice which never occurs and is not tolerated at St. Luke's. The administration of corporal punishment in the public school is attested to by both the teachers and the parents of the children in these schools. It has been witnessed by our own observers and by both present and former pupils in these schools. Pupils of St. Luke's who formerly attended public school have reminisced in their autobiographies how "rough" one or two of their former teachers were.[12] There are no city or state regulations prohibiting

[11] See Marian Kennedy *et al.*, "Should the Rod be Spared?", *National Parent Teacher*, vol. 51, no. 5 (January, 1957), pp. 16–18, where four people, a mother, teacher, school superintendent and guidance counsellor, give their views on corporal punishment in the schools. Two of them are in favor of it, at least in extreme cases.

[12] In the Taft public school, 44.7 per cent of the boys, and 31.5 per cent of the girls, in the three upper grades felt that some of the teachers "have it in for" pupils. The comparative figures for St. Luke's were 19.0 per cent and 24.2 per cent.

the corporal punishment of school children. Usually the teacher inflicts it only in the presence of the Principal or of some other teacher.[13]

Parents and Homework

Do parents want their children to study at home, whether or not any formal homework is assigned by the teachers? Almost all parents agreed that children ought to do some studying outside of school,[14] but they pointed out also that there are now study periods in the school itself and that in some instances "the teacher does not believe in giving homework." Mrs. Edwards, in the third grade, said she does not like to give homework "because the parents do it for their children," and the Principal, Sister Roberta, like several public school teachers, flatly declared, "I do not believe in home study."

The fact is, however, that the great majority of children in both schools actually do some studying at home, but there is a difference in that only 4.8 per cent of St. Luke's pupils, as compared to 20.2 per cent of the public school children, do no homework at all. This difference in numbers helps to explain also the average amount of time given to homework by the children of each school, about four hours per week for St. Luke's children and a little less than three hours per week by the public school children. The following table shows the dis-

Grade	Average hours and minutes per week of homework done by: St. Luke's	Public School
Eighth	4:30	4:30
Seventh	5:24	4:42
Sixth	4:11	2:12
Fifth	3:54	3:36
Fourth	3:45	3:30
Third	3:30	3:06
Second	3:36	1:30
First	2:48	1:24
School Average	4:02	2:57

[13] During the course of our study a public school teacher in another part of the state made newspaper headlines by paddling eleven pupils in his sixth grade without the presence of an adult witness. This brought no protest from the parents of the children involved, and was publicly approved by several of them. For the disciplinary measures in use at St. Luke's, see above, chap. 6, "Social Conformity and Conduct."

[14] See V. M. Schumann, "Is Homework on the Decline?" *Catholic Educational Review,* vol. 51, no. 2 (February, 1953), pp. 88–98, who gives the replies of seventy-six diocesan superintendents of schools concerning the amount of homework given in elementary schools.

tribution, in hours and minutes, of the homework done by each grade during the course of the week.

Whether this is too much or too little homework, is a question that was not settled by the parents. St. Luke's children in the upper grades who wrote autobiographies for us, occasionally commented on a teacher, past or present, who "gave too much homework." This is not, however, a constant or general complaint by the pupils. In our interviews with former St. Luke's pupils, now in high school, the opposite complaint was made, particularly about Sister Roberta. They said it was a real problem to get used to the heavy homework of high school after having had so few home assignments during their last year at St. Luke's.[15] It must be remembered that the above table represents the amount of studying the child does at home every week, what he does "on his own" as well as for school assignments.

The attitudes of parents toward their children's schooling can be seen from the fact that the majority help their children in their home study.[16] The parents help 80.7 per cent of St. Luke's children, as compared to 67.2 per cent of the public school children. The instructions of the superintendent of parochial schools, as printed on the report cards, note that any homework assigned by the teachers (in grades four to eight) "will require no help from those at home." Nevertheless, the parents do help the children in their home study, and the extent of this assistance, as well as its source, is shown in the following table.

Who helps child with homework	St. Luke's	Public School
No one	16.4%	31.9%
Both parents	40.6	31.9
Mother	30.0	27.7
Father	10.1	7.6
Others (older siblings, grandparents)	2.9	0.9

Helping with home study is one of the few direct ways in which a parent can enter the school experiences of his child, and it appears that most parents are happy to enact the combined role of teacher-

[15] Brother Basil, "Homework in the Elementary School," *The Catholic School Journal*, vol. 52, no. 4 (April, 1952), pp. 131 and 62A, says that homework is necessary to develop various skills and virtues in the child, that teachers should give it intelligently and that parents should encourage it.

[16] Harold G. Shane, "Do Parents Teach the Three R's?" *National Parent Teacher*, vol. 51, no. 2 (October, 1956), pp. 4–6, gives hints on how to educate the child, and warns against the parents either doing the assignment or confusing the child.

parent when it is possible.[17] The parents of St. Luke's children are more concerned about helping with homework than are the parents of the public school children. This may be partly due to the fact that St. Luke's children, not having so much free, supervised study time during the school day, have to do more home study than the public school pupils. Whether this indicates also more ambition and interest and higher motives on the part of the parochial school children, cannot be determined here.

In an effort to discover what was of greatest interest to parents in their children's studies, we asked them in what subjects they helped their children most. The following table does not answer this question completely, because we may assume that regardless of the parents' interest, the child was helped most in those subjects in which he had the greatest difficulty and the most homework. At any rate, it appears that arithmetic requires and receives the most attention from parents and that the father helps in this subject more than in others.[18] It is likely also that the element of competition enters here. Homework is often done, and helped by parents, so that the child can "do well" in school. When a report card shows low marks, the parent often assumes that the child can really earn better grades and decides that "something must be done about it." The result is supervision of homework and new rules about "you can't look at TV till your homework is done."

Subjects in which parents give help for homework	St. Luke's	Public School
No subject	16.9%	31.9%
All subjects	9.0	2.5
Arithmetic	29.7	31.1
Spelling	14.6	13.5
Reading	14.6	11.8
English	4.5	1.7
History	4.0	2.5
Other subjects [19]	6.7	5.0

[17] Estelle R. Roddy, "Whose Homework Is It Anyway?" *Parents' Magazine*, vol. 30, no. 1 (January, 1955), pp. 40–41 and 68, implies that the parent should help the child but not do the homework, that is, leave the actual teaching to the teacher.

[18] Arithmetic is also the favorite subject of the children in both public and parochial school. See below, chap. 17.

[19] These "other subjects" were mainly geography and writing. Only 2.4 per cent of the parents of St. Luke's children said that they helped their child with the study of religion at home, and these were parents of children in the second

Outside Activities

Various extracurricular activities are now considered almost an integral part of the whole process of elementary schooling. Some educational authorities and writers have come to the point of calling these activities "co-curricular," on the assumption that teaching and learning occur in them as well as in the classroom subjects. The public school has more, and a greater variety, of these outside activities than does St. Luke's. In an effort to find out what the parents thought about these programs, we asked "what further non-academic (or 'outside') activities would you suggest that the school provide for your child?" The parents of public school children seemed to be more satisfied in this regard than were the parents of St. Luke's children; 84.9 per cent of the former, and 67.1 per cent of the latter, felt that enough was already being done along this line. In fact, some of the parents remarked that "children nowadays get too much."

It is difficult to make a comparison between the parents of the two types of school on their attitudes toward outside activities. If the parents at St. Luke's want something more for their children they have to organize and work to raise the money for it. The public school system simply dips further into public funds, contributed partly by the taxes of Catholic parents, and thus finances the extracurricular programs. The parochial school has to "go to the people," that is, to the parents and parishioners themselves, for the extra funds to provide these programs. It must also derive the necessary personnel from among volunteers of the parish, instead of hiring professionals or more teachers. Thus the realistic attitudes of Catholic parents are colored by the fact that they themselves supply both the money and the talent to run these extracurricular activities.

Both types of parents are overwhelmingly in favor of the organized teams that compete with teams of other schools, 94.2 per cent of St. Luke's parents, and 95.8 per cent of public school parents, favoring this form of activity. Because there would be no athletic program at St. Luke's unless there were parental support of it, the actual participation of these parents is greater than that of the parents of the public school children—for whom the public school, as a matter of course, supplies all of the financial support and staff for athletics. From this point of view it appears that parochial school parents have a more intense interest in sports for their children.[20] They unquestionably put

---

grade preparing for the reception of first Holy Communion; although those who helped with "all subjects" helped also with religion.

[20] See above, chap. 8, on "Organized Sports."

a great deal more effort into providing it for them. At St. Luke's however, 15.9 per cent of the parents felt that the athletic program and physical education could be improved.

Besides the athletic program, all other extracurricular activities at St. Luke's school are also sponsored, organized, financed and maintained by the parents and parishioners themselves. This includes the parties and picnics provided by the PTA, the whole Scouting program run by an adult committee, and the very successful program of the Blue Birds and Camp Fire Girls, managed by the mothers. "Field trips" for the children, to the meager extent that they exist at St. Luke's, are also conducted under the initiative of the parents themselves. The fact that all of these activities find widespread favor among the parents of St. Luke's, does not imply that their personal and financial support is as widespread. Nevertheless, their existence is proof that the parents want this kind of program, for without the parents' support of them they would not exist at the school.

We may assume from all that has been said above that the parents in general of St. Luke's school are satisfied with the elementary training their children are receiving. Since learning is the primary objective of any school we asked the parents the question, "do you think your child is learning as much as he should in school? If not, what is the reason?" Here again we found that satisfaction of the Catholic school parents is somewhat higher than that of the public school parents. The following table shows the comparison of the answers to this question.

	St. Luke's	Public School
Child learns enough	79.1%	71.4%
Child does not learn enough	20.4	26.9
No opinion	0.5	1.7

When we asked for the reason for the child's failure to learn sufficient in school, we found that most of the parents put the fault on the child for being lazy, or distracted or slow to learn. Only a few of them thought it was because the teachers were incompetent or the school inferior. The distribution of this "blame" shows an interesting contrast in the parents of the two types of school. The parents of St. Luke's children tend to place the blame on the child much more than on the school or the teachers. This is a further indication of their general satisfaction with the work the school is doing for the child. The parents of the public school children find a considerable amount of fault in the school and the teacher as a reason for the failure of their child to learn enough.

Reasons why child does not learn enough:	St. Luke's	Public School
Fault of child	78.5%	53.1%
Fault of school	21.5%	46.9%

Schooling For What?

It is commonly supposed that parents know what they would like their child to be when he grows up, that they have some vocation or occupation in mind for him, and that they are guiding the child's growth along the lines of this anticipation.[21] What future did they envision for the children, as a result of all the time, energy and money they were expending for this education? Our interviews show that the parents definitely believe in education, but that the great majority have no notion of the specific life work to which this education should lead. The following table shows the distribution of answers to this question.

	St. Luke's	Public School
Never thought of it	11.7%	9.2%
No answer	5.8	15.1
Up to child	47.2	36.1
Specific answer	35.3	39.6

It is probably expected in our kind of culture that the decision for a future occupation or vocation be "left up to the child," or that encouragement along a specific line be deferred until the child demonstrates certain talents or inclinations. That the children have these inclinations, and that they think about their own future, was shown in the results of our questions to them. Most of them knew what they wanted; some gave an alternative vocation. It is, of course, likely that some of them will change their minds either voluntarily or from necessity. The important point here is that the children do have aspirations for the future, which the parents either do not know about, or do not take seriously.[22]

[21] See James J. Cribbin, "A Critique of the Philosophy of Modern Guidance," *The Catholic Educational Review,* vol. 53, no. 2 (February, 1955), pp. 73–91; also Florence Hiesler, "An Elementary School Background for Vocational Guidance," *The Elementary School Journal,* vol. 55, no. 9 (May, 1955), pp. 513–516; also the booklet, *Guidance in the Elementary Schools,* Publication no. 439 (Office of Superintendent, Los Angeles City Schools, 1948).

[22] For a discussion of the vocational interests of boys and girls, see Lester D. Crow and Alice Crow, *An Introduction to Guidance* (New York: American Book, 1951), chap. 14, "Guidance in the Elementary School." "Much of the guidance

In answer to the question, "what do you want to be when you finish school?" the boys in the sixth, seventh and eighth grades at St. Luke's School answered as follows: engineer 15, priest 14, armed forces 10, medical 8, business and sales 6, mechanic or factory worker 6, policeman, fireman or postman 6, athlete or entertainer 5, lawyer 4, artist 2, biologist, greenskeeper, teacher, trapper (one each), undecided 5.

The boys from the same grades in the public school answered as follows: engineer 28, armed forces 16, medical 10, mechanic or factory worker 7, business and sales 4, athlete or entertainer 4, scientist 3, teacher 3, conservation work 2, architect, farmer, lawyer, policeman, undertaker, writer (one each), undecided 15.

The outstanding difference between the boys of these two schools in any single chosen occupation is that of priest and engineer. There are a few Catholic boys among the public school pupils, but none of them suggested the priesthood as a vocation of the future. The boy from St. Luke's selects most often between engineer and priest, and the boy from the public school selects engineering as his first choice. If we rearrange these occupational choices into broader categories, we find that the largest number of St. Luke's boys are divided between the technical and the liberal professions, while the public school boys choose overwhelmingly in favor of the technical and hardly at all for the liberal professions.

Chosen occupation	St. Luke's boys	Chosen occupation	Public School boys
Undecided	5.9%	Undecided	15.3%
Technical profession (biologist, engineer, medical)	28.2	Technical profession (architect, engineer, physician, dentist, pharmacist, undertaker, scientist)	43.9
Liberal profession (artist, lawyer, priest, teacher)	24.7	Armed services	16.3
Services (athlete, entertainer, police, fireman, postman)	12.9	Manual workers (farmer, conservation, mechanic)	10.2
Armed services	11.8	Liberal profession (lawyer, teacher, writer)	5.1
Manual workers (greenskeeper, mechanic, trapper)	9.4	Services (athlete, entertainer, policeman)	5.1
Business and sales	7.1	Business and sales	4.1

We asked this same question of the girls in the three upper grades in both schools and found expected distinctions between their aspirations and those of the boys. The girls in St. Luke's school answered as follows: nurse 32, office worker 16, nun or sister 12, housewife 6, teacher

---

the elementary school child needs and receives can be experienced indirectly as he engages in classroom and school activities with his teacher and fellow pupils" (p. 225).

6, medical 3, artist, airline stewardess, librarian (each 2), model, beautician (each 1), undecided 7.

In comparison to these choices of the girls at St. Luke's, the girls in the same grades in the public school are aspiring to the following vocations: teacher 21, office worker 20, nurse 19, airline stewardess 7, medical 7, entertainer 4, artist, social worker, model, housewife (each 2), beautician, laboratory technician, engineer, science researcher (each 1), undecided 10.

Here again, the fact that the religious vocation of nun is open to the Catholic girls makes a difference in choices between the female pupils of the parochial and the public school. It is probable, however, that the girls at St. Luke's tend to equate nun with teacher and that if these two vocational categories were combined there would be about the same proportion of prospective teachers in both schools. Nursing attracts twice as many girls as office work does at St. Luke's school, but in the public school nursing is about equally attractive as office work and teaching, each of these occupations attracting about the same number of girl pupils.

Chosen occupation	St. Luke's girls	Chosen occupation	Public School girls
Undecided	7.8%	Undecided	10.1%
Nurse	35.6	Liberal profession (artist, social worker, teacher)	25.3
Liberal profession (artist, librarian, nun, teacher)	24.4	Business (typist, secretary, stenographer)	20.2
Business (typist, secretary, stenographer, receptionist)	17.8	Nurse	19.2
Housewife	6.7	Services (beautician, entertainer, model, stewardess)	14.1
Services (beautician, model, stewardess)	4.4	Technical profession (engineer, laboratory technician, physician, science research)	9.1
Technical profession (physician, veterinarian)	3.3	Housewife	2.0

It is not clear from what source the children derive their notions about future careers. The large majority of parents confess that they have "nothing in mind" for their children. No vocational guidance is given to the children on a group basis in the public school. In the parochial school talks and movies are occasionally presented about the career of the professional religious functionary, but apparently little is said concerning other careers.[23] "Sister explains what the future will be for us. The world outside is like a dark road leading everywhere but

[23] "The real work of vocational guidance as a particular program is best utilized in the upper grades." See Brother Arthur Philip, "Vocational Guidance by the Classroom Teacher," *Bulletin* of the National Catholic Educational Association, vol. 52, no. 1 (August, 1955), pp. 376–382.

nowhere. Now in the eighth grade it is well to plan the future, to see what state of life we want. The main states of life that Sister talks about are the religious and the marriage state." The choices the children actually make appear to meet the general cultural attitudes and expectations, and in the absence of direct guidance and counselling, we can assume that the children of both schools simply "pick up" their ideas about future occupations.

We had hoped through our interviews to find out why people favored certain careers for their children and what the parents themselves are doing to foster these aspirations. Since nearly two-thirds of the parochial parents and over sixty per cent of the public school parents could not give a definite answer concerning the future occupation of the child, we could not pursue further the questions of motivation and techniques. This negative approach to future careers does not mean that parents are unaware or uninterested in their children's upward mobility,[24] or that they do not want the best for their children. It seems that the "wide-open possibilities" of the American society, as well as the fact that children "should not be pushed" into careers, combine to make the parents reticent about specific aspirations.

Future School Plans

The desire to give the child more education, thereby improving his occupational potentialities, seems to be the extent of most parents' plans for their children's future. There was no doubt in the minds of these parents that their children would attend high school. This was true whether the parents themselves had gone to college, or to high school, or had not gone beyond elementary school. It is the expectation of the urban culture that children continue on to high school, and all of the eighth graders in both schools actually registered for high school toward the end of their final year in elementary school. The following table shows the amount of formal schooling enjoyed by the parents of the children from both schools.

	St. Luke's		Public School	
	Fathers	Mothers	Fathers	Mothers
Attended or finished college	34.8%	23.6%	33.6%	12.6%
Attended or finished high school	53.3	68.4	59.7	77.3
Attended or finished elementary school	11.9	8.0	6.7	10.1

[24] At the graduation Mass on Sunday, June 2, the Pastor told the children in the presence of their parents, that "your parents have reached certain standards.

Since all of these children are Catholics, both in the parochial and the public school, we were interested in knowing whether the parents intended to send them to a Catholic high school. In the city where St. Luke's is located there are two Catholic high schools, one coeducational and one exclusively for girls. The following table shows the difference in the intentions of parents concerning the school to which they would send their children.

Send child to:	St. Luke's	Public School
Catholic high school	64.4%	23.5%
Public high school	16.2	58.8
Don't know	19.4	17.7

About the same proportion of parents in both categories had not yet made up their minds about the type of school to which their child would go for secondary education. In the remaining families the generalization can be made that once a child starts in one type of school he tends to continue in it. Many of the parents remarked that the child "wants to go where his friends are going," but there was also the economic problem of the cost of sending a child to the Catholic high school as compared to the public school.

Since all of the children in the eighth grade had to register for high school admission in the spring of their last year in school we were able to compare this actual registration with the statements their parents had made in the interviews. We could also compare the intentions as expressed by the eighth graders themselves with the high school to which they actually registered. The following table shows this three-way comparison.

Type of high school	Intentions of parents	Intentions of eighth graders	Actual high school registration	
Catholic high school [25]	37	47	41	68.3%
Public high school	15	13	19	31.7
Undecided	8	0	0	0.0

The above information pertains only to the eighth-grade children and it shows that these pupils knew quite definitely what they wanted in the choice of high school. Not all who expressed a desire to attend a Catholic high school were able to do so, yet more of them actually went than the parents had anticipated. The eight parents who were unde-

---

You ought to go at least that far. Some of you can go further than your parents."

[25] This includes eight boys who went to the minor seminary, and three girls who became postulants for the religious sisterhood.

cided at the time of the interviews finally made up their minds in the spring, half sending their children to the Catholic high school and half to the public.

When we asked the parents about the future college plans for their children we found that the majority of parents of St. Luke's children were uncertain about the answer, (also 45.4% of the public school parents). Most of them were cautious because they did not know whether they could afford to send their child to college, some of them because they were not sure that the "child could make it," that is, whether or not he had the talent to succeed. The following table shows the comparisons in their answers to the question: "do you intend to send the child to college, and if so, where?"

	St. Luke's	Public School
Catholic college	34.2%	37.0%
Non-Catholic college	2.4	4.2
Not going to college	6.6	13.4
Don't know	56.8	45.4

There was a slightly higher percentage of public school parents who would send their children to Catholic colleges, but there was also twice as high a percentage saying that their children definitely would not attend college. We were able to obtain a partial confirmation concerning the intentions of parents regarding the future education of their grade-school children by noting where the older brothers and sisters of these children actually attend high school and college. The 632 children in St. Luke's school have 121 older brothers and sisters in high school and eighteen in college. The 181 Catholic children in the local public schools have thirty-four older brothers and sisters in high school and four in college. The following table shows the type of high school and college these older children in the family are attending.

Type of school attended	Older siblings of St. Luke's pupils		Older siblings of public school pupils	
Catholic high school	64	52.9%	2	5.9%
Public high school	57	47.1	32	94.1
Catholic college	7		1	
Non-Catholic college	11		3	

Since the numbers of high school and college students involved in these families of St. Luke's parish are so small we cannot draw any conclusive evidence from them. There is a clear indication here, and an expected one, that the parochial school child goes to a Catholic high school in much larger numbers than the Catholic child in the public school. Although about a quarter of the parents of public school children now intend to send their children to Catholic high schools only six per cent of those with children of high school age actually do so. It is true also, that the stated intentions of the parochial parents fall short in this regard; still more than half of their children of high school age are actually in Catholic high schools.

One final comparison may be made concerning the college aspirations of the children themselves. Here we compare the pupils of the sixth, seventh and eighth grades in St. Luke's school with children in the same grades in the nearby public school. Since most of the latter children are non-Catholics we make no comparison on the basis of the type of college, denominational or otherwise, they say they would like to attend. The following table gives also the sex differences in the choices of these pupils.

	St. Luke's				Public School			
	Boys	Girls	Both		Boys	Girls	Both	
Will go to college	73	56	129	73.7%	87	86	173	87.8%
Will not go to college	12	20	32	18.3	7	10	17	8.6
Undecided	0	14	14	8.0	4	3	7	3.6

From all of these data certain generalizations can be made concerning the parents' ideas about education for their children. While it is true that parents are rather vague about education when asked general questions, their opinions can be pieced together from answers to specific questions. Unlike a question about house furnishings or kinds of automobiles, where the parent "knows what he likes" and usually the reasons why, the question about the schooling of the child seems to indicate that they feel themselves on unsure ground. Since all of the parents had gone through the process of at least some formal schooling, one might expect more definite opinions and attitudes. Since the days when these parents were themselves elementary school pupils many changes have occurred, both in schools and in the world for which children are schooled. These rapid and complex changes seem to have decreased the parents' ability to comprehend the objectives and directions of their children's education.[26]

[26] On this question of change see Margaret Mead, *The School in American Culture* (Cambridge: Harvard University Press, 1951); also Richard Wysong, "Education for a Changing Society," in Bernard Meltzer, Harry Doby, Phillip Smith, eds., *Education in Society* (New York: Crowell, 1958), pp. 127–136.

To sum this all up, the typical parent of our study is sending his child to school—parochial or public—because he trusts that the school will somehow prepare his child for the future. The parent is quite willing to let the school authorities decide what the essential nature of the schooling will be, and to let the child decide what the schooling will be used for in future life. The parent enters the picture, and makes suggestions, mainly in those areas of school life that are similar to home life, like health, safety, play and discipline—and he leaves the curriculum and the teaching methods up to the school. He learns about and enters into the central educational process mainly when he helps the child with homework, which he does more often than not. Aside from this, the goal of schooling is rather vague in the vision of the parents. It is usually limited to the hope of some further education for the child—as much as money can buy and the child's abilities can take.

Generalizations

1. Parents sending their children to St. Luke's school do so mainly because they want them to have a Catholic training. Catholic parents who send their children to public schools do so mainly because it is more convenient; the school is closer to the home. The former have a religious and educational reason, the latter a reason of comfort and convenience.

2. Most of the parents of elementary school children appear to be satisfied with the school their child is attending: more than half in each category, parochial and public, think that the school is above average. About four out of ten in both groups have no suggestions to make concerning the improvement of the school. In comparing the present school with the school previously attended by the child, the parents of parochial school children have a somewhat higher regard for St. Luke's than the parents of public school children have for theirs. Certainly they consider St. Luke's better than the public school.

3. Parents of children in both schools expect the teachers to maintain discipline. The parochial school teacher is looked upon as somewhat more strict than is the public school teacher. Parents from St. Luke's think the teachers should use detention and written tasks as punishment for those children who misbehave. Parents of public school children suggest detention and corporal punishment as the best means of keeping children in line. The parents of public school children seem to want a stricter school than they now have, while the parents of parochial school children seem satisfied in this regard.

4. Children from St. Luke's school spend about twenty-five per cent more time per week in home study than do the public school children.

Whether or not parents are in favor of homework they tend to help their children with it in the majority of cases. The parents of parochial school children help their children considerably more with homework than do the parents of public school children. Both sets of parents help the children more in arithmetic than in any other subject. This may indicate the difficulty of the subject, but perhaps also the interests and preferences of the parents, especially the fathers.

5. The most enthusiastic and almost unanimous agreement between both sets of parents is found in the area of sports and athletics. In other forms of extracurricular activities, the public school parents seem to be more satisfied than the parochial school parents, but the latter spend much more time, energy and money on them than do the parents of public school children.

6. Parents in both categories appear to be fairly well satisfied that the children are learning enough in school, St. Luke's parents somewhat more so than the others. When the child is not learning enough, however, the latter tend to place the blame on the school more often than do the parents of St. Luke's.

7. The significance of present elementary education for the future careers and occupations of the children seems to be largely lost on the parents. Roughly two-thirds of them in both categories appear to have formulated no aspirations for their children in this regard. The children themselves have thought much more about this question, the goals of boys being set higher in the occupational structure than those of girls.

8. Parental plans for the child's high school training are more definite in both categories. Most of the pupils in St. Luke's will continue on to a Catholic high school in even higher proportions than their older siblings. Most of the Catholic children in public school will imitate their older brothers and sisters by attending a public high school.

9. More than half of the parents in both categories are either unsure about college plans for their children or have decided that the child will not attend college. But those who have made a choice intend for the most part to send the child to a Catholic college. About three-quarters (73.7%) of St. Luke's pupils intend to go to college, as compared to 87.8 per cent of the public school children. Catholic boys intend more than girls to go to college.

Chapter

THIRTEEN

PARENTS AND TEACHERS

THE DATA of this study show quite clearly that St. Luke's parochial school is the joint enterprise of priests, teachers and parents. There are numerous ways in which this multiple cooperation occurs, and also factors by which the school itself becomes the focus of solidarity for the whole parish.[1] The role of the parents in the operation of the school is of great importance, and it deserves a detailed analysis. Without the direct support of numerous parents there would not be an elementary school in this parish. The parents, however, do more than provide and support the school; they cooperate with the teaching staff.

That communication between parents and teachers is both necessary and desirable is hardly brought into question by expert educators.[2] It must be obvious that communication for its own sake cannot be a significant objective of the association between parents and teachers. The school child must be the main reason for these conversations. It is important to discuss the child, if the child needs help. It is important for the parent to know something about the school, and the teacher something about the home, if this knowledge will benefit the child. The by-product of such social intercourse may be increased understanding and even cordiality between teacher and parent, but this is only secondary. The kind and frequency of contacts cannot be so significant as the content of the contacts.

Experienced practitioners in this field, both parents and school administrators, agree that the three most important objectives of parent-teacher communication are the following: to bring about an improvement in child development, to clarify the parents' role in modern

[1] See below, chap. 17, "School, Parish and Community."

[2] All the teachers at St. Luke's agree to this need for parent-teacher contact. Sister Noel Marie, "Statistics of Religious Educators," *The Catholic Educator*, vol. 27, no. 5 (January, 1957), pp. 291, 292, 344, found that eighty-eight per cent of religious teachers were in favor of parent contact, eight per cent against it, and four per cent did not reply.

education, and to cooperate in the solution of problems of learning.[3] Agreement on these joint objectives does not mean that there is also agreement on the relative status and function of the two participants, the home and the school. There can never be complete equality between them because the primary and legal right of the parent to educate his own children must always keep the teacher and the school in a subordinate position. Similarly the functioning of the school, and particularly its policies, must always be subject to revision by the parents. The latter cannot be expected to agree to a policy of "noninterference" with the administration of the school.

The relationship between the parents and the public school is complicated by the fact that the parental function can be merely an advisory one, while the legislative and executive functions have been usurped by the public school authorities. This has been institutionalized over the years to the point that parents do not seem aware of the incongruity of the situation. It has been formalized, accepted, and even written into the by-laws of the National Congress of Parents and Teachers. The relationship between the parents and the parochial school is complicated for other reasons. Catholic parishioners do not have legislative and executive functions in the ecclesiastical structure, and they have an advisory function only in so far as the Pastor cares to listen to them. In the case of the parochial school, however, it seems that the parents cannot morally and completely relinquish their advisory, legislative and executive functions in the education of their child.[4] In practice, however, there is much confusion because there is a tendency to identify the educational structure with the religious structure by molding the former into the latter.

A Catholic authority in the field of elementary education points out that parents and teachers should cooperate, first, because they have similar God-given vocations; secondly, the child's personality is indivisible, and thirdly, the child's education is enriched by such collaboration. The fact that both parents and teachers are educators is recognized in the aims of an organization embracing both: "to coor-

[3] See Ward G. Reeder, *An Introduction to Public-School Relations* (New York: Macmillan, 1953), p. 142.

[4] In his Lenten Pastoral on education the Bishop of the diocese wrote that "the Church has always taught that parents have the first right and the first obligation to educate their children. That simply goes with the pride and joy of being parents. It is not the primary business of Church or State to take over this responsibility. The best they can do—and must do—is to help to provide the means by which children can be wisely and well educated for their double citizenship in this world and the world to come."

dinate and consolidate the educational activities of home and school by developing and deepening a mutual understanding of the objective of Catholic education and by cooperative action to achieve them." [5]

Another Catholic educator feels that very little has been done on the elementary level of Catholic schooling to acquaint the laity with its programs and to draw parents into its activities. "Our own Catholic principles seem to demand such participation. We have been the only group in this country that has consistently defended the principle that the parents have the primary right to determine the type of education their children shall have. Nevertheless, we have laid ourselves open to the retort that we are the only group that does not carry it out in practice." This diocesan school superintendent makes the further admission that "we as Catholic educators have too often taken the stand that once the children are turned over to us, it is up to us, and us alone, to determine all questions about the school." [6]

Pre-arranged Interviews

Communication between parents and teachers can occur in many ways, one of which is the formal, pre-arranged interview in which one of the parties asks the other for an opportunity to discuss a child in the school. During the school year, from September to June, the fourteen teachers at St. Luke's had pre-arranged interviews with parents concerning fifty-six of the 632 pupils. This represents only 8.8 per cent of all pupils about whom the interviews were held, and 14.8 per cent of all the parents with whom the interviews were held. Thus, through this device the teachers had contact with about one-seventh of the families, sometimes only through one parent, represented in the school. In about seven out of ten of these cases the parents initiated the interview by asking to see the teacher. In about one-eighth of the cases the problem under discussion was one of behavior and discipline.

In order to have a basis of comparison we interviewed fourteen teachers from the nearby public school, and found that they had pre-arranged interviews with parents concerning 542 of their 848 pupils. These 848 children are in twenty-four different classes since the teachers in the upper grades are specialists teaching the same subject to three or four different classes. In about three out of five of these cases the parents requested the interview. In 27.5 per cent of the cases the

[5] William McManus, "Essentials of Home and School Cooperation," *Bulletin* of the National Catholic Educational Association, vol. 51, no. 2 (November, 1954), pp. 11–23.

[6] Carl J. Ryan, "Catholic Education and the Laity," *The Catholic School Journal*, vol. 51, no. 4 (April, 1951), pp. 141–143.

teacher and parent discussed the behavior and discipline of the child. The public school teacher averaged thirty-eight interviews with parents during the year, or about one every week. In contrast, the teachers of St. Luke's averaged only four interviews during the year, although one had none and another had ten.

The following table gives the comparative statistical facts, an overwhelming evidence that the public school teachers have much more pre-arranged, formal communication with parents than do the teachers of St. Luke's parochial school.

	Parochial School		Public School	
Pupils	632		848	
Teachers	14		14	
Classes	14		24	
Average pupils in class	45.1		35.3	
Average pupils per teacher	45.1		60.5	
Pupils discussed	56	(8.8%)	542	(63.9%)
Interview requested by:				
Parents	40	(71.4%)	314	(57.9%)
Teachers	16	(28.6%)	228	(42.1%)
Subject of interview:				
Behavior problem	7	(12.5%)	149	(27.5%)
Studies	49	(87.5%)	393	(72.5%)

The expressed goal of the public school Principal is that each teacher should have at least one interview with the parents of every pupil once every semester. Although the Principal himself has interviewed the parents of almost every pupil from the third to the eighth grade, he has not been able to make sufficient time available during the day so that the teachers can imitate his example. The public school teacher must be at the school from eight to four, with an hour and a quarter off for lunch, and can arrange an interview before or after class hours, or at a free period during the day. Even with these advantages of time and opportunity the public school teacher averages only about one interview every week.

At St. Luke's school it is physically impossible for a parent to have an interview with a teacher between eight in the morning and three-ten in the afternoon. Every teacher, including the Principal, has a full schedule of classroom work and playground supervision, and has no free period in which to relax, much less talk to parents.[7] If Sister

[7] On registration day just before the beginning of school in September, the parents receive a list of "regulations," one of which reads as follows: "Sisters are avail-

Roberta were a full-time Principal and if the teachers did not have such a tightly packed schedule it would be possible to expand the amount of interviews with parents. Her present ideal is to have interviews whenever necessary and helpful.

It is clear that the public school teachers take the initiative more often than the parochial school teachers in arranging an interview with parents. Our reports show also that in a higher percentage of cases the public school teacher is concerned about a behavioral problem in the child. One teacher has the child dial his home phone number to make the first contact with the child's parent. From this and other comparative evidence between the two schools, it appears that St. Luke's does not have as many problem children as the public school, and that the parochial school teachers have an environmental advantage in handling the problems of discipline and behavior.

The pre-arranged interview is only one form of contact between the parents and the school,[8] and it is focused upon the child. We have no way of knowing how many complaints pour over the public school Principal's telephone about the teachers and the school, or how many parochial school parents phone in to complain to Sister Roberta after school hours or to Father Albert almost any time of the day or night. When asked about this matter, both reply, "we don't get so many complaints," or, "once in a while somebody calls up and gets mad."

Parents' Night

Unlike the pre-arranged interviews, the purpose of Parents' Night (sometimes called "Dads' Night" and "Open House") is not to discuss the abilities, problems and progress of the pupil. A certain amount of this is done in the informal conversation that takes place. In both the parochial and the public school the main purpose is to give the parents an acquaintance with the school, what the program is, what activities are performed, what the physical plant looks like. Most parents, even those with four or five children in the school, spend less than a half-hour at the school on this occasion. In the light of these facts, the communication between parents and teacher can at best be a casual one.

The Parents' Night takes place in the first week of November, at

---

able for interviews with parents the following hours: 3:30 to 4:30, 6:00 to 7:30. Telephone for an appointment."

[8] See Mary Nona McGreal, *The Role of the Teaching Sisterhood in American Education* (Washington: Catholic University Press, 1951), chap. 5, "Parent-Teacher Cooperation," pp. 80–101, for a discussion of such relations in 122 elementary and high schools operated by the Sisters of Saint Dominic.

the end of the first nine-weeks' period of school work.[9] The children prepare for it in advance by assembling samples of their school achievements, which are put on display on each one's desk. On top of this is a short note to the parents written by the child and explaining the contents of the folder. The parents come in, have a chance to look around the classroom, to examine the work of the child, and to chat briefly with the teacher who is present. All are asked to sign their names on a register provided on the teacher's desk and supervised by a room mother of the PTA. Because of the numbers present and the shortage of time, the conversation usually consists of the teacher praising the child and the parents praising the teacher.

At the end of the evening there are certain desks in each classroom where the child's folder of work lies untouched and unexamined. These represent the children whose parents did not appear for this special occasion. The percentage of parental absentees is greater at the public school than at the parochial school. The following table shows the comparative distribution of attendance at Parents' Night.

	St. Luke's	Public School
Both parents present	41.3%	25.1%
Fathers only	11.8	2.4
Mothers only	20.6	37.2
Neither parent present	26.3	35.3

The mothers fulfilled this duty of attending Parents' Night better than the fathers at both schools. Practically the same percentage of mothers appeared at the parochial school (61.9%), as at the public school (62.3%), but in the latter case most of them came without their husbands. The representation of fathers at the St. Luke's Parents Night (53.1%) was almost twice as great as that of the fathers at the public school event (27.5%). On this occasion, at least, the fathers of parochial school children have more communication with the teachers of their children, and perhaps also show a more immediate concern about the school work of their children, than do the fathers of public school pupils.

Organized Communication

In 1937, St. Luke's was the first parochial school in the city to affiliate itself officially with the National Congress of Parents and Teachers. It was followed by only three others of the fifteen local parochial schools.

[9] The pupils in the upper grades, fifth to eighth, had received their first report cards from the Pastor on October 15, since their reports are issued every six weeks.

This was at a time when a certain amount of controversy was going on among Catholics concerning the advisability of joining this organization.[10] Occasionally during the years there has been talk at St. Luke's of withdrawing and setting up a separate parochial unit, or of establishing a city-wide Catholic Home and School Association. But the Bishop and the Pastor and most of the parents continue to be in favor of maintaining the present organizational arrangements.

The PTA was originally established through the initiative of the laity, particularly of Mrs. Charles Birdsall, who was then chairman of the Parish Council of Catholic Women. She called a meeting in the spring of 1937, but only a few parents responded. In October, the first meeting was held and fifty-three women enrolled as charter members. They decided to join the National Congress and "to work with a group which was already well organized and working for the benefit of home, school, church and community. We felt, too that such an established group could help us more efficiently than if we groped along alone." [11]

The women knew what they wanted, but they realized too that they were operating within a parochial framework which included clergy and teaching Sisters. "At this time, of course," continues the historian, "we consulted our Pastor as to any objections he might have in regard to this association and he had none, provided the Sisters were willing to work along with us. We gained their consent, although we felt that they were a little skeptical of us and afraid we were going to interfere with the routine and place a burden on their already burdened shoulders. It was our duty to show them that we were only willing to aid them in their work and not hinder them."

[10] Warnings against affiliation were issued in an unsigned article, "Catholic Parent-Teacher Associations," *Catholic Action* (NCWC), vol. 21, no. 1 (January, 1939), pp. 14–15; and by Sister Mary Clare, "The Sister and the Home and School Association," *The Catholic School Journal*, vol. 40, no. 7 (September, 1940), pp. 220–221. A more sympathetic view, however, was expressed in an unsigned article, "Catholic Parent-Teacher Associations," *Catholic Action* (NCWC), vol. 21, no. 6 (June, 1939), pp. 16–17. Why the term "Home and School Association" is preferable is explained in an editorial note, *The Catholic School Journal*, vol. 40, no. 7 (September, 1940), p. 220, "it suggests the close relations between the home and the school, and emphasizes the importance of the home."

[11] An enquiry of 340 parochial parent-teacher organizations in sixteen states showed that only 5.3 per cent of them were affiliated with the National Congress of Parents and Teachers (some of these were also connected with the Catholic group), 73.5 per cent only with the National Committee on Home and School Associations of the National Conference of Catholic Women, and most of the rest were unaffiliated with either. See Theophane Power, *Home and School Relationships in the Catholic Elementary Schools of a Number of Selected Dioceses* (Washington: Catholic University Press, 1950), p. 42.

The structure of St. Luke's PTA includes a board of directors which appears to be honorary and never meets.[12] It is composed of the Pastor, the assistant pastor, the Principal and two members of the organization. The executive board, which meets monthly on the first Friday, is made up of the officers and the committee chairmen. The most important person is the president, who has always been a woman, assisted by first and second vice-presidents, a secretary and a treasurer. All of the officers, except the president, are also committee chairmen.

The PTA functions through a committee system, the whole work of each committee being performed usually by the chairman alone. Of the twenty-seven official committees, one, on study group and publication, was inactive during the year, and had no chairman. Three were headed by laymen and three by priests. Two were headed by Sisters, one by a husband and wife team, and one by a team of two female co-chairmen. The remaining sixteen committees were each in charge of a woman. As is usual in such organizations the actual work of the committees varied from those which did hardly anything to those which were very busy and successful.

The ideal proposal for the membership of St. Luke's PTA was that the parents of every child in the school would belong to the organization, and that the total membership would be subdivided into these committees, the size of which would depend upon the extent of its function. The fact is, of course, that the total potential was never realized although the membership committee this year reported the largest number, both absolute and proportional, of members in the history of the association. The following table shows the membership of St. Luke's parents in its PTA, as compared to that of the parents of Catholic children attending the public school.

Membership	St. Luke's	Public School
Both parents	65.0%	62.2%
Mother only	17.8	24.4
Father only	1.0	0.8
Neither parent	16.2	12.6

Paid membership by the fathers of St. Luke's pupils was something quite different from their active participation in meetings and in the functions of the PTA. The dues of thirty-five cents were quickly and easily paid by most of the fathers, who helped merely to swell the membership totals. If this situation is similar in other schools throughout

[12] For the model structure see *Parent-Teacher Manual* (Chicago: National Congress of Parents and Teachers, 1953), Part I, "Structure of the Parent-Teacher Organization."

the country (and it most likely is) the total of over ten million members claimed by the National Congress constitutes more than twice the number of active members. The fact is that about a half dozen men attended the first two meetings; but for the rest of the year there were never more than two men at any regular meeting. In previous years the meetings had always been conducted in the afternoon. This year they were deliberately changed to Tuesday evenings so that the men could attend.

The teachers likewise failed to participate in the meetings and programs of the PTA. Although Sister Roberta was chairman of the school education committee, and Sister Cecelia of the music committee, they and the other teachers attended only the meetings in September and October. It was no accident that both the men and the teachers absented themselves. The October meeting was marked by a lively discussion in which the men questioned a new scholarship up for the consideration of the PTA. Their questioning was interpreted as insolence; the president thought they should apologize to the teachers; the feelings of a number of people were ruffled; and the consequence was that most of the male parents and all of the teachers stayed away from meetings for the rest of the year.[13]

One committee, that of the room mothers, was ideally intended to comprise all of the women in the organization. Thus, since every woman had a child in one or another of the school grades she was nominally a member of the room mothers' committee even though she may also have been active in some other committee. As it worked out in practice a room mother was responsible for each of the fourteen classes, and whenever her room was responsible for an activity she telephoned down the list of women with children in that class until she had enough volunteers for the work.

Theoretically all sports in the school were under the committee on recreation, and the Parish Athletic Committee should have been merely an extension of this committee. The men were most active in this function and could in this sense be considered working members of the PTA. The fact is, however, that this group operated independently of the PTA,

[13] Theophane Power, *op. cit.*, found that in 340 Catholic elementary school parent-teacher organizations, the Principal and Sisters attend regularly in forty-six per cent of the cases, sometimes in 8.2 per cent, and never in 45.8 per cent. Most of the latter (37.6%) could not attend because meetings were held during school hours, the rest (8.2%) because they were cloistered. "Undoubtedly the religious rule of these Sisters necessitates their non-attendance, but such a rule seems inconsistent with the program of Catholic education to which these Sisters have dedicated themselves" (p. 59).

having its own treasury, raising its own funds, and making its own decisions. At times it appeared that the PTA was mainly in support of the Athletic Committee, and that the latter had only loose and friendly connections with it. During the basketball season the PTA offered to contribute one thousand dollars for improving the gymnasium, but this project was later dropped.

Another group, technically under the chairman of the committee on budget and finance, became so large and unwieldly that it finally divorced itself from the PTA and took the name of the Patrons of St. Luke's. The women who operated this group were also all members of the PTA, and their fund-raising was for the benefit of the school, but it had its own officers and another series of committees each with a chairman. It planned and reported its activities at the PTA meetings, and for most of the year it worked like an organization within the parent organization.

Problems of Communication

The PTA of St. Luke's parish is the only formally organized channel of contact and communication between parents and teachers. The focus of its communication system is the school pupil. The by-laws of this organization state clearly among its objectives that it is "to bring into closer relations the home and the school, that parents and teachers may cooperate intelligently in the training of the child." Among its policies there is also the statement that "this Association shall not seek to direct the administrative activities of the school or to control its policies."

A comparison between the objectives of the PTA and the activities it performed at St. Luke's during the year forces a consideration of two important questions: first, what is the function of parents in an elementary school? and secondly, what is the role of teachers in a parents' club? The first question finds an answer in the statement that "the Parent-Teacher movement is fundamentally a declaration, friendly but firm, of parental rights and duties. It has its rise in the very sound thought that the child belongs to the parents; that if they choose at times to share their prerogatives with others they never surrender them. School or no school, parents are still the educators of their offspring with claims to this high distinction that are grounded in natural law."[14]

The assumption that parents should in no organized way attempt to influence the administration and policies of the school, appears to be

[14] Mary C. Ryan, "The Purposes of a Parent-Teacher Organization," *The Catholic School Journal,* vol. 36, no. 8 (August, 1936), pp. 205–206.

more acceptable to the PTA in public schools than to that of parochial schools.[15] It is to be supposed that Catholic parents generally know that they may not morally relinquish to any school the primary right and duty to educate their own children. In so far as they allow the professional, full-time teachers to become parent-surrogates in this regard, they are obviously going contrary to the teachings of their own Church. This defection from responsibility seems most serious in the delicate area of religious instruction. The "hands off" policy of parents and the emphasis on the organized parochial school tend to make parents forget "that the primary, natural and ordinarily irreplaceable school of religion and the moral virtues is the home; that the principal, natural teachers of religion and morals are the parents; and that the parochial school and the religious teacher can serve only as aids, not as substitutes, for the home and the parent in the religious formation of the child." [16]

The only serious dissension that arose in the PTA occurred when some parents attempted to realize their responsibilities concerning practices and policies of St. Luke's school. The time of the monthly meeting had been moved to the evening so that teachers and male parents could attend. At the beginning of the year, a small group of men, coming to PTA meetings for the first time, participated in vigorous debate about three "academic" matters: The new report cards, the granting of two scholarships to eighth graders, and the introduction of a visual aid program. Whether these men were too blunt in their expression of opinion, whether the teachers were too sensitive about the problems, whether there was fear that the by-laws forbidding interference with the school administration were being violated, or fear that the traditional practices of the lay parishioners [17] in relation to the religious

[15] Although there is also a movement in this direction among some public school administrators. See Paul J. Misner, "Citizens and Teachers Plan the Curriculum," *National Parent-Teacher,* vol. 50, no. 9 (May, 1956), pp. 26–27.

[16] John L. Thomas, "Parental Responsibility Left At The School Door?" *The Homiletic and Pastoral Review,* vol. 57, no. 9 (June, 1957), pp. 814–819.

[17] See the eloquent arguments for lay participation by Carl J. Ryan, "Ghosts of Trusteeism," *The Homiletic and Pastoral Review,* vol. 57, no. 8 (May, 1957), pp. 705–714; also an older statement by a Catholic college president, Arthur M. Murphy, "Parent-Teacher-Pastor Relationships," *The Catholic School Journal,* vol. 42, no. 6 (June, 1942), pp. 187–190. "In my own case I have seldom, if ever, been asked an opinion concerning the care of any parish temporalities in any parish in which I have lived. Yet I am naturally always included when it is time to pay for these activities. Like most men in a democracy, we parishioners like to know where and how our money is being spent, even our parish school contributions" (p. 189).

teachers were being interrupted—whatever the reason or combination of reasons, the result was dissension within the PTA.

The new system of report cards had been suggested by the diocesan superintendent of schools in the previous year. It had been fully described in the diocesan weekly paper and introduced in more than half of the parochial schools. At St. Luke's, however, there was still a supply of old report cards to be used up, and when the new ones were introduced some of the parents complained that they did not "understand" them. The principal revision was simply the substitution of one set of symbols for another; in place of A, B, C, there now appeared the letters VG (very good), G (good), S (satisfactory). Some parents were irked because the change had not been "properly explained" to them.[18] The result of the controversy was that the Pastor was commissioned by the PTA to write a letter to the diocesan superintendent expressing the dissatisfaction of the parents and requesting a clarification.

The temporary scholarship committee made its report at the October meeting and started a controversy that carried over to the November meeting and probably would have continued if the chairman had not ruled to shut off debate and to cancel the business meeting in December "so that we can all be friends at Christmas time." The scholarship for one hundred dollars was to be awarded to one boy and one girl in the graduating class, who had attended St. Luke's for three consecutive years, and intended to go to a Catholic secondary school. The debate arose over the point system of selection, based on scholastic average, attendance and social adjustment, the two latter items counting for one-tenth of the total points. It was remarked by some opponents of the new report cards that "the letters will have to be changed back into numbers after all." The conditions for the scholarship could be changed only by a two-third majority vote at a monthly meeting. An amendment suggesting that ten-days' written notice be given the membership prior to any meeting when the conditions would be discussed, was defeated by a close 38–36 vote. Another objection was expressed that only one lay person was on the permanent scholarship committee, besides the Pastor, assistant Pastor and Principal.

By the time the January meeting of the PTA was held the contro-

[18] Bess Goodykoonts, "A Report on Report Cards," *National Parent-Teacher*, vol. 50, no. 2 (October, 1955), pp. 11–13 and 37, discusses various types of report cards from the points of view of both parents and teachers. See also Brother Columban of Mary, "The Functional Value of the Report Card," *Bulletin* of the National Catholic Educational Association, vol. 51, no. 1 (August, 1954), pp. 524–529; and Jerome V. MacEachin, "The Home-School Report Card," *ibid.*, pp. 530–533.

versy over the scholarship awards had died down. In spite of all the debate and acrimony over the matter, the actual selection of the winners was a relatively simple procedure. Sister Roberta merely listed the ten children with the highest I.Q. in the eighth grade. Six of these eliminated themselves by registering for public high schools. This left two boys and two girls. One boy was eliminated because he was absent from school for eleven days and was not an altar boy. The remaining boy, Walter Pattison, and the girl with the highest I.Q. and the least absences, Dorothy Ellis, were granted the scholarships. When these names were announced on Award Night, May 28, no recognition was given to the fact that three other graduates had higher scholastic averages than the two pupils chosen for the scholarships. This caused some "communication" of a relatively unpleasant nature the next day between the mothers of these children and the Principal.

The proposal to improve the visual aid facilities for the children of St. Luke's was also a question of scholastic import and, as one of the officers remarked, "the PTA does not interfere in the curriculum." The husband-wife chairmen of the visual aid committee had spent considerable time in analyzing the whole program, checking on models and prices of projectors, the availability of slides and films from local and state centers, and the various ways of operating the program. They objected strenuously to the purchase of a large daylight screen at a cost of six hundred and fifty dollars. "If we pay that much we might as well go to a down-town movie." They wanted the school to introduce a special course in audio-visual aid for the slower children, and also to use the services of the city schools' audio-visual department. Both of these suggestions went unheeded and the feelings of the chairmen continued to be ruffled during the ensuing months so that they took little further part in the PTA program.

The Absence of Communication

It is obvious that if parents and teachers are to communicate with one another in a formal organized way they have to be present at the principal meetings of the organization. In actual practice during most of the year this formal contact between the two parties through St. Luke's PTA was not possible because the organization was mainly a mother's club. The teachers in general were in favor of the organization, received practically anything they asked from its members, but appeared to be reluctant to attend meetings. In answer to questions about their continued absence, they replied that attendance is voluntary ("Father Albert leaves us free to attend or not attend,") that the meetings run past their eight-thirty curfew, and that they are under no obligation to participate in the PTA.

In contrast, the PTA in the nearby public school enjoys the active, if sometimes grumbling, support of the teachers. Attendance at PTA meetings by the public school teachers is also voluntary, but the Principal expects them to attend and they rarely ever miss a meeting. The vice president of the group, as well as the chairmen of several committees, are teachers. The activities of the organization are a cooperative venture of both parents and teachers, although the latter sometimes complain that the parents initiate projects and then leave them for the teachers to carry out and complete.

At any rate, the PTA in the public school represents an area in which the parents and teachers communicate about the educational problems and progress of the children. At St. Luke's school this is not the case. The failure in communication here is not entirely on the part of parents. In our interviews with parents we asked their opinion of the PTA and asked specifically what suggestions they would make for improving the organization. The suggestion mentioned most frequently was that the teachers should attend the meetings. The failure of the teachers to appear is frustrating to the parents in general and to the active officers of the organization in particular. The latter are forced to find other means of contacting the faculty in order to discover the needs of the school which they can help to fulfill.

It must be pointed out, of course, that many parents also fail to attend the PTA meetings, or even to belong to the organization. This neglect occurs among the parents of both public school and parochial school children, and more among fathers than among mothers. The participation of fathers is so negligible that the following table refers only to mothers, 82.7 per cent of whom are members of the PTA at St. Luke's as compared to 86.5 per cent at the public school.

Meetings attended:	St. Luke's	Public School
No meetings	36.3%	27.7%
One or two	24.1	25.2
Three or four	14.3	18.4
Five or more	25.3	28.7
Average meetings per mother:	2.7	2.9

These statistics show that even if the teachers of St. Luke's school were to attend the meetings of the PTA they would have the opportunity there to meet less than two-thirds of the mothers of their pupils.

A small nucleus of mothers (8.0%) faithfully attended every meeting of the organization, and these are the women from whom the leadership comes and with whom the teachers have the most contact outside the operations of the PTA. Only one-quarter of the mothers attended more than half of the meetings during the school year; but more than one-sixth (17.2%) of them do not even belong to the PTA.

There are, of course, many other ways, outside the PTA, in which contact and communication can be established between parents and teachers.[19] One exceptional young teacher of the first grade in the public school tries to visit the home of every child in her class. Aside from this interesting example there is also the fact that parents are permitted (not encouraged) to visit the classrooms of the public school during school hours. Because of the involved red tape of getting both the Principal's and the teacher's permission, relatively few mothers avail themselves of this opportunity, and then usually only when their children are in the early grades of the school. In St. Luke's parish there is neither visiting of the homes by the teachers nor visiting of the classrooms by the parents.

It is possible for parents to have contact with the teacher or the Principal by telephone, making a complaint, asking for information, inquiring about the child's progress or failure. We have no way of knowing how many parents had this kind of communication. We were interested in knowing, however, the frequency of personal contacts, whether and how often the parent "saw and talked" even briefly with the teacher. The following table, referring only to mothers of pupils, shows the percentage distribution and comparison of these personal contacts.

Number of times mother saw and spoke with teacher of her child	St. Luke's	Public School
Never	15.4%	24.4%
Once or twice	66.0	52.9
Three or more	18.6	22.7
Average per mother	1.8	1.9

Most of the contacts of mothers who met the teacher only once were

[19] The plan used in the elementary schools of the Lansing diocese is one of these. Both teachers and parents give the child marks on a series of eighteen traits, and when the marks differ greatly a conference is arranged. See Jerome V. MacEachin, "The Home-School Report Card," *Bulletin* of the National Catholic Educational Association, vol. 51, no. 1 (August, 1954), pp. 530–533.

made at the annual Parents' Night in the classroom. Even though about one-quarter of the mothers of public school children had never even met the teacher of their child, the remaining mothers had a greater frequency of contact with the teacher than did the mothers of St. Luke's pupils. This is probably due to the fact that the public school teacher and parent have many more pre-arranged interviews than do those from St. Luke's. In our interviews some of the parents who had never met the teacher felt themselves competent, probably through the interpretation of the child, to make a judgment upon her. While 15.4 per cent of St. Luke's mothers had not met the teacher, only 11.7 per cent of them refused to rate the teacher. In the public school, 24.4 per cent did not meet the teacher, and 18.5 per cent did not pass judgment upon her.

It is in the area of casual and occasional contacts that the teachers of the parochial school communicate more with the parents than do the teachers of the public school. The important difference seems to be that at St. Luke's the teachers and parents are both members of a Catholic parish that transcends the school. Throughout this book we discuss many instances of this personal and informal relationship, but it must be noted that this communication, especially by the religious teachers, is with a nucleus of parishioners who are closest to the main operational phases of the parish and the school.[20] These nuclear parishioners have easy and friendly relations with the teachers. They constitute less than ten per cent of the parents but they account for over ninety per cent of the contacts with teachers.

There is also a kind of "mass communication" through which the teachers sometimes use the children as messengers to the parents. For example, Sister Roberta sent a mimeographed letter asking the parents whether they wanted caps and gowns at the graduation ceremony. The parents agreed unanimously, but some of them had second thoughts about it when they had to pay the rental fee of seven dollars and fifty cents. At another time a letter prepared by the PTA asked the parents to vote on whether they wanted the children to wear uniforms to school. This proposal was defeated by a 73 to 180 vote, but a minority of parents still favors the use of uniform school clothes. The children were used as messengers on many other occasions, for the Bazaar, the Style Show, various card parties and fund-raising drives for the parish and the school.

[20] For an empirical elaboration of this concept, see Joseph H. Fichter, *Social Relations in the Urban Parish* (Chicago: University of Chicago Press, 1954), chap. 3, "Nuclear Parishioners and Leaders."

Raising Money

One of the complaints made by some of the parents was that St. Luke's PTA focused too much attention on raising money and not enough on raising children. This problem is, of course, a matter of relative emphasis. While the experts maintain that the gathering of money is not a primary purpose of parent-teacher groups,[21] or at least that such activity should be de-emphasized, the fact remains that every PTA in the city, in both public and parochial schools, engaged in fund-raising activities during the school year. Aside from its need to meet its annual budget, amounting to $758.75 this year, St. Luke's PTA annually has an "extra project" for the school. This project is the provision of some physical equipment for the use of the children, and no one has yet devised a way of getting necessary parochial school equipment without also devising some way of paying for it.

At the first meeting of the year, on Tuesday, September 18, the priests, teachers and ninety-two lay members of St. Luke's PTA discussed the several projects that were proposed.[22] The visual aid chairman suggested the purchase of a projector, slides and films, that could be moved from room to room as the teacher required. The Principal favored a public address system with outlets in every classroom, so that she could make announcements without leaving her eighth grade or sending a pupil with a message. The committee in charge of first Friday breakfasts suggested new tables, or at least new formica tops on the old tables, in the school cafeteria. The chairman of the recreation committee proposed that a large daylight screen be purchased for the school auditorium. (In the previous year the PTA had expended $749.25 for black-out curtains in the auditorium.)

No vote was taken at this meeting and the four proposals were again discussed at the meeting of the Executive Board, of which fifteen members were present, on the morning of Friday, October 5. The Pastor

[21] William McManus, "Essentials of Home and School Cooperation," *Bulletin* of the National Catholic Educational Association, vol. 51, no. 2 (November, 1954), pp. 11–23, says that this organization is not a grievance machinery for aggressive parents, nor a fund-raising society primarily interested in entertainment, nor a mothers' club, regarding fathers as incompetent and uninterested (see p. 17).

[22] Theophane Power shows that in 83.5 per cent of the Catholic parent-teacher organizations the main project was to buy equipment for the school and playground. See *Home and School Relationships in the Catholic Elementary Schools of a Number of Selected Dioceses* (Washington, D.C., Catholic University, 1950), p. 67. The equipment most frequently provided (43% of the cases) was a projector (p. 85).

spoke in favor of the first proposal, to purchase a projector for the use of all the children. Most of the ladies present were of the opinion that the public address system would be even more useful, but the Pastor remarked that "they've gotten along without it for years, and they can continue to do without it." The two remaining proposals were also discussed, but since the function of the Executive Board is to clarify and explore issues, and not to decide them, the members reformulated the suggestions to be submitted for a vote at the next plenary monthly meeting of the PTA.

This meeting was held on Tuesday, October 16, and it proved to be one of the most exciting of the year. It also marked the parting of the ways for most of the men and all of the teachers. So much time was lost in wrangling about the new report cards and about the method for selecting the recipients of the PTA scholarships, that the proposals for fund raising had to take second place on the agenda. The chairman of the visual education committee was also one of the most vociferous in the argument about report cards and scholarships; his attitude seemed to be interpreted as antagonistic by the membership, and this unfortunate human reaction led to a disregard of his proposal to buy a projector for the use of the school.

The Pastor ended the argumentation by suggesting that they "get on with the business" of the annual project. Ignoring the proposal for a slide projector, he then outlined the other suggestions, giving his own opinion about them. The public address system, he felt, was unnecessary and expensive. The daylight screen would be a great help but it too is very expensive. Providing new tables for the cafeteria would be the most practical project. "We could get these tables, with plywood tops, for $26.70 apiece; and they'd be good for twenty years. We don't want formica tops because it wears off and the kids can cut into it. But after all, these are just my ideas; it's up to the group to decide." Immediately the motion was made to buy the tables, seconded and passed unanimously by the membership, without any consideration of the other proposals.[23]

In preparation for the October meeting, the PTA officers had sent a mimeographed letter home to the parents through the school children. It opened as follows: "Dear Parents: The purpose of this letter is to familiarize each parent with our budget and projects for the year. Our goal for the year is $1,500.00, consisting of our regular budget of

[23] At the meeting of the executive board on the first Friday in November Father Albert reported that "people are complaining about the plywood cafeteria tables. Everything is left to me, and then nobody likes what has been done."

$654.75."[24] The letter then mentioned the projects to be voted on and the activities planned for the year. It stated further that "this year we are dispensing with one of our card parties. We hope to have the co-operation of all, to make our one card party, February 28, a big success."

This card party, the feature of which was a fashion show, was the principal money maker of the year. In early years the PTA sponsored small monthly card parties in the homes of parents. This gradually evolved into a system of two large card parties held annually in the parish meeting hall. The new combination auditorium and gymnasium provided the setting for a single all-out effort, a card party and style show which made a profit of more than eighteen hundred dollars.[25] (Exactly $1,844.06, with income at $2,480.44, and disbursements at $636.38.) The first style show, held in the previous year, had netted slightly over fifteen hundred dollars. At the final meeting of the group after the style show when all reports were turned in, our observer asked what was to be done with the money for which they had worked so arduously. No one seemed to have a ready answer. It was as though they had never thought about why they were raising money. Finally, the chairman said, "Well, I don't know. I suppose it goes into the school fund; or at least the parish can use it."

The amount and type of planning that went into this fund-raising affair are a measure of the success which it achieved. The work had started with a small meeting in the previous July.[26] They met again, separate from the PTA, once a month until January when two meetings were held; and in February there were three meetings. The group had its own chairman, treasurer and secretary, besides chairmen for committees on publicity, favors, decorations, ushers, drinks, tickets, raffle, kitchen, models, and door prizes. Publicity items appeared in the society section of the local newspaper once a month from July to November, twice in December, three times in January, seven times in

[24] At a later meeting the budget for the year was finally fixed at $758.75. The largest items on this budget were: two hundred dollars for the scholarship fund, one hundred dollars for the visual aid supplies, seventy-five dollars to send two delegates to the state convention, seventy-five dollars for the programs and notices, fifty dollars for the school's youth groups, fifty dollars for supplies used in textbook repairs.

[25] A television set was raffled in conjunction with this card party and style show, and the profits from the raffle alone were nine-hundred and eighty-five dollars.

[26] In preparation for next year's style show, the Patrons of St. Luke's School held its first small meeting on May 24, at the home of last year's treasurer who will be next year's chairman.

February, with a final lengthy description and pictures on the first day of March.

The decision to separate the Patrons from the PTA was made because of "commercial" reasons rather than because of fund raising. The local PTA in the public schools frequently sponsors affairs with the sole purpose of raising money for school projects. Gambling devices and raffles are not fully approved by the organization but are more often than not employed. The commercial aspect of the style show consists of the fact that a certain amount of advertising comes to the women's shop that provides the clothes worn by the models and described by the mistress of ceremonies. The ladies know also where the hats and shoes displayed are for sale, and they are drawn to make purchases at these commercial establishments. The business men who donate the various door prizes are also mentioned when the prizes are awarded. This too is advertising and adds to the commercial aspects of the event.

The PTA at St. Luke's had started the year with a bank account of slightly over nine hundred dollars, and ended the year with this reserve fund at about thirteen hundred dollars. Besides spending the whole budget of $758.75 and paying the amount of $312.00 for the special project of repairing the cafeteria tables, the PTA also voted to give one hundred dollars to the Mother House of the teaching Sisters, and eight hundred dollars for the following items: a set of encyclopedias for the eighth grade, eight sets of maps and eight large dictionaries for each of the classrooms from the fourth to the eighth grade, a four-drawer steel cabinet for the school files, and a portable screen for the slide projector in visual aid.[27]

Feeding the Children

The PTA provides a hot dog luncheon for the children monthly on the second or third Wednesday, whichever falls nearest the middle of the month. The room hostesses for the month are in charge of this function—the same ones who are hostesses for the monthly meeting. The room mothers of the first and second grades, most of whom have had little experience in this function, are not called upon to serve until March and April. The eighth-grade mothers served the September luncheon and were able to muster twenty-six women for the occasion.

[27] This affluence is in contrast to the problems of St. Luke's PTA in its first year of existence, when the repair of the Sisters' typewriter was discussed at three consecutive meetings, and finally accomplished when one of the mothers, a former stenographer, fixed it without expense to the organization.

In subsequent months no other grade had more than twenty women present for the luncheon. The fare consists of one hot dog, a bag of potato chips, and a cup of chocolate milk. Each child pays twenty-five cents for the lunch, and ten cents for an additional hot dog.

The grade mothers also provide breakfast for the children who have received Communion on the monthly first Fridays. Two ladies, Mrs. Heller and Mrs. Gibson,[28] constitute the committee in charge of these breakfasts. They purchase all the supplies, come to the cafeteria before Mass and supervise the setting of tables by the particular room hostesses of the month. Since the breakfast is followed by the monthly meeting of the executive board, some members of the latter are also usually present to help out. Thus, there were always more women present to help at the breakfast than at the monthly hot dog luncheon. The meal consisted of doughnuts, sweet rolls and hot cocoa, for which each child was charged twenty cents.

Unlike the luncheon arrangement, when the noon recess is staggered for the higher and the lower classes, the breakfast had to provide at one time for all the children from the third to the eighth grade who had received Communion that morning. For the first two months of the year an arrangement was made whereby the third- and fourth-grade children took their breakfast in the classroom, while those from the fifth to the eighth grade used the cafeteria, where only about two hundred and fifty children could be seated at one time. Carrying the food and drink to the classrooms and serving it there proved too inconvenient for the ladies. For the rest of the year they arranged that the cafeteria would be used to capacity, and the overflow of children ate in the auditorium adjacent to the cafeteria. The children were supervised by some of the teachers and although they were permitted to talk were never boisterous.

The simultaneous serving of breakfast to all children was devised only this year because in previous years the younger children, being served last, sometimes did not get their breakfast until nine-thirty. Some of the parents thought that the delay was due also to the fact that the Pastor added Benediction of the Blessed Sacrament, Litany of the Blessed Virgin and "lots of other prayers" after the eight o'clock Mass. A few of the more "progressive" parents have suggested that the Pastor institute a daily Mass at eleven-thirty o'clock.[29] This would allow the

[28] On Award Night in May for the graduation class, these two ladies were singled out for special awards (gift certificates) from the PTA, for their "work in the kitchen."

[29] While this has not yet been done at St. Luke's or any other parochial school in the city, it appears to be spreading in several mid-western places. See Gerard

children to eat a regular breakfast at home, start school at eight o'clock and still enjoy the noon recess. Under this plan the PTA would serve luncheon instead of breakfast on the first Fridays.

The feeding of children at the Wednesday lunch and the Friday breakfast was also part of the fund-raising function of the PTA. The income from the former netted about forty dollars a month and from the latter about twenty dollars a month. Most of the parents appreciated the fact that this was a small monthly contribution to the PTA; some of them jocularly, called it a "racket," but one mother complained seriously, "Why do we always have to charge for things and make money? Why can't we just *give* more to the children?" Ultimately, of course, the profits from these meals went to the school and were for the benefit of all the children.

It must not be thought that the children were charged a price every time they were given something to eat. The Christmas party for the school children was sponsored by the PTA on Friday afternoon, December 21. The sixth-grade mothers did the work of packaging candy in half-pound bags, the organization contributing twenty-five dollars to the cost, with the Pastor paying the rest. At the Christmas party for the parents on December 18, the seventh-grade children offered an entertainment and afterwards received a collation in the cafeteria. The eighth graders likewise had a snack on their Award Night in May, and enjoyed large quantities of food on their special graduation picnic. The two athletic banquets were paid for by the attending parents, and no item of expenditure appeared for this in the records of the PTA.

Educating the Parents

Besides helping the children, one of the objectives of the PTA is also to help the parent achieve a better understanding of the world for which he is educating his child. "To improve relations within the family, parents must learn to understand themselves. Good family relations develop when parents perceive their own needs and limitations as well as the needs of the child. To the good will that is cultivated by character and spiritual education must be added the clear perceptions that are developed by parent education." [30] In previous years

Sloyan, "The Eucharist and the Aims of Christian Education," *Worship,* vol. 31, no. 6 (May–June, 1957), pp. 312–319; also "Noontime Masses in Schools," *ibid.,* pp. 362–366, which is a reprint of Archbishop Cushing's "Answers to Anticipated Objections;" see also "Late Morning Masses for School Children," *Homiletic and Pastoral Review,* vol. 58, no. 2 (November, 1957), p. 210.

[30] *Parent-Teacher Manual* (Chicago: National Congress of Parents and Teachers, 1953), p. 216. Theophane Power, *op. cit.,* p. 74, finds that the topics most fre-

this objective was attained through the formation of study groups, modeled on the study courses outlined in the National PTA magazine; but during the current year this approach has been abandoned and no one was appointed as chairman of the study group committee.

It appears that some Catholic parents' clubs are geared more to this objective than to the direct assistance to school and pupils. "The real aim of the Home and School Association is to help parents to be better parents. As a corollary, the schools will be better schools." [31] This is an interesting form of adjustment between the school and the parents. It replaces communication between parents and teachers by a system in which parents become adult pupils, not of the parochial school teachers, but of the experts who are brought in to teach them how to be parents. The members of St. Luke's PTA have never accepted this passive role and have focused their meeting programs on much broader topics.

The national theme for the year in the PTA was "Progress through Cooperation Between Homes, Schools, Communities." The "liturgy" adopted by St. Luke's group was "Look upon your child as To-morrow's Citizen." These guiding slogans helped the chairman of the program committee, Mrs. Egan, to arrange for speakers and subjects. As soon as she was elected to this position she started on the program, and had it completed and published before the opening of school in September. She was guided also by the various themes for each month of the school year. It was part of the agenda of every meeting, after the business at hand had been concluded, to conduct this program for the enlightenment and education of the membership.

At the September meeting the theme was "Operation Cooperation." The Pastor elaborated this topic in welcoming the new mothers to the PTA and in pointing out the necessity for cooperation of all members in learning to understand the home, the school and the parish. Police Chief DeBram (whose wife is chairman of the safety committee) then gave the principal talk, asking the parents to cooperate particularly with the traffic department of the city police. He praised and explained the work of the patrol boys of St. Luke's school.

"Progress in Government" was the theme of the October meeting, at

---

quently presented in parent education programs of Catholic parent-teacher organizations are: religion in the home, child psychology, library reading, recreation in the home, selection of radio programs, and mental hygiene.

[31] Sister Mary Clare, "The Sister and the Home-and-School Association," *The Catholic School Journal,* vol. 40, no. 7 (September, 1940), p. 220; see also a case history of this kind in Sister M. Beatrice, "School *Versus* Home," *Education,* vol. 73, no. 4 (December, 1952), pp. 245–247.

which Mrs. Chadwick, chairman of the committee on international relations and legislation, showed a film entitled, *Government Is Your Business*. She is an active member of the League of Women Voters, and in her speech made an enlightened, liberal and non-partisan plea on the importance of intelligent voting in the forthcoming elections. It was partially through this inspiration that the parish Boy Scouts took an active part in a "Get out the vote day." Some of the teachers, present at this meeting for the last time, also took the cue of political interest. Later in the month they held a mock presidential election among the pupils from the fifth to the eighth grade (the incumbent Republican being returned to office by a "landslide").

At the November meeting the educational program was late in starting. The controversy over report cards and the manner of selecting candidates for the high school scholarships had been carried over from the October business meeting. The result was that the panel discussion on the theme, "No Nation is Stronger than its Homes," did not get under way until nine-fifteen and lasted till after eleven o'clock. This was the longest PTA meeting of the year. At any rate, the first speaker was Father Martin, who said that unlike the public school, the parochial school prepared the child for both his life on earth and his eternal destiny. Professor Comstock regretted the fact that Catholics do not have a representative percentage among the intellectuals of the country. Mrs. Curry pointed out that the child's lack of responsibility is frequently nothing more than a reflection of parental irresponsibility. Professor Goebel stressed the importance of guiding and developing the emotions of love and security in children.

In December the theme was "Progress for Peace," but the Christmas party with its entertainment by the seventh-grade choir displaced the educational program. "International Relations," the theme for January was exemplified in the form of a discussion by a visiting University debate team. Their topic was the discussion of economic aid to foreign countries. None of the members participated except as a listening audience to this program.

The February meeting was given over to the annual "Founder's Day" program, honoring Alice Birney and Phoebe Hearst, the originators of the movement, and commemorating the sixtieth anniversary of the National Congress of Parents and Teachers. Featured speakers at this event were the president of the City Council of the PTA, a non-Catholic, who congratulated St. Luke's as "one of the best groups in the city," and gave a historical account of the parent organization, and Mrs. Heaton, St. Luke's representative on the City Council, who devoted most of her talk to an explanation of the Christian Family Movement. The traditional candle-lighting ceremony was also performed this evening.

Although the theme for March was "The Citizen Child," the election of new officers for the following year was the main business of the meeting. Probably as representative of the future citizens being groomed by the school, the Boy Scout Troop performed two skits and the Camp Fire Girls gave recitations and sang songs. The April meeting had as its theme "Living Peacefully." This appears to have been interpreted by the officers as a question of contentment and recreation. A member of the State Conservation Commission was invited to show a film and to give a talk about the State Parks. This was the most poorly attended meeting of the year since only fifteen persons were present, and the officers were embarrassed that they had invited an "outsider" to speak that evening.

The May meeting was replaced by the annual breakfast, a custom started in 1943. There was no advertence to the theme of that month, "Progress—A Better Tomorrow," although the tone and content of the breakfast program pointed to progressively better relations between the public and the parochial schools. The presidents of both the state and the city PTA, as well as their immediate predecessors, were there. The public school superintendent was an honored guest, and the superintendent of public schools of the neighboring city was the featured speaker. His informative talk entitled, "The PTA can change the future" must be included among the best of the efforts made during the year for the education of parents.

Special Services

A full understanding of the contribution of the PTA to St. Luke's school cannot be obtained merely by attending its meetings and observing its programs. There were almost innumerable services performed, many of them in an informal way, which indicate that these women consider themselves an integral part of the parochial school. They pay the association dues and subscriptions for the priests and Sisters; they underwrite the Sisters' expenses at the annual teachers' institute. Some of the women act as chauffeurs whenever the Sisters have to go to the doctor or wish to go to their Mother House or elsewhere.

At the end of August each year, before the Sisters return to the school convent, a group of mothers gives their residence a thorough cleaning. The PTA contributes twenty-five dollars worth of groceries for them to start the year, and many families make voluntary contributions of foodstuffs. This form of "assistance in kind" continues throughout the year, with parents sending gallons of ice cream, bushels of fresh fruits and vegetables, cartons of canned goods, and many other items of food to the convent. The deep freezer and the shelves in the basement are kept constantly stocked by the throughtful and generous members of the PTA so that the Sisters need buy hardly anything for their table during the school year.

The registration for next year's first graders was done on Wednesday, April 24, and was also handled by four members of the PTA. The date was announced in the church bulletin and from the pulpit on the two previous Sundays. Two ladies were present in the school library from ten till noon and two others worked from one till three in the afternoon. On this one day, seventy-seven children were registered for the first grade, and two other prospective pupils' names were taken. Since the teachers were in the classrooms during these periods the PTA mothers handled the whole procedure, checking the age and residential qualifications and getting the signature of the responsible adult.[32]

Several members of the PTA are also at hand on the opening day of school. The class lists were made out before the end of the previous school year, and the women's function is mainly that of shepherding the pupils to their assigned classrooms. The possibility that the mothers might give more assistance along these lines was discussed at several meetings. The committee of room mothers held a separate meeting on Tuesday, October 2, at which it was suggested that some of the mothers rotate in supervising the first- and second-grade pupils at the noon hour in the school yard.[33] The teachers who have "yard duty" have to eat lunch in two shifts, and the eighth-grade girls also take turns looking after the youngest children. No decision was reached on this matter. The mothers living nearest the school felt that they would soon have to carry the whole burden; the mothers of older children in the school felt that the children were being adequately supervised; and the mothers of the youngest children were not numerous enough to take on this daily routine.[34]

The book-mending project is another form of service that the PTA renders the school. The chairman of this committee is Mrs. Egan, who

[32] This registration indicates a smaller first grade for next year, but the Principal remarked that "we usually have about twenty more drifting in between April and September."

[33] The youngest children use the northwest section of the school property as their play ground and are thus adequately protected from the play of the older and "rougher" children.

[34] The suggestion that the tuition be raised so that someone could be hired for this duty, was vigorously opposed by the Pastor who said that "we want to do away with tuition, not increase it."

is also first vice-president, chairman of the program committee and traffic patrolwoman for St. Luke's school. She has been in charge of textbook mending for two years. In previous years the mothers attempted to perform this function during the last week in August, but never succeeded in repairing all of the books before the school term started. On three occasions during the year, in November, January and March, the chairman contacted the room mothers and suggested that each ask three mothers from each room to come to the school library on Friday afternoon for two hours of book repair. Out of a potential of forty-two invited mothers the largest number of members ever to appear for these sessions was twenty-three.

Since 1948 all textbooks have been purchased out of parish funds and rented to the pupils of St. Luke's. Before that time the PTA had set up a kind of used-book service, through which the parents could sell the textbooks no longer needed by their children. Supervision of the book rental system was gradually taken over by the PTA through the work of Mrs. Heaton and Mrs. Buchert. Theoretically, the children and their parents were supposed to keep the books in repair. In practice, however, the PTA, while still maintaining that the first responsibility is that of the parents and children, set up the book mending service in 1950.

The teachers try to observe the condition of each child's textbooks, and when a book needs immediate repair, Mrs. Egan does it in her spare time. At the regular book-mending sessions, however, the committee attempts systematically to cover the whole school, class by class. The children are notified the day before by their teacher, and told to check their books for needed repair and to insert a note indicating what is to be done. Toward the end of the school year, there were still many books that had not been repaired. A call for volunteers was made from the pulpit. Daily sessions were held during the third week in May until all books had been satisfactorily repaired and prepared for the opening of the following school term.

Another occasion of service by the room mothers was the annual Parents' Night, or "Open House," sponsored by the school and promoted by the PTA on Wednesday, November 7. The first report cards of the year had just been given to the pupils of the first, second and third grades, and since a new system of reports was being introduced, this was felt to be a stimulus to the appearance of parents at the school. The teacher of each class was present to meet the parents, and a room mother was at each teacher's desk to register the names of parents and to indicate to them where the child sat in the classroom. At the main entrance of the school a table was set up to accept new members of the PTA, and their dues. At another table some of the mothers were selling tickets for a basket of groceries to be raffled that night.

The mothers of the PTA also gave assistance for the various entertainment programs offered by the children. Some of this was done in conjunction with the skits and programs offered by the Boy Scouts, Camp Fire Girls and the seventh-grade choir. The most elaborate pupil entertainment was the annual operetta, written and directed by Sister Cecelia, in honor of the Pastor's feast day. This was presented on Friday morning, May 10, for the school children and on the following Sunday afternoon for interested adults. Preparation included the purchase of material and the sewing of costumes by small groups of mothers under the direction of Sister Cecelia.

As one of the numerous parish societies of St. Luke's, the PTA does its share at the annual Bazaar which was conducted on the four days of November 17–20. Officially the organization was in charge of the Bingo games, but its members were scattered throughout the auditorium working in a number of booths and with the various other parish groups. This event was open also for teachers and pupils on Sunday afternoon from two to five. Games of skill and chance were played in great variety, and most of the children present were accompanied by their parents. The receipts from this annual festival are credited to the building fund for the new church, which will be erected in the next few years.

Generalizations

1. The parents of St. Luke's tend to be servants of the parochial school rather than its superior, partner or representative. Although parents have the responsibility of educating their own children, even prior to that of the school, most of them work for the school rather than with the school. There is a studied effort, especially among the officers and more experienced members of the PTA, never to "interfere" with the curriculum or the teachers. This relinquishing of parental authority follows the pattern set in the urban public schools; it is formalized in the constitutions of the National Congress of Parents and Teachers; and it appears to be fortified at the parochial school level because of a failure to distinguish among familial authority, educational authority and religious authority.

2. The public school, with a full-time Principal and with teachers who have free periods during the day, has an overwhelmingly larger percentage of pre-arranged interviews between parents and teachers, than does the parochial school. In the public school these interviews are requested more frequently by teachers, and they deal more frequently

with behavior problems, than is the case in the parochial school. More of St. Luke's parents attend Parents' Night, and about twice as many Catholic fathers participate in it, than is the case at the public school.

3. For the first time in its history, the St. Luke's PTA held its monthly meetings at night so that teachers and male parents could attend. The "walk-out" of the teachers after the second meeting, and the failure of the fathers to attend, left the organization essentially what it had always been, a mothers' club. The fathers cooperated in many ways, direct and indirect, in the activities of their wives. Four of them were officially chairmen of the committees on civil defense, character education, visual education and recreation (the last two being husband-wife teams).

4. Communication between parents and teachers broke down, and dissension arose within the PTA, only when matters of a curricular or academic nature came up for discussion. It was judged a case of "interference with the school" when some of the male parents raised questions about the new report cards, the scholarship awards and the visual education program. After this, none of the teachers came back to the meetings, and more than one-third (36.3%) of the parents never attended a meeting. Even outside the PTA, some of the mothers (15.4%) never met and spoke with the teacher of their children (as compared to 24.4 per cent of the public school mothers.)

5. The central preoccupation of St. Luke's PTA is on the physical aspects of education and school maintenance. Its most successful function was that of fund-raising. At one time or another it has contributed practically everything in every classroom, except the desks and the blackboards. Its annual projects are worked out in terms of purchasable equipment that will aid in the educational function of the school. The parents, as members of the PTA, stand merely on the periphery of the learning process of their children as this process is understood in a formal, traditional way. They submit to lectures, discussions and programs for their own education as parents, but for the children's schooling they provide equipment, mend textbooks, serve breakfasts and luncheons.

6. The three priests of the parish take an active interest in the PTA, but permit and encourage a wide latitude of decision-making among the parents. The Pastor is slow to give his own opinions until he has heard and weighed those of the lay leadership. He heads the committee on spiritual education and maintains close working relations with officers and other chairmen. A similar evaluation can be made of Father Martin, who teaches religion in the school, attends the PTA meetings, and holds the official position of director of recreation. Father Thomas

headed the temporary committee on scholarship awards, did most of the work connected with it, and later became a member of the permanent committee together with the other priests, the Principal and one lay woman from the organization.

7. A high degree of organizational ability, and even of executive leadership, is demonstrated by some of the women in the PTA, and in its sister group, the Patrons of St. Luke's. They exhibit a genuine talent and capacity to plan meetings, run them smoothly, reach decisions that are satisfactory to the majority, and follow through successfully on the chosen programs. Although they are all volunteers, unpaid participants, they perform their roles in a relatively professional manner. Part of this success is due to the organizational structure of the PTA, which encourages the greatest amount of participation by the largest number of members. The techniques of allocating specific functions to specific committees, and then demanding monthly reports from them, tends to increase both responsibility and activity among the members.

8. An important latent function of St. Luke's PTA is its use as a channel of communication with the non-parochial community. Far from being separatist, the group is an integral unit in the City Council, State and National Congress of Parents and Teachers. The newly elected president of the City Council is a member of St. Luke's PTA. Frequent, reciprocal and cordial relations exist with the three neighboring public schools and with the representatives (parents, teachers, principals, superintendents) of the whole public school system.

Chapter

FOURTEEN

FINANCING THE SCHOOL

THE MAINTENANCE of a parochial school plant like that of St. Luke's parish is a serious financial burden for both the priest and the laity. The Pastor must find means of raising the necessary money, learn how to husband the resources of the parish, devise ways of economical spending, and make annual financial reports to the Bishop. Father Albert has been doing all these things successfully since he first came to the parish in the middle of the Depression to find it saddled with a staggering debt. He lived frugally in a barn-like structure, became practiced in staving off creditors, and had his share of disillusioning experiences with the moneylenders. The years of struggle have left their mark on him and have made him very cautious in the handling of parish finances.[1]

Problems of Financing

The Pastor and people of St. Luke's have worked together for a quarter-century in building up the parish.[2] The original debt was paid off, a new priests' rectory was built, an auditorium-gymnasium with cafeteria and meeting rooms has been added to the school, and a drive has just been conducted to build a new church, and to move and remodel the Sisters' convent. The Pastor's financial acumen is indicated in his reminiscences about the new gymnasium. "The architects gave us a cost estimate of $350,000. They'd thumb through those magazines they have and when they'd see something nice, they'd say 'you need this too,' and would write down the price. I told them that

[1] Some of the parishioners joke about his personal frugality and simple tastes. When the new priests' residence was completed the parishioners insisted that he throw out the old furniture. He protested with the remark, "there's lots of sittin' left in them chairs."

[2] For a general discussion of the problems of church financing see two unsigned articles, "Complexities in Financing," *Church Property Administration*, vol. 17, no. 6 (November–December, 1953), pp. 66–70, and 98–102; and "Catholic Financing," *ibid.*, vol. 18, no. 2 (March–April, 1954), pp. 134–136.

was too much. So I bought the plans and specifications from them and started cutting down the price. We would shop around and buy a little here and a little there. Finally, we had the whole thing built, and it cost us around $200,000."

During this quarter-century, of course, the current operating expenses for the school and the parish have been met. These expenses have increased with the growing population as well as with the expansion of the parish plant. The cost of maintenance increased as more rooms and buildings were added, and as the use of fuel and light multiplied. Even though the southern section of the parochial territory has been cut off to form a new and separate parish, St. Luke's has grown from 1,668 people in 1933, when Father Albert took office, to 5,175 at the last census count at the end of our study.[3]

The annual financial report of the parish, published in January, shows that a total of $20,352.21 was expended out of parish funds for the maintenance of the school and the teachers' residence. This is a per capita cost of $32.20 for the 632 children in St. Luke's school.[4] During the same period the per capita cost for the elementary public school child in the same city (excluding kindergarten) was $283.14. If St. Luke's school were operated on this scale of expenditure it would cost the parishioners $178,944.48 per year. Obviously, the parochial school saves in many ways, and it can and must operate far below this cost.[5] The services of religious teachers bring the amount of salaries far below that of the public schools. The school as such does not pay the costs of the athletic teams, or of the numerous other "fringe" activities provided in the public school.

Since the financing of the parochial school is such a great burden and since this burden is borne by the parishioners themselves, and is of particular interest to the parents of the school children, we asked

[3] The current statistic includes 916 dormant Catholics, 17.7 per cent of the parochial population.

[4] There appear to be some "hidden costs" absorbed by the general parish funds, the inclusion of which would slightly increase this per capita figure. St. Luke's does not employ the "scientific" cost accounting advised by some experts. See Rowland E. Gannon, "The Challenge of Finance in Catholic Schools," *The Catholic School Journal,* vol. 51, no. 9 (November, 1951), pp. 287–289.

[5] See the detailed break-down of the study of costs of a Milwaukee parochial school, showing that the per capita cost was forty-three dollars. "Tell How Much It Costs to Teach Johnny!" *The Catholic School Journal,* vol. 52, no. 9 (November, 1952), pp. 273–274. Concerning the cost to parents of public school children, see L. B. Ezell and Paul Coleman, Jr., "Free Public High Schools Are Expensive," *School Review,* vol. 62, no. 7 (October, 1954), pp. 420–423.

these parents how they thought the costs of the school should be borne. The following table shows their answers.

Suggested Sources of Finances for St. Luke's School:

All or part from public taxes	59.4%	All from taxes	19.4%
		Part from taxes	40.0%
Parents, parish, or both	34.2		
All or part from diocese	4.3		
Other suggestions and no answers	2.1		

It is interesting to note that about one-fifth of these parents suggest that the parochial school be fully supported from public funds and that another two-fifths want at least partial support from the public funds. About one-third appear to be in accord with the present state of affairs—the main source of income for the school being from the parish and the parents. The notion that the diocese might be a source of support seemed strange to them, but this is precisely what the Bishop proposed later in the year.

On the fourth Sunday of Lent, March 31, the Bishop of the diocese brought the problem of school finance before all the people in a letter read from the pulpit and printed in the diocesan weekly. He proposed an annual diocesan collection during Lent as a "Catholic Education Fund," on which he could draw to help newly formed parishes in the construction of parochial schools. He pointed out that Catholic education has now become a "common cause," and that such school buildings can no longer be termed the "private enterprise" of the individual parish. The need for this new approach to school financing was further explained by the Bishop.

"There was a time, not so long ago, when tuition fees, paid by the parents, together with special parish school collections and various other sources of income, came pretty close to meeting the expense of our school system. The cold fact is that we have now got beyond that stage. The rapid and steady increase in the birthrate, the necessity of building more and larger schools, of employing an increasing number of lay teachers, of putting into our school program many services and facilities that were hardly dreamed of a generation ago—these conditions call for a new approach to the whole problem. They make Catholic education a *common cause*. They make it the concern of *all Catholics*, whether or not they have children in school, whether or not they have any school at all." [6]

[6] Edward A. Fitzpatrick, "The Financial Weakness of the Parish School," *The Catholic School Journal*, vol. 48, no. 6 (June, 1948), p. 201, made a similar proposal, comparing "diocesan aid" to poor parishes with "state aid" to poor public school districts.

This concept of sharing the wealth from the richer parishes for the assistance of recently established and poorer parishes is relatively new. Less than ten years ago a prominent Catholic educator pointed out that "parish obligations remain obligations of the parish. It is not customary for Pastors who fail to collect the necessary amounts to maintain the parish plant to look to the Bishop for assistance. The parish unit is expected to be self-contained and financed." [7] There were pleas for clearing the financial jungle of school maintenance, for setting up separate school budgets in parishes, for getting the Pastors to make clear financial statements on school costs to the parishioners.[8] Diocesan aid to parochial schools was clarified. "In short, must some larger unit than the parish, collecting from the whole body, come to the aid of the weaker parishes? Obviously we might use, in a preliminary way, the principle of redistribution so as to improve the capacity of poor parishes." [9]

Where the Money Comes From

The tuition at St. Luke's school is lower than that of any other parochial school in the city. The basic cost per family (not per child) is ten dollars a year. Added to this is the book rental of five dollars, another dollar for subscription to the *Little Messenger*, a charge of one dollar for art materials, and twenty-five cents for activities fee. Thus, the total tuition per family is $17.25 per year for the first child, and $7.25 for each additional child. Any family sending a child from the neighboring parish, where the new school has only five grades, must pay an extra five dollars. Any family unable to pay these amounts may send the child to St. Luke's school tuition-free.

The Pastor hopes that St. Luke's will some day be a free school. At a meeting of the room mothers of the PTA on Tuesday, October 2, a lady suggested that the tuition be raised so that people could be hired to supervise the playground during lunch periods. Father Albert objected to this with the remark, "I hope for the day when we can eliminate tuition completely." The tuition at the local public school appears to be extremely high. Children living outside the city limits, or who are not permanent residents of the city, must pay $125.00 per year in tuition to attend the public school. The total amount taken in

[7] Frederick G. Hochwalt, "Financing Catholic Education," *The Educational Record*, vol. 30 (April, 1949), p. 200.

[8] William E. McManus, "Financing Catholic Education," *The Catholic School Journal*, vol. 51, no. 4 (April, 1951), pp. 137–140, points out that the techniques of "fee enterprise," and the notion of fund raising as an adventure rather than as a science, are no longer tenable.

[9] Edward A. Fitzpatrick, "Parish Schools and Finance," *The Catholic School Journal*, vol. 50, no. 9 (November, 1950) p. 290.

from tuition during the year at St. Luke's was less than four thousand dollars, an obviously inadequate income on which to operate a school of 632 pupils.[10] In fact, this amount was not even sufficient to pay the salaries of the lay teachers at St. Luke's, an indication of the small segment of school expenses that can be met by tuition.[11]

Father Albert has the reputation among the parishioners as a man who "never talks money from the pulpit." He praises the loyalty of the people and wants them to think of the parish as something belonging to them. "They cooperate generously without any prodding on my part, and they give well in the Sunday collection." He employs the envelope system for collections, these envelopes going to 1,224 adult parishioners during the year of our study. A mimeographed report was distributed on the third Sunday of Advent, listing the names of contributors and the amounts they gave. The Parish Bulletin announced that "this does not include your Lenten offerings. Mistakes do creep in, but on the whole, the accounting is correct. For corrections, please get in contact with Father Martin and our records will be adjusted."

This "contributors' list" shows that seventy-three persons did not use their envelopes and that the remaining 1,151 persons contributed $58,224.55 in the weekly collection. This is an average weekly contribution of ninety-seven cents for each envelope user. But there were also 642 persons listed who contributed $6,792.80, which is an annual additional average of $10.58 for those who used the bi-monthly envelopes. Some parishioners object to the use of envelopes and particularly to the publication of names and amounts at the end of the year. They contribute anonymously by simply putting cash in the collection basket, and an indication of these amounts can be had from the financial report published in the Parish Bulletin on Sunday, January 13.

In keeping with his general attitude of treating the laity as partners in the parochial enterprise, the Pastor publishes this categorized report of receipts and expenditures every year.[12] It showed that the

[10] The total possible income from tuition and fees for the year was $8,325. This is combined from 377 "oldest" children paying $17.25 each, equaling $6,503.25, and 255 "younger" children paying $7.25 each, equaling $1,848.75.

[11] Concerning the question of lay teachers' salaries, see Joseph J. Panzer, "The Administrator's Approach to the Lay Teacher Problem Regarding Salary, Tenure and Pensions," *Bulletin* of the National Catholic Educational Association, vol. 52, no. 1 (August, 1955), pp. 267–272.

[12] "Intelligent action in connection with the financing of the school can be taken only in the light of information. It therefore becomes the responsibility of the

parish had received from all sources $112,403.11, and had paid out for all expenditures $70,925.82. With this favorable balance, the parish was thus able to add forty-one thousand dollars to the fund for the building of a new church. A one-day campaign was run on a house-to-house basis on Sunday, May 19, to raise the building fund to four hundred thousand dollars, and most of this amount has been pledged.

The bulk of the parish income for current expenses is, however, derived from the Sunday collections, but other sources of income are also tapped.[13] One of these is the annual parish festival, or Bazaar, held on the days of November 17–20, which netted $10,211.82. Except for the building fund campaign, this is the only joint money-raising effort of the whole parish, in which all the parochial societies participate. The PTA was in charge of the Bingo games, the Athletic Committee ran the raffles, the Camp Fire Girls and the Boy Scouts each had charge of a booth, and there was a special Sunday afternoon of games for the school children. Turkeys and TV sets were raffled off, poker and roulette drew many customers. The Bazaar brought many of the "old reliable" parishioners together in operating it, and most of the other parishioners in attendance.

In previous years the featured prize at the Bazaar was an automobile. This has been discontinued, says Father Albert, because "it's just one drawing and that's all. One person is happy and that's the end of it. The let-down is too quick." The raffling off of large home appliances, like refrigerators and deep freezers, has also been discontinued because of the inconvenience and dissatisfaction connected with it. "Most of the people already have these things.[14] The person winning a refrigerator would want the parish to buy it back—at retail prices, not at the wholesale price we paid for it. We would never do that; and now we don't have such prizes." The main prizes now are Government Savings Bonds totaling eighteen hundred dollars, ranging from the first prize of a one-thousand dollar bond down to a number

---

parish priest to report periodically the finances both as to income and expenditure of the parish school." Edward A. Fitzpatrick, "Parish Schools and Finance," *The Catholic School Journal*, vol. 51, no. 1 (January, 1951), p. 16. This was the fourth in a series of editorials dealing with the same subject.

[13] Joseph L. Bernardin, "Revenue Procurement in Catholic Schools," *The Catholic Educational Review*, vol. 49, no. 6 (October, 1951), pp. 514–523, gathered information from 214 elementary school Principals in twenty-three archdioceses, showing that 65.4 per cent of the schools got all or part of their revenue from general parish funds. Three out of ten (29.6%) would prefer to get revenue from tuition alone, and 52.8 per cent from parish funds alone.

[14] In our interviews with 496 families of elementary school children we found that only eighty-two, or 16.5 per cent, had deep freezers.

of twenty-five dollar bonds. Most of the people wanted the cash instead of the bond, and the parish would then give the cash equivalent.

It must be noted that the money raised through Sunday collections and from the annual Bazaar cannot be dedicated solely to the maintenance of St. Luke's school. These are general funds through which the whole parish plant must be operated, only part of which is used for the school. The fund-raising activities of the PTA are exclusively for school purposes, and their most profitable venture during the year is the Style Show, or "Dessert Bridge," as it was also called. Here also there was the raffle of a TV set, which accounted for almost half of the profits made. The PTA also profits from the monthly hot dog luncheon and the monthly breakfast on first Fridays. All of these sources accounted for more than two thousand dollars which were spent directly on school needs.[15]

In previous years the PTA had conducted a special children's bazaar. It had been held in the classrooms, with the room mothers in charge, on a Sunday afternoon. While the children themselves were the best customers on these occasions, many of them brought their parents, who had an opportunity to see the school, meet the teachers, and spend money for the benefit of the school. Each classroom had a different kind of booth, and there was a certain amount of rivalry among the classroom mothers. This had been discontinued for two years but will be resumed next year, with the hope of surpassing the usual net of about five hundred dollars.

Money for Athletics

The Athletic Committee of St. Luke's school also raised funds to equip the teams in football, basketball, baseball and volleyball. They used several devices for raising money. A dance was held on Saturday, October 27, at a public hall in the immediate community. Two tickets were sent home through the school children with a covering letter to each family, asking support of the venture. In spite of this, the attendance was small and the net profits were only one hundred and forty-two dollars. In the previous year the Ushers' Club had staged a dance at the same place, and made over six hundred dollars profit which they turned over to the Athletic Committee for the school teams. "This year," says the Pastor, "the men didn't get out and sell tickets; and you can't make money unless you do that." He suggested that they run a "Feather Party" (at which only live poultry is raffled off) "but they don't like all the work connected with it."

[15] See above, chap. 13, "Parents and Teachers," for an account of these activities.

The Rosary and Altar Society had also contributed a hundred dollars in the previous season, and the men in the Athletic Committee thought that each parish society ought to contribute to the support of athletics. Father Albert remarked "they want to do it the easy way, without working for it." The men then decided to conduct a house-to-house canvass of the parish, asking for personal donations. Father Martin provided a set of mimeographed cards with all parishioners' names and addresses, but this scheme was also dropped. "My wife and I spent about two days," said Donald Maestri, "planning the campaign, sorting the cards by blocks and sections; they were spread all over the living room. Then the committee changed their minds and decided to have a fish fry instead. Well, the work wasn't wasted anyway, because the Holy Name Society used the cards for their program."

The women of the parish are also interested in athletics, and it was not until they practically "took over" the fund-raising that the group had some success. Donald Maestri, the former football coach, said that "the women just go out and start projects and raise money without talking too much about it." Mrs. Bowman, the secretary of the Committee, said in January, that "the treasury is down to one hundred and seventy dollars, and we have to do something about it." The women planned a fish fry for Friday, February 22, but when they discovered that a dispensation from abstinence had been granted by the Bishop because of Washington's Birthday, they decided on a Chicken Fry. Although a group of six women worked the better part of two days, although they paid only twenty-five cents a pound for four hundred pounds of chicken, and although more than a hundred prospective diners had to be turned away, the Chicken Fry netted the group only two hundred and ten dollars.

The women were dissatisfied that so much labor had brought in such small returns, and immediately started plans for a Card Party to be held on April 22, Easter Monday. Meanwhile, all of these people were also busy working for the Fashion Show, held on Thursday, February 28. A "new plan" was instituted by the women whereby each committee would be headed by husband and wife as co-chairman. Mr. and Mrs. Andrew Heller were in charge of the affair and appointed the numerous committees. As early as March 17, a letter was sent to all parents through the children in the school, enclosing two books of raffle tickets and two entrance tickets for the party. "The proceeds from this affair," it stated, "will be used to further the athletic activities for your children. Therefore, we hope to have the full support of all the parents. The fathers are particularly encouraged to attend this party."

As the date drew nearer, it was clear that the women were the real workers for this affair. An organizational meeting was held on Monday, April 15, at which thirty women and only eight men appeared. On the night of the card party the weather was inclement and less than four hundred players attended, about four-fifths of them women. They raffled off a dinette set, donated by Mr. Weston, a Hi-Fi set donated by Mr. Pitre, and a mix-master donated by the City Electric Company. The ladies were pleased that they "cleared almost eight hundred dollars," and the men were pleased that the treasury was replenished so that they could buy more sports equipment for the school athletic teams.

The ingenuity of St. Luke's parishioners in "making things pay" was demonstrated at the two athletic banquets. Tickets were priced at one dollar fifty, but this was not enough to cover the meals for the "dead heads," as the coach called the invited, non-paying adult guests. To recover this deficit they "picked up about forty dollars" in raffling a football and a basketball, autographed by all of the team members. Another device was the "St. Luke's booster tags" distributed by the uniformed football players outside the church on Sunday, September 16. The boys up-ended their helmets and gave a tag to anyone who dropped money into the helmet. In this way they netted $141.00.

In a sense, all of this fund-raising for the athletic program is "extra income." The Pastor has stated numerous times that the school would not have any teams, and that it could not afford an athletic program, unless the parents found some way of contributing the money. The original fifteen football uniforms and equipment cost seven hundred and fifty dollars. "When he saw the size of the bill," said one of the men, "he almost fainted; but he had promised to pay it, and he did." Then, for two or three years, the Athletic Committee came to the Pastor whenever they needed money. "We would go in and ask him for a hundred dollars, and he would give us fifty. Then we figured we'd better ask him for two hundred when we wanted a hundred; but he was wise to us and we'd still get only fifty. Finally, we started our own treasury and got his permission to spend all we could raise."

Supporting the Sisters

The eleven religious teachers of St. Luke's school live in a frame house of sturdy construction adjacent to the church and across the yard from the school. It is a converted private residence which was enlarged for their use. Each Sister has her private room. The former sun porch is used as a repository of school records. The former living room and dining room are now used for entertaining visitors and for giving piano lessons by Sisters Cecelia and Ruth. The community chapel, refectory and recreation and study room, as well as the kitchen are all on the first floor. The basement under the "old house" contains the laundry and storage rooms.[16]

The bills for the upkeep of this convent—for heating, lights, and repair—are paid by the Pastor from the general parish funds.[17] He also presents a monthly check to the Principal for six hundred and fifty dollars, which she immediately endorses and sends on to the Mother House of her congregation. This fulfills the official obligation of the Pastor, through the parish, which is fixed in the regulations of the diocesan synod. Since the Sisters must meet their current living and other expenses it is obvious that they must have support other than this.

The voluntary generosity of the parishioners is again evidenced in the manner in which they pour gifts and help upon the Sisters. Sister Roberta says, "we have the vow of poverty, but we certainly never go hungry for want of food." Most of the parents send gifts through the children to the individual teacher at Christmas, and some at Easter. "It's hard to know what to give the Sisters," said one mother. "They get more candy, cake and nuts than they can eat. They must have handkerchiefs, gloves, rosaries, pen and pencil sets piled up to the ceiling." Knowing that it is difficult to select a personal gift for a Sister, and that any cash given to them will be turned over to the Mother House, many of the parents present to them gift certificates, which can be redeemed with merchandise at the downtown stores. They simply pool these certificates and each individual draws on them when she needs to make a purchase.[18]

[16] During the summer months following our study, the convent was moved to a new foundation, enlarged again so that there are now private rooms for fourteen Sisters. The whole building was faced with brick to match the priest's residence in appearance.

[17] Since there is one fuel bill, one light bill, one heating system, one janitor, etc., for the whole parish plant, it appears that some of the school costs are absorbed by the general fund for parish upkeep. Frederick G. Hochwalt, "Financing Catholic Education," *The Educational Record,* vol. 30 (April, 1949), says that "Pastors are not wont to look upon Catholic education as an independent entity that has to be maintained and operated; for most Pastors the school is but one part of the parish organization and is treated accordingly on the parish records. In nearly all cases school costs are not apportioned to the one or other but may be carried as one general item" (p. 201).

[18] It is obvious from this description that the teaching Sisters at St. Luke's are well regarded and well treated by the Pastor and the parishioners. In a study of 181 teaching communities, it was found that among the unsatisfactory features was "insufficient financial compensation, particularly when medical care, retirement, replacement, and community expansion are considered." See Kenny Cox,

It is the custom among Catholics physicians, surgeons, and dentists to treat the religious Sisters free of charge, or for a merely nominal fee. Transportation to the doctor's office, to the hospital, to the Mother House, to teachers' institutes, is provided by a list of twenty-five volunteer mothers of the PTA, particularly by Mrs. Egan, Mrs. McWellon, Mrs. Noto, Mrs. Heller and Mrs. Bowman. During the course of the last few years numerous larger gifts have been supplied by the parents of the school children: a TV set, a deep freezer, a laundry machine, an electric mangle, a clothes dryer.[19] The latter was installed as a "surprise" for Sister Roberta while she was at the eighth-grade picnic in May.

The Sisters also have several small "enterprises" in the school, the profits of which the Pastor lets them keep. St. Luke's does not have a financial subsidy for milk or for hot lunches.[20] The eighth-grade boys take turns bringing milk around to the other grades, and the eighth-grade girls sell candy, as well as orange and grape drinks, to the other children at recess and lunch time. They sell about seven dollars worth of candy daily. There are always more volunteers for these jobs than can be used, and a sanction on behavior is to threaten to take away this "privilege." Some of the parents grumble about the children eating between meals and spoiling their appetites.[21] Others approve because "otherwise the children would be running to the candy store or the corner drug store." At any rate, these enterprises are quite successful and the profits go to the Sisters.

In this sense, St. Luke's parish is a source of revenue for the Mother House of the teaching Sisters, and the people are contributing financial

---

"The Conditions of Service of Religious Teaching Personnel in Diocese and/or Parochial Schools" (dissertation in Library of Catholic University of America, 1953).

[19] Several men in the parish are in the home appliance business, and donate these objects. One of them, a non-Catholic, insists that the Sisters "don't tell anybody who gave you this."

[20] Several of the parents remarked that with a subsidy the children could get milk for three to five cents, instead of the ten cents they now pay, and they could also have good lunches at reasonable prices. The Pastor points out two objections to the lunch program: "there are not enough volunteers from the PTA to run it; and you have to adhere to a prescribed diet; and that's not good."

[21] "School Opinion Poll," *The Nation's Schools*, vol. 54, no. 6 (December, 1954), p. 54, showed that ninety per cent of the school superintendents queried objected to the sale of candy, carbonated beverages, soft drinks or gum in the school cafeteria. About three-quarters agreed that such sales may be permitted on special occasions.

assistance for the training of their future parochial school teachers. Sister Roberta said that in the year previous to our study she had been able to send over fourteen hundred dollars "extra" to her Superioress. Her "project" during the current year was to gather about six hundred dollars to pay for bedside tables in the new Mother House. Her next project is even more ambitious, to provide mattresses for all the new rooms at the Mother House, "just like the ones we have at St. Luke's convent." Father Albert thinks this is too big a promise to make. "It'll run into thousands of dollars."

Children's Fund Raising

The pupils of St. Luke's school are the ultimate beneficiaries of most of the fund-raising done for the school. Occasionally, they are used as emissaries, or channels of communication, through which the PTA or the Athletic Committee sends notices, tickets and raffle books home to their parents. Generally speaking, the children are not used by the adults in an exploitive way. The priests and teachers discourage any scheme which may turn the children into solicitors in door-to-door selling of tickets or chance books. The Pastor has warned the parish organizations that he would not tolerate this kind of practice.[22]

Nevertheless, there is a certain amount of volunteer money-raising done by the children. The Camp Fire Girls had one "bake sale" during the year. They sold some of their baked goods to relatives and neighbors but most of it to the parishioners on Sunday morning, March 3. The girls realized profits of one hundred and six dollars on this sale, using it to help defray expense of their own organization. The boys in the school participated in two paper drives during the year, but most of the work was done by adults. The drive was announced from the pulpit and in the Church Bulletin on the previous Sunday. The people brought bundles of papers to the school yard on Saturday and Sunday, January 5 and 6, and May 18 and 19, where they were loaded into a truck by Mr. Noto, Mr. Nordman and Mr. Buchert. The profits from these drives, one hundred and forty-three dollars, were split equally between the Boy Scouts and the Athletic Committee.

[22] In writing about the "ideal parish school," Paul E. Campbell, "The Pastor Ponders the School," *The Homiletic and Pastoral Review*, vol. 41, no. 11 (August, 1941), pp. 1112–1118, said that "the pastor will curb all solicitation of funds from the pupils or through the agency of pupils. Frequent drives make his school odious. The Mother House must have support, the missions need funds and more funds, but we jeopardize Catholic education when we make the school a mechanism for collecting money" (p. 1115).

The Boy Scouts also hawked tickets for the annual Scout-O-Rama. The athletes sell season's tickets to the basketball and volleyball games and the proceeds are turned over to the respective leagues in which they play.

A certain amount of pressure was put upon the children to sell tickets to the Easter Monday Card Party for the benefit of the Athletic Committee. The expectation was, as expressed in the letter to the parents, that each family (not each child) would purchase at least one ticket in support of athletics. The Athletic Committee then had it announced in all the classrooms that those children, whose families bought at least one ticket, would be invited to see a movie in the school auditorium on Friday, April 26. The children were reminded by the teachers "If you want to see the movie bring in the money for the card party ticket." The Athletic Committee rented the movie, a travelogue in color, and Father Martin operated the projector. Despite the threats of exclusion, all of the children attended this movie.

In previous years the PTA had sponsored a regular movie program on Sunday afternoons. The admission fee was ten cents, and the pupils of St. Luke's could invite their friends from other schools. The Daylight Screen, about which there was much discussion in the PTA meetings,[23] was for this purpose. The Pastor did not have a high opinion of this arrangement and noted that the movies shown "were old and streaky." He thought the screen should be used for good educational movies, which could be obtained from the State University and from the Visual Aid Department of the public school system free of charge. Since there is no neighborhood movie theater within the limits of St. Luke's parish, most of the PTA members thought this was a good way of raising money and furnishing entertainment at the same time. The chairman of the Visual Aid Committee of the PTA was not interested in this commercial aspect, and the plan for Sunday afternoon movies was abandoned for the year.

In our interviews with parents we were interested in knowing their comments and complaints about the children "pestering" them for money for school purposes. The parents were almost unanimous in saying that "very little of this is done at St. Luke's." Some of them had had experience in other parishes, or had heard about the practices in some parochial schools, and invariably compared St. Luke's school favorably with these others. They were unable to pin-point exactly how much money per week the child takes to school. "Once in a while a nickel or dime for paper; maybe a little money for the

[23] See chap. 13, "Parents and Teachers."

March of Dimes, or teacher's Christmas gift, or Father's feast day present."[24]

The Christmas gifts for teachers were presented on an individual basis from the parents through the children, and gifts brought for the lay teachers were as numerous and as varied as those given to the Sisters. Collecting for the priests' Christmas gifts required some "organization" which was provided by a committee of eighth graders, who visited the lower grades for this purpose. After the collection was made in early December, they returned to these grades to announce that the pupils were giving seventy dollars and a biretta to the Pastor, forty dollars and some recordings to Father Martin, and forty-five dollars and personal linen to Father Thomas. This distribution of gifts, measured according to the status of each priest, was worked out in consultation with Sister Roberta.

The teachers themselves were responsible for a certain amount of money collection in the classroom. At the end of October the children were reminded to bring fifteen cents each to pay for the large blue folders in which their prepared school work was to be displayed for the parents on "Dad's Night." Also in October tickets were sold through the teachers for the recital of the Boys' Town Choir, held in the local Catholic high school.[25] The sale of Holy Childhood Seals, of Christmas cards, and of Easter seals, was also handled through the teachers.[26] The eighth graders, however, organized a collection of nickels and dimes on May 1, and were able to present a feast day gift of one hundred dollars to the Pastor on Friday, May 10. Each child pays twelve cents a year dues in the Holy Childhood Association, and the eighth-grade pupils pay twenty-five cents monthly dues for membership in their St. Robert Bellarmine Club.

[24] According to the statement of the children themselves in St. Luke's sixth, seventh, and eighth grades, 21.4 per cent of the boys and 15.4 per cent of the girls, receive no spending money from their parents. The comparative percentage for the children in the same grades of the public school was 7.4 per cent for boys and 4.3 per cent for girls.

[25] A little girl in the second grade burst into tears after telling the teacher that her parents could not attend the recital because they just had a new baby. The teacher soothed her with the assurance that no one was obliged either to buy tickets or to attend the recital.

[26] The teachers act also as a channel of distribution for various kinds of advertising "literature" like that for the different Catholic summer camps in the area, leaflets announcing the opening of the summer session in the local public school and in the one private Catholic school of the city, advertisements for Saturday morning showings for children at two of the city movie theaters, and many others.

This eighth-grade club had numerous plans for "making money" so that they could "build up their treasury." They intended to make and sell pop corn during the school hours, but this was dropped because it interfered with the candy concession. In early November they raffled a football, donated by Matthew Kronlage, who had received it as an award in his newspaper boy activities. Chances were sold at ten cents a piece during the recess periods at a table set up in the school yard by the enterprising eighth graders. They made twenty-one dollars on this raffle. Most of the work was done by the boys. Then the girls decided to raffle off a doll, donated by Kathleen Duvic, and dressed by her mother. The nine dollars netted from this were also added to the club treasury. The members voted to spend the money in the following way. They spent fifty dollars for a set of green vestments, reserved ten dollars for each of the assistant pastors, and bought a gift certificate for Sister Roberta. All of these were presented at the Award Night, May 28. The residue of the treasury was contributed to the PTA to help defray the expenses of the picnic on the following day, May 29.

One of the "painless" ways of raising funds was that of a rag drive held in the entire school for two weeks in March. The commercial enterprise behind this drive informed the teachers that "this method of fund raising is very popular with teachers, as it takes so little effort and time. The major effort is the passing out of bags and letters to parents; however, your enthusiasm is important." Other motives, besides "raising money without asking for money," were the elimination of fire hazards by ridding homes of rags and discarded clothing, and making the child conscious of the value of salvage.

At any rate, the campaign was conducted according to the instructions of the professional rag gatherers. Large paper bags were distributed to the children on Monday, March 4, together with a letter to their parents explaining the drive. On the final collection day, Thursday, March 21, one hundred and forty-seven bags full of rags were stacked in the school "library," for which Sister Roberta expected to receive about fifty cents a bag. The total weight was about a half ton, 1,005 pounds, for which the company paid two and a half cents per pound. The whole drive netted the disappointing sum of twenty-five dollars and thirteen cents.

One of the most interesting school-wide campaigns for funds was the drive for "adopting pagan babies." The Holy Childhood Association officially set the dates for this campaign during the whole month of May. "In many pagan areas today it is estimated that the sum of five dollars will take care of a child over a period of several months.

This sum, then, has been set as the individual 'adoption alms.'"[27] The pupils at St. Luke's contributed enough money ($195.00) for the adoption of thirty-nine pagan babies, voted in each class on the names to be given to these children, and eventually received the "certificates of adoption" showing that they were "God-parents by proxy."

The campaign for pagan babies was held at St. Luke's school during the first two weeks of February, culminating on St. Valentine's Day. The teachers in the upper grades hit upon this as a clever device for breaking up the "expensive and foolish habit of exchanging gifts and cards on St. Valentine's Day." Sister Roberta suggested to her eighth grade that they save all the money they would have spent on such things and contribute it for the pagan babies. The class voted on the proposal, passed it unanimously, and took charge of distributing the small cardboard "mite boxes" to all of the classrooms. Each time a class reached the five dollar mark a meeting was held during the recess period to vote on the name of the baby.[28] Of the thirty-nine babies adopted, three were paid for individually by a boy from the first, fourth and sixth grade. Twenty-three boys were adopted, three of whom were named Luke after the parish, four were named after Father Thomas. Sixteen girls were adopted, and four of them were named after the teachers in the classrooms, Sisters Roberta, Cecelia, Justin and Martha.

At a soiree interview with a group of parents on the following evening there was general agreement that the substitution of this campaign of charity and sacrifice for the "annual nonsense" of Valentine exchanges was a very beneficial change.[29] It had at first been the custom for children to make Valentine cards for every other child in the classroom. By the time the children reached the fourth and fifth grades they were no longer satisfied with these amateur expressions and used "store-bought" cards which were "mailed" in a box in the front of the room, and then distributed to the children. The parents thought that the gift of one hundred and ninety-five dollars

[27] Editorial, "Adopt a Pagan Baby," *Our Sunday Visitor,* May 12, 1957.

[28] At the end of the campaign each class had a small amount of cash left over. For the fourteen classes in the school this residue amounted to $13.50. Sister Roberta donated this to a fund for a chapel being built in honor of Father Daniel Lord, at the Carmelite monastery in Jackson, Mississippi.

[29] We inquired informally among the pupils in the seventh and eighth grades and found that almost half of them actually received Valentine cards through the mail, practically all of them comic and anonymous. See also above, chap. 10, 'Boys and Girls Together."

for the mission was "much more sensible" and they were pleased that also on that day more than two hundred and fifty children received Communion as a "Valentine Offering" for the spiritual welfare of the pagan babies.

Selling Magazines

The most highly organized and intensive campaign of the year was the drive for magazine subscriptions, held during Catholic Press Month, from February 4 to 20. On the first day a mimeographed letter, addressed to "Dear Parents, Relatives and Friends," and which ended "Cordially yours, Sisters of St. Luke's," was distributed throughout the school, several copies to each pupil. This letter announced the "Catholic School Magazine Plan," sponsored by *The Sign, The Catholic World, Information, The Messenger of the Sacred Heart,* and *The Catholic Boy*. It authorized the pupils to accept subscriptions to one hundred and thirty magazines, fifty-four of which are "the very finest Catholic magazines." The school receives fifty per cent commission on some magazines and thirty per cent on others. "All profits realized from this campaign will be used for worthwhile school projects. Students are requested to limit their selling to relatives and immediate friends."

The campaign was professionally organized and supervised by a publisher's representative, whose sole occupation it is to conduct such drives in Catholic schools. The goal was set at three thousand dollars worth of subscriptions, to surpass last year's total of $2,247.00; [30] the pupils from grades five to eight were to average five dollars, those in the lower grades somewhat less (about $4.60). In the final result the upper grades averaged $6.45 per child, the lower grades $2.56 per child. Highly specialized techniques of competition were employed in this campaign. Grace Kleppner was general manager, and Walter Pattison assistant manager. The pupils in the eighth, seventh and two sixth grades elected their own class captains. The eighth graders then elected five girl classmates to be captains for the lower classes. The returns were counted early each day and the class having the largest amount was allowed to display "Zippy," a toy chimpanzee modeled after J. Fred Muggs. The child selling the most subscriptions to Catholic magazines was allowed to keep this toy at the end of the campaign.

[30] Roberta Suhor erroneously informed us that this amount was "profit for the school" in the previous year, a notion which seemed to be misunderstood also by other pupils.

There were many other incentives to keep this campaign alive. The top salesman, Carl Deroche of the eighth grade, won a table model clock-radio;[31] the second best salesman, Pauline Maurer of the sixth grade, received a "sales trophy." The most successful classroom, eighth grade, won a tape recorder, and its teacher, Sister Roberta, a Parker Pen Set. A daily prize, a Paper-Mate Pen, was given to the child selling the most subscriptions on that day. Every child who sold at least two subscriptions received some kind of prize. These prizes were worked out on a complicated credit system, the salesman getting a full credit for a dollar's worth of some magazines, and a half-credit for other magazines. The team captain calculated these credits every day for the members of his class. "These awards are offered through the courtesy of your school," says the campaign propaganda, and they ranged from a radio at 153 credits, a wristwatch at seventy-seven credits, down through cameras, binoculars, and sporting goods, to various kinds of charms and trinkets at five or six credits.

The final "push" into competition for all those who sold at least one subscription, was the movie *Man With a Million,* starring Gregory Peck, and shown in the school auditorium on the Friday following the campaign.[32] Some of the mothers did not believe that the teachers would actually prevent the unsuccessful salesmen from attending this movie. Yet, during the movie there were one hundred and thirty-six pupils remaining in six classrooms under the supervision of the three lay teachers and of Sisters Cecelia, Agatha and Justin. The children in the upper grades sat quietly studying or reading, and one of the seventh-grade girls said later, "we can see a lousy movie any time on TV." The children in the lower grades were happily busy cleaning out cupboards, re-arranging decorations and washing blackboards.[33]

[31] He sold $115.50 worth of magazines. Because of all the credits he made he won also an identification bracelet, a jack-knife, a flashlight and two wood-carving sets. "I divided this stuff with John Trammell, who helped me. We went mainly to people we know in the neighborhood; and we did a lot of business in the downtown building where John's father has his office."

[32] Our observer notes, "this movie wasn't much of an award. The acoustics were bad and the light worse. The projector, run by Father Martin, broke down twice, the children talked among themselves, and the Principal slept nicely for about an hour."

[33] The teachers had announced that the children not going to the movie would be allowed to do this clean-up job, an occupation they eagerly vie for. This psychology worked. A child in the second grade told his mother, "I'm sorry I have to go to the movie tomorrow; the other kids are going to have fun." His brother in the first grade was asked later how he liked the movie; he replied in a tone of disgust, "aw, they kissed three times."

There were mixed attitudes among the parents concerning this magazine campaign. Even the star salesman's mother later said, "I was furious with him for going around bothering people like that," and she complained to the Pastor about it. A few parents refused to allow their children to sell subscriptions. One of these children, an eighth-grade girl, remarked, "It doesn't make any difference. The other kids think you're trying to sell subscriptions and can't get any." Some of the parents thought that missing the movie "was a shame," and "too drastic to penalize the children for the failure of the parents to take subscriptions." Most of the parents, however, felt that the campaign was good experience for the youngsters. "It teaches them how to keep records, to take responsibilities, meet people and talk business with them." [34] Some of the children have gained "regular customers" over the years who promise to take subscriptions only from them. Any child selling thirty dollars worth of subscriptions received a "Certificate of Achievement," carrying the seal of the publishing company and the signature of the Director of its Vocational Division. This document is seven by nine inches, "suitable for framing" and "you will find this Certificate of Achievement helpful when applying for a full-time or part-time position."

The goal of the campaign, three thousand dollars, was not reached. Nevertheless, the pupils of St. Luke's (416 of them) collected $2,591.99, which was more than their elders did even in the successful Style Show. They sold 685 subscriptions and turned in a profit of $740.23. Although the original letter to the parents said that all profits will be used "for worthwhile school projects," Sister Roberta said at the conclusion of the campaign that "Father Albert received the profits as the children's contribution to the building fund for the new church." [35]

The final evidence of the children's interest in fund-raising was given at the graduation Award Night, when the eighth graders presented twenty dollars to the Pastor for the new church fund. These were the profits on the sale of the *Yearbook of Memories,* an eleven-page mimeographed account by various graduates of their experiences at St. Luke's school. It was originated by Clare Johnson, typed

[34] From the sophisticated level of the senior high school class one of the former girl pupils of St. Luke's looked back with distaste at her childish enthusiasm for magazine drives and pagan babies.

[35] In previous years the Pastor had allowed the Sisters to keep half of the proceeds from the magazine campaign. Because the teaching order had failed to provide the promised twelve Sisters, and one lay teacher had to be added to the staff, new expenses had been incurred by the Pastor. Sister Roberta decided to give the whole proceeds of the drive to the Pastor.

by Peggy Neumann; the paper was donated by the Pastor and the stencils by the school. On Sunday afternoon, May 19, five of the girls met at the school and ran off this impromptu publication. They produced a little over two hundred copies and sold them all before the following afternoon at ten cents a piece.

Control of Finances

The Pastor of any Catholic parish is ultimately responsible to the Bishop of the diocese for the management of parochial funds. There are certain limitations on the size and type of expenditures he is permitted to make. Certain fixed costs, like the salaries to be paid the religious teachers, are prescribed by the Bishop. Buildings and additions to existing construction must be approved by the Bishop.[36] In the actual expenditures at the local level, however, the Pastor is expected to exercise care and diligence—even shrewdness—so that the parish may be run in a financially economical manner.

In all of these matters Father Albert has a reputation among his parishioners as a cautious and frugal person. He is careful to itemize all large bills, and is constantly "looking for ways to save money for the parish." His own personal tastes are simple. The rectory in which he lives with Father Martin and Father Thomas is tastefully furnished with equipment that was bought new at the insistence of the parishioners. His annual vacation is an auto trip to his native town to visit his relatives about two hundred miles from the parish. The parishioners say that "he doesn't like flashy things," and that "he never throws anything away until it is worn out."

Theoretically, the Pastor is the "super-president" and the "super-treasurer" of every parish organization. This is part of his general administrative role, and the successful Pastor allows it to be a pliable role in which there is much discretionary subdelegation of role patterns. "In the power structure of the Catholic Church the appointed priest must exercise a supervisory functional relationship with all the parochial societies." [37] Father Albert seems to have worked out a happy combination of pastoral supervision and lay responsibility.

[36] Wide studies and detailed programs are available as guides. See Lawrence A. Griffin, "Twelve Major Steps in the Educational Planning of a Catholic School Building," *Bulletin* of the National Catholic Educational Association, vol. 52, no. 1 (August, 1955), pp. 324–326. The striking aspect of this carefully prepared program is that there is no place in it for the expression of opinion by the parishioners, who will pay for the building.

[37] Joseph H. Fichter, *Social Relations in the Urban Parish* (Chicago: University of Chicago Press, 1954), p. 129; see also whole of chap. 10, "Social Roles of the Parish Priest."

He actually delegates authority to officers of the organization and acts in their regard more often as counsellor than as decision-maker.[38]

In discussing the financial arrangements of the various parochial groups he said, "I let them have their own treasuries and I never interfere with them, but I tell them that if they have anything left at the end of the year and want to contribute to a worthy cause, they should not forget the parish treasury." The empirical evidence during our whole research project shows that he carries these words into practice. The PTA, for example, had a budget of $758.75 for the year. This figure was arrived at in the executive board meetings and then submitted to the membership for voting, discussion and approval. Father Albert is a member of the executive board and was present at all the general membership meetings, but he did not dictate or interfere with the making of the PTA budget.

It is customary in some parishes for the laity to keep the books but for the Pastor to keep the money. This means that each parish society has a record of its income and expenditures in the treasurer's book, but that the actual money is in the general parish fund.[39] This means also that all checks must be signed by the Pastor (and in some instances countersigned by the treasurer). In St. Luke's parish each organization has its own checking account at the bank, and the deposits made by the treasurer, as well as the checks written by him, are authorized not by the Pastor but by the president and officers of the particular group. In a strict sense, Father Albert does not exercise any direct control over this money gathering and spending. He does, however, supervise the financial activities.

This pattern of "supervision without control" requires some explanation, because it varies with the competency of the lay treasurer and with the degree of cooperation existing between the Pastor and the particular organization. In relation to the school, the most smoothly operating financial group is the PTA. The books are always in order,

[38] It must be pointed out that the more reflective parents consider educational expenditures as one of the best ways they can spend income on their families, and they are personally involved here as investors in their children's future. From the point of view of investment in national economic welfare, see Leslie L. Chisholm, "Is Education a Public Expense or an Investment?" *Education,* vol. 77, no. 6 (February, 1957), pp. 336–339.

[39] "The weakest point in the Catholic elementary school is the insecurity, uncertainty, and indefiniteness of its financial support. The support of Catholic schools depends entirely on the generosity of the Pastor. Practically no funds are collected or earmarked for the parochial school." See Edward A. Fitzpatrick. "The Financial Weakness of the Parish School," *The Catholic School Journal,* vol. 48, no. 6 (June, 1948), p. 201.

receipted bills are filed, every penny is accounted for, the check book balances, and the treasurer seems to take pride in her willingness to show the books to the Pastor at any time. Another example of smooth financial operation is the Patrons of St. Luke's school, the identical twin, or "other self," of the PTA. The annual Fashion Show and Dessert Bridge was handled by them as a completely separate enterprise.[40] At the meeting on January 11, the ladies decided to open a separate checking account at a bank other than the one the PTA uses. This account was closed on March 12, the day after the final meeting of the Patrons; a check for the full deposit was made out to the PTA and transferred to the latter's account at the other bank.

Father Albert's comment on the Style Show was that it was "too mammoth," similarly he thought that the operations of the Athletic Committee were "on a big time scale." He was pleased with the success of both groups, but the men involved in the latter were not so meticulous in their book-keeping as were the women of the PTA and Patrons. Adult females of St. Luke's appear to be more business-minded and financially careful than are the men. The Pastor wanted to see the bills contracted for by the Athletic Committee, "so that I know where the money goes," but the men were careless about receipted bills and had to be prodded into "keeping the books straight." After the men had failed to make enough profit at their November dance, the women took over and conducted the successful Chicken Fry and Easter Monday Card Party. The financial accounts of these two affairs were kept in excellent order by the ladies.

The Camp Fire Girls and the Boy Scouts also keep separate treasuries, which are obviously on a much smaller scale. Here again we find the female adults cooperating better with the Pastor than do the male adults. The girls collect their dues, make a little money on the side through bake sales, and use the treasury for running expenses and the occasional hikes and encampments. The Pastor approves of what they do and does not check their books. The cooperation between the Boy Scouts and Father Albert in this regard is not quite so smooth. He is "kept in the dark" about their finances although he has asked several times for an accounting. One of the adult committeemen is convinced that the Pastor "wants to know how much money we've got so that he can control our treasury," a conviction which could easily have been dispelled by an investigation of the manner in which the Pastor works with the other organizations.

In the actual operation of St. Luke's school, the Principal acts in

[40] See chap. 13, "Parents and Teachers."

the capacity of treasurer only in the sense that she keeps a careful itemized account of all expenditures. The bills for regular supplies and equipment are given to the Pastor, who also pays the salary of the janitor, and for the light, heat and maintenance of the school. In the case of the school itself Father Albert directly handles the cash and controls the treasury.[41]

Generalizations

1. Although about three-fifths of the parents of St. Luke's pupils are in favor of support from public funds, the total support of the school comes out of the parish itself, without help from the city or the state. It is the parishioners themselves who have built the school and who are paying all the costs for its maintenance and operation. A small percentage (4.3%) suggests that the diocese might give some financial aid, but the majority do not seem to have thought of this as a possibility.

2. Tuition and the expenditures of pupils for "incidentals" are, in the opinion of the parents, abnormally low at St. Luke's. The complaint, made in other parishes, that "it costs too much to send a child to the parochial school," is not made here. The Pastor plans to lower the tuition still further, and even to eliminate it eventually. Income from tuition is not even sufficient to pay the salaries of the lay teachers.

3. The bulk of the school expenses is drawn from the regular Sunday collections taken up at all the Masses. This means that all of the parishioners give financial help to support the school, and this includes the large percentage (68.5%) of wage-earners and envelope-givers, who are not parents or do not have children attending St. Luke's school. In this sense the school is an enterprise of the total parish.

4. Supplemental income for the school is gained through organized fund-raising. The PTA is the largest and the most successful gatherer of money for the school. (This includes the Patrons' organization, which will hereafter operate separately.) The next most successful is the Athletic Committee, although its contribution is limited only to the support of athletic teams and not to the general maintenance of the school. The pupils themselves are also enthusiastic and successful

[41] William E. McManus, "Financing Catholic Education," *The Catholic School Journal*, vol. 51, no. 4 (April, 1951), pp. 137–140, thinks there is a need for "greater lay participation in the management of school finances," and that this will come about "when the clergy become more aware of their limitations as financiers and of the great untapped resource of lay ability and experience in financial matters."

fund-raisers, not only for the school but also for the new church fund, pagan babies, and other worthy purposes.

5. The mothers of St. Luke's pupils are better fund-raisers than the fathers. They expend much more time and energy than their husbands and are also more successful in raising money, even in the Athletic Committee, where the interest and the enthusiasms of males are supposed to predominate. The talent of the women in handling money, keeping records, and performing the treasurer's function, is also clearly superior to that of the men.

6. The Pastor is the financial manager of the whole parish, as well as of the school, but he allows full freedom to the treasurers of the various school-connected organizations. He has complete confidence in the organizations and their officers and does not attempt to control their income or disbursements. The measure of this confidence is seen in the fact that each group has its own checking account.

7. The financial generosity of St. Luke's parishioners is evidenced in the abundant and "extra" support which they give to the Sisters' convent. For the most part this is a contribution in kind, in food and furniture and wearing apparel, but part of it represents also an outlay of cash in the numerous gift certificates presented to the Sisters.

8. The Sisters are also vigorous in their own support, or rather, in the support of the religious congregation to which they belong. Their new Mother House is being constructed at a cost of approximately $800,000; and all cash income they receive, including their salaries, the profits made from milk and candy sales, and all personal donations of money, are sent to the Mother House. Thus, the parishioners are helping indirectly to support this congregation from which the future teachers of their children will be drawn.

Part

IV

SOCIAL CORRELATES OF THE PAROCHIAL SCHOOL

Chapter

FIFTEEN

RELIGION AND PUBLIC SCHOOL CHILDREN

THE CATHOLIC parish is established for the sanctification and salvation of all its members. Its principal agencies, and this must include the parochial school, are intended to reach all who can possibly gain benefit from them. "No Catholic school faculty may say that its work is done when it has cared for only its student body." Catholic schools must be utilized "to provide systematic religious instruction and extracurricular activities for Catholic public school pupils."[1] St. Luke's parish attempts to reach these children, and the school property is used for Sunday instructions, but neither the teaching personnel nor the PTA has any direct connection with this work.

Who Goes to School?

As a matter of fact, the Pastor has handed over the administration of the Sunday school classes to the two catechist Sisters who live in the parish. Since Father Martin, however, teaches the eighth-grade public school children, there is still a direct communication between the priest's rectory and the Sunday school. During the school year 190 of these children received religious instruction (that is, were present for at least one-third of the classes given). There are about two dozen more known "border-line" cases who have stopped coming to instructions. There are undoubtedly more of these uninstructed children in St. Luke's parish, but their numbers cannot be accurately ascertained because their parents have not made known to the Pastor their religious affiliation.[2] Some of these "unknowns" we discovered

[1] William E. McManus, "Ten Points for Catholic Education," *Catholic Mind,* vol. 52, no. 1104 (December, 1954), pp. 710–717 (p. 714).

[2] Although the catechist Sisters maintain a "live census," there still remains the problem of criteria of Church and parish membership. See Joseph H. Fichter, "What Is A Parishioner?" *Theological Studies,* vol. 13, no. 2 (June, 1952), pp. 220–227.

because they were listed as Catholics in the public school records.

As an immediate and direct question, the problem of teaching religion to these children is not involved in the controversy over religion and the public schools.[3] Nor is there any question in the minds of teachers and priests whether it is "good" to reach these public school children with religious instruction. It is the stated duty of the Pastor to provide religious teaching for all children in the parish. The central problem is how shall this be done effectively and to what extent is the parish now carrying on this function?

Given the potential physical facilities of St. Luke's school, it is probable that these "extra" children could be accepted there.[4] A problem greater than classroom space, however, is that of supplying sufficient teachers for these children in the parochial school. The other parochial schools of the city are facing a similar shortage; some of them have unused classrooms, some have overcrowded classes; all of them are limited in the number of Sisters available and pressed for the money needed to hire lay teachers.

It is generally agreed upon by discerning religious leaders and by concerned parents of all religious denominations that Sunday school and released time programs are a second-rate substitute for the ongoing religious day school.[5] "Recently Protestants and Jews have evinced greater interest in the religious school as the instrument of general education. Many turn to it with reluctance because of a deep devotion to the public school. But it seems to them that if the public school must be maintained at the price of a thorough-going dualism

[3] For a general discussion on religion and the child see Florence G. Robbins, *Educational Sociology* (New York: Holt, 1953), chapter 8, "Religion in Child Living"; the religious educational number of *Education* (H. H. Meyer, editor) vol. 71 (February, 1951); the series of symposia in *Religious Education*, vol. 48, nos. 2 and 3 (1953); Ernest V. Johnson (ed.), *American Education and Religion: The Problem of Religion in the Schools* (New York: Harper, 1952). For an outspoken opposition to the teaching of religion in public schools, see Vivian T. Thayer, *Religion in Public Education* (New York: Viking, 1947).

[4] In its four highest grades St. Luke's is still caring for pupils from the recently established nearby parish, whose school is adding one grade per year. St. Luke's could put into use three, and possibly four, more classrooms. See, however, the question of overcrowding, below, chap. 16, "Problems of Elementary Education."

[5] See the forthright and somewhat pessimistic appraisal of Protestant Sunday Schools by Wesley Shrader, "Our Troubled Sunday Schools," *Life*, vol. 42, no. 6 (February 11, 1957), pp. 100–114; and the relatively optimistic discussion on the same subject by Ben Bradford, "Rebirth of the Sunday School," *New York Times Magazine* (September 19, 1954), pp. 30 and 60.

between the religious and the secular, the cost is too great."[6] Regardless of the desire of religious-minded parents, it appears that the present system will continue for an indefinite period. For the urban Catholic parents the problem will become greater as their parishes find it impossible to keep up with the expanding child population and the increased costs of maintaining parochial schools.[7]

At the beginning of the school year the catechist Sisters had the names of 202 public elementary school children on their lists, as either registered or prospective pupils of the Sunday school classes. These were ninety-four boys and 108 girls, who were known to be living in St. Luke's parish, and most of whom (with the exception of the newly enrolled first graders) had been in attendance at the instructions during the previous year. When the instructions actually got under way on Sunday, September 16, some of these had already "dropped out." Four boys and two girls, who were supposed to be in the eighth-grade class did not appear during the whole year. Instead of the expected seventeen pupils, Father Martin instructed only six boys and five girls. He contacted the others and their families several times, but to no avail.

A certain amount of family mobility, just as was the case in the parochial school, accounted for some slight shifts in the population of the Sunday school. Some families moved away, but others moved into the parish. The catechist Sisters, who also maintain the census of the parish, were alert to contact these newcomers as soon as feasible. At the end of the school year Sister Genevieve's records showed that 190 public school children came for at least one-third of the thirty-three classes that were conducted. These children came from 124 families, of whom we were able to interview only 119. The remaining five families, with nine children among them (two families with three children each, and three families with one child apiece) refused to be interviewed for our study. Thus, our completed interviews cover 119 families, who have 181 public school children attending the religious instructions.

[6] F. Ernest Johnson, "Church, State and School," *Education*, vol. 71 (February, 1951), p. 354. See also the Special Issue on Religion in *School and Society*, vol. 82, no. 2069 (October 1, 1955).

[7] This shortage of school facilities was dramatically high-lighted in May in Park Forest, a suburb of Chicago, when Catholic parents tried to register 550 children for the first grade which had a capacity of only 110. *Cf. Chicago Daily News*, May 25, 1957. See also "Diocesan Schools Across the Nation," *America*, vol. 95 (September 8, 1956), p. 523, for a report of crowded conditions in parochial schools at the beginning of that school year. See also Sister De Lourdes, "The Five-Year-Old Comes to School," *Bulletin* of the National Catholic Educational Association, vol. 52, no. 1 (August, 1955), pp. 387–392.

The following table shows the sex and grade distribution of these children, and it excludes those who were absent more than twenty times during the year.

Grade	Teacher	Boys	Girls	Both
Eighth	Father Martin	6	5	11
Seventh	Sister Dolores	8	6	14
Sixth	Mrs. Gray	9	6	15
Fifth	Miss Ulmer	7	12	19
Fourth	Mrs. Mayfield	11	9	20
Third	Miss Reickert	15	19	34
Second	Sister Genevieve	17	21	38
First	Miss Tuminello	15	24	39
Totals		88	102	190

The Teaching Staff

St. Luke's is unique among the city's parishes in having the services of two Sisters catechists, who do not teach in the parochial school, but who organize and operate the Sunday school. These Sisters, or their predecessors,[8] have been serving the parish since 1941. Besides supervising the religious instructions for public school children, they maintain a current census by visiting every home in the parish once every two years, make regular monthly visits to sixteen parochial "shut-ins," make contacts with dormant Catholics, instruct prospective members of the Confraternity of Christian Doctrine, and teach catechism to rural children on Saturdays. They live in their own convent, next to the school, and have the use of an automobile for their work.

From several points of view this Sunday school of St. Luke's parish appears to have the ingredients for successful operation. In comparison to the somewhat overcrowded parochial school, where there is a pupil load of 45.1 per teacher, the Sunday school instructs 190 children in eight grades, for a comfortable ratio of 22.6 pupils per teacher. This represents an uneven distribution, as shown in the above table, with the largest classes concentrated in the lower grades.

The school is also exceptionally well staffed. Father Martin teaches

[8] Originally five Sisters of this congregation lived here at the invitation of the Bishop to conduct a city-wide survey of Catholics, which required three years to complete. The expenses were pro-rated among the various parishes, but St. Luke's has continued to support the two nuns who remained in the parish. Two years ago they were "out on loan" to make a census of a newly constituted parish. Of this incident Father Albert remarked, "I had to foot the whole bill—and it wasn't even my parish."

the eighth grade, and expects these children to be prospective members of the Junior Newman Club which operates for high school students. Sister Dolores handles the seventh grade, and Sister Genevieve prepares the second graders for the reception of their first Holy Communion. The remaining grades in the school are taught by five devoted and trained lay women. The problem of obtaining the services of trained and dependable lay teachers seems to plague most parochial Sunday schools.[9] Sunday morning is a more propitious time for women who have to work during the week, but it is also an awkward time for women who have the management of a household, the members of which must also attend Mass and get their breakfast afterwards.

The background training of these five lay catechists varies considerably. The two more mature married catechists, one of whom has grown children, have had the advantage of a course in theology taught weekly by the Dominican Fathers over a period of three years. This was a popularized version of theology, attended more by men than by women, in which there was a great deal of discussion, but no examinations, credits or certificates. During its three-year existence it was held first at the Knights of Columbus building, then at a Catholic Book Store, and finally at one of the parochial schools. From the point of view of doctrinal content it was more than adequate, but it did not treat at all the teaching techniques so essential to catechetical work.[10]

The city in which St. Luke's parish is located does not provide the regular organized program of the Confraternity of Christian Doctrine, leading to an instructor's certificate for lay catechists. Sister Genevieve and Sister Dolores are experts in this field, however, and they personally

[9] William E. McManus, "How Good Are Catholic Schools?" *America,* vol. 95 (September 8, 1956), pp. 522–527, asked the question "Will some Sisters be released from parochial schools to engage full-time in the religious instruction of public-school children?" (p. 527). A few weeks later at the tenth National Congress of the Confraternity of Christian Doctrine (in Buffalo, September 26–30) Bishop Edward McManaman pointed out that nine-tenths of our professional religious teachers work with only that half of Catholic youth who are in our parish and private schools, and that the generous and able services of the laity must help the Church meet this pressing demand for teachers.

[10] See the discussion of methodological skills in catechetical work by Francis J. Connell, "Standards for Religious Teachers of Confraternity Classes," *Catholic School Journal,* vol. 52, no. 2 (February, 1952), pp. 37–39. For a somewhat broader survey of the types of lay persons who engage in catechetical work, see Thomas J. Frain, "A Survey of the Lay Catechists Teaching Public School Pupils," *Catholic Educational Review,* vol. 53, no. 4 (April, 1955), pp. 238–254. This is a report on a questionnaire returned by 566 lay persons who teach public school children.

conducted the "Introductory Course for Confraternity Teachers" for the benefit of the three younger and unmarried women who are teaching in the parochial Sunday school.[11] Besides the necessary contact every Sunday morning, the Sisters also meet occasionally with the five lay teachers in order to discuss the work, plan programs and improvements.

With the exception of Mrs. Gray, all of the teachers, lay and religious, in this Sunday school are themselves the products of parochial schools. They realize, and talk about, the sharp contrast between their own religious instruction at the elementary level and that which they are presently able to give to the public school children. Their attitudes toward the whole program range from discouragement (in the younger teachers) to optimism (in the older teachers). Above all, they are serious about the teaching process and the content of learning. "We are not providing a baby-sitter service, or an entertainment program, or even a study period for the children, while their parents attend Mass.[12] We are trying to teach them the elements of the Catholic religion."

As is to be expected of any school staff, the teachers differ in talent and in their abilities to arouse interest in the children. Aside from Father Martin, who is a teacher of rare ability, the most competent among the women teachers is Sister Genevieve. She assumes the serious responsibility of preparing the second graders for their first Holy Communion. Sister Dolores always teaches the seventh grade, while Miss Tuminello, an extremely patient and maternal person, handles the beginners in the first grade. The remaining teachers, in the third, fourth, fifth and sixth grades, have devised a system whereby they remain with the same children through these four years of Sunday school.[13] Thus they are able to develop a personal knowledge and interest in the children, and also to learn something of their family background and to make contact with their parents.

[11] *An Introductory Course for Confraternity Teachers,* a twenty-four page pamphlet in outline form, covering six sessions of two hours each, is published by Confraternity Publications (Paterson, 1955). See also, Sister M. Rosalia, *The Adaptive Way* (St. Paul: Catechetical Guild, 1955) and *Manual of the Parish Confraternity* (Paterson: Confraternity Publications, 1957).

[12] The nursery room for pre-school children is maintained every Sunday all year long by the Legion of Mary during the eight and nine o'clock Masses. Some small attempts are made here to teach the four-year-olds the elementary forms of prayer, the Sign of the Cross, the genuflection and so forth. Two eighth-grade girls from St. Luke's regularly assist the older women in this work.

[13] This is, of course, an "ideal" that cannot be fully realized. For example, the third-grade teacher, Miss Reickert, has since married and moved to a distant city.

Family Background

Among many other difficulties in the operation of St. Luke's Sunday school, the parent-teacher relation is a peculiar one. Sister Genevieve remarked that "some of the parents think they are doing us a favor by sending their children to Sunday school." She and Sister Dolores visit the homes during the course of their census-taking and try to induce reluctant parents to have their children instructed. "Some of the parents," she says, "are not really concerned about the religious instruction of their children even when they send them to Sunday school." The lay teachers from the third to the sixth grades tried to bridge this teacher-parent gap by making telephone contacts and by occasionally meeting with the parents before or after Mass. Many of the parents cooperated willingly and intelligently in these efforts.[14]

It is the general impression of the teachers that the family background of the children constitutes one of the main problems of the Sunday school. One of the factors at work here appears to be the greater proportion of mixed marriages among the parents who send their children to public school. The following table shows the comparison in this regard between public and parochial school children.

Religion of spouses	119 families of Sunday School pupils	377 families of St. Luke's pupils	1065 families[15] in whole parish
Both parents Catholic	66.4%	86.5%	79.4%
Mother Catholic	25.2	10.3	15.8
Father Catholic	8.4	3.2	4.8

To state this in another way, we note that in approximately one-third of the families of Sunday school pupils one of the parents is a non-Catholic. The fact that there are more Catholic mothers than fathers among these mixed marriages is, in part, a reflection of the general statistics. Catholic women who marry non-Catholics stay in the Church and perform their religious duties more often than is the case with Catholic men who marry non-Catholic women.[16] This, of course, does not account for the fact that 13.5 per cent of the parents of St. Luke's school send their children to the parochial school.

[14] See Sister M. Rosalia, "Cooperation Between Confraternity Classes and the Home," *The Catholic School Journal,* vol. 52, no. 6 (June, 1952), pp. 174–175. For the more detailed family background of St. Luke's pupils, see above, chap. 2, "The First Ten Years."

[15] This figure does not include 229 invalid marriages, forty-one of which are between two Catholics, and 188 are between a Catholic and a non-Catholic.

[16] See John J. Kane, *Marriage and the Family* (New York: Dryden, 1952), p. 154.

Converts to the Catholic faith are also present among the parents in both categories, and there are also some invalid marriages. Whether or not the convert shows eagerness to have his child receive religious instruction, and especially to attend the parochial school, is a matter that cannot be decided here. The following table shows the distribution of converts in the two categories.

Religion of parents	119 families of Sunday school pupils	377 families of St. Luke's pupils
Both "born" Catholics	45.4%	57.0%
Both converts	1.7	1.1
Mother convert	14.3	15.9
Father convert	5.0	12.5
Mixed marriages	33.6	13.5

If we consider the religion of the 754 parents in these 377 families of St. Luke's children, we find that 588 (78.0%) of them are "born" Catholics, 115 (15.2%) are converts, and the remaining 51 (6.8%) are non-Catholics. In contrast to this, we find that among the 238 parents of the Sunday school children, 171 (71.9%) are "born" Catholics, 27 (11.3%) are converts, and the remaining 40 (16.8%) are non-Catholics.[17]

The knowledge and practice of the Catholic religion among the parents of these children undoubtedly influence both the attitudes of the parents themselves and the practices of the children. Among the families of St. Luke's children there are eight (2.1%) invalid marriages, while among those of the Sunday school children there are six (5.0%). A considerable portion of the Catholic parents of these children are also lax in the performance of their religious duties, like attending Sunday Mass, making the Easter duties and receiving the sacraments.[18]

Although the overcrowding of the parochial schools is one of the reasons why parents sometimes send their children to the public school this is probably not a serious excuse among the parents of St. Luke's Sunday school pupils. It is difficult to escape the implication that the parents of these children are not so interested or concerned about the religious education of their children as are the parents of St. Luke's

[17] These statements are not all valid in the present tense, because some of these families have been broken by death. In the parochial school nine families are fatherless, one is motherless, and two have lost both parents. In the Sunday school there is only one child whose father is deceased.

[18] There are still others within the parish boundaries who are even more lax. They do not even send their children for religious instruction, and never attend Mass and the sacraments themselves. Of all married couples in the parish known to the Pastor, 17.7 per cent are in invalid marriages.

parochial school pupils. One of the elements to be considered here is the type of education which the parents themselves have had, particularly on the elementary school level. The following table gives the comparison among three categories of parents: those who never attended a Catholic school, those who never attended a non-Catholic school, those who attended both types of schools.

Total education of parents	754 parents of St. Luke's pupils	238 parents of Sunday school pupils
All Catholic	20.0%	7.6%
All non-Catholic	34.6	52.5
Mixed schooling	45.4	39.9

The comparisons of the elementary school education of these parents are shown as follows.

Elementary education of parents	St. Luke's pupils	Sunday school pupils
All parochial	49.6%	29.0%
All public	38.3	56.7
Mixed schooling	12.1	14.3

These two tables show quite clearly that the parents of St. Luke's children have had much more Catholic schooling than those of the Sunday school pupils. A large number of them (65.4%) have had some Catholic schooling as compared to 47.5 per cent of the parents of public school pupils. Similarly, on the elementary school level, 61.7 per cent have had all or some schooling in parochial schools, as compared to 43.3 per cent of the public school parents. It is probable that the shared educational experience of both husband and wife in the same family has an influence on their decision concerning the schooling of their children. The following table shows the contrast where both parents had the same type of elementary schooling.

Elementary education of parents	377 families of St. Luke's pupils	119 families of Sunday school pupils
All parochial by both parents	24.9%	8.4%
All public by both parents	12.7	29.4

There are no other important distinctions in the family backgrounds of these two categories of children. They are practically all third and fourth generation Americans, with approximately the same range of ethnic origin and mixture. We do not find the lower class families sending their children to one school and the upper class families to the other school. The occupational range of the fathers of these two categories of families is roughly similar. Thus, the main factors at work in the decision to choose one school rather than the other appear to be the religion, marital status and educational experience of the parents.[19]

A comparison of the amount of education completed by these two categories of parents shows that the parents of St. Luke's children have a greater proportion of both college people and people who attended only elementary school than do the parents of the public school children. This may indicate that St. Luke's school is more representative of all educational classes in the community than is the public school, but it appears to have little influence on the question of religious background.

Amount of parents' education	754 parents of St. Luke's pupils	238 parents of Sunday school pupils
Attended or finished college	29.2%	23.1%
Attended or finished high school	60.9	71.9
Attended or finished grade school	9.9	5.0

School Problems

The background, interests and preoccupations of the parents appear to be partial explanations of the major problems which beset the Sunday school at St. Luke's. This school is operated as an agency of instruction and like any other school requires the cooperation of both parents and children. The expectation of the teachers is that the pupils have done their homework in the form of studying catechism during the week. This expectation is more often disappointed than it is satisfied. While mere rote memorization has gone out of fashion, even in Sunday school, a certain amount of "memory work" is required in all aspects of the learning process. The basic truths of religion, and especially the more frequently used prayers, have to be memorized.

The teacher in the third grade remarked that "after the summer vacation a lot of the children remember almost nothing of what they learned last year. Some of them even forget the Our Father and the Hail Mary." It is the practice in the families of nuclear Catholics to say some prayers in common, at least the grace before and after meals, sometimes night prayers, and even the recitation of the Rosary. Thus

[19] See below, chap. 17, "School, Parish and Community," for the points of similarity among the children going to the two different schools. Numerous other comparisons are made *passim* throughout this book.

the children learn at least the Lord's Prayer and the Hail Mary even in their pre-school years.

The following table shows the comparison of parents' answers to our interview question in this regard. We asked whether the child knew any prayers before going to school and who taught these prayers. This parental duty was neglected completely by nine per cent of the parents of St. Luke's pupils and by 12.6 per cent of the parents of Sunday school children.

Teaching of prayers by:	St. Luke's pupils	Sunday school pupils
Both parents	38.2%	24.4%
Father	1.8	3.4
Mother	48.3	53.8
Others (older siblings, grand parents, aunts and uncles)	2.7	5.8
Nobody	9.0	12.6

During the first month of school, even before we had asked the parents the above questions, we tested the first grade children in both the parochial and the Sunday school, to discover what prayers they knew. The following table shows the results.

Prayers known by first graders	84 St. Luke's pupils	39 Sunday school pupils
Sign of the Cross	57.1%	43.6%
Hail Mary	51.2	30.8
Our Father	17.9	10.3
Short "night prayer"	89.3	82.0

In all fairness to the children it is likely that these percentages should be scaled upwards. The child who says prayers in the familiar surroundings of his home, and often with another member of the family saying the prayers with him, is likely to be confused and to have a "short" memory when asked to recite by strangers in the school surroundings. Even when all of this is taken into consideration, however, there is still a noticeable difference between the two categories of parents in the attention given to children's prayers.[20]

Not all of the blame for the Sunday school's problems can be placed

[20] John L. Thomas, "Religious Blackout of the Pre-School Child," *America*, vol. 36 (March 8, 1952), pp. 608–610, says that fifty per cent of the children entering the parochial schools do not know how to make the Sign of the Cross; less than one-fourth know the Our Father; about one-third know the Hail Mary; about one out of seven know the prayer to the Guardian Angel or the grace at meals.

on the lack of interest by parents or on the lack of study by pupils.[21] Parents know that it is difficult to get children to do any studying at home in most instances, and this difficulty seems to increase when the studying is something "extra" like that of the Catechism. The shortage of actual instruction time is an even greater problem. From Sunday, September 16, to Sunday, June 2, the Sunday school met thirty-three times. It must be obvious that this one hour a week (with school cancelled for the Christmas and Easter holidays), even if a child had perfect attendance, can hardly be termed adequate religious instruction. Yet, this is all these children receive, with the exception of the second graders who come for an extra period taught by the Pastor on Saturday afternoons for the three months immediately prior to their reception of first Holy Communion. The parochial school children receive not only five times as much formal instruction; they have also the tremendous advantage of the informal spiritual atmosphere of the religious school.

It is the Pastor's responsibility to test the adequacy of religious knowledge which the children have before he can permit them to receive Holy Communion. Up till this year he had insisted that they must attend the Sunday school for at least two years before he tested their knowledge of the Catechism. He has changed this rule to permit those who may have been taught by parents and others, so that the child who knows enough may receive the Sacrament, even though he may not have attended the Sunday school regularly. The number of public school children receiving their first Communion this year was twenty-eight (thirteen boys and fifteen girls). Among these, however, were one girl from the sixth grade and one from the third grade. The remaining children in the second grade were not considered "ready" for the Sacrament because of their lack of knowledge. All of the children in St. Luke's second grade received the Sacrament on schedule.

The content of the Sunday school classes is mainly that of the ordinary Catechism. The simplest and shortest form (*Baltimore Catechism No. 1*) is used for the first four years and then a larger edition is used during the remaining grades. The lesson from the previous week is "heard" by the teacher and then as much time as possible is given to the explanation of class material. The children were expected to study and remember the answers to five or six Catechism questions every week, and to explain these "in their own words." This meets with only indifferent success except among the more faithful and studious children.

[21] See above, chap. 12, "What Parents Want in Education."

A much more successful teaching device is the *Catholic Messenger* with its stories, current events and discussion questions.[22] This became a kind of workbook of weekly tests on the contents, completed and turned in every Sunday by the children. The children appeared to like this "homework," and the record chart kept by the teachers shows that more than ninety per cent of the children performed this task. They seemed to fill out the answers to the ten questions willingly without urging or help from their parents. The material appearing in this magazine during the year was written around the theme of the sacraments and the sacramentals. No report cards are issued to the parents, but several of the teachers turned in formal grades for each child in their attendance books. On the last day of Sunday school, June 2, the teachers in each class gave awards to the best pupils, and a medal or holy picture to each of the children.[23]

The teachers feel that, given the general difficulties involved in running a Sunday school program, the attendance of the pupils is fairly good. They say that only sickness, or some other serious reason, keeps the children away, once they have begun classes in September. The average number of absences is 6.45 per child, with the girls having a slightly higher average (6.48) than the boys (6.3). Actually, the attendance is fairly regular for the first few months until January, and then it tends to become irregular, especially for the younger children. The following table indicates the distribution of absences.

Number of times absent	88 Boys	102 Girls	190 Both	Per cent
None	7	9	16	8.4%
1–3 times	27	26	53	27.9
4–6 times	20	28	48	25.3
7–9 times	12	13	25	13.1
10–12 times	8	11	19	10.0
13–15 times	7	7	14	7.4
16 or more times	7	8	15	7.9
Average absences	6.30	6.48	6.45	

[22] This is published on three age levels: *Our Little Messenger, Junior Catholic Messenger,* and *Young Catholic Messenger* by George A. Pflaum, Publisher, Dayton. Each child pays the subscription price averaging ninety-five cents per year, and also pays forty-five cents for the Catechism.

[23] These awards were plastic statuettes, rosaries, children's book of saints. They were supplied from the "work fund" of the catechist teachers. Several of the teachers asked the children in the class, "Who do you think should get the awards?" and found that the pupils recognized and voted for the most diligent and competent children in the class.

It must be remembered that there were only thirty-three meetings of the Sunday school classes. Almost two-thirds (63.7%) of these children missed four or more classes, which means that they missed more than ten per cent of the instructions. One-quarter of them were absent ten or more times, which means that they missed one-third or more of the instructions. Certainly this is a worse record of absenteeism than that compiled by the parochial school children during the year, and it is probably also worse than these children themselves compiled in their own public school attendance.[24]

Perhaps the best that can be said about these children is that they at least receive some formal instruction in their religion. Some of them are excellent and conscientious students. More than a third of them can be said to do very well both in their lessons [25] and in attendance. A much more serious problem is the progressive absenteeism as the children grow older, those who stay away completely from religious instructions. The first and second grades have the largest number of pupils in attendance because these two years of study are required for the child to prepare for the reception of the sacraments.

Membership in the third grade continues fairly high, but from then on the numbers gradually drop off each year until the eighth grade, when about one-third of the original members of the class no longer attend Sunday school.[26] Some of the parents feel that the child has learned "enough religion" in the first few years to suffice for the rest of his life.[27] Some of the older children are simply unwilling to continue in Sunday school, and their parents accede to their wishes. When the catechist Sisters check up on former pupils of the school the most frequently given excuse of the parents is "he just doesn't want to go any more."

Running through all of the school problems mentioned above is the fact that Sunday morning is probably the poorest time that could be chosen for religious instruction to Catholic elementary school children. This may not be a problem among Protestants among whom Sunday school "counts" as going to church. The Catholic child who reaches

[24] For the absenteeism of St. Luke's pupils, see above, chap. 6, "Social Conformity and Conduct."

[25] In the final "test" in the fourth grade, three of the twenty students made a perfect score, and eight others earned a mark of ninety or better.

[26] This figure is computed by comparing the catechists' records of eighth-grade enrollments for 1957–53 with the first-grade enrollments for 1950–46. The growth of St. Luke's parish population in this period, 1946–57, distorts the figures somewhat, so that an accurate estimate would require a downward revision.

[27] At the end of the last class of the year a fourth-grade boy taunted the teacher with the remark, "ha, ha, my mother said I don't have to come back any more. I know enough Catechism."

the age of reason is obliged to attend Mass on Sundays, and so are his parents. The parents have to bring the youngest children either before or after they have themselves attended Mass, and then have to make an extra trip to pick them up. The lay teacher has her own Mass obligation to fulfill, and also often enough obligations to her home and family. Sunday is a holiday, and children dislike "going to school" on that day. Everything conspires against Sunday morning as a time for serious school work.

Second Class Parishioners

One of the most subtle problems in the Sunday school program is that the public school children tend to be categorized as second class parishioners. While no parent, teacher, Sister or priest intends deliberately to treat them in this way, the fact is that the children do not "fit in" with the regular pattern of parochial school training. Early in our study we had complaints from the parents of some of these children which centered mainly on the practice of segregating the public from the parochial school children at the first Communion services. On this occasion the children line up in the school, with St. Luke's boys first, followed by St. Luke's girls. Then the public school boys are followed by the public school girls. They file into the church, take their places in the pews, the Catholic school children in the front, with two Sisters from the parochial school behind them; then the public school children with the two catechist Sisters.

There is no "children's Mass" on Sundays at St. Luke's parish church although the seventh-grade choir sings at the eight-thirty Mass. The Pastor believes that families should go to church together whenever possible and that a special Mass for the children would separate the family on Sunday morning. Similarly, there is no check-up by the teachers on Mass attendance either on Sunday or on the following day in the school.[28] The result is that one cannot learn from observation whether the public school children fulfill this weekly obligation. The Sunday school teachers have made spot checks at Sunday Mass during the year and they observe that "frequently the children come to Sunday school but do not go to Mass." At the beginning of the school year some of them ask the children whether they have received Communion during the summer months and find that about half of them have not received the Sacrament at all.

The training of the children for their first Holy Communion consists

[28] Keeping an attendance record of the children at Sunday Mass is done in other places. See *Southern Parish* (Chicago: University of Chicago Press, 1951), pp. 144–145.

of more than the religious instructions by the Sunday school teachers. The public school children have to come to the parish on Saturday afternoons, just after lunch, during the three months before they receive Communion. They are given separate instructions by the Pastor. This sets them apart even further from the parochial school children. Like the latter they go to confession several times before receiving Communion.[29]

This means that the training is also done separately. The children practice separately on how to line up and make the procession from the school to the church, how to genuflect before going into the pews, how to go up to the altar steps, which way to turn on the way back to the pews, and finally how to file out of the church. The catechist Sisters and the school Sisters agree ahead of time about the type of dress the girls will wear, the color of the tie, suit and shoes of the boys. They assemble the so-called "Communion Kit," consisting of prayer book, rosary, medal and statuette, which is purchased by the parents for the child.[30] Thus the children have roughly the same appearance in dress and clothing, and carry the same "equipment." But in preparation for all this, the parents of the Sunday school pupils deal with the catechist Sisters, while those of the parochial school children deal with the school Sisters.

The First Communion experience is simply the most obvious example of the fact that the public school children are "different" from the parochial school children. Since they are in the minority they are more conspicuous as being "exceptions to the rule." They do not know as much about their religion, they are not caught up in the general patterns of religious practices or in the spiritual atmosphere which exist in the parochial school. In the higher grades they seem to become more conscious of this "lower status," of having to do "something extra" on Sunday mornings while the other Catholic children simply attend Mass. They do not participate in the parish processions on religious occasions, in the Forty Hours Devotion, in the choir singing and altar serving. In a sense, because of the circumstances in which they find themselves, they are "outsiders" to most of the experiences which St. Luke's pupils have.

In a minor way, the status of the public school pupils reflects the

[29] See above, chaps. 2 and 4, for the description of the First Communion preparations of St. Luke's school children.

[30] An enterprising photographer in the city presented a gift booklet to the parents of each prospective communicant three weeks before the Holy Communion Sunday. This is an illustrated child's booklet, Demetrious Manousos: *First Holy Communion for Little Catholics* (St. Paul: Catechetical Guild, 1955).

parochial status of their parents. This is to be expected since it is the decision of the parents ultimately, and not that of the child, which puts the latter in the status of second class parishioners. The following table shows the amount of membership in church groups by the Catholic parents in both categories and thus indicates their organizational activity as Catholic parishioners.

Memberships of Catholic parents in church groups	Saint Luke's[31]		Public school[32]	
	320 Fathers	363 Mothers	84 Fathers	109 Mothers
None	65.0%	58.9%	76.2%	81.7%
One	20.3	29.5	17.8	17.4
Two	8.4	8.5	4.8	0.9
Three	3.8	1.7	1.2	0.0
Four or more	2.5	11.4	0.0	0.0

The largest majority of all of these parents do not belong to any church group, but the percentage comparison shows that both mothers and fathers of St. Luke's pupils belong to more groups than do the parents of public school children. The most popular groups among the men are the Holy Name Society and the parish Ushers, and among the women the Rosary and Altar Society. The statistics above do not include the PTA at St. Luke's, even though it is a parochial group, since it its obvious that the parents of public school pupils, when they are members, would belong to the public school PTA.

The percentage of non-members of church groups is higher among the fathers than among the mothers of St. Luke's pupils, but the reverse is the case among the parents of public school pupils. The comparison between the mothers in the two categories shows the greatest difference, about two-fifths of St. Luke's mothers being active in church societies, as compared to about one-fifth of the public school mothers. The presence of a child in the parochial school tends to attract the mother closer to the parish.[33] It may well be said that these

[31] In the 377 families of St. Luke's pupils, thirty-nine fathers are non-Catholics, ten are deceased, and eight live separately; among the mothers twelve are non-Catholics and two deceased.

[32] In the 119 families of Catholic children in the public school, thirty fathers are non-Catholics, one is deceased, and four live separately; among the mothers ten are non-Catholics.

[33] See below, chap. 17, the section on the school as a focus of parochial solidarity. It is difficult to determine, of course, whether the mother's parochial group activity inclines her to send the child to St. Luke's, or whether the child's presence in the school draws the mother into more parish organizations.

mothers of St. Luke's pupils have a more intimate connection with the parish itself, and thus develop in their children a sense of "belonging" to the parish. On the other hand, the public school mother's lack of contact with parish organizations may be part of the explanation of her child's second-class status in the parish.

A final index of the second-class status of the Sunday school children is the lack of an adult organization to work for them, particularly to bring the home and the school closer together. The PTA of St. Luke's parish is not concerned with the Sunday school pupils because its members feel that the parents of the children attending instructions have the primary obligation to look after them. Ordinarily this adult support would come from the organized Confraternity in the parish or city, but this organization does not exist locally. During the course of the year, however, the Bishop of the diocese urged all Pastors to establish this Confraternity in their parishes, and it is likely that this lack will be filled in the ensuing years at St. Luke's.

Generalizations

1. The Pastor fulfills his obligation to provide religious instructions for public school children by operating a Sunday school and by giving special weekly instructions for three months preceding the reception of First Communion. The parochial school Sisters do not participate in any way in this program. The Sunday school is under the direction of two catechist Sisters, who maintain their own convent at St. Luke's and perform various other services for the parish.

2. The pupils who attend Sunday school are often considered the "surplus" children for whom there is no room in the parochial school. Although St. Luke's is relatively overcrowded this condition is due more to a shortage of teachers than of room, and it is probable that all of the Catholic children in the public school could be accommodated there. Thus, the reasons why these children do not attend St. Luke's seem to reside mainly in themselves and their families.

3. The Sunday school program presents a particular educational problem for the teachers in that the motives and sanctions effective in the parochial school cannot be easily applied. This is largely because the whole program is voluntary for the children and their parents. Religious instruction in this setting is a kind of "extracurricular" activity, and the teachers are unable to make even normal pedagogical demands on the pupils in either knowledge or behavior.

4. Sunday morning is probably the most awkward "school time" of the week for all involved in the program. The pupils are constrained to attend class at an hour when other children, from both the parochial

and public schools, are free. The parents who send their children to Sunday school have their own religious obligations, and also other duties to their families at this time. The teachers too, particularly the lay women, are inconvenienced because of their other religious and family obligations.

5. The religious knowledge obtained by the Sunday school pupils is relatively meager. Even the small percentage attending faithfully throughout the school year received at most only about one-fifth as much instruction as the pupils of St. Luke's. Because attendance was voluntary and interest sporadic, little could be expected in the way of homework, or studying the Catechism during the week. Only thirty-three sessions were held in the Sunday school during the school year, and the interruption of the long summer vacation forced a constant repetition of previously learned material.

6. The progressive dropping-out of children as they go into the higher grades of elementary school is an outstanding defect of the whole system. About one-third of them cease attending Sunday school before they reach the eighth grade. This means that they go into adolescence, youth and maturity with a small child's partial knowledge of their religion. Unless they later attend a Catholic high school or college, they will continue throughout life with an incomplete understanding of the faith they profess.

7. The family background of these children in the Sunday school is in many ways similar to that of the parochial school pupils, especially along the lines of social class and of ethnic, economic and occupational status. The major difference seems to lie in the religious background. Their parents teach them fewer prayers at home and appear to be less interested in their religious education than are the parents of parochial school pupils. Parents in about one-third of the families are in mixed marriages. About three out of ten of the parents attended full-time in a parochial elementary school, as compared to half of the parents of St. Luke's children. Their parents are also much less active in the parish organizations.

8. The Sunday school children form a kind of second-class citizenry among the children of the parish. They do not have the "normal" Catholic child's experiences like serving at the altar, singing in the choir, partaking in the processions and the liturgy. They are segregated in many of their activities, in the time and place for learning about religion, even in the public and formal reception of the first Holy Communion. They have no adult organization in the parish, similar to the PTA, to look after their needs.

Chapter

SIXTEEN

PROBLEMS OF ELEMENTARY EDUCATION

THERE ARE many points of view from which the elementary school can be studied, pedagogically, philosophically, financially, theologically, politically, and otherwise. Our study has focused on the sociological aspects, the areas of social relations, groups, functions, structures, leadership and communication. We have seen certain points of stress and strain, other points of efficient and smooth operation. Fortunately in this research project, we have had the full-hearted cooperation of public school officials, administrators and teachers, so that we were in many instances able to make comparisons between St. Luke's parochial school and the neighboring William H. Taft public school. These comparisons show that many school problems are shared by both systems.[1]

It is seldom, however, that a published comparison can be made, or accepted by readers, between the parochial and public school in an objective clear-headed way. The very terms, "public school" and "parochial school" have become value-loaded words to the partisans and professionals on both sides. Traditional ways of thinking across the school lines have developed a number of stereotypes, so that some Catholics have distorted notions of public schools and some non-Catholics have similarly erroneous notions about parochial schools. Most of the problem areas we discuss in this chapter are common to the elementary school, both parochial and public. They are common to both, not in the sense that they are equally intense, but in the sense that each must find its own approach to them.

Within the boundaries of St. Luke's parish there are three public elementary schools with 2,958 pupils. This school population cannot be adequately compared statistically with the number (632) of children attending St. Luke's, because the boundaries of the three public

[1] See Samuel Brownell, "Unsolved Problems in American Education," *The School Review*, vol. 62 (December, 1954), pp. 519–522.

school districts are not co-extensive with the boundaries of St. Luke's parish. One public school is near the southern edge of the parish and the district from which it draws its children extends out beyond the parish lines. In the larger city there are eighteen public elementary schools with an enrollment of 15,113 pupils.[2] The fifteen parochial schools on the elementary level have a total enrollment of 6,723 pupils. There is also a private Catholic school with 519 children. Thus, more than two-thirds (67.6%) of the city's children attend the public school, a minority of 2.3 per cent the private school, and the remaining 30.1 per cent attend the parochial schools.[3]

Public Relations

At this stage of its development in most parts of the country the public school does not have a real problem of "selling itself" to the general population. Most adult Americans have at one time or another had experience as pupils of the public school, and are "sold" on universal education at the elementary school level. This does not mean that the function of public relations is either unnecessary or dispensed with by public school officials.[4] The most sensitive area appears to be that of spending the tax-payers' money. The elected school board has to satisfy the people that a new bond issue for building or expanding schools is justifiable; a proposed salary raise for teachers becomes a partisan issue; the Principal of the school is sometimes harried by irate parents. As one Principal and several teachers told us, "the greatest problem is interfering parents."

The controversy that has raged in the post-war era over "why Johnny can't read" indicates that the general dissatisfaction with the public elementary schools goes beyond the question of thrift and expenses. The public schools have been attacked from many angles, and several scorchingly critical books have become near best-sellers.[5] The delicate

[2] The city also operates a small school for fifty-three handicapped children.

[3] This is higher than the national average. The U.S. Office of Education (release of February, 1957), points out that in 1899–1900 the non-public schools accounted for 8.02 per cent of total elementary and secondary school enrollment, in 1953–54, this had increased to 13.08 per cent, and is expected to increase to 14.6 per cent by 1965.

[4] See Leslie W. Kindred, *School-Public Relations* (Englewood Cliffs: Prentice-Hall, 1957), Part III, "Personal Public Relations;" also Scott Winfield and Clyde Hill, eds., *Public Education Under Criticism* (Englewood Cliffs: Prentice-Hall, 1954), and V. T. Thayer, *The Attack Upon The American Secular School* (Boston: Beacon, 1951).

[5] See Rudolf Flesch, *Why Johnny Can't Read* (New York: Harper, 1955). Other books on the subject range from the highly critical Arthur E. Bestor, *Educa-*

question of the teaching of religion and moral values has not been settled in these schools.[6] These criticisms became so vigorous and acute that the Educational Policies Commission of the National Educational Association felt constrained to publish a defense of the public school system in 1955. This was advertised as a reappraisal at a time of decision, but was in reality a confident reiteration of the assumption that the public schools are the correlative of the democratic society.[7]

The public schools in the city where St. Luke's is located have not been the subject of such severe criticism. The public relations aspect has been handled quite smoothly from the school superintendent's office, and the Principals of the individual schools appear to be quite competent in handling relations on the immediate local scene. One exception stands out in the person of a woman Principal who refused for twenty-six years to allow the formation of a PTA in her school. Her successor, a male Principal, says that he is about to "capitulate" to the parents' demands.

The problem of the parochial school in this regard is that of interpreting itself, and sometimes defending itself, to the general American public. One study along these lines elicited the remark, "these schools are regarded by the public school educator and Protestant layman as cloistered. I have been in the school business forty-six years and have never been inside a Catholic elementary or high school." [8] The apologetic value of public relations appears to be more and more realized by Catholic educators. The superintendent of a large diocesan school system remarks that "Public relations should not only aim at

---

tional Wastelands: The Retreat from Learning in Our Public Schools (Urbana: University of Illinois Press, 1953), to the wildly angry Albert Lynd, *Quackery in the Public Schools* (Boston: Little, Brown, 1953).

[6] The "official" policy of the American Council of Education is that the public schools should teach factually, not dogmatically, *about* religion, without teaching religion. This policy is laid out in the following reports: *Religion and Public Education,* 1944; *The Relation of Religion to Public Education; The Basic Principles,* 1947; *The Function of the Public Schools in Dealing with Religion,* 1953. The same policy is expressed in *Moral and Spiritual Values in the Public Schools* (Washington: National Educational Association, 1951), and is discussed by Randolph Crump Miller, *Education for Christian Living* (New Haven: Yale University Press, 1956).

[7] *Public Education and the Future of America* (Washington, National Educational Association, 1955). See also George Williams, "Religion in the Public Schools of Our Democracy," *Religious Education,* vol. 51 (September–October, 1956), pp. 374–377.

[8] Sister Mary Pauline, "Interpreting Catholic Schools to the Community," *Catholic Educational Review,* vol. 51, no. 8 (October, 1953), pp. 547–550, suggests that Catholic teachers participate more in professional and community activities.

reaching our Catholic people, it should also reach non-Catholics. Most Americans are fair-minded people. To the extent to which they know our schools and the work of our schools, to that extent they have a higher regard for them. This is important for our own Catholic people. When they find that non-Catholics have a high regard for Catholic schools, it increases the confidence of Catholics in their own school system."[9]

Father Albert has been Pastor of St. Luke's for almost twenty-five years and has acted as prominent spokesman for the parish and for the school. He is one of the best known men in the city, having served on civic committees, cooperated with social agencies and attended hundreds of luncheons and banquets. He encouraged the formation of the PTA in 1937, and its continuous connection with the city, state and national administrations and programs of this organization, even when some of his parishioners asked "what do we get out of it?" or claimed that "Catholics don't get a voice in their programs." He maintains a personal relationship with the local public school Principals and with public school officials like the superintendent of city schools. Father Albert encourages the parishioners to take an interest in public school questions precisely because of the deficiencies of these schools and because alert citizens should be concerned about good education for all children.

From the more immediate viewpoint of the school itself, Sister Roberta is the main "contact person" for St. Luke's.[10] All communications from all agencies having any interest in the pupils must come through her. We must remember that she is a full-time teacher and superioress of the convent, as well as the Principal. The amount of communication she has with non-parochial agencies, and the activities into which this brings her, are almost incredible. This is aside from the normal contacts required in ordering supplies, buying books, paper, pencils, and so forth. A partial list of these further contacts are: U.S. Marines, City Health, Fire and Police Departments, Knights of Columbus, Pilot Club, Sons of the American Revolution, Christmas Seals,

[9] Carl J. Ryan, "Parochial Schools Rest on Good Will," *The Catholic Educator,* vol. 27, no. 8 (April, 1956), pp. 493–494 (p. 494). See also the very practical comments of another diocesan school superintendent, John J. Voight, "Improving Cooperation Between Diocesan Superintendents and Business and Civic Groups," *Bulletin* of the National Catholic Educational Association, vol. 51, no. 1 (August, 1954), pp. 471–474.

[10] See Sister M. Fridian, "The Functions of the Principal in Catholic Elementary Schools," *The Catholic Educational Review,* vol. 53, no. 8 (October, 1955), pp. 433–440.

Easter Seals, March of Dimes, Serra Club, Magazine Subscription Drive, Rag Gathering Campaign, Paper Drive, Pagan Babies, Bishop's Lenten Drive, local radio stations, bicycle registrations, high school registrations, Summer Camps, and many others.[11]

The public with whom the other Sisters deal is made up mainly of the parents of their pupils. But there is a differential of contact in this regard. Aside from the Principal, the other persons making most frequent contact are Sister Cecelia and Sister Ruth, through the entertainment and music programs, and Sister Justin, through her work with the altar boys and the sacristy. The teachers do not attend the PTA meetings, the Principal does not have an office room, and parents are not welcomed to visit the classrooms during school hours.[12] When the incoming president of the PTA suggested that an orientation meeting be held for parents in early September "in order to discuss problems" the suggestion was turned aside as unnecessary.

This description does not imply that there are no cordial and frequent relations between the teachers and the parents of St. Luke's pupils. Our analysis leads us to the conclusion that parents are contacted both as friends of the teachers and as individuals who may have some particular problem concerning their children. This means a kind of personal relationship, but it does not focus upon the parents as representatives of the parish and the community. Since most of the teachers are religious Sisters, and since their direct communication with the larger community is thus inhibited, it is the parents of the school children who can best act as representatives of the community. It is mainly through them that the community is contacted and informed of the work and program of the parochial school.[13]

It must be pointed out here that St. Luke's school becomes known and is publicized to the general community in a variety of informal ways. Many of these ways are not intended as "means of publicity" for the school, but they do in effect provide public knowledge of at

[11] For a study of the numerous tasks of teaching Sisters see Mary Canice Werner, *An Analysis and Evaluation of the Problems Arising from the Extra-Class Activities Assigned Religious Teachers in Parochial Schools* (Cleveland: St. John College, unpublished thesis, 1956), especially tables 10–14.

[12] See Urban H. Fleege, "Participation, the Key to Good School-Community Relations," *The Catholic Educator,* vol. 24, no. 4 (December, 1953), pp. 242–245; also Virginia Marie Frain, "Parents' Share in the School's Public Relations," *The Catholic School Journal,* vol. 53, no. 10 (December, 1953), pp. 299–301.

[13] This point is well developed by M. Genevieve Hauber, "The Principal and Public Relations," *The Catholic Educator,* vol. 26, no. 10 (June, 1956), pp. 616–617.

least some aspects of the school's program. In this sense, "all activities are public relations." [14] The general public may not hear of the scholastic achievements of St. Luke's pupils, but the teachers and Principals of the high schools which some of the graduates later attend know about them. The newspapers carry accounts of the athletic prowess of the teams, of the programs and awards in Scouting and Camp Fire, of the style show by the Patrons of St. Luke's, the card parties of the Athletic Committee, the meetings of the PTA. In fact, some of these organizations have a publicity chairman among the functionaries, and the result of these activities appears to be publicity in an informal sense rather than public relations in a formal sense.

Our interviews with parents indicate that there are certain areas of ignorance concerning St. Luke's school, and it may be assumed that this ignorance is even broader and deeper among the non-Catholics of the community. Whether through their own negligence or through the failure of the school to supply information, some parents know nothing about their child's teacher or her qualifications. They know nothing about the facilities of the school or the extracurricular activities open to the children. Many of them believe vaguely that both the instruction and the behavior of the children are better in the parochial than in the public school, but have little factual knowledge of either school on which to base their belief. The way in which this information may be supplied and the extent to which the parents and others actually desire this information cannot be discussed at this point.[15]

The Role of Parents

The position and function of parents in relation to St. Luke's school are quite different from those of parents of public school children. The Catholic parents are "owners" of the parochial school in a more immediate and personal way than the way in which they, as well as the parents of public school children, "own" the public schools. It is said that the tax-payers and citizens own the whole public school system, even though their control over their "property" is so remote that it is quite negligible. It is true, of course, that parents do not "have a say" in the operation and policies of the elementary school, either public

[14] Henry C. Ringkamp, "All Activities Are Public Relations," *The Catholic School Journal,* vol. 52, no. 8 (October, 1953), pp. 240–243, points out the various groups with which public relations should be maintained by the schools.

[15] See, however, the suggestions in John Schroeder, "Tell the Public About Your School," *The Catholic School Journal,* vol. 55, no. 4 (April, 1955), pp. 107–109, who advised Catholic educators that they should not "hide their light beneath a bushel."

or parochial.[16] The professional educators have seen to that; and the associations of parents and teachers formally acknowledge this "hands-off" policy in their published constitutions.

There is a curious comparison between the public and parochial schools in this regard. The rules of public school administrators have the force of civil law, and the same authority that makes regulations also controls the purse strings. In all of this the teachers have little to say, and the parents less. At St. Luke's school the parishioners supply the money, the Principal makes the regulations and the Pastor controls the purse strings. In this situation the parents are extremely important in that they can increase or decrease their financial support. The Principal's regulations are persuasive rather than compulsory. This three-way relationship of Pastor, Principal and parents, is a well-balanced, reciprocal triangle.[17] In practice, it works out in a fairly smooth process of cooperation because the persons involved recognize their dependence on one another. This kind of arrangement may not be in operation in some other parochial schools; it cannot be in the public schools where the parents have neither authority nor control.

There is, nevertheless, a difference in the degree and kind of possessiveness that the parents express when they speak of "our school." The parochial school belongs to the parish, and the parish is the people who belong to it. The money that has gone into the school building came directly out of their own pockets. They have put part of themselves into the maintenance of the physical plant. This feeling they do not have concerning the public school to which their money has also contributed. For the parents of public school children, the use of these tax-supported facilities is on the same level as the use of public libraries, parks, railway stations and highways.[18]

[16] This probably is not the case with parents who send their children to private schools and who may have undue influence over the school (particularly on the elementary level). There is, however, a growing literature on "Citizen Advisory Committees" for public schools. For a bibliography, see Leslie W. Kindred, *School-Public Relations* (Englewood Cliffs: Prentice-Hall, 1957), pp. 432–433.

[17] See the discussion of this point by Carl J. Ryan, "Parochial Schools Rest on Good Will," *The Catholic Educator,* vol. 27, no. 8 (April, 1956), pp. 493–494. See also above, chap. 14, "Financing the School."

[18] Even from the point of view of financing there is too much bureaucracy in the management of the public school, operating as it does in a "narrow official routine," and should be changed because "to the degree possible, people affected by decisions should participate in making them," says Paul R. Mort, "Bureaucracy in Business Management," *Teachers College Record,* vol. 54, no. 2 (November, 1952), pp. 59–62. See also Myron Lieberman, *Education As a Profession* (Englewood Cliffs: Prentice-Hall, 1956).

The result of this differential relationship is that the parents of St. Luke's children demonstrate a greater interest, devotion and responsibility toward their school than they, or the parents of public school children, show toward the public school. This can be measured, in a general way, by the amount of time and energy that the parents devote to the maintenance and improvement of the school. The parents of public school children belong to the PTA, and they conduct projects for the benefit of the school, but they are doing these things for the most part as parents of children and not as loyal members of a group of people who own and promote a school.

Another important difference is that between the voluntary and the compulsory relationship of parents to the school. From this point of view the parents of parochial school children are much freer than are the parents of public school children. In most instances the latter have no choice in the matter of the school attended; it makes no difference whether they give or withhold support; the school does not depend upon them. The parochial school is much more dependent upon the good will and cooperation of the parents. Without their support it would close down. If they are dissatisfied with the school they can still make the decision to send the child to the public school.[19]

Contrasting Bureaucracies

A comparative analysis of the two types of school shows that the local public school is caught up in a rigid, stratified, complex organization. The question here does not concern the number of levels in the hierarchy of each system, but the manner in which the people at each level operate in relation to the others. The public school is more bureaucratic than the parochial school. "The type of organization designed to accomplish large-scale administrative tasks by systematically coordinating the work of many individuals is called a bureaucracy." [20]

We must be careful not to confuse the varying types of personality in each school with the bureaucratic structure itself. Some of the public school teachers we interviewed considered their Principal a "tyrant" and a "dictator." It is possible, of course, to find a democratic personality in a rigid and formalized system, just as it is possible that an authoritarian personality may operate more or less successfully in a

[19] There is, of course, the intangible moral pressure and the traditional religious loyalty at work on the Catholic parents to give their children a Catholic education.

[20] Peter M. Blau, *Bureaucracy in Modern Society* (New York: Random House, 1956), p. 14.

flexible regime. The point here is that the public school system is relatively rigid and formalized, and that this system necessarily has an effect upon the social relations of pupils, teachers, and others within it.[21]

The systematic coordination of individual functions is the essence of a highly bureaucratic system. For example, the multiplication of rules and regulations, of offices and personnel, of experts and committees, is undoubtedly intended to make the public school operate more efficiently. It is not merely that the average public school is large in numbers (averaging 839.6 pupils each) but that each school is a unit in a much larger system. Multiplied functions within each school, so that the school is now performing many "extra" activities that were formerly supplied by the home and the community, extend the local bureaucracy as well as that of the city school system. Each school itself must be controlled "from above" and this means that decision-making for the most part is out of the hands of the lower functionaries.

It is an interesting fact that Max Weber's classic definition of the bureaucrat[22] can be applied to the Principal of the public school but not to the Principal of St. Luke's. These two Principals are similar in that their office gives them a distinct *social esteem,* and that both are *appointed* by a superior authority. Sister Roberta, however, does not have *tenure,* nor *pecuniary compensation,* nor is she a *career person.* The Principal of the public school has all five characteristics of the bureaucrat, and the public school system has all of the characteristics of the classical bureaucracy.

From this point of view, the Pastor of St. Luke's is a bureaucrat within the ecclesiastical bureaucracy, and holds a position analogous to that of the public school Principal within the educational bureaucracy. Even this, however, must be viewed as merely an analogy because the Pastor of a parish has much more freedom of decision in many more areas of decision than has the public school Principal. Although he has a much broader competency he must also depend much more upon the voluntary cooperation and good will of his subordinates, the

[21] A hopeful note is struck, but without the evidence of empirical studies, by Albert J. Huggett and T. M. Stinnett, *Professional Problems of Teachers* (New York: Macmillan, 1956), who write that "for the last decade or so the 'line-and-staff' philosophy in administration has been rapidly giving way to the teamwork idea, involving all members of the professional staff in the determination of school policies. And the trend is a fortunate one. For if education is to be democratic, that process must start with those who staff the schools" (p. 299).

[22] See H. H. Gerth and C. Wright Mills, (translators and editors) *From Max Weber: Essays in Sociology* (New York: Oxford University Press, 1946), pp. 199–204.

parishioners, than the public school Principal does upon his subordinates.

In one sense, the public school is a system of laws while the parochial school is a system of persons. This analogy is only partly true and it must not be pushed too hard. Both formal laws and personal decisions are operative to some degree in both types of schools. The public school Principal, for example, is more subject to the system of rules from above than is the parochial school Principal. The latter is much freer to make decisions, and the success of her personal and social relations with parents, teachers and children, depends more upon her competence than upon the standardized procedures in the filing cabinet.

A most important aspect here is that St. Luke's school is local and autonomous *in operation,* while the public school is not, and cannot be, in any real sense independent. We have seen this all during the year. The Principal, Sister Roberta, runs the school on the basis of her knowledge, competence and experience. St. Luke's is largely the result of her ideas and her ability to get cooperation from everyone involved. She was appointed to the position by her religious superior, with the approval of the Pastor. We have seen that the Pastor does not interfere with the school. The diocesan superintendent of parochial schools is also a Pastor in a distant city and has not even visited the school in the last two years.

In contrast to this, the Principal of the public school is appointed by his educational superior, the superintendent of the school system. He cannot, and does not, do anything on his own decision except purely routine matters and thus operates mainly on orders from above. The duties of the Principal have been highly regularized; they are spelled out in formal phrases printed in a booklet. Directives from the superintendent of schools, as well as numerous city and state regulations, confront the public school Principal at every turn. He is not permitted even to administer questionnaires to the pupils without the approval and permission of the superintendent's office. Whether this works for ultimate efficiency, or, what is even more important, for the benefit of the school children, is not the point here. It is typical of the organized bureaucracy.[23]

The clearest example of this contrast between the public and the

[23] Anyone familiar with the operation of larger colleges and universities will recognize the development of this same bureaucratic pattern. The highest developed form is, of course, in America's big business. Up till now, it appears that the Church represents the only major institution in America that has not yet been highly bureaucratized.

parochial schools is found in the use of "red tape." Whether or not red tape is irritating to people, whether or not it is in practice efficient, it appears to be necessary in the public school system.[24] An example of this routinization and complication is that of the selection of textbooks, which in the public elementary school becomes an elaborate annual ritual. A committee of teachers, from the public schools in the area, appointed by the superintendent of schools, reads and censors the new textbooks each year. The committee then prepares a list of approved books, two or three for each subject, and submits it to the superintendent. The list, when censored and approved by him, is published to all the Principals, who are then forbidden to choose any except an approved textbook.

In St. Luke's school, the selection of textbooks is a very simple procedure. If a change of text is desirable, the teacher talks it over with the Principal; the latter orders the books; and the Pastor pays the bills. Obviously, considerable investigation and examination of various textbooks precedes the decision, and the teachers are guided by an annual list published in *The Catholic Educator*.[25] This list offers additional guidance because after each textbook it provides the names of the dioceses in which the particular book is in use. The superintendent of schools in the diocese where St. Luke's is located does not issue a list of recommended texts to be used in the parochial schools, but this procedure appears to be followed in some of the larger Catholic centers of the country, where educational bureaucratization resembles that of the public school system.[26]

St. Luke's school, like parochial schools generally, has not been plagued by the wave of "book burnings" and "witch hunts" that has

[24] For a survey of attitudes on bureaucratic red tape, see Alvin W. Gouldner, "Red Tape as a Social Problem," in *Reader in Bureaucracy*, edited by Robert K. Merton, Ailsa P. Gray, Barbara Hockey and Hanan C. Selvin (Glencoe: Free Press, 1952), pp. 410–418.

[25] This periodical had previously been named the *Journal of Religious Instruction*, and in September, 1943 (vol. 14, no. 1), it published its first list of "Approved Textbooks for Catholic Schools." The implication that any agency could assume the right to "approve" texts for all American Catholic schools was resented by superintendents and other administrators. The word "approved" was later dropped from the title. For a discussion of teacher participation, see Paul S. Anderson, "How Teachers Share in Textbook Selection," *The Nation's Schools*, vol. 60, no. 3 (September, 1957), pp. 57–59.

[26] The *Book of Policies for Elementary Schools* of the Archdiocese of Chicago School Board (p. 20) states clearly that "the texts adopted by the Archdiocesan School Board must be used in all the schools of the Archdiocese. A list of these books is sent from the School Board each spring."

annoyed public school administrators in some American cities.[27] Except for tirades of the Blanshard type there have been no investigations or charges by anti-liberal groups concerning the content of textbooks used in parochial schools. The public schools in the same city have also been relatively free from such outside pressure, although the city itself contains its quota of highly and negatively critical citizens. Thus, both the local public and parochial schools have been able to pursue the stated ideals of liberal, open, honest and democratic teaching so highly valued in the education of American school children.

Conformity of Teachers

The effects of the expanding educational bureaucracy have invaded the classroom of the public school teacher. "I have so much paperwork," said one teacher; "I have so many reports to fill out; I'm in charge of so many things that have nothing to do with learning. I love to teach but on some days of the week I am lucky if I can squeeze in a good hour and a half of real teaching." [28] This complaint may be the exaggeration of a tired teacher; it may not be typical, but it is an indication that the public school teacher is suffering much more from the effects of over-organization than is the parochial school teacher. When these practices invade the classroom they affect and interfere with the central function of the school, the teaching of children.

The daily working arrangements of the public school teacher are also more strict and regimented than those of the parochial school teacher. She (or he) [29] must sign in at the Principal's office in the morning and sign out again in the afternoon after school. This practice is referred to by the teachers as "punching the time clock." The rule says that "All teachers should report to their respective building before 8:00 in the forenoon and may not leave before 4:00 unless excused by

[27] There are numerous articles on this subject. See Mark A. Hennessey, "Saving Los Angeles from the U.N." *The Reporter,* vol. 7, no. 10 (November 11, 1952), pp. 28–31; Benjamin Fine, "The Truth About Schoolbook Censorship," *Parents' Magazine,* vol. 27, no. 12 (December, 1952), pp. 46–47, 84, 86, 88; H. Apel, "Academic Freedom: Its Second Front," *Bulletin* of the American Association of University Professors, vol. 41, no. 3 (Autumn, 1955), pp. 518–530; Lloyd W. King, "You Can Trust Your Textbooks," *Education,* vol. 77, no. 6 (February, 1957), pp. 346–348.

[28] This is not a new complaint. Twenty years ago the Lynds quoted a Middletown teacher: "If we could only take a day off to teach!" Robert S. Lynd and Helen Merrell Lynd, *Middletown in Transition* (New York: Harcourt, Brace, 1937), p. 224.

[29] There are five male teachers in the Taft public school where we have made our comparative study. All teachers at St. Luke's are women.

the Principal." The forenoon sessions in the elementary grades are 8:30–11:45 and the afternoon sessions are 1:15–3:30. The printed regulations for teachers are accompanied by a note stating that they are "not to be changed unless special permission is granted by the Board of Education." This subjects the teacher to another and higher level of the hierarchy, even above the superintendent of schools.

There is a rather wide-spread complaint among public elementary school teachers to the effect that "we are ourselves treated like children." Brookover points out that "the attitude of the administrator or supervisor toward his subordinates is generally characterized by an authoritarian role and an unsympathetic identification with the teachers. No doubt such a pattern is, in part, a transfer of his former authoritarian role in relation to students to his present relations with the ordinary teacher." [30] It must be remembered, of course, that the public school Principal or administrator is caught up in a specific rank of a stratified system, and is himself subject to a series of authoritarian persons above him. Sister Roberta at St. Luke's does not suffer from this cramped position of stress from above. Furthermore, since she is herself a teacher she has a sympathetic identification with the other teachers.

The pressure of conformity on the teacher tends to be translated by the teacher in the form of pressure on the pupils. The authoritarian practices are more in evidence at the public school than at St. Luke's. We have seen a hint of this in the fact that corporal punishment is still used and that other forms of sanctions are more rigid and less intelligent than the practices employed in St. Luke's. The teachers in the latter school are not under the same "strict subordination," of which John Dewey wrote, as are those in the public school. Dewey surmises that "the dictatorial, autocratic attitude adopted by some teachers in the classroom is, in some considerable measure, a reflection of what they feel they suffer from." [31]

[30] Wilbur B. Brookover, *A Sociology of Education* (New York: American Book Company, 1955), p. 254. On the following pages he reproduces an actual example of school policies, rules and regulations for the school year in a particular community. See also Bernard Meltzer, Harry Doby, Philip Smith, eds., *Education in Society* (New York: Crowell, 1958), Part 5, "The Social Control of Education."

[31] "There is a disposition to pass on to those who are under the immediate jurisdiction of the teacher—namely, the children—the pattern of strict subordination which they themselves have to follow. . . . If these teachers had an opportunity to take some active part in the formation of general policies, they might well be moved to be less autocratic in their own domain." See John Dewey, "Democracy and Education Administration," *Official Report*, New Orleans Con-

The teacher certificate is another example of demands made upon the teaching personnel. Its requirements are not set by the Principal, the superintendent, or even the board of education. The hierarchy of authority in this instance reaches up into the remote area of state operations. Educational agencies far removed from the city in which the public school operates dictate both the kind and the amount of education the teacher must have.[32] St. Luke's, like other parochial schools in this area, is unaffected by these state regulations. Experience, competence and personality are the main requirements of the parochial school teacher. Like most public school teachers, she takes summer courses, but she is not pressured into "in-service training" or the desperate struggle for further "credits."

The important difference here is that an area of personal initiative exists for the parochial school teacher which the public school teacher has largely lost. In contrast to all of the superimposed and restrictive practices of the public schools, St. Luke's parochial school seems an island of freedom with a relaxed and informal atmosphere. The teacher can make decisions on the spot, and what is more significant, she can permit some freedom of choice to her pupils. If the class is strong on arithmetic and weak on spelling, she spends more time on spelling. If the children are bored and need relaxation she lets them sing a song or choose a story or other activity.

The popular stereotype of the parochial school teacher, especially the nun, as compared to the public school teacher, seems to arise from a confusion of the private and professional lives of these teachers. As a professional, that is, in the actual performance of the teacher-role, the parochial school Sister is freer and more independent than the public school teacher. In her non-professional role, that is, in the private and social life of the Sister, there are many voluntary inhibitions, which the public school teacher does not have.[33] This, however, is the

vention of the American Association of School Administrators (Washington, D.C., National Education Association, February, 1937), p. 54.

[32] See Lydia Stout, "What Strangles American Teaching," *The Atlantic Monthly*, vol. 201, no. 4 (April, 1958), pp. 59–63; also H. Otto Dahlke, *Values in Culture and Classroom* (New York: Harper, 1958), chap. 17, "Teaching and Bureaucracy."

[33] Inhibitions on the expected behavior patterns of public school teachers still exist in many parts of the country. Even in her private and non-professional life the public school teacher is not so "free" as the woman who has other kinds of occupations. Brookover, *op. cit.*, pp. 237–253, has brought together the more interesting examples of such inhibitions. See also Willard Waller, *Sociology of Teaching* (New York: Wiley, 1932), chap. 2–6. For the decrease in official discrimination against married teachers, see *Research Bulletin*, no. 30 (Washington: National Education Association, February, 1952), pp. 12–14.

difference between the lay person and the religious functionary. It is not a comparison of teacher with teacher.

Teacher Shortage

So much has been said and written during the post-war years concerning the "crisis" in schools that everyone is aware of the problem.[34] Basically, it is a question of unbalance between the growth of the school population on the one hand and the lack of personnel and buildings on the other. Expanding facilities have not been able to keep up with the expanding demand. This is a national problem. It is particularly pressing in the large urban and the growing suburban areas for the public schools. It is even more pressing in the parochial school system, which depends heavily on religious orders for its teaching personnel and on voluntary contributions of parishioners to finance its operations.

St. Luke's school has fourteen teachers for 632 children, for a teacher load of 45.1 pupils. In all of the parochial schools of the city the average load is 43.6 pupils per teacher. This contrasts unfavorably with the normal teaching load of 29.1 pupils for the public schools of the same city.[35] In the private elementary schools the ratio of pupils to teacher is even lower. The shortage and crowding are highlighted even further at St. Luke's by the fact that the school does not have a kindergarten and that the Principal is also the eighth-grade teacher.

Since this question is of vital concern to the parents of children who are crowding the schools we wanted to get their opinion and suggested solutions. We interviewed the parents of 813 elementary school children and asked them "What can be done about the teacher shortage?" We put the same question to forty-two teachers in the elementary schools, both public and parochial. We wanted to know what suggestions parents and teachers could make about providing more personnel for the grade school class room. A little over fifteen per cent of the parents had no comment to make, or had never thought of the matter, but all the teachers had something to say about it.

[34] As a sample of many discussions on this problem see Oscar Handlin, "The Crisis in Teaching," *The Atlantic Monthly*, vol. 198, no. 3 (September, 1956), pp. 33–37; also Frederick G. Hochwalt, "Catholic Education Today," *The Ave Maria*, vol. 85, no. 17 (April 27, 1957), pp. 12–15; and the national survey, "Back to the Three R's?" *U.S. News & World Report*, vol. 42, no. 11 (March 15, 1957), pp. 38–44.

[35] A Research Bulletin, "Class Size in the Elementary Schools of Urban School Districts, 1955–1956" (Washington: National Education Association, Research Division *Special Memo*, July, 1956), showed that 56.9 per cent of these classrooms contained thirty *or more* pupils each.

Suggestions	Parents	Teachers
No suggestion	15.1%	0.0%
Raise salaries	45.2	9.1
Encourage youth to teach [36]	16.1	14.8
Hire lay teachers in parochial schools	8.7	12.5
Improve working conditions [37]	7.1	38.6
Use teachers' aides	3.0	11.4
Other suggestions [38]	4.8	13.6

The solution most frequently suggested by parents is an economic one. Forty-five per cent of the parents suggested that the teachers' salary should be raised, and almost nine per cent said that more lay teachers should be hired for the parochial schools. Thus, the majority seem to feel that the teaching profession is grossly underpaid and that more personnel would be attracted if the salaries were increased.[39]

Parents have deep sympathy for teachers who have to "get along for twelve months on a ten-months' salary." Some suggest that arrangements should be made by local business and industry to employ the lay teachers during the summer months. The most frequent statement made by parents is: "the only way to get more teachers is to pay them more money." Some are even willing to contribute more taxes and tuition for this purpose. Almost nine per cent of the parents of parochial school children are willing to pay more money to get lay teachers into the parochial school.

The teachers themselves were less money-minded. None of them, of course, is averse to a "pay hike," but an unexpected response to our interviews with public school teachers was that none of them suggested a salary raise as the most important incentive for meeting the shortage. Of course, the married male teachers with children were less content with their income than were the unmarried female teachers, who felt

[36] This includes "encouraging Sister vocations."

[37] Includes "raising teacher status," "making teaching more attractive," and "improving advancement procedures."

[38] Includes "relax requirements," "get former teachers to return," and "influence public opinion."

[39] Frederick Moffitt, "What Teachers Want," *The Nation's Schools,* vol. 60, no. 3 (September, 1957), pp. 53–56, found that teachers themselves want most appreciation, acceptance and sympathetic supervision; school board members think that teachers want more salary, more security and more promotions; school administrators think that teachers want better equipment, smaller classes and better working conditions.

that their salaries compared favorably with the average income of other employed women in this city.[40]

The parochial school teachers (including the three lay teachers) logically focused their attention on the problem of teacher shortage within St. Luke's school. Most of them suggested two principal remedies: the encouragement of religious vocations for girls, and the employment of lay teachers. All of the Sisters at St. Luke's school are in favor of having more lay teachers, and they want them "to be accepted as equals, and not just tolerated as a necessary evil." The fact that a relatively small percentage of parent interviewees suggested the employment of lay teachers for the parochial school indicates that this is to most of them a novel and somewhat incongruous suggestion. The decision to employ lay teachers is up to the Pastor who must ultimately finance their salaries. Sister Roberta, the Principal, thinks that there should be at least one lay teacher for every five Sisters.

Status and Encouragement

It is a sociological axiom that status[41] does not just happen automatically and that the prestige attached to an occupation can be artificially increased. All kinds of jobs have been made more attractive simply by renaming them and spotlighting them. Janitors are sometimes called building superintendents, salesmen are called manufacturers' representatives. The humble function of airline stewardess has been glamorized with uniforms, training periods, and advertisements hinting at romantic and exotic experiences. Chiropractors and social workers have struggled for years to raise their occupations to the status of professions by raising qualifications and standards.

The status of teachers in the parochial and the public schools differs considerably. All of them in both schools are professional functionaries, and they share in whatever general esteem or disesteem the public holds this function. In the parochial school, however, the religious Sisters have another kind of status added to the teacher status,

[40] The starting salary of a public school teacher with a Bachelor's degree is $4,000, and with a Master's degree, $4,200. These salaries reach a maximum of $6,250 and $6,650 after seventeen years' service. Lay teachers in the parochial school start as low as $2,750 and have no prearranged guarantee of advancement in the salary scale.

[41] For a discussion of the worst problems affecting the professional status of teachers, see Louis Kaplan, "The Annoyances of Elementary School Teachers," *Journal of Educational Research*, vol. 45, no. 9 (May, 1952), p. 659. See also "The Status of the American Public-School Teacher," *Research Bulletin*, vol. 35, no. 1, National Education Association.

and sometimes confused with it, and based on their religious vocation. They enjoy the respect and prestige given by the Catholic laity. But this puts the lay teachers in a peculiar position. From the point of view of the teacher role, they are not lay people, but professionals. Thus, while the public school teacher is called a trained, professional teacher, her counterpart in the parochial school is constantly referred to as a trained, lay teacher.

Although parents often say that teaching is a socially important function, they still tend to underrate teaching as a profession. There appears to be an undercurrent supposition that "anybody can do it," that "it's a soft job with lots of time off," and that, for men, at least, "you teach when you can't get anything better to do." Since status depends largely on the attitudes of the people in the parish and the community, elevating the status of teaching requires a change in those attitudes. The so-called law of "supply and demand" seems to be at work here. Since teachers are scarce, the people are beginning to look with even greater respect on the work of the religious Sisters. Public school teachers suggest that they can change public attitudes by strengthening their organizations and increasing their demands.[42] They feel that teachers must mingle more with non-teachers and become active in the community.

The attempt to raise status by multiplying the technical requirements for teacher's certificates has not helped to relieve the teacher shortage. It is doubtful that it has helped to raise the prestige of teaching. Among the mothers we interviewed there were some who said they had entered college with the intention of studying to be teachers. They quit after a year or two, or switched to another degree program, because of the peculiar insistence upon formalistic, but often content-less pedagogical courses. This aspect of teacher-preparation was reflected in the opinions of many parents and teachers. They pointed out certain parishioners, especially women, who have bachelor's degrees from a liberal arts college but who are disqualified from teaching because of the technical requirements imposed by educationists.[43]

[42] The public school teachers in the city have weakened their position of bargaining by being split in two professional groups. The Teachers' Union is composed of the more alert, aggressive, and progressive teachers, while the Teachers' Association, connected with the National Education Association, contains the tradition-minded, slow-moving people. It is mainly female in membership.

[43] Eugene B. Elliott, "Teacher Demand, Teacher Supply," *The Nation's Schools*, vol. 60, no. 3 (September, 1957), pp. 77–78, reporting a study of the prospective teacher supply, says "it is forecast that one-third of the elementary children will be taught by teachers with less than a college degree."

Parents and teachers in both schools felt that there is a great need to "sell teaching" as a profession and an occupation, and that young people should be encouraged to enter the teaching field, and that the teaching profession should be made more attractive. The fact that these suggestions are not now being followed is indicated by another aspect of our study. We asked the children in the sixth, seventh and eighth grades in both schools to write down what they want to be when they finish their education. Approximately one-quarter (27.0%) of the girls in these three classes said they want to be nurses, and about one-fifth (20.6%) were looking forward to becoming nuns or teachers.[44] When we asked the parents what they wanted their children to be when they grow up, 11.6 per cent said they wanted the girl to be a nurse, and 10.9 per cent indicated teaching or the Sisterhood as a future career for their girl.

The prospect of becoming a stenographer, typist or secretary was more attractive to the school girls than that of becoming a teacher. Certain female occupations appear to have been "glamorized" through television, radio, movies, and even in deliberate advertising. This has not been the case with school teaching.[45] The physician, lawyer, clergyman and government employee still rank higher than the elementary school teacher. Although there is also a great need for men teachers at the elementary level, only four boys in the upper grades of the two elementary schools look forward to teaching as a career, and no parent suggested this for his son.

The source of the future teaching profession is in the school itself at the present time. A larger proportion of the children who are now learning must somehow be persuaded to become teachers themselves.[46] But the attempt to induce them to think along these lines runs into two difficulties. First, many of them come from economic-minded families in an economic-dominated society. They are impressed with the notion that income is the measure of success and that teachers' incomes are

[44] Of the 189 girls in the three upper grades of both schools, fifty-one intend to be nurses and thirty-nine teachers or Sisters. See above, chap. 12.

[45] See Robert Richey, William Fox and Charles Fauset, "Prestige Ranks of Teaching," *Occupations,* vol. 30 (October, 1951), pp. 33–34; see also Myron Lieberman, *Education as a Profession* (Englewood Cliffs: Prentice-Hall, 1956), pp. 477–478, where he writes about the decline of status of the teaching profession.

[46] Clarence Fielstra, "An Analysis of Factors Influencing the Decision to Become a Teacher," *Journal of Educational Research,* vol. 48, no. 9 (May, 1955), pp. 659–667. The most influential factors found in this study were: "(1) an inspirational teacher; (2) a friend or relative; (3) newspaper accounts on the need for teachers; (4) leaflets, magazine articles, and books on teaching and education; and (5) their parents."

low. Secondly, the child is with the teacher five or six hours a day and this realistic relationship cannot compete with the glamor of more distant and well-known forms of occupation.

Still there are suggested ways in which the child can come to appreciate the value of the teaching profession. Children always love to play adult roles. At St. Luke's the older children are given an opportunity to perform some of the tasks ordinarily performed by the teacher. The honor patrol boys supervise the children's exits and entrances to the school. The honor patrol girls help to supervise the smaller children during the recess and lunch periods, and sometimes give help to particular children during a study period. In a sense this is a kind of miniature apprenticeship, like that of the "cadet teachers" who are high school students. Just as the child learns the elements of the paternal roles by being allowed to help around the house, so also can he or she develop an interest in teaching by performing some of the minor tasks of the teaching role.[47]

To some extent the teachers themselves may be charged with neglect in failing to recruit future members of the profession. Their contacts with the children are close, personal and extended. The children are ready and eager to "help teacher" and are constantly asking to be allowed to perform chores. The Sisters at St. Luke's take every opportunity to talk to the children about becoming future priests or nuns. Implied in the latter vocation is the fact that most members of this particular order are *also teachers,* besides being nuns.[48] Many of these children feel that they have to be at the top of their class or have to "know everything" before they could even begin to think about being teachers. The girls do not have this attitude about being nuns.

Several of the public school teachers make a deliberate effort to arouse interest among the school children in teaching. They talk to likely individuals among their pupils about the importance of teaching and about the intangible rewards of dedication to the profession. They try to inspire and attract them and even encourage them. Thus, recruit-

[47] Robert H. Anderson, "The Principal Faces Overcrowding," *Educational Leadership,* vol. 13, no. 1 (October, 1955), pp. 18–23, suggests, among other practices, the use of paid "teacher aides," as experimented with in Bay City, Michigan.

[48] In our observations we have never heard a teacher at St. Luke's praise any vocation or occupation other than the priesthood and the sisterhood. Our interviews with the children confirmed this observation. One of our research assistants, a married man, told an eighth-grade boy who is planning to study for the Franciscan priesthood, that he had himself thought about the same vocation as a grammar school boy. The Sister who overheard the conversation turned to him and said, "Don't you wish you had done it?"

ment starts at the elementary level even while certain minor aspects of the apprenticeship are put to use. These same teachers, however, complain that the attitudes of parents tend to frustrate their efforts. Families do not encourage their children to become teachers, and this fact reflects again the need to raise the social status of teaching in the minds of parents.

Working Conditions of Teachers

There is a widespread interest in improving the working conditions of teachers which is seen as a means to making teaching more attractive and also raising teacher status.[49] This is a kind of "complaint department" into which the teachers pour their distasteful experiences. The teacher shortage is demonstrated, and perhaps even accentuated, by the fact that most teachers in elementary schools are overworked. This is seen not only in the crowded classrooms, but also by the large amount of peripheral tasks they have to perform. The public school teachers particularly are irked at this arrangement. As one woman said, "We ought to let the teachers teach and the parents parent." She explained that the school has absorbed many functions that belong in other hands. Her list of such functions included the following: instruction in health, safety and athletics; supervising study, lunch and recess periods; taking care of behavior problems, performing extra paper work and serving on Scout committees. Another teacher said that she has so much "extra work" to do that "I feel more like a secretary and file clerk than a teacher."

One of the frequent complaints of teachers is that of overwork. The public school teachers must be at the school from eight in the morning till four in the afternoon, and besides this bring "homework" that consumes about two hours more. They suggest that the actual hours in the classroom be limited to a period from nine in the morning till two in the afternoon. This could be done by eliminating the study periods or by having parents come in to supervise the study period (since this has practically taken the place of "homework" which parents used to supervise at home). This suggestion is not acceptable to most parents, who seem to feel that the school is the place for study as well as for learning.

There is a whole litany of further grievances which the public school teachers have, and which they feel should be removed if teaching is to

[49] For a discussion of recent trends in this area, see Albert J. Huggett and T. M. Stinnett, *Professional Problems of Teachers* (New York: Macmillan, 1956), chap. 9, "Professional Working Conditions for Teachers," pp. 199–242.

be made attractive. They complain about too much clerical and paper work and about extra duty on the playground and in the cafeteria during recess and lunch time. They are often dissatisfied with their lack of authority regarding discipline and with the peculiar attitudes of parents toward discipline.[50] There is too much extracurricular participation and they object that the parents and the PTA meddle in their classroom functions.

The teachers at St. Luke's also have a long day and are overworked. In contrast with some public school teachers who complain that they do not "have enough teaching to do," the teacher at St. Luke's sometimes complains of "having too much teaching" to do. Their classes are somewhat larger than those of the public school teacher. Their day starts with Holy Mass for the children at eight o'clock in the morning. Thus, the Sisters' "working day" has this extra hour in the morning as well as the usual period for supervised study during the day. Besides this, some of them also have extra duties like sacristan work, teaching music after hours, directing the choir, as well as the normal domestic tasks in the convent. It has even been suggested that the rules of the cloister be changed in order to fit the exigencies of the teaching role.

This question of possible conflict between the religious and the educational roles of the Sisters is one of delicate proportions. There appears to be no problem at St. Luke's from the point of view of content of classes, techniques of instruction, or attitudes of teachers and pupils. The question here is whether rules which hinder the Sisters from full participation in the PTA, or from devoting "extra hours" after the official bedtime to reading and study, or from participating in a professional way in the community, detract in any way from the professional role of teaching. The teaching order to which St. Luke's Sisters belong, seems to have heeded the hint of Pope Pius XII, that the urgency of the times demands, as well as justifies, an adjustment in the accidental structure of religious life itself.[51]

From the point of view of effective teaching within a particular school the religious teachers have the great advantage of participating in

[50] The laws in this state permit teachers to "paddle" pupils, but public school Principals discourage the practice. One second-grade girl told her teacher, "my mother just dares any teacher to lay a hand on me."

[51] See the balanced discussion on this point by Aumann Jordan, "Religious Life and Modern Needs," *Review for Religious,* vol. 13, no. 4 (July, 1954), pp. 169–178. See Pius XII's exhortation to teaching Sisters at Rome, September 15, 1951, "On Educating Youth," *The Catholic Mind,* vol. 50, no. 1074 (June, 1952), pp. 376–380.

group activity outside the classroom. Living in the same house together gives them an opportunity to exchange knowledge about the school's problems and about the children they have in class. Communication among the teachers is carried on in a way that is outside the possibilities of the public school teachers who can perform this valuable function only in short informal sessions or in occasional contrived teachers' meetings. From a professional point of view, this community living approximates the ideal working conditions of the educational role, and is perhaps the single greatest advantage the Sisters have over the public school teachers.

Teacher Wastage

The remarks made above are a summary of interviews with parents and teachers and of observation in and around the school. They are focused mainly upon the question of how to get more young people to enter the teaching profession and also how to keep people from leaving the profession. To meet the immediate problem at hand, however, there are certain short-term, or stop-gap, arrangements that are possible. Some of the parents suggested that the crisis could be alleviated if teachers' aides were employed just as we employed nurses' aides during the war. St. Luke's Parent-Teacher Association tried to get this scheme under way at the beginning of the year, but it never eventuated.[52] The plan was for mothers to come at the noon-time recess to supervise the children on the playground and on the return to the school rooms. Others were to assist in distributing paper, pencils and other supplies, and in checking the simple written work like spelling and arithmetic. With this kind of assistance it was believed that the teacher could easily handle as many as fifty children in the same classroom.

The teachers point out that there is a certain wastage of the actual teacher talent which is now available in the community. Former teachers who are willing and able to return to the classroom are discouraged because they do not have the formal requirements for the teacher certificate. Since these requirements are not necessary for teaching in St. Luke's school, these former teachers constitute a pool from which substitute teachers can be drawn.[53] Since the salary for lay teachers,

[52] The following announcement and appeal appeared in the Parish Bulletin on Sunday, September 30: "School Ground Supervisors—The PTA is calling for some women to assist during noon recess, from 11:30 to 12:30. Are you willing? Get in touch with the chairman of the Room Mothers."

[53] Sister Roberta has also a list of the certified and qualified public school teachers who are Catholic women of the parish. This list was supplied by the public school board.

however, is so low, it is difficult to attract these women to the parochial school. The three lay teachers now at St. Luke's exemplify the highest spirit of dedication and loyalty in returning to the classroom under these conditions.

In another way there is wastage in the public school system. In the city schools relatively large numbers of teachers are drawn from the schoolroom to do administration work which could easily be done by social workers or other trained personnel. This "proliferation of bureaucracy," found so widely on the college and high school level, has extended down even to the elementary school. The question is not whether these administrative positions and "paper jobs" are necessary but whether well-qualified teachers should be taken from the classroom to perform them. It is an interesting fact that the ordinary parochial school like St. Luke's by sheer necessity cannot indulge in this apparent luxury of extra administrative function.[54]

There was a vague notion among some of the parents that the teacher shortage could be relieved by a kind of "G.I. Plan" which would subsidize future teachers through college. It was pointed out that certain voluntary organizations already do this; for example, the Red Cross provides scholarships for future social workers on the agreement that they will work for the organization for a specified period of time after graduation. Whether the city, county, state or federal government can develop a workable teacher's program along these lines is still open to question. The possibility of setting up a diocesan fund for the training of future lay teachers for the parochial school was also hinted at by some of the teachers.[55]

Overcrowding

The teacher shortage is closely allied with the problem of overcrowded schools. From the point of view of physical space St. Luke's has the opportunity of expanding into several available classrooms that are not now in constant use. These include the music room, and also the former high school library, which could be converted into two more classrooms. The fourteen classrooms now in use are uniform in size and they average 747.5 square feet per room. The experts in school design and construction seem to agree that one thousand square

[54] Administration, as a recognizable function of the Principal, is a kind of "sideline" with Sister Roberta. The school employs no secretaries or clerks, and has only the part-time services of the parish janitor.

[55] An NCWC news release of June 9, 1957, reported that "at their fifty-eighth annual state convention, the Knights of Columbus announced a $50,000 scholarship program to help provide lay teachers for the state's expanding parochial school system." The state in question is Ohio.

feet are essential for an elementary class with an enrollment of about thirty pupils.[56] A study of twenty American cities in 1950 showed that the median size of all elementary classrooms was 880 square feet. The experts say also that each classroom should have no less than thirty square feet of space for each child. For all the pupils in St. Luke's school the average classroom space per child is 16.55 square feet.

As we have seen in discussing this question with the teachers, overcrowding is a relative situation. If thirty square feet per child were taken as a minimum space requirement, each of St. Luke's classrooms could accommodate twenty-five pupils. The following table ranks the classrooms by this physical measurement and compares the results with the individual teacher's opinion of overcrowding in her classroom.

Grade	Children in class	Square feet per child	Measured extent of overcrowding	Teacher's measure of overcrowding
Eighth	60	12.45	35	20
Two-B	52	14.37	27	22
Seventh	52	14.37	27	17
Three-A	52	14.37	27	12
Two-A	51	14.65	26	16
Four-B	50	14.95	25	10
Four-A	46	16.25	21	16
Three-B	46	16.25	21	6
One-B	45	16.60	20	10
One-A	39	19.16	14	9
Five-B	38	19.67	13	—7
Five-A	36	20.76	11	1
Six-B	33	22.04	8	—2
Six-A	32	23.36	7	—3
Totals	632		282	127
Average	45.1	16.55	20.1	9.1

In the composite opinion of the teachers, they could handle 505 pupils at St. Luke's school, which means that in their opinion the school is overcrowded by 127 children. From the point of view of the "experts," however, we see that the fourteen classrooms now in use should contain an average of twenty-five pupils, or a total of 350 children. This means

[56] Some of the studies on this question are as follows: James D. MacConnell, *Planning for School Buildings* (Englewood Cliffs: Prentice-Hall, 1957); New England School Development Council, *The Elementary Classroom* (Cambridge, May, 1950), N. L. Englehardt, N. L. Englehardt, Jr. and Stanton Leggett, *Planning Elementary School Buildings* (New York: F. W. Dodge, 1953).

that St. Luke's school has an excess of 282 pupils. According to the teachers, the average class has about nine pupils too many; according to the ideal demands of physical space the average class contains about twenty excess pupils.[57]

Quite aside from the ideals expressed either by the teachers or by the designers of school buildings, we may say that the crowded classrooms at St. Luke's are due to both an insufficiency of teachers and a lack of schoolroom space. We felt, however, that this question should be included in our interviews with both parents and teachers. From the point of view of numbers answering, or of agreement of answers, the results were disappointing. To our question, "what can be done about the problem of overcrowding?" 17.1 per cent of the parents and 15.8 per cent of the teachers had no answer to give; about sixty-four per cent of the parents and thirty-five per cent of the teachers could suggest nothing better than an expanded building program.

Most of our interviewees seemed to be puzzled by the problem of overcrowding or had never previously given it any serious thought. Usually, the answer that "more and larger schools should be built" was accompanied by some discussion concerning the sources of finances or construction costs. One parent, who is an architect, suggested that school building plans be standardized and that all schools should be built on the same basic plan, thus saving large architects' fees. Another parent, who is in the building business, said that smaller, cheaper and more practical schools should be built so that every neighborhood could have a school. He added that a gymnasium could be built for the common use of four or five such small schools. A teacher suggested that neat small temporary buildings should be erected, which could be transported and set up again elsewhere to meet population shifts.

The great majority of St. Luke's parents believe that the elementary school teacher can handle fairly large classes, considerably larger than the "ideal" number suggested by experts. While the teachers think that an average of about thirty-six pupils is a proper number, 38.7 per cent of the parents think they could handle thirty-five to forty-four pupils, and another 35.5 per cent of parents think that thirty to thirty-four pupils "about right." One parent boasted that when he went to school "there were fifty kids in the class, and after we graduated we could compete with anybody in high school." Granting a top limit of pupils,

[57] See above, chap. 11, "Teachers of St. Luke's." For a broader picture of overcrowding see "Nearly 40 Million in School," *School Life*, vol. 38 (October, 1955), pp. 5–6.

even educators have questioned the dictum that a small class is better than a large class, or that "the teacher's ability to give more time to individual pupils results in superior achievement by the pupils." [58] There is positive proof in the high school records of St. Luke's graduates that their crowded schoolrooms did not lessen their learning achievements.

Other ideas about overcrowding centered on the children rather than on the physical plants. St. Luke's has no kindergarten, and some of the parents felt that perhaps the first and second grades could also be eliminated. This helps to solve both the teacher shortage and the overcrowding in parochial schools but simply amplifies these problems for the public school system. Sending the children to school in shifts, which was widely practiced throughout the large cities, and which is still true of some kindergartens and first grades in the local public schools, was mentioned as a temporary aid. One teacher proposed a twelve-month school year on a rotation basis, so that the present available personnel and facilities could take care of all overcrowding.

In one way or another the notion of better selectivity of pupils was suggested as a means of both decreasing crowding and improving the quality of teaching. Several public school teachers felt that the backward and uninterested pupils in the sixth, seventh and eighth grades could well be taken out of the normal elementary school and sent to some sort of vocational training school. This, of course, would still require the city to provide buildings and teachers for the overflow. St. Luke's can practice selectivity on various criteria, eliminating the children who now come from other parishes, those who do not live up to the minimum scholastic standards, as well as those who do not follow the rules of good conduct.

In the last analysis the administrators of the parochial school have a tremendous advantage over those in the public school. Teacher shortage and overcrowding are not static items, and there seems little like-

[58] This common opinion was tested and found false by Robert F. Spitzer, "Class Size and Pupil Achievement in Elementary Schools," *The Elementary School Journal,* vol. 55, no. 2 (October, 1954), pp. 82–86. This study shows that third grade pupils in larger classes (thirty or more children) were superior in each department except arithmetic skills. An earlier work by Earnest Horn, *Methods of Instruction in the Social Studies* (New York: Scribner, 1937), concluded that "class size is not an important factor in determining achievement as commonly measured" (pp. 68–72). Similar conclusions were drawn by Howard Blake, in his unpublished doctoral dissertation, *Class Size* (New York: Columbia University Library, 1954). See, however, the opposite opinion by William McLaughlin, "Class Size Affects Learning Ability," *The School Executive,* vol. 75 (March, 1956), pp. 91–92.

lihood that they can be completely solved within the parochial school system. This means that the overflow of pupils from the parochial school to the public school is increasing in volume. Since most Catholic parents cannot afford to send their children to private schools this overflow must be absorbed by the public schools.[59] This is a crucial clue to the future of the elementary school system. The present desperate expansion of the parochial school building program cannot possibly keep pace with the expansion of the Catholic child population trying to get into these schools.

While the situation can be controlled in the parochial school, that of the public school promises to get worse. More than half of the Catholic children of elementary school age in the United States are now in public schools, and within the next decade this proportion will probably increase to two-thirds. This imminent invasion of the public school by large numbers of Catholic children has practically compelled a re-examination of the position of the parochial school in the larger community. "Attacks" on the parochial school tend to come now from national committees, from leaders of pressure groups who are unrealistically removed from the local scene. One seldom hears derogatory remarks about the parochial school on the part of local officials and administrators and educators who are responsible for the maintenance of the public school system.[60] The climate of public opinion in the city where St. Luke's is located is one of admiration, gratitude and even support of the parochial school. This change of opinion and this increase of good will are, like so many other American attitudinal changes, based on hard economic facts. It is costly to provide schooling for all our children.

The Exceptional Child

A child may be an exceptional "case" in the elementary school from many points of view. Some children are handicapped physically, and

[59] See, however, the contrasting estimate in Fred F. Beach and Robert F. Will, *The State and Non-Public Schools* (Washington: Office of Education, 1958), p. 1. This report calls non-public schools "important educational resources of the nation" and gives an account of both regulations and responsibilities of the various States in regard to non-public schools.

[60] This change is significant because it is on the local level where people must live together in the same community. The change is also quite recent and quite different from the statement that "the animus I have found against religious schools has been more marked at the elementary level than at any other." See Frederick G. Hochwalt, "A Catholic Educator's View," F. Ernest Johnson, ed., *American Education and Religion: The Problem of Religion in the Schools* (New York: Harper, 1952), pp. 61–76.

others may be mentally retarded. Others may be exceptional because they are far above the normal in intelligence and aptitudes. Parochial and public schools appear to have different approaches in handling the exceptional child. The public school system has established a special small school for the physically handicapped children of the city. The Catholic schools have no provisions of this kind. There are no professional facilities for mentally handicapped children with the result that these attend both the public and the parochial schools for a few years and then drop out of school.

The Taft public school, neighboring to St. Luke's, which we have used in many ways as a control group, has instituted a special fifth grade class for its more talented pupils. This exceptional group is urged to go as far as it can in mathematics and English, and has also started the study of French. It is an experimental class and is taught separately from the other classes. Nothing of this kind has been tried at St. Luke's and, although this attempt is contrary to the "levelling" function of the public school, it was continued on into the following school year.

Both parochial and public schools have the problem of variant abilities within each grade and within each class.[61] Both schools divide the grades alphabetically, the parochial school identifying them with the letters A and B, the public school with the room number of the class' "home room." Thus, by the law of averages each class has about the same range from bright to dull students. Within the class, however, and for certain subjects, there are further subdivisions. In the lower grades, each class is subdivided into at least three "reading groups" according to their degree of "readiness," and on the assumption that children of the same ability perform better when they read together. Similarly in arithmetic, a slow group may be sent to the blackboard and given more attention than a more competent group.

Beside the handicapped and the gifted children, and the normal range within any classroom, there are also children who are maladjusted to the classroom routine for other reasons. Some of these may become disciplinary problems for the simple reason that they have no interest in the kind of school work the other children are doing. At St. Luke's

[61] See Theodore A. Opdenaker, "The Parochial School and the Exceptional Child," *The Catholic School Journal*, vol. 55, no. 1 (January, 1955), pp. 1–2. See also Sister Noel Marie, "Statistics of Religious Educators," *The Catholic Educator*, vol. 27, no. 5 (January, 1957), pp. 291–292, 344, who found that of 230 religious educators queried only twenty-one per cent said that there was an organized effort in their schools to divide pupils according to individual differences. The practice, however, of arranging groups within the same class according to their abilities is almost universal.

school the few children of this type coming to our attention were advised to find another school to attend. The public school is able to absorb children of this type into its own curriculum because it already provides the kind of activities—shop work, manual arts, cooking classes—that are usually attractive to these children. The normal parochial school cannot revise its curriculum and improve its physical facilities to absorb these children.[62]

There is still another type of child who requires special attention. In the parochial school this is the child who comes from a religiously inadequate family background. Children of this kind are looked upon as pupils who deserve special help from the school to make up for that which they are not obtaining at home. The parochial school teachers know their family circumstances; they know the parents who attend Mass irregularly or seldom receive the sacraments. They attempt the delicate function of bringing religious balance into the child's life; to have the child accept the approved patterns of religious conduct without at the same time condemning the parents' failure in this regard.[63]

While the Catholic child with poor religious family life may come from a middle-class and even upper-class home, the analogous problem of poor home life for the public school pupil is usually that of the lower class. The upper-class child is often in the private non-Catholic school, tends to learn easily, but is also less submissive and less respectful to teachers. Our interviews with public school teachers confirm the generalization that lower-class children are often the "lost sheep" for them. This type of child tends to be unruly, to lose interest in school work especially in the higher grades, and requires more attention than other children.[64] The three public schools within the boundaries of St. Luke's parish have relatively few of these lower-class children, but several other public schools within the city have large numbers of them.

[62] Sister Noel Marie, *op. cit.*, pp. 291–292, found that thirty-four per cent of her respondents approved sending this kind of child to the public school, while sixty-four per cent believed that the parochial school should find a way of taking care of them.

[63] William E. McManus, "Ten Points for Catholic Education," *The Catholic Mind*, vol. 52, no. 1104 (December, 1954), pp. 710–717, suggests that in many instances these children are the "lost sheep" for whom the teacher must exert tender and maternal care.

[64] See Howard S. Becker, "Social-Class Variations in the Teacher-Pupil Relationship," *Journal of Educational Sociology*, vol. 25, no. 8 (April, 1952), pp. 451–465; also Robert Havighurst, W. Lloyd Warner, Martin B. Loeb, *Who Shall be Educated?* (New York: Harper, 1944), "The Social Role of the Teacher," pp. 107–109.

The question of the exceptional child, in whatever way he may be categorized, indicates again the differing functions of the parochial, the public and the private school. In so far as the exceptional child requires special physical facilities, specialized classes and curriculum, the normal parochial school is unable to take care of him. The public school, with its deliberate policy of mingling, normalizing and levelling of children, is also inhibited from taking care of these pupils. The private school, to the extent that the parents are willing and able to pay for specialized care, is usually best equipped to handle these children, "problem cases" of all kinds, the mentally retarded as well as the brilliantly gifted.

Generalizations

1. Good public relations at St. Luke's parish are the result of numerous informal techniques. The Pastor is well-known about the larger community in which he has been a long-time resident and participant. The Principal makes the most contacts with formal agencies of various kinds. The parents themselves are "boosters" for the school. In the public school this general function is performed from the superintendent's office, and no important statement can be made by the Principal without clearance from this office. The public school Principal is, however, the most important link between the school and the parents in the immediate community.

2. From the aspect of "ownership and control" the parents of parochial school children have a much larger stake in St. Luke's school than the parents of public school children have in the public school. The parent-school relationship at St. Luke's is voluntary and informal; that at the public school is compulsory and formal. The regulations at St. Luke's are persuasive and generally acceptable; those at the public school have practically the force of civil law and are generally considered bearable rather than acceptable by the parents.

3. While every large-scale, efficient social organization has tendencies toward bureaucracy, the public school is much more bureaucratic in operation and administration than is St. Luke's school. This fact is particularly demonstrable in the comparative position of Principal, the public school Principal embracing all of the characteristics of the classical bureaucrat. In an analogous sense the Pastor may be termed a bureaucrat within the ecclesiastical structure, but the Principal of St. Luke's school cannot be termed a bureaucrat within the educational structure.

4. The pressure to conformity is much greater among public school teachers than among the teachers at St. Luke's. Public school regula-

tions are less flexible, more detailed and more numerous than parochial school regulations. The whole process of teaching in the public school is more institutionalized and standardized; the teacher has less freedom and initiative than the parochial school teacher. The common stereotypes concerning both kinds of teachers seem to arise from a confusion of professional roles and from a comparison of the religious role of the teaching Sister with the educational role of the public school teacher.

5. The teacher shortage, as measured by the number of pupils per teacher, is more acute in the parochial school than in the public school. Parents of the children in both schools look upon this as an economic problem and suggest that salaries be raised. The teachers themselves tend more to think of it as a problem of the working conditions in the school. Teacher shortage is a greater economic problem for the parochial school than for the public school because the hiring of more lay teachers in the parochial school means that more money must be raised through the voluntary contributions of the parishioners.

6. The recruitment of teachers is hampered by the fact that both parents and children anticipate more lucrative occupations for the boy pupils and more glamorous occupations for the girl pupils. It appears that the percentage of female teachers will increase on the elementary level. The status of teacher seems to be more in conformity with the cultural expectations of the female sex than of the male in our society. Thus the encouragement of girls to become teachers gets a certain degree of response absent in the case of boys. The teachers at St. Luke's encourage the girls to become nuns, and since teaching is the largest single function of nuns, this is tantamount to encouragement of the teaching career.

7. From the point of view of personal satisfactions and of effective group function, the working conditions of St. Luke's nuns appear to be more conducive to good teaching than are those of the public school teachers. The former are more resilient to the demands of the classroom, willing to accept the burdens of teaching as part of their life's offering to God. Their personal wants, as culturally defined by their religious role, are less broad than those of the public school teacher. They have the further advantage of belonging to a residential community of teachers, associating almost like family members in their private lives after school hours.

8. There appears to be a reserve of teacher talent among the women of every large community and this is largely wasted as far as the needs of the public school are concerned. The bureaucratic regulations of the public school system prevent these women from teaching because

of set requirements in formal educational courses and other training procedures. The parochial school is not hampered by these regulations and is free to employ any woman of talent and education, whether a former teacher or not. A further wastage in teacher talent in the public school arises from the siphoning off into administrative positions and from the classroom a certain number of experienced teachers.

9. The overcrowding of elementary schools is a matter of insufficient school buildings rather than of insufficient teachers, although the two problems overlap. St. Luke's has three available unused classrooms, and if there were three more available teachers the problem of overcrowding could be solved. Because of financial considerations, the expansion of the public school system is going on more rapidly than that of the parochial schools of the city. This indicates that in the coming years the overflow of Catholic children from the parochial school will tax even further the classroom facilities of the local public schools.

10. St. Luke's school is competent to handle the normal range of urban Catholic children, but has no facilities to care for the exceptional child, the physically or mentally handicapped and the obviously maladjusted. The public school is inhibited from doing much for these children because of its stated policy of normalizing and standardizing as many as possible of the great varieties of child personalities seeking education. The exceptional child is sometimes taken care of in a special school at public expense, but more often in private schools to which parents can afford to send them or in private schools endowed and supported by religious and other philanthropic groups.

Chapter

SEVENTEEN

SCHOOL, PARISH AND COMMUNITY

THE STUDY of a particular parochial school in a modern American city confirms a fact that is apparently missed by many observers. The school belongs to the parish and the parish belongs to the larger community in which it exists. This concept of "belonging" does not refer to ownership or authority, but to the fact that the teachers, parents and pupils involved in the parochial school, are integral members of the neighborhood and the city, even while they are identifiable as Catholic parishioners. The parochial school is obviously different from the public school, and the parish is not the same as the Main Street Businessmen's Club, or the political wards that it embraces. But parishioners are citizens, and the school and parish do not set them apart from the community.

Cultural Pluralism

The pluralism of the American socio-cultural system implies the profound sociological principle that there is unity in diversity. We are a people of many diverse backgrounds—ethnic, racial and religious, and even economic and political—but the strength of the American democratic culture lies in the very recognition of the importance of protecting these differences. Paradoxically, this pluralistic culture implies that the diverse pluralities are integral segments of the total society.[1]

From a socio-cultural point of view one of the necessary preoccupa-

[1] One of the clearest applications of this concept to the American culture is that of Robin M. Williams, *American Society: A Sociological Interpretation* (New York: Knopf, 1952), especially, chap. 14, "The Integration of American Society," pp. 528–529. See also John Courtney Murray, "The Religious School in a Pluralist Society," *The Catholic Mind*, vol. 54, no. 1125 (September, 1956), pp. 502–511.

tions of our study of St. Luke's was to analyze its position and function in the larger community in which it operates. In what ways is it different from, and similar to, other elementary schools? Does the difference necessarily imply that the school is separatist? Does the similarity necessarily imply that the school is indistinguishably participant? The persistent notion, raised in some quarters, that parochial schools help to "promote divisive tendencies among children," forces a re-examination of these questions on the local scene.[2]

In trying to arrive at the answers to these questions we came almost immediately to a fundamental distinction that is seldom recognized in the literature on this subject. Parochial schools are almost everywhere classified as "private" schools, but our empirical evidence forces us to make a clear distinction between the parochial school (which is semi-public), and the private school (which is not parochial). In other words, there are three kinds of elementary schools: public, parochial and private.[3] St. Luke's is a parochial school, and it differs from those schools in which children obtain private expensive education as well as from those schools in which children receive free public education.

Perceptive social scientists have, through independent research, come to this same conclusion. "The parochial type of private school is usually quite similar to a public school in its relation to social class. Most parochial schools are Roman Catholic, and the Catholic Church in most communities is fairly representative of the population as regards social class." Private schools, on the other hand may be operated by Catholics, by other denominations, or by no denomination. "The independent private schools cater to families of upper and upper middle class and perform special functions in relation to the social structure." [4]

[2] Writings on this subject can be found almost anywhere. See, however, Robert C. Hartnett, *The Right to Educate: A Symposium* (New York: America Press, 1949); Blaine E. Mercer and Edwin R. Carr, eds., *Education and the Social Order* (New York: Rinehart, 1957), chap. 13, "The School and Moral and Spiritual Values," pp. 459–487; also Joseph H. Fichter, *Social Relations in the Urban Parish* (Chicago: University of Chicago Press, 1954), chap. 13, "The School and the Parish," pp. 165–177.

[3] Gerald Schnepp, *Leakage from a Catholic Parish* (Washington: Catholic University, 1942), uses throughout the odd term, "religious public school" for the parochial school, as contrasted to the "state public school."

[4] Robert J. Havighurst and Bernice L. Neugarten, *Society and Education* (Boston: Allyn and Bacon, 1957), p. 239. The official statement of the Presbyterian General Assembly, *The Church and the Public Schools* (Philadelphia: Board of Christian Education, June, 1957), though heavily biased against church schools, makes this distinction of the three educational patterns of private, parochial and public schools (p. 6). See, however, the Special Issue on Religion of *School and Society*, vol. 82, no. 2069 (October 1, 1955).

Thus, parochial schools are characterized by religion while private schools are characterized by social class.

Beyond the essential functions of transmitting the culture and socializing the child, the well-financed private school can perform certain functions that are very difficult of achievement by most parochial schools. First, the private school is able to experiment educationally. Unlike the parochial school it has the means to do so, and unlike the public school it has the independence to do so. Secondly, the private school, being selective in its teachers and pupils, can establish high educational standards, and act as a "yardstick" of achievement for other elementary schools. Thirdly, the private school can enact a creative role through its experimentation and normalization; and finally, because of all these advantages it can also exercise leadership in the whole field of elementary education.[5] The ordinary parochial and public schools are not in a position to perform these functions, even though there have been some remarkable instances of experimentation in both systems.

Whether a school is parochial, public or private, the very nature of the educational institution forces it to perform two inseparable functions: (a) to transmit to the younger generation the culture with its patterns, institutions and values, and at the same time (b) to supervise the socialization process whereby the child actively "receives" the culture, that is, adapts himself to, and is adapted to, the socio-cultural system in which he lives. No school exists merely on the abstract level of the transmission of culture and the supervision of socialization. Every other major cultural institution, in so far as children participate in it, performs these functions, at least in an ancillary fashion.

In the concrete, day-to-day operation of the elementary school certain more specific functions are discernible. Every elementary school, whether parochial, public or private, is directly and immediately concerned with the pupils' (a) intellectual improvement, (b) character development, (c) social adjustment and (d) bodily and physical welfare. In reading the literature produced by educators one is a little puzzled by the great "controversies," especially among the philosophers of education, concerning these objectives of education. There appears to be no confusion about them among the actual teachers of elementary school children. They are striving for all four objectives—mental,

[5] Dan W. Dodson, "Foreword: Democracy and Private Education," *The Journal of Educational Sociology*, vol. 30, no. 8 (April, 1957), pp. 337–338. See also Sister Mary Dorothy, "Are Catholic Schools Progressive?" *The Catholic Educator*, vol. 21, no. 2 (October, 1950), pp. 116–119, who describes the integration of certain progressive elements into the Catholic school system.

moral, social and physical—and while there may be varying emphases on one or the other of them, no school excludes or belittles any one of them.

Multiple Functions

The realistic understanding of the operation of St. Luke's school requires us to go a step beyond this. The school does not operate in a cultural vacuum. As the active expression of the educational institution it coexists and cooperates with two other major cultural institutions: the familial and the religious. These latter transmit aspects of the culture that are complementary to, and often overlapping with, those transmitted by the school. "Without questioning the potent force of education, it can be stated that, in so far as producing or maintaining a culture is concerned, it is only one such force. Education cannot be expected to carry the whole burden of cultural transmission and change." [6] Major institutions in conflict or in contrast with the educational institution tend to disrupt the function of the latter.

In the empirical study of St. Luke's parochial school we have found the educational, religious and familial institutions inextricably interwoven. In this concrete situation the school and the family—in addition to performing their specific functions—also perform the basic function of the religious institution: (a) the sanctification of people, that is, the provision of means through which people may become better persons, both as individuals and as social beings, and (b) the salvation of people, that is, giving assistance so that they reach their eternal destiny with God in heaven. Teachers and parents, as well as the parish priests, pursue these religious objectives when they work with the elementary school children.[7]

It is a demonstrable fact too, that the parental function within the family institution, which aims at the mental, moral, social and physical development of the child, is duplicated, amplified and formalized in the parochial school.[8] Not only the parents, but also the teachers and

[6] Scudder Mekeel, "Education, Child-Training and Culture," *American Journal of Sociology*, vol. 48, no. 6 (May, 1954), pp. 676–681.

[7] In his Lenten Pastoral on Education the Bishop went even further than this, insisting that the school is a common cause of all Catholics, "whether or not they have children in school, whether or not they have any school at all."

[8] A discussion of the various ways in which the familial and the educational institutions can cooperate is given by Sister Bernard Francis, "Home-School Partnership," *The Catholic Educational Review*, vol. 52, no. 6 (June, 1954), pp. 361–371. See also the dissertation by Leonis Kirane, "A Survey of Home and School Relations in Catholic Elementary Schools in the Archdiocese of Chicago" (Washington: Catholic University Library, 1953).

priests are deeply concerned about this multiple and "well-rounded" development of children. This is no novel discovery, and it is probably observable, in some degree or other, in every elementary school in the country.[9]

Roughly then we may say that the family, the school and the church are doing the same things in slightly different ways. We may say also that the aim of Christian education is also the aim of the Christian family and parish: "to provide those experiences which, with the assistance of divine grace, are best calculated to develop in the young the ideas, the attitudes, and the habits that are demanded for Christ-like living in our American democratic society." [10] In providing these experiences, the parochial school is a joint enterprise of parents, teachers and priests. It is the setting in which family, school and church co-operate for the benefit of the child.

In the practical operation of St. Luke's school there is no perceivable confusion in the simultaneous and multiple functioning of educational, religious and familial aspects of socialization. Certainly, the religious "atmosphere" is discernible in the persons of nun-teachers, in the artistic decoration of the classroom, in the prayer practices before and after class periods, in the references to religious examples in various subjects of study. Also clearly discernible, and subject to empirical testing, are the various educational techniques, the ways of getting children to study, understand and learn, the experience and abilities of the teachers, the receptivity of pupils, the comparable results of the learning process as evidenced by report cards and awards. The familial "atmosphere" is seen too, in the titles of "Sister" and "Father" used for the nuns and priests. It is seen in the numerous concerns which the school seems to have "taken over" from parents, the correction and disciplining of children, the instilling of habits of cleanliness, self-control and health.

This simultaneous performance of logically distinct institutionalized patterns blends together so well and so "naturally" that the participants themselves seem unaware of any distinctions. Children, however, who had previously attended a public school are aware of the difference. Some of them have pointed this out. "My new school was a

[9] See the extended remarks of Frederick Mayer, "The Aims of Education," *Education*, vol. 76, no. 10 (June, 1956), pp. 633–636. For the transfer of functions from the family, see I. L. Kandel, *The New Era in Education* (Boston, Houghton Mifflin, 1955), pp. 55–57.

[10] From the Preface by George Johnson in Sister Mary Joan and Sister Mary Nona, *Guiding Growth in Christian Social Living* (Washington: Catholic University Press, 1944), p. 5.

friendlier and warmer sort of place than the public school." "I guess I was the only one in the fourth grade who didn't know the name of the tall lady dressed in black. I soon found out that it was Sister." "At first I didn't understand why there was so much about God and religion, but afterwards I wondered how I ever got along in the public school without all this." [11]

St. Luke's school is not "just" an educational system that performs the basic functions of the educational institution; nor is it "merely" a religious system that performs the basic functions of the religious institution; nor can we say that the school is nothing more than a parent-surrogate, supplying that which the family fails to do. The process is not an equation of cathechism plus secular knowledge plus child training. "Catholics can never be content to cultivate a system whose aim is keyed no higher than to intellectual excellence cultivated in a religious atmosphere. This would reduce education to secular training plus catechism, a system that is highly artificial, to say the least." [12]

This joint enterprise of home, school and church may be viewed in other ways. One may say that the Catholic families "employ" the parochial school, rather than the public or private school, to provide elementary education for their children. Or, one may say that the priests of the parish establish and maintain the school in order to inculcate religious and moral training into the children of these families. Or, finally, one may say that the teachers operate the school in order to integrate the familial and religious aspects of the child's life, and to act as a kind of bridge between the parish and the families of the parish.

Each of these is, of course, a one-sided and therefore partial view of the parochial school. The fact is that the school is a cooperative effort of priests, teachers and parents for the benefit of the child. Thus, if we focus upon the child as the central reason for the school's existence, we note that the cooperation of adults on his behalf is not of a mechanical and "equally balanced" kind. Parents are more numerous than teachers, and teachers are more numerous than priests. Teachers are full-time functionaries in the school; the priests are general supervisors and part-time teachers; parents contribute mainly "extracurricular" efforts to the school. The priests worry about the finances and

[11] These are remarks of the pupils written in their autobiographies, done by the children in the fifth, sixth, seventh and eighth grades.

[12] Frederick G. Hochwalt, "A Catholic Educator's View," in F. Ernest Johnson, ed., *American Education and Religion: The Problem of Religion in the Schools* (New York: Harper, 1952), pp. 61–76.

are responsible for "raising the money;" parents make the heaviest financial contribution to the school; the teachers are the day-to-day immediate custodians of the instruments and properties of the school.

In a complex system like a parochial school cooperative effort is necessarily multiphasic and unequal. Whether it is viewed from the numbers of persons involved, the time consumed, the function performed, the financial outlay, or from some other aspect, the parochial school shows variations of cooperative effort. Sociologically, however, these variations are not nearly so significant as the fact that cooperation does exist among parents, priests and teachers, and that there is an integrative effect which this cooperation has on the parish.[13]

Focus of Parochial Solidarity

Up to this point in our analysis we have seen what the three agencies of socialization, the family, school and church, do *for the child.* The kinds of action performed by the adults, and their degree of success or failure, have been discussed in various places in this book.[14] If we focus only on the child, however, as the purpose and product of the cooperative effort of adults, we may overlook the important sociological fact that the parish as a social system is also a beneficiary of this cooperative effort. In other words, the parochial school has consequences *for the parish* because it acts as a locus of social solidarity, cohesion and integration at the adult as well as the child level of parishioners.[15]

In simple words, this means that the parochial school "brings together" in cooperative action more lay parishioners in a more intimate and functional way than any other program, agency or group in the parish. This valuable integrative function of the parochial school is frequently overlooked even by interested participants in the system. The significance of this fact is appreciated if we try to visualize St. Luke's parish *without* its parochial school. Perhaps other agencies of adult cooperation and parochial solidarity could be devised as a substitute for the parochial school but they are not presently in practice in the parish.

[13] For a well-reasoned analysis of one aspect of this problem, see Donald McNassor, "Barriers and Gateways in School-Community Relationships," *Journal of Educational Sociology,* vol. 28, no. 1 (September, 1954), pp. 1–10.

[14] See below, for example, the whole of Part III.

[15] M. Laurina Kaiser, *The Development of the Concept and Function of the Catholic Elementary School in the American Parish* (Washington: Catholic University Press, 1955), pp. 112–113. See also the discussions on "Catholic Schools and Public Relations," by Mary Sparks, Francis Lally, Sister Mary Canice, *Bulletin* of the National Catholic Educational Association, vol. 54, no. 1 (August, 1957), pp. 269–276.

This concept is worth pursuing somewhat further.[16] At the present time there are five nuclei, or "rallying points," toward which the parishioners gravitate, and which may be termed centers of parochial solidarity. They are the altar, the pulpit, the rectory, the meeting rooms and the school. The first three are the locus of the pastoral role, where the priests perform their duties in service to the people. The meeting rooms including the auditorium or gymnasium, are the scene of activities of the various parish societies. The school itself, as a physical plant, at first glance looks simply like a place where teachers and children get together five days a week.

A brief comparison of these five nuclei of solidarity indicates immediately that social integration is something more than the mere assemblage of people or the mere "attendance at" a program. It is expressed not merely by individual participation but by group participation in a program.

The altar is the center of parochial worship. Without the Mass and the sacraments the existence of a Catholic parish would have no meaning. The six Masses on Sundays and holy days of obligation unquestionably draw larger numbers of parishioners together. When the church is completely occupied there are approximately 850 persons present at any one Mass. The extent to which any individual participates in this religious service depends partly on his own piety and partly on the canonical limitations placed on the Catholic laity. Although the Catholic Church recognizes a supernatural unity, through divine grace, in its members, the extent to which social bonds and relations are developed, or the extent to which people function together at Mass, is sociologically questionable.[17]

The pulpit of the parochial church appears to be going out of fashion as a "drawing card" for the people. The essential task of preaching the word of God is still performed in St. Luke's pulpit, as it is in every parish in the country. But "great preaching" no longer brings large crowds to the local church and appears actually to have passed over to other channels of communication, like radio and TV, and seems also to have been supplanted by the more quiet indoctrination given in retreats and days of recollection. From the sociological

[16] See Joseph H. Fichter, "Conceptualizations of the Urban Parish," *Social Forces,* vol. 31, no. 1 (October, 1952), pp. 43–46.

[17] See the more detailed discussion of this question in *Social Relations in the Urban Parish* (Chicago: University of Chicago Press, 1954), chap. 4, "Social Solidarity and Modal Parishioners." It must be noted, of course, that certain groups—the choir, acolytes, Altar and Rosary Societies—direct their functions toward the altar, and exist because of it.

point of view, in the last analysis, the audiences for even the greatest preachers in the Catholic Church are passive participants, and their listening does not constitute a solidaristic function.

The rectory is the "command post" of the parish in the sense that from it emanates the supervision and general direction of the whole parish.[18] As a locus of parochial solidarity it depends more upon the personality of the priest and his abilities as organizer and administrator than it does upon any other facet of the pastoral role. Contact with the rectory by mail, phone or in person, and the response of the priests to this contact tends to be primarily on the level of individual relations and only secondarily on that of group relations. The Pastor unquestionably tries to foster the spirit of unity and to develop an attitude toward the parish as "one big happy family," but this is of its nature the type of objective that no one person can achieve.

The meeting rooms of the parish are the locus of programs and activities of the numerous parish societies. "There is something going on here every night," says the Pastor. The Junior Newman Club, the Holy Name Society, the Boy Scouts, the Altar Society, and other parochial groups, hold their meetings there. These groups are limited in numbers and kinds of members, being either male or female, young or adult, single or married. Thus they tend to function toward the unity of only certain categories of parishioners and not of the parish as a whole. They are also intermittent organizations, some of them meeting only once a month, and the specific program of each is attractive to only a limited number of people.

When we note that none of these four at the present time replaces the school as a focus of parochial solidarity, we do not mean to imply that they contribute nothing to solidarity or that they cannot be improved as solidaristic factors. Each of them—the altar, the pulpit, the rectory and the meeting rooms—attracts people and gets them together. They vary in the intensity and duration of the interest they arouse, and they appear to be limited too, in the amount of cooperative effort they can muster.

Pupils, Parents and Parish

St. Luke's parochial school is an on-going operation which absorbs most of the interest and energies of 632 children for the greatest part of each year. These children come from 377 families, which constitute 35.4 per cent of all the families in the parish and 45.6 per cent of the

[18] For a sociological account of religious patterns on a parochial level see Joseph H. Fichter, *Southern Parish* (Chicago: University of Chicago Press, 1951).

parish population. Involved in these families are, by actual count, 1,924 persons—omitting uncles, aunts and grandparents of school children, who may be presumed to have some interest in the children and who actually do participate in some school functions.

The school child is the focus of, the channel for, and the ultimate reason for, the greatest amount of lay adult parochial solidarity. The fact of children in the school brings together numerous adults in the program of the Parent-Teacher Association, 542 persons on the membership list; 149 members who attended three or more meetings during the year.[19] The school entertainments attract former students now in high school as well as the friends and relatives of the children now in school.

St. Luke's Athletic Association is concerned about the football, basketball, baseball and volleyball teams of the school. This means not only that adults come out as spectators for the games, but also that they participate in card parties, dances, style shows which raise money for the teams, and also in the two annual banquets honoring the athletes. The Cubs and Boy Scouts involve certain adults in cooperative activities; and the Blue Birds and Camp Fire Girls also bring together many parents in the parish who would otherwise remain strangers to each other.[20] The Patrons of St. Luke, who have organized mainly for the support of the school reach out to many adults who do not have children in the school.

For the most active and interested parents this participation extends over the eight years spent by the child in the school, and over an even longer period of years for the family with several children.[21] When the child himself enters the school he "begins to make contacts with more fellow-parishioners and is developing his new social relations and bonds." We have empirically verified a conclusion from an earlier study to the effect that "the children themselves are morally and

[19] The PTA has to rebuild its membership every year by collecting dues from parents. This year, 542 was the highest number on its membership list. In our interviews we found 561 parents claiming membership, and some of these were undoubtedly previous, or unpaid, or merely intended, memberships.

[20] See the discussion on adult participation above, chap. 7, "Youth Movements," and chap. 8, "Organized Sports."

[21] At the annual breakfast of the PTA, a visiting speaker told a joke about the lady whose youngest child was in the eighth grade and who expressed dismay when her obstetrician informed her that she was again pregnant. The Doctor was surprised at her reaction and reminded her that she had always previously been overjoyed at the prospect of having a child. "It isn't that, Doctor," she said. "It's just that I can't bear the thought of going through the PTA all over again."

socially closer to the heart of the parish at this time than at any later period of their lives."[22] Thus, the future adult parishioners are able to develop at this early stage an appreciation and loyalty for the parish.

Up to this point we have seen that three institutions—the religious, educational and familial—are necessarily involved in the operation and maintenance of St. Luke's parochial school. This means that the basic institutional functions of these three are being performed. Secondly, the elementary school is the joint enterprise of three sets of people—the priests, teachers and parents; and this means a certain amount of cooperative effort by all. Thirdly, the school is an instrument of parochial solidarity in the sense that it brings together numerous parishioners in performing activities which they consider worth doing.

This question of the elementary school as a factor for parish solidarity must be analyzed somewhat further. Does the school actually develop social solidarity, or does it simply help to maintain an already existing parochial solidarity, or does it do nothing more than reflect the group cohesiveness that "naturally" prevails in St. Luke's parish?

We must be careful not to reach the conclusion that the elementary school is the only instrument of parochial solidarity, or that without the school this solidarity would not exist among the parishioners. As a matter of fact we have found here a relatively high degree of parish loyalty and social solidarity, as measured by the words, attitudes and actions of people, and as compared with other parishes we have studied. The fact that the people of St. Luke's have common religious values and practices is at least a partial explanation for some of their social cohesiveness. This is an aspect of the group-mindedness fostered from the altar and the pulpit.

Ethnic Mingling and Solidarity

It is sometimes said that the ethnic and national loyalties of immigrant Catholics were the most important bases for their parochial solidarity. "There is apparently an intimate connection between the cultural backgrounds of American Catholics and their success in establishing and maintaining a mass educational enterprise."[23] The

[22] See the discussion on this point in *Social Relations in the Urban Parish* (Chicago: University of Chicago Press, 1954), pp. 170–172.

[23] "The parochial schools furthermore served as an important institutional device for maintaining group attachment over time. Even today the parochial schools still play very much the same role, particularly for the Irish and French Canadians in the New England States." Peter and Alice Rossi, "Background and

common culture, which "happened" to include Catholicism, kept these immigrant groups strongly cohesive in the traditional "national" parishes. The notion here is that the parish which was composed almost exclusively of Irish, or of Germans, or Italians, or Poles, already possessed a solidarity rooted in the common national and ethnic background. It would be argued from this that a German Lutheran congregation maintained its group spirit and solidarity more because it was German than because it was Lutheran. The "huddle" of immigrant families possessed and maintained solidarity in the same neighborhood, talking the same language, preparing the same kinds of food dishes, following the same family customs. In this hypothesis, the fact of common religion was at best a secondary cause, and the presence of the parochial school was merely an expression or reflection of already existing group cohesiveness.

St. Luke's parishioners possess the common Catholic religion and they maintain a parochial school, but they do not have a common "foreign" ethnic background or culture. From this point of view, the composition of the population is of major importance. It contains no single dominant ethnic group and has never been either in reputation or in fact a "national" parish. Only 4.5 per cent of the parents of the school children are foreign-born, as compared with five per cent of the people of this age level in the city (and 6.7 per cent of foreign-born in the total American population). The people are already "well mixed." In almost three-quarters (72.2%) of the families of school children, the mother and father are of different ethnic background, and many of these individuals are themselves the product of mixed ancestry. The national ancestry of the paternal grandfathers shows that 19.8 per cent are German, 19.0 per cent Irish, 15.5 per cent Polish, 10.7 per cent Hungarian, with the remainder scattered among Austrian, Belgian, English, French, Italian and others. The largest majority of the elementary school children are already fourth-generation Americans.

With this empirical evidence in hand, we cannot attribute the solidarity of St. Luke's parishioners to the quick and easy factor of similar (foreign) ethnic background. In so far as common culture is a factor of group solidarity it is in this case the common American culture. From the point of view of ethnic composition, St. Luke's appears to be the Catholic parish of the future. The acceptance of American cultural values and behavior patterns, the continued urban-

---

Consequences of Parochial School Education," *Harvard Educational Review*, vol. 27, no. 3 (Summer, 1957) pp. 168–199.

ization of life, the tendency to intermarry, the pursuit of American economic and political goals, are removing these people further and further from their immigrant ethnic background. This urban parish has reached a point of assimilation at which the dominant cultural influence is the American urban influence.[24]

There is another aspect in which the parish, and therefore, the elementary school children, are representative of the emerging American Catholic population. These people are both urban and urbanized. Just as they have no recent foreign background, so also are they lacking in recent rural background. Most of the poor, ill-educated, rural migrants, who since the first World War came to the city where St. Luke's is located, have been Protestants. Since the American Catholic population has always been urban (with the small exceptions of parts of rural Louisiana and Maryland) this Protestant swelling of the urban masses has given a different dimension to the traditional socio-religious class structure of the larger city.

In so far as these characteristics are applicable, the same can be said concerning the socio-cultural background of the priests and teachers. They too, are the products of the American urban culture. None of these influential leaders in the educational process is an "import" or an immigrant foreign missionary. What was once validly stated about the influence of various foreign ethnic leaders among the Catholic clergy and religious Sisters, is not true of St. Luke's parish and school.[25]

Social Classes and the Parish

By their ethnic background and place of birth the people of St. Luke's, and their children, are indistinguishable from the larger community in which they live. They are an integral part of the rising and expanding urban middle class. They blend into the general population on all the criteria of Americanism. Except for one small corner in the southeast of the parish, in which some well-to-do families live,

[24] This fact does not deny the earlier importance of Irish, German, French, Spanish and other national influences as a factor of group solidarity in various regional areas of the Catholic Church in America. But the historical development necessarily dilutes these influences.

[25] Several years before our study began there was an Irish nun, Sister Virginia, teaching the fourth grade for one year. She played Irish songs on her concertina, taught the children to do the Irish jig, and directed their attention to the importance of St. Patrick's Day. This foreign oddity was a unique experience for the pupils in her class, and practically all of them mentioned it in their life stories.

and one small corner in the northwest portion, where the residences are sub-standard, St. Luke's parish exhibits the middle class social structure of the typical midwestern American city.

The educational background of the fathers of St. Luke's school children shows that they had more schooling in general, than the males, thirty to forty-four years old in the same city. Considerably more of them went to college, and considerably fewer of them attended only elementary school. The following table gives the comparison.

Amount of schooling	Fathers of St. Luke's pupils	Males 30–44 yrs. old in the same city
Attended or finished college	34.7%	19.2%
Attended or finished high school	53.3	52.8
Attended or finished elementary school	12.0	26.1
Not reported	0.0	1.9

The fact that these Catholic parents were better educated than the general category of men in roughly the same age bracket, helps to explain why they are also in the professional and white collar occupations. The occupational status of the fathers of these Catholic school children represents an urban range from professional to unskilled. The percentage distribution in the following table indicates that about fifteen per cent of these families are in the lowest income bracket, and about sixty per cent are in the middle economic class. Here the comparison is made with all employed males of the city, without reference to their age, and this fact is also a partial explanation of the occupational differences.

Occupation	Fathers of St. Luke's pupils	Employed Males in same city
Professional	11.6%	8.3%
Manager or owner	13.8	10.2
Sales	17.7	6.6
Clerical	7.3	7.8
Craftsmen	20.7	19.7
Operatives	13.5	34.4
Service	12.6	5.7
Unskilled	2.8	5.9
Unreported	0.0	1.4

It is obvious to any student of social stratification that education and occupation, taken separately or combined, do not suffice as reliable criteria of social class. While we could not obtain data for the whole city in which St. Luke's exists we were able to classify almost five hundred families of the parish having children of elementary school age. These families were placed in social classes according to their rank as measured by six different criteria of social status. These criteria were as follows: (1) residential areas, as divided into five grades by real estate experts in the community, (2) type of occupation, as graded in standardized categories, (3) amount of education, as ranked in six categories, (4) birthplace of four grandparents, determing native or foreign-born status, (5) condition of residence, graded as excellent, standard or sub-standard, (6) crowding of dwelling unit, as measured by the number of persons and the number of rooms.

As measured by these criteria, the 496 families of St. Luke's parish, with 813 children of elementary school age, are distributed percentagewise in the following social classes. When ranked separately, the families of Catholic children in the public school had a lower percentage in both the upper-upper class (2.5%) and the lower-lower class (3.4%), but the numbers involved are so small that we omit the complete comparison.[26]

Social class	496 families of St. Luke's parish			
Upper-upper	26	5.2%	18.1	Upper class
Lower-upper	64	12.9		
Upper-middle	142	28.6	50.4	Middle class
Lower-middle	108	21.8		
Upper-lower	118	23.8	31.5	Lower class
Lower-lower	38	7.7		

In so far as the use of these criteria can objectively pinpoint the social status of families, they show that slightly more than half (50.4%) of these parochial families are in the middle class. Another segment of them, almost one-quarter (23.8%) of the families, is pushing upward toward the middle class. There were the normal, and often subtle, expressions of class consciousness among the adults, even within the PTA, the Athletic Committee and the Patrons, where persons of different class positions worked smoothly and efficiently to-

[26] See above, chap. 2, "The First Ten Years," for the class status of St. Luke's pupils.

gether for the benefit of the parochial school. Social class position as such, however, was hardly detectable among the parochial school children themselves. It appeared to make no difference in the choice of friends, working on projects, playing on teams, voting for leaders or selecting the most popular pupils.[27]

In evaluating these evidences we are forced to the conclusion that St. Luke's parochial school is typically American because it exists in an urban parish that is typically American. The existing solidarity of St. Luke's parishioners, exhibited in their group loyalty and in their cooperation for the benefit of the school, is being maintained and reinforced by the common socio-cultural background of the people. Similar cultural attitudes and beliefs combine with the sharing of a common religion and a common interest in the school, and this combination of factors tends to erase the earlier internal differences due to ethnic divergences among the immigrant ancestors of these people. The family life and community background, as well as the school experiences of the children, are in continual process toward group cohesiveness; and the Catholic religion and the Catholic school are partial factors in this development.

Parochial and Public School Pupils

The influence of the common urban culture is seen most strikingly in the similarity of tastes and preferences shown by the elementary school children. We were able to replicate in the sixth, seventh and eighth grades of the Taft public school a series of tests and questionnaires which we administered to children of the same grades at St. Luke's school. These experiments demonstrated a remarkable similarity between these two categories of children in all cultural areas which did not deal directly with religious questions or personalities. Except for religious background, these children appear to be immersed in the same socio-cultural milieu. There was only a handful of non-Christians (1.9%) in the public school, and no Negro pupils in either the public or the parochial school. Their mean scores on the *California Test of Personality* were remarkably similar.[28]

We asked the children in both schools to write down the name of their favorite movie and TV star. A relatively long list of different persons came out of this question, indicating that there are many favorites in the minds of the children, but there was sufficient con-

[27] See above, chap. 9, "Cliques and Clubs," for a discussion of friendship groups.

[28] For a comparative analysis of parts of this test see chap. 5, "Social Attitudes and Standards."

centration on the following persons to indicate that the same stars are "most popular" in both schools. The following list gives the order in which the six most popular stars were chosen in both schools.

Parochial School Choices	Public School Choices
1. Tab Hunter	1. Tab Hunter
2. John Wayne	2. John Wayne
3. Debbie Reynolds	3. Rock Hudson
4. Elvis Presley	4. Elvis Presley
5. Rock Hudson	5. Jerry Lewis
6. Grace Kelly	6. Debbie Reynolds

Since these children have no choice except to look at the movies presented in theaters and on television, it is to be expected that they would have a similar knowledge of the best-known actors and actresses. From this point of view, the influence of these media upon them is not likely to be altered by the school they attend. There appears to be a difference, however, in the frequency with which these children attend the movies. Forty-four per cent of the parochial school children did not attend the movies during the month previous to the questionnaire, as compared to 33.5 per cent of the public school children. The average monthly attendance at the movies by the parochial school children was 1.1 per child, as compared to 1.3 per child in the public school.

We asked the children in these same grades to write down the titles of their favorite TV programs, and here again the answers showed a great similarity in preferences. One difference, however, the choice of the Bishop Sheen program, is traceable in part at least to the teachers at St. Luke's school. The Sisters themselves viewed this program regularly in the convent. They discussed it in the classroom on several occasions and recommended it to the children and their parents. They also watch the Perry Como Show, but we have never heard them discuss it with the pupils. The following list gives the order in which the children from both schools chose TV programs.

Parochial School Choices	Public School Choices
1. I Love Lucy	1. I Love Lucy
2. Bishop Sheen	2. Disneyland
3. Navy Log	3. Navy Log
4. Lassie	4. Lassie
5. Disneyland	5. Air Power
6. Perry Como	6. West Point

These extracurricular interests and activities, like movie-going and television-watching, are obviously more under the influence of the home and neighborhood than they are under that of the school. The similarity in tastes and preferences is simply another indication that Catholics tend to do what their neighbors do. It shows also that the recreational institution has become highly stylized in our culture and that the behavior patterns of the people in this regard have become quite regularized.[29]

We felt, therefore, that we should question the children further, and particularly on matters that are pertinent to the school itself. To this end we asked them what subjects they liked best in school and what subjects they liked least. Here again we found a similarity in that mathematics ranked the highest among the favorite subjects of both schools. Among the children of the three highest grades in St. Luke's school, the favorite subjects—in this order—were mathematics, spelling, social studies and religion. The favorite subjects in the same grades in the public school were mathematics, social studies and science. When we isolated the eighth grade, however, we found that there was a considerable difference. There were sixty eighth graders in each school. At St. Luke's twenty-seven of them chose mathematics and ten chose social studies; at the public school this was practically reversed, with twenty-eight choosing social studies and eleven mathematics.[30]

It appears, however, that some of the same subjects are disliked by some other pupils. When we asked the children to write down the names of the subjects they liked least, the pupils at St. Luke's picked social studies, English and mathematics, while those in the public school most disliked science, music and social studies. Here again we compared separately the eighth graders in both schools, and found that twenty-four of them in St. Luke's dislike social studies and eleven English,[31] while in the public school thirty-one do not

[29] See the factual and informative article, Katherine Mahony, "Elementary School Pupils' TV Habits and Choices," *Catholic Educational Review*, vol. 51, no. 4 (April, 1953), pp. 234–245. Three-quarters of the children looked at TV daily from two and a half to three hours; about half said that TV programs are discussed in school, and forty-five per cent said they have complete freedom of choice in selecting programs.

[30] The influence of Sister Roberta is probably at work here. When asked what she liked best about her teaching position at St. Luke's she replied, "the teaching of mathematics."

[31] Some of the high school students who had graduated from St. Luke's recalled that they had been drilled constantly in the fundamentals of English grammar

like science and eight music. In making these comparisons on the likes and dislikes of the pupils we must remember that science is not taught in St. Luke's school and religion is not taught in the public school.

Since the elementary school is a source of knowledge about world events, both historical and contemporary, we wondered whether there were significant differences in the things that the children learned. It was felt, at least, that the different interests in the two schools would produce different impressions and emphases in the minds of the pupils. We asked them to write down the names of the greatest persons in history. Both schools chose the same three men in the same order of importance: George Washington, Abraham Lincoln and Christopher Columbus. This indicates that American history is taught more fully than world history, and that historical figures associated with America are more important than others.[32] In the fourth place the public schoolers chose Benjamin Franklin and the parochial schoolers Julius Caesar. Jesus Christ, as a historical figure, gained fifth place among the Catholic school children, and was also mentioned by some of the children in public school.

We felt that the answers given by the children concerning historical personages merited further investigation, particularly at St. Luke's school. We asked the same children in the upper grades to write down the "three greatest things that ever happened in the history of the world." The following events were named most, and they are listed here in order according to the number of times they were mentioned: the discovery of America, the birth of Christ, the death of Christ, the Resurrection, the creation of the world, the Declaration of Independence. This question was administered to the children in the third week of Lent, and at the same time we re-tested them on the greatest persons in history. This time Christ moved from fifth place to third place, and the Blessed Virgin took the place of Julius Caesar on the list.[33]

---

but had not spent much time in the analysis of English literature in the eighth grade. They appreciated the former and deplored the latter when they reached high school.

[32] The question asked by D. R. Penn, "Can Catholics Teach History?" *The Catholic Educational Review*, vol. 50, no. 7 (September, 1952), pp. 475–479, may be answered only indirectly here by the statement that Catholic children learn some ancient history, as well as the ordinary modern history taught in the public schools.

[33] The fact that Jesus was not mentioned in first place as the greatest historical person caused considerable interest among the teachers. The explanation seems to be that the children consider Him somehow "above history." To them, a historical person is one you read about in a history book.

We did not ask the question about the greatest historical events of the public school children.

There is a difference between the two categories of children in their selections of the "greatest men living today." [34] The choices made by the children appear to be a reflection of the conversations of their parents, peers and teachers. St. Luke's children chose in this order: Pope Pius XII, President Eisenhower and Cardinal Mindzenty. These names were mentioned repeatedly by the teachers in the classroom and they appeared frequently in the current events section of the *Messenger* which all the parochial school children avidly read. Among the pupils in the three upper grades in the public school, the opinion is that the greatest men living today are: President Eisenhower, Vice-President Nixon and Elvis Presley. It must be noted here that the choice of the President and Vice-President was so heavy among these children that there were not many votes left to distribute among the "also rans," and the third place choice could have been almost anybody in the public news.

Relations with Public Schools

The fact that St. Luke's school is an autonomous social unit does not mean that it has no relationships with, or does not cooperate with, other educational agencies. To suggest that the school is either separatist or participant, is to over-simplify the whole dynamic existence of the parochial school in the middle of the community. The vital concept of pluralism in the American society is meaningless unless separately identifiable segments of the society, like the parochial school, are also cooperative participants with other school units.[35] The participation of St. Luke's school in the larger community means that the school both takes from and gives to the broader community. In actual fact, there are many forms of interrelated activities with

[34] Roger T. Lennon, "A Comparison of the Educational Achievement of Public and Parochial Elementary School Pupils," *The Catholic Educational Review,* vol. 46, no. 10 (December, 1948), pp. 647–652, showed that the worst subject for Catholic pupils was science, and the best subjects were history and civics. Catholic children had slightly higher IQ's than public school pupils and were about two months younger.

[35] The dynamics of pluralism are completely missed by men like Randolph C. Miller, *Education for Christian Living* (New Haven: Yale University Press, 1956), who replaces empirical research with imagination when he says that ". . . it is easy to imagine what would happen if Protestants should support parochial schools with the same effectiveness as Roman Catholics. Each denomination having its own school would divide every neighborhood into factions and aggravate the divisions that already exist" (p. 114).

various public and tax-supported agencies in the city.[36] They are so numerous that only a few can be mentioned here.

The city in which St. Luke's school exists appears to exhibit cordial relations between the public and parochial school systems. On the third Saturday of August, the Chamber of Commerce sponsors a luncheon for all new primary and secondary teachers. About forty parochial school teachers and almost 150 public school teachers, who were to start their duties in September, were invited to the luncheon. At each guest's place was an "apple for teacher" with the recipient's name attached to it. The Mayor of the city, the public school superintendent and the Catholic dean gave short addresses of welcome to the newcomers. There was no contrast made between the public and the parochial schools, and no mention of competition between the two systems. The city officials warmly accept and praise the parochial school teachers.

The relationship of St. Luke's school with the public school officials is one of the ways in which mutual cooperation occurs.[37] The Pastor keeps in contact with the public school superintendent and the local Principals. Even though the diocesan superintendent sends a tentative schedule for the year, the Pastor outlines the program of school days and holidays as closely as possible to that of the local public schools. He does not want St. Luke's children to "run the streets" on days when the public school children are in class, so that St. Luke's was the only parochial school in the city that took the spring vacation during the first week in April instead of during Holy Week. This coordination of school days was not perfect, the public school pupils having two days off while their teachers attended an institute, and the parochial school children having a holiday in honor of the installation of the new Bishop, and another because of the confirmation ceremonies in May.

There are cordial and continuous relations within the whole Parent-Teacher movement. St. Luke's is one of the four parochial schools in the city sponsoring an official PTA joined with the city council and the state and national congress of parents and teachers. Delegates from St. Luke's regularly represent the school at the city and state programs.

[36] See William E. McManus, "The Catholic School and the Community," *Catholic Action,* vol. 33, no. 11 (November 1951), pp. 6–8 and 18, who takes up the charge of divisiveness of parochial schools.

[37] See Mary Myles, "Relations with Public Schools," *The Catholic Educator,* vol. 25, no. 7 (March, 1955), pp. 416–417, 420, 442, who suggests numerous ways of keeping the channels of communication open between the parochial and the public schools.

During the year of our study the president of the City PTA Council was elected from St. Luke's. The highest state and city officers of the PTA attended the annual breakfast in May which took place in St. Luke's auditorium, and three of them gave short but enthusiastic speeches. The superintendent of the city public school system was an honored guest, and the principal speaker was the public school superintendent from a neighboring city.

Another connection between the two school systems is found in athletics. While each has a separate league for the main sports, football, basketball and baseball for boys and volleyball for girls, the teams from St. Luke's occasionally play a practice game with the teams of the local public schools. A large number (46.2%) of St. Luke's children have one or more public school children as their best friends. The football and baseball teams practice on the public school fields, and until St. Luke's gymnasium was completed two years earlier, the school teams played their indoor engagements in basketball and volleyball at the gymnasium of the nearby public school. The director of the city recreational department encourages and invites the pupils from St. Luke's to participate in the summer park program.

Other activities of both pupils and parents of St. Luke's are also closely interrelated with those of people from other schools. The Boy Scout Troop is as active as any in the district and city programs. Mr. O'Toole, of St. Luke's, is the district chairman of the committee on special events. The Blue Birds and Camp Fire Girls participate regularly in all of the larger organization's activities, and Mrs. Johnson has been elected as general chairman of the Camp Fire District.[38] The children from St. Luke's take their regular part in the public program of song and prayer sponsored by the city at the Court House on Thanksgiving Day and in the carol sing at Christmas time.

St. Luke's school participates equally with all other schools in numerous health and safety programs of the city. The school receives fire protection in the form of practice, lectures, drills and supervision by the city's fire department. Similar help is rendered in matter of health and sanitation. The parochial school children fill out the same health certificates, get the same shots, and meet the same standards as the public school children. The city health department assigns a registered nurse to look after the pupils at St. Luke's.

The safety of the children from traffic hazards, and of the school property from vandalism, is assured through cooperation of the city police department. A woman traffic officer is employed by the city,

[38] For further details on these activities see above chap. 7, "Youth Movements."

and the patrol boys get the same recognition as those from public schools. The pupils of St. Luke's participate in the numerous drives sponsored by civic organizations; they sell Christmas and Easter seals, donate to the Red Cross and the Heart Fund, as well as to numerous other agencies. The public transportation system arranges to run special busses at reduced fares during the busy time before and after school hours. The school property itself is, of course, tax free.

Contributions to the Community

The contributions that are made by St. Luke's parochial school to the larger community in which it exists are also numerous and significant. As the city superintendent of schools remarked, "this city needs the parochial schools, and they are doing a tremendous job of education." Many people are realizing for the first time that the parochial school contributes something more than citizens to the community. In the city where St. Luke's is located, the per capita cost for public school children in the elementary grades in the 1955–56 school year was $283.14. This means that the 632 children in St. Luke's, since they are not being educated at public expense, are saving the community $178,944.48 per year. The sixteen parochial schools of the city are now educating 6,611 children. Thus, they are contributing annually to the city the amount of $1,871,838.54, which would have to be raised through taxes if these children attended public schools.

Besides these annual savings made for the community by the parochial school, there are also notable contributions in capital investments and buildings. For example, in this mid-western city it now costs about $30,000 per classroom to build an elementary school (not including cafeteria, gymnasium or the cost of the land).[39] This means that the fourteen classrooms of St. Luke's school would cost the city more than $420,000 to replace, *after* the land had been acquired and *before* the cafeteria and gymnasium are built. To replace approximately 150 classrooms in all the parochial schools of the city would cost more than four and a half million dollars.

Furthermore, at practically no expense to the taxpayer, the parochial school is offering the services of trained teachers who would otherwise have to be supplied by the community. Practically all of the teachers in the parochial school were educated at private and

[39] During the year of our study the construction costs of three schools in the city were as follows: (a) $556,882 for fifteen classrooms and a gymnasium, (b) $575,453 for fourteen classrooms and a gymnasium, (c) $601,214 for a second-story addition to a school of twenty-one classrooms and a cafeteria.

Church expense, while most of the teachers in public schools have been educated in state colleges and universities. It is difficult to estimate how much it costs the state and the community to educate a public school teacher. Whatever this cost is, a considerable saving is made to the public when the teacher is educated at private or Church expense.[40]

This financial saving is in one sense, however, the least important contribution made to the community by the parochial school. Less tangible, but more important, is the fact that the parochial school is, by definition, training and educating a "better" citizen. The basic assumption and justification for the parochial school is that the religiously educated person is a better moral person. It is difficult, and perhaps invidious, to make comparisons along this line while the children are still in school. One crude comparison is that of the rates for juvenile delinquency. Over a two-year period, 486 children were committed to the city reform school, only sixteen of whom were from parochial schools.[41] None of these children was from St. Luke's school.

If the quality of its future adult citizens is of concern to any community, the parochial school is here again making a contribution. St. Luke's is able to maintain a relatively high level of moral and social conduct on the part of its pupils. Its selectivity in the admission and dismissal of pupils is not based on class or ethnic status (as happens often in private schools), or even on standards of intelligence, but on norms of behavior. It is a fact, that can be confirmed by any objective observer, that these children behave in a courteous, orderly and polite manner.[42] There are, of course, incipient roughnecks and problem children among them, but these are reduced to a minimum because there is a clear understanding of the accepted and expected patterns of behavior.

Another important contribution of the parochial school is that of an example of successful voluntary association. This grouping of people (parents, priests, teachers) represents an effort to do for themselves that which the larger community cannot, or will not, do. The whole parochial school system represents the best tradition of self-

[40] See above, chap. 14, "Financing the School."

[41] This represents only 3.3 per cent of all cases, even though Catholics represent about forty-five per cent of the total city population. Exactly half of these Catholic delinquents came from one parochial school.

[42] In the previous year the local newspaper printed a feature article with photographs, describing the patrol boys of St. Luke's school and demonstrating the orderly way in which the pupils made their exit from the school building. This was meant to be an "example" for other elementary schools.

reliance, initiative and responsibility, through which Americans have historically made great progress over tremendous obstacles. Catholics have voluntarily assumed this educational enterprise as a matter of moral principle.

In an era when secondary groups and association are gradually replacing primary groups, the parochial school acts as a focus of local, face-to-face, primary solidarity and cooperation. The preservation and extension of such groups is considered by social scientists as a basic requirement for the maintenance of the larger society.[43] To the extent that they flourish and multiply they are performing an intangible but significant service to the American society.

It may be said further of St. Luke's school (and this appears to be typical of the normal urban parochial school) that it is contributing heavily to the middle-class mores of our society. It teaches the virtues of respectability, cleanliness, conformity, ambition, patriotism. By the very composition of its population it avoids the class consciousness which develops in private schools as well as the minority consciousness which is often a part of the public schools in racial and ethnic neighborhoods. St. Luke's is clearly part of the stream of culture which goes into the molding of the middle-class consciousness, the broad attitudinal basis of the American urban democracy.

Generalizations

1. The parochial school differs from both the public and the private elementary school. Like the public school, it draws from all classes in the community, the Catholic Church being more representative of the total community than any other Church. Unlike the public school, religion is at the center of its total function. Unlike the private school, the parochial school does not select its pupils on a basis of social class and family income. On the one hand, it cannot afford the many "fringe" programs of the public school, and on the other hand, it cannot afford to act as educational experimenter as the private school can.

2. Every elementary school acts as an important instrument for the transmission of the culture and for the socialization of the child. In performing this two-fold function, it attempts to develop the individual child along mental, moral, social and physical lines. It is unrealistic to suggest that the modern urban elementary school, whether parochial, public or private, neglects any of these needs. The parochial

[43] George C. Homans, *The Human Group* (New York: Harcourt, Brace, 1950), pp. 456–457, discusses the relation between the breakdown of small groups and the breakdown of society.

school has no monopoly on the moral training of children, just as the public school has no monopoly on teaching social adjustment to the children, or the private school on intellectual development.

3. The formalized educational institution is unable to carry the whole burden of educational functions. Other major institutions can and do transmit the culture and socialize the child, and provide for its mental, moral, social and physical training. In the case of the parochial school there is an intimate inter-functional system which coordinates the three major institutions—educational, familial and religious. Of central concern to school, family and church, is the sanctification and salvation of the recipients of education. This spiritual objective is the main reason for the existence of the school.

4. An important latent function of St. Luke's parochial school is the fact that it acts as the largest single focus for cooperation and solidarity among the parishioners. This is not performed by the mere presence of the child in the school room, but by the acknowledged fact that the school could not exist without the contributions of parents and parishioners in time, money and energy. In making these contributions the adult parishioners necessarily meet with one another, work together toward ends they value highly, and develop a consciousness of group cohesiveness.

5. The pupils of St. Luke's school are representative of the typical urban, mid-western, middle-class Catholic. This is seen particularly in the mingling of ethnic ancestry of the children themselves and the fact that the parish represents no particular ethnic category. They are not distinguishable from the population of the larger community by social class. Their fathers' education ranges from college completion to partial elementary, and occupation ranges from professional to unskilled jobs. About half of them come from white collar and professional families, while about one-third of the employed males in the city population are in these occupational categories.

6. Children from parochial and public schools are quite similar in their tastes and preferences. They share with other children of their age in the same cultural milieu the popular choices of movie stars and of television programs. The only exception is a specifically Catholic program advertised and encouraged by the parochial school teachers. In the choice of school subjects, mathematics was the favorite in both schools; the parochial school children most dislike social science, and the public school children science.

7. Although the parochial children study Church history, they nominated exactly the same great historical persons in the same order as did the public school children. These personages, Washington,

Lincoln and Columbus, were all connected with the events of America's past. This may indicate an emphasis on patriotism in both schools, or it may indicate a lack of knowledge of world history. The greatest living persons mentioned by the children in both schools are those who are prominent in the current news, and the difference here was that the Catholic children selected two Church leaders, a Pope and a Cardinal.

8. Multiple relations exist for both pupils and parents between the public and the parochial school system. This is shown on the child level through the various organized programs in which children from both schools participate, and on the adult level through the PTA and the adult committees of the youth movements. St. Luke's children share in the numerous health and safety measures maintained by the various departments of the city government.

9. The parochial school participates in the community through the hidden and indirect financial contribution it makes to the city. It is contributing future citizens who have been trained to high norms of moral and social conduct. It is contributing also the example of successful voluntary association of people expressing initiative in the traditional American manner.

Appendix

HOW TYPICAL IS ST. LUKE'S?

IF ST. LUKE's parochial school is completely unique, if it is an "unusual" or "ideal" elementary school, the data we have gathered and the conclusions we have drawn will suffer the same limited utility of any sociological case study. The practical value of a case study of this kind is greatly enhanced if the system under study is fairly representative of most other systems that bear the same title. How valuable, then, as a source of knowledge and as a standard of comparison, is St. Luke's school? To what extent can we project our findings? Are there enough common elements, are there enough practices and programs similar to those of other parochial elementary schools, so that we can consider St. Luke's a "typical" school?

It is physically impossible to study simultaneously a large number of these schools with the same detailed methods of research employed at St. Luke's. In order to test our major conclusions we found it necessary to use questionnaires and thus to obtain information from other American urban parochial schools. We drew up a list of questions based on our findings at St. Luke's which we submitted to a sample of parochial school teachers and of parents who send their children to parochial schools. The answers to these questionnaires provide basic information concerning 433 parochial elementary schools in twenty-nine states.[1]

Is this a valid and adequate sample? Parents reported on 192 different schools at the annual convention of the Christian Family Movement. The type of person who attends a convention of this kind probably represents the more dedicated, active and interested Catholic parishioner. For this reason he is probably more knowledgeable and more honestly critical of the school his child attends than is a less interested parent. Teachers reported on 241 different schools while they attended the regular summer session of the University of Notre Dame. There is no reason to believe that this is a skewed sample of

[1] A total of 512 completed questionnaires was received, including duplicates from the same school, which were rejected.

parochial school teachers, or that these women are biased in a way that other similar teachers would not be. These data were gathered from both parents and teachers during the summer after the end of our research program and refer only to the previous school year. The results are, therefore, strictly contemporaneous with the study of St. Luke's.

These 433 schools contain 245,292 pupils from the first to the eighth grade, averaging 566.5 pupils and 12.1 teachers per school. The pupil load per teacher was 46.7 children. Three-quarters (75.3%) of the faculty members were religious Sisters, and the remaining teachers were lay women. Because all of these schools are in urban areas they are larger than the national average. While the parochial schools in this sample range from those with less than a hundred pupils to those with over thirteen hundred, they are somewhat larger than the national average of 390.1 pupils and 8.5 teachers per school. The teacher load, however, is quite similar to the national average of 45.9 pupils per teacher.[2] St. Luke's school has 632 pupils, eleven Sisters and three lay teachers, and a teacher load of 45.1 pupils.

In a sense, every elementary school is unique because it exists at a definite time and place and involves specific children, teachers and parents. Nevertheless, all elementary schools have some elements in common since they can be conceptualized as belonging to the same social category. In a few items, St. Luke's is an exceptional parochial elementary school. It has an adult supporting organization that is affiliated with the National Congress of Parents and Teachers. It provides a formal, organized course in sex instructions for the seventh- and eighth-grade pupils. The Sisters of St. Luke's do not teach Catechism to the public school children of the parish. In almost all other particulars, however, St. Luke's fell into the largest statistical category with the schools of our sample.

The extent to which St. Luke's school follows the "majority practices" of American parochial schools can be seen by comparing the text of this book with the following sections. This comparison with the representative sample of 433 schools indicates that St. Luke's may be called "a modal statistical type" of the American parochial elementary school. From this point of view the findings on St. Luke's can be projected to most other schools, and the practical value of the study is greatly enhanced.

[2] The national statistics are taken from the *Catholic Directory* (New York: Kenedy, 1957).

The Faculty

All of the schools are run by local authority with practically no interference from diocesan officials. In more than half (52%) of the schools, the diocesan superintendent of schools did not even visit the school during the year. In twenty-nine per cent of the schools he made only one visit, and in the remaining schools he came from two to five times during the year. In almost seven out of ten (69%) schools, however, the school superintendent provides a list of the textbooks to be used and also sends a recommended time schedule for the subject matter of the classes.

In only twenty-one per cent of the cases studied does the Pastor himself operate the school. In most of the parochial schools the function of the Pastor seems to be whatever he wants to make it. In ten per cent of the schools he does nothing at all. His most frequently performed role, in seventy-three per cent of the schools, is that of giving out the report cards to the children. In two out of five schools (39%) he teaches religion. In twenty-two per cent of them he acts as ultimate and chief disciplinarian of the pupils. In relatively few instances (7%) does the Pastor visit the classrooms frequently and regularly. There are other isolated activities mentioned in the reports, like judging contests, coaching teams, hearing first Friday confessions.

The Sister Principal, either alone or with one of the parish priests, actually directs the parochial school in more than three-quarters of the cases studied. The full-time Principal, however, is something of a luxury in the parochial school system, existing in only sixteen per cent of the schools.[3] Nine per cent of these schools have part-time Principals, who do some teaching. In the great majority of schools the full-time teaching Principal handles either the eighth grade, or in the smaller schools, the combined seventh and eighth grades. One-fifth of the teaching Principals, however, teach in the lower grades.

Sisters outnumber lay teachers three to one on the faculties of the parochial schools. But fourteen per cent of the schools have no lay teachers at all, and these are relatively small schools, averaging only 245.7 pupils and 6.1 teachers, with a teacher load of 40.3 pupils per teacher. The lay teacher receives an average monthly salary of $252.90. The lay teachers appear to be more popular with parents than with the Sisters, forty-seven per cent of the former, and only thirty-one per cent of the latter, being in favor of hiring more lay teachers.

[3] All of these schools with full-time principals have more pupils than St. Luke's.

The teacher shortage is evidenced almost everywhere, especially in handling the problem of sick or absent teachers. Fifty-three per cent of these schools make provisions for substitute teachers in the event that a regular teacher is absent. In one-quarter of them, however, the teachers double up their classes, or the part-time Principal takes over the class. In the remaining schools an eighth-grade girl is pressed into service or a mother of the parish is called upon to substitute for the teacher.

Most of the teachers (63%) in these elementary schools had a full parochial school education in their own childhood. Twelve per cent had never been in a parochial school as a child and the remainder had a mixed education in both parochial and public schools. Forty-eight per cent of the religious Sisters and forty-seven per cent of the lay teachers have a bachelor's degree. Fifty-six per cent of these women think that the school in which they are now teaching is superior to the elementary school that they themselves attended; nine per cent think that it is inferior, and the remainder see no significant difference.[4] Twenty-one per cent rate their present school above average; and only four per cent consider it below average. The parents think more highly of the parochial school than do the teachers. Forty-six per cent of the parents rate their child's school above average, and one of them considers it below average.

In all of these schools the teaching Sisters have some extracurricular work to do in the church and parish. The most frequent (73%) function of this kind is that of choir director; next in frequency (70%) is that of training the altar boys. The Sisters are also sacristans in thirty-eight per cent of the parishes and organists in twenty-three per cent of them. They do a variety of other jobs like counting the Sunday collection, doing typing and office work for the parish, mimeographing bulletins and teaching catechism to public school children. Besides these activities they all have the routine housework and chores to perform around the convent.

Ninety-five per cent of the parochial schools have some kind of faculty connection with teachers' institutes, and about three-quarters of these institutes are operated in conjunction with the diocesan school system. They do not, however, appear to place a great burden on the

[4] Fifty-one per cent of the parents had had a full parochial elementary schooling, and nineteen per cent had been in both parochial and public elementary schools. Forty-six per cent of the parents said that the present parochial school of their children is better than their own elementary school. Eight per cent said the child's school is not so good as theirs.

teachers. Seventy-eight per cent of them met only once during the school year; twelve per cent met twice; and the remainder (10%) met three or four times.

Parents and Teachers

The organized interest of parents in these parochial schools appears to be mainly a female activity. Thirty-one per cent of the schools had some kind of women's organization, mostly Mothers' Clubs, but also others like the Rosary Society or the Sanctuary Society, that worked in support of the school. One-third of the schools had no type of lay adult organization connected directly or indirectly with the school. The remaining thirty-six per cent of the schools sponsored organizations called Parents' Clubs, and sometimes Home and School Associations, in which the parents and teachers could meet for the benefit of the pupils and the school.

In the great majority (74%) of these parishes having groups in which both parents and teachers were members, the teachers themselves did not serve on the executive board, hold office, or act on committees. Thus, the formal government of the organization was mainly in the hands of the laity. The teachers, however, seem to have attended meetings fairly consistently, almost three-quarters (73%) of them having attended five or more meetings during the school year. This is a fairly good record since in only forty-six per cent of the cases is the attendance of teachers compulsory; in the remaining schools the teachers are under no obligation to come to the meetings.

The laity, of course, is the heart of any parent-teacher group since the parents must necessarily outnumber by far the teachers in any school.[5] Here again the mothers are predominant. They outnumber the fathers three to one in attendance at meetings. They hold most of the offices in the organization and they perform most of the functions of the group. These functions may be roughly divided into three main categories: fund-raising, the supply of equipment, and the giving of service.

The main fund-raising programs of the parent-teacher groups, mentioned in order of frequency, are: bazaars, card parties, rummage sales, fashion shows, bake sales, fish fries and candy sales. The main kinds of equipment purchased were for athletics and the playground; but numerous other items were also provided like film projectors and audio-visual aids, new desks and bookshelves for the classroom, public address systems, radios and television sets. The services performed by

[5] For example, at St. Luke's there are fifty-three parents for each teacher.

the parents (almost exclusively the mothers) for the schools are varied and extensive: helping in the library and in the school health program, giving Christmas parties and Easter egg hunts, supervising the cafeteria at lunch time and providing breakfast on first Fridays, promoting school picnics and graduation parties, doing clerical work and substitute teaching.

Communication with the teachers is most frequent on the part of those mothers who do the most work for the parents' club. This is not the same as pre-arranged interviews in which the parent and teacher discuss the child and its problems. The teachers answering our questionnaire claimed an average of 21.7 pre-arranged interviews during the year, an average of better than two every month. The frequency of interviews ranged from those teachers who had none at all during the year to those who interviewed the parents of every pupil in their classes. According to this report, a little less than half (47%) of all the pupils attending these parochial schools were discussed in an interview by their teacher and their parents.[6]

Parents and teachers appear to be more concerned about the academic problems of the pupils than about any other aspect of school life. Fifty-three per cent of these interviews were arranged in order to discuss the child's schoolwork; in thirty-seven per cent of them some behavioral problem was under consideration; and the remaining ten per cent concerned both the behavioral and scholastic activities of the child. These proportions are only roughly accurate, because although the purpose of the interview is usually quite clear on any given occasion, the parent almost always asks the teacher also about the "general" progress and behavior of the child.

More often than not it is the teacher who initiates these interviews, since it is the teacher who has to face the problem child every day in the schoolroom. About three out of five times (61%) the teacher asked the parent to come for an interview. In seven out of ten cases (69%) the interviews were held in the school building, mainly in the classroom, while the rest were conducted in the Sisters' convent. Exactly two-thirds of these interviews were held between the teacher and the child's mother in the afternoon after school hours. The rest were at times when the father could be present, about three out of ten (29%) in the evening after supper, and the remainder on Saturdays and Sundays.

[6] About two-thirds of the parents (64%) said that they had had interviews with the teacher during the year discussing their "oldest child" attending school. The teachers, however, were reporting on all their pupils.

It is reported by both teachers and parents that in about two-fifths (39%) of these elementary schools the parents are permitted to visit the classrooms of their children during school hours. In every case where this is allowed, however, it is necessary for the parents to obtain previous permission from either the teacher or Principal, or from both. In actual practice it appears that little visiting of classrooms is done by the parents. In those schools where such visits are permitted only seventeen per cent of the teachers had had parents visiting the classroom during the year, and only eighteen per cent of the parents said that they had taken advantage of this opportunity.[7]

The Spiritual Life

The practice of having a special children's Mass on Sundays seems to have waned in most of the parishes where elementary schools are located. Sixty-three per cent of the schools in this study do not follow this practice, and the children are expected to attend Mass with other members of their family. In those parishes, however, where the custom is followed, the favorite times (69%) for the children's Mass are at nine, nine-fifteen or nine-thirty o'clock. In one-fifth of these places the children's Sunday Mass is at eight, eight-fifteen or eight-thirty o'clock. In the remaining parishes there are two Masses for school children, usually at eight o'clock for the upper grades, and at nine o'clock for the younger pupils. In more than half (54%) of the schools that provide a children's Sunday Mass, the teachers check up on the attendance and absence of their pupils.

The majority of these elementary schools (78%) start the school day with Mass for the children, but in only twenty-two per cent of them is Mass attendance compulsory. Practices vary concerning the pupils for whom the daily Mass is provided. Sixty-two per cent of those schools having morning Mass expect all of the grades, from first to eighth, to attend; while most of the other schools have only the pupils from the fourth to the eighth attend. These parochial schools have varying success in the actual attendance of the children at daily Mass. In eighteen per cent of the schools, less than one-quarter of the children come to daily Mass; sixteen per cent have between one-quarter and one-half; twenty-three per cent have between one-half and

[7] The more exact statistics are 17.3 per cent for teachers, and 17.7 per cent for parents. This similarity indicates that both the teacher sample and the parent sample for this study are fairly representative of the elementary parochial school system.

three-quarters; and the remaining forty-three per cent of the schools claim that more than three-quarters of the pupils come to Mass every day.

The school children are encouraged to receive Holy Communion frequently, but those who do so must in most cases (77%) bring their breakfast to school with them, and in a few instances (5%) they are permitted to go home for breakfast after Mass. In most of the other schools the cafeteria is opened for a short time after Mass and before the start of schoolwork, and the child is enabled to purchase a light breakfast. Usually however, the schoolwork starts immediately after Mass and the children must eat their breakfast in the classroom. In a few rare instances the daily Mass is celebrated at eleven-thirty o'clock in the morning.

In the great majority of these parochial schools it appears to be the belief that the religious teaching of the sixth and ninth commandment and the occasional talks on modesty constitute sufficient sex instructions for the pupils. Formal and separate instruction in sex knowledge is provided in only fifteen per cent of these schools; and in more than half of these cases the instruction consisted of only one lecture period during the year. Most of the time the parish priest gives the instructions, sometimes the teacher, and only rarely a doctor or nurse. In practically all schools the instructions are limited to the pupils in the seventh and eighth grades.

Every parish in which there are public school children makes some arrangement for the religious instruction of these children. Ninety-three per cent of the schools studied in this survey have Sisters in charge of this catechism teaching. In twenty-one per cent of the parishes assistance is given by lay persons, and in eighteen per cent of them the parish priest also helps in the teaching. If the proportions are arranged according to the total personnel involved in these programs, we find that eighty per cent of the teachers are religious Sisters, twelve per cent are lay persons, and the remaining eight per cent are priests.

The traditional time for the teaching of catechism to public school children has been on Sunday mornings, and this practice is still followed in fifty-three per cent of the parishes studied. Eighteen per cent of the parishes arrange for this instruction on weekdays after school hours; fifteen per cent take advantage of the released time program of the public schools. The remaining fourteen per cent teach the public school children on Saturday.

Schoolwork

Most of the teachers in these elementary schools are in favor of giving homework to the children, and actually do so. The majority of them (82%) are also in favor of the parents giving the child some help in his home study. The opinion of teachers ranges from a few who think that the child should not study at home at all, to a few who think that the child should study at least two hours daily. The composite teachers' opinion, however, is that the child should average about fifty-five minutes daily, or about four and a half hours per week. The teachers believe that the children actually study a little over a half-hour daily, or about two hours and thirty-five minutes a week.

The majority of parents (92%) also believe that they should help the child with his home study, and in eighty-five per cent of the cases both parents give this help. In a small number of instances (six per cent) the child receives no help at all; and the remaining children get more assistance from their mothers than from their fathers. The subject in which the parents help the children most (49%) is arithmetic, with spelling, reading and history following in the order of the amount of time devoted to them. The parents think that a child should study about an hour a day, and this coincides closely with the average opinion of the teachers. The parents testify, however, that the actual home study of their children averages one hour and two minutes daily, or about twice as much as the teachers think the children actually study.

About half of these schools (51%) have a separate library room, while about one-sixth (16%) have bookshelves in each room with a small collection of books for the use of the class. Almost half (48%) of the schools having separate libraries keep them open all day, but none of them has a full-time person exclusively in charge of the library. Most of the elementary school libraries are run by the teachers, some by the eighth-grade girls and some by adult female parishioners. Books for these libraries are provided mainly (49%) by the donations of parishioners. In one-quarter of them (24%) the school itself buys the library books; in seventeen per cent of the cases the parents' organization or mothers' club does so. In the remaining one-tenth of the parochial schools there is a regular arrangement with the public library for the temporary loan of large numbers of books.

The large majority (89%) of the parents claim that their children hold borrowers' cards at the public library, and that this makes up for the absence of, or the poor selection of books in, the elementary school library. Almost half (49%) of the parents whose children have library cards say that they themselves help the youngsters in the selection of books; twenty-four per cent of them say that the public librarian advises the child. In very few instances, three per cent, does the parochial school teacher give any reading guidance; and all of the remaining children make their choices of public library books without adult assistance.

Most of these parochial elementary schools (71%) do not have field trips of any kind as part of the education of their pupils. Even in schools where these outside trips are conducted they appear to depend mainly upon the special interests of the particular teacher, and they averaged a little less than two per year for each class. According to the frequency with which they were mentioned by parents and teachers, the most popular attractions for these trips were: public parks, zoos, museums, factories, fire stations and dairies.

Discipline and Conformity

Almost two-thirds of the teachers failed to answer the question, "Is corporal punishment allowed in your school?" Those who did answer, however, gave exactly the same proportion of affirmative answers, forty per cent, as the parents (of whom almost all answered the question). Four out of five of the teachers express disapproval of corporal punishment of pupils, and the others qualified their approval with statements like, "sometimes it is necessary," or "only the Principal should administer it," or "it should be permitted only rarely." The parents, however, do not show such reluctance to have their children spanked or paddled, seventy-two per cent of them approving of corporal punishment in the elementary school.

The common attitude of school teachers concerning the "laxity" of parents is corroborated in this study. About seven out of ten (71%) of the teachers said that the parents are more lenient in the disciplining of the child than is the teacher. All of the rest, with one exception, stated that the teachers and parents are about the same in the degree of strictness they exhibit toward the children. The parents think differently. Only twenty-four per cent of them agree that they are themselves more lenient than the teachers. The majority (65%) believe that they handle the child in about the same way as the teacher does. The remaining eleven per cent feel that they are even stricter than the teacher.

While the teachers in general are not in favor of corporal punishment, they do apply various forms of sanctions and threats in order to maintain discipline or to punish breaches of the rules. Informing the parents of the deviant child is the practice mentioned most frequently (27%) by teachers. Other threats, sanctions and practices are the following, in order of frequency with which they are mentioned: assigning a written task (18%), detention after school (17%), detention at recess (11%), speaking privately with the child (11%), depriving the pupil of various privileges (7%), and several other practices (9%), like changing the seating arrangements, assigning a manual task, having the child pay a fine to the mission collection, "giving a stern look."

The parents were also asked their opinion about the most effective devices employed to preserve order in the schoolroom, and they too mention most frequently (36%) that the parents should be contacted. Other sanctions that they approve of are the following: giving the child a written task (28%), detention at recess (14%), detention after school (13%), and other practices (9%), like sending the child to the Principal, "reasoning" with the child, depriving the child of something he wants to do. It may be said from this comparison that the teachers and parents are in general agreement about the ways of keeping order in the schoolroom.

These parochial elementary schools appear to have a remarkable record for retaining the pupils they admit. Most of them (74%) did not expel even one child during the year; and the remaining schools averaged only 1.3 pupils expelled per school. Most of the expellees (72%) were dismissed because of misbehavior (stealing, fighting, "serious" disobedience), and the others for a variety of reasons, mainly the inability to keep up with the academic standards. One-third of the schools (34%) had problems of absenteeism and truancy. They made use of the city attendance officer to check up on an average of three children in each of their schools. A somewhat larger percentage, two out of five of the schools studied, had an average of 3.1 pupils who were "in trouble" with the police during the year.

Athletic Programs

Thirty-five per cent of these parochial elementary schools have a gymnasium either for the use of the school itself or one that was built for the general use of the parish. Seventy-four per cent of the schools, however, do not have a regular physical education program for the children. In fifty-seven per cent of the remaining schools the classroom teacher herself conducts the physical education period. In other places college students perform this service for the school. All of the grades, from the first to the eighth, get this physical training in seven out of ten (68%) of the schools having such classes. In the other schools only the upper grades receive it.

The boys are favored much more in the athletic program than are the girls; and this appears to be a typical pattern in elementary schools. Only sixteen per cent of the schools have no organized teams for the male pupils, while more than three out of five (62%) have no athletic teams for the girls. This imbalance of emphasis is seen more clearly when we analyze the kinds of sports played by boys and girls in the parochial schools. The following table shows that boys' opportunities to play on organized teams are greater than girls'. The boys play more in organized school leagues, and also more against public schools, than do the girls.

	Per cent having teams	Per cent playing in leagues	Per cent competing with public schools
Boys Sports			
Basketball	74.1	45.8	16.0
Baseball	48.6	26.4	8.5
Football	47.6	33.0	8.0
Track	11.8	5.7	2.3
Girls Sports			
Volleyball	18.4	11.8	1.9
Basketball	17.9	8.7	0.5
Softball	11.8	8.5	1.0
Track	2.8	0.9	0.5

In those schools having athletic teams the cost of the program is borne roughly by three main categories of support. In forty-five per cent of the cases the cost is absorbed by the parish school itself. In thirty-nine per cent of the schools there is a men's group, most often a Boosters' Club, sometimes the Holy Name Society, and occasionally the Knights of Columbus, paying for the athletic teams. In the remaining sixteen per cent of the schools the Mothers' Club or the parents' organization pays the bills.

In most of the parochial schools that have teams the coaching is done on a volunteer basis by lay persons in the parish. Fourteen per cent of them, however, have the assistant pastor as the coach, and nine per cent have the priest and a lay person together coaching the teams. There are some instances (13%) in which the coaching is done by the teachers in the school. Financial remuneration is given to coaches in only about one-sixth (16%) of the schools that have athletic teams.

There is greater equality of the sexes in these schools in the matter of extracurricular youth movements. The Boy Scouts and Cubs exist in fifty-seven per cent of the schools, while the girls are in Scouts and Brownies, or in Camp Fire and Blue Birds, in fifty-five per cent of the schools. The participation by female pupils is, however, slightly larger than by males. Forty-eight per cent of the girls in these schools belong to these youth groups, as compared to forty-six per cent of the boys. These differences obviously are not great, and they indicate that while the boys are favored in the athletic programs, there is not much sex discrimination in the Scouts and similar movements.

Parties and Dances

It appears to be typical of the parochial elementary school that it does not promote the various "frills" of education found in some other school systems. We have seen that "field trips" are not widely encouraged. This is true also of parties and dances. In only twenty-eight per cent of these schools is any instruction provided so that a child can learn to dance, and this instruction is mainly in the form of group activity, like square dancing and folk dancing. Only three out of ten of the schools permit dances for the children on the school property, or sponsor dances for the upper grades. In some places this activity is forbidden by the Pastor, or even by the diocese, and in some instances our respondents said that they "used to have dances."

There is a similar lack of interest, and a certain amount of control exercised, concerning parties attended by both boys and girls. In nine per cent of the cases mixed parties of pupils are forbidden by the school authorities. In those schools where such parties are tolerated, according to the parents' reports, seventy-three per cent of the children did not attend a mixed party during the school year. Those children who did go to mixed parties attended an average of two during the year.

As may be expected in this area of behavior, the girls were more often the "party-givers" than were the boys, the former accounting for sixty-one per cent of the parties, and the latter for the remaining thirty-nine per cent. According to the teachers' reports in schools where such parties took place, the girls gave mixed parties on an average of 4.1 times per year, while the boys gave them on an average of 2.9 times. It appears that the parents encourage parties for the youngest grades, while the pupils themselves want parties in the highest grades—the smallest number of mixed parties was given in the fourth and fifth grades.

School Finances

About two out of five (42%) of the elementary parochial schools are "free schools" in the sense that they do not charge tuition. Eleven per cent of those that charge tuition do so on a family basis, charging an average amount of $33.66 per family per year. The remaining schools require a definite amount from each child, usually slightly higher for the oldest child in the family. This individual pupil tuition ranges from a high of one hundred dollars per year to a low of five dollars per year, with the average at twenty-four dollars per child. In some of these schools book rental is included in the tuition, and in some schools an extra charge of as much as forty dollars is made for bus transportation. Only two of the parents said that the tuition is too high, and both send their children to schools that charge one hundred dollars. Only two teachers also said that the tuition was too high, one at a school where it is forty-five dollars per child, and another where it is ten dollars.

The majority (76%) of these schools use a rental system for the pupils' textbooks. In only fourteen per cent of the schools must the children buy their own books, while in the remaining schools some books are rented and others are bought. The charges for book rental vary so greatly that it is difficult to discern a pattern. Some schools fix it at one-fifth or one-fourth of the original cost of the book; some charge twenty-five cents, others fifty cents per book; some schools include the rental charge in the tuition. In those schools where a definite amount is charged per child, the book rental varies from a high of fifteen dollars per year to a low of a dollar and a half, with the average at $6.04 per year per child.

Every elementary school, public and parochial, is used in some way as an instrument of fund-raising. The parochial schools usually have their pupils contribute not only to civic drives, as do the public schools, but also to various kinds of religious and charitable campaigns. Eight per cent of the parochial schools, however, refuse to participate in civic drives. When asked about kinds of fund-raising campaigns his child's school cooperates with, one parent answered, "You name it; we have it!" The following list is given in the order of frequency in which both parents and teachers mentioned them: Red Cross, mission contributions, pagan babies, Bishops' Relief, magazine subscription drive, March of Dimes, sale of Christmas cards, sale of bazaar books, Polio Drive, Community Chest, sale of Christmas seals and the Heart Campaign. Besides these, however, are numerous scattered and local fund-raising campaigns.

The financing of the parochial school is becoming more problematic, and both parents and teachers appear to be more concerned about it than ever before. The following table shows the comparative distribution of answers by teachers and parents to a question about suggested sources of finances for the parochial school.

Suggested Source of Income	Teachers	Parents
All from taxes	14.3%	3.5%
Part from taxes	32.1	43.0
Parents, parish, or both	39.3	24.4
All or part from diocese	14.3	29.1

When asked whether they were in favor of receiving financial aid for the schools from some public agency, fifty-four per cent of the teachers and sixty-one per cent of the parents answered affirmatively. Those who were opposed to such public aid and support gave as their main reason the fear of government control and the loss of freedom. Some felt that even if the schools did not lose their independence the teachers and administrators might be inclined to favor unduly the interests of the state. Others thought that there might be a hindrance to the religious training of the child, the main reason for which the parochial school exists.

The above table shows that the parents and teachers are not quite sure what form public financial aid to schools should take. When asked specifically about the proposed sources for financing the schools, a lower percentage of both parents and teachers suggested that all or part of the expenses should be supplied from public taxes. The others were probably thinking of indirect aid, like textbooks, and health programs. The parents would like to get more help from the diocese, an idea which seems to be growing in favor, while the teachers are more in favor of support from the parents and the parish.

Desired Changes

Most of the above material has been centered around questions of "fact," asking what the teachers do, how the children behave, and so forth. There were also some questions of opinion, asking what the parents and teachers thought about various aspects of the parochial school system. From these questions of opinion one can deduce the areas in which changes from present practices would be desirable.

In order to specify the most needed changes we put a final question to our respondents: "If you had the power to make *only one change* in this parochial school, what would that change be?" The fact that eighteen per cent of the teachers and eleven per cent of the parents did not take the trouble to answer this may indicate that they are more or less satisfied with the school as it is, that they could think of nothing to improve the school. It may also indicate, however, that they did not wish to voice any criticism. As we have seen above, twenty-one per cent of the teachers, and forty-six per cent of the parents, rate their school above average. Forty-nine per cent of the parents rate their child's teacher above average; and only six per cent rate her below average.

The most frequently mentioned change desired by the parents centers around the teacher shortage and the overcrowding of classrooms. Since the teacher load in these schools is 46.7 pupils per teacher, it is easily understandable why the first request of the parents would be for smaller classes, more classrooms and more teachers. A second suggestion, however, was made almost as frequently by the parents. This was the widely-expressed desire for better understanding and cooperation between teachers and parents. Most of the parents who made comments on this item felt that the lack of cooperation was on the part of the school and the teachers.

The suggestions for change made by the teachers were so varied and specific that it is practically useless to attempt to categorize them. The most frequently made suggestion (though not made nearly so frequently as by the parents) also had to do with overcrowding and teacher shortage. Smaller classes were a desideratum among the teachers. Some in the larger schools suggested that the Principal be relieved of teaching duties and that a replacement be hired for her. Some want the extracurricular activities of the children to be curbed, and others want better janitorial service in the schools. Presumably, these two latter improvements would permit the respondents to concentrate more on the central function, that of actual classroom teaching.

The Intangibles

It must be pointed out in conclusion that a sample of this kind, no matter how accurate and representative, cannot take the place of daily observation, personal interviews, frequent testings and first-hand contacts in the local group. For example, the amount and kind of cooperation that exists among priests, teachers and parents in the functioning of a parochial school, can best be appreciated when the researcher is actually "on the ground" and watches carefully what goes on. The "spirit" of cooperation is an intangible; it cannot be studied at a distance; it cannot be accurately interpreted with statistics.

The area of authority and decision-making is another intangible of this sort. We know from our respondents that the Pastor "runs the school" in about one-fifth of the cases, and that the Pastor has a "hands-off policy" in one-tenth of the schools. In between these extremes there is a great variety of policy and functions on the part of the Pastor. From first-hand observation we have seen precisely how Father Albert acts toward the teachers and pupils of St. Luke's. This is a behavioral pattern, with overtones of attitudes, that can best be appreciated when one watches what he does and says, and what the reactions of people are to his behavior.

Sister Roberta falls into the modal category of the parochial school Principals since like most of them she is in direct charge of the school and she also teaches. Unlike most other schools, however, she and the other teachers hardly ever attended meetings of the Parent-Teacher organization. We have seen, both at St. Luke's and in our sample of parochial schools, that pre-arranged conferences between parents and teachers discussing the school child occur less frequently than they do in public schools. Nevertheless, there exists at St. Luke's a distinctive cordiality between parents and teachers. Here again is a quality of social relations that is not statistically tangible and that can be fully discerned by the researcher who is constantly on the scene.

The function of parents in the parochial school may be roughly described as "extracurricular"; and this is borne out both in the sample and in the study of St. Luke's. The degree to which the parents share in decision-making cannot be clearly discerned from a large sample study. For example, the pupils wear uniforms in forty-nine per cent of the parochial schools, and sixty-eight per cent of the parents are in favor of this arrangement. At. St. Luke's school, the parents were given an opportunity to vote on whether or not they wanted the children to wear uniforms, and they voted against it. In eighty-seven per cent of the schools, however, this decision is taken out of the hands of the parents. They had "nothing to say" even in this extracurricular matter, about the making of the decision.

The attitudinal relations existing between the parents and the school authorities may be paralleled by similar relations existing between the children and their teachers and among the pupils themselves. Any particular study may be useful in measuring the "school spirit" among the children, their friendliness toward one another, the degree of class consciousness within the school population. We have seen that at St. Luke's the discipline is not rigid; that the pupils show no signs of repression, and that the relations between teachers and pupils are for the most part considerate and cordial. The immediate observation of a social system in operation can lead to reliable conclusions about these relatively intangible items.

This fact in itself may lead one to question the "typicality" of St. Luke's school. As we said above, there is a unique, as well as a typical, aspect of a school of this kind. It may well be that a personality like Sister Roberta accounts for a central and important difference which distinguishes St. Luke's from all other parochial schools. Perhaps there is no other Pastor quite like Father Albert in his relations to children, teachers and parents. Pastors and Principals who read this account of St. Luke's may conclude that the parents here "make all the difference." From the point of view of social science, however, these comments tend to be oversimplifications. The individual is still compelled to work within a social system.

In the last analysis we are faced here with the central problem of sociology, as a science. From a sufficiently wide and representative sample of parochial schools we discover generalized patterns of behavior. Without these valid universals one could not talk of a science of social behavior. When performing the same general social function, and when striving for the same general social goal—as in the educational system—the participants must logically act in similar ways. There are also always certain differences, and these differences are frequently attributable not only to the unique personalities involved in the system, but also to local circumstances and conditions. These are the aspects that help to "bring alive" the detailed study of a particular school in a way that the representative sample of many schools cannot succeed in doing.

INDEX OF NAMES

INDEX OF SUBJECTS

The Library of Congress has cataloged this book as follows:

Fichter, Joseph Henry, 1908–
Parochial school, a sociological study. [Notre Dame, Ind.] University of Notre Dame Press, 1958.

495 p. 24 cm.

1. Catholic Church in the U. S.—Education. I. Title.

LC501.F5 377.5 58–13614 ‡

Library of Congress

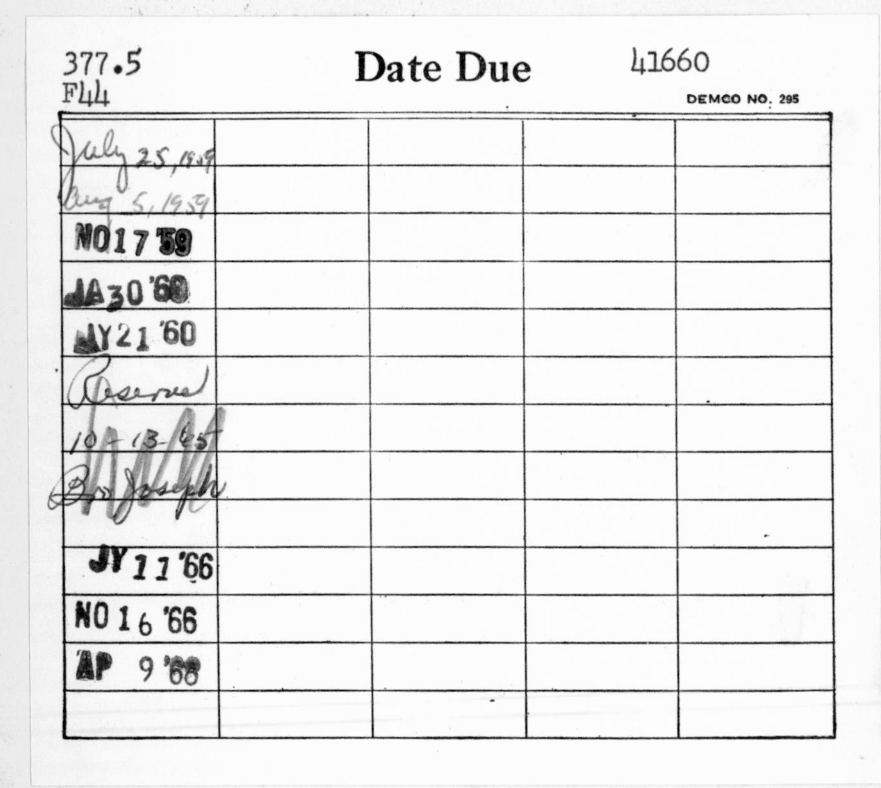

Date Due

41660

DEMCO NO. 295

July 25, 1959				
Aug 5, 1959				
NO 17 '59				
JA 30 '60				
JY 21 '60				
Reserve				
10-13-65				
Bro Joseph				
JY 11 '66				
NO 16 '66				
AP 9 '68				